Brand.new

V&A PUBLICATIONS

Brar

d. new

First published by V&A Publications,
2000

V&A Publications
160 Brompton Road
London SW3 1HW

Designed by Stephen Coates, August
Cover designed by Agenda Design
Associates

Specially commissioned photography:
Graham Brandon, V+A Photography
studio and Andrew Cross

ISBN 185177 324X

A catalogue record for this book is
available from the British Library

Printed in Singapore

Every effort has been made to seek
permission to reproduce those images
whose copyright does not reside with
the V&A, and we are grateful to the
individuals who have assisted in this
task. Any omissions are entirely
unintentional, and the details should
be addressed to the publishers

CONTENTS

ACKNOWLEDGEMENTS

In the course of the preparation of both this book and the exhibition Brand.New, the curators have received invaluable advice and assistance from many varied quarters. My first thanks must go to my co-curator, Gareth Williams. His contribution to this book extends far beyond the chapter that bears his name. Secondly, the exhibition organiser, Anna Gustavsson, who has worked tirelessly to make the entire project possible, and Mike Malham, who deftly co-ordinated the design work. We have all been ably assisted by Poppy Hollman from the Exhibitions Department and researchers Emmie Kell, Debra Dawson and Catharina Holmberg.

I would like to thank all the contributors, who offered their expertise and scholarship not only to the book but also to the exhibition during the course of its development. Their details are on the following pages. Thanks are also due to the numerous people from companies, press and publicity offices, business archives and photographic agencies, who helped us in the search for images and information, and took the time to talk with us. In particular, I would like to mention: The London Business School; Phil Mooney and his team at the Coca-Cola Archive; Lynn Downey, Levi Strauss & Co Archive; Antonella Viero, Diesel; Siamack Salari, BMP DDB; Masuhiro Yamaguchi and Yasuhiro Masuda, Sanrio GmbH; Angela Gleinicke, Greenpeace; Amanda Sandford, Action on Smoking and Health; Allan MacDonald, The Media Foundation; The John Lewis Partnership Archive; Harrods Archive; Woolworths Archive; The Anti-Counterfeiting Group; Manchester United Football Club; Liz Lowe, Coca-Cola Great Britain; John Sorrell of Interbrand Newell and Sorrell; Caroline Lynch and Gillian McVie, Purple; George Pincus; Shubhankar Ray; Dave Morris; and Tony Hayward.

The team at V&A Publications have been patient and supportive during the preparation of this book, in particular Mary Butler, Head of V&A Publications, Miranda Harrison, Mary Wessel, Helen Armitage and Geoff Barlow. I am grateful to John Styles and Jonathan Woodham for helpful comments on various drafts of the text. I would especially like to thank Stephen Coates and August Media for the design of the book, and Agenda Design for the cover and the Brand.New logo. The photographs specially commissioned for this book are the work of Graham Brandon, V&A Photographic Studio, who has contributed enormously to this project, and also Andrew Cross. Special thanks also must go to the exhibition design team: Thomas Heatherwick, Kieran Gaffney, Tom Chapman Andrews, Richard Greenwood and Stephen Coates, who have given creative form to our ideas.

Many colleagues at the V&A have offered help and advice with Brand.New: particularly Linda Lloyd Jones, Head of the Exhibitions Department, and Paul Greenhalgh, Head of the Research Department, who have guided the project. All members of the project team for Brand.New have contributed enormously, especially Eithne Nightingale, Francis Pugh, Jane Rosier, Emily Owen, Sarah Gray, Brian Griggs, Lucy Morrison and her team in the Development Department, and Michael Cass and staff of V&A Enterprises. Thanks also to members of the Research Department and the Furniture and Woodwork Department, and to the numerous colleagues and friends who sent us photographs and press clippings, told us their 'brand' preferences, and thought of us whilst out shopping: in particular, Tessa Hore, Andrew Bolton, Ghislaine Wood, Susan McCormack and John Strand. My personal thanks also go to the University of Brighton and the British Academy, who have supported my time at the V&A in the form of a six-year research fellowship, and last but especially not least, Tim Burne.

Jane Pavitt

PAOLA ANTONELLI is curator in the Department of Architecture and Design at the Museum of Modern Art, New York. She has curated a number of exhibitions, including *Mutant Materials in Contemporary Design* (1995), *Thresholds: Contemporary Design from the Netherlands* (1996), *Achille Castiglioni: Design!* (1998), and *Projects 66: Campana/Ingo Maurer* (1998–9). She is currently working on a cycle of exhibitions about the MoMA collection from 1960 to today, in collaboration with Kirk Varnedoe and Josh Siegel.

PATRICK BARWISE is Professor of Management and Marketing, Director of the Centre for Marketing and Chairman of the Future Media Research Programme at London Business School. His publications, with various co-authors, include books on *Television and its Audience*, *Accounting for Brands*, *Strategic Decisions*, *Predictions: Media and Advertising in a Recession*, as well as numerous articles. He is currently writing a book with Andrea Dunham on *The Business of Brands*, to be published by Harvard Business School Press. He is Deputy Chairman of the Consumers' Association and Joint Managing Editor of *Business Strategy Review*.

RUSSELL W. BELK is the N. Eldon Tanner Professor of Business Administration and Professor of Marketing in the David Eccles School of Business (University of Utah, USA). He has also had regular, visiting or honorary university appointments in Canada, Romania, Zimbabwe, Hong Kong, Australia and elsewhere in the United States. His areas of expertise are consumer behaviour, qualitative research, and marketing and development. He is past president of the Association for Consumer Research and current president of the Society of Marketing and Development. He is a Fellow in the Association for Consumer Research and the American Psychological Association. He has published more than 250 books, articles and videotapes, including *Collecting in a Consumer Society* (1995).

AARON BETSKY is Curator of Architecture and Design at San Francisco Museum of Modern Art. He has curated a wide range of exhibitions including *Icons: Magnets of Meaning* (1997). He has published, taught and lectured extensively, and is currently an Adjunct Professor at the California College of Arts and Crafts (CCAC) and a Contributing Editor of *Architecture*, *Metropolitan Home*, *Blueprint* and *ID* magazines. He has published eight books on architecture and design, including *Violated Perfection: Architecture and the Fragmentation of the Modern* (1990), *James Gamble Rogers and the Architecture of Pragmatism* (1994), *Building Sex: Men, Women, Architecture and the Construction of Sexuality* and *Queer Space: The Spaces of Same Sex Desire* (1997).

ANDREW BOLTON is the Joint London College of Fashion/Victoria & Albert Museum Contemporary Fashion Research Fellow. Formerly an assistant curator in the Far Eastern Department of the V&A, much of his research centres on East Asian fashion, on which he has published several essays and articles.

RACHEL BOWLBY is Professor of English at the University of York. Her books include *Just Looking* (1985), *Shopping with Freud* (1993) and *Carried Away: The Invention of Modern Shopping* (2000).

ALISON CLARKE lectures at the Royal College of Art, London, and as Visiting Professor at the University of Applied Arts, Vienna, in the field of material culture and design history. She has published numerous articles around the consumption of everyday artefacts, and is the author of *Tupperware: The Promise of Plastic in 1950s America* (1999).

CHARLOTTE COTTON is an assistant curator of photographs at the Victoria & Albert Museum. She is part of the team there responsible for the national collection of the art of photography and the programme of exhibitions and events for the Canon Photography Gallery. She is curator of the V&A exhibition *Imperfect Beauty* (2000) and author of the accompanying book.

ANDREA DUNHAM is President of Unique Value International, Inc., a New York based management consultancy with global clients. She is co-author of *Unique Value: The Secret of All Great Business Strategies* (1993) and *Building a Global Image*, a 1991 report published by the Economist group. She is currently writing a book with Patrick Barwise, *The Business of Brands*, to be published by Harvard Business School Press. She is a Fellow of the Royal Society of Arts.

KENT GRAYSON is on the marketing faculty at London Business School, where he researches deception and trust in marketing and branding. He also studies a type of direct selling called 'network marketing'.

HELEN JONES is a freelance writer, curator, researcher and lecturer. She is a graduate of the Victoria & Albert Museum/Royal College of Art MA in the History of Design, where her specialist subject was petrol-station design. She was co-curator with Deyan Sudjic of *The Architecture of Democracy* (1999) and is currently visiting lecturer in Design Studies at Goldsmiths University.

GUY JULIER is employed in the School of Art, Architecture and Design at Leeds Metropolitan University. His previous books include *New Spanish Design* (1991) and the *Thames & Hudson Dictionary of 20th-century Design and Designers* (1993). The discussion of branded leisure that appears in this publication is developed further in his forthcoming book *The Culture of Design* (2000).

SHARON KINSELLA is a researcher and lecturer in contemporary media, culture and society in Japan at the University of Cambridge, UK.

CELIA LURY is a Reader in Sociology at Goldsmiths College, University of London and has a DPhil in Sociology from Manchester University. She has written widely on consumer culture, the culture industries and visual culture. She is currently researching a book on brands. The pieces in this book are based on research conducted as part of an RSRC-funded project 'Global Culture Industries:

The Biography of Cultural Products' with Deirdre Boden, Scott Lash, Vince Miller, Dan Shapiro and Jeremy Valentine.

STEFANO L. MARZANO is Managing Director of Philips Design. He was born in 1950 in Italy. He holds a doctorate in Architecture from the Milan Polytechnic Institute. During the early part of his career, he worked on a wide range of assignments for several design firms. In 1978 he joined Philips Design in The Netherlands, as Design Leader for Data Systems and Telecommunication products. He returned to Italy in 1982 to direct the Philips-Ire Design Centre (Major Domestic Appliances), becoming Vice President of Corporate Industrial Design for Whirlpool International (a joint venture of Whirlpool and Philips) in 1989. In 1991 he took up his present post in The Netherlands.

JANE PAVITT is University of Brighton/Victoria & Albert Museum Senior Research Fellow in Product Design & Museology, based in the Research Department at the V&A. Formerly a senior lecturer in design history at Camberwell College of Arts (The London Institute), she has written widely on aspects of design and design history. She is co-curator of the major exhibition Brand.New at the V&A in autumn 2000. She has curated several design exhibitions including *Designing in the Digital Age* (1999) and *The Shape of Colour: Red* (1999). She is the author of *Buildings of Europe: Prague* (2000).

MARK RITSON is an Assistant Professor at London Business School and has a PhD in Marketing from Lancaster University. His research focuses on branding, advertising and consumer culture. His most recent article, 'The Social Uses of Advertising', appeared in the December 1999 edition of the *Journal of Consumer Research*.

GARETH WILLIAMS is co-curator of the major V&A exhibition Brand.New in 2000 and an Assistant Curator in the Department of Furniture and Woodwork at the Victoria & Albert Museum, London, where he specialises in twentieth-century and contemporary furniture. For

the academic year 1999–2000 he was the V&A/University of Sussex Exchange fellow. He has written numerous articles about aspects of furniture design and collaborated with the design group Inflate on their book *Swell* in 1998. He has curated several V&A displays including *Green Furniture* (1996), *...not so simple* (1997), *Swell* (1998) and *Ron Arad, before and after now* (2000). He is the author of *Branded? Products and their Personalities* (2000), also published to coincide with Brand.New.

JONATHAN WOODHAM is Professor of the History of Design at the University of Brighton. He is also Director of the University's Design History Research Centre, which seeks to promote the discipline nationally and internationally, and holds a number of important design archives, the most significant of which is that of the Design Council. He has written widely on the history of design, including *Twentieth-century Design* (1997) and serves on the editorial boards of a number of periodicals, including the *Journal of Design History and Design Issues*.

From cornflakes to cars, our daily lives are increasingly dominated by branded goods and brand names; the brand is the prefix, the qualifier of character. The symbolic associations of the brand name are often used in preference to the pragmatic description of a useful object. We speak of 'the old Hoover', 'my new Audi' or 'my favourite Levi's' – not needing to qualify them with an object description. The brand is at the heart of this process for many of the goods we buy and sell.

The concept of the brand is central to our society. Media interest in the subjects of branding, marketing and corporate concerns has been substantial in recent years, and the fortunes of global corporations such as Microsoft make for regular news features.

The subject of brands is also one that crosses over a diversity of interests. Recent studies in sociology, anthropology, business, marketing and design have chosen to focus on the relationship between brands and consumer behaviour.

In the light of this, we have brought together writers and commentators for whom the brand is the 'point of entry' to their subject approach. As well as the five main chapters that form the body of the book, there is a selection of writings that provide snapshots of brand and consumer behaviour. The contributors range from observers and critics of brand-culture to the 'image-makers' themselves. The subjects cover products, locations and social practices, as they all fall within the matrix of branding.

CHAPTER ONE

IN GOODS WE TRUST?

JANE PAVITT

"The logo is the point of entry to the brand."

Milton Glaser, designer, *Graphis*, 1995

The origins of the term 'brand' in its contemporary sense are relatively new. The term derives from the practice of indelibly marking or stamping property, usually with a hot iron. Cattle or sheep would be marked in this way, but it was equally a means of signalling disgrace. Criminals would be 'fixed with a mark of infamy' using a hot iron or tattoo. Branding therefore signalled a loss of esteem that could not be restored and could be publicly recognised. We still talk of people being 'branded a liar'. Branding is principally the process of attaching a name and a reputation to something or someone.

The most recognisable feature of a brand is a name, logo, symbol or trademark that denotes a product's origin. A person, corporation or institution will own the rights to the brand name and employ it as a means of distinguishing their product or service from others. The ways in which this is done is described as branding, the process by which the values of the brand are attached, both physically and by suggestion, to the product. The brand, however, is much more than a

name or trademark. As Patrick Barwise, Andrea Dunham and Mark Ritson propose in their chapter, 'Ties That Bind', the idea of the brand also encompasses the associations that the name has for consumers. The brand image, or brand value, results from the 'dialogue' that takes place between producer or brand owner and the consumer or user. A brand's strength rests upon a close correlation between the image the brand creates through the process of branding, and the reception of that message by the consumer. Any distortions to that message tend to result in a weaker brand – for example, a brand that promotes itself as 'cheap and cheerful' may actually be read as poor quality if the message is mismanaged.

A brand name can be both that of the company or product owner and that of the particular product or product range. A family of branded products, all owned by the same company, may share certain features of their brand image, while still possessing a distinctive character or potential market. Jane Frost, Brand Manager of the BBC, has described this as a kind of 'brand DNA'.[1] Despite their individual character, each brand depends upon the image of the parent-brand. The brand structure of the BBC

(or any broadcast network) is a good example of this. The BBC has a powerful and globally recognised brand image and heritage, associated with quality broadcast, drama and news. It is seen as a reassuring voice heard all over the globe – particularly through the BBC World Service. Its brand values are an asset. Associated with it is a host of family members: Radio 1, 2, 3, 4 and 5live, regional radio stations, two TV channels and so on, not forgetting recent forays into digital broadcasting. Radio 1 and Radio 2 have markedly different brand values (both subject to considerable repositioning in recent years). On each station or channel are a multitude of programmes and personalities, each again with their own brand values. These values and associations are bankable assets, both for the Corporation and individuals associated with it.

So how is brand value established? The invention of a new brand overnight with subsequent rapid marketing is unlikely to be a success. Brands with strong images are the product of a successful nurturing of the relationship between producer and consumer. They also require economic investment, marketing and corporate nurturing. The most recognisable brands tend to maintain their position by establishing loyalty and ubiquity, by becoming the market standard. Early branded products often literally embodied the brand's promise within its name, such as the 'Thorough Washer', an early washing machine, patented in England in 1871. In some cases, the brand name becomes the generic name for that product, such as Hoover, Coke, Walkman or Rollerblade. For certain products, what started out as a brand name has become so generic that it can not be protected by trademark: aspirin, yo-yo, thermos and escalator are all terms that began life as brand names. The familiarity of names such as these demonstrates the rise to prominence of the brand in the last century. Brands are a part of twentieth-century mythology.

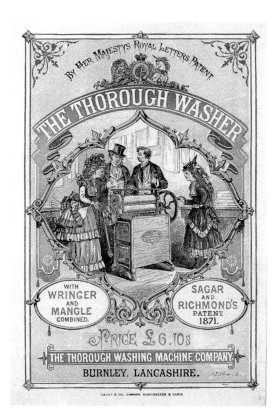

Opposite page: Winston Churchill, BBC broadcast, June 1942 (with current BBC logo below).
Above: Advertisement for the 'Thorough Washer' by the Thorough Washing Machine Co. of Burnley. English, nineteenth century.
Right: Advertising hoarding in Bolton, Lancashire, by Alec Davis. English c. 1898.

EVERY GARMENT GUARANTEED

LEVI STRAUSS & CO'S

TWO HORSE BRAND

TRADE MARK

PATENTED   MAY 20 1873

COPPER RIVETED CLOTHING

BLOUSES, JUMPERS, COATS, VESTS, MENS YOUTHS
AND BOYS OVERALLS. WITH OR WITHOUT BIBS
CARPENTERS APRONS AND SPRING BOTTOM PANTS

ALSO MANUFACTURERS

OF

SUN SET SHIRTS

EL REAL
HOSIERY
AND UNDERWEAR FOR
MEN WOMEN CHILDREN
AND DISTRIBUTORS FOR
RUGBY STOCKING
FOR CHILDREN
"THEY WEAR AND WEAR AND WEAR"

"In 19 out of 22 product categories, the company that owned the leading American brand in 1925 still has it today – Nabisco in cookies, Kellogg's in breakfast cereals, Kodak in film, Sherwin Williams in paint, Del Monte in canned fruit, Wrigley's in chewing gum, Singer in sewing machines, Campbell's in soup, Gillette in razors."[2]

The historical development of branding and branded goods is bound up with changes to the production, distribution and retail of goods, and to related demographic and economic shifts. Equally important, however, is the way in which the social history of a brand is often mythologised to become part of that brand's image. The respective histories of Coca-Cola and Levi's parallel neatly the rise of the American mass market, and the biography of each company is an exercise in the making of the American myth. Both products exemplify the ideal of American individualism. Levi's have successfully exploited the image of the American cowboy or rock'n'roll hero in generations of advertising.[3] Coca-Cola's association with the Free West in the post-war period has been, until recently, unshakeable. Images of Coca-Cola drinking American soldiers during the Second World

War summed up the idea of America as a land of plentiful consumer products (along with silk stockings and cigarettes). Less tangibly, Coca-Cola may have been a nostalgic reminder of home for homesick GIs, and even of the values for which they might feel themselves to be fighting.[4] This image was successfully re-deployed during the Korean and Vietnam wars, when Coca-Cola kept American troops supplied with the drink, even building extra bottling plants in Vietnam to maintain the 'demand'.[5]

However successful a brand image might be, significant social and even political shifts can result in a loss of popularity. For brands that trade on heritage or national identity, for example, attempts to reposition them can be dangerous. Both Levi's and Coca-Cola, however, have in the past achieved significant 'comebacks' using advertising campaigns that combine the emotional appeal of the product with current concerns. In 1971 Coca-Cola made a successful appeal to a post-Vietnam, post-Woodstock generation of youthful consumers, who could conceivably have been ill disposed to Coke's image of all-American patriotism. The 'Hilltop' advertisement of that year featured a crowd of peace-loving people of all creeds and colours in a natural setting, all enjoying a Coke, and singing a song that was to become famous: 'I'd like to teach the world to sing in perfect harmony … I'd like to buy the world a Coke and keep it company.' The song was subsequently released as a single to huge success, although with its references to Coke

Previous pages: Cover of brochure, 'Evolution of a Pair of Overalls', showing Levi Strauss & Co.'s Two-Horse Brand, c.1907.
Right: Levi Strauss & Co. original jeans label.

American soldiers serving
overseas were supplied
with Coca-Cola during the
Second World War.
Overleaf: Coca-Cola
reinvented their image
with the memorable 'Hilltop'
TV commercial of 1971.
'I'd Like to Buy the World
a Coke' Words and music by
B. Backer, B Davis, R. Cook
and R. Greenaway.

I'd like to buy the world a home
with apple trees and honey bees
I'd like to teach the world to sin

I'd like to buy the world a Coke

I'd like to teach the world to sin

I'd like to buy the world a Coke

I'd like to teach the world to sin

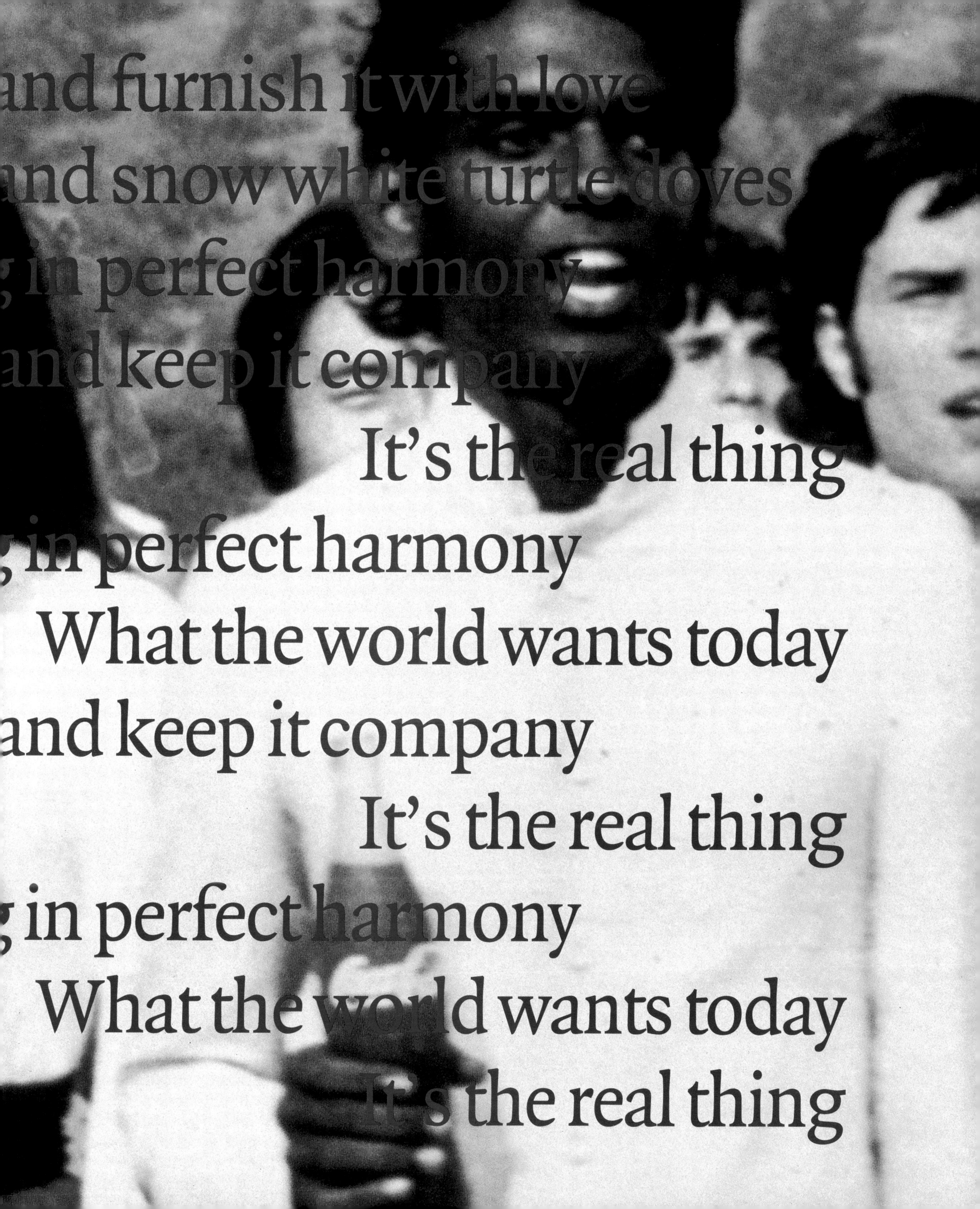

and furnish it with love

and snow white turtle doves

in perfect harmony

and keep it company

It's the real thing

in perfect harmony

What the world wants today

and keep it company

It's the real thing

in perfect harmony

What the world wants today

It's the real thing

Top: Coca-Cola Soda
Fountain, USA, c. 1920.
Above: Coca-Cola bottling,
Junction City, Kansas, USA,
c. 1910.
Right: Cover of Sears,
Roebuck & Co. catalogue,
no. 102, 1896.
Opposite: The Eiffel Tower,
illuminated by Citroën,
Exposition des Arts
Décoratifs, Paris, 1925.

removed.[6] The song and its related imagery became part of Coca-Cola folklore, so much so that the Corporation attempted to revisit the success of the ad in 1989, using the children of the original cast.[7] The success of Levi's television advertising in the 1980s, with their famous 'Laundrette' campaign and others, once more demonstrated how the popular-music charts could be used to reinforce the image of brand. Like most of Levi's advertising, this campaign again utilised the image of a mythologised America.

It is no accident that a number of familiar companies promote themselves as the brands that 'built' America. The growth of national networks of goods circulation and distribution in mid-nineteenth-century America and the increasing regulation of products created a climate where brands could flourish. In a more mobile society, the familiarity of branded goods quickly became an important selling point. Companies rushed to register patents on new products and brand names, as others were quick to move in on the popularity of a new idea. Patent or proprietary medicine was one particularly burgeoning area for brand names. Coca-Cola started life in 1886 (and was patented in 1887) as a medicinal product or 'nerve tonic', sold as a general pick-me-up at a time when a host of similar products were appearing.[8] Available first through cafés or 'soda fountains' and only later as a bottled (and then canned) product, it achieved rapid success by investing in the value and image of its name. In fact, patent-medicine makers were early exploiters of newspaper and billboard advertising and among the first to trade on image above product,[9] by a range of promotional activities and related merchandising. By the late 1890s, Coca-Cola was being claimed in the States as the 'national drink'.[10]

Aside from the growth of advertising, other channels for branded goods were developing, and retail outlets developed into brands in themselves. Large multiple stores, such as Woolworths and J. C. Penney's in America and Thomas Lipton's stores in Britain, began to standardise the quality of service in their outlets. British companies W. H. Smith and John Menzies took control of a network of railway-

station news-stands. Mail Order giants like Montgomery Ward and Sears, Roebuck offered American consumers the opportunity to purchase the same goods regardless of location. All of these companies, founded in the 1870s, 1880s and 1890s, are among the major national (and sometimes international) brand-name retailers today.

Promotion of branded items often focussed on the lifestyle attributes of the product: health, beauty or social status. Goods and their messages contributed to the establishment of popular concepts of self-identity and individualism. In his history of American advertising, Jackson Lears has argued that advertising by the early twentieth century had become 'dominated by the ethos of personal efficiency'.[11] Perfectionism, both physiological and psychological, was inculcated into its messages.[12] Advertising was just one of the mechanisms that helped brands to succeed in establishing the association of physical and social ideas with particular brands. Beauty brands, for example, benefitted from the range of promotional and distribution channels for goods: 'By 1880 a spider's web of establishments – pharmaceutical houses, perfumers, beauty salons, drugstores, wholesale suppliers, the incipient mail order trade, and the

Top: Tradecard of Mowbray
& Son, Tea Dealers & Grocers,
High Street, Newport,
1850-1900.
Above: Tradecard of Hope
Insurance Company, Ludgate
Hill, by John Girton,
1800-1825.

department stores – provided the infrastructure for beauty culture.'[13] Female entrepreneurs such as Helena Rubinstein and Elizabeth Arden established companies that grew into international brands by the mid-twentieth century.

Although we may associate the idea of globalisation in business with the information culture of the late twentieth century, many companies were operating transnationally by the early twentieth century. Coca-Cola resisted international expansion for some time, only agreeing to a European venture in the 1920s,[14] and found different degrees of difficulty in establishing their brand in other countries. Ford began with exporting cars to Britain from America but quickly moved to set up a production plant in Manchester as early as 1911.[15] The prominence of brand names at international expositions in the late nineteenth and early twentieth century contributed to the transnational recognition of some companies. Citroën's 'branding' of the Eiffel Tower at the International Exposition des Arts Décoratifs in Paris in 1925 may well have contributed to the consumer perception of Citroën as not only a manufacturer but also an embodiment of Frenchness.

But at some point in the twentieth century branding became pervasive. The maintenance of brand image and value was the driving force for producers and brand-owners and national – even global – brand names came to dominate local markets. In the post-war West, against the backdrop of the Cold War, to be an active participant in a consumer society became increasingly regarded as a basic human right. The idea of citizenship becomes framed around the idea of consumership and this 'redefinition of rights and obligations articulated itself in the seemingly innocuous language of soft drinks, cars and household appliances'.[16] Critics of this materialist society also tended to see 'Americanisation' as the driving force behind such consumer demands. We may classify this post-war society as the apogee of consumer culture, but the origins of such social and business practices can be traced back much further.

Changes in retail practices and relations in the eighteenth century in Britain heralded the rise of

branded goods. But in Britain, as in other European countries, the full development of branding was inhibited until the later nineteenth century by the absence of legislative protection against piracy for trademarks, packaging and the like. The shift from barter to fixed pricing, the increasing use of advertising and even the embryonic use of the 'brand' as an assurance of quality can be found in late eighteenth-century Europe.[17] Tobacco branding, to give just one example, evolved from the use of trade cards, first used by tobacco merchants in the seventeenth century. In the early nineteenth century, some tobacco importers differentiated their products using different brand names.[18] Trade cards for wholesalers, importers, retailers and service businesses, although not brand names, used descriptive imagery to embody the practices and promises of their trade.

There is certainly evidence for the emergence of retail brands, as opposed to branded products, prior to the mid-nineteenth century. Consumers were more likely to identify goods with the retailer or distributor than with the manufacturer, with the exception of some early manufacturer brands such as Wedgwood. In 1780s' Paris a fashionable and expensive boutique, Le Petit Dunkerque, sold goods at fixed prices and promoted the shop's good name as a kind of brand so that, 'as with today's designer jeans, the label on his goods was more important to his customers than the products themselves'.[19] Wide-scale distribution was well established in Britain by the eighteenth century, as was a consumer taste for novelty and an increasing diversity of product ranges, such as in printed fabrics. The development of new marketing and advertising strategies such as handbills, newspaper advertisements and other promotional activities was underway. However, this is a long way from 'the extensive advertising of branded products characteristic of the end of the nineteenth century, or the concern with the mental processes of the consumer, with empathy and therapy, that has become widespread in advertisements by the mid-twentieth century'.[20] The idea of modern branding had yet to emerge.

As historian and anthropologist James Carrier has

pointed out,[21] until the late 1800s consumers were unlikely to associate goods with the name of the manufacturer, importer or distributor. Goods were more likely to be thought of in terms of the retailer or the place of origin – French lace, Scotch whisky and so on. Retailers had traditionally traded in loose dry, fresh and cured goods, blending, weighing, bottling and wrapping purchases on the premises. Increasingly, manufacturers or importers started to package their own goods, standardising the size of purchases in paper parcels, jars and later tins. This was partly due to the rise of regulation, which fuelled the perception among consumers that packaged and tinned goods were cleaner and protected from impurities. The US Food & Drug Administration, for example, was established in 1906 to regulate corporations selling such goods. Regulation also meant that large and profitable enterprises could flourish, less hampered by rivals with inferior products.

Packaging also allowed manufacturers to standardise pricing, rather than leaving it to the retailer (thus ensuring a regularised percentage of profits, too). As packaging became more distinctive, shoppers learnt to distinguish goods by their brand name and ask for them by brand. According to a survey of Chicago grocers in 1920, more than three-quarters of their customers asked for baked beans by brand name.[22] In a more mobile society, the reliability of finding a familiar brand in stores all over America compensated for the increasing anonymity of shopping. It also meant that retailers began to stock more than one brand of sugar, tea, cereal and so on, so that packaging had to compete on the shelves. Dry goods were more likely to be packaged initially – particularly tea, coffee, spices, sugar and soap. Among the first, and still familiar, brands were Bovril, Cadbury, Rowntree and Oxo.[23] The packaging of butter, ham and other cured foodstuffs started soon after 1900.[24]

As pre-wrapped merchandise eclipsed loose goods, so the role of the retailer changed too. Pre-packaged cigarettes had emerged in Britain in the 1880s with the launch of brands such as Woodbines, and by the 1930s the cigarette dominated the tobacco retail market. The tobacconist, who had once been the purveyor of an assurance of quality to the consumer, now found this role increasingly being played by the brand:[25]

The brand became the new expression of assurance. It laid the foundation for the modern confidence of the purchaser when buying commodities which he could neither try nor test before use. This applies in particular to articles for which a guarantee is given; the branded article means, more or less, a direct relationship between the consumer and the producer.

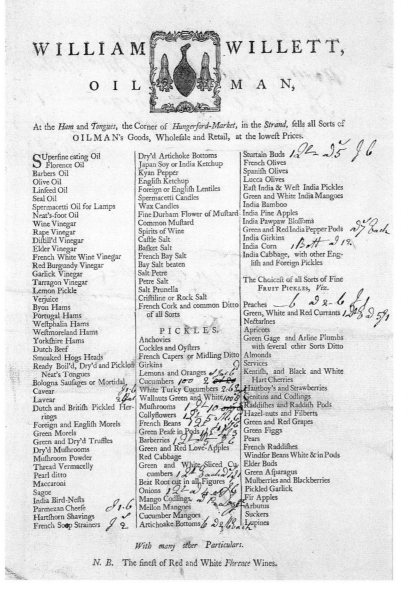

Right: Advertisement for a grocer. William Willett, Oilman's goods, At the Ham and Tongues, the Corner of Hungerford Market, in the Strand, sells all sorts of Oilman's goods, Wholesale and Retail, at the lowest prices: 4 May 1765.

Willings
BESSEMER
gave us
Steel
Give me
OXO
GTH LIKE THAT
NESTLÉ'S
MILK
RICHEST IN CREAM

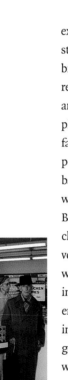

Many of the early food and drink brands that still exist today came from strongly paternalistic company structures. Company philosophy was equivalent to brand values, and the advertising slogans tended to reflect this. The names of Kellogg, Cadbury, Rowntree and Mars are associated with the kind of company philosophy that embraced puritan ideals, conservative family values and moderation in all things (except perhaps profit). These, and other early brand owners, based their company behaviour upon issues such as worker welfare and education, health and temperance. Benign organisations, which formed their own worker clubs, schools and social events, tended also to be vociferous opponents of trade unionism and organised worker politics. Ford, Rowntree and Cadbury all invested in education, welfare and housing for employees and their families. Health and goodness, in fact, were frequent early selling points for branded goods, trading on the concerns of shoppers, which were in turn fuelled by an increasingly visible system of regulation. Soft drinks, cigarettes and chocolate often carried the association of being 'good for you'. The Mars Bar slogan 'helps you work, rest and play'

is a variation on a message that had been sold with the product since the 1930s. Forrest Mars Snr, who arrived from the States to set up a confectionery company in England in 1932, marketed his new product to appeal to a depression-hit society that was wary of indulgence. The Mars Bar was therefore promoted as a nutritional product.[26] The consistency of such messages gives these early brands a common identity: they all aimed to inspire trust and loyalty, the first principles of branding.

From the 1930s onwards, almost inevitably beginning in America, as Aaron Betsky points out in 'All the World's a Store', the supermarket became one of the main locations for engagement with the brand. Like its older sibling, the department store, the supermarket created a retail environment where the shopper could look without buying and enter without prejudice. Unlike the department store, the supermarket's image was one of utility, with 'a vaunted lack of display: here it is, nothing fancy, no extras'.[27] Packaged goods could vie with one another on the shelves for the shoppers' attention. The advent of the shopping trolley and self-service meant that the

shopper would select her goods (it almost invariably was 'her') without the direct intervention of the sales assistant. Over-the-counter purchases meant that the 'eye-appeal' of a product or package was less significant. Once in the supermarket, however, the package had to do the work of the shopkeeper and make the sale. Faced with an array of choices, the well-known brand name is a constant upon which the shopper would rely. It is a means of making the choice on behalf of the shopper. Therefore, 'Kellogg's cornflakes' or 'Heinz baked beans' offer reassurance.

The association of the brand name with the product turns the purchase into an engaging experience – packaged with the cornflakes is the promise that this is the authentic product. It carries a feeling of reliability and communicates a sense of care to the family. Advertising, of course, plays on the knowledge that choices made when shopping for the family are bound up with both fear and love.[28]

These are the messages that carry through all the channels for engagement with the brand. Billboards, TV and radio advertising, product placement and

status, desire, fear and need, condensing more complex thoughts into short signals that can be read instantly from a billboard or in moments from a television commercial. It relies upon a vocabulary of emotional triggers that can be commonly understood: art, nature and classical music are reliable indicators of the mood of a certain ad and product. Humour, celebrity endorsement or the use of 'real people' are other well-known narrative strategies. What can not be determined is the range of responses to ads. We may understand the message and the associations, but a level of more personal association is likely finally to determine our response. We may enjoy the ad, admire it, laugh at it, discuss it, but still not buy the product. Consuming the ad may even enable us to have the product experience without needing to consume the product. As Patrick Barwise, Andrea Dunham and Mark Ritson propose in 'Ties That Bind', advertising is a weaker force than we imagine. Particularly with household goods and consumables, the advertisement presumes a prior relationship to the well-known brand and tends to focus on keeping the brand name in consumers' minds.

The package and the ad are not the only outward manifestations of brand value. Brand owners often seek to control the experience of engaging with the brand and encourage us to see purchase as only one aspect of the 'brand experience'. Brand values are also played out in the service offered by companies, and the places in which we encounter brands. Indeed, retail environments are now so completely dominated by the signs of branding that the formal architecture of such spaces disappears, a point expanded upon by Aaron Betsky in 'All the World's a Store'. The creation of brand-specific environments – from NikeTown to Disneyland – is an indication of this. A clearly definable shift in advertising has been the move from a product-centred message (ads that outline the purposive benefits of the product) to an experience-centred message (ads that determine a relationship between the brand and a perceived lifestyle, by association).[31] Guy Julier suggests in his snapshot piece (p. 148) that the emphasis in branding is shifting 'from object to experience', so that our time,

endorsement are all conduits for reinforcing the value of the brand. Advertising is often seen as an alchemic process, taking our emotional weaknesses and fashioning them into demands and desires for goods. The development of the advertising industry and its corollary, marketing, is generally assumed to be based on the dominant American model of the 1950s. In Britain, large American advertising agencies moved in to control a vast proportion of the industry during that decade.[29] As Gareth Williams suggests in chapter five 'The Point of Purchase', totemic publications such as Vance Packard's *The Hidden Persuaders* (1957) confirmed the view that the advertisers and marketers were the key agents of change in the post-war society and the architects of what Tibor Scitovsky called 'the joyless economy'.[30]

Much more recently, studies of advertising have presented it as a polysemous process, where there is a diversity of readings and responses, rather than the manipulator–victim relationship between advertiser–consumer implied by early critics. Advertising makes use of already established codes of

ARMANI

eau pour homme

as well as our goods, is becoming branded.

Brands are 'designed' in a multitude of ways, and this is part of the branding process. Products, whether sportswear or electronic goods, can have the brand values of the company literally 'built-in'. Just as the process of designing is not simply styling but also development and innovation, so branding is not just the addition of a company's logo or corporate colours to a designed product. Some branding is, of course, just that, when unbranded goods are bought and repackaged with the brand name, but this tends to be seen as a relatively unsuccessful example of brand development in the long term. However, when the brand company develops new products, either designed in house or by consultants, the brand image is of significant importance to that development.

Brand image had become so central to the success of a product that it is now as important if not more so than product innovation.[32] In fact, the relationship of product, marketing and branding is so close that it becomes impossible to distinguish the character of an object from that of its branded image – they are one and the same.[33] The design of the product is actually a vehicle for brand value, rather than the other way around. Rather than brands existing to sell more of a product, products are developed as a means of extending and consolidating the brand. A good example of this is the relationship between the couture collections produced by designers for established fashion houses, and the success of house fragrances and cosmetics. The publicity garnered by the seasonal couture collections is crucial for the sales of branded merchandising, which may have little to do with the designer or the fashion house itself: what counts is the name.

This is not to say that companies do not invest in design and product development, as many clearly do. A branded company will tend to develop goods that have a clear relationship to their brand image. Tracking the histories of established industries, one usually finds the reason for a line of development lies in manufacturing knowledge and technical ability. Nokia, the Finnish telecommunications company, has its roots in three nineteenth-century industries:

paper making, rubber and synthetics and the manufacture of cables for telegraph and telephone networks. Outside of Finland, the brand has achieved global recognition only in the last decade, and its origins are largely unknown.

Consumer-goods companies with a strong brand image and awareness often move into areas of product development where the brand values carry across successfully. Richard Branson's empire, Virgin, has tested out the strength of its brand value on everything from clothing to mortgages. When moving into areas of business activity where it has no previous experience, Virgin is relying upon the image of Branson as 'the consumer's friend' who brings personality to faceless industries and business practices. The success of the Virgin brand is firmly tied to the cult of personality. What Branson offers is a specific character of service and a reputation for challenging authoritative brands (for instance, his public battles with British Airways). Virgin makes ironic use of the 'rules' of branding as part of its brand image; when Virgin cola was first launched, the company parodied the myth that the famous 1930s' Coca-Cola bottle was based on the voluptuous curves of Mae West. Virgin produced a similar curved plastic bottle, coloured red, and christened it the 'Pammy', after surgically enhanced *Baywatch* star Pamela Anderson.

Corporations are now more than ever involved in the manipulation and control of image, over and above the production of 'real' things. Sociologist Don Slater has characterised contemporary culture as 'the domination of information, media and signs, the disaggregation of social structure into lifestyles, the general priority of consumption over production in everyday life and the constitution of identities and interests'.[34] This is the idea that we all engage in 'lifestyles' literally fashioned from commodities and forms of entertainment and information gathering, rather than from more traditional providers of identity such as family and work, religious and political belief. As goods take on this greater symbolic function in our lives, so their aesthetic content increases. The roles of the image-makers, including designers, ad agencies and

brand managers, take centre stage. Consuming is defined as a more romantic, hedonistic and emotional act. The product is promoted as a 'sign of me' – a signal to others of our status, aspiration or personal values. This is what has been called 'the aestheticisation of everyday life'.[35] Contemporary society is 'saturated' with images and signs, where the aesthetic and symbolic appearance of goods becomes the primary means of everyday experience. The prime role of commodities becomes to express emotional and symbolic value – as signs to be decoded by ourselves and others. Branding is one of the processes by which products become signs. A pair of jeans becomes associated with youthful sex appeal, or a particular bar of chocolate signals the exotic.

Two 1999 ad campaigns present a very literal view of the symbolic properties of objects and their function as indicators of status and fashion. The campaign for the IBM ThinkPad shows the product on a clothes hanger and the Nokia 8810 mobile phone is photographed variously in a perfume bottle, sunglasses case or shown as a powder compact. Both ads employ the qualities of perfume or cosmetics ads – sparse white background, photographed in a way that indicates the casing of the object is somehow 'precious' and stylish. Both campaigns were run in the lifestyle press. Although no person is shown with the products, the implication is that these items are about adornment rather than utility. They are to be worn on the body, like make-up or clothing. A marked tendency in current advertising is to associate a wide diversity of products with the fashion system, so that all goods are seen as 'accessories' to our lifestyle or personality. Signs of sexual or emotional gratification are often used, for example, to advertise everything from ice cream to cat food. Branded products are used to signify our emotional relationships to those around us: friends, families, pets.

We are encouraged by advertisers and the media to see the acquisition of goods as a means to constructing a social persona, and we are all likely to make certain high-risk purchases at certain times as a means of sending signals to others. A sleek and expensive car is a pretty straightforward indication of wealth and career success. In choosing from the bracket of executive cars, however, the signalling becomes more complex. Two cars in the same price range may be associated with very different values, such as successful sex appeal or reliable family values. Volvo is a car that has variable brand associations – a residual image as rather staid, dull and kindly, and a newer brasher one that has been stressed in the ad campaigns for several years. The success of Volvo currently implies that the second brand image is being received and understood, but the residual one is still evident.

Stuart Ewen has called the appropriation of personality by the acquisition of goods 'the assembling of the commodity self'.[36] American artist Barbara Kruger, whose work deals with the relationship between identity and consumerism, expressed this in more ironic terms with her phrase 'I shop therefore I am.' The reading of character through personal goods is the staple practice of a good deal of advertising and also magazine editorial, with features on celebrity shopping habits, favourite car brands, designer labels and even the contents of famous refrigerators. American beer label Schlitz parodied this in its press advert featuring a rummage through celebrity dustbins and the tagline 'You are what you trash.' As Celia Lury has commented: 'Is garbage, the husks of a personal selection of consumer goods, to be understood as a self portrait?'[37]

Although undoubtedly consumption is bound up with a sense of self and group identity, it is not simply enough to think that commodities are a way of telling others about ourselves. Objects do communicate certain accepted social truths, but as the British Conservative Party leader William Hague demonstrated when he wore a baseball cap to the (predominantly Afro-Caribbean) Notting Hill Carnival in London, the signals may be different to those we wish to send out. Hague's appearance at the Carnival was an exercise in the acquisition of what French sociologist Pierre Bourdieu has termed 'cultural capital'. By associating himself with some signs of 'hip' and youthful popular culture, and with an event that is seen, in cultural and racial terms, as highly 'authentic', Hague should have made political capital

out of his actions. Instead, his behaviour was ridiculed in the press, and Hague's projected, personal 'brand' image went somewhat awry.

The use of branded goods to send signals to others is rarely as self-conscious as it might appear. We tend to imbue branded goods with a significance that is out of proportion to their everydayness. Take the sight of President Clinton giving testimony during the 1998 investigation into his relationship with Monica Lewinsky. The President sipped from a can of Diet Coke, an act that was analysed in detail by the world's media almost instantaneously. The President is known for his love of junk food, and the sight of the packaging (rather than a glass) could be taken as a sign of his 'ordinary Joe' Americanness. But Diet Coke rather than ordinary Coke? Some saw this as a sign of emasculation, others as a sign of penitence. In choosing a low-calorie drink, the President perhaps unwittingly presented the world with an image of pleasures denied, a form of calorific sobriety.

The idea that goods act as a kind of language is a precarious one.[38] First of all, the assembling of commodities in one place or on one person is not like constructing a sentence, as there is no apparent grammar. There is rarely a consensus about what is 'in fashion' and 'out of fashion' among more than very selective groupings of people.[39] Branding is an attempt to fix the codes attached to certain goods and to make for a more reliable form of communication. However, once control over the reception of the branded message is lost, the brand itself is weakened. The recent and on-going controversy in Britain over 'grey goods' was more than simply an argument about profit

and loss – it was a battle for control over brand image. Two large supermarket chains, Tesco and Asda, began stocking 'designer brands' at discount prices. The goods on sale were legitimately purchased but from sources other than the brand owners. Genuine label goods, bought at end-of-line ranges, could then be sold at much lower cost than in the 'brand-sanctioned' outlets. However, the availability of discounted brand names on supermarket shelves might be seen to devalue an established luxury brand.

The significance of branded goods to our concept of lifestyle is dependent upon a speedy turnover of product types and brand innovations. Fuelled by flexible systems of goods production and circulation, manufacturing is increasingly responsive to fluctuations of taste and meaning within the market and is, in turn, able to promote fluctuations in order to increase turnover. In the 1950s and 1960s, as Gareth Williams describes in 'The Point of Purchase', critics of industry argued against what they saw as 'planned obsolescence' in consumer goods, against products that were deliberately designed only to last several years. Planned obsolescence is now more applicable to the meaning rather than the functioning of the object. Signs are increasingly unstable and more quickly superseded by new ones than ever before.

The shift from a production- to a consumption-oriented economy is indicative of this. Increasingly, branded companies place the emphasis on service and marketing, rather than on manufacture, which is clear from a look at the 'image industries' involved in the production of highly symbolic goods. In the early years of mass production, producers looked to forge new markets and demands for their products. Production systems were more rigid, and tooling and assembly relatively inflexible. Developing standardised products for mass markets and driving down prices to make goods more attractive were the core aims of most manufacturers. The American mass market was built on this method, as were the beginnings of the Japanese 'economic miracle' after the Second World War. However, Japan was able to develop a more flexible and adaptable system of production, which kept better pace with changes in consumer behaviour and

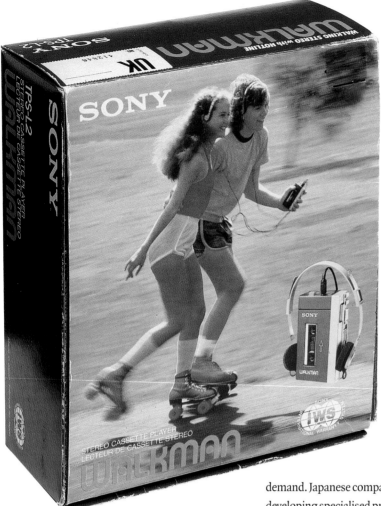

demand. Japanese companies had great success from developing specialised products for niche markets, or generating new market demands, with products such as the Sony Walkman.

In the 1970s, when many large-scale industries foundered due to their cumbersome and inflexible structures, some smaller-scale ones found their ability to adapt made them able to respond to shifts in niche market demand. As economic historians Piore and Sabel have described it 'the spread of flexible specialisation amounts to a revival of craft forms of production.'[40] The practice of flexible specialisation means the production of short-run, specialised goods, often with a high design content. It often develops around an interdependent community network of similar producers, suppliers and creative industries. This in turn supports a community of skilled workers and ensures that the required expertise, materials and

technologies are on hand. Often with a high level of 'crafting' or skill involved in the creation of products, such companies tend to be in the 'luxury goods' bracket. In Italy, the manufacture of home wares, furniture, ceramics, leather goods and other 'lifestyle' products works according to this system. Alessi is perhaps the best example of a local company with global brand recognition. These Italian industries may be the result of a centuries-old tradition of manufacture in the region, but flexible specialisation does not always refer to the transformation of existing forms of production. The same model can also be applied to two localities for production in California. 'Silicon Valley', so called for its predominance of electronics and information technology industries, and Hollywood, the home of the film and entertainment industry. Both rely upon a network of highly specialised and skilled producers, and a supporting community of creative talents. Both are also outstandingly successful in the art of brand management and image creation.

As markets for new consumer goods became saturated, and demand more sophisticated, specialised and fragmented, so the emphasis on production changed too. Nowadays, manufacturing is characterised by the high level of out-sourcing, where companies no longer own the means of production but sub-contract or buy in from other manufacturers. By maintaining a flexible production or service base, shorter life cycles for goods and constant (but low-cost) product innovation, companies maintain a dynamic image. Often, this innovation will concentrate on marketing, advertising and styling alone. Mass customisation refers to the greater range of product or service variants that companies now offer. When purchasing a car or a mobile phone, for example, the range of 'optional extras' may be such that the customer feels that he or she is creating a unique product from the characteristics on offer. Mass customisation also employs the device of offering 'special' limited editions that are a variation on the basic purchase. The 'theming' of items by fast-food outlets to tie in with a major film release (usually children's cartoons) is a good example of this.

A dominant model of brand behaviour has been termed 'McDonaldisation' after the global fast-food chain. Whilst McDonald's may appear at first as a paradigm of mass production and standardisation – the Henry Ford of Hamburgers – it is an organisation capable of rapid and continuous innovation. On one level, uniforms, recipes, interior architecture and the character of service are similar across the world. The 'Big Mac' has become an economist's unit of value to analyse the difference in the economic status of nations. McDonald's is based on a system of franchising restaurants, where the parent company owns the brand values but not the real estate. McDonald's also create local products for different locations – the infamous 'Maharajah Big Mac' in India or the 'McTeryaki Burger' in Japan. As Russell Belk explains in 'Wolf Brands in Sheep's Clothing'

(pp. 68-9), global brands such as McDonald's nurture their relationship to a particular locality in a number of ways, in order to become 'naturalised'. To quote Edward Rensi, President of McDonald's USA: 'People have a vision of McDonald's being identical in 12,000 restaurants.... We've got products in Texas that we don't have in Boston. There's a lot going on at McDonald's all the time.'[41]

The stereotype of the modern consumer lifestyle is set against a backdrop of global culture. Terms such as 'globalism' and 'globalisation' abound in any discussion of brands and branded consumer goods, and the mythological power of these terms needs addressing. One assumption is that 'über-brands' such as Coca-Cola and McDonald's have achieved such a global penetration of the market that one can almost expect to encounter them on a Himalayan

Opposite: Packaging for Sony Walkman, c. 1979.
Right: McDonald's, Shanghai, 1999.

mountain pass or a military base camp in the Antarctic. A second assumption is that globalisation is an entirely new phenomenon, borne out of late twentieth-century cultural and economic shifts, rather than a longer historical process. In fact, it can be argued that the roots of modern globalisation can be found in the early fifteenth century, and that the most dramatic period of global expansion, until now, covered the years 1880–1925.[42] That period, which saw the setting up of the first global competitions such as the Olympics, was also a fertile period for the establishment of today's most familiar brands, including BMW, ICI and HMV.

Despite these precedents, however, it seems we are now more self-conscious about our place in a globalised culture than before. Since Marshall McLuhan's influential concept of the 'global village' first appeared in the 1960s,[43] the idea of an homogenised global culture has been seen as one of the chief characteristics of the late twentieth century. Signs of cultural homogeneity include the rapid advance of new technologies such as the Internet, allowing near instantaneous communication across the globe. The international language of brand names and branded goods, and the presence of Microsoft or McDonald's in towns and cities from Calcutta to Cincinnati, support the view that we are all citizens of a single, Americanised and commodified culture.

Brands are the signifiers of this vision of contemporary culture, with Coca-Cola, McDonald's, Versace, Gucci, Nike and Tommy Hilfiger presented as icons of a homogenised international language of goods. In the global village, shopping, eating and entertainment are products packaged identically in any high street, mall or entertainment park. In the words of one cultural commentator: 'Eclecticism is the degree zero of contemporary general culture: one listens to reggae, watches a western, eats McDonald's food for lunch and local cuisine for dinner, wears Paris perfume in Tokyo and "retro" clothes in Hong Kong.'[44] The brand acts as quality control, reassuring us that a hamburger in Moscow will be the same as in Manchester. Globalisation, it seems, offers the kind of market saturation of which corporations once only dreamed and suggests the domination of market forces over all other cultural practices.

Whereas advertisers present an image of the modern consumer as unfettered global traveller, free to pick and choose from a range of lifestyles, the reality of our everyday lives is very different, and in a series of scenarios we should consider some of the implications of the 'globalised experience'. First of all, the process of globalisation has to be observed through what has been called 'the prism of the local'.[45] Local contexts and local consequences all offer variations on the experience of the global paradigm. In fact, the abstract concept of a truly globalised experience is a construct of advertising alone. All our experiences of global culture, whether through community life, media or travel, are tempered by the local context of ourselves and others.

Furthermore, instead of creating homogeneity, it can be argued that globalisation promotes and sustains difference and plurality in everyday experience. Anthropologist Arjun Appadurai has described this as a series of imaginary landscapes, where our view depends upon our location within that landscape.[46] These landscapes are formed by ethnicity, by technology, by finance, media and ideologies. Popular culture (as the primary form of contemporary expression) feeds off the intrusion of different cultural forms. Pop music, with its borrowing, sampling and recycling, is the best example of how imported tastes are indigenised, creating new and different forms. The new global cultural economy, according to Appadurai, 'has to be seen as a complex, overlapping, disjunctive order'.

The interweaving of global and local contexts is made more possible by developing networks of data and communication. The expansion of telecommunications means that different kinds of information can be transported across the globe in an instant (voices, text, pictures, sounds and moving images). These means of communication are also increasingly more cheaply available to a wider range of people. Contact between communities of people, between families, ethnic groups, shared-interest groups and so on can be maintained on a daily basis.

This can even mean the creation of 'virtual' communities. As people become more mobile and migratory while staying in contact across distances, there is a greater tendency to view the world as a single place. This shift to a global perspective has been called 'space–time compression'[47] and results in nation-state borders and institutions becoming less significant in people's worldview.

Rather than talk of a global culture, it is therefore more appropriate to talk of global flows and global relations – suggesting the fluidity and diversity that globalisation encompasses. However, this should not be taken as a utopian view. The late twentieth century has witnessed the rise of religious fundamentalism alongside the decline of nation-state frameworks. Social mobility and the migration of populations are more often enforced or reluctant than the result of personal choice. The kinds of compression that result from mobility and technology are not available to everybody – economic and educational factors restrict this to those who have the means to exploit them.

Just as globalisation has prompted new social formations and encounters, so has it affected the production and distribution of goods around the world. Again, this is crucial to an understanding of how branding operates. Few truly global corporations exist. The idea of a multinational company without a preferred geographical locus is hard to imagine. Many companies that operate globally still exhibit the signs of a latent national or cultural specificity. Coca-Cola is inseparable from its carefully nurtured image of the American 'good life' as global exemplar. Microsoft, whose branded interfaces appear on most desktops in the world, is synonymous with its founder, Bill Gates, and spends much legal time fighting allegations of monopolisation on home territory. National legislative controls are used to curb the global freedoms of transnational companies.

There are also few truly global products. Again, both state legislation and cultural differences mean that goods tend to be 'adapted' to suit local conditions. Consumables are produced in localised sites (bottling plants, packaging and assembly sites). There are technical restrictions on producing a homogenised product (think of the difficulties in getting electrical products to work when travelling without adapters). There are language and cultural barriers to instructions and ingredients, as well as sometimes problems with the name of a product. Despite the claims of a few companies, such as the Italian fashion and lifestyle business Diesel, advertising is more likely to be tailored to local conditions than a global advertising campaign used. In the case of multinational advertising agencies, 'there is no tendency towards globalisation in the production and transmission of the ads themselves'.[48] There are far too many different possible readings both between and within social and cultural groupings (consider how assertions of sexuality and female individuality are not acceptable in Muslim cultures).

The only constant, it appears, is the brand itself. Product names and specifications may vary, but the brands of Ford, Unilever, General Motors, Toyota and Sony are global standards. Protecting the value and image of that brand, then, becomes paramount. It is the vehicle for the placing of goods in certain market contexts and niches, and the means of differentiating the product in the absence of a 'home-grown' context. However, as both company and consumer behaviour indicates, brand image is a vulnerable concept, susceptible to social and local interpretation, which can be good or bad for the value of the brand.

The vulnerability of brands means that brand owners invest considerably in consumer research. Patterns, behaviours and preferences are minuted in an attempt to anticipate our purchasing habits.

Unsolicited mail shots are targeted by postal or zip codes, and also by subscriptions and mail ordering. Our choices of newspaper, magazine, bank and supermarket all apparently indicate other kinds of consumer preference, such as the shampoo, washing powder or holiday we might buy. With the advent of digital and pay-per-view television, we are likely to find in the future that TV advertising is tailored more directly to us as individuals. A preference for watching animal programmes and sports channels may mean that the ads that appear most frequently on our screens are for cat food and sportswear.

Our identity as consumers appears to be our chief mode of existence. State and cultural services, government, education and even the law see us as citizen–consumers.[49] Consumer rights organisations, television programmes, advice lines and charters are all signs that the right to purchase is now seen as the means by which we gain representation. Those who can not or choose not to engage with consumer culture might appear disenfranchised.

Yet, as Gareth Williams shows in 'The Point of Purchase', consumption is also politicised. Consumer protests and boycotts, acts of consumer terrorism and subversion, the appropriation of branded goods to convey alternative messages are all powerful ways of communicating political messages to a world primarily focused on consumption. Similarly, there are environments for the exchange of goods that are mediated by the consumer, rather than the brand owner. Barter and labour exchange, second-hand networks, car-boot and jumble sales, children's toy libraries, all form part of an alternative system for exchange and consumption.

Within this map of company and individual allegiances and behaviours the brand acts as chief navigator. It is the vehicle for both corporate messages and personal appropriation, and we go on now to explore the wide diversity of both brand behaviours and consumer interventions. The object of this journey is to assess the cultural significance of branding and look at some of the ways in which brands have been fetishised, eulogised and demonised in recent years.

"The signature is part
of the identity of
a product or brand."

PAOLA ANTONELLI

Signature value

Below left and right: Michael
Graves Design™ Collection
blender and Collection
toaster, both Target Stores,
1999.
Opposite: Good Goods by
Starck.
Following pages: Frank Gehry,
Guggenheim Museum, Bilbao.

Among all the promises that brands make to consumers, the 'signature' of the designer is seen as a particular mark of distinction. Signature and editioned goods are promoted as an alternative to the 'mass market', as they target closely identified audiences and lifestyles. The value of the signature is such that it can represent a contract between the named designer and the consumer, and an endorsement of the goods on sale. The signature is part of the identity of a product or brand.

The development of corporate identities in the twentieth century has involved the creation of distinctive visual devices, logos and colours that can be applied across a wide range of products, packages and locations. In this way designers were being used to create the company signature, rather than 'sign' the goods themselves. Some of the oldest successful examples of corporate-image design like AEG, Olivetti and Campari are European. The integrated designs by Peter Behrens for AEG, which comprised products, buildings and advertising campaigns, spoke the supernational language of neoclassicism. By hiring such artists as the Futurist Fortunato Depero, Campari became a patron of the arts, and its campaigns became awaited cultural events. Olivetti employed renowned Swiss designers of the century as art directors and created a top executive position that dealt with the company's influence on the arts. These three companies, which remain shining examples of corporate communications skills, could invariably count on a smaller and homogeneously sophisticated audience.

Rather than targeting such distinctive audiences, many American designers aimed to create brands identified with universal appeal. Raymond Loewy, for example, engineered identities for some of the most distinctive brands of the century. Loewy's Lucky Strike and Shell brands, much as other designers' Coca-Cola, McDonald's and Levi's, are branding masterpieces, as well as live organisms that to this day employ thousands of designers striving to keep them current and powerful. Branding has also been the key to success for a host of American non-denominational designed goods: those traditional low-cost, everyday objects that carry a brand, like Swingline, Tupperware or Black and Decker, but do not need an established author's name to enter the firmament of good design. At least not in the past.

The demands of consumerism, however, have also changed. Increasingly, brands offer differentiated products designed to particular lifestyle groups. The democratic ideal of the universal product is disappearing. The star system of designers and architects that has emerged in recent years has been particularly noticeable in the American market. The popularity of names of influential twentieth-century figures such as Charles and Ray Eames and Frank Lloyd Wright generates a myriad of merchandising opportunities for, among others, museums. The star system has also encouraged more mainstream manufacturers and retailers to call on the services of living 'celebrity' designers.

In the late 1990s, large American retail companies such as Target, K-mart and 7-11 have revamped their image by signing on celebrities to provide

'quality' products at affordable prices. Philippe Starck, for instance, has designed a range of basic items for the Japanese division of the 7–11 chain, including stationery and personal products, such as toothbrushes and hairbrushes, that retail for less than $10. Martha Stewart, a woman who made her name into a commercial empire, has been involved with K-mart since 1987 as a lifestyle consultant. Two years ago she initiated 'Martha's World', a store within K-mart featuring 'Martha Stewart Everyday' and based on her unmistakable concept of quality and ability to provide her public with an attainable status promotion through their purchases. In 1997, the sales of bath towels alone were forecast at $500 million.

Similarly, the Minnesota-based Target has produced a range of more than 200 products, ranging in price between $3.99 and $479.95, for the home, designed by architect Michael Graves. They were introduced in September 1998 under the slogan 'Michael Graves Targets Everyman'. The common denominator – be it lower or higher – are coquettish petlike shapes and sweet knobs and handles. The collection flew off the shelves. Architects, too, have become brand signatures as exemplified by the use of Richard Meier by the Getty Museum and Frank Gehry by the Guggenheim Museum.

Once again, Americans are succeeding at the game, this time by personalising it. Through a person's eyes, the public learns to notice objects and architecture for what they are – carriers of function, beauty and meaning, personal choices that define each person's universe. Ultimately, the shrewd commercial operation has a positive outcome in our contemporary world, the opposite of a suffocating standard for everyday living. With or without a signature.

> "Some of the methods used by global companies to manage their corporate identities can be usefully taken up to ensure clarity and consistency for the whole corporate image of the UK." *Britain™ Renewing Our Identity*

JONATHAN WOODHAM

A brand new Britain?

During the 1990s both commercial and state-sponsored organisations looked to the idea of branding to create a 'New Britain'. In Mark Leonard's Britain™ *Renewing Our Identity*, a report commissioned by Demos, a left-wing independent think-tank, funded by the British Design Council and published in 1997, the conclusion reached was that Britain's national identity was for most people largely associated with history, heritage and tradition. It was sorely in need of radical rejuvenation.

For much of the twentieth century, official projections of Britain's national identity embraced the past, usually with a strong English inflection. In 1932, writer Stephen Tallents identified Oxford, Bond Street, the English Countryside, the English Home, English servants, gardening and tailoring as essential ingredients of identity. Such retrospection was echoed in many of the displays in British Pavilions at international exhibitions. It was not until Expo '67 in Montreal that much official space was given to the portrayal of dynamic contemporary British culture. Designer James Gardner created an evocation of '60s Britain, featuring a BMC Mini against a Carnaby Street-influenced display of urban chic that was peopled by mannequins dressed in clothes from Mary Quant and Biba.

By the 1990s a number of British companies had found that overt identification with 'Britishness' was rarely advantageous in the global marketplace. British Telecom, which re-branded itself as BT after privatisation in 1984, found that the 'British' label had ceased to be associated with technological expertise. However, not all internationally oriented British companies found the position so straightforward. The most notable commercial re-branding exercise was that of British Airways, which invested in a £60-million corporate facelift in June 1997. Cast aside was the red, white and blue of the 1984 Landor Associates' Union Jack aircraft tail-fins in favour of a series of eye-catching artworks that represented the cultural diversity of the airline's global passengers, ranging from Celtic illumination to Aboriginal designs. The aim was to commission more than 50 world images from artists and designers to appear on 300 aircraft, thus promoting the idea of British Airways as a 'citizen of the world'. However, such global aspirations found little favour with the nationalism of the British public. Indeed, domestic chauvinism asserted itself so strongly that after a mere two years, it was announced in June 1999 that British Airways would once again fly the national flag.

After New Labour swept to power in 1997, an updated version of 'Swinging London' was championed by the new administration. Cultural patriotism assumed a fashionable guise with the advent of 'Cool Britannia,' and the promotion of cutting-edge and popular British fashion, design, arts and music. Indeed, the origins of 'Cool Britannia' may be seen to derive from the 1967 song from the Bonzo Dog Doo-Dah Band's *Gorilla* album ('Cool Britannia/Britannia you are cool/ Take a trip/Britons ever, ever, ever shall be hip'). Britain's then Prime Minister Harold Wilson lost favour with some in the 1960s when he invited the Beatles to his official residence at No. 10 Downing Street. Tony Blair's receptions for media celebrities were similarly criticised as showing a preoccupation with style rather than substance. Not helped by the 1998 launch of Ben & Jerry's 'Cool Britannia' brand of ice cream, New Labour soon began to

Above: Traditional Britain: the Country Set display in the British exhibition at Expo '67, Montreal, designed by James Gardner, figures by Astrid Zydower.
Below: Rebranding Britain in the 1960s – 'Swinging London': the Carnaby Street display in the British exhibition at Expo '67, Montreal, designed by James Gardner.
Opposite: The 1997 re-branding of British Airways.

distance itself from the associations with over-hyped notions of 'Cool Britannia'.

'Cool Britannia' notwithstanding, the Blair government continued in its efforts to re-brand Britain as a dynamic and diverse economy with a wealth of creative talent in design, fashion, science and technology. The powerhouse::uk exhibition in London in 1998, housed in an inflatable pavilion designed by Nigel Coates, was a showcase for creative Britain, including fashion designer Alexander McQueen and products by Tom Dixon and Jasper Morrison among others. Simultaneously the Foreign Office launched Panel 2000, which comprised people 'at the cutting edge of industry, design, the media and the Government itself' whose 'creativity and energy show what modern Britain is about'. The creative industries are still an essential ingredient of a re-branded Britain. Embracing design, fashion, publishing, digital technology, the performing arts and music, this sector was estimated to be worth £60 billion per year, generating £7.5 billion in annual exports and 1.4 million jobs. Millennium Products, another scheme launched by Blair in September 1997, sought to identify and promote ground-breaking products and services created in Britain and feature them in exhibitions and publications around the world until the year 2000 and beyond. The Millennium Dome is perhaps the finale to this reinvention of Britain through design.

The extent to which these and many other initiatives to 're-brand' Britain will succeed remains to be seen. As the new Millennium unfolds it will soon become clear whether such projections of a creative, dynamic and exciting new Britain will influence those in the global marketplaces or whether the weight of history, heritage and tradition will remain the most potent brand of 'Britishness'.

Right: Xenium™ Dual Band
cellular phone.
Far right: Philishave Cool
Skin 620.
Below: Hopper SV10 Virtually
Silent Multimedia Projector.
Opposite: 'Precision' kitchen
scales.

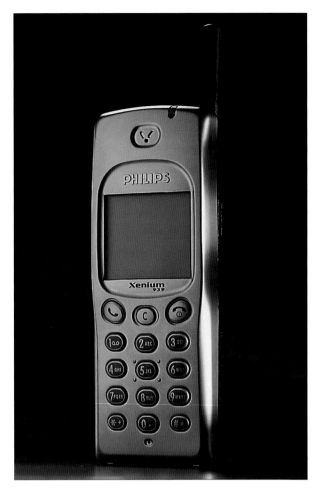

STEFANO MARZANO Philips Design

Branding = Distinctive authenticity

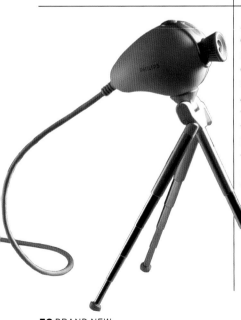

A successful brand is ultimately a question of authenticity. It needs to reflect transparently the values of the company behind it. In this respect, it is not unlike an individual. My name, indeed any name, calls up in the minds of those who know me a certain set of qualities or values. Those associations have been built up over time, abstracted from the totality of their experience with me. If I promise to do something that is in line with those values, they will trust me to carry it out. If it clashes with those values, they will be sceptical.

It is not easy, either as a brand or an individual, to make sure you are authentic in this sense. As individuals, our personalities are composed of a number of values that determine our ethical framework - our self. When these core values govern our behaviour, we are behaving authentically. When one of our sub-personalities gets the upper hand, however, we behave 'out of character'. This unbalanced state can occur by accident, but it can also be deliberately induced, as when we put up a façade, behaving in accord with values that do not belong to our core. Such situations become untenable.

People

How does the company make sure that there is a perfect match between values and behaviour? Products, buildings and machines - even ideas - can be copied, but the only unique elements in a company are its people. They constitute

the soul of the brand. The first step to creating brand authenticity is therefore to ensure that its core values are clear and have been fully internalised by those who work within the company. That is not to say everyone has to be identical - that would be impossible and undesirable. But there should be certain values that they share as part of their own core values.

Role of Design

Our primary role at Philips Design is to create the aesthetic of the values behind the Philips brand. Given the enormous range of products that bear the name and the many countries around the world where they are sold, we can only do our task if we have properly internalised the company's core values. Of course, we can - and do - try to lay down guidelines for

"A successful
brand is ultimately
a question of
authenticity."

designing packaging, say, to make sure that wherever they are produced they reflect the right values. But rules only take us so far: general principles are better, and internalised ones are better still, because they ensure the right decisions are taken automatically in new situations. Such principles or values give us a touchstone to help us produce any brand expressions that are consistent and authentically reflect those values. This applies at all levels, from decisions on product features and form language, to packaging, advertising and displays – everything, in fact, that brings the brand into contact with the consumer.

The role of design in representing the brand is greater than ever before. Technologies are increasingly shared among companies, so that the real differentiating factor is the way technology is shaped. This is more than a question of styling. To design is to shape the future. The Italian for design is *progetto*, or *architettura* - project, or architecture. These expressions clearly convey how design gives physical shape to ideas that will affect people's lives. Viewed in this way, design is a continuous attempt to create future civilisation – no small undertaking.

Continuity
The set of values that forms the self takes shape over time. The same applies to a company: its values do so as a result of the values of the individuals who work there, particularly those who guide it. In the autobiography of Frits Philips, the son

of one of the founders and a former chairman, the personal principles of the Philips family can be clearly discerned – from their refusal to buy black market food during the German occupation to their support of the first collective labour agreement with the unions. And then to the inclusion (decades before others got round to it) of a statement of the company's responsibility to society in its articles of association - what is now called 'stewardship'.

In many respects, Frits Philips was very much a 'people's industrialist'. His values were the universal ones of civilisation. Although they remain constant, the way in which they are applied at different periods and in different circumstances varies. In his day, during and after a

devastating war, the main needs of people were those relating to the lower rungs of Maslow's scale: food, shelter, work. Today, in our age of relative prosperity, Frits Philips would be a 'cultural industrialist', an agent of the future whose objective is to advance people's self-actualisation, to enhance their cultural well-being, by creating ways of helping them towards the highest levels of Maslow's hierarchy.

This is what we at Philips Design are aiming at today, and I hope that by internalising core values we will be able to do so in the same spirit – though in different form – as our predecessors at the company. To me, this continuity of core values is what constitutes the essence of successful brand design.

Brand associations through advertising

This page and opposite: Levi's 'Original Levi's' campaign, August–November 1996. Published in magazines including *The Face, i-D, Dazed & Confused, Sky, Arena* and *FHM*. Photographer: Nick Knight; Stylist: Simon Foxton; Casting: Jason Evans and Stefan Ruiz; Concept creators: Steve Hudson and Victoria Fallon.

Brands that aim for mass-market appeal nevertheless also target more narrowly identified market sectors through localised campaigns. Such campaigns might employ a more unconventional brand image, but one that is still in keeping with the core values and image of the brand in question. In 1996 Steve Hudson and Victoria Fallon at the UK-based BBH advertising agency were given the role of concept creators for the British magazine advertising for Levi's original jeans. Their brief was a campaign that would authenticate the brand's 145-year heritage as the original workwear-jeans manufacturer and clearly distinguish Levi's from long-term market rivals and the growing number of new jeans brands. The aim of the campaign became to trade on the idea of 'age' and authenticity, using older models in the context of youth-oriented advertising. In broader terms, it was felt this idea held the potential to highlight attitudes to ageing within the fashion and advertising industry. Such a campaign would also create a more radical edge to Levi's well-established brand image.

British photographer Nick Knight was chosen to work on the campaign. Knight had not worked for a 'high street' brand before, and his commercial image making had been for the editorial pages of magazines and campaigns for fashion designers including Yohji Yamamoto and Jil Sander. Knight said in interview:

What I was getting frustrated about was that I work with my heart, using real feelings that take into account the world around me. There was a division between the work that I was producing of supposedly beautiful women in supposedly beautiful clothes doing supposedly beautiful things and real contemporary issues. The Levi's project was the first time that I was being paid to have a social agenda to my work.

While the setting for the ad played on the traditional associations of the Levi's brand with the American cowboy, the approach to the subject was highly unconventional for fashion advertising. The proposed campaign was not market tested by BBH, and as Hudson acknowledges: 'I think that if they had asked young kids they would have said, "I don't want to see some old people in Levi's," and blown the idea out.'

Jason Evans and Stefan Ruiz undertook the casting for the campaign over a six-week period in Colorado. Their search centred on the senior rodeo circuit. Ironically, the rodeo had been sponsored by Levi's competitor brand, Wranglers, since the early post-war period. Well aware that the American West had been a rich source for American photographers throughout the twentieth century, the team set out to reflect the grandeur of the Midwest in both the choice of models and setting. Knight wanted to explore some of the issues around the conventional representation of the American West. The significance of Afro-American cowboys, who made up one third of cowboys in the nineteenth century, but whose history has remained relatively hidden, was one area highlighted by the campaign.

The fashion shoot took place over a period of a week in Colorado. Simon Foxton, who has played an important role in the shaping of the identity of Levi's during the 1990s, styled the shoot with a minimal approach. The models brought their own clothing and props, which were mixed with items collected by him. Knight used a large-format camera positioned low with the models posed on a platform in front of a neutral white backdrop. In the printing process, this backdrop was given a stylised coloration of the high, flat plains of Colorado. Although the staging of the shoot was carefully planned, there were last-minute changes such as the inclusion

"In a society where we don't need another pair of jeans or trainers, there is very little chance to redress this unless you give your work a political angle."

of the only female model in the campaign, Josephine. The ambiguity of age in fashion imagery is especially apparent in the casting of this female model.

The media response to the Levi's' original jeans campaign moved beyond the more typical appraisal of technical and aesthetic accomplishment to focus on the social issue that the campaign raised. It was flagged as the start of a re-evaluation of the way advertising portrays older people in light of an ageing and affluent population of consumers. It was also credited as the most influential mainstream fashion campaign to politicise its overt and central narrative. The campaign was produced within a climate of growing popular desire to see our commercial image making, our collective fantasies, reflect real social concerns. As Nick Knight says: "It felt like I was engaging with people. In a society where we don't need another pair of jeans or trainers, there is very little chance to redress this unless you give your work a political angle. Fashion photography is by its very definition shallow but in a good sense - it can be changed. "

JANE PAVITT

Diesel
for successful branding?

The Italian fashion and lifestyle brand Diesel was launched in 1978. Beginning life as a jeans and clothing company, the Diesel brand has grown to include licensed fashion goods such as eyewear, footwear and scent, and a distinctive and subversive advertising campaign. Diesel is now a global brand, retailing in over 80 countries in Europe, Asia and the Americas. Here Renzo Rosso, its President and Founder, Wilbert Das, Creative Director and Head of Design, and Maurizio Marchiori, Advertising and Communications Director, discuss the value of the brand and the relationship between design and communication.

RR: Diesel means being international, innovative and fun. Our brand's values are our own just as much as the clothes we produce are those we like and wear. Every product has to have its own brand image and values built. For consumers, brands and brand values are a way to 'feel' the product as part of their own personalities. Consumers need more subtle motivations than ever to buy a certain brand. They have to identify themselves with the product they are buying, with its lifestyle, its attitude.

Being global is essential for a brand like ours: young people worldwide are more and more one group, disregarding their nationalities. They are furthermore divided into several 'tribes', centred round a particular kind of music, or habit or taste. During my travels I have the chance to meet kids from Tel Aviv to Los Angeles, from Helsinki to Tokyo, and I regularly find evidence of this. Global distribution is obviously a means and a necessary condition. Therefore we have a large international network of subsidiaries and distributors who

work extremely closely with us in order to project our brand consistently and accurately to the far corners of the world.

WD: Diesel is not made to be a local brand, by its very nature it is meant to be global. We believe that our ideas of design and communication are border-less and can be shared across all cultures, by like-minded people all over the world. Our design team is made up of young people who share a lot of the same ideas and sense of imagination. They blend together well, travelling the world constantly in pairs or small groups in search of new inspiration and ideas, which they bring back to our style office and share with the other designers. After all ideas are collected, the real design process starts. Although we produce a single worldwide product line, it is so large and diverse that it gives consumers abundant options to dress themselves. We offer them the possibility to define their own style within our range and this aspect tends to play well across all markets of the world.

One thing that consumers possess abundantly today is choice. They have countless options for everything they could possibly want, so that often the single reason a consumer will choose one item over another is the perceived values of the brand behind it. We therefore have to make Diesel goods 'different' from others, not just in consumer perception gained through branding and communications but also in product characteristics such as design, manufacture and distribution techniques. This is particularly important and relevant today because the tendency in fashion seems to be that branding and showing off logos and labels is diminishing. Consumers now want to have clothes that can stand out naturally, without being overtly

branded. This doesn't mean, of course, that the brand is not important, it still is, but the perception of consumers now is that you shouldn't have to 'shout' what brand you're wearing, others should be able to recognise it naturally.

MM: In the beginning the product in Diesel advertising played the same role that costume plays in movies. Brand awareness was key, but now product quality has become more important. We must give back to the product what has been neglected in the past for the sake of brand awareness and without forgetting the historical values of our brand. Our communication respects the brand's style and personality. In today's 'jungle of communications' it is more and more necessary to stick your head out and to walk close to the border sometimes. Consumers are free to explore the meaning of our ironic advertising campaigns.

The basic concept of the FOR SUCCESSFUL LIVING campaign is a kind of mockery of the idea that brands such as ours can 'sell' people better

lives. By playing the 'bad brand' or laughing at ourselves, we distance ourselves from big corporate brands and bring ourselves closer to the attitudes of young-minded consumers. Big brands try so hard to portray themselves as sincere and well-intentioned but it doesn't come across as real, and you can almost always feel the monstrous corporate structure behind it.

RR: For companies, brand image and brand values are priceless; they are increasingly the field upon which future battles for market survival will be fought. Every brand must have a mission, but what is more important is the company's added value. The more people realise that wearing is a way to communicate, to express their personality, the more companies must increase and protect their brand's awareness. During the '80s, brand logos were enormous, people liked uniforms and identifying oneself within a social group was so important. Nowadays people look for an individual and personal look and the world of fashion has [to] come to terms with this.

This page and following pages:
images from the 'FOR
SUCCESSFUL LIVING' campaign

"THANK'S DIESEL, FOR MAKING US SO VERY BEAUTIFUL."

BRUCE, HERB, STEVEN, PATRICK & PETER.

The DIESEL Formula 1 Team.

"For consumers, brands
and brand values are
a way to 'feel' the
product as part of their
own personalities."

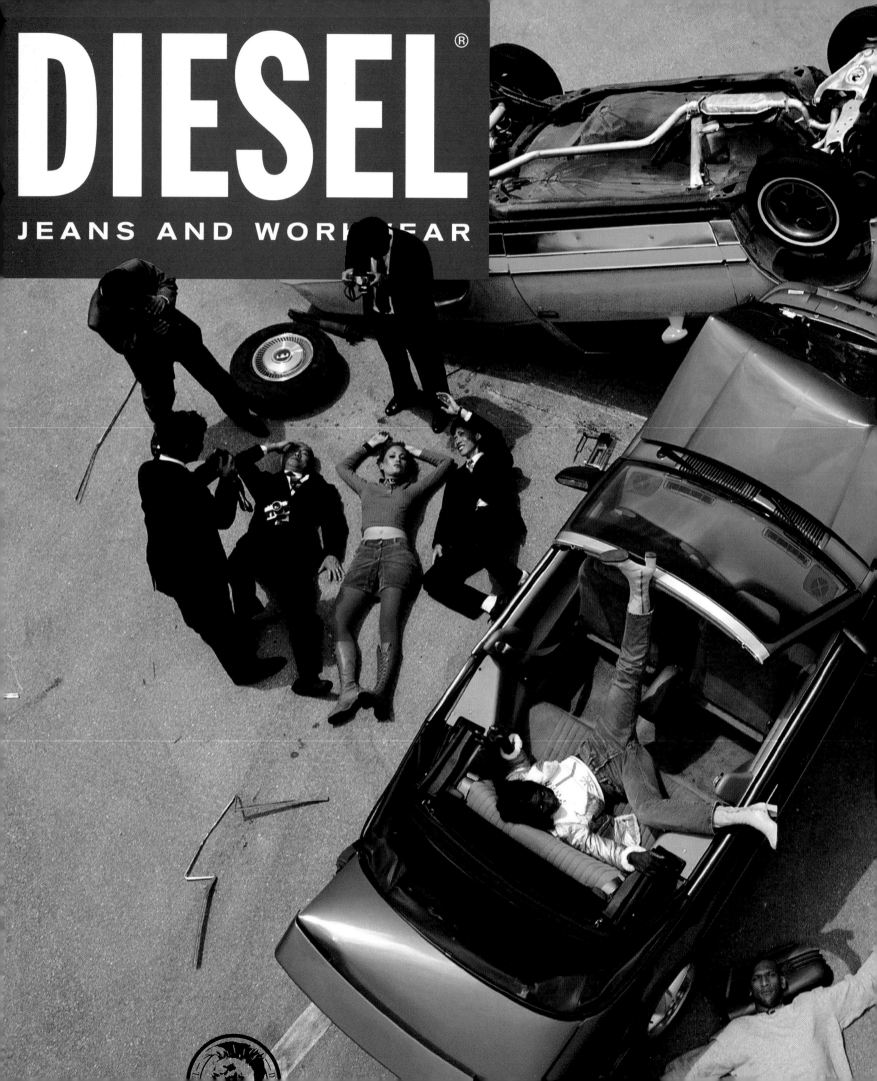

Left: Promotion for Iftar meal at McDonald's, Ankara, 1990s.
Below: Chinese New Year promotion at Singapore McDonald's, 1992.
Bottom: *Hongbao* envelope from Singapore McDonald's, 1992.

福祿壽禧賀新春

FOUR FESTIVE MONKEYS FOR THE NEW YEAR.

小福猴
LUCKY LUCY

小壽猴
LONGEVITY LARRY

小祿猴
RICH RICHIE

小禧猴
HAPPY HARRY

一年复始，万象更新，麦当劳祝您猴年如意，事事顺利。
现在，买任何汉堡包，多付80￠，送一只贺年小猴。∕收齐四只，
把福祿寿禧，带回您家里！
Now when you buy any burger, one of the four Festive Monkeys is yours for just 80¢. Collect all four and greet the New Year with Fortune, Prosperity, Longevity and Happiness.

RUSSELL W. BELK

Wolf brands in sheep's clothing

In the global marketplace competitions between local and multinational brands are often regarded as David and Goliath battles, with sympathies clearly on the side of the local brand hero. Such is the story that Daniel Miller (1997) tells about Trinidadian soft-drink brands fighting the multinational American and British giants. With local, national and even ethnic sentiment favouring the domestic, one countervailing strength of multinational brands is their ability to represent what is modern, hip, and (most likely) Western. But in the last quarter of the twentieth century multinationals found another way of defeating domestic offerings by clothing their brands in regional costumes. In so doing, they maintain their strengths as giant

multinationals while co-opting local sympathies by making the global brand appear to be immanently local. Their ingenuity in doing so is sufficient that a group of Japanese Boy Scouts travelling in the United States were amazed to find a McDonald's in Chicago (Safranek, 1986), while many young people in Hong Kong are also unaware of McDonald's foreign origin (Watson, 1997).

How are the disguises that help global brands pass as local created? In the case of McDonald's, conscious efforts are made for neighbourhood franchises to support popular community causes, to establish local Ronald McDonald houses for hospitalised children, to choose façades that fit the neighbourhood and employ decor that reflects sources of

pride in the vicinity. Menus often adapt to regional tastes in cuisine. As Watson discovered, McDonald's serves teriyaki burgers in East Asia, Maharaja Macs (mutton burgers) in India, McLaks (salmon burgers) in Norway, McHuevo (egg burgers) in Uruguay, pasta and espresso in Italy, and frankfurters and beer in Germany. McDonald's varies its menu as well for some occasions, as with free soup with Iftar (post-sundown) meals during Ramadan in Ankara in 1996. Not only are local cuisines incorporated into the menu, but rituals and holidays as well. During the celebration of the 1992 year of the Monkey in Singapore McDonald's offered for 80-cents Singapore, any of four plastic monkeys: Lucky Lucy, Longevity Larry, Rich Richie and Happy

> "Multinationals have found some clever
> ways of co-opting local sentiment. How
> can we feel anything but warmth toward
> a clown who promotes regional traditions?"

Harry. In these figures Chinese virtues combine with Western names in order to insinuate McDonald's into the local celebration. Singapore McDonald's also transformed traditional plain red *hongbao* (gift) envelopes for Chinese New Year into branded versions featuring Ronald McDonald, the Hamburgler and the Fry Babies. Ronald McDonald's observation of local rituals helps McDonald's become a part of local culture.

Coca-Cola, the quintessential global marketer, also forgoes totally global brand promotion in order to cultivate a local image. In southern Africa, its Sparletta Creme Soda is green and comes in a green can. On 1998 cans from the Namibia bottler much of the front of

the can is taken up by a hip green hippopotamus dressed in a suit, hat and wingtips. On the back of the can he introduces himself: 'Hi, I'm Mr Big, the Hippo. I come from Manzini [in Swaziland] where everything is green. That is why Sparletta Creme Soda is my favourite drink. While I may wear a suit, underneath it all, I am a hippo and I haven't forgotten my roots.' The appeal to urbanised Africans with strong links to the villages from where they come could hardly be clearer.

Sometimes Coke must play conflicting roles in order to create a local identity. During the 1996 Atlanta Olympic summer games, the brand was billed in the USA as an 'official food service partner' and was widely seen as a sponsor of the US

Olympic Team. But in their corporate museum at Circular Quay in Sydney, a booth invited proud Australians to 'send a [videotaped] message to our athletes in Atlanta'. One of the items for sale at Circular Quay, but not at the main Coke museum in Atlanta, is an advertisement featuring an outline of Australia draped in a Coke logo. These emblems try to evoke a strong nationalistic feeling that Coke is indigenous to Australia.

As these examples suggest, multinational brands have found some clever ways of co-opting local sentiment. How can we feel anything but warmth toward a clown who promotes regional traditions, helps community causes and waves national flags? It is increasingly common to see packages of global food

products bearing promotions for local sports teams, theme parks, museums and entertainments. Sponsoring neighbourhood events, contributing to regional charities and hiring resident employees are among the other ways that global brands indigenise themselves. Rather than being seen as a corporate giant, such tactics help to make the global brand seem familiar, friendly and an integral part of local traditions.

CHAPTER TWO

TIES THAT BIND

PATRICK BARWISE, ANDREA DUNHAM AND MARK RITSON

BRANDS, CONSUMERS AND BUSINESSES

Opposite: Branded shopper,
London, 1999.
Top right: Ford logo
Bottom: The FA Premiership
trophy, sponsored by the
brewers Carling.

We live in what anthropologist John Sherry has called 'brandscapes', places in which brands are an integral part of our everyday existence.[1] Yet, the prevalence of brands goes almost unnoticed in today's world. Because there are so many of them around us, we rarely question their nature and function. They are simply there.

Such is the power and prevalence of branding that a variety of organisations are increasingly adopting the methods and language of brands to describe themselves and their activities. The recent successes of Manchester United have seen the football club 'brand' itself across a range of products from sports clothing to tomato ketchup. In an age of global media, celebrities from sports stars to opera singers are also increasingly packaged and managed as brands. We hear of political parties and even politicians being 're-branded'. We may even find that we brand people and things in our day-to-day personal life. The woman who chooses one boyfriend over another because the first is a real 'Armani man' and the other is 'man at C&A' is bringing the philosophy of brands to bear on her most intimate relationships.

Brands have been around for a long time,[2] though their nature has changed significantly. Traditionally the brand was a symbol of production. It represented the type of ingredients, the method of manufacture and the skill of the manufacturer to any prospective consumer.[3] Yet it is clear that many brands today represent more than just production qualities. Often a particular brand logo on a product or service can enhance the consumption experience.[4] The Nike brand worn by many says little about the nature of production, and few wearers could say where or how their clothing was made.

The primary reason why brands exist is economic.

Brand names and other trademarks are still used to identify a supplier's products or services, distinguishing them from those of its competitors. This, at the very least, makes life simpler and less risky for the consumer. Although their symbolic role plays an increasingly important role in consumers' lives, most brands are still sold on a straightforward set of benefits, such as familiarity, predictability and value. In image-rich categories like cosmetics and fashion, the brand image and associations may also, in themselves, be an important part of what the consumer is buying. Because a successful brand has value for the consumer, it allows the firm to sell more, or at a higher price, than if the product were unbranded. It therefore rewards the company for developing and promoting new products and services, and for their consistent quality and image.

What exactly is a brand? It is a word that is so over-used that we rarely stop to consider what it actually means. The brand concept is complex, and different people define brands in different ways. Some focus on the brand as trademark, such as David Aaker from the University of California, Berkeley, for whom it is: 'A distinguishing name and/or symbol (such as a logo, trademark, or package design) intended to identify the goods or services of either one seller or a group of sellers, and to differentiate those goods or services from those of competitors.'[5] Others, such as Jean-Noel Kapferer at the HEC School of Management in Paris, fix on what it means to the consumer: 'A brand is not a product. It is the product's essence, its meaning, and its direction, and it defines its identity in time and space.'[6] This is a view to a large extent supported by Stephen King from the J. Walter Thompson advertising agency: 'A product is something made in a factory; a brand is something bought by a customer. A product can be

copied by a competitor; a brand is unique. A product can be quickly outdated; a brand is timeless.'[7]

But a full definition of the brand surely encompasses both perspectives. It is a combination of a set of trademarks (brand name, logo etc) as well as consumers' perceptions and expectations of products or services branded with these trademarks. For example, Coca-Cola Inc owns a range of trademarks and registered designs, including the shape of the traditional Coke bottle, and employs intellectual property lawyers, whose job is to ensure that no one else can use any of these symbols except – with permission and by paying a royalty – under licence. But the underlying reason why the Coca-Cola brand is so valuable is because of the perceptions and expectations about Coke that consumers carry in their heads. In the words of one Coca-Cola executive:[8]

"If Coca-Cola were to lose all of its production-related assets in a disaster, the company would [survive]. By contrast, if all consumers were to have a sudden lapse of memory and forget everything related to Coca-Cola the company would go out of business."

Because millions of consumers have built up positive perceptions and expectations about Coca-Cola over a period of time, most will choose it instead of another brand if they are both on the same shop shelf, even if the other one is cheaper (and often partly because it is cheaper). Customers' perceptions and expectations are sometimes called 'brand equity'. If these are strong and positive for large numbers of valuable customers, the brand is said to be 'strong' or to have 'strong brand equity'. A strong brand like Coca-Cola, Sony or Mercedes-Benz can have huge financial value because it can support profitable sales of both existing and future products. Unlike most of the tangible assets owned by a company, such as factories and computers, brands can have indefinite lives. In fact, increased usage of a brand – over time and over different products – can raise its value, if properly managed. Sony (the company) is constantly launching

new products to replace its existing ones, but the Sony brand lives on, potentially strengthened by every new product.

A striking feature of brands is their potential longevity. Except in industries such as personal-computer software, where the whole product category is only about 25 years old, most big brands are at least 50 to 100 years old. Coca-Cola was launched in 1886, Gillette in 1902, Kodak in 1888, Shell in 1897, Sony in 1958.[9] A brand like Coca-Cola is older than not only the physical plant and equipment used to produce it but also the consumers who carry its value in their heads. A crucial feature of the business of brands is to manage these potentially valuable intangible assets for the long term and nurture their relationship to successive generations of consumers.

Paradoxically, to understand what a brand is it is helpful to consider what it is not. Commodities are like faceless brands – products or services that achieve their primary functional aim but do so without any distinctive characteristics or identifiable differences. Flour is a commodity. Beer is a commodity. A plane journey is a commodity. To understand what a brand is we must juxtapose Coca-Cola (a brand) against a carbonated-caffeinated beverage (a commodity). When this juxtaposition is performed it is possible to grasp the added value that brands confer on the consumer. This consists of the symbolic associations that the consumer attributes to the branded good – attributes they may not associate with a rival or store brand. People may buy cola because they are thirsty, but some may choose a Coca-Cola because they see it as the 'real thing'. When we talk of brand equity, we are really talking about the differential associations between a brand and a commodity.

Where does this equity come from and what does it consist of? Kevin Keller, a leading expert on brands and branding, breaks brand equity down into two dimensions: awareness and image.[10] Awareness represents the ability of a customer to recognise a particular brand. Most people when asked for some examples of brands will immediately recall a list of

Changes to the design of the
Coca-Cola bottle, 1899-1994.
The classic contour design,
which is still current today,
was first used commercially
in 1916.

famous brand names, which, typically, might include Coke, McDonald's, Disney or Microsoft. On a day-to-day level, brand awareness is usually prompted by need. Thus when a consumer realises that they have run out of washing powder or when they decide to grab some fast-food while out shopping, they will usually recall between one and three brands for which they have high brand awareness. For most manufacturers this 'top of mind' position is an important place to be. Using advertising, sponsorships, huge zeppelin-style balloons, store designs and so on, the managers of brands fight an ongoing battle to reinforce their brand in the consumers' consciousness.

More complex is the second dimension image, which can include any association that a consumer has for a brand. Coke may make us think of America, The Real Thing, red and white. Microsoft suggests Windows, Bill Gates, or their slogan, 'Where do you want to go today™?' These brand images can take any number of forms. At their simplest level they come from the products and services with which a brand is associated. McDonald's main brand image is simply their restaurants and their burgers. A successful advertising campaign may add the images featured in the ads to the brand image. A 1999 British TV advertising campaign for the fast-food chain featured soccer star Alan Shearer visiting his local McDonald's. The 'values' attributed to Shearer – English football hero, down to earth, Northern, working class – are equated in the consumer's mind with McDonald's, and so its image becomes more 'local' than global. But this is not all

one-way traffic. Ideally the manufacturer could simply flick switches in each consumer's mind and have them associate the brand with whatever was its most positive brand image. But unintended and negative images can be linked with a brand and may even be prompted by a particular ad. Not everyone likes Alan Shearer, England, football, the North or the working class.

One of the biggest challenges of brand management is to control and channel the image. With the help of advertising, PR and marketing, most major organisations attempt to do just this. They monitor the current brand images that exist in the minds of different types or 'segments' of consumers and try to highlight some and sideline others, while continuously introducing new, positive associations. A key challenge is to find brand images that are different from those of competitors' brands. Many successful brands have been built around a unique connection with a particular place, individual or process, and this distinctive image has become the cornerstone of their business. Saab created a successful brand image around the world for its cars partly by exploiting its brand associations with aircraft manufacturing. Saab cars were imbued with associations such as safety, precision, speed and technological advance because these links already existed with aircraft manufacture.

Three key concepts contribute to the brand equity of any particular brand. Irrespective of the kind of target market, the nature of the product or service, or the origins of the manufacturing company - all brands depend upon trust, familiarity and difference. A brand is a badge of trust. Consider the difference between an unbranded packet of headache tablets and a well-known brand such as Nurofen. The presence of a visible and recognised brand name is likely to engender confidence in the mind of the consumer.

It is one thing to describe the brand concept, but quite another to explain its prevalence and popularity. For consumers a brand plays several interrelated roles, from familiarity and reassurance through to a range of symbolic devices.[11] The business of branding

Above: Shopping centre
signage, London, 1999.
Below right: Discount
clothing store, London, 1999.
Opposite: Unbranded goods
on sale, London, 1999.

is to position the brand favourably in one or more of these roles. To do this, understanding brands from a consumer perspective is essential. Familiarity is vital to success, and regular exposure to brand names over a period of time will go some way to fixing them in the consumer's mind.[12] A brand provides a source of identification. In doing so it is able to transform a unique act, such as going for a meal, into a familiar one: going to McDonald's.

It also acts as a guarantee of quality. The brand represents a connection, or a promise, from the manufacturer to you. The absence of such association in non-branded items partially explains why branded goods almost always cost more. With purchases such as gifts for others, or for highly symbolic products such as clothing, this visible signal of quality can be particularly important.

A brand offers insurance against many different kinds of risk that we, as consumers, try to avoid. Perhaps the most obvious one is functional risk: the fear that a new product might not meet our expectations. A trusted brand name might be enough to reassure most of us. This is important when consumers do not know much about a product, where experience of the brand in other contexts may reassure them. Then there is physical risk, an even more basic fear that a purchase will result in a threat to the consumer's (or their family's) health or wellbeing. Again, brands can offer assurance, a familiar airline being the classic example of this. Some consumers will prefer to pay a premium to fly with a well-known branded air carrier than risk a lesser-known operator (or one with a tarnished reputation). The planes, journeys and on-flight services may be exactly the same, but the brands are different, and this and its impact on risk perception is enough to persuade people to pay more for a known brand.

Financial risk is the fear that what is being purchased is not actually worth its price. Again brands reassure us here with their associations of trustworthiness. Faced with an unknown product, we have no reference point against which to calculate whether the price is good value or not. A branded

product, however, offers us reassurance that we will get what we are paying for. We can even check this by comparing the price of the same brand across different stores to make sure that the price is constant or nearly so. Paradoxically, this price may be considerably more than we would pay for a non-branded product. Yet many consumers would prefer to spend more, assuming that they are getting value for money by buying a familiar brand.

Finally, social risk describes the threat of enduring social contempt or rejection as a result of a particular purchase. In a world in which we increasingly form opinions of others based on what we buy, this form of risk is becoming more prevalent, particularly among the young. In many cases brands today offer us a reassurance that what we purchase will be accepted by others. Indeed, in especially intense social contexts, such as the school playground, this need to avoid social risk is heightened to the degree where a child feels it has to have a specific brand or face public humiliation. Psychologist Judith Harris argues that peers are an even stronger influence on children and teenagers than has traditionally been assumed.[13] If so, we are likely to see even more brands targeting the young, often with imagery that consciously excludes adult consumers. Demographic trends will encourage many other brands to target the fast-growing segment of well-off, active over-50s.

Brands do not just have a role to play in the expensive, fashion-conscious buy. Most purchases we make are mundane, repetitive and not at all interesting to us. Yet we still want to make sure that we get the best product to meet our particular needs. The consumer behaves like a 'cognitive miser': they

want the best without having to commit to the thinking energy associated with buying a car or a new suit. It is here that brands can again play a useful role in the consumer's life. Rather than reading every package and comparing every price in the supermarket, we simply look for the brand that we want. Because of the other roles that brands play in our lives (identification of source, quality assurance, risk reduction) we can make a cognitive short cut and simply pick the one we like. This 'brand preference' is actually a complex gestalt reflecting many different factors such as advertising, past experiences and word of mouth. It allows us to make a choice quickly. In many cases the wheels of our shopping trolley hardly stop while we do so. We may be tempted to assume that brands are popular because of their symbolic value, their luxury and their ability to communicate to others who we are. All these factors play a role, but ultimately the main reason we populate our houses with familiar brands is because they are easier to buy. Brands simplify our lives.

The final and most complex role for brands in the consumer's life, however, is the symbolic role. They are often used as a signal or measure of personality. We might assess others on first meeting by the car they drive or the clothes they wear. We do the same interpretative job on our own sense of self. We go through life trying to find answers to existential questions: What does it mean to be young? What does it mean to be a mother? Respected? Professional? Increasingly as a culture we have used brands to help us answer these questions. Wearing Diesel jeans rather than Levi's emphasises my youth. Buying a Volvo rather that an Alfa-Romeo reinforces my identity as a father. When we consume a product or service we do not just consume its physical properties. We also consume it on a symbolic level.

Brands are important in this cultural sense because they stand for things – often for things that are arbitrary and unnatural yet we accept them. Consider Häagen-Dazs ice cream, one of the more sexually suggestive brands you can buy. The meanings of adultness and sensuality that have been associated with it have been developed through a decade-long advertising campaign and can now come to mind when we consume the product. Anthropologist Grant McCracken calls this process the 'meaning flow'.[14] In essence meanings and symbols are created by advertising, then transferred to the product that is featured and finally celebrated through its consumption by the consumer. Brands are used symbolically in two different directions: inward and outward. Outwardly, to communicate to others the kind of person we are. Inwardly, to bolster our sense of self. These twin roles are perhaps the most influential factors in explaining the increasing numbers and popularity of brands within the last two decades. All of us are now all fluent in the language of brands. In addition, we are defined, and we define ourselves, as much by the brands we do not buy as by the ones that we do.

These are the building blocks of brand equity from a consumer viewpoint. From a business perspective, however, a brand only has value to the extent that it influences customer purchases, by making more people buy (and more often) at a given price, or the same people pay a higher price, than if the product or service were sold under an unknown brand. Although there is an extraordinary number of brands on the market, really valuable ones are relatively few. For individuals, only a proportion of these will be relevant, and even the most brand-aware consumer knows only a few hundred.

What we buy and use is not a brand and a product/service but a combination of the two, neither of which is clearly separate from the other in our minds. When Coca-Cola launched 'New Coke' to compete with Pepsi in 1985, it forgot the value of Coke's own reputation as the original and unique cola. Coke drinkers did not want this changed.[15]

In the event, it was able to retain and eventually increase its market share, but at enormous expense. The financial value of the brand and of the total corporation ('shareholder value') were reduced and, without the remedial action taken at the time, might have been even more so.[16]

The functional price-performance of the physical product is usually only part of what customers are buying. When computing was dominated by mainframes, IBM's competitors would often launch models with 15 or 20 per cent better price-performance. But none could match IBM's service reputation or its range of compatible hardware and software. Nor was it easy to recruit staff to program or operate systems that were not IBM-compatible. Nor was there any risk of IBM pulling out of the business as General Electric, Xerox and other major players did. No wonder 'No one ever got fired for buying IBM', despite the higher price.[17]

Maintaining the reputable associations of a brand is of huge importance as these are the predominant source of brand value. Think, for example, of what the BMW brand tends to bring to mind. What associations do you make? Typical links with BMW might be: German; one or more of its car models, or perhaps a general idea of upscale, fast saloons ('sedans' in America); good engineering; driven by successful yuppies. You might also recall the blue-and-white four-quadrant logo, although perhaps not as readily as Mercedes-Benz's even better known three-pointed star. Interestingly, with a strong, global brand like BMW, millions of consumers around the world would have these same associations in their heads. Most of them might not be able to afford a new BMW. Even among those who could buy a BMW if they wanted, most may never do so because they prefer other marques or because they dislike Germany or fast cars or yuppies or the particular styling of BMWs. They may not wish to associate themselves with the BMW brand. But many will do so – BMW is a large and growing brand – and this will be partly because of the mixture of functional and emotional associations of the BMW brand in their heads.

BMW (the company) does not own these associations, but its shareholders are richer because they exist. Most of the value of the BMW brand derives from its strong brand equity (in consumers' heads), not from its trademark *per se*. This is an interesting situation, because BMW (the company) owns the trademarks but not the brand equity. It could, if it wished, sell the trademarks, but the extent to which it could sell the brand equity is unclear – and would depend greatly on which firm was the buyer. If a manufacturer of cheap, volume cars bought BMW and used the BMW marque to rebuild its own sportier saloon models, consumers would not suddenly start thinking of these cars as BMWs. More likely, they would see the change as mere 'badge engineering' probably weakening their perceptions of the BMW brand as a whole. With a well-known brand like BMW, each individual may have many more associations than the listed core ones. Someone interested in cars or brands may know more details about BMW: its history, design and engineering. Most consumers will also have personal ties with the brand, for instance, people they have known who drove a BMW.

Consumers buy branded products and services; they do not buy trademarks. A trademark is a symbol, and its value derives from what it symbolises. If consumers' beliefs about that underlying reality change, so may the value of the trademark. An extreme case of this occurs if the consumer believes

'Beckham Delivery, Guaranteed Anytime – Anywhere'. The celebrity footballer David Beckham is shown as a brand, in this poster campaign for adidas, 1999.

that the seller is trying to 'pass off' an inauthentic product such as a fake Rolex watch.

A less extreme example occurred in the late 1980s when Mars started a policy of standardising on a limited portfolio of global brand names. In spring 1990 the well-established Marathon trademark was dropped and replaced by the global Snickers trademark in the UK (at that time almost unknown there). Before the change, the strapline 'Internationally known as Snickers' was printed in smaller type below the Marathon trademark. Again, for some months after the change, the strapline 'The new name for Marathon' was printed below the Snickers trademark, and another strapline 'All that's changed is the name' printed on the packaging along the side of the bar. Also, the overall 'look and feel' of the before and after packaging was very similar. Mars slightly increased its advertising for the brand and made it a priority for the sales force selling to the retailers. The result was that, far from losing sales, the brand actually increased its market share. Changing the brand name from Marathon to Snickers had no significant effect on consumers' perceptions of the brand: in their minds it still exists, under a new name. This is a clear illustration of the fact that the concept of brand-as-trademark (name, logo etc) fails to capture the full concept of what brands mean to consumers and therefore to businesses.[18]

From a company perspective, we are moving into an age in which management is increasingly about 'intangibles'. Companies no longer look at their tangible assets (cash, factories, machinery, inventory and land) as the markers of their success. Instead, they now view the intangible aspects of their business as the central indicators of the value of their firm. Brands represent an important example of this shift to 'weightless' assets. The 'weightless' part of a modern economy includes not only other intellectual property (patents, copyrights) but also knowledge and know-how, libraries and databases, information and communication systems, research and so on.[19] Many would include employee, customer and supplier loyalty.

Successful brand management starts with a deep understanding of what the brand means to customers and what drives choice. It then becomes clear that the role of the brand is to raise expectations in consumers' minds of specific benefits. These must be delivered on a consistent basis in order to build a franchise of satisfied loyal customers – the translation of brand choice into predictable and steady income for the firm, year in and year out. Since firms are valued by shareholders on the basis of their predictable income over a five- to ten-year period, the role of the brand in driving customer choice can be central to a corporation's strategies for increasing 'shareholder value', that is the financial value of the company to its shareholders.

Businesses survive, grow and make money by profitably meeting customers' needs better than the competition. More precisely, customers buy products and services because they are seeking functional and emotional benefits that they expect a category of products or services to provide. The main benefits promised and provided by the brand provide the key to management decisions about the firm: competitive strategy, innovation and technology and marketing.

Valuable brands reflect the development of positive brand perceptions, usually over a long time period. Firms seek to establish a virtuous cycle whereby people choose the brand and use it, and the benefits delivered by usage lead to high customer satisfaction. This in turn leads to both positive word-of-mouth recommendations to other potential customers (especially important for infrequently purchased products and services) and positive brand perceptions in the mind of the consumer. In the case of frequently brought items like groceries or fast food, it is these positive brand perceptions leading to repeat purchase of the same brand that establish it with long-term value. Repeat-buying constitutes a positive feedback loop, in which brand choice and usage lead to satisfaction, which feeds through to reinforced commitment to the category, brand preference and brand choice. Repeat-buying also reinforces top-of-mind awareness, which, as already noted, has a direct link with brand preference, and is, itself, a predictor of brand choice and therefore stable revenue streams. At this stage, repeat-buying becomes more of a habit than a conscious choice. This type of repeat-buying is what is normally meant by brand loyalty.

Big brands enjoy two advantages over small ones: in any given time period, more consumers buy big brands and do so more often. This type of pattern was first observed in a study of radio announcers by Columbia University sociologist William McPhee in 1963 and labelled the Law of Double Jeopardy (from the perspective of the less popular brand, which

suffers twice over).[20] It has also been found in a wide number of other contexts.[21]

For high-involvement, infrequently purchased goods such as cars or holidays, and to a lesser extent new products and brands, customer satisfaction can also be communicated by word-of-mouth. This is the most trusted source of information about brand benefits, apart from the consumer's own direct experience, because, unlike advertising or promotion, it is not seen as commercially self-serving. Customer dissatisfaction is even more potent for service businesses: such customers seldom complain, but often tell their friends and acquaintances, other potential buyers, about their bad experience.

Perhaps the single most important role for brands within an organisation is their ability to spawn loyalty; this is akin to a long-term relationship between brand and consumer. Because the brand identifies itself and because it is able to stand for certain meanings, it is sometimes able to impact upon a consumer over several purchases to form both a practical and symbolic part of that consumer's life. At its most extreme a brand-loyal consumer will specifically ask for the brand by name if it does not appear on a grocery shelf and will defer their purchase until it becomes available.

In the UK one example of long-term brand loyalty is the relationship between British consumers and MG sports cars. When the new MGF was launched in the mid-1990s, some people had to wait months before their car was available. Yet wait they did. Indeed, such was the power of the MG brand that for several years after its launch, the second-hand price of an MGF was significantly higher than its original list price. Such loyalty is rare, especially in today's markets where the consumer is seen as increasingly fickle. However, the more fickle the consumer becomes in general, the more valuable brand loyalty becomes in particular. In a fascinating study of nostalgia and brand loyalty Barbara Olsen[22] suggests that the latter may exist for several lifetimes. She described one Italian-American family who 'inherited' their brand loyalty for the household brands Gold Medal flour and Domino sugar from their mother whom, in turn, had adopted it from her mother. The value to the firm of such loyalty patterns is enormous. If manufacturers can build brand loyalty at an early stage in the consumer's development they may reap a lifetime's benefits.

Marketers increasingly try to demonstrate not only how much of the total market they currently service but also how much of each single consumer they will service in a lifetime. The key is to win over the consumer while they are still developing their preferences and then try to ensure that they will remain loyal. This strategy has proved successful for many high-street banks that specifically target new students with attractive packages to draw them in at the start of their financial lives. This is equally the case with Sony's range of goods produced for children: 'My First Sony'.

Brand strategy is about managing the manufacturing, distribution, communication and economic mix to develop consistent perceptions of the brand among certain customer segments, so as to maximise how often it is chosen at a price that pays. This involves choosing the most profitable target

market and making sure that these customers see the brand as likely to provide more core benefits than competing brands. It also means ensuring that the brand (or strictly the combination of brand and product/service) is priced and distributed to maximise long-term sales and profits. In a competitive environment, brand perceptions, prices and 'availability' (how and where the product can be bought) are always relative to the competition, not absolute.

Relatively small differences in brand preference – if shared widely among consumers – can therefore lead to large differences in brand choice and therefore in the value of brand equity to the firm. That is, a brand need not be 'powerful' (in the sense that consumers believe it dramatically superior and refuse all substitutes) to be extremely valuable to the business.

There are large systematic variations between the branding strategies of different industries. Most industries (industrial products, industrial services, consumer services, infrequently bought consumer products) market largely under a single corporate/umbrella brand, often with sub-brands

Right: 'My First Sony', 1992.

Advertising hoarding in
a London car park, 1999.

Above: Supermarket
shelving, Tesco, West
Kensington, London, 1999.
Below: Harrods carrier bag.

and other detailed product descriptors. The main exception to this is with anything that is bought infrequently, in which case the same firm may market two or more distinct product lines/ranges at very different price levels. Portfolios of brands may cover a range of products within a single category, such as whisky, marketed to different social groups and purses.[23] In this case, a separate brand name may be used for each of these. General Motors was established after the First World War with a portfolio of five main brands at different price points and other positionings or attributes, such as sportiness: Chevrolet, Buick, Oldsmobile, Pontiac and Cadillac.[24] These brands, and their relative market profiles, continue today.

Toyota, Nissan and Honda have all launched luxury-car ranges under separate brand names from their volume-car brands. GM and Ford have acquired European manufacturers such as Saab and Jaguar, and a large part of their motive for doing so appears to be to gain control of the brands that are valued for luxury or style. Part of BMW's rationale for buying Rover was the latter's portfolio of mostly dormant classic British car marques, such as Morris, Triumph, Riley, Wolsley and especially MG. Until BMW pulled

out of Rover in 2000, the main reason for the takeover was for BMW to acquire Land Rover, the only serious 4x4 manufacturer in Europe with a very strong brand name. Another current example of a car-brand portfolio is VW's four-brand strategy (Audi, VW, Seat, Skoda) using a limited number of platforms shared across the brands.

One of the most obvious aspects of brand strategy is advertising, which can have many roles in building and maintaining brand equity.[25] It can be used to create awareness of a new brand or product; to encourage trial purchase (for a low-ticket item) or a request for more information (for example brochures and a test drive for a car); to reinforce repeat-buying of a familiar, frequently purchased product, perhaps just by reminding or 'nudging' the consumer; or to strengthen and develop consumers' positive long-term perception of the brand.[26]

Advertising is pervasive, but perhaps less powerful than many people believe. Quite a widespread attitude is that it influences – even manipulates – other people, but not oneself. The evidence is that it is both less powerful and less sinister than this. Most advertising focuses on trying to influence consumers' choice of brand, such as Ariel versus Persil, not on trying to persuade them to buy more of the product category.[27] This is not clear-cut. For a dominant brand in a growth market, such as BSkyB in pay TV or Coca-Cola in the Chinese soft-drinks market, advertising may be as much aimed at bringing new consumers into the market (and encouraging existing consumers to buy more) as at capturing or protecting market share from other brands. Again, if the product category is defined very narrowly, brand advertising will tend to increase category sales, by 'capturing' consumers from other brands.

Even at the brand-choice level, advertising is a weaker force than many people believe, and firms' investment in it more of an act of faith. Most major advertisers can roughly measure the impact of their advertising on short-to-medium-term brand sales – up to two or maybe three years. This sales impact varies greatly between brands and advertising campaigns, but it is rarely big enough to cover the

Below: Nestlé
products, 1999.

THE WORLD'S MOST VALUABLE BRANDS

	Brand name	Country of origin	Brand value $US billion	Company value $US billion	Brand value as % of co-value
1.	Coca-Cola	US	84	142	59
2.	Microsoft	US	57	272	21
3.	IBM	US	44	158	28
4.	General Electric	US	34	328	10
5.	Ford	US	33	57	58
6.	Disney	US	32	53	61
7.	Intel	US	30	144	21
8.	McDonald's	US	26	41	64
9.	AT&T	US	24	102	23
10.	Marlboro	US	21	112	19
11.	Nokia	Finland	21	47	44
12.	Mercedes	Germany	18	48	37
13.	Nescafé	Switzerland	18	77	23
14.	Hewlett-Packard	US	17	55	31
15.	Gillette	US	16	43	37
16.	Kodak	US	15	25	60
17.	Ericsson	Sweden	15	46	32
18.	Sony	Japan	14	29	49
19.	Amex	US	13	35	35
20.	Toyota	Japan	12	86	14

Source: Interbrand/Citibank 1999

cost – or even half the cost – of the advertising. Most of the mass-media advertising for established products and brands is therefore defensive, which is to say that it is aimed at maintaining brand equity. However, firms' ability to measure how much this actually works is limited because the effects are not strong, and there are so many other influences on brand choice: product improvements, price, promotions, retail presence, the state of the economy and, especially, competitor activity. To decide the long-term value of advertising, there would need to be an estimate of what sales might have been without it. This is rarely possible.[28]

Nor is advertising essential to the development of brand equity. The customer franchise of brands like Microsoft, IBM, Mercedes-Benz, Boots or Harrods has little to do with advertising in a traditional sense. A market such as petrol is dominated by the number, location and quality of outlets with price a secondary factor and branding probably only third. Similarly, with infrequently bought items such as cars or white goods, the product itself, its price and availability, and the firm's general reputation ('corporate brand equity') are considered to be more important than advertising.

As a result of some significant corporate takeovers during the 1980s, the concept of brands on the balance sheet came very much to the fore in UK corporate finance.[29] Brands had always been an important topic within the marketing departments of manufacturing organisations. Very rapidly they became crucial for the financial departments of these organisations, too, as the value of a particular company became as much associated with its intangible brand assets as with its more tangible ones, such as plant and machinery. Perhaps the best example of this sea change in British business was the Rowntree takeover. In early 1988 the stock market valued British confectionery company Rowntree at a little over £1 billion. Much of this stock-market valuation was based on the perceived value of Rowntree's familiar and well-loved brands (Kit-Kat, Aero, Lion Bar, Rolo etc). The tangible assets of the company (land, plant and equipment) were worth well under half of the overall market value of the firm – about £0.4 billion. During this period, Swiss company Jacobs Suchard made a 'dawn raid' on Rowntree, buying its shares at an inflated price in a race to gain control of it over their larger Swiss rival, Nestlé. During the next few frenzied weeks of competitive bidding, the price of Rowntree's shares more than doubled. Nestlé eventually paid £2.3 billion for Rowntree. Most of this was to secure (and stop Jacobs Suchard from getting a hold over) Rowntree's strong established brands. Nestlé believed not only that Rowntree's brands were strong and valuable but also that they would be even more so under their ownership, because of the strength of their international distribution. This example – from a solid, dependable, Swiss company – highlights the important financial value of strong brands in today's business environment.

According to brand consultancy Interbrand, the most valuable brand in the world is Coca-Cola, which they valued at $84 billion in 1999, over half the total $142-billion financial market value of the Coca-Cola Corporation. As the table on the previous page shows, the top 20 most valuable brands in 1999 are dominated by global US brands.

Brand valuation is controversial. For instance, Interbrand has arguably overvalued technology brands like Microsoft, Intel and Nokia, whose brand equity has shallow roots in fast-paced markets in which this year's winner may be a loser in two years. But these huge values nevertheless reflect an important truth for businesses today. Brands can represent enormously important assets that need to be carefully nurtured and exploited.

Now we have entered the new millennium what will become of brands? Their story is a long one. It has also taken some recent twists. In particular, the growing awareness of the financial value of brands stands out as one of the most important changes in recent business history, and their strategic management has emerged as one of the most important challenges for companies in the twenty-first century. Recent technological advances, and

in particular the emergence of electronic or 'e-commerce', are already changing the way in which businesses operate and consumers make their decisions and purchases.

Inevitably we will witness new major brands emerging in the first few years of the new century. Nobody yet knows who will be the next Amazon or Microsoft, but its emergence is certain. Equally likely is the fact that some of the power brands of the twentieth century will fall by the wayside. Those that have not been updated and made to move with the times will suffer and perhaps even die. The recent problems of Levi's, Marks & Spencer and even Coca-Cola emphasise how rapidly the once mighty can stumble in the modern marketplace. Obviously the market context of the twenty-first century will be different. As consumers, we are already beginning to glimpse the kind of markets that e-commerce is creating for us. These are without national boundaries and have unlimited information, markets that provide us with an almost limitless array of choices from which to select with a simple 'click'.

Yet within these brave new markets the part that brands will play in the life of the consumer is unlikely to change fundamentally. Consider the consumer roles for brands discussed earlier: identification of source, signal of quality, risk reducer, search-cost reducer and symbolic device. These will continue because they concern issues that consumers will always need to address, regardless of the particular purchase in which they are involved or the market and technology context in which that decision has to be made. For example, the identification of the source of a product that brands can provide for consumers and the familiarity that this confers will prove vital as we begin to make decisions in on-line markets with an even greater menu of options. The more we are faced with familiar choices, the stronger the attraction for the brands that we know and trust.

Similarly, the role brands play in assigning responsibility and signalling quality will remain equally important in the next century. Consumers will be faced with online decisions in which their choices increase, but where direct, tangible access to the

products from which they must choose will decrease. We shall buy bananas that we will not be able to squeeze or smell before we click them into our baskets. In situations like this the role of brands in guaranteeing quality will only serve to increase our dependence on them and their importance to us.

One implication of e-commerce is that new markets will offer more choices than ever before. While this may be a positive result for the consumer, many of the purchases will remain mundane. Once more, the role of brands in reducing search costs will prove crucial in ensuring their worth in the next century. Finally, and perhaps most importantly, no matter how we select and purchase goods and services in the future we will continue to consume many of them conspicuously. The role of brands as symbolic devices that feed our self-concept and our lines of communication to others will continue through the age of e-commerce and into whatever age may follow it.

While brands continue to exert a significant influence on consumer decision-making in the digital age, it is clear that online shopping offers the consumer a unique and unprecedented combination of features.[30] First, until now, most category and brand choice has been at a retail outlet – supermarket, travel agent or car showroom. Firms with big, strong established brands have had a huge advantage in making their products easily available to consumers – and sometimes ensuring that new competitors are excluded from the best retail outlets. But on the Internet, a one-person business can make its electronic shop window available to as many online consumers as Sony or The Gap.

Second, the Internet knows almost no boundaries of time and space. A website can be accessed at low cost at any hour and from anywhere. We are still at an early stage of assessing the future impact of what financial journalist Frances Cairncross has called 'the death of distance'.[31] Third, online shopping combines the real-time interactivity of the telephone with some of the best features of catalogue shopping. It lets the consumer evaluate and compare competing brands using pictures and text. Finally, online

technology allows the consumer not only to compare brands easily (as with a catalogue) but also, and increasingly, to use the power of the computer to do the hard work of searching for alternative supplies of a brand, comparing features and prices, highlighting special offers and so on. Bill Gates, Chairman of Microsoft, has suggested that we are moving towards a 'shopper's heaven'.[32]

The reverse of this coin is potentially a 'shopper's hell'. Firms too are able to use competing power to optimise their relationships with consumers, especially those about whom they have a stream of data from loyalty-card transactions, online interactions and so on. In principle, this will also aid consumers, since it will enable suppliers to tailor their products, services and communications to each individual to the benefit of both parties.[33] In practice, this kind of 'one-to-one' marketing (or 'mass customisation') is hard to do well – most consumers feel they now receive more junk mail than ever – and also raises other societal issues: the invasion of privacy, the tendency to focus only on the better-off, increasing social exclusion and so on.[34]

Digital technology is of course especially well suited to producing and distributing information products and services. Nicholas Negroponte, Director of the MediaLab at MIT, regards the distinction between 'bits' (information) and 'atoms' (physical products and services) as the key to understanding the digital age.[35] Some information products such as classified advertising and encyclopaedias, are especially well suited to digital media. Others, such as television programmes, newspapers and novels, are less so. But it is clear that digital technology will have a huge impact on some product categories, for example the travel-agency business.[36]

What impact will all this have on brands? As with everything to do with the Internet, the short-term impact on most consumer markets (as opposed to businesses selling to other businesses) has been over hyped. Although it is true that any online consumer in the world can access a one-person-business website, with no brand equity it will remain largely unvisited.

This is why all the Internet start-up businesses, often known as 'dot coms', are spending millions on advertising to create brand equity, mostly on traditional print and broadcast media. In practice, most e-commerce is being done by established brands – although there are many exceptions to this pattern. Some Internet-pioneer companies set the pace and have held it in their category, such as Amazon.com in the book market, but older brands, the venerable American book store Barnes & Noble for example, now online, are starting to catch up fast.

This is not to say that reputable businesses can be complacent. Almost every company is at risk from nimbler competitors finding new ways to reach the customer using this technology. The empowered consumer, helped by increasingly powerful software, will be more likely to find the best buy – or at least, the cheapest place to purchase the preferred brand – so price competition will intensify in many markets. But the fundamental reasons why brands exist will not disappear. In fact, in an information-laden society, their role in saving time and assuring quality will be as great as ever, as will their symbolic role. We may even have to extend our definition of brand equity to include information held in computer memory as well as human memory: if I and my computer are both geared to buy groceries online from Waitrose@work, our brand loyalty to that retailer will be higher than ever.

In addition to the influence of technology, brands will need to adapt to other consumer and societal trends. Some of these, such as the age profile of the population – with a higher proportion of retired people, many of them active, healthy and with high disposable income – are relatively predictable. Others are less so. For instance, US economists in the 1960s worried about how people would spend all their extra leisure time in the 1990s. In the event, Americans today – especially women of working age – have less leisure than then, not more.[37]

Now we are in the twenty-first century, the forces that have made brands such a feature of modern society and business – market economies and consumerism, globalisation, consumers who are money-rich and time-poor, information overload – seem set to continue. Even those who advocate a 'third way' – neither communism nor free-market capitalism – stress the importance of competitive markets and consumer power.[38] On this basis, we might expect the role of brands to become even greater during this century.

If present trends continue, huge populations in today's emerging markets – Asia, Latin America, Eastern Europe – will be able to afford branded products on an unprecedented scale. The evidence is that they will become enthusiastic consumers of brands, including global ones. In the developed world, as Gareth Williams confirms in 'The Point of Purchase', a small minority is saying, 'Enough.'[39] There are also signs of ethical considerations influencing brand choice, at least among a minority of consumers. Body Shop, one of the few global British brands launched in the last 50 years, has built its brand positioning in consumers' minds on its moral principles for developing and sourcing products.[40] Recently, Nike, McDonald's, Shell, Monsanto and Wal-Mart[41] have all been subject to aggressive campaigns by groups critical of the wider societal impact of their corporate policies.[42]

Campaigns along these lines seem likely to continue and, at least in some cases, will have enough influence on brand equity and therefore brand choice to persuade firms to adapt their policies. One prediction, therefore, is that the ethical dimension of brands will become more important to consumers and therefore to businesses. But this development should not be overstated: a trend, not a revolution, in the world of brands.

Many categories of the twentieth century have been dominated by the same brands for more than 50 years with remarkably little change in the competitors and their relative popularity with consumers. Some of the power brands that we encounter daily will disappear as competitive forces and market changes take their toll. Brands may well be promoted using innovative, as yet unheralded, techniques, but as long as people feel the need to produce things and to consume them, brands will remain with us.

KENT GRAYSON

Why do we buy counterfeits?

From breakfast cereals to luxury hotels, what we like to hear about our favourite brands is that they keep their promises. Strong brands tell us what to expect from them and then deliver on those expectations. No brand can keep its promises all the time but building a strong brand image takes time, commitment and not a small amount of money.

So it is hardly surprising that some companies do not even try to keep their promises – instead, they pretend to keep somebody else's. Customers will be lured into buying inferior products by the illegal use of another company's well-established logo, packaging and reputation. This practice is about as ethical as using someone else's credentials to get a job, and in most countries it is illegal.

Counterfeiters earn millions every year selling not only the familiar fake watches and knock-off handbags but also bogus children's toys, sporting goods, car parts, even pharmaceutical products.

Because legitimate manufacturers want customers to spend these millions on the real thing instead, companies will often hunt down and prosecute those who manufacture counterfeits. But while those who make and distribute counterfeit goods frequently are blamed for creating the market for fakes, it is important to recognise that this market is kept alive by supply *and* demand. So it is useful to ask why do we buy counterfeits?

Perhaps when people buy fake goods they are really being fooled by a clever imitation and believe they are purchasing the genuine article. Some counterfeiters are so effective that only an expert might notice the difference – the only dissimilarity between some Cuban cigars and their counterfeits, for example, is the way the paper is folded at the ends. On the other hand, even when a fake looks like the original, the way in which it is sold will be entirely different – usually by street vendors or temporary discount stores. The customer might be wary, but such goods are usually traded cheaply with the justification that 'They're factory seconds' or even 'They fell off the back of a truck.' Most customers, however, do not ask for an explanation and will happily buy knowing that the goods are fake.

Are these customers just good bargain hunters? Do they buy counterfeits because they believe they are getting the same quality for a lower price? A 1993 American study, by Bloch, Bush and Campbell, explored people's perceptions of fake versus real goods. Setting up a table in a shopping area, the researchers sold three types of shirt, all of the same quality and colour. The first shirt had a designer logo on the pocket, and customers were told it was a genuine designer shirt. Price: $45. The second shirt also had a designer logo, and customers were told it was a counterfeit. Price: $18. The third shirt had no designer logo, but the label inside showed it to be from a well-known retailer. Customers were told it was genuine. Price: $18. By the end of the study 38 per cent of the consumers had bought the counterfeit. In a similar survey in Britain, 40 per cent of those asked said they too would knowingly buy a counterfeit if the price and quality were acceptable.

After the customers in the first survey had bought their counterfeit shirts, they were taken aside and asked to rate the quality of the three types on offer. Although all the shirts were of the same quality, those buying the counterfeit rated it lower than the 'real' designer shirt, but higher than the retailer's. It is clear that the 'designer' shirt was rated highest, because customers generally believe a fake to be of lower quality than the real thing. But why did people rate the supposed counterfeit higher than the shirt without the logo, even though it was said to be from a reputable retailer? Seemingly, even the counterfeit logo sends an unconscious message of quality. The customers know they are getting a fake, but the logo on the pocket, with its carefully cultivated brand image, offers subtle reassurances. If that is the case, then even customers knowing they are getting a fake are being deceived.

Not only that, but these customers may also be engaging in a deception of their own. They recognise the logo gives them fashion value and a certain status in the eyes of others. But for many, this value only remains as long as the customers keep quiet about the origin of their goods. Admitting to purchasing a fake 'bargain' affects the status of both the product and the wearer.

So maybe we buy counterfeits because we are fooled by a clever imitation – though in many cases we might instead be trying to fool others, or even ourselves.

"When people buy
counterfeit goods,
are they really
being fooled by a
clever imitation?"

MARK RITSON

Consumer proactivity

To consume or not to consume? Is that the question? When we find ourselves drawn into a shop by a particularly enticing window display, we are being consumers. When we buy a new brand of toothpaste because the packet informs us that it will whiten our teeth, we are being consumers. When we show our spouse an advertisement for walking holidays in India from the Sunday paper, we are being consumers. The act of consumption has been characterised as the flow of goods from producers to consumers. Consumption is what we do in response to the activity of retailers, manufacturers and advertisers. Consumption begins with the actions of the organisation and ends with some impact on people.

Of course there is an alternative. We can choose not to consume. We can dismiss the temptations of the window display and keep walking. We can scoff at the claims of the new brand of toothpaste and return it to the supermarket shelf. We can decide not to read any of the advertisements in the Sunday papers. In these instances we see ourselves as non-consumers. We may even derive as much satisfaction from these acts of non-consumption as we do from consuming; we may feel we have resisted temptation, or that we have acted with discernment. Of course, even in these acts of non-consumption we are still reacting. By choosing not to buy a product, not to enter a store or not to read an ad, we are still responding to the marketing efforts of organisations.

To consume or not to consume appear to be our only choices. Yet, when we dichotomise consumer behaviour in this way we assume that the only available option is consumption reactivity. But there is a third way, which represents the activities of people who attempt to reverse the classic causality of

consumption. This can be called consumer proactivity, and under its banner appear any acts that originate with people and are targeted at marketing organisations. Consumer proactivity questions our traditional assumptions about consumption. Thus, instead of asking what advertising does to people, we have to ask what people are doing to advertising. Rather than examining the impact of brands on people, we have to examine the impact of people on brands. The consumer becomes the active player in this new relationship, and the organisation is faced with the question of how they will respond.

Consumer proactivity is by no means a singular activity. Like the standard consumption behaviours that flow in the opposite direction, it can take many forms and exhibit varying levels of involvement. At its most superficial level it exists as a sudden, almost instinctive desire to break free from the passivity that most people experience on a day-to-day basis in their roles as consumers. Consider exhibit 1. An anonymous commuter waiting in the underground for their train is offended and angered by the explicit promotion of smoking as 'sexy' in a poster ad on the walls of the station. The traditional consumer dichotomy of consuming or non-consuming does not, in this case, present our commuter with an acceptable response. Instead, they turn to proactivity and deface the ad. It is a crude gesture, but one that illustrates the power of the consumer as proactive. The ad is now for ever changed. What's more its message is not weakened by the fact that it originally represented a medium of traditional consumption. Indeed, the very power of this new message derives from this origin and its subsequent transformation. The ad was designed to have an impact on people.

Now a person has had an impact on the ad, and its original intent, message and effect have been superseded by an act of consumer proactivity.

Consider exhibit 2. We see a familiar brand, Nike, transformed. A brand that looks the same yet now communicates the word 'Dike' - or dyke, a slang word for lesbian. Nike is a brand that is popular among all sections of the population and includes a significant number of lesbian consumers. Unlike some of the rest of the mass market, however, Nike do not explicitly acknowledge this group. There are no ads featuring a lesbian couple working out in Nike sports gear, there are no lesbian celebrity endorsers for Nike, Nike does not sponsor specifically homosexual events and activities such as the Gay Games. Yet the Nike brand is as popular with these consumers as it is with the rest of society. The dichotomy of being a consumer or non-consumer is again insufficient for some gay women. They like Nike products; they use and consume them. However, they do not like the way in which their relationship with this brand is ignored by its manufacturer. As a result, some resort to consumer proactivity to allow them to redress the lack of explicit representation that they experience at the hand of Nike. Rather than letting the brand impact upon this market, the market is impacting itself upon the brand. Once again, the power inherent in this act of consumer proactivity derives from the transformation of a traditional, expected medium of consumption, and thus altered, its purpose is subverted.

Most buying will continue to be represented by a singular arrow of causality that flows from organisations to consumers and non-consumers. Yet, in these early days of the twenty-first century it is possible to glimpse more and different examples of consumer proactivity taking place. In this post-modern age of reflexivity and playfulness all the cultural indicators suggest that as consumers we will become increasingly predisposed to it. Standard consumption media such as advertising, branding and retail spaces that have typically assumed consumer passivity may need to evolve greater degrees of interactivity in order to enable them to engage with increasingly proactive markets. Only time will tell exactly how creative, constructive and subversive we shall become.

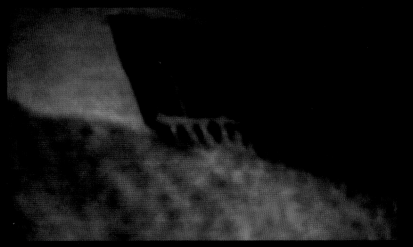
Barcode tattoo.

"I wanna get rich"

"Sell"

SHARON KINSELLA

Japanese high-school girl brand

In the 1990s a new brand appeared not on the shelves but on the streets of Japan: *joshi kōsei*, the schoolgirl brand. It brought to the consumer the essence of authentic spontaneity and youthful naivety. It was all part of an idea that was current in the media of the time that Japanese schoolgirls had become brand-name goods in their own right (Miyadai, 1994). Time spent in their company had become a commodity that men could buy. What was purchased was not always sex but the elixir of youth. For producers, editors and intellectuals, who were aware of the trends, the company of these girls became a voguish and risqué entertainment that could be flaunted or presented as a gift.

BURUSERA
News attention began in 1993 when the media became aware of the idea that schoolgirls were selling their school uniforms, knickers, even gobs of their saliva, to the proprietors of makeshift shops. *Burusera* or 'bloomer sailor' shops catered to men with a sexual fixation on the paraphernalia of schoolgirl uniforms (Miyadai, 1994). Titillating TV documentaries brought the *burusera* issue to the attention of the Japanese public. Images of Japanese schoolgirls began to be sold on-line to men in other parts of the world.

URI
Buying, acquiring and selling became referred to at that time by two extremely fashionable words: *getto* ('get') and *uri* ('sell') These words derived their pleasing frisson from the fact that they explicitly blurred any distinction between shopping for goods and shopping for people. 'Getto' can mean 'being good at flirting' and 'getting a boyfriend' as well as 'acquiring something'. Both terms seemed to symbolise exciting elemental forces uniting as one all human and financial activity. An immense electronic stage-play acted out by high-school girls was being conducted across the interface of the media. Media workers and intellectuals struggled to write the script for a story about a people threatened with disappearing into the interstices of financial exchange.

ENKŌ
In 1994 the *burusera* phenomenon bled into a new and greater scandal. Not only were schoolgirls selling off their uniforms, but apparently they were also throwing themselves into a new kind of amateur prostitution. This was called 'assisted dating' – *enjo kōsai* – but it was widely referred to by the cuter abbreviation 'enkō' (Kuronuma, 1996). For the media and for schoolgirls *enkō* became a keyword of the mid-90s. The media featured images of schoolgirls on the streets; using their PHS handsets or borrowed mobile phones and dialling in to *terekura* (telephone chat lines) to find male customers for their dates.

Such stories were frequently featured on television for the next three years.

「援助交際」を希望しています

"I'm looking for an assisted date"

> "Schoolgirls seemed to merge physically with the technology of the electronic screen and telephone network. They became the *joshi kōsai* brand."

Schoolgirls in uniform peopled the news, documentary and educational programmes, chat and game shows. One journalist reported in the *Japan Times* on 22 October 1997 that 40 per cent more print space was devoted to discussing schoolchildren in Shibuya than to all domestic and international affairs combined. Their faces and voices were frequently disguised with screen pixelation and voice synthesisers so that the girls appeared as vague and shifting impressions of bodies with squeaky, computerised voices. Schoolgirls seemed to merge physically with the technology of the electronic screen and telephone network. They became the *joshi kōsai* brand. Time spent with them could be bought by men.

It was said that money raised from dates was used by schoolgirls to fulfil their only desire – to own brand-name goods, namely designer clothing and accessories. Journalists stood in theatrical awe of the ignorant gluttony of the girls. They were filmed clutching 10,000 yen notes. The viewing public were enthralled with the spectacle of an open, amoral and limitless pursuit of the symbols of corporate wealth.

KOGAL
The phenomenon of the schoolgirl-sex industry had influenced the style and mannerisms of ordinary schoolgirls, who customised their school uniforms in a sexually provocative manner. Known as *kogal*, these girls rolled up the waistband

of their school skirts to turn them into miniskirts, and instead of regulation school socks *kogal* wore 'loose socks' crumpled around their shins. Their dishevelled style resembled the images of semi-naked schoolgirls featured in *burusera* pornography for men. *Kogal* played games with the dominant and fetishistic image of the schoolgirl as a sex object.

CHŌ-KAWAII
Beyond school uniforms *kogal* had another style, variably identified as *chō-kawaii* (super-cute), *shitagi-kei* (lingerie-style), *ō'share* (showy) and kitsch. *Kogal* wore cheap imitations of silk, fur and leather, such as silky acrylic shirts in prints reminiscent of Hermès silk-scarf

designs and full-length coats with fur collars. Their gaudy look was accessorised with salon suntans, elaborate manicures and hair heavily streaked with whitish-blonde flashes. New fashion magazines were launched, aimed specifically at *kogal* culture. Utilising cameras, mirrors and accessories, *kogal* made heavy-handed performances of vanity and preening on the streets. The conspicuously staged materialism that was part of *kogal* style mimics the media images, in what was almost a parody of the notion of 'consumer lifestyle' itself.

JANE PAVITT

At home with the Joneses

Next time you make a cup of instant coffee or feed the cat, think about how you do it and why. You never know who may be watching. Bar-code scanning, credit-card usage, the prevalence of CCTV and surveillance technology are all used for monitoring the social and demographic nature of consumption. The means of analysing contemporary consumer behaviour are literally embedded into the fabric of our technological society. An understanding of how consumers' preferences are formed and articulated provides vital information for marketers and brand owners. Major corporations have used market research and the observation of consumer behaviour as a means of understanding our responses to brands

since, at least, the 1930s. Current brand research also now demands an even more intimate access to our personalised choices and private behaviours around brands. The London-based advertising agency BMP DDB has an experimental consumer-research department called Culture Lab, run by Siamack Salari. Working with householders and shoppers, Salari builds profiles of consumers that focus on their habits, routines and personalised use of products. Salari explains:

Culture Lab is a context-based observation research unit. Our premise is that no action or occasion can be understood in isolation or as a discrete event. Context is the unexplored frontier in marketing services. Consumers

are increasingly unpredictable and less likely to be persuaded by advertisers' messages. Their responses to brands are more likely to be based on how they relate to family and friends, and the contexts in which they encounter goods. By gathering this data, we can tell our clients how their brands fit into people's lives, and how their brand values are interpreted.

Our method is to set up relationships with individuals and households, documenting the random and inconsequential instances of their daily lives, to build up a picture of them as consumers. Subjects are also given cameras and encouraged to film themselves. Because we do not describe our findings as objective, they are made as transparent as possible to both client and subject. Households are actively involved in the

"Brands are like chess pieces – the moves we make with them are an indication of our relationship to others."

research process, and the researcher becomes a participant in the process of discovery. The emphasis with observational research is to keep the subjects as animated and comfortable as possible. Their behaviour is affected by the presence of the observers, but the way we explore decision-making processes is by telling households, at opportune moments, about our own habits and traits.

The home is where most things happen. We cook, write shopping lists, save vouchers sent by post, plan our finances, read magazines, watch television and discuss the near and distant future with our families and friends. The home, therefore, is a decision-making backdrop against which most buying choices can be understood. It is impossible to explain a mode of behaviour,

without understanding its context.

A tired parent may choose a frozen or ready meal to prepare for the family after a hard day. Only, before she places it in the oven, she adds her own grated cheese, some extra pepper, onion or tomato. By the time the pizza is ready, the preparation time is the same as it would have been to make it from scratch. The reality of the scenario is that her choice took her less thinking time, but her actions personalised the family meal.

Home is also where we organise our relationship with brands, and each household has a nerve centre for the management of this – by the phone, on a pin board, where the bills and money-off vouchers are kept. It is where we choose to read or throw away junk mail. Whatever the location, it is here

we can discover an individual's brand preferences and observe decisions being made that the buyer may not be conscious of when acting on them.

Sometimes the most insightful data comes in the form of stories that we are told concerning a particular subject. These can be sad, funny, angry ones or even lies. They reveal an enormous amount about an individual and his or her realities; the way we perceive the world around us. We observe activities and naturally occurring conversations in order to decode everyday behaviour and understand how brands fit into people's lives. Brands are like chess pieces – the moves we make with them are an indication of our relationship to others.

CHAPTER THREE

ALL THE WORLD'S A STORE

AARON BETSKY

THE SPACES OF SHOPPING

The world is not just a stage, but also our shopping mall. We put together our identities by buying bits and pieces of consumer culture. We identify ourselves and others by how we dress, what music we listen to, which brands we sport. The places in which we do this are our temples of consumption, where we learn some of the rituals of belonging. These are the locations of desire and the home of branding. The shopping mall is our church and our palace, our mirror and our agora.

The question we need to ask is to what degree both we as consumers, and the brands we buy, are connected to and affected by the nature of the spaces in which that buying and selling takes place. At a time when marketers want their customers' buying experiences to be 'seamless', from the first time they see the advertising to the day they purchase the product, how well do the forms of the selling space reflect this desire?

The architecture of contemporary selling spaces is difficult to pin down. We expect buildings to reflect the abstract values we hold, in structures that are both literal and metaphoric. The architecture of the shopping environment, however, disappears into the background as much as it can. Retail environment design is dominated by engineers of various sorts. Retail consultants, store planners, security specialists as well as designers all work together to create the spaces in which we encounter brands. Their task is to make the building, as a physical form, as invisible as possible. All the shopper should find is the products and the brands – appearing as if by magic and floating free from constraints – in a space that we can inhabit by reference to them. We are never supposed to be aware of the systems that make all of this possible. This would open our eyes to an order that is larger than us, something that by implication we cannot purchase. The logic of shopping is that we are fully able to make, and control, our own world.

This is the importance of the shopping environment. The store and the mall offer an alternative to many traditional types of architecture that have largely led to dead ends. Traditional architecture was concerned with the central institutions of a society, whether temples or palaces, offices or museums. Architects set out to build fragments of perfection that stood out against the realities of everyday life. These moments of order always represented the values of those in control. Architecture in such cases became the concrete expression of an abstract and alien order, to which we, the common consumers, could only aspire.

An architecture that appears to remove itself from the arena of power offers an alternative to such a traditional vision. This would be an architecture that allows us to assemble the fragments of everyday life into a continually changing collage. As sociologist Anthony Giddens says:[1]

> The self established a trajectory which can only become coherent through the reflexive use of the broader social environment. The impetus towards control, geared to reflexivity, thrusts the self into the outer world in ways which have no clear parallel in previous times. The disembedding mechanisms intrude into the heart of self-identity; but they do not 'empty out' the self any more than they simply remove prior supports on which self-identity was based. Rather, they allow the self (in principle) to achieve much greater mastery over the social relations and social contexts reflexively incorporated into the forging of self-identity than was previously possible.

By weaving together a tapestry of forms, we can cloak ourselves in a pleasing and ever flexible representation of our reality. To a certain extent we have always done this with our interiors, where furniture, mementoes and other fragments of our lives come together to form a highly personal and always changing composition. We can also find a momentary sense of this 'collage' environment at festivals, concerts and other expressions of collective enjoyment and exploration. Such a woven architecture also exists in our memory, which we are constantly reordering so as to make sense of our current situation. Conversely, we also project our sense of a flexible and modular reality into the future, imagining a better world in which we may some day live.

Superficially, the places where we shop seem

to provide us with just such a free space. The displays change constantly. We can see ourselves reflected not only in the scenes and mannequins the stores show us but also in the shop windows themselves. These thus become tools for social connection and seduction. We gather in malls and stores to promenade, socialise and construct a social sphere. The architecture of these places reconstructs the past in pastiches of bygone eras, as well as presenting the future; and the very absence of fixed form seems to liberate us to make anything we want of this world. As Margaret Crawford has said: 'In a city of endless atomisation, infinite individual ecologies are available.'[2]

But it is all a fiction. We are not truly free in our shopping environment. We have to buy into this world – literally. Many of us cannot even enter this scene, either because social or economic disadvantages exclude us, or because we do not possess what has been called the 'artefactual literacy' required to interpret and enjoy it.[3] We may also exclude ourselves by choice, if we recognise how our behaviour is being manipulated. For those who

can enter, however, it appears to be a beautiful world, and one that appears to set us free to create our own scenarios. This is the central paradox of the shopping environment: it is both a place of freedom and the ultimate expression of a society in which we are all composite constructions controlled by the laws of ownership, production and demand.

To understand the potential and the dangers of our contemporary retail architecture and brandscape, we must look closely at the new shopping spaces. This is not something we usually do, since we consider the store, the mall or the market to be a place that offers little to hold our attention apart from the things we want to buy. Yet this very lack of imposed order can make these spaces liberating.

What is more, the vestiges of the physical frame that these spaces provide can actively help to prevent the goods on sale from disappearing into the background. Without this spatial influence, what we are buying would vanish into a seamless continuum: a collection of properties that can only assemble themselves as branded products through the production and consumption processes. As the

Right: Shop window, London, 1999.
Following spread: French Connection store, London, 1999.

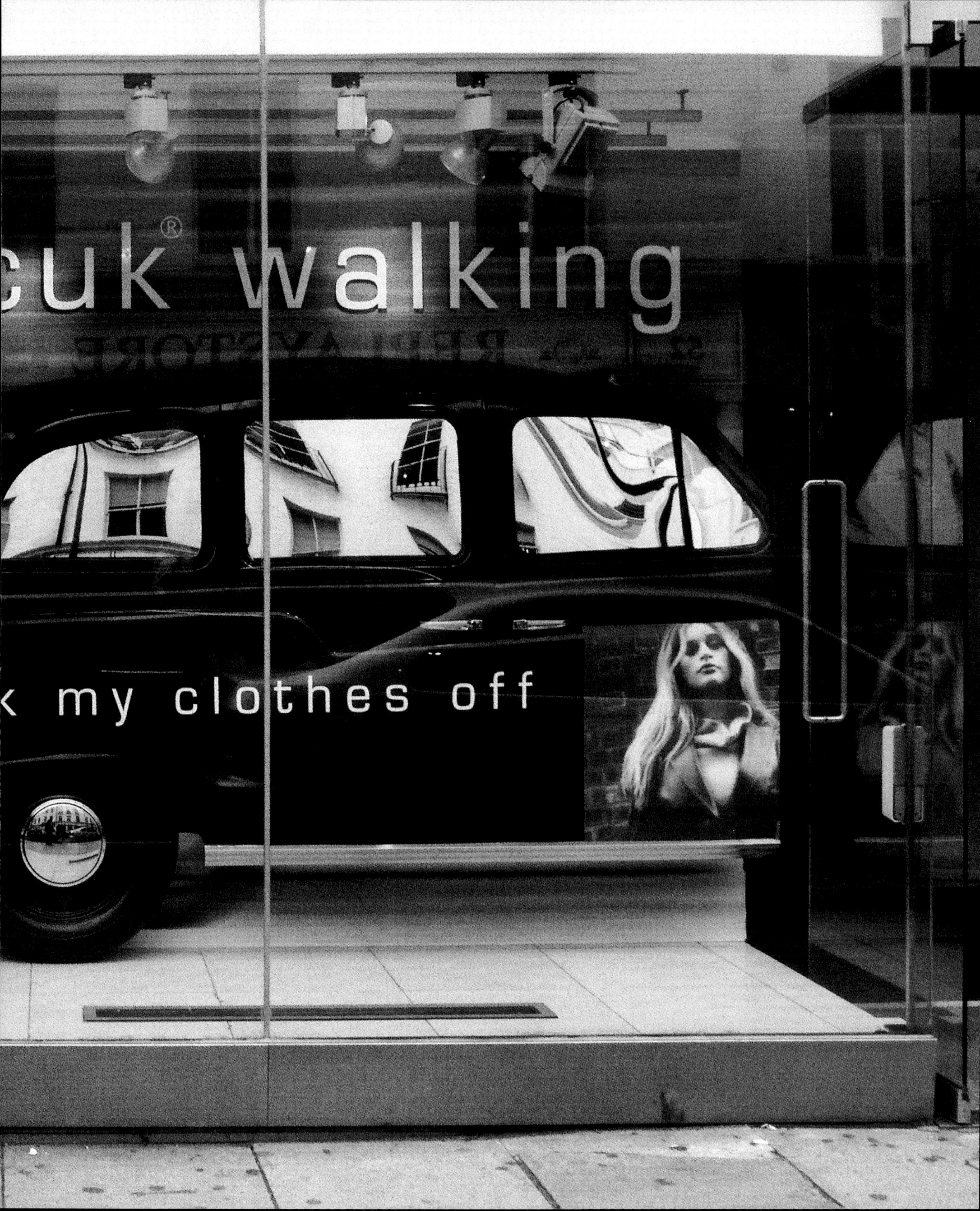
cuk walking
my clothes off

things we buy turn into brands *into which* we buy, the physical distance to the goods, the social space in which we buy them, and the difference between the physical thing and its projected appearance all disappear. We can no longer understand the spaces of shopping as places that assemble the riches of the world into a collage of colours and materials, within a choreography of spatial sequences amid the rituals of buying. With a *swoosh*, the spaces themselves disappear into brands.[4]

This situation is deeply rooted in the past. The history of retail spaces is one in which the presentation of goods is always thinly framed. Yet in the past, this structure always offered a 'third scene' – an alternative prospect both of the goods themselves and to the civic structures in which they were being sold. Brands mediate between object and ideology, while architecture offers a cut, a division or a critical break between them. The architecture of shopping is always characterised by openness, opening up within the city and around the product.

Democracy began in the agora, an outdoor market.[5] In much the same way, even the Roman Forum was originally a place to shop, rather than a place to adore ancestors or debate matters of state. The open space at the heart of any city was, and still is, an empty void that implies order and control. But it is only of use when it is filled with cafés, stalls and other accoutrements of commercial life.[6] Cities congealed not just around defensive points but also around crossroads, river crossings and harbours: places where goods arrived, were displayed and bought.[7] As Jane Jacobs has pointed out, the city starts as an open space where we display our artefacts, the products we create from the raw materials that surround us. It is from trading in such things that culture arises.[8]

The logic of the open-air market provides us with the first order of commercial architecture. The formalisation of the selling space offers a rhythm, a hierarchy and an increasingly complex form of organisation. Each stall is one small part of a scaffold, constructed from simple materials. It gives us a defined area, shelter from rain or sun, and an arena for social interaction. Midway between the tent that was our first and moveable home, and the rigid walls of our houses, the open-air market suggests a notion of order that is still sufficiently flexible to contain the changing displays of the products and allow them to offer themselves to us.[9]

As time passes, these stalls are arranged into rows or other geometric forms that imply a stronger rhythm. As proto-streets, these sequences of stalls blend into each other to form a concatenation of sticks, cloth or whatever material we can string together into a sequence. We observe each stall in order, and yet each has a relationship to the other. This is the space of appearance of those goods that mediate our relationship with the larger world; and their display is halfway between an abstract order (the rows of stalls) and the collage of individual forms with which, for example, we dress ourselves.

In a larger sense, the marketplace is also a spectacle. This is where we have traditionally acted out alternatives to the official reality, where we gather to dramatise innovative realities and viewpoints that we would not otherwise see. Here we find the comedies and tragedies, the Punch-and-Judy shows, the carnival acts, the grotesques and the magic tricks, mixing in with the real goods we purchase to provide the unorthodox alternatives, the ob-scene to the scenes of everyday life. The marketplace is the stage for freedom of ideas and expression. Here law and order dissolves, licentiousness appears, tricks are played on the unsuspecting, property is bought, sold or liberated by sleight of hand, and we give and take freely of our commentary on each other.[10]

The architecture here is almost invisible. The appearance of the marketplace stands midway between forest or field and the formality of the city. In Greece and Rome, where it was at the heart of the urban scene, the marketplace was an opening that recalled the countryside outside the walls. In medieval Europe, where the fairs first knitted together an economy that was to conquer the world, the great cities were as often as not generated around a clearing or crossroads.

In other cultures the shopping space was darker and less open. The souk or bazaar was a labyrinth that

XIV.
Der Metzger oder Fleischer.

Nächst dem Brod ist auch das Fleisch des Rindviehes, der Kälber, Schafe und Schweine eins der ersten Bedürfnisse unsrer Tische. Der Metzger oder Fleischer kauft dieses Vieh von den Landleuten, die sich mit der Viehzucht beschäftigen, schlachtet solches und verkauft das Fleisch wieder, entweder in seinem Wohnhause, oder an einem öffentlichen Ort, welcher die Fleischbank genannt wird. Unsre Tafel stellet eine solche Fleischbank vor, wo die Frau eines Metzgers Fleisch an eine Köchin auswiegt. — Es ist ein wichtiger Artickel für eine weise Polizey, dahin zu sehen daß kein anders als gutes und gesundes Fleisch zu Markte gebracht, und die Fleischbänke möglichst reinlich gehalten werden. Die Stadt Nürnberg übt diese nützliche Polizeyanstalt in demjenigen Grad der Vollkommenheit aus, daß selbst auswärtige Tadler ihr in diesem Stücke einen nahmhaften Vorzug vor andern grossen Städten einräumen müssen.

Below: The grand staircase
of the Bon Marché, Paris,
c. 1870, engraving by
Karl Fichot.

middle classes, where they were surrounded by the goods that defined them.

Department stores became increasingly elaborate and developed their own spatial order. The sequences of counters mimicked the old stalls, while the atrium became the void at the heart of this activity. The grand stairs offered performance stages on which the shoppers stood in for the actors. The dressing rooms became places of liberation and transformation in which mirrors reflected a new self being born, while the tea rooms and restaurants became sites for the construction of a new set of social relations. The

stores even introduced many people to such technical innovations as the elevator. Here was a whole new world in one building.[17]

The new stores also brought a sense of uncertainty as new forms of social order that replaced the concerns of the individual with those of the mass. The freedom of entry meant that in theory the department store was accessible to all sectors of society; although in practice some were excluded or at least discouraged. The department store was more than likely to be seen as a middle-class, feminised space.[18] During the much publicised opening of Selfridges in

London in 1909, for example, the store was declared as 'dedicated to woman's service first of all'.

While the great department stores that arose at the beginning of the twentieth century helped reform and renovate cities, they also lost their power to amaze and liberate.[19] Although certain of them remained Meccas, such as Harrods or Selfridges in London, Bloomingdales or Macy's in New York, the march of advertising and branding meant that goods were also available everywhere – even by mail order. The diffusion of the buying public into the suburbs created an audience that depended on advertising more than the physical framework of the store to convince them to buy. As a result, stores became integrated once more into the fabric of the city. Occasionally, architects would use commercial environments as places to build a vision of the new – one thinks of German architect Erich Mendelsohn's Schocken department stores, such as in Stuttgart (1928) and Chemnitz (1929). But in general, the store became just a place to buy goods. It now existed in urban environments that were so thoroughly dominated by middle-class structures and advertising that there was little sense of memory or aspiration for

the architecture to embody.

It was only when the middle class began leaving the city and making a place for itself on the fringes of the city that stores regained their function. They became focal points in the new, artificial landscape the middle classes were making for themselves. The suburb, that place between the city and nature where the middle class constructed its meandering, uncertain and technologically driven homeland, found its heart in the shopping mall. Movement – roads, railroad lines – dominates the suburb, which has no clear order and is always changing as people shift within it or develop it. This is the logic of suburban spaces, which demand reinvestment of capital as quickly as possible for the purposes of further speculation and profit.

The basis for the suburban shopping space was the market stall. In this case, however, the new retail spaces were designed to service the automobile culture, and so they banded together to provide an aggregation of goods for the shopper on the move. They provided plenty of parking, thus creating a void that extended the street, and added large and prominent signs that could be read by people moving at speed. These soon overwhelmed the architecture.

Previous pages and above:
Macy's, New York, 1920s,
decorated for the Christmas
season.

These new, auto-friendly selling spaces also became the focal point of their community:[20]

> The drive-in was oriented not to recreational paths, but to routine ones of area residents. If enough people living within about a one-mile radius drove by the site on a regular basis, a respectable business could be sustained and, just as in more densely settled districts, other retail outlets might be attracted to the vicinity. The drive-in market thus helped to pioneer business locations within an urban context rather than standing as an outpost that would long remain isolated in more or less open surroundings... When the drive-in market was a catalyst for commercial development, the resulting aggregation often lacked the centralised structure of a neighbourhood business district, having no clear hierarchy of sites or functions. At a pivotal point in the metropolitan area's growth, when business owners were beginning to understand the implications of a mass motoring populace, the drive-in market demonstrated how even a place catering to mundane shopping needs could be an attraction in itself.

The supermarket grew directly out of these small strips, the first being opened in Memphis, Tennessee, in 1916 (it was called Piggly-Wiggly). Supermarkets were formalised in 1928 in Los Angeles by the store brand Ralphs. Here the model was not so much the interior market halls – it was the open world of the seasonal market made permanent: 'Ralphs created a new kind of space that was lofty, imposing, yet non-hierarchical and conductive to perambulation, allowing consumers to choose their own paths of movement as well as their own goods. In no previous instance had so large a retail space seemed so perceptually open and so liberating.'[21] After the Second World War, these techniques were adopted both by British retailers such as Tesco, and by the French with the growth of hypermarkets such as Carrefour. The latter became a supermarket blown up to a scale at which even the American chains could only wonder.

The real monument to suburbia, and the final scene where we see goods transformed into brands that float in an abstract retail environment, was the

Right: Display of household goods, Woolworths, Great Britain, 1960s.

shopping mall. The first of this new breed was Southdale , outside of Minneapolis, designed in 1954-6 by the Los Angeles-based architect Victor Gruen. Southdale was a meandering collection of modernist pavilions that fragmented and popularised the interlocking compositions demonstrated in both the buildings and the teachings of the German modernist design school, the Bauhaus. It was also a thoroughly American building that exalted space and movement. The shopping mall was, like rock'n'roll and the skyscraper, an American invention that spread to the rest of the world with the globalisation of commerce.

Leaving the parking on the outside, the shopping mall created a new version of the city street that ran between the stores themselves. The mall became an abstract version of the city that the middle class had left behind. It had gateways, streets, alleys, service areas, central squares and gathering spaces. What it did not have was a hierarchy. The biggest stores became anchors, rather than focal points. These big, windowless boxes signalled the beginning of a journey into the commercial world. They had few features that would distinguish them from other retail establishments. Those stores then marched

around whatever pattern the planners established in such a way as to get the shopper lost.[22]

The key moment in the shopping mall experience was the 'Gruen transfer'. This was where shoppers, who may have arrived intending to purchase a particular product, would become distracted by something else, deviate from their path and start wandering. Before long shoppers would be lost in a maze from which the only escape was to expose themselves to more chances to buy. One had to become lost in the world of artefacts to find one's self. The bazaar had merged with the marketplace stalls and the arcade to form a perfect shopping environment.

As shopping malls grew in size and importance, they became community focal points. This was where housewives and children gathered, where old people strolled, and where community activities took place. Since the mall was often the largest building in the landscape, it became the signpost by which the suburban resident could identify different parts of an amorphous and changing world. Ironically, the mall lost most of the crystalline nature of the marketplace, the arcade or even the strip mall. It became a featureless box whose interior was as often as not

Right: Northland Shoppping Center, Detroit 1954. Architect: Victor Gruen. Gruen's plans for both Northland and Southdale Center (1954-6) defined the American shopping experience of the 1950s.

inarticulate. The core of the suburban experience was a place that did not offer visual hierarchies. It displaced the columned fronts and articulated facades of courthouses, city halls and banks that had previously been the focal point of communities. As a result, civic traditions were no longer embodied in its architecture.[23]

The shopping mall that evolved in the three decades after 1945 was the endpoint for the development of the marketplace. From a temporary construction of stalls that appeared as needed, it had become a closed box that defined a completely artificial realm of shopping. The commercial scene now excluded the ob-scene, the informal and vulgar culture, as much as it could. As brands and store chains gained importance over the goods, even the reality of the object of desire dissolved into nothing but signs of seduction. Since at least the second half of the nineteenth century, advertising had striven to create a sense of cohesion across time and space by breaking through the physical barrier of the store. The end result was that the rise of branding had reduced the chaotic variety of commercial images to a set of singular and iconic graphic identifiers. The panoply of merchandising devices that recalled the advertising campaign could then disappear from the selling space. The store environment needed fewer and fewer features, just as the goods themselves became more and more abstract carriers of meaning.

Malls have become the same all over the world, with only minor regional variations.[24] In Asia, many are underground, and are part of large railroad or subway stations. Here the lack of exterior becomes literal. In Europe, they have tended to be smaller and often integrated more carefully into existing urban situations. While some projects are also underground and part of large railroad or subway stations – for example, Les Halles in Paris – others are more complex and seamless parts of the city. The model here is the Lijnbaan, the 1954 mixed-use project in Rotterdam, designed by Bijvoet and Duiker. The Lijnbaan plays off open-air shopping arcades against housing slabs set in small parks, and an anchor department store designed by Marcel Breuer. As both developers and designers have increased their global reach, however, regional distinctions that might extend from their organization to differences in colour schemes and signage have disappeared.

Similarly, as the science of shopping and its finance have gone global, the organisation of malls has developed into a series of quite closely matched variations. The most common malls are still those that connect two or three anchor stores with a dominant corridor and several smaller cross-corridors. Food courts and cinemas are usually located either at the heart of the building or on a higher level. They form a public square within the maze of corridors. The entry is not usually taken as an opportunity to make a major statement: the developers do not want shoppers hanging around admiring the architecture, when they should be progressing into the active shopping environment as quickly as possible.[25]

Though tastes and architectural styles have changed, the overall structure of the elements within the mall's spatial organisation has not.[26] Stores are very narrow (usually no more than 20 to 30 feet) and long, so that as many stores as possible can announce themselves to shoppers. The storefronts are almost completely glass, with frames that are meant to validate the merchandise: wood for a bookstore, marble for a jewellery store. Lighting is bright.

Signage – or 'way-finding systems', as the experts like to call them – dominates these spaces. These signs create a rhythm akin to that of trees, they establish focal points, and they combine the images that tell us what to do (road signs) and what to want (commercial advertising) into singular structures. In recent years, these systems have come to dominate the malls so completely that they have merged with the architecture. They form continual arcades, strips along the centre of the mall and frameworks for planting, seating or other decoration.

There are few right-angled turns or orthogonal grids in shopping malls. This is not so much because designers wish to make a statement, as because developers want the experience of shopping to be seamless. All barriers and all possible

stumbling-blocks have to be removed. Shops rarely
have visible doors and corridors angle into each
other; even the lines between soffits and ceilings
dissolve to where a skylight or the coving hints at
nothing but a nebulous other realm. A good example
of this 'classic' shopping mall design is the Beverly
Center in Los Angeles, designed by Welton Becket
& Associates in 1982.

In recent years, the stalls that sparked all this have
reappeared as carts – 'incubators' where individual
retailers can try out their merchandising ideas before
they invest in a store or are taken over by a large chain.
They give the mall a sense of reality and diversity,
though they are only temporary way-stations that lead
us to the mall proper. Just as any architectural style
quickly disappears into the fabric of the mall, so these
expressions of commercial innovation soon fade into
the background.

By the mid-1980s, the mall had become stagnant.
In their perpetual need to entice shoppers into the
next experience, developers had created ever larger
malls ever further removed from urban centres. Some
developers turned to tricks such as opening up malls
to the outdoors again whenever possible, or

propelling them vertically upwards in the centres of
city in their willingness to try anything that might
upgrade the appearance of their buildings. However,
they were caught out by the fact that the mall had
become utterly formulaic, dominated by chain stores
and a gloomy sense of familiarity. It was felt that there
was little room for growth. After the Reagan
recession, retail developers began looking at ways out
of the tomb they had built for themselves.[27]

In the last two decades, the shopping mall has
begun to fall apart. It has dissolved into mini-malls
and convenience centres, Big Box retail centres,
hybrid entertainment and shopping environments,
and quasi-malls that have become reintegrated into
the city. Each of these new types points the way
toward a potential re-deployment of the marketplace
into a form that might be either more liberating or
even more constricting. The appearance of the
electronic mall, whether on the World Wide Web or
through television shopping and catalogues, further
extends these possibilities.

The mini-mall condenses its big brother into a
form that both minimises its importance and
reintegrates into our daily lives. It was a type that
emerged in the south-western states of America in
the mid-1980s, when environmental regulations and
rising gas and real-estate prices conspired to put
many urban gas stations out of business. Their corner
lots became the sites for L-shaped commercial
developments. These mini-malls combined the auto-
oriented configuration of the strip mall with the
contours of the urban grid. They made use of the
rhythm of the city, determined by traffic lights and
pedestrian crossings, to form nodes of shopping.
Though the original malls were one-storey tall, a few
two- and even three-storey variations have emerged.

Some developers have tried to turn their mini-
malls into giant signs or have adopted stylistic devices
such as colonnades to distinguish them. But the vast
majority of these buildings are indistinguishable
from their surroundings, to such an extent that it is
difficult to identify any particular architectural
element. Beyond the number of storeys, these malls
exhibit other variables such as the inclusion of a fast-

food outlet or drive-through box (either for a bank or for services such as dry cleaning, photo developing or coffee). Other variations include the way in which signage is incorporated into the building or vertical circulation appears as exposed and articulated.

There is little to say about such structures as buildings. They are no more and no less than the intensification of those parts of the city's fabric in which shopping has become practically the only element in the public realm. This is true to such an extent that we now equate vast stretches of empty road only as the space between commercial developments. And yet they are somehow unnoticed: it is only when something calamitous happens, as it did following the civil unrest after the Rodney King verdict in 1992, that these commercial nodes become visible: during the riots, it was the mini-malls that burned.

The Asian variation provides us with the vertical mini-malls found all over Japan, Korea and other developed nations. Here an open sliver of circulation leads up, and down, to floor after floor of stores and restaurants. As in the West, there is little to distinguish these developments from the overall texture of the city. Just as the traditional shopping malls of Japan are underground expanses spreading out from railway stations, so the mini-malls are invisible intensifications of an immensely dense urban grid.

The other interesting point about mini-malls is purely economic: they serve as points of entry for small entrepreneurs into the mainstream economy. Many of the shop owners belong to ethnic minorities, and these relatively cheap stores give them a chance to establish their own commercial ventures. The presence of many different cultures and languages further fragments the appearance of these shopping spaces. An assortment of typefaces, signs from a variety of ethnic visual traditions, and different approaches to what makes a store an attractive space are all in vigorous competition. From brightly lit interiors to an explosion of advertising signs, everything undercuts the homogeneity the shopping mall has imposed on the commercial environment during the last few decades.

A European variant on the mini-mall is the small-scale 'local shopping centre'. British versions of these small strips of around ten to twelve stores, built on what was previously unused space at the edge of traditional High Street shopping areas, have become adept incubators for entrepreneurial immigrant store owners.

Big Box retail centres go the other way. They are huge structures, often further removed from population centres than traditional malls. They are constructed to house collections of large chain stores that specialise in bringing a series of related goods together under one immense roof: Home Depot, Ikea, Maxis and Toys'R'Us are good examples. The mall becomes a collection of immense boxes standing in vast expanses of parking. There is no room here for the Gruen Transfer – only for the piling up of more and more goods in ever greater bulk. There are no public spaces, other than an occasional food court, and no sense of a promenade. Here the space of shopping has become larger, more directed and less a part of the fabric of everyday life.

Ironically, this has given architecture an opportunity to get back into the picture. The big blocks give designers a chance to create grand monuments to shopping. Though their clients usually restrict their freedom, designers have occasionally created some rather striking structures.

Right: Mini-Mall,
Atlanta, USA, 2000.

Opposite: Horton Plaza, San
Diego, California, 1985,
Architect: The Jerde
Partnership International,
Inc.
Previous pages: Faneuil Hall
and Quincy Market, Boston,
1990s. The Rouse
Corporation.

A good example is the intensely coloured, almost surreal landscape Ricardo Legoretta created for the Tustin Center in Southern California. The architect made good use of the fact that here the parking lot and approaches do not surround a singular object, but comprise a more complex landscape that connects an assortment of nodal points. Lines of palm trees, tilted rock planes and geometric fragments take the place of way-finding systems and give the development a strong sense of place.

In Europe, the mode for Big Box retailing started with the enlargement of supermarkets such as Maxis and Carrefour. These grew to such gigantic proportions that they began to take on the character of an enclosed market, offering a wide variety of goods and acting as a regional centre. Ikea made its forms recognisable by turning their stores into abstract blue sculptures, and providing day care and decent food in their interiors. Here the Big Boxes became abstracted and interiorised versions of the agora.

The interiors of the Big Boxes can be overwhelming. Except in the case of companies like Ikea, which has divided up half of each of its stores into environments of domestic vignettes, almost all of these retailers present their spaces to the viewer without any modulation. The spaces are high, the aisles repetitive and the structure on which the goods present themselves are evident. These are places that resemble the vast archives of which the architects of the Enlightenment dreamed. All is clear, available and at hand. Machinery for stocking and moving goods mixes with both the scaffolding for construction and display, and with the human beings making use of these technologies. So they resemble the kind of city architects Fred Koetter and Colin Rowe called for in their seminal Collage City.[28] This is about as modern as architecture can be. There is no decoration, no hint at hierarchy and no sense of the real world. In this artificial world, the shopping environment has become a total experience.

A variation on these Big Box retail centres is the outlet mall. Here stores present their goods in warehouse-like settings, the size of which approaches that of the Big Box retailers but the arrangement of which borrows from aspects of the traditional mall. Most of them are outdoors, and thus they also have some of the direct nature of the older strip centres. The emphasis on cheap construction (not only to save the developer money but also to give the customer the sense of a bargain environment) again allows designers to experiment with forms less reserved than those permitted in a traditional mall. Though the quality of the graphics and the materials used for the stores is often rather harsh, the primitive quality of the concrete, block or stucco construction has given some designers an excuse to experiment with forceful forms.

Shopping in these spaces is divorced so completely from the experiences of everyday life that it has little connection with the tradition of the marketplace. These are destination points that resemble a strange hybrid of the cathedral of commerce and democratic versions of the king's or priest's warehouse of wealth. They are placeless spaces where technology reveals itself in all its naked glory, alongside the abandonment of packaging and other forms of seduction that habitually enclose objects at the core of our consumer society. Their scale approaches the point at which people become almost insignificant – a utopia of which some architects have always dreamed – while any chance of experiencing the hidden, the secret or the oppositional space has completely disappeared. Here shopping, architecture, storage and space have come together to create ex-urban magnets that seem to have no particular meaning.

When the branded goods, stacked high in eerily immense spaces, do not speak for themselves, architecture provides its own brand that dissolves the product brand from the outside in. The opposite of such stripping down of form, in which shopping becomes an experience of the goods in an abstract landscape, is the entertainment architecture of the themed malls. The prototypes for these spaces were the urban renovations performed by the Rouse Corporation in Boston (Faneuil Hall), Baltimore (Harborplace) and New York (South Street Seaport),

as well as by John Jerde, whose San Diego Horton Plaza was the first and in many ways remains the most sophisticated themed environment. The precedents, however, were Disneyland and its Florida cousin, Disneyworld. These gave birth to the idea that one could go somewhere for an experience that was neither religious nor transforming, but merely enjoyable – and then further merged this with the evocation of other times and places. The fair became permanent, and the experience consumable.

In the earliest themed-shopping environments, the mall re-invigorated itself by turning back to its own history. Faneuil Hall was a marketplace repackaged as a mall, which was meant to resemble a marketplace. It also used a historic structure that made people feel as if they were coming to that quaint place of memory, the city. The location of almost all of these early re-developments was at such edges of the old city as the docks. Here the old order used to break down and the freedom of the open seas crept into the city's mores along with the wares that arrived there. These locations reinforced the artificial sense that the new selling space was a place of freedom. The themed environment offered the ability to capture the past and then to use it as a place of liberation from the control of the present.

Architects such as John Jerde justified their work by claiming that they were providing the public with a space that rediscovered the values of community, dense housing and public space – elements for which the renovation movement of the 1970s had fought so hard. Jerde borrowed the forms of the Italian Renaissance to dignify his malls, then gave them bright colours and abstracted their outlines in the manner of Charles Moore. The results were stage-sets, the operatic overtones of which became more evident because of the combination of their large scale and flimsiness. It took a while for the retail establishments to catch up with the visual pandemonium Jerde produced, but soon the balance between the architectural and retail packaging was restored. What remained was the scale of Jerde's gestures; their evocation of a language that was primitive in its cartoon pastiche of a child's idea of home or official building, yet still able to indicate some form of public space.[29]

Jerde also mastered the use of the curve as an alternative to the corridor. In an era in which the importance of department stores was waning, fragmenting the retail experience along with most other elements of the economy, Jerde and his followers came up with a simple gesture. The curved

BORDEN MAIN STREET ICE CREAM PARLOR
MAGIC KINGDOM–WALT DISNEY WORLD

Above: Ontario Mills, California, 1997. One of a series of retail sites selling discounted brands, developed by the Mills Corporation. Designer: Communication Arts Inc. Following pages: Bluewater, Kent, England, 2000.

paths and fragments of paths, leading to and from nowhere in particular, let shoppers promenade past the retail establishments without seeing any hierarchy in what they encountered. Food courts and cinemas, plazas and cul-de-sacs interrupted these fluid lines as places for gathering, rest and reflection, where shoppers would find themselves completely surrounded by signs and symbols of retail.

Many of these themed environments were also open to the outside, so that they began to resemble something like a 'real' city. Other architects made this reference even more clear by adopting closer approximations of classical architecture. They might sometimes create storefronts to make the mall appear like a New England, French provincial or vaguely Spanish street. British examples such as Bluewater, on the edge of London, wear their theming rather lightly and concentrate on creating an overwhelming, festive environment in which we can become completely immersed.[30]

Only a few architects chose themes outside of the more-or-less traditional urban repertoire. In the Orient especially, a few high-tech environments appeared, as they did in Renzo Piano's Bercy shopping mall in Paris. Only in airports, which soon began to rival malls as locations for mass retailing,

did the language of glass and steel connections, streamlined into vaguely futuristic fragments of angular geometries by the likes of Helmut Jahn, become truly popular.

Disney and its theme-park imitators took the themed shopping environment to its logical extension by creating complete villages that were both tourist destinations and stores. Disney's original stores were recreations of a mythical American Midwestern small town constructed at 5/8th scale. When they became more adventurous they designed French, British and even 'Japanese' villages. In Hollywood, Universal Studios worked so hard to recreate the eclectic architecture of a Los Angeles located only a few miles away, that one executive exclaimed: 'If I have to get bums to make it seem more like a real city, I'll just call central casting.'[31] —

Though some critics predicted that such theming would come to dominate all retail environments, most developers chose not to be too specific.[32] Instead of definite references, designers chose to evoke a generic past that was also modern enough to promise a better future through acquisition. As a result, many themed environments began to blend with their more conventional predecessors. They offered just a hint of a specific atmosphere, just enough to distinguish one

Opposite: Canal City Hakata,
Fukuoka, Japan, 1996.
Architect: Jerde Partnership
International, Inc.
Right: Bellagio, The Resort,
Las Vegas. Architect:
Jerde Partnership
International, Inc.

mall from another. It was the way-finding systems that became the principal repository of such themes. The master of such binding elements is Communication Arts. This Colorado-based firm, headed by Henry Beer, a former employee of Charles and Ray Eames, manages to give each of the malls in which they are involved a specific flavour without making them too specific. The Ontario Mills project, for instance, pays homage to local agricultural traditions, a Hispanic heritage and a vague notion of California modernism – all without offering literal references to any of these.[33] Companies such as Jerde and Communications Arts are becoming brands in themselves, and imposing their themed abstractions on cities everywhere: Jerde's design for a 'shopping ditch' in Rotterdam has essentially the same form and elements as his giant Canal City in Fukuoka.

The only time when theming dominates is when shopping becomes part of an overall entertainment experience. Here New York-based architect David Rockwell, designer of restaurants for the likes of Planet Hollywood and Nobu, as well as of the Foxwood Casino in Connecticut, excels at creating a place in which customers are made to feel they are simultaneously on, behind and in front of the stage. These fairy-tale lands invite participation not only through consuming but also by playing games or taking rides. Though most of the theming concentrates on such restaurant franchises as the Rainforest Café, in certain places it does seep into

the more traditional retail environment. The most obvious example of this is in Las Vegas, where the Forum Shops – the most successful shopping mall in the United States in terms of per-square-foot sales – intensifies the theme of the Caesar's Casino. The Bellagio pretends to be a village on Lake Como, the Venetian offers gondola rides past the stores, and the Parisian focuses on a scale model of the Eiffel Tower.[34] In Tokyo, planners are trying to imitate the Forum Shops with a new mixed-use development in Tokyo Bay.

One innovation that the theming movement has given the development of the mall is a more complete divorce of appearance and space. In Disneyland, though all the shops look separate, they are in fact one large department store. Behind small storefronts, the shops actually sprawl out and interconnect. The Limited, an Ohio-based brand, has picked up on this idea of an alternative to the department store. It lines up its various 'products' (or brands) in sections of malls. There is The Limited, The Limited Too, Victoria's Secret, Bath and Body Works and Compagnie Aérospatiale, all of which seem to be distinct stores, each with its own theme. In fact each is selling differently targeted versions of the same merchandise. The most amusing of The Limited's subdivisions is Structure, a store aimed at young men themed around architecture. Market research informed them that their target audience considered architects their role model, so these sections of the quasi-department store display quotes from Mies van der Rohe and Louis Sullivan, and are furnished and furbished with Le Corbusier 'cube' chairs and fake metal beams. Here, retail

Above: Rainforest Café
Interior, Trafford Centre,
Manchester, 1999.
Right: The Changing Sky,
Forum Shops at Caesar's,
Las Vegas.

architecture has disappeared into its own theme.

In other instances architecture has vanished into the fabric of the city. Many of the world's traditional shopping streets have become de facto malls. The same stores line up along Fifth Avenue in New York, the rue du Faubourg-Saint-Honoré in Paris or Bond Street in London. The theming here is more related to the economic class to which these streets have usually catered; the forms take and adapt whatever architecture is at hand. As in the traditional mall, it is the way-finding system that makes sense of it all. Business Improvement Districts (BIDs) create a graphic identity for shopping areas that extends from street signs to the uniforms of the private security guards they hire. Here the vestigial hierarchy of the department store disappears in the tumult of urban form, while the artificial public spaces again become one with the public street. Ironically, however, the city becomes a facsimile of itself. The BIDs clean up the storefronts, regulators control the appearance of buildings, and those aspects of the city that are not for sale disappear around the corner. The city itself is now for sale.

Today even suburbs, influenced by the New Urbanists theorists and the success of BIDs, are creating imitation urban centres. Existing village streets that had lost their stores to highway-convenient strips are revitalised, and retail villages are created on the same 'cornfield sites' that once sprouted malls. Behind the stores, parking structures offer convenient access. The anchors for such retail villages are, as is now the case in most malls, cinema complexes combined with restaurants and clubs for night-time attraction and bookstores with their own cafés to cater for the daytime crowd. Once again, it seems we can only establish a community in our culture if we focus not on shared institutions, but on the things we can buy.

Both The Limited's strategy and the reintegration of the mall into the city point to the place into which the architecture has actually disappeared: into the brand itself. Henry Beer has said that he wants 'the experience of the shopper from the moment they see the Nike commercial on TV to the point where they are wearing the shoes when they come out of the store to be completely seamless'.[35] In some of the projects he designs he has come close to achieving this ideal. The walls have become so thin and abstract as to be almost invisible; and way-finding systems have merged with the stores' individual signs. In urban malls today, Big Box retail, the department store and the advertising environment all merge into such 'superstores' as NikeTown or Old Navy. Here commercials and projected images assault the viewer, while the logo ties all manner of otherwise only lightly related products together. The most extreme example of this is the emergence of stores such as those devoted to Microsoft, which has few tangible goods to sell.

But to most shoppers, even such a concentrated statement of the brands they buy is usually not necessary. Increasingly, they seem to base their retail decisions on the advertising that sells a particular lifestyle to a 'cohort group' through a logo the company extends into its packaging. To these logos it adds narrative images that show the kind of scene in which they hope their customers would like to be actors. Brands are the uniforms for the tribal nomads, who buy them at whichever caravanserai they find themselves.

The obvious extension of this movement is the disappearance of shopping into the ethereal realm of the electrosphere. The tremendous growth of catalogue shopping around the world has already increased the retail space to the point where it almost completely infiltrates both home and office. In the 1980s, catalogues branched out on to television through such cable channels as the Home Shopping Network. Now the Internet promises to make it ever easier to acquire goods without even the luxury of a catalogue framework or a disembodied salesvoice at the other end of a toll-free number. With a drag and a click, the object of desire is yours.

While the space of retail thus shrinks to the thickness of a screen, new spaces appear. These are mainly located in the area of distribution. Immense new warehouses and trans-shipping centres are growing up in strategic locations. One of the largest of these in the western United States ironically dwarfs Ontario Mills, one of California's largest shopping malls, which sits just across the freeway. Indeed, it is many years since the landscape critic J. B. Jackson pointed out how the architecture of delivery services has shaped our cities.[36] Now the needs of large and small trucks, the warehouses and the control centres continue to erode what we think of as traditional architectural form. The appearance of double-stacked containers has required the rebuilding of thousands of bridges and roads all over the United States to create the necessary clearance for trucks and trains. The warehouses and the clerical centres that service the invisible shopping networks are often the largest buildings on the ex-urban landscape.

The new landscape of shopping is one of completely anonymous volumes, which can house either goods or people. The only articulate elements we can distinguish are the containers, *their* containers (ships, trains and automobiles) and the methods of loading and unloading them. Logos (FedEx, UPS) tie together these eternally moving components. The back of the store has not only survived the disappearance of the shop as a physical artefact but also completely overwhelmed its original *raison d'être*.[37]

There is a logic to the architecture of the electrosphere. I asked Jim Bezos, founder of Amazon.com, why the 'splash page' for the firm's 'store' appears to be so chaotic. He pointed out that every square inch of that page, when viewed on a 13-inch monitor, was worth about $1 million in revenues through advertising and product placement.[38] Each element the viewer sees on the screen has an active and continually changing relationship to the viewer's desires and actions. The site appears as a collage changing in space and time as compositions and messages arrange themselves on pages and across the screen. They are animated by Java-activated programs to become ever changing images. The only thing that remains constant (more or less) is the scaffolding of the site or virtual store. This structure consists of a relationship of typography, fields of colour and abstracted forms.[39] Here the space of

retailing, the company carrying out the retailing, the packaging of the goods and the logo all become one. The only thing missing from this merger is the product itself. Indeed, some science-fiction writers would have us believe it is only a matter of time and miniaturisation (or incorporation of technology into the body) before this final step takes place.[40]

We should be careful not to overestimate the scope of the electrosphere. Though boosters claim huge growth in this sector, in reality it is still only a very small part of the retailing experience. Most people, it seems, continue to prefer to visit a physical location when they want to shop. They go to such sites because they can discover a direct relationship between themselves and the goods they consume in a social setting defined by a certain kind of architecture. They still go to the marketplace because it is still the scene of their social activity.[41]

If it is true that our most profound work as human beings is to construct ourselves to appear on a stage of our choosing, then the activity of acquiring the costumes and props, building the stage-sets and acting out our roles is not just a secondary one.[42] We need brands, and the spaces in which they and we appear now seem to be melded together. We may not like the fact that the engine behind all these developments is a form of capitalism that both creates and (though never quite fully) fulfils desires, but that is the situation, and one that we cannot ignore. We can only try to understand its mechanisms – the ways in which it operates through the appearances of product, brand and architecture in the selling spaces in which we act – so that we can enlarge our own roles and take control of our destiny. As retail environments become places of fantasy and convenience, be they bare-bones bulks or fancy forums for commercial creativity, they present us with a varied set of scenes that can help us understand our desire to live through objects and appearances, and integrate this with some notion, however momentary and however mercenarily conceived, of a public space. We may not want to shop till we drop; but we can construct meaning in, and through, the retail environment.

Following pages: 'Wal-Mart' goods train, USA, 2000.
Below: Amazon.com website.

HELEN JONES

Packaging
petroleum

As we drive along our highways, the petrol station is one example of what American architect Charles Jencks describes as '60-mile-an-hour architecture' – its aim to signal the presence of the station to a driver travelling at speed. Roadside architecture is an architecture of branding. The marketing priority of the station is to inform the driver of not merely its existence but also the particular brand on offer. The gas station has attracted the attention of American architects other than Jencks: for Robert Venturi 'its buildings are small and cheap, the signs are big and expensive', while Hitchcock and Johnson sum it up as: 'Dominating roof plane over transparent screen wall. Colors: Brilliant red and white for advertisement. A design easy to standardise'. This was in 1932.

Indeed the methods of branding petroleum have changed only slightly in the last 100 years. The corporate identities of the major oil companies have remained remarkably consistent during this time ('You can be sure of Shell'). Petrol stations have become a unique building type, evolved through the interface between architecture, engineering and industrial design, together with signage and advertising graphics. In its totality it is a giant-scale advertisement. Global brands, such as Shell and Texaco, take a monolithic approach to their global presence, using, according to Wolff Olins (1980), 'one simple name and one visual look wherever they go'. By standardising their image across the globe, oil companies are also reinforcing the brand promise of consistent quality and reliability.

Increasingly the 'brand experience' is supplemented with the offer of consumable services: fast food, supermarket shopping, news agencies and car valeting. The future of the world's most powerful oil companies lies not so much in their oil products but in the success of their branding strategies. After all, petrol is petrol, but a brand must promise much more.

Top: Esso, Birchanger, England, 1999.
Left: Texaco, Route 271, PA, USA, 1999.
Opposite: Shell, Yakima Valley, WA, USA, 1999.
Following spread: Total, Stansted, Mount Fitchet, England, 1999.

"Petrol is petrol, but a brand must promise much more."

TOTAL

premium unleaded per litre	**69·9**
star per litre	**77·9**
diesel per litre	**72·9**

Alldays
your local store

TOTAL

Shop

No-one TOPS our rewards

Now there's an easier, smarter way to collect TOPS Points

RECRUITING NOW ASK INSIDE FOR DETAILS

CAMBRIDGE ROAD

From object to experience

Left: 'Skegness is SO Bracing', UK. First published in 1908 by Great Northern Railway; reissued by LNER, c. 1925.
Below: Legoland, Windsor, England, main entrance, August 1997.

Cadbury World, Legoland, Heron City, Center Parcs, Warner Village. These are all places to relax, enjoy yourself, spend time with friends and family. But they are also products. We have been parting with our hard-earned cash to have a good time in increasing amounts since before the Industrial Revolution, but the way we do it has changed dramatically.

In the nineteenth century, the growth of railways provided easy access to the tourist destinations of the seaside and spas. Subsequently, entire industrial towns would close their factories for specific fortnights, known as 'the wakes', while its workers and their families headed *en masse* for Blackpool, Bridlington or Bognor. Seaside entertainment - music hall, amusement parks and piers - developed to cater for the concentrated demand for pleasure that they brought with them. Just as work became increasingly rationalised and regulated by industrialisation, so, then, did leisure.

Holiday resorts would compete with each other by promoting their attractions - the length of their piers, the quality of the air - often through advertising. In this way, leisure spaces began to be conceived of as brands. The seaside resort of Bridlington, for example, was marketed as 'Bright, Breezy, Bracing'. The Butlins holiday camps, established in 1936, were, then, a more tightly orchestrated commercialisation under a single brand of what seaside towns had been doing for a century.

The growth of the Spanish costas in the 1960s and the development of charter-flight operations ensured a more flexible attitude to when and where holidays could be taken. In this system, the basic offer of sun, sea and sand was the same for most resorts. Tour operators had then to compete on price and the strength of their brand. The

greater flexibility of tourist demand in choosing destinations and activities is thus met by the development of 'off the peg' tailored holidays.

In *Capitalism and Leisure Theory*, published in 1985, sociologist Chris Rojek identified four key features of contemporary leisure. First, it is a more privatised affair increasingly focussed on the home, rather than the public sphere. No doubt this has been encouraged by the development of radio and television, then teletext, video, Internet and computer games. Thus it is the job of leisure entrepreneurs not only to get people out of their homes but also to give their leisure spaces the same security, exclusivity and, paradoxically, 'buzz'. Second, leisure is more individuated; more subject to personalisation. Leisure spaces must deliver a menu of choice without destabilising the core values of the brand. Third, Rojek believes that leisure has become more commercialised, evolving into a major industry in itself. Currently more money is spent on leisure and tourism in the UK than on food, rent and rates. Finally, leisure is more pacified: it entails more complex and encultured expression through activities that require learning, practice and mastery. Whether it is appreciating high cuisine or trying out a new sport, leisure activities are, in fact, more restrained and regulated than ever.

As work patterns in the late twentieth century have become more fragmented and varied, so has leisure. While there has been an overall decline in the length of the working week, for those in employment the total amount of leisure time - that is hours spent in unproductive activities - has paradoxically diminished. Leisure entrepreneurs increasingly take seriously the notion of 'time-squeeze': in a consumer-research survey by the Henley Centre, a London-based British

"The distinction between leisure and retail is increasingly blurred."

consultancy, which was published in 1998, 59 per cent of respondents agreed that 'I have never had enough time to get things done.' This is particularly so among women who work, who report only 13.5 hours per week free as against the 60 hours average. This time-squeeze has given rise to the development of one-stop leisure complexes, or so-called E-zones (for entertainment), which incorporate a variety of leisure activities into one branded site. This allows consumers the most efficient use of their precious leisure time as they move from cinema to pizza restaurant to bowling alley or from swimming pool to tennis court to health spa. Much design-consultancy work is dedicated to achieving the right 'fit' between the retail and leisure brands situated within a single branded space.

If this makes such centres sound like shopping malls then it underlines the point that the distinction between leisure and retail is increasingly blurred, as in so-called 'retail-tainment' sites. Thus Tesco Extra at Pitsea in Essex offers a fast-food and takeaway area, mooing cows and roller-skating customer-services assistants. Specific brands have also extended into the leisure sphere: the Volkswagen Autostadt in Wolfsberg, Legoland in Windsor or Cadbury World in Bournville, NikeTown in New York and London all provide visitor attractions that subsequently reinforce their brand identity, whether that is based on technological innovation, play or heritage. Significantly, investment for these 'brandlands' comes from global advertising budgets rather than capital-revenue.

In bringing together a range of activities and identities in leisure spaces, content has to be arranged to build a narrative flow, to give the visitor a sense of moving through a set of activities or sensations to make up a complete story. Small wonder, then, that designers increasingly talk of 'scripting' leisure spaces. They ascertain the message and effect of its overall structure before mustering design components around this that will frame the desired consumer response. The emphasis thereby switches from the design of objects to the creation of experiences.

**Above: Cadbury World.
Right: Center Parcs, Longleat, England, forest subtropical swimming paradise, 1990s.**

Left and right: Branded street signs, Hong Kong, 1999.
Below: Li-Ning Trainers, 1999, V&A Museum.

ANDREW BOLTON

Great mall of the people

In China today people are faced with an inexhaustible supply of consumer products from around the world. But what are they buying and what are their aspirations? Some answers to these questions can be found in an analysis of the range of goods on sale in department stores and shopping malls in major cities throughout China. Limiting my field of enquiry to the arena of fashion, I will focus on the mammoth Sun Dong An Plaza in Wangfujing, one of Beijing's most popular shopping districts.

The Sun Dong An Plaza, which opened in 1998, offers a diverse range of fashion, by which I mean world or cosmopolitan fashion, everyday dress that is often referred to as 'western' but is in fact worn by people in both the eastern and western hemispheres (Eicher, 1995). Customers to the Plaza can choose from an assortment of tailored suits, jackets, trousers, skirts, shirts, blouses, jeans and T-shirts. Sold in boutique-style shops arranged over seven floors, customers have access to a wide range of fashion labels, both international and local. The type of labels available is significant and a close look at their scope and profile provides subtle and revealing insights into current consumer trends in modern day Beijing.

A large proportion of those on offer are local (about 70 per cent), which would seem to suggest a lower demand for international labels among customers to the Plaza. Quantity, however, is not necessarily a reliable indicator of taste.

Neither is it a particularly accurate reflection of the preferences and aspirations of shoppers. Indeed, an examination of the building's infra-structural rhetoric indicates a definite hierarchy of fashion labels. Shops selling international western labels are given a much higher profile on the ground and first floors of the building, while those selling local Chinese labels are less prestigiously situated on the remaining five floors. Arguably, it is the prominent placement of the former rather than the profusion of the latter.

It is not just any western label that shoppers aspire to wear. Generally speaking, people living in Beijing dress in a relatively conservative manner and favour international labels that

many westerners might consider conventional. The British label Burberry, for example, is popular among professional men and women. Considered an 'exclusive label', the shop is situated on the ground floor with its own off-street entrance. To satisfy the conservative taste of its customers, Burberry limits its product line to the Burberry Traditional collection. The more avant-garde Preview or Prorsum collections, designed by Robert Menichetti and popular in Europe and America, are entirely absent. Nike is extremely popular among younger customers to the Plaza. Its high-profile status is confirmed by its prime location on the ground floor, again with its own off-street entance. Almost all (about

Above: Sun Dong An Plaza,
Wangfujing, Beijing, 1999.
Right: 'Pye' fashion brochure,
Hong Kong, 1999.

"It is not just any western label that shoppers aspire to wear."

99 per cent) of Nike shoes are manufactured in Asia, with a large proportion made in China by independent firms (Skoggard, 1998). Other major western sports companies that produce their shoes in China include Adidas, Puma and Reebok. Nike, however, is the preferred choice among many Chinese. Its popularity can be explained less by the localisation of its merchandise than by its image, since Nike often uses Chinese sports personalities to front its advertising campaigns, such as the football hero Cheng Siu Chung. In fact, so popular is Nike that the Chinese sports company Li-Ning, has appropriated and slightly adapted its Swoosh logo. Perhaps because of this brand association,

Li-Ning has become one of the most popular Chinese sports companies in China.

As well as western labels, customers to the Plaza also aspire to wear those from Hong Kong, which, on the whole, are also located on the ground and first floors. Pye is one of the most popular among professional men and women. Part of the Esquel Group founded by Y. L. Yang in 1978, Pye is one of the few Hong Kong labels with an instantly recognisable, albeit westernised, Chinese logo π. Popular among a younger audience are Bossini and Baleno. Similar in style to the Gap, their clothes often display no visible logo. This invisibility explains why Bossini and Baleno appeal to the brand-

conscious youth of Hong Kong. The absence of any logo means they can be mixed with more prestigious in their own right western labels such as Calvin Klein and DKNY to give the overall impression of an internationally designed ensemble. While some young people in Beijing may buy Bossini and Baleno for similar reasons, the majority look upon labels from Hong Kong as prestigious.

There are, of course, several Chinese labels that are considered desirable among customers to the Plaza. Popular among professional men are Ying Weng and Lan Bao situated on the ground floor and among professional women Yingdak and Sanong, located on the first floor. On the whole, though, customers to the Sun Dong An Plaza prefer wearing western

labels and those from Hong Kong. The internal dynamics of other department stores and shopping malls in major cities throughout China reflect similar hierarchies of labels, such as Parkson in Shanghai. Until Chinese labels are successful in penetrating the international fashion market this trend is likely to continue. The Hong Kong label Episode, which belongs to the Toppy Group, has managed this successfully. For a Chinese label to do so, Chinese consumers need to develop more confidence in their own brands, which, by necessity, would have to entail a mental shift away from the superiority of international western fashion labels to those that are locally produced and consumed in China.

Supermarket futures

In 1962 the British trade journal *The Grocer* published a centenary number, which included a fanciful feature on 'The Grocery Shop of the Future?'. The accompanying illustration, a black-and-white drawing, shows mother, daughter and dog returning from the supermarket in their flying saucer-shaped helicopter. Outside a ranch-style suburban dwelling, father and son stand waving a welcome in the distance. This private helicopter fantasy had some currency at the time: in France, René Uhrich, in a book also published in 1962, imagines that in the United States at least, 'the civilisation of the automobile', will soon give way to 'the civilisation of the helicopter'.

In *The Grocer*, author Howard Fox runs through possible prospects for stores that in the 1970s will move from rectangular to circular designs, perhaps with 'a series of little personal shops' round the perimeter. The customer stands on moving aisles, getting off whenever she wishes. In the dim distance that can be glimpsed beyond the 1970s, the shoppers have come to a complete standstill as the goods circulate to offer themselves for inspection: 'Eventually, the entire perimeter of a store may be arranged in lounges, with the shopping area a huge revolving island. The housewife would sit, talk with her friends

"We all have our special trolleys now, thoughtfully provided to meet our aisle-cruising needs from Pampers to eternity."

Above: Woolworths fruit and vegetables display, c. 1960. Below: 'Back from a trip to the grocers! Future stores will be designed to accommodate new trends in transport. "The Grocery Shop of the Future"', *The Grocer*, 1962. Opposite: Tesco supermarket, West Kensington, London, 1999.

and pick items as they pass by.'

This passage is quoted from an American source in another trade journal, on which the whole article is based; characteristically, the future of supermarket shopping is imagined in an American mode. And in numerous respects, the piece returns us to earlier histories, of supermarkets themselves, of their antecedents and of the first projections of their futures. With those little shops round the edge, the old High Street is back, now inside the single store. Shopping, we learn, is to be 'a pleasure rather than a chore', the same term that generations of store operators had imagined from the start of the century.

From the perspective of 1990s Britain, these 1960s fantasies, in their own time echoing futures past, become strange in another way, comfortably and uncomfortably familiar in their partial anticipation of our own present. There is the out-of-town site reached by private transport; the deli and fresh fish and bakery counters round the edge to signify service alongside self-service, the best of all worlds under one roof; the place to sit and talk. Supermarkets may not have changed their structure, to transform themselves into circles with moving aisles. But in certain ways, they have almost gone further than Fox's projections. It is as though they were turning the wheels of retailing revolutions full circle, coming to be all shops to all people, to recapitulate all the phases of retailing history under one roof.

Evoking the fonder memories of the high street and the market they have supplanted, supermarkets parade their counters with personal service – the baker, the fishmonger, the butcher, the dry cleaner, and even the Post Office. In the wake of their general up-marketing, as they come to sell more and more expensive, recherché lines, they loudly proclaim their fidelity to their cheap origins, still piling it high and selling it low with ranges of minimally priced own-brand goods. At the same time, like the grand department stores, they now sell fashion as well as cheapness. Where the department stores collected the exotic products of the colonies, supermarkets sell 'ethnic' cuisine and plant out the

former colonies to supply them with esoteric tropical vegetables. And where they were once associated solely or primarily with the selling of food, supermarkets as superstores have extended their range of non-food lines so far that they have come to resemble the department stores in contents as well as in forms. The introduction of cafés, inviting the slower time of an outing, puts an end to the identification of food shopping as a definite task to be completed as quickly as possible. Now, you can be doing the shopping and going shopping, getting the basics and enjoying yourself, all in one place and one time.

Or indeed, it might seem, at all times and everywhere. For supermarkets in Britain have risen in the 1990s to a position of unprecedented prominence in that blur between media representations and actual behaviour that makes up the fabric of our daily life. They seem to be occupying every possible space and time, from daytime and prime-time TV advertising to Sunday morning family shopping, in the wake of the relaxation of the laws on opening hours in 1994, and now all-night shopping as well. In their metamorphosis into out-of-town superstores, they have become the focus for a new environmental argument about the decline of urban centres and the growth of a car-dependent culture. The 1960s image of the supermarket shopper as a female zombie has given way to a much less identifiable figure, anyman, anywoman and especially anybaby – for we all have our special trolleys now, thoughtfully provided to meet our aisle-cruising needs from Pampers to eternity. The future of supermarkets in the twenty-first century is in one sense anybody's guess, anybody's choice. Yet it sometimes appears that the future itself is envisaged in the image of a great supermarket in which citizen-consumers move about making their more or less informed and random individual choices. Whether that image draws on a hope or a fear depends on the persuasions of the speaker. But it is perhaps not irrelevant that in the UK stores are often designed so that customers start with the fresh fruit and vegetables on the left and exit, after the drinks, on the right.

BRANDING
THE
Jane Pavitt
INDIVIDUAL

"It's a marketing given by now that the consumer defines the brand. But the brand also defines the consumer. We are what we wear, what we eat, what we drive. Each of us in this room is a walking compendium of brands."[1]

This observation by Sir Michael Perry, Director of Unilever, may sound sinister. Is it true that brands define us? We are often told that as consumers our 'rights to choose' are paramount, and that the success or failure of brands is in our hands. Yet we also know that a vast economy is devoted to the investigation of consumer preferences, so that brand promises and advertisements may closely match (and fuel) our fears and aspirations. We use branded goods in a myriad of different ways. At times, these will be the same as or close to those suggested by brand owners. What we wear might make us feel powerful, happy or reassured. At other times, they may be different from those anticipated or implied by brand owners – and more personal, localised or closely connected to family or social situations.

Anthropologists Mary Douglas and Baron Isherwood have proposed, 'the most general objective of the consumer can only be to construct an intelligible universe with the goods he chooses.'[2] We can use goods to locate ourselves and establish a sense of belonging. We might also employ them to individuate ourselves, both in terms of how we see ourselves and how others see us. This means that branded goods can be simultaneously our anchors and our springboards.

Most often, shopping is a relatively mundane activity, but there is a difference between 'going shopping' and 'doing the shopping'.[3] We may enter a store to buy something several times a day, without attaching a great deal of significance to the purchases we make or the reasons for them. 'Doing the shopping' means provisioning for the household, buying food, visiting the supermarket, stocking up on staple household goods. We say we are 'going shopping' when we mean we are out for pleasure, browsing or making special purchases. Going

shopping might be an adventure, doing the shopping a chore. We attach much more significance to the purchases we make when we are shopping for leisure; these are the goods that may give us identity or bring to us a sense of belonging. A third kind of shopping – 'shopping around' – is implied by the kinds of purchases that involve time, research and planning, such as buying a car or a house.

Of course, brands are involved in all of these activities. Sometimes, choosing a particular one can be a way of not having to think hard about the purchase. Selecting or rejecting brands can also be part of the process of defining our lifestyles and of presenting an identity to the world. Some are selected to make a statement to others about ourselves as a form of communication, and branded goods are specifically designed to speak to us on an emotional and associational level. In turn, we use them to speak for us.

Sociologist Zygmunt Bauman has argued that the consumer is involved in 'self construction by a process of acquiring commodities of distinction and difference'.[4] Buying an identity, the idea of the 'commodity self', is a useful way of looking at the relationship between people and things. 'Is that me?' is a question often addressed to not only certain types of goods, particularly clothing, but also leisure and entertainment activities, such as choosing a restaurant, a film or a holiday. Goods can be a means of differentiating oneself in order to belong. Bauman also argues that consumption has become the primary means of formulating and expressing personal identity, arguing that: 'the same central role which was played by work, by job, occupation, profession, in modern society, is now performed in contemporary society, by consumer choice.'[5]

The image of the consumer is fraught with anxiety

Previous spread: Adidas wearer, London, 1999.
Below: Waitrose supermarket, promotion of washing powders with washing machines, supplied by Caleys of Windsor, Slough, England, c.1958-63.
Opposite: Shopper, London, 1999.

and contradiction. For most of this century
consumption has been associated with not
individuality or the 'authentic' self but mass culture
and a loss of self. A substantial literature of the
twentieth century has been devoted to a critique of
the consumer as victim, who willingly succumbed to
the persuasive messages of advertiser and marketer.
The packaged delights of mass culture, from lipstick
to tinned salmon, were frequently derided by inter-
war cultural observers. The leisure pursuits of the
majority, such as cinema-going, popular fiction
and theatre, and, of course, shopping, were seen
as tawdry and unfulfilling. Even now some critics
persist in arguing that we are purely the products
of media manipulation. One recent 'exposé'
pronounced: 'It was advertising that taught us to
define ourselves by what we consumed … and we
would never have been so sheep-like compliant if
it had not been for television.'[6]

Class and gender prejudices tended to lie at the
heart of these criticisms. The irrational or imaginative
consumer so often depicted is feminine,
irresponsible with money or the spender rather than
the begetter of wealth. Although leisure shopping is
usually defined as a feminine activity, the female
consumer was also likely to be portrayed as the frugal
or careful shopper, holding the purse strings and
stretching her husband's wage to cover household
expenses. Supermarket choices, the evaluation
of one brand of soap powder over another and the
search for bargains are usually skills assigned to
women.[7] Consumer culture plays a role in the
creation, maintenance and occasionally the
subversion of assigned gender roles, just as it does
with class or with definitions of sexuality. Take this
example of the male writer's characterisation of
women's spending and leisure activities in 1938,
from a piece by the Irish writer Louis MacNeice:
'Suburb-dwellers, spinsters, schoolteachers, women
secretaries, proprietresses of teashops, all those,
whether bored with their jobs or idleness, go to the
theatre for their regular dream-hour off. The same
instinct leads them which makes many hospital
nurses spend all their savings on cosmetics,
cigarettes and expensive underclothes.'[8]

Much more recently, however, a more celebratory
image of the consumer has predominated. Instead
of a victim, the consumer has been depicted as a free-
thinking creative individual, who constructs a sense
of self out of their consuming culture, in ways that are
regardless of such 'limitations' as class, gender or
even geography. Modern consumer society has been
depicted as a spectacle of goods and experiences, an
exciting and adventurous terrain. Consumption is
viewed in terms of fantasy and personal exploration
rather than subjugation. The post-modern subject, it
has been argued, constructs him or her self through
the appropriation of goods, 'surfing' through style
cultures and 'trying on' personal identities like
clothing. The myth of the post-modern consumer
is as unfettered global traveller, socially mobile and
regarding material goods as the chief indicator of
culture, ideology and status. In such a scenario,

Above: Passer-by, posters, London, 1999.
Right: Billboards, London, 1999.

individuality is defined as having the freedom to pick and choose from a range of commodified lifestyles. The contemporary consumer is pictured as 'the isolated individual, juggling with assorted signs and symbols in a never-ending attempt to construct and maintain identity in a fragmented and ever-changing environment'.[9]

In short, the consumer has tended to be depicted as either pleasure seeker, motivated by hedonistic desire, or victim, manipulated by cynical advertisers and corporate interests. Consumption is either a tool for the 'invention' of self, or a process that strips away our individuality. Both of these views are problematic.[10] There are as many different types of consumption and consumer behaviour as there are

traditions of defining consumption. The idea of the 'rational' consumer does not allow space for an imaginative and emotional engagement with goods.[11] Many of us purchase for reasons that are not immediately rational, nor simply a response to the persuasions of a glossy advertisement or package.

Modern consumerism has been defined as when 'the individual's interest is primarily focused on the meanings and images which can be imputed to a product'.[12] In other words, we are not simply buying and using things because of functional or rational justifications but for the range of emotional and social meanings they can also embody for us. Furthermore, to want something for these reasons does not necessarily mean that the gratified wish will satisfy once the purchase is made, as such desires are relatively fluid and transient. Longing is an important part of our relationship to goods. This constant deferral of gratification is one of the hallmarks of modern consumerism and identity.

The consumer may at times be a pleasure seeker, but this is only one guise among many others.[13] We use different consuming strategies for different kinds of goods, occasions or locations. Sometimes we might be very self-conscious about the strategy we use (for example, if we choose to boycott a product or brand), other times we take a more passive and less time-consuming approach. Consuming choices are not made in isolation; even if we feel free to choose, they say much about our cultural and familial background. Identity, therefore, is much more than the sum total of an individual's possessions. Rather, the crucial building blocks of identity, such as gender and ethnicity, shape our attitudes to consumption.

The French philosopher Michel de Certeau has argued that, as consumers, we are also producers of meaning, because we make meaning with the goods we buy.[14] We might display a concept of personal identity through our association with particular goods, cultural preferences, leisure activities and, inevitably, brands. We call this 'style', which is, in the words of one critic, 'a tool for constructing personhood'.[15]

But how do we individualise ourselves through the

Right: Passage de L'Opéra
Debouchant, Boulevard des
Italiens, Bibliothèque de la
Ville de Paris, late 1800s.

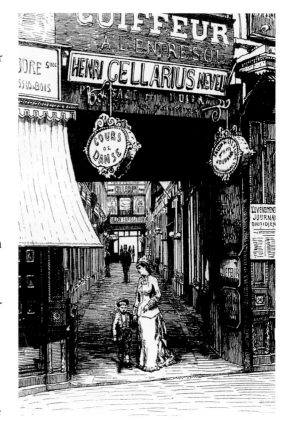

mass of consumer goods and brands that are, in fact, widely available? After all, the nature of brands is to offer up images that are purchased 'off the peg' rather than bespoke. Mass-produced commodities are impersonal and may not appear even to offer the space for personalisation. As Celia Lury says in her contributions to this book, the pervasiveness of brands is such that there is less space left for us to 'think with things'.

The collective appeal of brands, however, is such that to identify with one is a way of identifying with a particular social group. These practices of self-definition through branded goods are more common among some age groups than others. Close identification with fashion and lifestyle brands is most often found among teenagers and young adults. Brands are useful because they also provide ways to belong. To take one example: 'I have to shop at Wal-Mart to buy clothes. I try my hardest to fit in but my clothes don't say Abercrombie & Fitch or Gap. They don't say anything.'[16] This is a comment from Nicole, a respondent to a website discussion forum about the American clothing company Abercrombie & Fitch in July 1999.[17] She explained how her family could not afford the brands with which she wanted to be associated. Nicole wants to align her own identity to the fashion brands she mentions rather than the discount store Wal-Mart. By not being able to do this, she does not feel a sense of belonging – she says elsewhere that 'my friends make fun of me'. Nicole sees clothing as a form of communication but feels that the clothes she can afford 'don't say anything'. The brands she wants are ubiquitous American ones, Abercrombie & Fitch and Gap, found in every mall in America and, increasingly, worldwide.

During the same period, the American boy band LFO had a hit both in Britain and the USA with a song ('Summer Girls') that included the chorus line: 'I like girls that wear Abercrombie & Fitch.' The band sang also of preferences for fast food, TV stars and other 'consumables'. The list, which included Coca-Cola and the former teen star and actor Michael J. Fox, echoes the preferences of many teenagers. Lists like these, of favourite brands and bands, are posted on

thousands of personal websites. Fashioned into a vocabulary of collective significance, they are meant to communicate to others and invite correspondence from those with similar tastes. In this way, brands are used as a means of expressing personal identity and identifying with a collective taste.

Differentiation and belonging are two of the main driving forces behind what has been termed 'conspicuous consumption'. At the end of the nineteenth century, the American theorist Thorstein Veblen identified social emulation as the impetus behind what he saw as most 'unnecessary' consumption. For Veblen, 'conspicuous consumption' meant the acquiring of goods in emulation of one's social 'betters'. Goods were markers of social status for the leisure classes; their symbolic function one of ostentatious display. The traditional codes of luxury and wealth in goods, for example, were used as a means of indicating one's status to others. Even now, brands use luxury and opulence, such as gold, silk or exotic references, to sell consumables like chocolate, coffee or cosmetics.

As well as material goods, leisure itself was evidence of one's economic status: [18]

> Goods are produced and consumed as a means to the fuller unfolding of human life; and their utility consists, in the first instance, in their efficiency as a means to this end. The end is, in the first instance, the fullness of life of the individual taken in absolute terms. But the human proclivity to emulation had seized upon the consumption of goods as a means to an invidious comparison, and had thereby invested consumable goods with a secondary utility as evidence of relative ability to pay.

Veblen's idea of emulative spending was one means of explaining the system of fashion in modern society. The competitive nature of the leisure classes, according to him, meant that fashions changed with increasing fluidity. The function of wealth in modern society was not only to emulate one's social superiors but also to differentiate oneself from one's social inferiors. In Veblen's view, the dynamic nature of fashion is due to the 'natural' process of society, which dictates that habits in food, leisure, dress and etiquette are formed by the aristocratic classes and from there filter down the social ranks. Veblen suggested that the symbolic purpose of goods was to demonstrate our place along that chain and perhaps to assist in moving us upwards. He also implied that certain tastes and fashions become debased after a time, as they become diffused throughout the social hierarchy. Although Veblen establishes the vital link between consumption and class, it is also clear that fashion does not simply work in the 'top-down' manner he describes. Rather, tastes and fashions circulate around class, age and cultural boundaries, being transformed from many different directions.

Veblen was writing at a time when modern consumerism appeared to be revolutionising America. The origins of such behaviour have been traced back to the seventeenth and eighteenth centuries in Europe[19] and even further.[20] However, many of the institutions and experiences that have shaped consumerism in the twentieth century originated in the nineteenth.[21] The character of

Right: Household Linen Department, Harrods, London, early 1900s. Following pages: Corner of the Costume Salon, Harrods, London, 1902.

Above: Street stall,
London, 1999.
Right: Yves Saint Laurent
shop window, London, 1999.
Below: Shoppers in 'Peartree'
Stores, Welwyn Garden
City, England, c.1964.
Opposite: Closing-down sale,
London, 1999.

this consumer society was reflected in its desire to construct and consume symbolic meanings around goods, and to seek out personal fulfilment from things. The acquisition and display of material goods was one means of indicating social success and status. Investing in the construction of one's social self by consuming was a way for people to announce their membership of the bourgeoisie.[22] Whether or not such consumer practices and desires were new at this time is questionable, but for Veblen the idea of the conspicuous consumption of the bourgeoisie was the hallmark of his age. Others, too, identified the elusive nature of fashion as the sign of a society seeking social differentiation and 'betterment' through goods. 'The peculiarly piquant and suggestive attraction of fashion lies in the contrast between its extensive, all-embracing distribution and its rapid and complete disintegration,' wrote the German sociologist Georg Simmel in 1904.[23]

Veblen's theories were vital in establishing the idea of the value of goods as markers of social status. However, the uses of goods are far more varied that

his view implied. For instance, expensive luxury items gain their status because they are only affordable to a few, but other kinds of 'cult' goods will only appeal or even be known to a narrow band of consumers.[24] Social status is therefore dependent upon an ability to demonstrate not only wealth but also 'taste' to those of a similar lifestyle or social group.

According to some anthropologists, 'all material possessions carry social meanings,' and therefore we must think of goods as 'communicators'.[25] Material goods are often seen as insulation against one of the inherent dangers of the modern world: social embarrassment or exclusion. They are a way of representing social relationships, and they help us to 'pin down' values and meanings in society. As well as being used to communicate, consumer goods are used to regulate our lives, perhaps to compensate for any feelings of inferiority, even to confirm status or reward success. Wrapped up in the logo, the product, the ad and the name lies a promise of emotional satisfaction – branded goods are saturated with this meaning.

The ways in which we acquire goods and the places in which we shop can also be said to be 'socially meaningful'. Do we view shopping as pleasurable or routine? Do we think our approach to shopping is based on thrift and the search for 'bargains'? Do we choose to shop in local stores, second-hand markets and shops or large out-of-town shopping malls?[26] These kinds of decisions are not simply a matter of free choice, as they are clearly governed, if not solely determined, by economics. If there is little pleasure to be had from 'doing the shopping', for instance, then a large and convenient supermarket might be felt to

be an economical choice, in terms of time spent. In contrast, while shopping for second-hand goods is for many an economic necessity, others might view it a pleasurable and alternative (as well as cheaper) means of buying clothing, for example in the shops that advertise 'designer labels for less'. Buying counterfeit or imitation branded goods involves another complicated set of social relations – we might congratulate ourselves on buying a 'name' more cheaply, but do not want to be seen by others as having done so, as Kent Grayson observes in 'Why Do We Buy Counterfeits?'.

Below: Fruit and vegetable stall, London, 1999.
Right: Boots from Timberland.

The ways in which we choose to shop as well as the goods we choose to buy (or not to buy) are an indication of the social groups to which we belong (as well as those with which we might choose to identify). Traditionally we might have viewed this as a straightforward distinction between classes or ethnic groups. However, working both within and against these residual hierarchies is the concept of lifestyle, another form of social differentiation. It can be defined as 'the ways in which people seek to display their individuality and their sense of style through the choice of a particular range of goods and their subsequent customising or personalising of these goods'.[27]

The formation of taste is a product of social patterns as much as it is of individual choices. Assuming that taste is a social as well as a personal mechanism, however, does not discount the role of the individual in asserting his or her independence from the taste-distinctions of his or her background. Social mobility, particularly since the Second World War, has tended to be made most visible in the changing taste and lifestyle patterns of different generations. The proliferation of a variety of lifestyles within the broader social divisions of class and ethnicity is another indication that consumption has become our primary mode of living. What appear to be rather arbitrary, subjective and even whimsical demonstrations of taste – a preference for one soap opera over another, or for particular cooking ingredients – are signs of social positioning.

In Britain, for example, an increasingly broad range of activities has been drawn into what we might term the 'fashion system'. Food – both eating out and cooking at home – is now more than ever a focus of the lifestyle industry. Interior design, sports, gardening and home entertaining are popular subjects for television and print journalism. Although it is true that all of these subjects have generated a consistently popular literature for at least a century or more – from Mrs Beeton to Delia Smith – they now appear to saturate our media more than ever. The popularity of a new or alternative sport, such as snowboarding or surfing, will result in the quick emergence of lifestyle goods, TV programmes and magazines devoted to that subject. These may even become popular with a segment of consumers who have no intention of taking up that particular sport, but identify with its associated media images and musical or fashion preferences.[28]

In his influential study of French tastes and cultural preferences in the late 1960s and 1970s,[29] sociologist Pierre Bourdieu argued that what we take for granted in terms of our own taste is actually an indication of our familial, educational and professional background. Bourdieu called this our 'habitus'. While we are generally unaware of its actions, habitus is embodied in all our daily lifestyle choices. It does not impose a straightjacket, for example making us replicate our parent's preferences, but is malleable according to other environmental factors. As new cultural forms emerge, whether in music, literature or fashion, our preferences will adjust. Whatever we prefer, however, our choice will be a means of differentiating ourselves from other groups and identifying with our own.

Our cultural preferences are thus indicators of a social hierarchy of taste. Tastes are not merely a sign of economic status but also of what Bourdieu terms 'cultural capital' – the expression of social difference through value judgements. A preference for fine art, classical music or repertory theatre, for example, demonstrates cultural capital and is a vital part of an individual's identity, as it marks them out socially. Social distinction is an important factor in our commodity preferences and patterns of consumption will reflect this. In his discussion of sports preferences and sports gear, Bourdieu considers the kinds of goods that are promoted as appealing to a particular social preference for country walking:[30]

parkas, plus-fours, *authentic* Jacquard sweaters in real Shetland wool, *genuine* pullovers in *pure natural* wool, Canadian trappers' jackets, English fisherman's pullovers, U.S. Army raincoats, Swedish lumberjack shirts, fatigue pants, U.S. work shoes, rangers, Indian moccasins in supple leather, Irish work caps, Norwegian woollen caps, bush hats – not forgetting the whistles, altimeters, pedometers, trail guides, Nikons and other essential gadgets without which there can be no natural return to nature.

The emphasis on 'genuine', 'authentic' and 'natural' products is an important selling point for this kind of sports wear, appropriate to the kind of lifestyle such an activity is meant to evoke. The goods described above might appeal to someone who actively wants to reject branded sports clothing, preferring instead to exhibit a kind of 'cultural capital' by their consumption of unbranded, handmade, locally crafted goods or perhaps even army surplus. The 'unbrandedness' of these goods actively reinforces their value as 'authentic'. At the same time, the codes at play in them are also found in brands that trade on an image of outdoor pursuits and rugged individualism, such as Timberland, Karrimor and Range Rover. Lifestyle is not merely a product of advertising and branding, nor is advertising a straightforward reflection of readily available lifestyles. Rather, they are dependent upon one another.

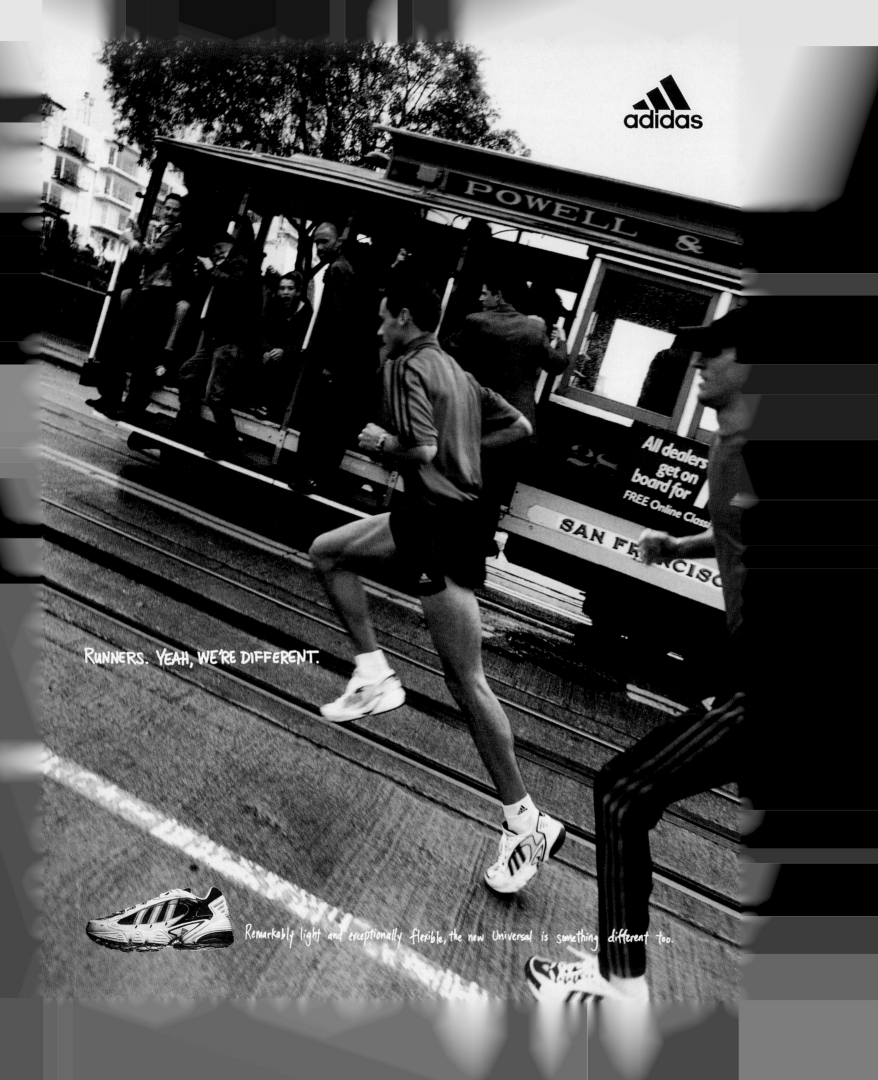

How do brands fit in with the view of goods as signifiers of social meanings? They represent very well the ways in which things become encoded with social values. Advertising may successfully turn a social message into a brand value over time – such as the established association of 'whiteness' with cleanliness in ads for washing power, which has traded on this metaphor for most of this century. In a mobile and fragmented society, the marketing of consistent and reliable values is seen as a benefit by the consumer. Throughout this century, brands have been marketed with the message that they can reassure us in a world that is not always comforting or familiar. Famous historical marketing campaigns such as the slogan for a Strand cigarettes: 'You are never alone with a Strand', and the long-running 'If Only Everything in Life Was as Reliable as a Volkswagen' spoke to consumers of their need for reassurance.

The late twentieth century saw an increased focus on the meaning and image-value of goods, sometimes referred to as the 'aestheticisation of everyday life'.[31] Aesthetic considerations are now applied to a much broader range of goods, services and experiences than before, so that any selection is seen as an expression of taste, a sign of style. The corollary of this, of course, is the expansion of the professional sector devoted to 'style' and image-rich products – advertising, design, fashion, media and other creative industries. Lifestyle industries such as these tend to promote the idea that goods are part of the process of individuation. A 1999 series of ads for Adidas running shoes used the strapline 'Runners. Yeah, we're different.' Another successful campaign for L'Oréal hair products always ends with 'Because you're worth it' or even 'Because I'm worth it'.

The function of advertising is to sell us things, by telling us that one brand of jeans, T-shirt, cigarettes, marmalade or soap powder is more suited to our daily lives than another. Advertising shows us, by implication, that our loft apartment, kitchen, workplace or dining table is the right location for a particular commodity, one that can be slotted in among others to create a coherent sense of self or place. Furthermore, lifestyle ads suggest that, while we may only be able to aspire to the loft apartment, we can at least own the type of goods associated with it. Assigning particular brands to people, places or actions is part of the process of defining lifestyle.[32]

Advertising is successful in linking particular brands and goods with lifestyles and experiences, but it does not construct those lifestyles in the absence of other processes. Advertisements, like the goods themselves, can act as the vehicle for a message. They are a means of embodying social and cultural values, and of temporarily fixing an experience to a brand, such as a sporting activity to a soft drink, or a mode of family life to a ready-prepared meal. Some critics of advertising in the twentieth century characterised it as deceptive, devoted to the encouragement of a wasteful lifestyle.[33] Yet the content of much of it is also moralistic and conservative, providing us with idealistic images of stable family life, the importance of cleanliness and order, the reassurance of safety and authority. Advertising is often a relationship between innovative form and conventional content, sensuous surface and serious undertone.[34]

Advertisements contribute to our desire to project

Opposite: 'Runners. Yeah, We're Different'. Poster campaign for Adidas, 1999.
Right: 'Kellogg's Corn Flakes Can Now Help Ease Stress and Aid Relaxation', poster, 1998.

Above: Still from Ronseal television advertisement, 1998-9.
Below: Billboard with Nike Swoosh, USA, 2000.

ourselves as purposeful and fulfilled, and 'continue to construct a separate striving self in a world of fascinating but forgettable goods'.[35] Branding and advertising together encourage us that goods are the means by which we differentiate ourselves from others and communicate a sense of personal identity. Advertising might provide a set of normative images of identity in a period when concepts of identity are fluid.[36] Most brand messages are based on essentially conservative values such as reassurance, authority and reliability (no better expressed than in the British advertisement for Ronseal paint and varnish products – 'It does exactly what it says on the tin'). Others, such as fashion and sports goods, as previously discussed, promote self-assurance and the autonomy of the individual. The 'separate striving self' is told to 'Just do it'™, suggesting that human will and strength of character are the means to success. The same 'self' is asked the question by Microsoft 'Where do you want to go today?'™, intimating that a world of possibilities is freely available and within the grasp of the individual. We are sold goods that are promoted as both a means to success and a reward for it. Yet do brands really leave space for the personalisation of goods?

The autonomous and successful individual, presented in various ad-guises, is typically male – fit, energetic, over-achieving, a 'winner' in either sports or business, but with a softer, gentler side usually intimated by the ad-presence of either children or animals. The female individual is far less likely to be presented as autonomous – her identity is forged in her association with others, as mother, girlfriend or wife, friend and successful businesswoman. This difference in the gendering of the autonomous self was epitomised by a Nike campaign of 1991, which featured lines like 'You were born a daughter. You looked up to your father, ' and ended with the line 'You became significant to yourself.' The campaign targeted what Nike saw as a kind of female empowerment, although the message was that Nike was 'giving the female consumer permission to fashion her own identity'.[37]

Brands exemplify the idea that what the modern consumer buys is experiential as opposed to functional. We need a toaster, for example, to make toast and might choose a Dualit because we think it is stylish, smart and of significant social value. It is also very costly. Unable to justify the expense of one, we suggest it for a wedding list, conferring another meaning upon it, as it comes to signify an important event and remind us of the giver. Once acquired, the toaster might continue to be referred to by its brand name alone, as the 'Dualit'. We perhaps do not need to worry that visitors to our home will wonder why we have this kind of toaster – it feels like a relatively secure purchase, having maintained its status for some time now, still a familiar product in style magazines and advertisements for stylish living. In years to come, however, the Dualit toaster might become rather unfashionable (due to its ubiquity and a number of cheaper imitations). Once that happens, we can smile and say, 'The Dualit? Oh, that was a wedding present' – thus deferring a judgement on our taste.

The Dualit toaster is therefore symbolic of a certain lifestyle, but its meaning is liable to change or be 'misread'. There is a certain amount of social risk

attached to such a symbolic purchase. The pleasure gained from it is perhaps only temporary, and the consumer might then move on, seeking to replicate the experience in the desire for, or purchase of, other experiences.[38] But purchasing experiences packaged up in branded goods is not the only means of identifying with a particular lifestyle. The idea that personal identity has become so reliant on commodities and advertising messages that the 'self' is merely an assemblage of bits appropriated from media imagery is rather reductive.[39]

All commodities, including brands, gain their meaning from their place within a greater lexicon of goods, images, services and social activities. The value of one brand name is relative to others, and complex social categorisations of goods result in the need for the consumer to understand and participate in its organisational structure. The grouping of certain brands may be site specific, such as in the department store, shopping mall or style magazine, or it may be socially implied, as with the class and status-based hierarchies of 'exclusive' fashion brands. Both, of course, are related, so that exclusive stores such as Prada and Hermès are found in similar locations together in different cities. Social categories of goods are found in individual consumer behaviours, so that (in Britain) driving a Range Rover and doing the weekly grocery shop at Marks & Spencer's food store are all (rather clichéd)

signifiers of a well-heeled, conservative lifestyle. Similarly, we can play associative games with well-known brand names, perhaps placing a BMW with a Rolex watch, a Montblanc pen and a Psion organiser. The hierarchy of brands, therefore, can be treated as a cultural barometer. The brand name is a short cut to a complex cultural idea or social image.

The brand also acts as a bridge between the world of people and things, and can connect the individual to the collective. Brands are used for framing relationships – they are also like a vocabulary, and we construct phrases and meanings by linking certain ones together in particular ways. In specific times, locations and social groups, brands can make sense as an established 'grammar' – we understand that some brands make sense together, but others are mismatched. We often talk of clothing and goods as language. But, as anthropologist Grant MacCracken has argued, the communicative function of goods is too limited, too arbitrary for it to constitute a language. The use of that term is best meant as metaphoric and is frequently used in this way, as with 'Nicole' who felt her clothes did not 'say' anything.

However, goods do communicate, if not in the specific way implied by the language analogy. Their communicative abilities are also context specific. A pair of trainers worn with a business suit in the street, for example, would not be felt to be unusual, as it could be assumed that the wearer was going to change once in the office and was wearing them for practical reasons. Trainers worn with the same suit in a boardroom meeting of a traditional finance company, though, would be less usual. While a woman combining trainers with a fashionable suit in the offices of a media or arts company would, at least in 2000, be identified as having made a conscious style choice, even if only by her peers. The 'putting together' of branded goods, the assembling of the fashion self, is only successful if the message is understood by others.

This underlines the importance of 'localisation' and context for global products. The homogeneity suggested by the de-personalised mass of branded goods available worldwide is countered by the

Above: Brands in Bond Street, London, 1999. Right: Dualit four-slice toaster.

which consumer behaviour is politicised is more deeply explored by Gareth Williams in his concluding piece 'The Point of Purchase'.

The tendency to emphasise the relationship between identity and consumer behaviour eclipses another crucial relationship – with those employed to produce the goods we consume. The parts of the world identified by brands as the most lucrative potential markets tend to be in those areas that have become the centres for production, such as the Far East, South East Asia and South America. The manufacture of sports footwear is concentrated in Indonesia and China, where cheap labour is plentiful.[46] Arguably, their personal identity is

just as determined by their relationship to the brand, although we are unlikely to see this identity in terms of personal freedom, longing and desire, rather the opposite. How should we evaluate the attitudes to brands of these consumers in the future?

It is without doubt that consumer choice forms an important part of our sense of individuality and social belonging. Inability to take part in consumer culture can result in an exclusion from the practices of everyday life. However we choose to 'choose' brands, we do so on the basis of a set of power relations that are corporate, political and economic. The brand is revealing of some social relationships, but it keeps others very well hidden.

Nike wearers,
Venice Beach,
Los Angeles.

CELIA LURY

Moving things

We are sitting on the beach, observing two boys playing in the waves. Both are wearing Nike shorts, the letters NI and KE on each leg. The shorts make the boys larger and smaller versions of each other. Their shorts give a flickering message as they run in and out of the water. This is a visual message, but it has an aural accompaniment like a crowd chanting: NI-KE, NI-KE. The brand communicates using the whole of their bodies: the use of profiles, sound, shapes and the body in movement.

In the shopping malls we visit the next day, I notice the careful positioning of Nike logos. They are often situated on the body in a proper three-dimensional space: the marks and logos at right angles to one another.

I observe someone sitting down, the ankle of one leg resting over the knee of the other, with a Nike Swoosh on the sole of the shoe. Others walk by in shorts and socks, the Swoosh riding high on the side of their ankles. Yet although their legs move in sequential time, while they are clearly in three-dimensional space, they are simultaneously repositioned by the logos or marks. It is as if the mark of the brand collapses the foreground into the background and slides now into then. These Sunday shoppers are moving into and out of multiple planes in space and dimensions in time. The mark, as a conceptual outline or trace of movement, seems pressed against the boundaries of space and time, and

concurrently far away *and* near, right here *and* already gone. In short, the mark of the brand re-calibrates time and space.

In these observations, the brand redefines the limits of the human body by placing it in a newly extended field, as space that is both material and imagined, objective and subjective, mechanical and embodied. The space in which Nike moves is one that we are in and at a distance from; in which the gap between the individual and the mass might be closed, the space of 'life on the screen' (Turkle, 1995). In it, the brand presents observers with manifold ensembles of signs; the observer can attend to the whole of the frame and then its parts or

"This is a visual message, but it has an aural accompaniment like a crowd chanting: NI-KE, NI-KE."

vice versa. In the movements I have described, on the beach or in the mall, the signs are in sequences. These sequences operate not only in three-dimensional space and linear time but also in the articulated frames of the extended field of multiply mediated space. Indeed, the presence of brand logos co-ordinates the articulation of these frames. They organise how the observer sees the movement from one frame to another. In other words, the brand is a form of phatic communication.

In linguistics, the term 'phatic' is given to the signals that maintain dialogue or discourse but have little or no intrinsic meaning, for example, the question 'How are you?' In comics and

strip cartoons, for example, the phatic refers to the panels or framing devices such as lines and balloons, and motifs such as arrows or speed lines. These direct the observer's attention, showing the relationship between one frame and the next. They maintain movement and direct the action. The Nike Swoosh directs my viewing and positions me in relation to its use. It shows how to move and how to see movement in space. Moreover, through empty demonstration of effect, it creates a community. The brand is thus also a form of phatic communion or identification. As a phatic image it constitutes the subjective capacities of people and the objective properties of things in new ways.

Buzz Lightyear,
Ultimate Talking
Action Figure,
made in China
(Disney, 1997).
1999 Disney
Character © Disney
Enterprises, Inc.

CELIA LURY

Thinking with things

As companions to the mundane routines of daily life – alarm clocks, drinking mugs, key rings, pencil cases, clothes and bags – branded merchandise reminds us of our childlike ability to lose ourselves in play. Its design, the use of scale, colour, contour, line and other surface qualities , separates it from any immediate association with utility (Miller, 1987). In this playfulness, there is the suggestion that the routines of waking up, of gulping down breakfast and leaving home to go to work or school are not necessarily one dimensional. There is a pleasure to be found there that lies above and outside the necessities and seriousness of everyday life.

Perhaps then, branded merchandise, with its emphasis on image and style, contributes to the elaboration of concrete thinking. Concrete, as opposed to abstract thinking, involves thinking with things, not concepts: it is immediate, synaesthetic and situated. It is also conventionally associated with a stage in childhood development, one identified and described by Piaget in *Dreams and Imitation in Childhood*. It is a stage, so Piaget argues, that is superseded by adults, formal thinking, thinking that can be done without things. But in *Life on the Screen*, her study of the use of computers, Sherry Turkle suggests that with the rise in importance of the interface in contemporary consumer culture, there has been a re-evaluation of this kind of thinking with objects. Concrete thinking, therefore, is no longer confined to childhood.

In considering this suggestion, let us take the example of the computer-animated film *Toy Story*, released by Walt Disney and Pixar and distributed by Buena Vista in 1995, and the associated popular merchandising campaign of children's toys and other branded consumer products. In the film itself, computer-generated images are rendered tactile. As Thomas Schumacher, President of Walt Disney Feature Animation, points out (Lasseter and Daly, 1996):

> The tactileness of this world, even though it has never existed – the sense that you can reach out and hold what you see on the screen – is very significant to the appeal of the film. If you tried to make it look like real life, you would fail, because it will never look like real life, but it can be touchable life.

The toy-objects, who are the main characters in the film, are given personalities. The film's director, John Lasseter, says of them: 'The task of bringing *Toy Story* to life began with thinking through each toy's physical and conceptual essence. How is it made? What was it built to do? What are its physical flaws and limitations?' Each of the toy's personalities, he goes on to explain, was derived from the traits of the physical construction, and respected the 'physical integrity of the object'. Mr Potato Head, for example, is a 'natural malcontent'. As Lasseter says, 'you'd have a chip on your shoulder too if your face kept falling off all day.'

This description implies an understanding of the image as the surface of the object, recognised by touch, recalled in habit or renewed in gesture. Certainly, this understanding is given a new solidity of sense in the process of 'imagineering', a combination of imagination and engineering, that is deployed by Disney in the creation of the fantasy environments of Disney theme parks, where the cartoon and the real world are one. As branded merchandise, objects are so designed to be (re)-inserted in the ongoing stories that comprise our everyday worlds. They offer, as *Toy Story* character Buzz Lightyear attests, the possibility

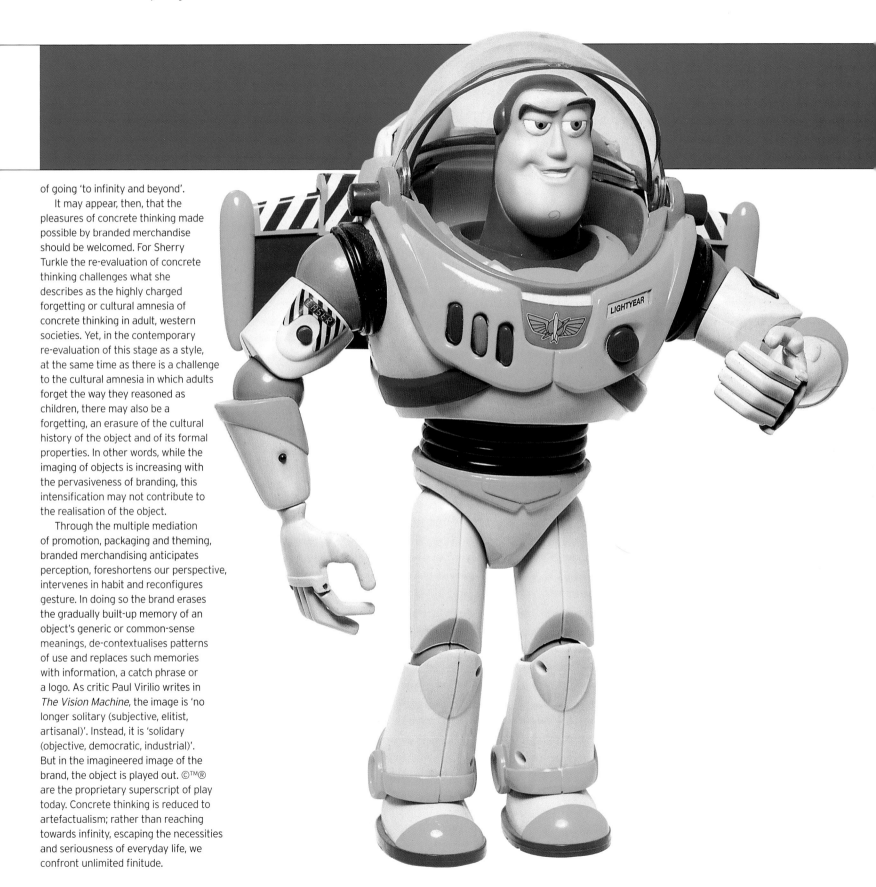

> "Branded merchandise reminds us of our childlike ability to lose ourselves in play."

of going 'to infinity and beyond'.

It may appear, then, that the pleasures of concrete thinking made possible by branded merchandise should be welcomed. For Sherry Turkle the re-evaluation of concrete thinking challenges what she describes as the highly charged forgetting or cultural amnesia of concrete thinking in adult, western societies. Yet, in the contemporary re-evaluation of this stage as a style, at the same time as there is a challenge to the cultural amnesia in which adults forget the way they reasoned as children, there may also be a forgetting, an erasure of the cultural history of the object and of its formal properties. In other words, while the imaging of objects is increasing with the pervasiveness of branding, this intensification may not contribute to the realisation of the object.

Through the multiple mediation of promotion, packaging and theming, branded merchandising anticipates perception, foreshortens our perspective, intervenes in habit and reconfigures gesture. In doing so the brand erases the gradually built-up memory of an object's generic or common-sense meanings, de-contextualises patterns of use and replaces such memories with information, a catch phrase or a logo. As critic Paul Virilio writes in *The Vision Machine*, the image is 'no longer solitary (subjective, elitist, artisanal)'. Instead, it is 'solidary (objective, democratic, industrial)'. But in the imagineered image of the brand, the object is played out. ©™® are the proprietary superscript of play today. Concrete thinking is reduced to artefactualism; rather than reaching towards infinity, escaping the necessities and seriousness of everyday life, we confront unlimited finitude.

This page: Hello Kitty branded goods: TV and video recorder, calculator, toaster and coffee-maker, 1999.

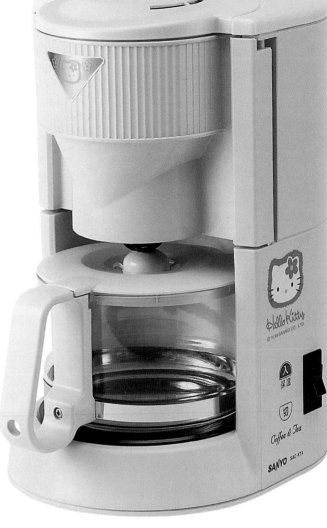

GARETH WILLIAMS

Hello Kitty

Sanrio ♥

"small gift, big smile!"

From key rings to cars, Kitty adorns over 3000 products, and along with fellow characters produced by Japanese company Sanrio, its products and licences are worth $9 billion annually. Created originally for greeting cards by Sanrio president Shintaro Tsuji in 1974, as a recognisable, patented character Hello Kitty adds commercial value to the most commonplace product,. The company quickly expanded the use of the brand into merchandising: specifically giftware and clothing for children. Sanrio describe their products as 'small gifts that bring big smiles', and as such they play a part in the complex protocol of gift giving in Japanese culture. Like a great deal of merchandising, Hello Kitty products also have a collectors market, which

targets items that are rare or no longer in production.

Kitty's progress has been somewhat different to that of her brand-rivals Mickey, Donald and other cartoon characters. In what we might call 'Disneyfication' in reverse, Kitty began life as a merchandise creation and only recently made it on to the screen in her own animated TV series. She does, however, have her own theme park, Puroland in Japan, which is shared with the stable of other Sanrio brand characters.

Although Hello Kitty is principally marketed at children, in Japan many consumers (particularly women) have grown up with the brand and still identify with it in adulthood. The merchandising available confirms this

view. The product range reflects what Sanrio see to be the main stages of growing up and socialisation for their consumers: there are toy household and beauty products, for example, but these are also available as full size, 'proper' working domestic products, such as toasters, vacuum cleaners and microwaves. In order to produce these, Sanrio entered into a licensing deal with Sanyo, the Japanese consumer-electronics corporation. Hello Kitty is a brand that marks out some of the rituals and behaviours of a contemporary lifestyle: the character appears on credit cards, mobile phones and even wedding dresses. Arguably, in this context, the Hello Kitty brand sells itself as a form of transitional safety for the

"Hello Kitty is a brand that marks out some of the rituals and behaviours of a contemporary lifestyle."

young woman, where the equipment necessary for adult domesticity is reminiscent of the accoutrements of childhood.

Although Hello Kitty is principally marketed for children, she gained a cult following in European club culture. The image of the character and the range of merchandise, including girl's T-shirts, hair grips, small purses and handbags, seemed ripe for ironic appropriation. Sanrio have significantly expanded their global reach, targeting fashion stores like Top Shop in Britain, who cater to the teen and pre-teen market. With such market penetration and greater control over the brand image in the UK, less space will be left for the ironic appropriation of 'Hello Kitty'.

Above: Hello Kitty collectors at home, Japan
Right: Hello Kitty promotional event, Top Shop, Oxford Street, London, 1999.

ALISON CLARKE

Brand not-so-new

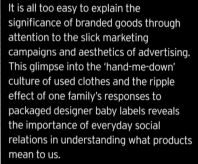

Above: Assorted second-hand children's clothes. Opposite: Child's *101 Dalmatians* pyjamas and *Aristocats* hand bag, Disney characters © Disney Enterprises, Inc.

It is all too easy to explain the significance of branded goods through attention to the slick marketing campaigns and aesthetics of advertising. This glimpse into the 'hand-me-down' culture of used clothes and the ripple effect of one family's responses to packaged designer baby labels reveals the importance of everyday social relations in understanding what products mean to us.

Children's toys, from Barbies to Game-Boys, are frequently in the firing line from the critics of consumerism, given as prime examples of the extent to which we and our children have become embroiled in the world of branded goods. So how do parents make sense of a market full of expensive Disney merchandise and Telly-Tubby jigsaw puzzles? The term 'brand new' connotes a pristine, packaged and mass-produced commodity distinguished only by the mark of its manufacturer. But what happens to branded goods once they have become part of everyday lives and social worlds? This ethnographic snapshot of the second-hand, informal economy in children's wear provides a colourful insight into the post-sale 'lives' of ambiguous branded commodities. In this example popular and familiar branded goods are re-evaluated and interpreted through the particular moral economies of households on an average street in north London.

Jane, a mother of three young children, regularly receives a consignment of second-hand clothes from relatives who live in suburban North America. Along with other 'hand-me-down' clothes given by friends and neighbours Jane sorts through the various articles judging their appropriateness in relation to the values of her own household. Certain items, such as a sequinned party dress and a toddler's white real-fur coat, are rendered distasteful, anomalous or impractical within their new context. Other items, such as a pair of polyester *101 Dalmatians* pyjamas and a satin-pink fluffy miniature Disney handbag, prove more problematic.

In principle, Jane and her partner discourage their children's interest in branded merchandise, which they consider as exploitative and non-educational. Due to its stereotypical connotations the colour pink 'for girls' is also generally avoided. But as a mother Jane is fully aware of the desirability of the pyjamas among girls her daughter's age. For six-year-old Sophie they hold a special premium, operating, as they do, outside the rules that constitute the value system of this household. Certainly Sophie does not need new pyjamas. A hand-made nightdress in 100-per-cent cotton, made by her grandmother as a Christmas gift, lies unused in her wardrobe. For a young girl, despite her affection for her grandmother, the attachment to the magic of a pink sparkly Disney outfit far outweighs the value of a handmade gift. Sophie and her girlfriends frequently covet such items, flicking through the pages of catalogues brought into the school playground. For Sophie's mother the dilemma of the Disney pyjamas is further compounded by its dubious status as a 'synthetic' garment, which she considers to be unhealthy. As a compromise, Jane allows her daughter to keep the pink, fluffy handbag and offers the pyjamas to her daughter, not for her own use, but as a potential gift for her best-friend Rachel (a seven year old living in the same street).

Unfortunately, allowing Sophie to present Rachel with the pyjamas might be construed as insensitive or insulting to Rachel's mother. Why would Jane try to pass off something deemed problematic within her own household to another mother? Both women frequent the local nearly new children's sales and thrift shops together and have often discussed their tastes and preferences as mothers and, in particular, their shared disinclination towards their children wearing branded goods and synthetics. Over a cup of coffee later in the week Jane pre-empts the 'problem' of the contentious pyjamas by assuring Rachel's mother of her own ambiguity towards them and explaining that if unsuitable, they 'can always be sent to the charity shop'. Through their shared views of 'brand' and 'synthetic' products the women generate consensus and sociality around such 'hand-me-down' articles and a particular understanding of 'mothering'.

A week later Jane discovers a pair of Osh-Kosh dungarees in a local charity shop. Overjoyed with her purchase ('fancy finding a designer label in there!') she washes the overalls and proudly dresses her 18-month-old toddler Jeremy in them. The status of the designer label for this particular low-income middle-class group resides in the very contradictions it poses. As a second-hand garment the brand's relation to the manufacturer and advertiser is neutralised to an extent that it can be re-enchanted as a 'bargain find' expressing the knowledge and skill of a wily and ethical mother.

Through swapping values and tastes around children's clothing women create and contest their values as mothers. Bombarded with brand names and designer labels, these mothers circumvent the full-price retail outlets and create an alternative set of values around branded products. Ultimately this trafficking of used children's clothes and the re-interpretation of brand and designer labels generates values (used to enhance the ethical role of mothering) that exist in direct contradiction to the intentions of the marketers and producers.

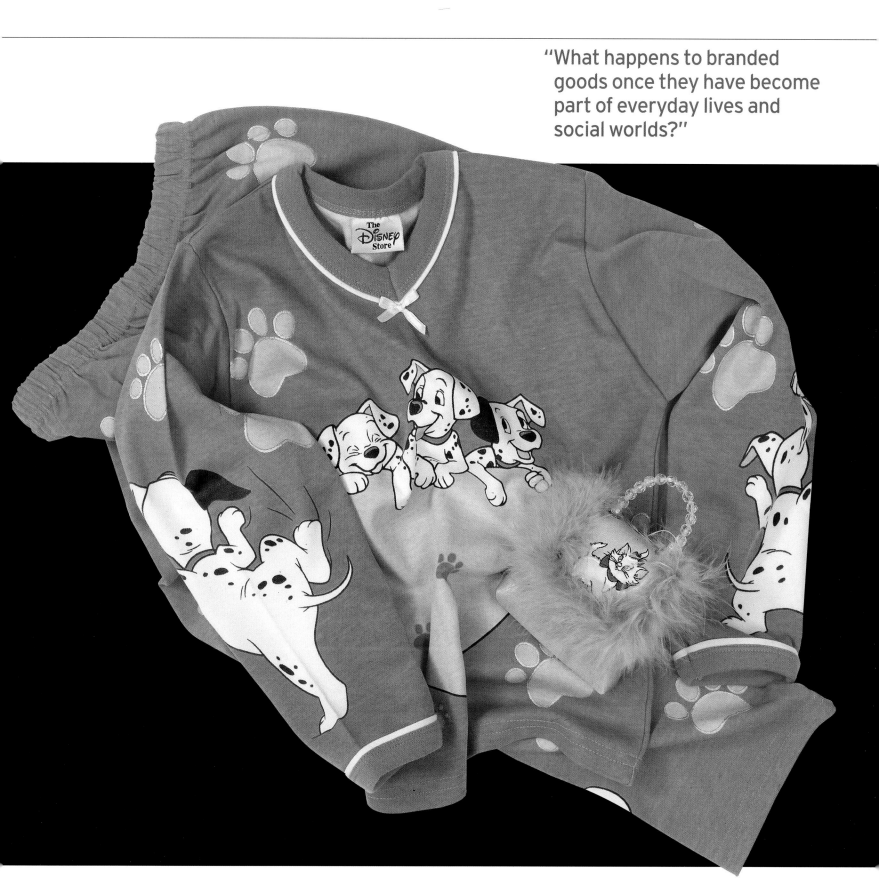

"What happens to branded goods once they have become part of everyday lives and social worlds?"

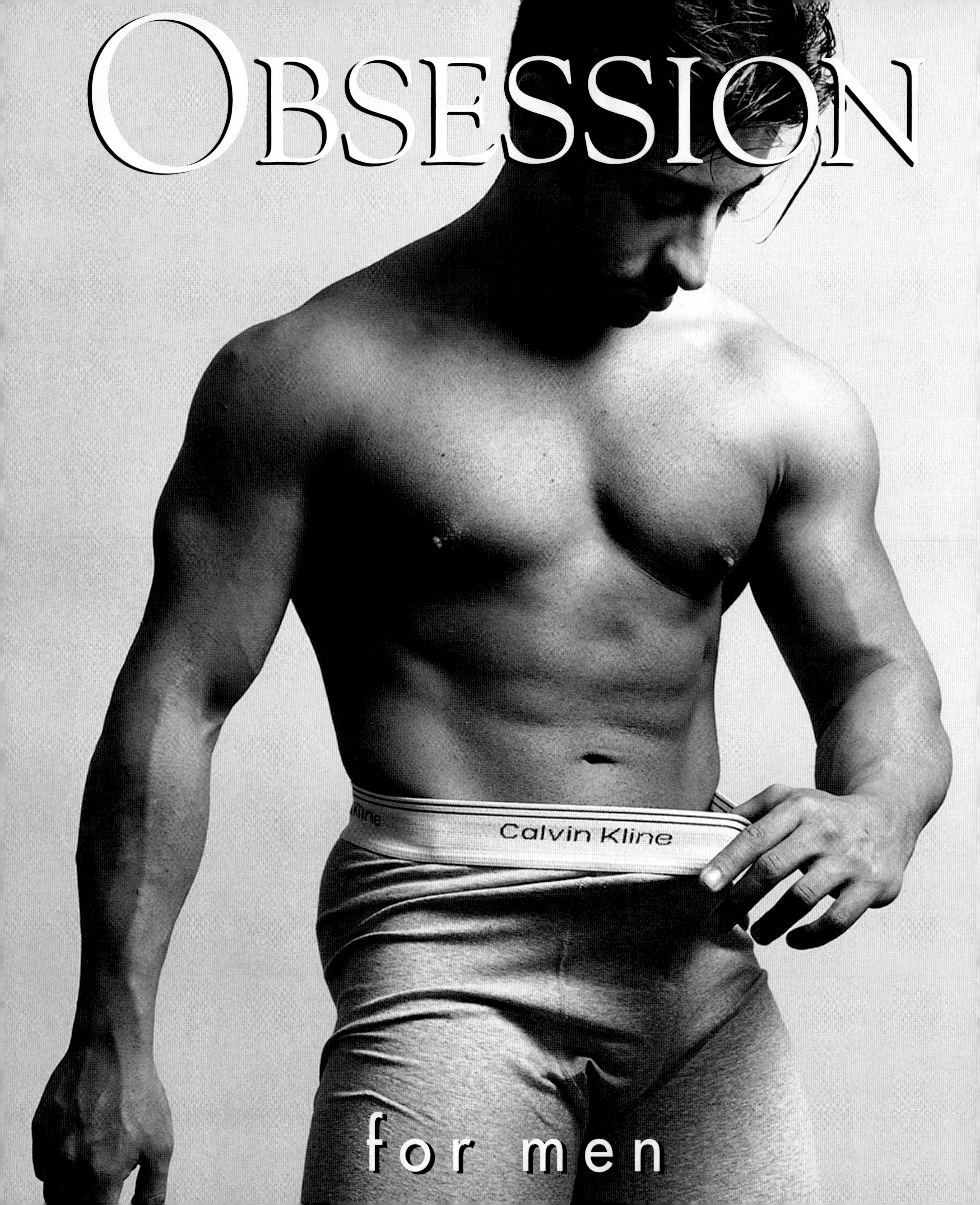

OBSESSION

Calvin Kline

for men

conventional political processes. Conversely, the right to consume has been asserted as evidence of democratic human freedom, as with the American gun lobby's support for carrying handguns. Consumer culture is far from neutral; it is a political arena, a battlefield for activists and ideologies, fraught with moral choices and ethical concerns.

A traditional target for consumer concern has been the advertising industry. Advertising surrounds us; it influences our aspirations and our choices. Its primary function is to create needs, but its important secondary function is to ensure these needs are not fulfilled, in order to guarantee continued, even escalated consumption. As the German philosopher and Marxist critic, Wolfgang Fritz Haug, writes: 'Appearance always promises more, much more, than it can ever deliver. In this way the illusion deceives.'[2] One way of being critical of branded culture is to question the validity of advertising.

The post-war economic boom was fuelled by consumer demand for new commodities. In 1957 Vance Packard, a popular sociologist and critic of American consumer society, wrote of 'the hidden persuaders' in his famous book of the same name.[3] These are the advertisers who make us want what we do not need and buy what we can not afford. Writing in 1950s America, the acme of the consumer society, Packard believed advertisers were manipulating public desire and demand for new goods, using techniques of motivational research learnt from psychoanalysis. According to Packard and other critics of this 'new' consumer society, the function of advertising was the creation of false needs, fed by the constant arrival of new products on the market. The 1950s saw the advent of rapid obsolescence in some manufacturing industries, whereby seasonal style changes encouraged consumers frequently to replace the models of their products, long before they may actually have ceased to function. Rapid obsolescence in the automobile production became a focus of criticism from a variety of parties including consumer journalists, insurers, safety experts and legislators who perceived that changes in style were not the

same as exponential enhancements to performance.[4] Ralph Nader, an important and vocal defender of consumer rights in the USA, went so far as to equate rapid obsolescence with 'designed-in dangers'.[5]

Yet even though there was a growing scepticism of advertising's claims, post-war American society was increasingly defined by its consumer goods. The emigré German philosopher of the New Left, Herbert Marcuse, wrote of commodity fetishism: 'People recognise themselves in their commodities; they find their soul in their automobile, hi-fi set, split-level home – social control is anchored in the new needs which [the consumer society] has produced.'[6]

If social control was exerted through the allure of material goods then perhaps happiness was found there too, particularly in contrast to what was felt to be the miserable austerity of Soviet socialism against which the American consumer society defined its values. While Packard believed 'free' Americans were as brainwashed as anyone inside the Iron Curtain was, he suggested advertising was as coercive as Stalinist politics.[7] American politics has always defined itself against external enemies, and from the 1950s to the 1980s this enemy was the spectre of communism and 'the evil empire' of the Soviet bloc. Advertising can be seen as expressing the power of pure American-style market economics, an ideology that underpins the 'land of the free'. Yet its critics viewed it not as a force for individual liberation (through the promotion of personal choice) but as a repressive agent of social control exerted by corporate powers. To misquote Karl Marx, perhaps we should view commodities, not religion, as the opium of the people, as they distract us from questioning the social and economic status quo. Packard viewed the American public as duped by advertisers, but the question remains whether, or to what degree, consumers have been convinced to buy products that could not fulfil the advertisers' promises of happiness?

Packard's criticisms were largely concerned with advertising, but other critics perceived the advertising industry as symptomatic of a greater social and corporate malaise. Wolfgang Fritz Haug

Below: Environmentalists
promote International Buy
Nothing Day in Seoul, South
Korea, 24 November 1999.
Below right: Adbusters'
Christmas Gift Exemption
Voucher, 1997
Opposite: Adbusters poster
for Buy Nothing Day.

argues that advertising is merely part of a larger exploitative system:[8]

> Since the vast majority of people can find no worthwhile goal within the capitalist system, the distraction industry appears to be a good investment for the system as a whole.... With shades and shadows the illusion industry populates the spaces left empty by capitalism, which only socialism can fill with reality.

Antipathy towards advertising is therefore, perhaps, a natural position for the political left that distrusts the motives of capitalism. Ralph Nader equates the consumer with the citizen but acknowledges the disillusionment many have in political processes.[9]

> Citizen cynicism is a corrosive asset of democracy. Yet democracy is the only instrument we know of that can comprehensively build a happier, more prosperous society. That's why a lot of people like democracy – in theory. But when they become cynical they no longer practice it. They don't join local groups. They don't participate in electoral campaigns.

Nader believes democracy demands engagement by the individual citizen. John Harms and Douglas Kellner have developed a critical theory of advertising and concluded, like Nader, that it is non-democratic as it promises to provide commodity solutions for all problems without the need for personal engagement in the political process.[10]

Critics of advertising, therefore, position their activity as the defence of the individual and democracy against the corporate machinations of big business and the state. 'Subvertisers' are critics of advertising who take on the advertisers at their own game, by defacing or spoofing 'real' advertisements. In so doing they are critical of a mass culture that has been dominated by big corporations.

The most famous of the 'subvertisers' is Adbusters, now a global organisation that grew out of anti-advertising actions in Vancouver, Canada. Adbusters publish a quarterly magazine with the twin goals of raising consciousness about commercial excess and elevating the media awareness and skills of the environmental movement.[11] Targeted brands include Camel cigarettes and Calvin Klein underwear. Rather than defacing existing advertisements, Adbusters produce elaborate spoofs mocking the values of existing ad campaigns and the inflated importance of the corporations that produce them. They challenge the advertisers on their own territory, using their own tools. Adbusters also promote the annual International Buy Nothing Day every November, exhorting shoppers to 'Participate by not participating' (that is to buy nothing, in protest

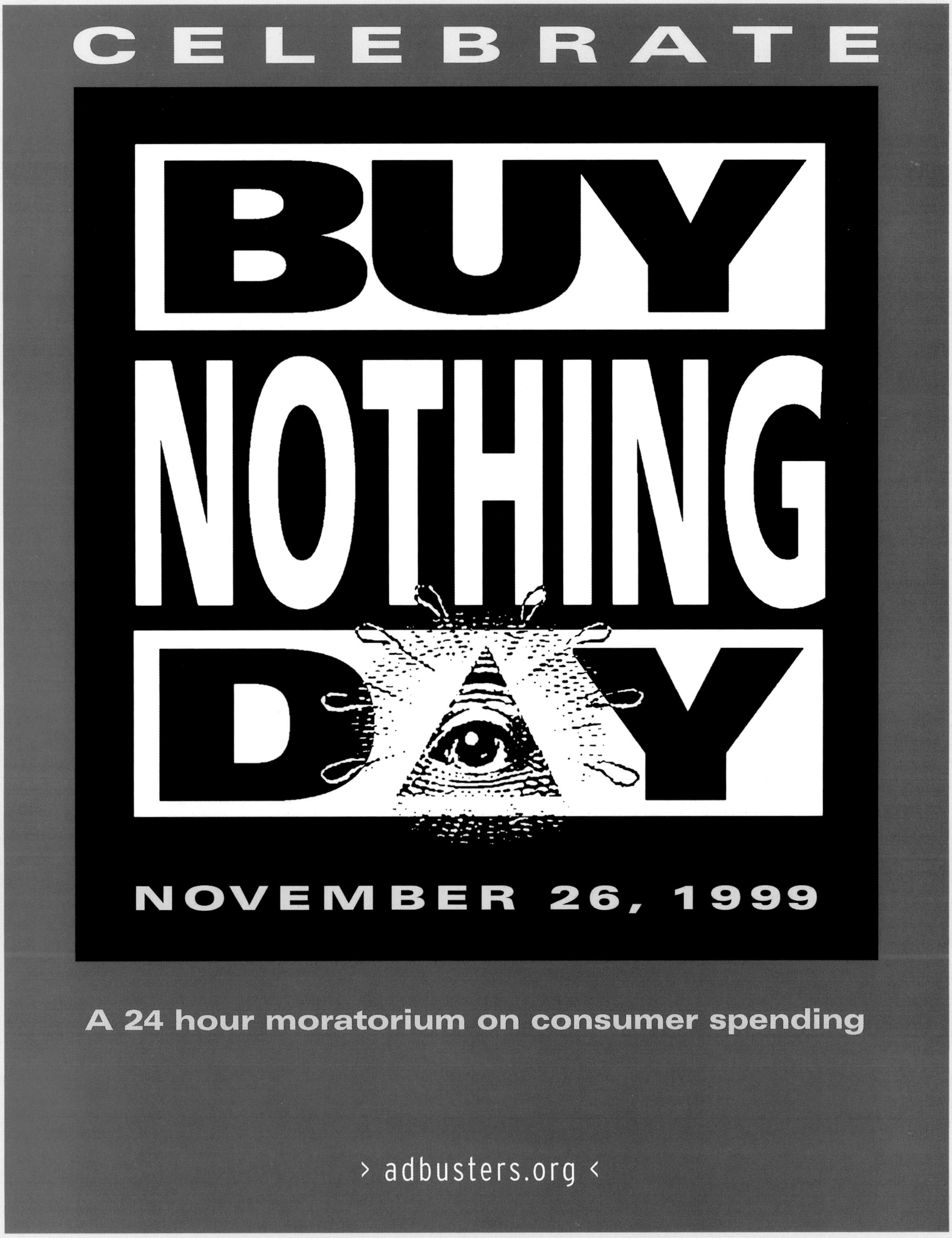
CELEBRATE
BUY
NOTHING
DAY
NOVEMBER 26, 1999
A 24 hour moratorium on consumer spending
› adbusters.org ‹

Impotent

WARNING: SMOKING CAUSES IMPOTENCE
California Department Of Health Services. © 1999 California Department of Health Services

OUTDOOR SYSTEMS

against the values and methods of the manufacturers of branded goods and the shops that sell them). In 1999 the day was celebrated in twelve world cities as far afield as Boston in the USA and Seoul in South Korea. Another strategy is to issue 'Christmas Gift Exemption Vouchers', which can be downloaded from Adbusters' website, for individuals to exchange in lieu of purchased gifts. In a sense, like Packard in the 1950s, Adbusters and the other 'subvertisers' believe that shoppers are powerless to resist messages in advertising.

Billboard-Utilising Graffitists Against Unhealthy Promotions (BUGA-UP), a movement formed in Australia in 1979 by a surgeon, Dr Arthur Chesterfield-Evans, targeted among others the tobacco industry. Supporters of BUGA-UP's aims defaced billboard advertisements for cigarette brands in protest against what Chesterfield-Evans described as 'a cold-blooded and systematic campaign of deception waged by monied interests against less-informed consumers'.[12] Like Packard and Nader, Dr Chesterfield-Evans clearly associates advertising solely with the interests of capital rather than society. He is now a member of the New South Wales parliament.

In parallel to the kinds of subversion practised by campaigners, some advertisers and brand managers have incorporated irreverence and even 'playful' criticism into their own marketing. Such promotional campaigns diffuse the 'subvertisers'' critique, at the same time exploiting the potential associations. Death cigarettes, for example, could be a creation of Adbusters, but it was in fact a genuine tobacco brand in the early 1990s that 'packaged' the criticism of the tobacco industry and sold it as novelty, appealing (it hoped) to the consumer's sense of irony. This approach invites the consumer to collude with the brand-owner in the subversion of the product.

A noteworthy recent twist in the fortunes of 'subvertising' and its relationship to cigarette advertising is the case of the famous 'Marlboro' Man' billboard in Hollywood. The billboard, a 'more enduring urban monument than almost any other building in Los Angeles'[13] has stood on the Hollywood hills for many years, a symbol of masculinity and part of American folklore. When the USA banned tobacco advertising in 1998, tobacco companies were also forced to hand over their remaining billboards for use by State health and education agencies but had to maintain payments on these sites until January 2000. The sites were to be used for creative work with a health message instead. The Marlboro' Man was transformed – instead of the Marlboro name running beside him, the word 'Impotent' was produced in an appropriate red type, and his cigarette hung limply from his mouth. The emasculated cowboy 'subvertised' the brand message, parodying the values of virility and Americanness that Marlboro' traditionally embodied.

The boundaries between the activities of marketers and the activities of consumer pressure groups are fragile. No longer perceived as the passive victim of advertising claims, the consumer has been 'repackaged' by the media in recent years as demanding, discerning and pro-active. In turn, this shift has provided ample opportunity for brands to target the consumer's conscience. In no other area of marketing and consumption has this been as clear as in the case of Green consumption, where grassroots politics have impacted upon product development and new directions in marketing.[14]

Green consumerism has clearly captured the popular imagination to an unprecedented degree. This is because it offers ordinary people access to a new and immediate democratic process: 'voting' about the environment can take place on a daily basis. People are not only not duped, they are able through their shopping to register political support or opposition.

During the last decade, Green issues have moved increasingly towards the centre stage of consumption debates. More and more shoppers are aware of complex ecological and social effects wrought by the manufacture and consumption of the brands they use. Their awareness affects their feelings toward the brands that they buy and ultimately demonstrates the political power of purchase.

The Annual Survey of British Green Activism, conducted by MORI in 1994, revealed the following behaviour by shoppers.[15]

> In answer to the question, 'Which if any of these things have you done in the last 12 months as a result of concern for the environment?' 45 per cent said they had bought products in recycled packaging, 52 per cent had bought products made from recycled materials, 35 per cent had bought environmentally friendly detergents or cleaners, and 33 per cent products in bio-degradable packaging. Overall, 42 per cent of people participating in the survey said they had selected one product over another because of its environmentally friendly packaging, formulation or advertising.

Above right: Packaging showing a range of Green symbols, c. 1992.
Right: Signage for organic food, Tesco, West Kensington, London 1999.

These figures reveal the broad extent of low-level green shopping in the UK by the mid-1990s. Other studies suggest a hard-core of some 10 per cent of British shoppers who integrate ecological issues very consistently into their buying behaviours, while a further 70 per cent occasionally consider the environment.[16] Green consumers' choice of one product over another is dependent on their level of awareness and their inclination towards Green claims by manufacturers. What affects this choice?

Shoppers' most immediate source of environmental information is on the packaging and products they buy. A panoply of symbols and marks are used to validate Green claims. The International Standards Organisation's Strategic Advisory Group on the Environment has identified two types.[17] The first are claims for the product made by a third party, often a governmental agency, but sometimes another body or a private company. Consumers International, a global network of consumers' associations from over 80 nations, sees the endorsement of products by independent specialists as generally a good thing but is doubtful of the efficacy of environmental marks. This is because the messages can be confusing to the shopper. For example, more than 30 schemes are run worldwide incorporating the Mobius loop used to mean 'incorporating recycled materials' or the converse 'recyclable'. National and transnational schemes include Germany's Blue Angel and the EU's flower symbol. However, the proliferation of these symbols, and the variety of criteria for their use, mean environmental marks are difficult to implement with any meaningful clarity.

A newly arrived marker upon products is the Humane Cosmetics Standard logo. Leading animal protection groups such as the British Union for the Abolition of Vivisection (BUAV) have joined forces to endorse the logo that identifies 'cruelty-free' cosmetic products and brands: companies will be independently assessed to judge their compliance. The mark is intended to help consumers to choose cosmetics that have not been tested on animals, and although this issue is aside from green consumerism per se, the logo will act in much the same way as ecological marks, an aide to ethical consumerism.

The second type of marker denotes the claims made by manufacturers themselves. A response to the Green shopper's arrival in the 1980s was a marked increase in the quantity and range of Green products. Advertisements making Green claims in the period 1985 to 1991 increased, while ecological statements have diminished through the rest of the 1990s.[18] Green claims have been most extreme in areas of intense competition, for example in the market for washing powders where environmentalism invigorated the tired advertising of such products. This leads to the sceptical view that the manufacturers were, after all, most concerned for their profit margins and market shares. Green imagery often includes trees, flowers, the Earth held in a pair of caring hands and the sun. They are clearly intended to reassure the consumer and, as it is virtually impossible to differentiate between quasi-official marks and manufacturers' own claims, the marks do not particularly aid the Green shopper. Imagery suggestive of nature's bounty and freshness, such as leaping dolphins, wild flowers and waterfalls are used in the design of much packaging to suggest a 'natural' or 'organic' basis for the product. Often the imagery is unconnected to the product's function, as with the inclusion of dolphins on the label for Reckitt & Colman's Down to Earth washing up liquid. Natural imagery employed in packaging extends to advertising, as with the use of waterfalls in the long-running campaign for Timotei shampoo. The

inference for the consumer in both these examples is that the products are non-polluting and derived from natural ingredients, and to use them re-connects the user with nature.

Many claims on packaging substantiate the manufacturers' efforts to ensure the sustainability of their products, indicating the ingredients or materials included, although most often those that they have excluded. CFC gases (chloroflouro carbons, alleged to contribute to ozone depletion and global warming) are now commonly understood by consumers to be undesirable. Although they have been phased out of aerosol production since 1989 manufacturers still boldly claim the absence of CFCs as a specific selling point. Additionally they may stress that the propellant in their aerosols is harmless compressed air, neglecting to point out this needs thicker, stronger cans using more material and energy to manufacture. Green claims reassure consumers, even if they are at best misleading and at worst economical with the truth.

Much eco-labelling on general household products now implicates the consumer, not the manufacturer, to take responsibility through recycling or safely disposing of waste. Cleverly, this strategy implies responsibility by the manufacturer without delivering it, while the social and economic networks for adequate retrieval of materials and commodities such as aluminium are not in place. Yet the potential of recycling post-consumer waste is enough to persuade most shoppers that they are contributing to improving the environment. A statement such as 'This carrier bag is biodegradable or recyclable' can only be effective if the consumer acts upon it. Little information is published to show that landfills, where most so-called 'biodegradable' waste ends up, are specifically managed to reduce biodegradation and so control the emission of harmful gases. The recycling advice alleviates the responsibility of the supplier, whether or not it is heeded, and using the Green product relieves the consumers' environmental guilt. Both parties in the transaction are vindicated by the green claims.[19]

Vague claims such as 'Environmentally Friendly'

Below: Humane Cosmetics logo, 1999.
Opposite: Packaging showing environmental imagery, 1999.

are even more effective at persuading consumers to buy products, although they may be meaningless in their non-specificity. UK trading and advertising standards inefficiently combat them, although the law in the USA and in other European Union countries such as Sweden has proved better equipped. Ironically it is rival manufacturers, not consumers, who often complain about the accuracy of Green claims for products, implying they perceive environmental responsibility as another marketing tool. In 1994 Lever Bros complained to the Advertising Standards Authority (ASA) about claims made by their rival, Reckitt & Colman, for Down to Earth washing-up liquid. The wording of Reckitt & Colman's advertisement was 'our washing up liquid … looks after rivers. We get independent experts to conduct stringent tests for biodegradability, on the whole product, to ensure we're reducing the harm to the environment.' Lever complained the advertisement implied that competitors' products were less biodegradable and therefore did more harm to the environment. Since Reckitt & Colman was unable to demonstrate its claims relative to

other products, the ASA upheld the complaint.[20]

Consumer confusion about and ignorance of Green issues plays into the hands of manufacturers and marketers. The supermarket shopper may find it near impossible to make informed, critical decisions about green claims, however concerned he or she is to make the right choices for the sake of the environment. Manufacturers employ tried and tested techniques such as the use of 'independent experts' to verify their environmental practices, perhaps as a way of countering cynicism about unendorsed product claims. Mostly, the shopper responds to the manufacturer's claims with complicity and is made to feel better about his or her environmental responsibility by buying what is ostensibly a 'natural' or 'eco-friendly' product. This relationship between the shopper and the brand is a collective mitigation of guilt, in which the palliative of Green consciousness assuages the environmental responsibility of the consumer and the supplier. It is a 'disacknowledgement' of environmental issues, where consumers match manufacturers' Green claims with tokenistic ecological responses. This Sheffield shopper typifies many consumers' approach to Green shopping; 'I don't mooch, ferreting for environmentally friendly ones. If they really stand out then I'll go for it and think, I've done my bit.'[21]

'Light Green' supermarket shoppers seldom deny themselves through their product choices, choosing to consume differently rather than reduce their consumption.[22] However, proactive consumption also takes the form of a refusal to buy certain goods and protest against their presence in the market. Increasingly, we are witnessing the targeting of brands by political activists. Boycotts, for example, are organised for reasons that often transcend the product or manufacturer to make broader social or political points, and they may inconvenience or even threaten those who undertake them. As one critic has put it 'consumer boycotts … have specific goals that do not necessarily operate to the material advantage of the consumer'.[23] Ultimately the environmental movement and economic boycotts combine high-

week we price check hundreds of everyday

BAG
FOR
LIFE

RECYCLABLE BAG, REPLACED FREE

level political concerns with low-level commercial ones. The consumer is political, and the 'vigilante consumer' can effect change.[24]

Not every boycott succeeds, and it is not the only method for consumers to register their criticism. One study of commercial boycotts found that they are most likely to succeed if the target organisation is highly visible and closely involved with the principal cause of the action. The bull's-eye is 'a consumer good or service, low cost, frequently purchased, branded, substitutable, perishable, distributed through retail outlets, and publicly (visibly) purchased and consumed'.[25]

The boycott of Barclays Bank was organised by the Anti-Apartheid Movement in the 1980s. The protest was against the bank's investment in what was perceived as the repressive South African regime. Its specific aim was to persuade Barclays to withdraw from South Africa, and the long-term goal was the overthrow of the apartheid system through the economic isolation of South Africa itself. The campaign encouraged potential customers, particularly students, not to have Barclays accounts. Therefore, boycotters were able to use commercial action to register political dissent, especially as the Anti-Apartheid Movement was also critical of the British government's reluctance to act on the issue. Barclays was not the only British institutional investor in South Africa, but as a prominent High Street brand it became the focus for the action.[26] A direct result of the boycott was a reduction in the bank's share of the student market from 27 per cent in 1983 to 17 per cent in 1985.[27] Barclays also largely withdrew from South Africa, although it claimed this was for a raft of economic reasons, not exclusively due to the sanctions.

A consumer boycott may be deemed a success if it damages a company's representation of itself (its brand image), forcing a fundamental public reappraisal of the corporation's activities. One such example was the action taken by a small pressure group known as London Greenpeace (not related to the environmental pressure group Greenpeace) against McDonald's in the late 1980s. From 1986

activists distributed a leaflet titled 'What's Wrong With McDonald's?' that entreated customers to boycott its fast-food restaurants and questioned the corporation's own environmental and labour relations claims. In this instance, it was not the boycott *per se* that became the focus of media attention or consumer action, but the resulting court case when McDonald's sued two of the activists for libel.[28]

At 313 days, the so-called McLibel trial became the longest court case in English legal history, and the media scrutiny this engendered worked against the successful image of McDonald's. Far from quieting criticism, as had been intended, the case sharply focussed public attention upon the corporation's practices and core values. The defendants, Helen Steel and David Morris, were found guilty of libel against McDonald's as they were not able to substantiate their claims that the corporation caused starvation in the third world, destroyed rain forests, lied about recycling, poisoned customers or maintained poor conditions for their workers. However, Justice Bell ruled that McDonald's had exploited children in its advertising, was cruel to animals, and that its restaurants paid low wages to British workers.[29] Despite the complexity of the case and the inability of the defendants to make it stick, McLibel can be interpreted as a public-relations disaster for McDonald's as it drew public attention to aspects of the corporations activities it did not wish to publicise. The fact that issues surrounding McDonald's activities were discussed openly in the media is evidence of the activists' success, even if they had to go to the High Court to defend their views. This was no 'light Green' consumer activity, therefore, but a committed, politicised action against the values and policies of corporate, branded culture.

For the McLibel activists, their court case symbolised the greater injustices of a world controlled by corporate interests, of which McDonald's was the metaphor. Their protest was essentially about freedom of speech, which they

What's wrong with McDonald's?

Everything they don't want you to know.

Above: Sainsbury's loyalty card and Unilever disloyalty card, 1998.
Below: 'No to GM Food, Yes to Organic Food', True Food campaign logo, Greenpeace, UK, 1999.
Opposite: True Food campaign, Greenpeace, UK, 1999.

felt to be suppressed by corporate interests. After the court case they wrote:[30]

> People should have the right to put forward their honestly held beliefs to draw attention to what they see as the problems with the way society is run. It is only through the expression of alternative views and ideas that injustice is remedied and society progresses. It is in the public interest that there be the widest possible dissemination of critical information about those institutions which dominate our lives and environment. There also needs to be vibrant public debate about what is really happening around us, and about the alternatives.

McLibel bears comparison with a previous, successful boycott of a multinational. In 1974 Nestlé, the world's leading manufacturer of powdered baby milk with half the global market, won a libel suit but lost valuable public support. The company was countering claims that their baby-milk products were being marketed in poor countries incorrectly and leading to 'commerciogenic malnutrition'. A full-scale boycott of Nestlé in the USA was organised in 1977 by a coalition of protestors under the banner of the Infant Formula Action Coalition (INFACT). The action of one boycotter illustrates how personal choices have a larger political and social dimension. Her letter to Nestlé read:[31]

> My children love Nestlé Quik. My husband and I are virtually addicted to Nescafé. But we will no longer be buying these or your other products. We have learned about the suffering your advertising of infant formula causes. You are a large company. Individually, we don't have much power over your actions. But our outrage joins with that of many others and together we will boycott Nestlé products until you change.

Like McDonald's, Nestlé responded initially with legal action to refute accusations. Under intense pressure from activists, who along the way recruited establishment support from the World Health Organisation (WHO), Nestlé eventually took on board the criticism aimed at it and amended its practice. The boycott was suspended in 1984 but demonstrated how effective consumers could be

when they call corporations to accountability, and it stands as the model for successful consumer action.

In the 1990s other issues with food have shaken consumers' confidence. So-called 'Mad Cow Disease' (Bovine Spongiform Encaphalopathy, or BSE) was connected to the fatal human degenerative condition Creutzfeldt-Jacob disease (CJD). The ensuing collapse of public faith in British beef, along with European boycotts of its products, led to the virtual collapse of the beef industry itself. By the summer of 1999 the BSE scare appeared to be gradually subduing,[32] only to be replaced in the public arena by a new food fear, that of untested genetically modified (GM) ingredients in processed food.

GM food raises ecological and ethical questions, ranging from potential damage to the ecosystem and human DNA, to concern about animal (and ultimately human) cloning and accusations of 'playing God'.[33] International corporate brands such as Monsanto have been accused of developing new strains of crops to withstand biological and other threats without thoroughly testing the environmental- and human-health implications. Monsanto identified a potential threat to its business activities and public relations from protests in Britain. Interestingly, the American general public have remained unconcerned by the inclusion of genetically modified ingredients in food, and the US agricultural industry has until recently embraced the new technology. By issuing full-page advertisements in the British national press in early 1999, Monsanto countered its critics, an action that has been identified as the strongest possible reaction to a boycott by a target organisation.[34] However, Monsanto is (or was, until the current public debate arose) an 'invisible' corporation, rather than a consumer brand, and consumer action has tended to focus on the better known makers and retailers of food. Unsurprisingly, therefore, the introduction of ingredients such as genetically altered pulses into familiar supermarket branded foods has raised intense criticism from quarters as diverse as dieticians, food writers, ecologists, middle-class housewives and advocate groups like the Consumers'

AVOIDING
GM FOODS
GREENPEACE
THE GUILD OF FOOD WRITERS
ACADEMY OF CULINARY ARTS
EUROTOQUES • SLOW FOOD

Association. In June 1999 even the conservatively minded Women's Institute voted to join more radical groups such as Friends of the Earth and Greenpeace in calling for a freeze in growing GM crops.[35]

Activism has taken the now familiar form of product boycotts. An affiliation of Green groups issued a 'Unilever Disloyalty Card' to shoppers outside a north London supermarket in 1998, to protest against that company's unlabelled use of genetically modified soya in brands such as Bachelor's Beanfeast meals. The activists' ironic appropriation of the supermarket loyalty card mocked a popular method of encouraging brand loyalty by incentives. Mimicking advertisers' own use of 'independent experts', the card quoted an influential food retailer (Malcolm Walker, Chair of Iceland Foods) as saying, 'This is Frankenstein Food.' This emotive image of a 'manmade' monster was an appropriate metaphor for the complexity of GM food science and has become an enduring but negative summary image in the debate. The debate crystallised around two issues: the demand to end GM testing and use of GM foodstuffs in Britain, and the more immediate request for efficient labelling of foods to enable shoppers to make informed personal choices. These issues result in lively debate between consumers, suppliers, scientists, government ministers and activists.[36] Supermarket retailers, attempting to pre-empt or deflect possible consumer action, began removing genetically modified products from their shelves before the debate has concluded. Unilever also bowed to pressure. Van den Bergh, the Unilever subsidiary that makes Beanfeast meals, and sister company Birds Eye Walls both announced the withdrawal of GM soya from their products in April 1999. On 28 April, Britain's biggest supermarket retailer Tesco announced it had banned GM ingredients from its own-brand food. Iceland was the first chain to ban GM foods, followed by Sainsbury's, Asda and Safeway. At the same time Tesco conducted a survey of customers and found that one in four wanted GM products removed from the shelves. A Consumers' Association survey found that 94 per cent of shoppers wanted food packaging to contain information on GM ingredients. European Union legislation may enforce the labelling of genetically modified ingredients, though it will not suppress their use. The British government advocates a cautious approach to the licensing of GM foods, but the environmental pressure group Friends of the Earth suspects commercial lobbying and political leverage from the United States are at play. 'If that type of pressure has occurred, as we expect,' said Charles Secrett, the executive director of Friends of the Earth, in the *Times* newspaper, 'then it helps to explain why the Government is doing all that it can to rush through these potentially very dangerous crops and foods before adequate testing has been carried out.'[37]

The furore about GM food embraces the integrity of science, commercial interests, political expediency and citizens' rights. The consumer is torn between these contrary positions. Critics of GM food express various social and ethical points of view, and come from all walks of life, from ordinary shoppers to the Prince of Wales.[38] 'Middle Englanders' have been encouraged by the tabloid press to band together against GM food with events such as 'The *Express* Great Organic Picnic', which took place over the August bank holiday in 1999 as a form of peaceful mass demonstration. Less peaceful was the destruction of a trial crop of genetically modified maize by Greenpeace, an action that resulted in the arrest of prominent activist Lord Melchett.

Consumption, it appears, has become the central metaphor, or leitmotif, of debate in modern society.

Charitable giving, like buying green products or boycotting companies, is a way of empowering people to express opinion over ethical, social concerns. There are approximately 180,000 registered charities in the UK with a total income in 1998 of almost £20 billion. But about five per cent of all the charities receive over 85 per cent of the total annual income, and a tiny percentage (271 charities, or 0.17 per cent of the total register) attract approximately 40 per cent of the total annual income.[39] The big charities, therefore, are big business, and they are increasingly behaving as major brands to attract and maintain their share of public and corporate support. Some have their own credit cards, issued by conventional financial corporations who pay a small commission on each transaction to the charities. These cards may also be vehicles for promoting a particular cause of the charity, for example the PVC-free card issued by Greenpeace. For many of the larger ones, charity shops have gained a major role in promoting their activities and in raising revenue. Dealing with both second-hand goods and new products from alternative sources, charity shops also represent an important alternative to shopping for branded goods usually found in conventional retail outlets.

Oxfam, the acronym of the Oxford Committee for Famine Relief, is one of Britain's best-known humanitarian charities dedicated to relieving hunger and poverty. Its annual income of £91.7 million in 1996/7 included over £17 million raised through its shops.[40] Oxfam shops have become the paradigm of charity shops. The first was opened in Oxford in 1948 and sold everything from feather boas to false teeth, the guiding principle being that the public donated all the stock. Mixing the thrift of the jumble sale with the commercial sparkle of the High Street boutique, Oxfam shops have more recently moved away from their bric-à-brac origins and are now managed as efficiently as other major retailers. With over 850 outlets in the United Kingdom and Ireland, Oxfam has become a branded retailer in its own right.

Oxfam has now created a number of niche outlets, dedicated to particular kinds of goods, such as furniture. Reflecting super-saver own-brands in supermarkets, Oxfam operates 100 Super Savings shops that sell only very low-cost clothes and household goods. Some high value second-hand goods, such as designer clothes, are creamed off for other more 'up-market' outlets. At the other end of the scale, Oxfam also operates Wastesaver in the English town of Huddersfield, a recycling plant that sorts all the unsold clothes from the charity shops. These goods that have failed to re-enter the market are recycled for their materials, earning nearly £2 million for Oxfam in 1997/8.

Traditionally charity shops like Oxfam only sold second hand-items given by the public. More recently the stores have included new goods such as decorative objects, candles, basketry and food, originated in the parts of the world where the charity's humanitarian aid is most active. Not only do the shops raise revenue for the charity but also public awareness of its core activity. The customers participate in the charity's work through purchasing goods. Most of these new products are part of Fair Trade schemes, which are intended to benefit the producer (often in the third world) as much as the consumer. The Green shopper expresses a concern for the natural environment and makes choices of products accordingly. As an extension of this sensibility, ethical shoppers choose products and services because of their impact upon other people. Often, green and ethical issues may co-exist or overlap. For example, at Oxfam coffee drinkers can buy CaféLatino, ground coffee supplied by Peruvian

Right: Greenpeace PVC-free credit card, 1997
Following pages: 'Oppressive Regimes', advertisement for the Co-operative Bank, 1999.

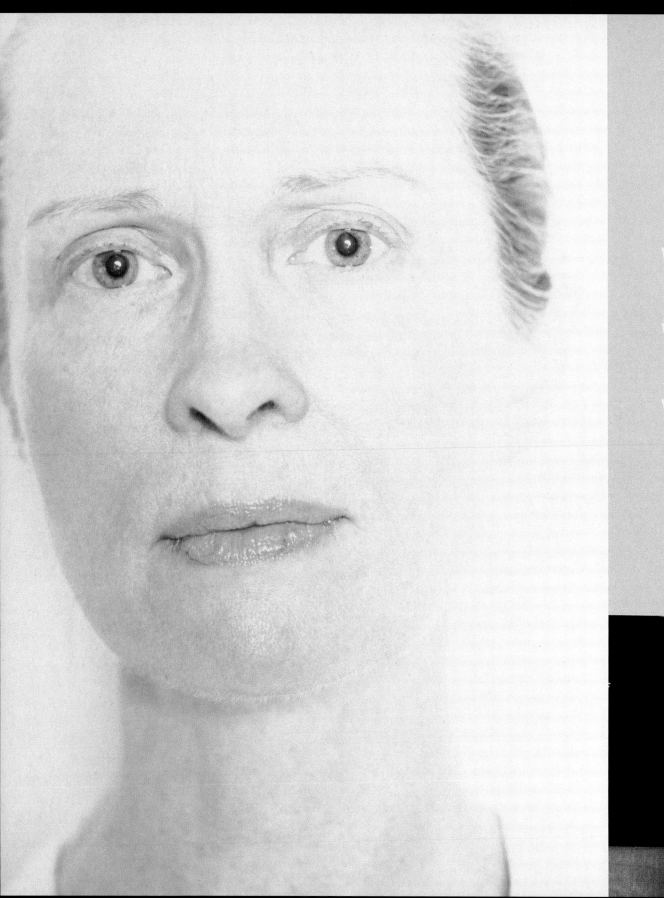

Who f

Who g

Who t

Not m

The COOPERATIVE BANK
After all, it's your money
ds these people?
es them money?
hell funds these people?
The Co-operative Bank will never invest its
customers' money in the finance of arms to oppressive regimes.
It's part of an ethical policy that states what we will and won't
do with your money. After all, it's your money.
0800 90 50 90
www.co-operativebank.co.uk

and Nicaraguan co-operatives made from organically grown beans.

One recent example of a service brand responding to the demands of ethical consumers is the Co-operative Bank in Britain. The bank grew out of the Co-operative movement of the nineteenth century, in which business enterprises were owned and managed by and for the benefit of customers or workers, but by the late twentieth century it was perceived as down-market and old-fashioned. The Co-op appealed to a new generation of customers by drawing upon its own humanitarian origins. The bank differentiated itself from its competition by promising its customers that it would not invest their money in ecologically harmful industries or oppressive regimes, a message forcibly made through advertising. This standpoint is in contrast to the activities that brought Barclays Bank into disrepute in the 1980s. Co-operative Bank customers, therefore, are able to express their political and social values through their choice of bank. Ethical consumption both empowers the consumer and reinforces the brand's image.

This is the context in which Fair Trade products operate. The Fair Trade Foundation is an independent body founded by a coalition of commercial producers and charities to oversee the awarding of the Fair Trade mark. Producers such as Gourmet Percol, who fulfil the criteria for ethical trading, are able to mark their

products. In theory the Fair Trade mark informs consumers who wish to purchase commodities ethically. In reality, as with the confusion about Green marks, officially sanctioned Fair Trade products can easily be confused in consumers' minds with those bearing imagery of one-world unity, or which claim to be 'fairly traded'. Co-operatives or their representatives market "Fair Trade" products and seek to guarantee the subsistence of regional growers and suppliers who are threatened by the economic and political might of global corporations. The best-known examples include Cafédirect in the UK and Max Havelaar in the Netherlands, brands of coffee produced in the developing world but sold in competition with global brands such as Nescafé in the first world.[41] Another example is Divine chocolate, 'Heavenly chocolate with a heart', produced by the Day Chocolate Company in London on behalf of cocoa growers in Ghana. The company claims to offer 'A fair deal for cocoa growers'. The African growers and workers own a part of the company that makes the chocolate. Profits are ploughed back into the community, rather than siphoned off for foreign investors and shareholders. Fair Trade products can be more expensive than more familiar brands (due to their economies of scale), but they offer the shopper the chance to make a purchase in the knowledge that

Top right: Eau No! product range, The Body Shop, UK, 1999.
Right: Kwabena Owusu holding a bar of Divine chocolate, Ghana, 1998. His family grow cocoa and are partners in the Day Chocolate Company that makes Divine.

Packaging for Gourmet
Percol Fairtrade Latin
American organic arabica
coffee, 1999.

the profits will reach the producer directly. Oxfam shops stock over 70 Fair Trade food products, including Swazi Hot Chilli Sauce made by an all women kitchen in Swaziland, organic honey from Zambia and Bolivian Pasta Twirls.

Beyond the range of charity shops and Fair Trade products, some retailers have strong ethical practices for their own-brand goods. The Body Shop, for example, aims to oppose the conventions of the mainstream cosmetics industry with highly visible policies on organic and ethical sourcing of products (including using Fair Trade suppliers), animal welfare and recycling. It purports to respect peoples in the third world, their traditions and products. This ethic is manifested in the 'Eau No!' range of travel products, available for so-called eco-tourists who go to 'places where water, not adventure, is in short supply', and includes dry shampoo and body wipes to reduce the need to use limited local water supplies. The range is backed-up by in-store pamphlets, published by The Body Shop in association with the Centre for Environmentally Responsible Tourism, that advise would-be ethical tourists to 'use locally owned transport, accommodation and services' and 'learn a few words of the local language'.[42] In the larger context of the first world's relationship to the third these products and suggestions may appear at best limited and at worst patronising.

Underlying the concept of ethical consumption, therefore, is a notion that consumers are citizens of the world with responsibilities to one another as well as to the Earth. However, taken to its logical end, ethical consumption is potentially the most critical practice of all. Ultimately it demands that we consume less in order to minimise the detrimental effects of our consumption on the planet and on society.

In some consumer societies, increasing signs of 'consumer fatigue' may mean that the call to consume less finds advocates and supporters. 'Voluntary simplicity' may also result from discriminating choices of purchase and from revised concepts of product and service development that build-in longevity, not obsolescence. Despite a

number of commercial initiatives that reflect a 'one-world' philosophy, the implications of globalisation for developing countries remain largely negative. Global brands are still likely to locate their production sites in areas where labour is cheap and conditions can be poor. Finding their markets in the developed world to be saturated with goods, international companies are seeking ways of penetrating potential new ones, such as China. Global sustainability may be achieved through a reduction in consumption in developed countries, and by investment in the economies of developing countries. However, the global call to consume less is fraught with risks of imperialist moralising. The Malaysian consumer activist Martin Khor says:[43]

The most important changes required are changes in mentality about happiness and pleasure. But this can only happen if the developed countries offer an example here, because they disseminate their culture to the developing countries. So massive change in consumption patterns, in motivation and in the meaning of life itself are very important. But that can only come about if we can change the distribution of commercial and therefore political power world-wide, between countries and within countries, so that the local communities can have their fair share of resources, so that they can vote in the marketplace or in their communities on how to fulfil their needs.

Many of the ethical consumption practices described so far are aligned to the politics of the left. But politicised consumption can also be an expression of right-wing politics, when the issue at stake is the right of the individual to choose to consume and to resist what is perceived as 'despotic' centralised governmental control. Consumer activism, and a claim to the moral high ground of consumer rights, is not only the preserve of the left. In the United States legislation that is seen as limiting the rights of the individual to consume is frequently criticised as being 'anti-American'. The National Rifle Association (NRA), for example, associates the right to own firearms with the 'American way.' Citing the Second Amendment of the American

Constitution, Charlton Heston, actor and President of the NRA, argued:[44]

> But our essential reason for being is this. As long as there is a Second Amendment, evil can never conquer us. Tyranny, in any form, can never find footing within a society of law-abiding, armed ethical people. The majesty of the Second Amendment, that our Founders so divinely captured and crafted into your birthright, guarantees that no government despot, no renegade faction of armed forces, no roving gangs of criminals, no breakdown of law and order, no massive anarchy, no force of evil or crime or oppression from within or from without, can ever rob you of the liberties that define your Americanism.

Each time we make a purchase, its effects ripple out like rings of water on a pond. Buying and owning goods may be viewed as an inalienable right and a demonstration of our personal autonomy. Beyond this, our personal consuming choices can have implications for others. Whether we are choosing the best value for ourselves or the best deal for the planet, the transactions described so far are predicated on an exchange of money and operate in a commercial environment. The alternative to this is the growth of alternative economies that do not rely on money at all.

In recent years Local Exchange Trading Systems (LETS) have proliferated with over 200 formed in the UK in the early 1990s. LETS originated in British Columbia in 1982, but the idea has spread to the USA, Australasia and Britain. These cashless economies trade services and commodities between members on a barter basis, using a notional currency (for example, the LETS scheme in the London borough of Camden uses 'Locks'). A related cashless economic system is Time Dollars, where different services are offered in exchange for time-equivalent labours. Such schemes provide invaluable services within the communities that support them. The citizenship of the consumer is central, and the trading of services and commodities, from baby-sitting to computer training, food and even architectural design, strengthens community relations. LETSLINK, the British development agency for LETS schemes, promotes them as social mortar:[45]

Capital flight deprives an area of a means of trade with itself. Many low-income areas, however, still possess skills, human energy and potential, and all kinds of material resources. All the components of real wealth are there, locked away, alongside a myriad of unmet needs. All that is missing, essentially, is a medium of exchange. We simply need a communication system, linking supply and demand.

The sociologist Zygmunt Bauman has examined the relationship of consumers to economic power and sees two types of consumers. The 'seduced' are those who have the economic power to make the choice to consume and who respond to the messages of brands and their advertising. The 'repressed' are those consumers who are subjected to the allure of brand messages through mass communications, but who are not able to partake in the consumer society because poverty disenfranchises them. Alternative economies might enfranchise Bauman's repressed consumers by circumventing the need for currency that underlies all other acts of consumption.

The boundaries between consumption and resistance to consumption are porous.[47] Most consumption relies on personal choices, affected by advertising and social convention. Economic power will also effect the ways in which a consumer is able to choose. A growing body of opinion, however, is arguing that our ability to exercise choice as consumers is now more than ever under the control of global corporations. In November 1999, the most serious organised critical action focussed against consumerism and corporate interest took place in Seattle. The World Trade Organisation (WTO), a coalition of 135 nations dedicated to promoting global free trade, met for talks in Seattle. A highly organised protest, combining a mixed coalition of anti-capitalist activists, anarchists, church leaders, human-rights and consumer-rights groups, successfully disrupted the conference and forced the city to declare a state of civil emergency. Whatever the future for global brands in the twenty-first century, it seems clear that they will have to deal with the actions of increasingly politicised consumers.

NOTES

CHAPTER 1: IN GOODS WE TRUST

1 Jane Frost, in interview with author, 1999
2 Bryson, p.288.
3 See later in this chapter, Charlotte Cotton, 'Brand Associations through Advertising', pp. 60–63.
4 Jean-Christophe Agnew questions the extent to which products such as Coke might inspire a loyalty 'beyond the market place' in his essay 'Coming Up for Air: Consumer Culture in Historical Perspective' in Brewer and Porter, pp.33–4.
5 Pendergrast, pp.292–3.
6 *Ibid.*, pp.305–6.
7 *Ibid.*, p.395. However, only a small percentage of the original cast could be traced.
8 *Ibid.*, pp. 56–60. Coca-Cola's name denotes its original ingredients – extract of coca leaf, or cocaine, with extract of cola nut. Although the traces of cocaine were completely removed from the recipe a few years later, the rumours of its cocaine content persisted, which both jeopardised sales and, in some quarters, encouraged them.
9 *Ibid.*, p.13.
10 *Ibid.*, p.64.
11 Lears, p.11.
12 *Ibid.*, pp.162–95.
13 Kathy Peiss, 'Making Up, Making Over: Cosmetics, Consumer Culture and Women's Identity' in de Grazia with Furlong, p.322.
14 Pendergrast, p.170.
15 Batchelor, p.72.
16 Agnew in Brewer and Porter, p.32.
17 Christina Fowler, 'Change in Provincial Retail Practice during the Eighteenth-century, with Particular Reference to Central-Southern England' in Alexander and Akehurst, p. 38. For a discussion of the development of branding in the seventeenth and eighteenth centuries, particularly proprietary medicines, see John Styles, 'Product Innovation in Early Modern London', *Past & Present* (2000).
18 Goodman, pp.99–102.
19 Cissie Fairchilds, 'The Production and Marketing of Populuxe Goods in Eighteenth-century Paris' in Brewer and Porter, p.239.
20 John Styles, 'Manufacturing, Consumption and Design in Eighteenth-century England' in Brewer and Porter, p.541
21 Carrier, p.101.
22 Strasser, p.52.
23 Gareth Shaw, 'The European Scene: Britain and Germany' in Benson and Shaw, p.31.
24 Carrier, pp.100–1.
25 Hermann Levy, 1942. Quoted in Matthew Hilton, 'Retailing History as Economic and Cultural History' in Alexander and Akehurst, p.119.
26 Martin Kettle, 'The Candy Man', *Guardian*, 6 July 1999, G2, pp.2–3.
27 Rachel Bowlby, 'Supermarket Futures' in Campbell and Falk, p.94.
28 Miller, 1998.
29 Frank Mort, 'Paths to Mass Consumption: Britain and the USA since 1945' in Nava *et al.*, p.24.
30 Scitovsky, 1976.
31 Pasi Falk, 'The Benetton–Toscani Effect: Testing the Limits of Conventional Advertising' in Nava *et al.*, p.68.
32 Celia Lury and Alan Warde, 'Investments in the Imaginary Consumer: Conjectures Regarding Power, Knowledge and Advertising' in Nava *et al.*, p.93.
33 The ideas put forward by the founder and creative directors of Diesel, in interview for this book, show how brand, product and advertising are seen as intertwined. See pp. 64–7.
34 Slater, p.193.
35 Featherstone, 1991.
36 Ewen, 1988, p.79.
37 Lury, p.232.
38 McCracken, 1990.
39 Colin Campbell, 'When the Meaning is Not a Message' in Nava *et al.*, p. 343.
40 Michael Piore and Charles Sabel, 1984. Quoted in Pine II, p.105.
41 Quoted in Pine II, p.41.
42 Roland Robertson, 'Mapping the Global Condition: Globalization as the Central Concept' in Featherstone, 1990, pp.26–7.
43 Marshall McLuhan and Quentin Fiore, *War and Peace in the Global Village*, 1968; repr. McLuhan, Fiore & Agel, 1997.
44 Jean-François Lyotard, quoted in Slater, p.196.
45 Miller, *Worlds Apart*.
46 Appadurai, 1996.
47 Harvey, 1989. See also Giddens, 1984 and 1991. Also Lash and Urry, 1994, pp.223–51.
48 Miller, *Acknowledging Consumption*, p.9.
49 Gabriel and Lang, pp.173–86.

CHAPTER 2: TIES THAT BIND

1 John E. Sherry, 'Marketing and Consumer Behavior: Into the Field' in Sherry, pp.3–44.
2 Peter H. Farquhar, 'Managing Brand Equity', *Marketing Research*, September 1989, pp.24–33.
3 Jones, 1988.
4 Richard Elliot, 'Exploring the Symbolic Meaning of Brands', *British Journal of Management*, 5, 1994, pp.13–19.
5 Aaker, 1991, p.7.
6 Kapferer, p.11.
7 Aaker, 1991, p.1.
8 Arvind Rangaswamy, Raymond R. Burke and Terence A. Olivia, 'Brand Equity and the Extendibility of Brand Names', *International Journal of Research in Marketing*, March 1993, pp.61–75.
9 Room, 1982. See also Tedlow, 1996.
10 Keller, 1998.
11 *Ibid.* Keller identifies five interrelated roles for brands from a consumer perspective.
12 Robert B. Zajonc, 'Attitudinal Effects of Mere Exposure', *Journal of Personality and Social Psychology*, 8, 1968, pp.1–29.
13 Harris, 1998.
14 McCracken, 1990.
15 Oliver, 1987.
16 Carol J. Simon and Mary W. Sullivan, 'The Measurement and Determinants of Brand Equity: A Financial Approach', *Marketing Science*, 12:1, 1993, pp.28–52.
17 Rodgers, 1970; Foy, 1974.
18 Tim Ambler and Patrick Barwise, 'The Trouble with Brand Valuation', *Journal of Brand Management*, 5:5, May 1998, pp.367–77.
19 Danny Quah, 'The Weightless Economy in Growth', *Business Economist*, 30:1, March 1999, pp.40–53.
20 McPhee, 1963.
21 Andrew Ehrenberg, Gerald Goodhardt and Patrick Barwise, 'Double Jeopardy Revisited', *Journal of Marketing*, 54,1990, pp.82–91.
22 Barbara Olsen, 'Brand Loyalty and Consumption Patterns: The Lineage Factor' in Sherry, pp.245–81.
23 Patrick Barwise and Thomas Robertson, 'Brand Portfolios', *European Management Journal*, 10:3, September 1992, pp.277–85.
24 Sloan, 1965.
25 See, for instance, Aaker, 1991; Kapferer, 1992; Keller, 1998.
26 Andrew Ehrenberg, 'Repetitive Advertising and the Consumer', *Journal of Advertising Research*, 14:2, 1974, pp.25–34. Demetrios Vakratsas and Tim Ambler, 'How Advertising Works: What Do We Really Know?', *Journal of Marketing*, 63, 1999, pp.26–43. Patrick Barwise, 'Advertising for Long-Term Shareholder Value' in Barwise, 1999, pp.1–8.
27 Andrew S. C. Ehrenberg and Neil R. Barnard, 'Advertising and Product Demand', *Admap*, 373, 1997, pp.14–18.
28 Demetrios Vakratsas and Tim Ambler, 'How Advertising Works: What Do We Really Know?', *Journal of Marketing*, 63, 1999, pp.26-43.
29 Barwise, Higson, Likierman and Marsh, 1989.
30 Patrick Barwise, 'Editorial: Brands in a Digital World', *Journal of Brand Management*, 4:4, spring 1997, pp.220–3.
31 Cairncross, 1997.
32 Gates, p.158.
33 Peppers and Rogers, 1993.
34 Barwise and Hammond, pp.45–51. Dyson, 1997.
35 Negroponte, 1995.
36 Shapiro and Variam, 1998.
37 Schor, 1991.
38 D. Mario Nuti, 'Making Sense of the Third Way', *Business Strategy Review*, 10:3, autumn 1999, pp.57–67.
39 Charles Handy, 'The White Stone: Six Choices', *Business Strategy Review*, 7:1, spring 1996, pp.1–8.
40 Aaker, 1996, pp.108–10.
41 See, for example, Ortega, 1999.
42 Clifton and Maughan, 1999.

CHAPTER 3: ALL THE WORLD'S A STORE

1   Giddens, 1991, pp.148–9.
2   Margaret Crawford, 'The Fifth Ecology: Fantasy, the Automobile and Los Angeles' in Crawford and Wachs, pp.222–3, 231.
3   The phrase derives from the work of Harvey Green, which is perhaps best represented in his *The Light of the Home*, though he uses the phrase not here, but in lectures.
4   For a wonderfully nostalgic recent evocation of the socialising power and its internal contradictions of the spaces of shopping, see Nicholson's novel, *Everything and More*.
5   The excavations of the agora in Athens have led to various interpretations of the uses of this space. For the most complete description of the nature of such possible activities, see Wycherley, 1978.
6   Wycherley, pp.91–103.
7   Girouard, p.17
8   Jacobs, 1984.
9   There has not to my knowledge been a thorough study of the history and character of traditional marketplaces with respect to their architecture. This is perhaps because of their ephemeral nature.
10 Hanawalt and Reyerson, 1994.
11 Weiss and Westerman, 1998.
12 Girouard, pp.18ff.
13 The most complete history and analysis of the arcade is to be found in Geist. For the social uses of the arcades, see Walter Benjamin, *Paris, Capital of the Nineteenth Century*, as well as the fragments of his *Passagen*, both in Benjamin, 1978.
14 Peter Gay, *Pleasure Wars*, volume 5 of *The Bourgeois Experience*.
15 Quoted in Buck Morss, p.292.
16 Miller, *The Bon Marché*.
17 For a discussion of Zola's attitude to the department store, see Miller, *The Bon Marché*. See also Zola's novel *Au Bonheur des Dames* (Paris, 1883), published as *The Ladies of Paradise* (trans. B. Nelson), OUP, 1999.
18 Crossick and Jaumain, 1999.
19 Barth, 1980.
20 Longstreth, p.11.
21 *Ibid.*, p.92.
22 There is still no monograph on Victor Gruen. He did write a short article, 'Shopping Centers: The New Building Type', *Progressive Architecture*, 33:6, 1952, pp.67–94, and *Shopping Town USA*, 1960. For a somewhat unscholarly survey of the emergence of the shopping mall, see Severini Kowinski.
23 The best review of the type is to be found in Rowe, pp.109–47.
24 For the relationship of malls to global culture, see Castells, pp.376–428.
25 For a review of the type, see Sudjic, pp.215–32.
26 For a review of the 'science' of mall planning, see Beddington, 1981, and Howard Gillette, Jr., 'The Evolution of the Planned Shopping Center in Suburb and City', *Journal of the American Planning Association*, 51:4, 1985, pp.449–60.
27 Ellen Barry, 'The Mall Doctor', *Metropolis*, May 1999, pp.21–5, 53–5.
28 Koetter and Rowe, 1984.
29 Jerde, 1999, and Anderton *et al.*, 1999.
30 Marcus Field, 'Tragedy in the Chalk Pit', *Blueprint*, 61, May 1999, pp.42–5.
31 Conversation with author, 21 April 1988.
32 See also Gottdiener, 1997.
33 I described this place extensively in 'Ontario Mills, California: Castle of Consumption in the Empire of Signs' in Moore, pp.192–203.
34 Allen Hess described with great verve and scholarship this world in *Viva Las Vegas*, but the city has developed at such a rapid pace that the book is already somewhat out of date.
35 Conversation with the author, 12 July 1998.
36 Jackson, pp.171–86.
37 For a recent speculation on how e-commerce will reshape both our virtual and our physical realities, see Mitchell, especially pp.85–97.
38 Conversation with the author, 24 February 1998.
39 The best description of such design parameters is to be found in Wurman's *Information Architects*, but it also already needs updating.
40 For example Kurzweil, 1999, and Stephenson, 1996.
41 The most recent analysis of the place of shopping is by Paco Underhill, though it has a profoundly pro-shopping bias. The result of Rem Koolhaas' five-year project at the Harvard Graduate School of Design, to be published this year, should offer a critical counterpoint to such analyses.
42 Giddens, 1991.

CHAPTER 4: BRANDING THE INDIVIDUAL

1   Sir Michael Perry, Director of Unilever, 1994. Quoted in Gabriel and Lang, p.36.
2   Douglas and Isherwood, p.65.
3   For a discussion of different types of shopping and shopping analysis, see Campbell and Falk, pp.1–14.
4   Zygmunt Bauman, quoted in Campbell and Falk, p.3.
5   Bauman, 1992, p.223.
6   Robinson, p.46.
7   There are a number of historical and social analyses of the female consumer, for example de Grazia with Furlong, 1996. Also Sparke, 1995.
8   Louis Macniece, 1938, quoted in Carey, p.52.
9   Colin Campbell, 'The Sociology of Consumption' in Miller, *Acknowledging Consumption*, p.101.
10 *Ibid.*, pp.21–30, for Daniel Miller's analysis of the myths of consumption in 'Consumption as the Vanguard of History'.
11 See the idea of the 'modern hedonist' in Campbell, 1987.
12 *Ibid.*, p.203.
13 Gabriel and Lang explore the representations of the consumer under the following 'guises': chooser, communicator, explorer, identity-seeker, hedonist, victim, rebel, activist, citizen.
14 De Certeau, 1988.
15 Ewen, 1988, p.79.
16 Message posted on chat site, 14 July 1999: http://wackywet.com/messages/4387.html.
17 The Abercrombie & Fitch brand is, in fact, a re-branding of a sportswear brand that has existed for 60 or 70 years. Now popular with high-school and college kids in the USA, it signifies a clean-cut, informal brand of clothing rather like its better-known rival, The Gap. Alongside Nike, Tommy Hilfiger and Old Navy, The Gap and Abercrombie & Fitch effectively constitute the standard apparel of many American teenagers.
18 Veblen, p.111.
19 See Brewer and Porter, 1993, and McKendrick, Brewer and Plumb, 1982.
20 Mukerji, 1983.
21 As outlined in the introduction to this book, pp. 18–51.
22 Leora Auslander, 'The Gendering of Consumer Practices in Nineteenth-century France' in de Grazia with Furlong, p.81.
23 Georg Simmel, 'Fashion' (1904) repr. in Levine, p.322; quoted in Gabriel and Lang, p.52.
24 Lury, 1996, p.44.
25 'It is standard ethnographic practice to assume that all material possessions carry social meanings and to concentrate a main part of cultural analysis upon their use as communicators,' Douglas and Isherwood, p.59.
26 For an analysis of five types of shopper and shopping, see Lunt and Livingstone, 1992.
27 Lury, 1996, p.80.
28 Hebdige, 1979.
29 Bourdieu, 1999.
30 *Ibid.* p.220.
31 As outlined in the introduction to this book.
32 See Pasi Falk's discussion of the 'experiential' nature of advertising in Nava *et al.*, 1997, chap. 4.
33 See Gareth Williams, 'Hello Kitty', pp.180–1 of this chapter.
34 As described by Lears, p.11.
35 *Ibid.*
36 See Kathy Peiss, 'Making Up, Making Over: Cosmetics, Consumer Culture and Women's Identity' in de Grazia with Furlong, pp.330–1.
37 Goldman and Papson, p.127.
38 Campbell, pp.85–9.
39 Kathy Peiss, 'Making Up, Making Over: Cosmetics, Consumer Culture and Woman's Identity' in de Grazia with Furlong, p.312.
40 As outlined in the introduction to this book.
41 See Caroline Humphrey, 'Creating a Culture of Disillusionment: Consumption in Moscow, A Chronicle of Changing Times' in Miller (ed.), *Worlds Apart*, pp.44–68.
42 *Ibid.*, p.61.
43 'The black market trade in jeans or nylon stockings are probably the best known examples of this phenomenon. (In the 1930s, Parker pens and imported cigarettes played a similar role in

Soviet culture.)' See Gronow, p.50.

44 Appadurai, 1996, p.174.

45 A historical example frequently cited is that of France in the 1950s, which resisted the expansion of Coca-Cola into the French market on the grounds that it 'diluted' French culture and threatened the wine trade. See Pendergrast, pp.241–4, and Richard Wilk in Miller, *Worlds Apart*, p.114.

46 'Whereas South Korea and Taiwan accounted for a combined 76 per cent of Nike shoewear production in 1987, by 1997 78 per cent of Nike's shoes came from Indonesia and China while the share produced by South Korea and Taiwan had shrunk to 7 per cent.' Goldman and Papson, pp.6–7.

CHAPTER 5: THE POINT OF PURCHASE

1   Bauman, 1998, p.30.

2   Haug, p.50.

3   Packard, 1957.

4   For example, *Consumer Reports* (1952) and the *Journal of Optical Society* (1955) criticised tinted windscreens as hazardous to night driving, even though General Motors continued to promote them as a safety feature until 1965. Woodham, p.228.

5   Nader, 1965. Cited by Woodham.

6   Marcuse, p.24.

7   'Americans have become the most manipulated people outside the iron curtain,' Vance Packard, preface 'To British Readers' of *The Hidden Persuaders*, Penguin Special Edition, London, 1960.

8   Haug, pp.120–1.

9   Ralph Nader, 'Upsizing Downsized Americans', quoted from the following website: www.fatdawg.com/ralph.

10 J. Harms and D. Kellner, 'Towards a Critical Theory of Advertising', www.uta.edu/english/dab/illuminations/kell6.

11 *Adbusters*, Adbusters Media Foundation, Vancouver.

12 Dr Arthur Chesterfield Evans, quoted in Millwood and Gezelius, p.14.

13 Aaron Betsky quoted in Thomas Sutcliffe, 'At Least He Died With his Boots On', *Guardian*, London, 20 August 1999, G2, p.9.

14 Mica Nava, 'Consumerism Reconsidered: Buying and Power', *Cultural Studies*, 5:2, 1991, p.168.

15 Smallbone and Sutcliffe, p.9.

16 Wagner, p.1.

17 Winward, p.13.

18 Smallbone and Sutcliffe, p.14.

19 For more detailed information about consumer responses to green claims described in the paragraphs above, see Smallbone and Sutcliffe, pp.43–54. For more detail about CFC markings see T. J. Olney and Wendy Bryce, 'Consumer Responses to Environmentally Based Product Claims' in R. H. Holman and M. R. Solomon (eds), *Advances in Consumer Research*, 18, Association for Consumer Research, Provo, UT, 1991, pp.693–6.

20 Smallbone and Sutcliffe, p.69.

21 *Ibid.*, p.45.

22 *Ibid.*, pp.50–2. 'Light green' shoppers are defined as those who are more knowledgeable than most shoppers about green and environmental products available in general retail environments.

23 Nava *et al.*, p.168.

24 Peter Lunt, 'Psychological Approaches to Consumption: Varieties of Research: Past, Present and Future' in Miller, *Acknowledging Consumption*, p.245; Gabriel and Lang, p.145.

25 Smith, p.253.

26 For a full examination of the Barclays' boycott see Smith. For an analysis of corporate strategies to combat boycotts see Dennis E. Garrett, 'The Efficacy of Marketing Policy Boycotts: Environmental Opposition to Marketing', *Journal of Marketing*, 51, April 1987, pp.46–57.

27 Smith, p.241.

28 For a full account of the trial proceedings see Vidal. www.mcspotlight.org contains analysis by supporters of the defendants in the case.

29 Reported in the *Daily Telegraph*, London, 20 June 1997.

30 Dave Morris and Helen Steel: quoted in Vidal, p.342.

31 Cited by Smith, p.249.

32 David Brown, Agriculture Editor, 'Barbecues Mark End of Nightmare for Farmers over EU's Export Ban', *Electronic Telegraph*, www.telegraph.co.uk, 1529, 2 August 1999.

33 Alan Simpson MP, 'A First Victory against Those Who Want to Play God', *Evening Standard*, London, 10 February 1999, p.13.

34 Dennis E. Garrett, 'The Effectiveness of Marketing Policy Boycotts: Environmental Opposition to Marketing', *Journal of Marketing*, 51, April 1987, pp.46–57.

35 John Vidal, 'Power to the People', *Guardian*, London, 7 June 1999, G2, pp.2–3.

36 'Tesco Bans GM Food in Own Brands', *Electronic Telegraph*, www.telegraph.co.uk, 1433, 28 April 1999; 'Tesco and Unilever Join High Street GM Boycott', *Metro*, London, 28 April 1999, p.15; '"Genetically Modified" must be on the Label', *Design Week*, London, 12 March 1999, p.6.

37 Philip Webster and Nigel Hawkes, 'Blair Resists Calls for Ban', *The Times*, London, 13 February 1999, p.10.

38 HRH the Prince of Wales, 'My 10 Fears for GM Food', *Daily Mail*, London, 1 June 1999.

39 Charity Commission, © Crown Copyright.

40 www.oxfam.org.uk.

41 Gabriel and Lang, p.167.

42 'Take Away Tips For Responsible Travelling', in-store leaflet, The Body Shop, 1999.

43 Gabriel and Lang, p.162.

44 Extract from the President's closing remarks at the NRA Meeting of Members, Denver, Colorado, 1 May 1999, www.nrahq.org.

45 Cited in Gabriel and Lang, p.147.

46 Zygmunt Bauman develops the notion of 'seduced' and 'repressed' consumers in *Legislators and Interpreters*. See also Alan Warde, 'Consumers, Identity and Belonging: Reflections on Some Theses by Zygmunt Bauman' in Keat, Whiteley and Abercrombie, pp.58–74.

47 Lisa Peñaloza and Linda L. Price, 'Consumer Resistance: A Conceptual Overview' in L. McAlister and M. L. Rothschild (eds), *Advances in Consumer Research*, Association for Consumer Research, Provo, UT, 1993, 20, pp.123–8.

BIBLIOGRAPHY

Aaker, D. A., *Building Strong Brands* (New York, Free Press 1996)
— *Managing Brand Equity* (New York, Free Press 1991)
Alexander, N., and Akehurst, G., eds. *The Emergence of Modern Retailing: 1750–1950* (London, Cass 1999)
Anderton, F., with Bradbury, R., Crawford, M., Klein, N. M., and Hodgetts, C. *You Are Here: The Jerde Partnership International* (London, Phaidon 1999)
Appadurai, A. *Modernity at Large: Cultural Dimensions of Globalisation* (Minneapolis, University of Minnesota Press 1996)
Appadurai, A., ed. *The Social Life of Things* (Cambridge University Press 1986)
Assael, H. Consumer *Behavior and Marketing Action* (Cincinnati, OH, South-Western College Publishing 1995)
Barth, G. *City People: The Rise of Modern City Culture* (New York, Oxford University Press 1980)
Barwise, P., and Hammond, K., eds. *Predictions: Media* (London, Phoenix 1998)
Barwise, P., ed. *Advertising in a Recession: The Benefits of Investing for the Long Term* (Henley-on-Thames, NTC 1999)
Barwise, P., Higson, C., Likierman, A., and Marsh, P. eds. *Accounting for Brands* (London, Institute of Chartered Accountants in England and Wales 1989)
Batchelor, R. *Henry Ford: Mass Production, Modernism and Design* (Manchester University Press 1994)
Baudrillard, J. (trans. Ritzer, G.) *The Consumer Society: Myths and Structures* (London, Sage 1998)
— (trans. Foss, Patton and Beitchman) *Simulations* (New York, Semiotext(e) 1983)
Bauman, Z. *Imitations of Post-Modernism* (London, Routledge 1992)
— *Legislators and Interpreters: On Modernity, Postmodernity and Intellectuals* (Cambridge, Polity 1987)
— *Work, Consumerism and the New Poor* (Buckingham, Open University Press 1998)
Beck, U., Giddens, A., and Lash, S. *Reflexive Modernization* (Cambridge, Polity 1994)
Beddington, N. *Design for Shopping Centers* (London, Butterworth Scientific 1981)
Benjamin, W. (trans. E. Jephcott) *Reflections: Essays, Aphorisms, Autobiographical Writing* (New York, Schocken 1978)
Benson, J., and Shaw, G., eds. *The Evolution of Retail Systems c. 1800–1914* (Leicester University Press 1992)
Benson, S. P. *Counter Cultures: Saleswomen, Managers and Customers in American Department Stores* (Urbana and Chicago, University of Illinois Press 1986)
Bhabha, H. *The Location of Culture* (London, Routledge 1994)
Bloch, P. H., Bush, R. F., and Campbell, L. 'Consumer Accomplices in Product Counterfeiting', *Journal of Consumer Marketing*,

10:4, 1993, pp. 27-36.
Bourdieu, P. (trans. R. Nice) *Distinction: A Social Critique of the Judgement of Taste* (London, Routledge 1999); first published in French as *La Distinction: Critique sociale du jugement* (Paris, Minuit 1979)
Bowlby, R. *Shopping with Freud* (London, Routledge 1993)
Brewer, J., and Porter, R., eds. *Consumption and the World of Goods* (London, Routledge 1993)
Brown, S., and Turley, D., eds. *Consumer Research: Postcards from the Edge* (London, Routledge 1997)
Bryson, B. *Made In America* (London, Minerva 1994)
Buck Morss, S. *The Dialectics of Seeing: Walter Benjamin and the Arcades Project* (Cambridge, MIT Press 1989)
Cairncross, F. *The Death of Distance* (London, Orion 1997)
Campbell, C. *The Romantic Ethic and the Spirit of Modern Consumerism* (Oxford, Blackwell 1987)
Campbell, C., and Falk, P., eds. *The Shopping Experience* (London, Sage 1997)
Carey, J. *The Intellectuals and the Masses: Pride and Prejudice Among the Literary Intelligentsia, 1880–1939* (London, Faber 1992)
Carrier, J. *Gifts and Commodities, Exchange and Western Capitalism since 1700* (London, Routledge 1995)
Castells, M. *The Rise of Network Society* (Oxford, Blackwell 1996)
Certeau, M. de. *The Practice of Everyday Life* (Berkeley, Los Angeles and London, University of California Press 1988)
Clarke, A. *Tupperware: The Promise of Plastic in 1950s America* (Washington and London, Smithsonian Institute Press 1999)
Clifton, R., and Maughan, E., eds. *The Future of Brands: Twenty-five Visions* (London, Interbrand/Macmillan Business 1999)
Corrigan, P. *The Sociology of Consumption* (London, Sage 1997)
Crawford, M., and Wachs, M., eds. *The Car and the City: The Automobile, the Built Environment and Daily Urban Life* (Ann Arbor, University of Michigan Press 1992)
Crossick, G., and Jaumain, S., eds. *Cathedrals of Consumption: The European Department Store, 1850–1939* (London, Ashgate 1999)
Debord, G. *Society of the Spectacle* (Detroit, Black and Red 1977)
Douglas, M., and Isherwood, B., eds. *The World of Goods: Towards An Anthropology of Consumption* (London, Allen Lane 1978)
Dyson, E. *Release 2.1: A Design for Living in the Digital Age* (London, Penguin 1998)
Eicher, J. B., ed. *Dress and Ethnicity* (Oxford, Berg 1995)
Ewen, S. *All Consuming Images: The Politics of Style in Contemporary USA* (New York, Basic 1988)
Ewen, S. *Captains of Consciousness: Advertising and the Social Roots of the Consumer Culture* (New York, McGraw Hill 1976)

Featherstone, M. *Consumer Culture and Post Modernism* (London, Sage 1991)
Featherstone, M., ed. *Global Culture, Nationalism, Globalization and Modernity* (London, Sage 1990)
Fine, B., and Leopold, E. *The World of Consumption* (London, Sage 1993)
Forty, A. *Objects of Desire* (London, Thames and Hudson 1986)
Foy, N. *The IBM World* (London, Eyre Methuen 1974)
Gabriel, Y., and Lang, T., eds. *The Unmanageable Consumer, Contemporary Consumption and its Fragmentations* (London, Sage 1995)
Gates, B. *The Road Ahead* (New York, Viking 1995)
Gay, P. *Pleasure Wars*, vol. 5 of *The Bourgeois Experience: Victoria to Freud* (New York, Norton 1999)
Geist, J. F. (trans. Newman, J. O., and Smitt, J. H.) *Arcades: The History of a Building Type* (Cambridge, MIT Press 1983)
Gendai Yogo Kisō Chishiki [Modern Terminology Basic Knowledge] (Tokyo, Jiyokokuminsha, 1997)
Giddens, A. *The Constitution of Society* (Cambridge, Polity 1984)
— *Modernity and Self-Identity: Self and Society in the Late Modern Age* (Stanford University Press 1991).
Gilmore, F. Brand *Warriors: Corporate Leaders Share their Winning Strategies* (London, HarperCollins 1997)
Girouard, M. *Cities and People: A Social and Architectural History* (New Haven, Yale University Press 1985)
Goldman, R., and Papson, S. *Nike Culture: The Sign of the Swoosh* (London, Sage 1998)
Goodman, J. *Tobacco in History: The Culture of Dependence* (London, Routledge 1993)
Gottdiener, M. *The Theming of America: Dreams, Visions and Commercial Spaces* (New York, HarperCollins 1997)
Grazia, V. de, with Furlong, E., eds. *The Sex of Things: Gender and Consumption in Historical Perspective* (Berkeley, Los Angeles and London, University of California Press 1996)
Green, H. *The Light of the Home: An Intimate View of the Lives of Women in Victorian America* (New York, Pantheon 1983)
Gronow, J. *The Sociology of Taste* (London, Routledge 1997)
Gruen, V. *Shopping Town USA: The Planning of Shopping Centers* (New York, Reinhold Winston 1960)
Hanawalt, B. A., and Reyerson, K. L., eds. *City and Spectacle in Medieval Europe* (Minneapolis, University of Minnesota Press 1994)
Harris, J. R. *The Nurture Assumption* (New York, Free Press 1998)
Harvey, D. *The Condition of Post-Modernity* (Oxford, Blackwell 1989)
Haug, W. F. *Critique of Commodity Aesthetics* (Minneapolis, University of Minnesota Press 1986)
Hebdige, D. *Hiding in the Light: On Images and Things* (London, Methuen 1987)

—Subculture: The Meaning of Style (London, Methuen 1979)

Hess, A. Viva Las Vegas: After-hours Architecture (San Francisco, Chronicle 1993)

Hitchcock, H. R., and Johnson, P. The International Style (New York, Museum of Modern Art 1932; repr. 1995)

Homer, T., and Wycherley, R. E., eds. The Agora of Athens (New York, American School of Classical Studies 1972)

Jackson, J. B. A Sense of Time, A Sense of Place (New Haven, CT, Yale University Press 1994)

Jacobs, J. Cities and the Wealth of Nations (New York, Random House 1984)

Jameson, F. Postmodernism, or, the Cultural Logic of Late Capitalism (London, Verso 1991)

Jerde, J. The Jerde Partnership International: Visceral Reality (Milan, L'Arca 1999)

Jones, J. P. What's In a Name? Advertising and the Concept of Brands (Lexington Books 1988)

Kapferer, J-N. Strategic Brand Management (London, Kogan Page 1992)

Keat, R., Whiteley, N., Abercrombie, N., eds. The Authority of the Consumer (London, Routledge 1994)

Keller, K. L. Strategic Brand Management (Saddle River, NJ, Prentice Hall 1998)

Klein, N. No Logo (London, Flamingo 2000)

Koetter, F., and Rowe, C. Collage City (Cambridge, MIT Press 1984)

Kracauer, S. (trans. Y. Levin). The Mass Ornament: Weimar Essays (Cambridge, Harvard University Press 1995)

Kuronuma, K. Enjo kōsai: jochūkosei no abundai na hōkago [Assisted dating: the dangerous after-school pursuits of middle- and high-school girls] (Tokyo, Bungei Shunjū 1996)

Kurzweil, A. The Age of the Spiritual Machines (New York, Viking 1999)

Lash, S. The Sociology of Postmodernism (London, Routledge 1990)

Lash, S., and Urry, J. The End of Organized Capitalism (Cambridge, Polity 1987)

— Economies of Sighs and Spaces (London, Sage 1994)

Lasn, K. Culture Jam: The Uncooling of America (New York, Eagle Brook, Morrow 1999)

Lasseter, J., and Daly, S. Toy Story: The Art and Making of the Animated Film (New York, Hyperion 1996)

Lears, J. Fables of Abundance, A Cultural History of Advertising in America (New York, Basic 1994)

Leonard, M. Britain ™ Renewing Our Identity (London, Demos 1997)

Levine, D. Georg Simmel: On Individuality and Social Form (Chicago University Press 1971)

Leyda, J., ed. Eisenstein on Disney (London and New York, Methuen 1988)

Lloyd-Jones, P. Taste Today: The Role of Appreciation in Consumerism and Design (Oxford, Pergamon 1991)

Longstreth, R. The Drive-In, the Supermarket, and the Transformation of Commercial Space in Los Angeles,
1914–1941 (Cambridge, MIT Press 1999)

Lunt, P., and Livingstone, S., eds. Mass Consumption and Personal Identity: Everyday Economic Experience (Buckingham and Bristol, Open University Press 1992)

Lury, C. Consumer Culture (Cambridge, Polity 1996)

Lury, G. Brand Watching: Lifting the Lid on the Phenomenon of Branding (Dublin, Blackhall 1998)

McCracken, G. Culture and Consumption: New Approaches to the Symbolic Character of Consumer Goods and Activities (Bloomington, Indiana University Press 1990)

McKendrick, N., Brewer, J., and Plumb, J.H., eds. The Birth of a Consumer Society: The Commercialization of Eighteenth-century England (London, Europa 1982)

McLuhan, M., Fiore, Q., and Agel, J. War and Peace in the Global Village (San Francisco, Hardwired 1997).

McPhee, W. N. Formal Theories of Mass Behavior (New York, Free Press 1963)

McRobbie, A. Feminism and Popular Culture (London, Routledge 1994)

McRobbie, A., and Nava, M., eds. Gender and Generation (London, Macmillan 1984)

Marcuse, H. One Dimensional Man: Studies in the Ideology of Advanced Industrial Society (London, Routledge 1964)

Marling, K. A. As Seen on TV: The Visual Culture of Everyday Life in the 1950s (Cambridge, Harvard University Press 1994)

Marling, K. A. ed. Designing Disney's Theme Parks: The Architecture of Reassurance (Paris and New York, Flammarion 1997)

Mauss, M. The Gift: The Form and Reason for Exchange in Archaic Societies (London, Routledge 1925, repr. 1990)

Miller, D. A Theory of Shopping (Cambridge, Polity 1998)

— Capitalism: An Ethnographic Approach (Oxford, Berg 1997)

— Material Culture and Mass Consumption (Oxford, Blackwell 1987)

Miller, D., ed. Acknowledging Consumption (London, Routledge 1995)

— Worlds Apart: Modernity through the Prism of the Local (London, Routledge 1995)

Miller, D., Jackson, P., Thrift, N., Holbrook., B., and Rowlands, M. Shopping, Place and Identity (London, Routledge 1998)

Miller, M. B. The Bon Marché: Bourgeois Culture and the Department Store, 1869–1920 (Princeton University Press 1981)

Millwood, D., and Gezelius, H., eds. Smart Promotions (Sweden, Konsument 1989)

Mitchell, W. J. E-topia: 'Real Life, Jim, But Not As We Know It' (Cambridge, MIT Press 1999)

Miyadai, S. Seifuku shōjotachi no sentaku [The Uniform Girls' Choice] (Tokyo, Kōdansha 1994)

Mollerup, P. Marks of Excellence: The History and Taxonomy of Trademarks (London, Phaidon 1997)

Moore, R., ed. Vertigo: The Strange New World of the Contemporary City (London, Laurence King 1999)

Mort, F., Miller, D., and Lowe, M.Lowe, eds. Commercial Cultures (London, Berg 2000)

Mukerji, C. From Graven Images: Patterns of Modern Materialism (New York, Columbia University Press 1983)

Nader, R. Unsafe at Any Speed: The Designed-In Dangers of the American Automobile (New York, Grossman 1965)

Nava, M., Blake, A., MacRury, I., and Richards, B., eds. Buy This Book: Studies in Advertising and Consumption (London, Routledge 1997)

Negroponte, N. Being Digital (New York, Knopf 1995)

Nicholson, G. Everything and More: A Novel of Shopping and Terrorism (London, Gollancz 1994)

Olins, W. Corporate Identity (London, Thames & Hudson 1989)

Oliver, T. The Real Coke, The Real Story (New York, Viking Penguin 1987)

Ortega, B. In Sam We Trust: The Untold Story of Sam Walton and How Walmart is Devouring the World (London, Kogan Page 1999)

Packard, V. The Hidden Persuaders (London, Longmans 1957)

Pendergrast, M. For God, Country and Coca-Cola: The Unauthorised History of the World's Most Popular Soft Drink (London, Phoenix 1994)

Peppers, D., and Rogers, M. The One-to-One Future (London, Piatkus 1994)

Piaget, J. Play, Dreams and Imitation in Childhood (London, Routledge and Kegan Paul 1962)

Pine, B. Joseph II, Mass Customisation (Cambridge, Harvard Business School Press 1999)

Piore, M., and Sabel, C., eds. The Second Industrial Divide: Possibilities for Prosperity (New York, Basic 1984)

Redhead, D. Products of Our Time (Basel, Boston and Berlin, Birkhäuser; London, August 2000)

Robinson, J. The Manipulators: Unmasking the Hidden Persuaders (London, Simon and Schuster 1999)

Rodgers, W. Think: A Biography of the Watsons and IBM (London, Weidenfeld and Nicolson 1970)

Rogers, M. F. Barbie Culture (London, Sage 1999)

Rojek, C. Capitalism and Leisure Theory (London, Tavistock 1985)

Room, A. Dictionary of Trade Name Origins (London, Routledge and Kegan Paul 1982)

Rowe, P.G. Making a Middle Landscape (Cambridge, MIT Press 1991)

Safranek, R. 'The McDonald's Recipe for Japan' Intersect, 2, October 1996, p. 7.

Schor, J. B. The Overworked American: The Unexpected Decline of Leisure (New York, Basic 1991)

Scitovsky, T. The Joyless Economy: An Enquiry into Human Satisfaction and Consumer Dissatisfaction (New York, Oxford University Press 1976)

Severini Kowinski, W. The Malling of America: An Inside Look at the Great Consumer Paradise (New York, Morrow 1985)

Shapiro, C., and Variam, H. R. Information Rules: A Strategic Guide to the Network Economy (Cambridge, Harvard Business School Press 1998)

Sherry, J. *Contemporary Marketing and Consumer Behaviour* (London, Sage 1995)

Shields, R., ed. *Lifestyle Shopping* (London and New York, Routledge 1992)

Skoggard, I. 'Transnational Commodity Flows and the Global Phenomenon of the Brand', in Brydon, A., and Niessen, S., eds. *Consuming Fashion – Adorning the Transnational Body* (Oxford, Berg 1998)

Slater, D. *Consumer Culture and Modernity* (Cambridge, Polity 1997)

Sloan, A. P. Jr. *My Years with General Motors* (London, Pan 1965)

Smallbone, T., and Sutcliffe, M. *Green Claims: A Consumer Investigation into Marketing Claims about the Environment* (London, National Consumer Council (NCC) 1996)

Smith, C. N. *Morality and the Market: Consumer Pressure for Corporate Accountability* (London, Routledge 1990)

Sparke, P. *As Long as It's Pink: The Sexual Politics of Taste* (London, Pandora 1995)

Stephenson, N. *The Diamond Age* (London, Roc 1996)

Stern, B., ed. *Representing Consumers: Voices, Views and Visions* (London, Routledge 1998)

Strasser, S. *Satisfaction Guaranteed: The Making of the American Mass Market* (New York, Pantheon 1989)

Sudjic, D. *The 100 Mile City* (New York, Harcourt Brace 1992)

Tallents, S. *The Projection of England* (London, Faber 1932)

Tedlow, R. S. *New and Improved: The Story of Mass Marketing In America* (Cambridge, Harvard Business School Press 1996)

Turkle, S. *Life on the Screen: Identity in the Age of the Internet* (New York, Simon and Schuster 1995)

Turkle, S. *The Second Self: Computers and the Human Spirit* (New York, Simon and Schuster 1986)

Uhrich, R. *Super-marchés et usines de distribution: Hier aux Etats-Unis, aujourd'hui en France?* (Paris, Plon 1962)

Underhill, P. *Why We Buy: The Science of Shopping* (New York, Simon and Schuster 1999)

Veblen, T. *The Theory of the Leisure Class: An Economic Study of Institutions* (London, George Allen and Unwin 1925)

Vidal, J. *McLibel: Burger Culture on Trial* (London, Pan 1997)

Vihma, S. *Products as Representations: A Semiotic and Aesthetic Study of Design Products* (Helsinki, University of Art and Design 1995)

Virilio, P. *The Vision Machine* (London, British Film Institute 1994)

Wagner, S. A. *Understanding Green Consumer Behaviour: A Qualitative Cognitive Approach* (London, Routledge 1997)

Warde, A. *Consumption, Food and Taste* (London, Sage 1997)

Watson, J. L., ed. *Golden Arches East: McDonald's in East Asia* (Stanford University Press 1997)

Weiss, W. M., and Westerman, K. M. *The Bazaar: Markets and Merchants of the Islamic World* (London, Thames and Hudson 1998)

Winward, J. *Environmental Labelling in Central and Eastern Europe* (London, Consumers International 1996)

Woodham, J. M. *Twentieth-century Design* (Oxford University Press 1997)

Wurman, R. S. *Information Architects* (New York, Watson-Guptil 1997)

Wycherley, R. E. *The Stones of Athens* (Princeton University Press 1978)

Zukin, S. *Landscapes of Power* (Berkeley and Los Angeles, University of California Press 1991)

Zukin, S. *Loftliving: Culture and Capital in Urban Change* (London, Radius 1988)

CREDIT LINES

INDEX

Page numbers in *italic* indicate a reference in an illustration caption

Abercrombie & Fitch 160
Adbusters *186*, 188–92, *188*
adidas *86*, 151, *156*, 169, *169*
advertising 30, 32–3, 37–8, 51, 140
  brand associations and 60–3, 80–2
  brand strategy and 92–3
  Green claims and imagery 194
  lifestyle and fashion 29–44, 169–74
  subversion of 102–3, *102*, *186*, 188–92
  tailored to local conditions 51, 68–9
  validity of questioned 187–92
  web pages 141, *141*
  see also billboards; hoardings; marketing; newspaper; radio; television
advertising agencies, multinational 51
Advertising Standards Authority (UK) 199
AEG 52
aerosol cans 194
aestheticisation, of everyday life 44
airports, mass retailing 135
Alessi 46
Alfa-Romeo 82
Amazon.com 94, 96, 141, *141*
American myth 26, 30, 78
Americanisation 32, 48
Anderson, Pamela 39
Anti-Apartheid Movement 200
Appadurai, Arjun, on globalisation 48
Apple, iMac and iBook *41*
arcades 116–17, *117*, 126, 127, 160
architecture
  brand signatures 53
  branded buildings *21*, 128, 144, *144*
  roadside petrol stations 144, *144*
  shopping environments 110–43, *110*, *126*, *132*
Arden, Elizabeth 32
Arena 60
Armani, Eau Pour Homme *39*
Asda 45, *45*, 204
Aaker, David, on trademarks 73
aspirin 23
Audi 92

Batchelor's Beanfeast meals 204
Baleno 151
Barclays Bank 200, 208
Barnes & Noble 96
Bauhaus 126
Bauman, Zygmunt 156, 211
bazaars 114–16, 126
BBC, brand structure 21–3, *23*
BBH advertising agency 60
Beatles 56
beauty products 30–2, 39, *39*, 73

  see also cosmetics
Beckham, David *86*
beef, and BSE 202
Beer, Henry (architect) 139, 140
Behrens, Peter (designer) 52
Bellagio, The Resort (Las Vegas) 139, *139*
Ben & Jerry 56
Benjamin, Walter, on Paris arcades 116–17
Bercy shopping mall (Paris) 135
Beverly Center (Los Angeles) 128
Bezos, Jim 141
Biba 56
Big Box retail centres 128, 129–32, 140
Bijvoet and Duiker (architects) 127
Billboard-Utilising Graffitists Against Unhealthy Promotions (BUGA-UP) 192
billboards 30, 37–8, *159*, *170*, 192, *192*
  see also hoardings
Birds Eye Walls 204
Black and Decker 52
Blair, Tony 56–7
Bloomingdales 121
Blue Angel symbol 193
Bluewater (Kent) *110*, 135, *135*
BMC 56
BMP DDB advertising agency 106
BMW 48, 83, 171
  Rover purchase 92
Body Shop 96
  Eau No! range of products *208*, 210
Boileau, L A (architect) 117
Bon Marché 117, *117*, *120*
Bonzo Dog Doo-Dah Band 56
Boots 93
Bossini *150*, 151
Boucicaut, Aristide 117
Bourdieu, Pierre, on
  'cultural capital' 44, 167
  taste 167
Bovril 33
Boycott, Rosie *204*
boycotts, by consumers 199–204
brand
  associations 60–3, 70–97, 171
  equity 75–8, 82, 83, 92–4, 95–6
  image *21*–3, 39–51, 64, 73–8
  loyalty 88–9
  portfolios 92
  strategy 89–93
  valuation 93–4
  value *21*–3, 33–8, 64, 169
  see also trademarks
branding *21*, 38–45, 73
  and authenticity 58–9
  consumer perceptions 75–88
  role in consumer choice 80–9, 94–5, 140, 170
  'brandlands' 149
brands

critical response to 186–211
  discounted designer brands 45, *45*
  individualisation and 159–66, 169–71
  as phatic communicators 176–7
  social signifiers 169–74
Branson, Richard 39
Breuer, Marcel (architect) 127
Britain, rebranding of 56–7
British Airways 39, 56, *56*
British Broadcasting Corporation *see* BBC
British Telecom, rebranding 56
British Union for the Abolition of Vivisection (BUAV) 194
BSE 202
BSkyB 92
Budweiser *175*
BUGA-UP 192
Buick 92
Burberry, in China 150
Business Improvement Districts (BIDs) 140
Buzz Lightyear 178–9, *178*

Cadbury 33, 36
  see also chocolate
Cadbury World 148, 149, *149*
Cadillac 92
Caesar's Casino (Las Vegas) 139
Cafédirect, Fair Trade coffee 208
CaféLatino, Fair Trade coffee 205–8
Cairncross, Frances, on online shopping 95
Calvin Klein 151, 188
Camel cigarettes 188
Campari 52
Campbell's soup 26
Canal City Hakata (Fukuoka, Japan) 139, *139*
Carling, sport sponsorship 73
Carnaby Street 56, *56*
Carrefour 125, 132
Carrier, James, on 19th-century advertising 32–3
cashless economies 211
catalogue shopping 95, 128, 140
  see also mail-order companies
CCTV surveillance 106
celebrities, branding of 73, *86*
Center Parcs 148, *149*
Centre for Environmentally Responsible Tourism 210
Certeau, Michel de, on consumerism 159
CFCs 194
chain stores 128
Chanel, counterfeit perfumes *99*
charities 205
charity shops 205
Charles, Prince of Wales 204
Cheng Siu Chung 151
Chesterfield-Evans, Arthur 192

Chevrolet 92
China 150–1, *150*, *151*, 174, 175, *175*
chocolate 36
  Fair Trade schemes 208
  see also Cadbury
Christmas Gift Exemption Vouchers *188*, 192
Churchill, Sir Winston S 23
cigarettes 33, 36, 169
  anti-smoking campaigns 188, 192, *192*
cinema complexes 140
cities
  de facto malls 140
  markets and 114–16
Citroën *30*, 32
Clinton, Bill *21*, 45
Co-operative Bank 205, 208
co-operatives 208
Coates, Nigel 57
Coca-Cola 23, 26–30, *27*, *30*, 47–8, 50, 94, 160, 174
  advertising 92
  bottle design *76*
  brand and logo 75–8, *75*
  corporate identity 52
  Diet Coke *21*, 45
  global marketing 69, *69*
  market value 94
  New Coke 82–3
  transnational expansion 32
  Virgin cola and 39
coffee, Fair Trade schemes 205–8
collectables 180, *181*
Communication Arts Inc 135, 139
communications, and global culture 48–50
concrete thinking 178–9
consumer choice
  branding and 80–9, 94–5, 140, 70–1, 175
  ethical considerations 96, 186, 205–11
  and Green issues 192–9
  in the home 107
  individualism and 158–60, 171, 175
consumer proactivity 102–3, *102*, 192, 199
consumer protests 51
consumer research 51
consumer response, to advertising 38, 102–3, *102*, 186
consumer terrorism 51
consumerism
  Green consumption 192–9
  and human rights 32, 51, 211
  identity and 44–5, 51, 156–75
consumers, behaviour analysis 106–7, 175
Consumers' Association 202–4
Consumers International 193
consumption, alternative systems 51, 166

North-Holland Series in
SYSTEM SCIENCE AND ENGINEERING
Andrew P. Sage, *Editor*

Conflict Analysis

Models and Resolutions

Conflict Analysis
Models and Resolutions

Series Volume 11

Niall M. Fraser

Keith W. Hipel

Department of Systems Design Engineering
University of Waterloo

North-Holland
New York • Amsterdam • Oxford

Elsevier Science Publishing Co., Inc.
52 Vanderbilt Avenue, New York, NY 10017

Distributors outside the United States and Canada:
Elsevier Science Publishers B.V.
P.O. Box 211, 1000 AE Amsterdam, The Netherlands

Library of Congress Cataloging in Publication Data

Fraser, Niall M.
    Conflict analysis.
    (North-Holland series in system science and engineering; 11)

    Bibliography: p. Includes index.
    1. Conflict management—Mathematical models. I. Hipel, Keith W.
    II. Title. III. Series.
HD42.F73 1984   658.3′145   84-7965
ISBN 0-444-00921-3

Manufactured in the United States of America

Contents

Contents

Preface

The purpose of this book is to present a general methodology for studying a wide variety of conflict situations that can arise in the real world. Conflicts can range from a small scale dispute between individuals, such as a landlord and tenant, to a large military confrontation where huge armies battle. However, the underlying philosophy and mathematical structure that describe the conflict process are identical, regardless of the size of the conflicting parties. Therefore, the comprehensive conflict analysis techniques developed in this book should prove to be valuable for anyone interested in disputes involving two or more opposing groups.

Table P.1 provides a list of the conflicts which are analyzed in the book using exactly the same general methodology, followed by the sections in which the conflicts are presented and analyzed. As exemplified by the application fields given in Table P.1, this systems design approach to conflict analysis should be useful for individuals such as:

Water resources managers	Labor–management negotiators
Environmental engineers	Politicians
Energy experts	Political scientists
Transportation engineers	Lawyers
Management scientists	Historians
Economists	Military strategists

The conflict analysis methodology provides two major functions. First, the particular conflict being considered is modeled by putting the available information pertaining to the dispute into proper perspective and systematically structuring the problem. Second, the conflict model is employed to predict possible solutions to the dispute. Based on the results of a

Table P.1 Real World Conflicts Studied in the Book

Conflict	Sections	Application Area
Cuban Missile Crisis	1.3, 3.2 6.6	Politics Military strategy
Garrison Diversion Unit	2.1–2.5	Water resources Environmental engineering International law
D-Day Invasion	3.3	Military deception
Fall of France	4.2	Military tactics Strategic surprise
Suez Canal Crisis	4.3	Politics Military strategy Strategic surprise
Zimbabwe	5.5–5.7	International negotiations
Watergate Tapes	6.2–6.5	Politics Law
Poplar River	7.2–7.5	Energy Scarce resource allocation Environmental engineering International law
Holston River	Chapt. 8, 9	Bargaining Negotiation

Hypothetical Conflicts Studied in the Book		
Conflict	Sections	Application Area
Afghanistan	6.5	Military tactics Acts of nature
Nuclear War	Chapt. 9, 10, 11, 14	Military strategy Game theory
Prisoners' Dilemma	12.6	Game theory
Naval Conflict	12.6	Game theory
Chicken	12.6, 14.4	Game theory
Cookie Conflict	12.6	Game theory

conflict study a decisionmaker can select a realistic course of action which would be most beneficial for his purposes.

The main approach used in the book for analyzing conflicts is the conflict analysis methodology of Fraser and Hipel (1979a), which is based on metagame theory developed by Howard (1971). In later chapters of the book, other existing conflict analysis methods are rigorously compared to the conflict analysis of Fraser and Hipel (1979a). However, as will be shown both from practical and theoretical viewpoints, the conflict analysis procedure of Fraser and Hipel constitutes the most realistic and comprehensive approach for studying conflicts. Consequently, the methodology of Fraser and Hipel (1979a) is referred to as "conflict analysis" throughout the book. An inherent attribute of conflict analysis is that the authors have found in practice that it can readily handle virtually any size of complex conflict problem that can occur (see Table P.1). Furthermore, the method of application of the technique is straightforward and easy to use.

Another major advantage of conflict analysis is that it is not necessary to understand any of the underlying theory in order to apply the technique to a real world dispute. As a consequence, the text has been subdivided into two major sections. The first group of chapters, consisting of Chapters 1 through 9, deals mainly with the method of application of conflict analysis and extensions thereof. The second part (Chapters 10 through 14) is concerned with the theory underlying conflict analysis as well as other related concepts from the field of game theory. The Contents delineates the chapters and sections constituting the two main parts of the book. A summary of the different topics covered in the entire text is presented in the first column in Table P.2; the second column lists equivalent terminology from conflict analysis that is employed in the text. From the third column, the reader can locate the chapters in which a particular topic is discussed.

Practitioners wishing only to apply the methodology to real world conflict problems need only concern themselves with the relevant sections from Part I. Chapter 1 provides a solid introduction to conflict analysis, which is reinforced and expanded upon in Chapter 2 through the analysis of the controversy surrounding the Garrison Diversion Unit, a complex international water resources dispute. Chapter 3 introduces and develops the idea of a hypergame where one or more of the participants misunderstand the true nature of the conflict situation.

If desired, the remaining chapters of Part I can be studied independently of one another, except for Chapter 9 which should be read after covering Chapters 6 and 8. In Chapter 4, the concepts of hypergames introduced in Chapter 3 are used to study historical situations in which one or more of the participants employ "strategic surprise." Chapter 5 discusses the techniques for ascertaining the sensitivity of the predicted possible resolutions of a conflict to changes in the conflict model describing the controversy. The forming of meaningful coalitions between two or more participants in a dispute is one way in which to determine how the possible solutions can be affected. In Chapter 6, methods are given for modeling a conflict as it evolves over time and for incorporating probabilistic information into a conflict study.

Although all of the necessary calculations needed for the procedures

Table P.2 Topics in the Book

Topic	Equivalent Terminology	Chapter
Simple conflict 2-Player conflict	Simple conflict	1
Complex conflict Multi-player conflict	Complex conflict	2
Deception Misinformation Misperception Very complex deception Levels of perception	Hypergames	3, 4
Strategic surprise	Hypergames	4
Imprecise information Risk	Sensitivity analysis	5
Coalitions	Coalition analysis	5
Changes with time	Dynamic Forms Supergames	6, 14
Probabilistic information	Dynamic Forms	6, 14
Computer assistance	Computer algorithms	7
Bargaining Negotiation	Bargaining Negotiation	9, 10, A, B
Game theory	Game theory	10–13, C–F
Metagame theory	Metagame theory	10–13, D

in Part I of the text can be done by hand, a computer can be utilized to store information and perform routine tasks. Consequently, in Chapter 7 algorithms are described that permit the conflict analysis methodology to be efficiently programmed on a microcomputer. Because a computer allows calculations to be completed almost instantaneously, the practitioner can devote his valuable time to executing extensive analyses and carefully interpreting the final results. A flexible conflict analysis program (CAP) and an accompanying instruction manual are available from the publisher. CAP is a "user friendly" program which allows for meaningful communication between the user and the program when constructing a conflict model for studying a specific real world dispute.

The final two chapters of Part I deal with bargaining and negotiation. Bargaining and negotiation commonly arise in areas such as business, labor management, pollution abatement and political disputes. Consequently, the extension of conflict analysis for modeling bargaining and negotiation is thoroughly described in Chapters 8 and 9, respectively.

In Part II the theoretical basis of conflict analysis is presented and rigorously compared to existing solution concepts from the field of non-cooperative game theory. An appealing feature of the conflict analysis tools developed in Part I is that the entire underlying theory is based on fairly elementary concepts from set theory and logic. These branches of mathematics are often referred to as the "mathematics of relationships" and they constitute a nonquantitative approach for realistically modeling the sociological and psychological properties inherent in conflict situations. Because conflict analysis is nonquantitative in nature, the preferences of each participant or player among the feasible outcomes in a conflict can be realistically modeled using a minimum amount of information. Only relative preference information is required when a given player decides whether he prefers one outcome over another. It is not necessary to know *by how much* a player prefers a particular outcome. Therefore, real numbers or utilities do not have to be assigned to each outcome for representing the preferences of a player. In many conflicts, the preferences of a player are ordinal and the feasible outcomes can be ranked from most to least preferred. However, a player's preferences may be intransitive in a particular situation, so that he may prefer outcome x to y, y to z, but z to x. A major advantage of conflict analysis is that it is mathematically designed to handle intransitive preference information where it arises.

The theory behind conflict analysis has been checked according to the scientific method by demonstrating that correct results are obtained when analyzing a wide range of historical and current conflicts plus experimental data. Therefore, in addition to academics and students, some practitioners may wish to peruse the appropriate sections of Part II in order to fully appreciate the diversity of situations in which conflict analysis methods can be applied.

Chapter 10 concerns the development of metagame theory as a consequence of some classical problems from game theory. The concepts that transformed metagame analysis into the practical methods for conflict analysis used in Part I are presented in Chapter 11. In Chapter 12, some philosophic considerations regarding conflict analysis are examined, and the idea of solution concepts is brought forward. Chapter 13 thoroughly examines the exact mathematical relationships among conflict analysis and other solution concepts from noncooperative game theory. In this chapter it is clearly demonstrated that where other approaches to conflict analysis are used to predict the possible resolutions to a dispute, the meaningful results are almost always members of the set of resolutions predicted by conflict analysis. Accordingly, practitioners who have previously employed other approaches to conflict analysis should have great confidence in the comprehensive and flexible techniques presented in this text. To further demonstrate the importance of conflict analysis, some advanced topics in dynamic modeling, including methods for modeling a conflict over continuous time, are presented in Chapter 14.

Six appendixes follow the text of the book. Appendix A covers some historical approaches to the bargaining problem; Appendix B deals with traditional concepts from the field of negotiation. These two appendixes can be used as companions to Chapters 8 and 9, respectively. Appendix C contains some classical ideas from game theory which are examples of other, less practical, analytic approaches to studying conflict. Appendix D is a proof of the Characterization Theorem, a key theorem used in the discussion on metagame theory in Chapter 10. Appendixes E and F support the mathematical material on solution concepts presented in Chapter 13. Using examples, Appendix E demonstrates the existence of relationships among solution concepts illustrated in Chapter 13; Appendix F continues the comparison of solution concepts by examining them all for the particular cases of no–conflict games and games of complete opposition.

The text is designed for use among three main groups. University instructors may wish to employ the book in courses for students at the senior undergraduate and graduate levels. Researchers concerned with both the development and application of conflict analysis methods will find many innovative and new results in the book. Finally, because all of the methods have been designed to solve a wide variety of actual conflict problems, consultants can use the techniques presented in this book to solve specific problems brought to them by their clients.

When the book is used as a textbook, the flowchart in Figure P.1 may be of assistance in deciding which topics should be included in the course. In this diagram, solid lines indicate recommended routes of study through the book; dotted lines represent alternative paths to follow. In all cases, it is recommended that at least Chapters 1 and 2 be included in any course, while Chapter 3 must also be covered if any of the chapters from 4 to 9 are used. If most of the book were covered there is enough material for a two–semester course. For instance, a two–semester course might consist of Chapters 1 through 6, 10 and 11, along with materials from the other chapters which are of particular interest to the lecturer and students. For courses in which the mathematical theory is not deemed important, appropriate chapters from Part I can be selected for a single semester course. When designing a one–semester course that is largely concerned with the practical aspects of bargaining and negotiation, Chapters 1 through 3, 5, 6, 8, 9, and Appendixes A and B could be employed. For technically oriented students from disciplines such as Management Science or a field of engineering, relevant chapters from both Parts I and II could be selected. Chapters 1 through 5, 10 and 11, for instance, could be employed in a one–semester course. In addition to some chapters from the first section of this book, mathematical students may wish to study all of the mathematical material covered in Chapters 10 through 14 in the second

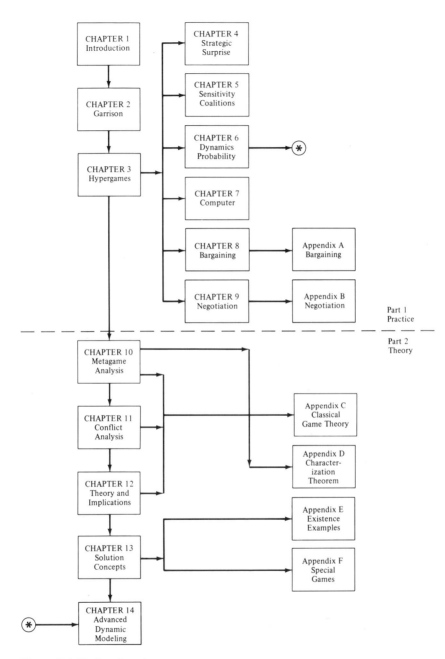

Figure P.1 Paths of study.

half of the book, plus Appendixes C, D, E and F. The first or the first few chapters could also be used as part of a broad course in operations research, game theory, systems engineering, political science, or other applicable disciplines. For the past few years, chapters from Parts I and II have been used for a course entitled "Conflict Analysis" within the Department of Systems Design Engineering at the University of Waterloo.

Each chapter of the book starts with an introduction outlining the structure and scope of the chapter, with perhaps some background material. All chapters in Part I include at least one complete analysis of a real world conflict to clearly demonstrate how various conflict analysis methods work in practice. In Part II, some hypothetical conflicts are employed for comparing different approaches to conflict analysis. At the end of each chapter there is a thorough summary of the important concepts introduced in the chapter, including equations (when deemed necessary) and references to the section numbers or tables in which algorithms or further information can be obtained. Concluding each chapter are a number of questions of varying difficulty. A book of answers to these questions is available from the publisher.

Thoughout the book it is never necessary to have a thorough understanding of the history behind the example conflicts in order to understand the conflict analysis techniques that are presented. Indeed, some of the examples have been developed solely for their pedagogical value. All of the applications are included to clearly explain how the conflict analysis methods are easily applied to actual problems. For each application, considerable effort was taken to obtain accurate information about the conflict. Nevertheless, if a reader possesses special information about a given application, he may wish to reformulate the problem and execute his own analyses using the conflict analysis techniques presented in the book.

This book presents numerous original ideas in conflict analysis that are unavailable in any other published text. However, many of the basic concepts have been previously published in prestigious international journals such as: *Advances in Engineering Software, Conflict Management and Peace Science, Energy, European Journal of Operational Research, IEEE Transactions on Systems, Man and Cybernetics, INFOR Interfaces, Journal of Conflict Resolution, Journal of the Operational Research Society, Journal of Policy Modeling, Journal of the Water Resources Planning and Management Division* (American Society of Civil Engineers), *Large Scale Systems, OMEGA, Political Methodology, Water Resources Bulletin,* and *Water Resources Research,* as well as articles in unrefereed publications and conference proceedings. The careful reviewing of the authors' research and subsequent dissemination of the authors' papers by the foregoing journals are gratefully acknowledged by the authors. Material from some of the published papers is contained within the text and is properly referenced wherever it appears.

Acknowledgments

The authors wish to express their deep appreciation to the many colleagues, students and friends who have contributed immensely to this book. Their support, advice, contributions and suggestions have made this book much more than just a compilation of previously published material. In addition to being a fine individual to have as a friend, Marc Kilgour is a most pleasant person to deal with from a professional viewpoint. Without Marc's sound understanding of mathematics, it would not have been possible to develop the extensive mathematical results found in Chapter 13 and some of the appendixes. The authors have enjoyed working with Rob Harvey in developing the computer algorithms of Chapter 7, the Conflict Analysis Program (CAP), and an instruction manual for using CAP on a microcomputer. Some of the hypergame results in Chapter 3 are based upon joint research executed with Allyn Takahashi. Bill Wright and Michael Shupe took part in the hypergame research on the Suez Canal crisis in Chapter 4. Peter Bennett and the late Robin Bussell furnished useful advice about the application of hypergame analysis to actual problems. In the development of the coalition analysis algorithm described in Chapter 5, Jon Kuhn worked diligently with the authors. Mike Meleskie's keen interest in the Watergate tapes conflict resulted in the application in Chapter 6; Jose del Monte analyzed the potential nuclear war conflict in Part II of the book. In his Master's research, Nigel Stokes clearly demonstrated the great import of conflict analysis in business and wrote the summary of the Characterization Theorem which appears in Appendix D. Peter Savich's Master's research involved the use of conflict analysis in energy, and Aldo Dagnino examined the application of dynamic games to international business. Christian Dufournaud has strongly promoted the use of conflict analysis in geography and water resources; Ian McLeod has included conflict analysis in his operations research courses. Chris Mitchell, Charles Benjamin and Charles Powell have studied international relations from a conflict analysis viewpoint. In his personal comments and also his own research, Steven Brams has stimulated the use of conflict analysis techniques. Likewise, in the role of editor of various international journals and subject editor for a book company, Andrew P. Sage has strongly encouraged the development of such methods as various conflict analysis procedures which can handle multiple objectives. Among many others, the authors would also like to thank Eric Burke, Martin Giesen, Nigel Howard, Nico Meijer, Jim Radford, R.K. Ragade, Steve Shevell, T.E. Unny, and Ying Xiong. Finally, the authors greatly appreciate the encouragement, support and patience of their lovely wives Peggy and Sheila, as well as other family members.

In addition to individuals, various organizations should be thanked. The National Science and Engineering Research Council of Canada provided funding for many of the individuals who were involved with research projects which are cited in the text. The International Joint Commission and the Department of External Affairs provided information about the Garrison Diversion Unit conflict in Chapter 2. All of the research in the book was completed within the Department of Systems Design Engineering at the University of Waterloo.

PART I
CONFLICT ANALYSIS
IN PRACTICE

Chapter 1
Introduction to Conflict Analysis

1.1 Types of Conflicts

A *conflict* is a situation in which there is a "condition of opposition" (*Funk and Wagnells*, 1974), and parties with opposing goals affect one another. Often conflicts involve the use of military force, and indeed a number of military conflicts are examined in this book. These include the Cuban missile crisis of 1962, which is discussed in this chapter; the fall of France in 1940 and the Normandy invasion in 1944, which are considered in Chapter 3; and the Suez crisis of 1956, an extensive study of which appears in Chapter 4. A potential nuclear war between the superpowers is studied in Chapters 10 and 11, and peace treaty negotiations for the Zimbabwe dispute are analyzed in Chapter 5. However, conflicts need not be military in nature. In fact, conflict is virtually inevitable whenever humans interact, either individually or in groups.

Business problems constitute another important area where conflicts often arise. Patent disputes between multinational corporations, such as the recent suit of IBM by Xerox claiming infringement of some of its photocopying patents, can be as complex as international military operations. The bargaining and negotiation procedures presented in Chapters 8 and 9, respectively, can be very useful in management and labor negotiations, where a wisely chosen strategy can save or make a great deal of money for the company or union. The carrying out of administrative duties can often be interpreted as a sequence of conflict decisions. For example, administrators in a large company may have to revise a budget continually in order to resolve the conflicting financial needs of various departments. Other examples of conflict situations in business include the development of retail marketing strategies and the assessment of one's competition within a business organization in order to plan for personal advancement.

Conflict analysis is of significance to engineers because of the increasing importance of social and political influences in engineering decision making. A large scale engineering project must be feasible not only physically, environmentally, financially, and economically, but also socially and politically. Although useful analytic techniques abound for the assessment of feasibility in many cases, only recently have comprehensive methods from conflict analysis become available that permit rigorous examination of the social and political factors. In the past many large engineering projects have been abandoned or stalled because of improper assessment of just these factors. For example, the Garrison Diversion Unit in the state of North Dakota is an immense irrigation project that could cause environmental damage by polluting rivers that flow into Canada. Political pressure by the Canadian government and environmental groups may eventually cause much of the proposed project to be canceled, even though millions of dollars have already been spent (Hipel and Fraser, 1980). This conflict is discussed in detail in Chapter 2. In Chapters 8 and 9 an environmental dispute illustrates how conflict analysis can be used in negotiations where both environmental and sociopolitical concerns must be satisfied. Another illustration of a large project adversely affected by political and social factors is the proposed Pickering airport, which was planned to be built north of Toronto, Canada. Thousands of acres of land were expropriated for a giant modern airport; then, just as construction began, the entire project was canceled owing to public disapproval.

In the modern world, national governments strive to attain high standards of living for their citizens. Consequently, there is stiff competition among and within nations for scarce natural resources. For example, the competition to gain control of ocean resources prompted the United Nations in 1980 to draw up the Law of the Sea agreement, which stipulates how the potential wealth of the oceans should be divided. The Poplar River conflict described in Chapter 6 is concerned with the allocation of water between opposing groups: the Canadians wish to use the water in the production of thermal electricity, whereas American Indians want the water for irrigation (Fraser and Hipel, 1980b). To maintain access to the oil supplies in the Middle East, the Western nations must compete not only with Russian interests but also with the nationalistic aspirations of the oil producing countries. As another example, the wheat exporting nations are considering forming a cartel in order to control the international price of wheat. All cartels are conflicts between those who control a commodity and those who need it.

The widespread use of natural resources in the production of industrial and agricultural products has put a severe strain on the natural environment and thus given rise to a wide range of environmental disputes. For instance, the production of energy from fossil fuels has caused the atmosphere to become severely polluted. The "acid rain" that results from this kind of pollution is killing life in the lakes and rivers of the affected regions. The problem of acid rain is quite complicated since the pollution spreads from the source across local and national boundaries. Consequently, regions that do not directly benefit from the energy production are adversely affected by the industrial by-products. Other types of environmental problems that are of great concern include the treatment of sewage, the disposal of radioactive wastes from nuclear power plants, the proper use of agricultural land, and the preservation of natural areas such as the Amazon rain forest in Brazil.

Conflicts occur in many types of social situations—both between individuals (such as landlord and tenant disputes or arguments between spouses or friends) and among groups. Consider the keen competition between sporting teams or academic departments within a university. Illustrations of social conflict between large groups of people are the disputes of political parties and of nations at war. A major role of politicians and military commanders is to assess and act in situations where a resolution of opposing views must be found. Legal disputes, which may involve large groups of people or only a handful of individuals, can also be modeled using techniques from conflict analysis. The legal and political conflict surrounding the Watergate tapes controversy is analyzed in Chapter 6 of this book.

Other applications of conflict analysis methodology to real world problems can be found in the published literature. For instance, Savich et al. (1983) have analyzed a North American energy controversy, Dufournaud (1982) has studied international river basin disputes, Stokes and Hipel (1983) and Stokes et al. (1984) have analyzed international trade disputes, and Hipel and Fraser (1983) have examined the Polish crisis of July 1982. Hipel (1981) has explained how conflict analysis can be employed in conjunction with other operations research techniques to solve problems arising in large scale engineering projects, such as a system of water resources reservoirs or nuclear power development.

Conflict resolution has long been primarily the field of political scientists, sociologists, economists, and psychologists (Steele, 1976), but the ability to understand and resolve conflicts is required by all decision makers. For lack of comprehensive models, it has been difficult for the participant in a complex conflict situation or for an interested observer to use all the available information to structure the problem systematically and to assess the likely or possible resolutions to the conflict. Approaches to the problem have made use of detailed case studies, simulations, and econometric and economic models (Steele, 1976), but the most useful recent developments have been in the area of game theory.

Techniques from game theory specifically designed to solve real world conflicts are often referred to as *conflict analysis* methods. The purpose of this book is to present a set of related comprehensive models and analytic techniques from the field of conflict analysis that permit the assessment of a wide variety of conflict situations. Although ideas from classical game theory (e.g., von Neumann and Morganstern, 1953; Luce and Raiffa, 1957) and hypergame theory (Bennett, 1977) are presented and used in this book, the basis of all the discussed techniques is a method for analyzing conflicts (Fraser and Hipel, 1979a) that is a reformulation and extension of metagame analysis (Howard, 1971). The conflict analysis method has inherent advantages. It is easy to use, and the practitioner does not have to know the underlying theory in order to employ the technique. The method of application of the technique for studying various types of conflict problems is explained in Part I of this book. The theoretical basis of the approach of Fraser and Hipel (1979a), along with other related topics in game theory, is presented in Part II. The present chapter is devoted to a step-by-step introduction to the conflict analysis of a simple conflict.

1.2 Modeling and Analysis of Simple Conflicts

The function of conflict analysis is to enable a participant to make better decisions. This is accomplished in two ways. First, the information the analyst already has about the conflict is presented in a systematic manner that permits consideration of the conflict as a whole, rather than as a collection of discrete facts. Because the historical details of the conflict are organized according to a formal structure, this step is called *modeling*. The great importance of the modeling stage in conflict analysis has been emphasized by a number of authors (Radford, 1980; Bennett and Huxham, 1982; Hipel and Fraser, 1984). Second, based on the model and the available data, possible resolutions to the conflict are determined. Since the possible solutions must be stable for all the participants involved in the conflict, this second step is referred to as *stability analysis*.

Figure 1.1 illustrates the general conflict analysis procedure. The real world situation is represented as an amorphous blob, with little apparent structure. It is complex and not amenable to analysis. The process of modeling imposes a structure on the real situation, making it more accessible to analysis. In practice, it is often advantageous to develop a range of simple models to describe the conflict. If deemed necessary, more complex models can be constructed based upon information gained from the simpler models. Furthermore, simple diagrams can be drawn to indicate the interactions among the players [see Hipel and Fraser (1984) for an example of an interaction diagram]. A given model is considered to be valid if it preserves the important characteristics of the real world

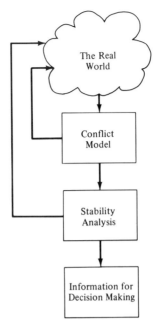

Figure 1.1 The general conflict analysis process.

conflict. One or more of the more promising models are then analyzed to provide stability results, which can then be compared to the real world. No matter how reasonable a model may appear, it can never be as complete or as complex as the real world situation; therefore, it can never be completely accurate. However, a well designed model can be a useful tool for the decision maker. The best verification of a model's accuracy is whether it provides reasonable answers to the actual problem. If it does not, the model should be reformulated and the process repeated.

Conflict modeling mimics the natural psychological activity that occurs when thinking about a conflict. For instance, when mentally analyzing the fall of France in World War II (see Chapter 3) one rarely considers the detailed intentions and interactions of all the individuals in the opposing countries; rather one thinks about the Germans and the Allies. This is a modeling process where millions of individual human participants are reduced to two combatants. Similarly, the actions that participants can take in a conflict are naturally reduced from the infinite to the countable.

Formally, a conflict or *game* is a situation where two or more groups are in dispute over some issue or resources. The participants in a game are called the *players*. The possible courses of action available to the players in the game are referred to as *options*. Any set of options that can be taken by a particular player is called a *strategy*. If there are k options available to a given player, that player has 2^k possible strategies since each option can either be selected or rejected. When each player has selected a strategy, the result is referred to as an *outcome*. In a game with a total of *m* options for all the players, there are 2^m mathematically possible outcomes. When it is logically impossible or highly unlikely for an outcome to occur, the outcome is *infeasible*. For instance, in a military conflict where an army is of limited size, it is unfeasible for the army to launch two major attacks simultaneously. After the infeasible outcomes have been removed from the game, the *feasible* outcomes can ordinally be ranked from most to least preferable for a given player in order to determine that player's *preference vector*. It is possible to allow for intransitivities in a preference vector, as well as for outcomes being equally preferred.

A game or *conflict model* consists of the players, their options, and their preference vectors. The *stability analysis* of the game is executed by determining the stability of each feasible outcome for every player. If an outcome is *stable* for a given player, it does not benefit that player to move unilaterally to any other outcome by a change in strategy. If such a change is advantageous for a given player, the avoided outcome is *unstable*. An outcome that is stable for all the players in the game model is an *equilibrium* and constitutes a possible resolution to the conflict. As the stability analysis stage is used to predict the possible equilibriums, it is sometimes referred to as the *prediction* or *forecasting* stage.

A formal conflict analysis offers a number of advantages over approaching a given conflict problem in an intuitive manner:

1. Available information about the problem is retained and structured so that the analyst can examine a complex problem in a realistic and objective manner.
2. Conclusions about the conflict can be verified and communicated easily.
3. Implications of information the analyst already has are discerned.
4. The areas where information is most needed become apparent.
5. The correct course of action for the participants can be determined.

1.3 The Cuban Missile Crisis

In order to present the steps required for the modeling and stability analysis of a conflict, consider the Cuban missile crisis of 1962, which has been studied by Fraser and Hipel (1983c) and Hipel and Fraser (1983). In this conflict, the USSR installed offensive missiles in Cuba, just 90 miles off the American mainland. Firm American reaction to this apparent threat led to the verge of nuclear war. The conflict is examined to determine whether the correct actions of the adversaries can be determined, and whether the results of these actions came about in the historical course of events.

1.3.1 Historical Background

Prior to 1957 Cuba had for many years been under the complete economic and political control of the United States. Many American companies had substantial investments in agriculture and tourism on the island, and the government of Fulgencio Batista heeded U.S. interests. Late in 1956 a revolution to overthrow the Batista regime was initiated by Fidel Castro, an educated middle class socialist. To the surprise of many Americans, Castro managed to take control of Cuba in 1959, resulting in the nationalization of all American property on the island. Subsequent to the revolution, Castro established a close relationship with the Soviet Union. The loss of a large economic investment and the perception of a communist threat close to the American mainland made Cuba a sensitive issue in the United States.

American pride was not improved by the failure of the Bay of Pigs invasion in April 1961. The Soviet Union had previously declared its willingness to aid Cuba in defending itself against the United States by supplying military aid, including missiles. When Cuban exiles invaded Cuba at the Bay of Pigs with the help of the U.S. government, the Soviets reiterated this intention, even, it was implied, should the result be nuclear war. Consequently, President Kennedy backed down, denying the invaders further assistance and thus ensuring their failure. Afterward, however, Kennedy publicly committed his administration never to tolerate offensive missiles in Cuba (Allison, 1971).

On October 14, 1962, American aerial reconnaissance discovered evidence of Soviet offensive missiles in Cuba. The USSR probably placed them there for a number of different reasons, which include (Allison, 1971):

1. Cuban missiles could be used as a bargaining tool in exchange for dismantling the U.S. missile bases in Turkey and Italy. From the point of view of the USSR, it was duplicity for the United States to maintain bases on the borders of Russia while objecting to offensive activity in Cuba. [Kennedy had already ordered the withdrawal of offensive missiles from Turkey. However his orders had not yet been carried out (Able, 1969, p. 176).]
2. If the United States were enticed into striking "little Cuba," world opinion would run against the Americans, and the Soviets could more easily move against West Berlin. Berlin was at this time a hotly contested pawn in the Cold War. The distraction of Cuba could permit action in Germany much as the Suez crisis of 1956 allowed Russia to invade Hungary.
3. The missiles fulfilled the Soviet Union's commitment to defend Cuba and reinforced Russia's credibility among Third World nations.
4. Confronting the United States with operational missiles in Cuba

would constitute a strong but risky move in the politics of the Cold War. If the United States reacted indecisively, all credibility of American commitments to other nations would be lost. The environment in which the Berlin problem could be discussed would be entirely different.

5. The establishment of missile bases in Cuba would immediately double the first-strike capability of the USSR and reduce the possibility of bold American employment of their superior nuclear power. Thus this was an efficient way of significantly equalizing the nuclear balance of power.

To generate alternative responses to the missile deployment, President Kennedy created the Executive Committee of the National Security Council. This included major cabinet and government agency officers with principal responsibility for political and military decisions, representatives of major segments of the public, and some special advisors. The Executive Committee formulated a number of possible actions, the most likely of which included the following (Able, 1969; Allison, 1971):

1. Perform no aggressive actions. This would result in the instant doubling of the Soviet Union's missile power, the outflanking of the American early warning system, and the loss of credibility in American foreign commitments. This could be mitigated by diplomatic pressure through the United Nations or Organization of American States (OAS) or by a summit meeting with Nikita Khrushchev, then Soviet chief of state. Hopefully this action would avoid the escalation of the conflict to full nuclear war.

2. Perform a "surgical" air strike. This would mean destroying the missile bases in a quick conventional air attack and could possibly require a follow-up invasion of the island.

3. Impose a blockade. The American Navy would enforce an embargo on military shipments to Cuba.

Essentially three courses of action were open to the USSR in this conflict:

1. Do not withdraw the missiles from Cuba.

2. Withdraw the missiles.

3. Escalate the conflict. This could be done by invading West Berlin, assaulting U.S. Naval ships, bombing southeastern American targets from Cuba, or commencing an ICBM (Intercontinental Ballistic Missile) attack on the United States.

As it turned out, the United States adopted a strategy of blockading military shipments, and the USSR withdrew the offensive missiles (Able, 1969; Allison, 1971).

1.3.2 Modeling the Cuban Crisis

The first step in performing a conflict analysis is to select a point in time. This is an extremely important consideration because a conflict is generally a dynamic phenomenon, and it is easy to get the players, options, and preferences mixed up because they may change over the course of the conflict. Consequently, the problem is modeled for one specific instant, and all results apply only to that instant. When more than one point in time is crucial for the analysis, modeling and stability analysis can be performed for each. Thus, modeling is analogous to a series of snapshots of the conflict, with a stability analysis performed for each one (The Suez crisis of 1956 is analyzed at two points in time in Chapter 3.) If the actual dynamic aspects of a conflict are critical, there are techniques for modeling these, as are covered in Chapter 6. *Dynamic analysis* is analogous to a motion picture of the conflict as it evolves over time. For the Cuban crisis, the courses of action for the United States and the USSR described in Section 1.3.1 became apparent around October 17, 1962, so this is chosen as the time for which to conduct the static analysis.

The next step is to determine the players and options for the model. At the chosen time, the two players are clearly the United States and USSR. In both countries, the political forces were undivided and dedicated. The crisis had not yet been made public in the United States, but later unanimity was expressed not only domestically but by its European allies and the members of the OAS (Able, 1969). Cuba had no relevant independent action it could take at this time. Later in the crisis, it unilaterally withheld some heavy bombers from the withdrawal of Russian weapons, but this independence was soon overruled by Russia.

The options available to the players correspond to the courses of action listed in the previous section. However, these can be expressed more economically. Each player's options for this conflict are listed in the first column of Table 1.1. Although the options listed below each player could be ordered in any desired manner at the start of the analysis, the chosen *meaningful ordering of options* is maintained throughout the analysis. As shown in Table 1.1, one US option was to perform an air strike on Cuba; another was to invoke a quarantine (blockade) of Cuba, which would prevent the importation of any military supplies into Cuba. The United States could have chosen either option *or both*. Alternatively, it could have chosen to pursue neither, seeking instead a resolution through diplomatic measures alone. The USSR could either dismantle and remove the offensive missiles (withdraw), react with renewed aggression (escalate), or perform no overt action (indicated by selecting neither of these options).

Following the notation of Howard (1971), the selection of an option by a given player is indicated by a 1 opposite it; a 0 indicates the option was

Table 1.1 Players, Options, and Outcomes for the Cuban Missile Crisis

Option	Outcomes											
U.S.												
Air strike	0	1	0	1	0	1	0	1	0	1	0	1
Blockade	0	0	1	1	0	0	1	1	0	0	1	1
USSR												
Withdraw	0	0	0	0	1	1	1	1	0	0	0	0
Escalate	0	0	0	0	0	0	0	0	1	1	1	1
Decimal	0	1	2	3	4	5	6	7	8	9	10	11

not taken. When either a 1 or 0 is written opposite all of the options for a given player this constitutes a strategy for the player. An outcome is formed by all of the players choosing a strategy; therefore in Table 1.1 each column of 1s and 0s constitutes an outcome for the Cuban missile crisis. In the text, these columns are written horizontally. In the seventh column from the left in Table 1.1, the 0 opposite the first US option indicates that there is no American air strike; the 1 opposite the second option means that there is an American blockade of Cuba. Thus, the United States has selected the strategy (0, 1). By withdrawing its missiles from Cuba and not escalating the dispute, the USSR has chosen the strategy (1, 0), which combines with the American strategy (0, 1) to form the outcome (01, 10). The decimal entries at the bottom of this and the following two tables are explained in Section 1.3.3.

Because each option can be either chosen or not, a conflict with m options has 2^m outcomes. As there are four options in the model of the Cuban crisis, there are $2^4 = 16$ possible outcomes in this game. However, in general not all outcomes are possible or likely to occur in a game. In the Cuban crisis it is considered highly unlikely, if not impossible, for the USSR to withdraw from Cuba and escalate at the same time. Consequently, the four outcomes (00, 11), (10, 11), (01, 11), and (11, 11) are infeasible and should therefore be removed from the model. This leaves the 12 feasible outcomes shown in Table 1.1. When there are a large number of options in a game, techniques are available for efficiently removing infeasible outcomes by hand (see Chapter 2) or by using a microcomputer (see Chapter 7). In practice, after outcome removal there are usually no more than 50 feasible outcomes left, even in very complex games.

The final step of the modeling process is to order the outcomes of Table 1.1 to reflect the preferences of the players. This has been done in Tables 1.2 and 1.3 for the United States and USSR, respectively, where the outcomes are ordered with the most preferred on the left and the least preferred on the right. Each preference vector embodies a great deal of _most preferred_ ———————— ▷ _least preferred._

Table 1.2 Preference Vector for the United States in the Cuban Missile Crisis

U.S.												
Air strike	0	0	1	1	0	1	1	0	1	1	0	0
Blockade	0	1	0	1	1	0	1	0	1	0	1	0
USSR												
Withdraw	1	1	1	1	0	0	0	0	0	0	0	0
Escalate	0	0	0	0	0	0	0	0	1	1	1	1
Decimal	4	6	5	7	2	1	3	0	11	9	10	8

information about the given player's viewpoint regarding the conflict. The development of preference vectors generally requires a substantial amount of careful research on the part of the conflict analyst. Also, since one's understanding of a conflict improves as the study evolves, the preference vectors selected for the players are likely to be refined.

The American preference vector in Table 1.2 is based on the overriding concerns that the conflict not escalate into nuclear war and that the Russians withdraw their missiles. Thus all outcomes in which the USSR withdraws appear on the left, whereas outcomes involving Soviet escalation are on the right. For example, the most preferred outcome for the United States is (00, 10) where the Soviets withdraw their missiles without any overt U.S. actions. The least preferred outcome is (00, 01): Soviet escalation without any U.S. response. If the USSR were to withdraw, the United States would prefer that they do so under the minimum amount of American coercion; if they were to escalate, the United States would prefer to be taking the most aggressive actions possible. In the situation where the USSR does nothing, the United States would prefer taking some action to doing nothing, but would also rather not provoke the Soviet Union unnecessarily.

As shown by the Soviet preference vector in Table 1.3, the USSR also wishes to avoid escalating the conflict to nuclear war. If the USSR is to escalate, it is preferred in conjunction with aggressive action on the part of the United States; consequently, (00, 01) is their least preferred out-

Table 1.3 Preference Vector for the USSR in the Cuban Missile Crisis

U.S.												
Air strike	0	0	0	0	1	1	1	1	1	1	0	0
Blockade	0	0	1	1	0	0	1	1	1	0	1	0
USSR												
Withdraw	0	1	1	0	1	0	1	0	0	0	0	0
Escalate	0	0	0	0	0	0	0	0	1	1	1	1
Decimal	0	4	6	2	5	1	7	3	11	9	10	8

come. Without escalation, the USSR would prefer that the United States not invade Cuba and not impose a blockade. In the event of either or both of these aggressive actions, the USSR would prefer to withdraw its missiles; without such American aggression, the Soviets would prefer to leave them in Cuba.

1.3.3 Stability Analysis

The notation using 1s and 0s is designed for convenient representation of each outcome, but in order to manipulate the outcomes easily, it is necessary to use shorter symbols. A symbol that has convenient mathematical properties is developed from the outcomes by considering them as binary numbers and then converting them to decimal numbers. A binary number is written as a string of 1s and 0s as is an outcome. Each digit of a binary number corresponds to a power-of-2 value; that is, the low-order (right-most) digit corresponds to 2^0, the next digit to 2^1, then 2^2 and so on. (In a decimal number the low-order digit corresponds to 10^0, the next digit to 10^1, then 10^2, etc.) To convert from binary to decimal notation, simply multiply the number (1 or 0) in each location by the power-of-2 value to which that location corresponds. Thus the decimal value of the binary number 1010 is calculated to be

$$1 \times 2^3 + 0 \times 2^2 + 1 \times 2^1 + 0 \times 2^0 = 8 + 0 + 2 + 0 = 10.$$

When considering outcomes as binary numbers, however, the most convenient approach is to let the top entry in a tabulated outcome be the low-order digit. This means that when the outcome is written in text, the ordering is reversed from mathematical convention and the low-order digit is on the *left* rather than on the right. Thus, outcome (10, 10), where the United States executes an air strike against Cuba and the USSR withdraws its missiles, is converted to decimal form as follows:

$$1 \times 2^0 + 0 \times 2^1 + 1 \times 2^2 + 0 \times 2^3 = 1 + 0 + 4 + 0 = 5.$$

The decimal values of all the outcomes are listed below each outcome in Tables 1.1–1.3. These tables can conveniently be used to translate decimal outcomes to their corresponding real world scenarios.

The decimal preference vectors of Tables 1.2 and 1.3 form the nucleus of the stability analysis tableau for the conflict, which appears in Table 1.4. Beneath some of the outcomes in the preference vectors are numbers labeled "UIs" (unilateral improvement). A UI is an outcome to which a particular player can unilaterally move by a change in strategy, assuming the other player's strategy remains the same. Under normal circumstances, UIs from an outcome are preferred by the player under consid-

Table 1.4 Stability Analysis Tableau for the Cuban Missile Crisis[a]

												U.S.
E	E	×	×	×	×	×	×	×	×	×	×	overall stability
r	s	u	u	r	u	u	u	r	u	u	u	player stability
4	6	5	7	2	1	3	0	11	9	10	8	preference vector
	4	4	4		2	2	2		11	11	11	UIs
		6	6			1	1			9	9	
			5				3				10	

												USSR
r	s	r	u	r	u	r	u	u	u	u	u	player stability
0	4	6	2	5	1	7	3	11	9	10	8	preference vectors
	0		6		5		7	7	5	6	0	UIs
							3	1	2	4		

[a]Simultaneous stability calculations:

$2 + 5 - 1 = 6$, preferred by both players over 1;
$2 + 7 - 3 = 6$, preferred by both players over 3;
$11 + 0 - 8 = 3$, preferred by both players over 8;
$11 + 5 - 9 = 7$, preferred by both players over 9;
$11 + 6 - 10 = 7$, preferred by both players over 10.

Outcomes 1, 3, and 8–10 remain unstable for both players.

eration and appear to the left of that outcome in the preference vector. For example, consider outcome 5 for the United States. From the binary interpretation in Tables 1.1–1.3, it can be seen that in this outcome the USSR has selected the strategy of withdrawing its missiles and not escalating; thus, this is notated as (1, 0). If the USSR maintains the strategy (1, 0), the United States could unilaterally change outcome 5 to either 4, 6, or 7 by appropriately changing its option selections from (1, 0) (air strike but no blockade) to (0, 0), (0, 1), or (1, 1), respectively. Of these, outcome 4 is most preferred by the United States, and is therefore placed immediately under the 5 in the American preference vector in Table 1.4. Outcome 6 is also preferred to 5, and is written under the 4 that has just been placed under the 5. Outcome 7 is not preferred to 5, and so does not constitute a UI for the United States from outcome 5. However, as can be seen in Table 1.4, in addition to outcomes 4 and 6, outcome 5 is a UI for the United States from outcome 7. In a similar manner all UIs for each player are listed under the appropriate outcomes in the player's preference vector in the stability analysis tableau.

For any given feasible outcome there are four types of stability that can be determined for a particular player (Fraser and Hipel, 1979a). The mathematical theory governing these properties is given in Chapter 10. The types of stability for a particular outcome being analyzed from a particular player's point of view are defined in Chapter 2 for a game with any finite number of players. The case for two players is given below:

1. *Rational*. In this situation, the given player has no UI to make from the outcome: the strategy already chosen is the best that can be taken given the strategy selection of the other player. A rational outcome is stable, and is denoted by r.

2. *Sequentially sanctioned*. This is the case when, for all UIs available to one player, *credible* actions can be taken by the other player that result in a less preferred outcome than the one from which the player is improving. A credible action is one that results in a more preferred outcome for the player taking the action. The possibility that a worse outcome could result from a player changing strategy deters the player from unilaterally attempting an improvement in position and induces a type of stability that is labeled s.

3. *Unstable*. Here the player has at least one UI from which the other player can take no credible action that results in a less preferred outcome for the given player. An unstable outcome is denoted by u.

The above types of stability can be determined for each player without regard to the stability results of the other one. However, the following form of stability does require knowledge of the stability of the outcome for both players. In practice, the following type of stability is calculated after the previous three types have been determined, and for the two-player game it is determined for outcomes that are unstable (u) for both players.

4. *Simultaneously sanctioned*. If both players change their strategies simultaneously from an outcome that is unstable for both players, it is possible that a worse outcome for one or both of them could result. If this is the case, it may deter the expected improvement and cause stability of the outcome for one or both of the players. This form of stability is not very common, but is important in the analysis of certain situations and so should be assessed in a thorough analysis of a conflict. Simultaneous sanctioning is denoted by slash ($/$) superimposed over the u that was previously written.

The procedure for determining the foregoing types of stability is quite straightforward. First, check in the tableau for outcomes in a preference vector that do not have any UIs listed under them. Since the player has no improvements to make unilaterally from these outcomes, they are rational and can be immediately marked with an r. Now proceed through each of the remaining outcomes in the preference vectors and assess their stability. This is generally done for each player sequentially. In Table 1.4, outcomes 4, 2, and 11 are rational for the United States, whereas outcomes 0, 6, 5, and 7 are rational for the USSR.

As an example of a sequentially sanctioned outcome, consider outcome 6 for the United States. The United States can improve from 6 to outcome 4. However, by examining the Soviet preference vector it can be seen that the USSR has an improvement from 4 to 0. As shown in the U.S. preference vector, 0 is less preferred than 6, and the United States is therefore deterred from improving from 6 because of the possibility that 0 could come about. Because the USSR would improve its position by unilaterally moving from 4 to 0, the sanction is credible. Consequently, outcome 6 is stable, and an s is written above 6 in the U.S. preference vector. In the actual conflict, this corresponds to saying, "The United States would not relax its blockade of Cuba if the USSR were to withdraw its missiles because the USSR might return the missiles to Cuba."

To demonstrate how instability is ascertained, consider outcome 5 for the United States. The United States has two UIs from 5: outcomes 4 and 6. Since 4 is more preferred than 6 it appears on top of the UI list below 5 and is checked first. The possible improvement by the United States moving to outcome 4 is sequentially sanctioned by the USSR moving to 0 as in the case of outcome 6; but note that if the United States improves from 5 to 6, the USSR can take no subsequent action—6 is rational for the USSR. The United States would therefore be undeterred in taking an improvement from 5 to 6, and to indicate this a u is written above the 5 in the U.S. preference vector.

As another example of a stability calculation, consider outcome 2 in the preference vector for the USSR. The USSR has a UI to outcome 6. From outcome 6, the United States has an improvement to outcome 4, which the USSR prefers more than outcome 2. Since no credible sanction has been found, outcome 2 is unstable for the USSR. The stability of all of the remaining outcomes can be determined in a similar manner.

After labeling all outcomes as r, s, or u for one player at a time, simultaneous stability can be calculated for each outcome that is unstable for both players. Consider outcome 1, which is unstable for both players in Table 1.4. In this outcome the United States has the strategy (1, 0), and to achieve a UI by moving to outcome 2 it must change its strategy to (0, 1). The Soviets have the strategy (0, 0) in outcome 1, and (1, 0) is their strategy choice in outcome 5, which is their UI from outcome 1. The new outcome formed by the United States and the USSR choosing UIs 2 and 5, respectively, is outcome (01, 10). In decimal form this is outcome 6. Since 6 is preferred by both players to outcome 1, 1 remains unstable for both players. If 6 were not preferred to 1 by one of the players, a slash would be placed through the u above outcome 1, indicating simultaneously stability for that player.

Rather than entertaining the binary form of the outcomes formed by simultaneous sanctioning, a more convenient approach is to perform a calculation based on the decimal numbers for the outcomes. Simply add the decimal values of the two UIs together and subtract the value of the original outcome. For the case of outcome 1, which was unstable for both players, the calculation is

$$2 + 5 - 1 = 6,$$

which is the result obtained when the binary form is considered.

When checking whether a given outcome with more than one UI below it is unstable for a particular player, it is only necessary to have at least one UI that is not sequentially sanctioned in order for the outcome to be unstable. If an outcome with more than one UI below it for one or both players in a two-player game is unstable for both players, then it is possible that stability may be induced by simultaneous sanctions. Consider carefully the logic behind simultaneous sanctioning. The UIs used in the simultaneous stability calculation are not necessarily the most preferred UI listed under the outcome, but rather the outcomes to which the players *could* improve. For example, if outcome 5 were to be unstable for the USSR, the UI used in the simultaneous sanctioning calculation for the United States would be 6 and not 4, because the UI for the United States from 5 to 4 is sanctioned by the USSR. Consequently, when checking for simultaneous sanctioning, only the initial UIs that determined the preliminary instability need to be checked as long as the outcomes remain unstable. However, if stability is induced, the next most preferred UI must be checked first for sequential stability and then for simultaneous stability, until all UIs have been exhausted or until instability has been determined. For example, outcome 9 is unstable for both players, and the simultaneous stability calculation is

$$11 + 5 - 9 = 7,$$

which is preferred by both players. Hence, instability for both players is assured, and the stability check is completed. In general, one must check all UIs that were not originally sequentially sanctioned until one that is unstable is found. A player whose most preferred UI is simultaneously sanctioned would naturally choose a less preferred, unsanctioned UI if one were available. In the example above, if the USSR preferred outcome 7 less than outcome 9, then stability would have been induced for the UI to 5 from 9 by the USSR. In this case, the UI to 1 from 9 is checked to see if it is stable due to a sequential sanction. If it is, since 1 is the last UI under 9 for the USSR, the outcome is stable (u). If 1 is unstable, simultaneous stability is calculated again. The new formula is

$$11 + 1 - 9 = 3.$$

In this case, since 3 is preferred by the USSR to 9, outcome 9 would remain unstable.

There are five outcomes in the Cuban conflict model that are unstable for both players (1, 3, 8, 9, and 10). In all cases the outcomes remain unstable after checking for simultaneous stability for the UIs that determine the initial instability. The simultaneous stability calculations for these outcomes are listed at the bottom of Table 1.4.

A summary of the procedure for the stability analysis of a single outcome q for player A in a game in which there are two players A and B is shown as Figure 1.2. In this figure the assessment of simultaneous stability is parenthesized to indicate that this phase of the stability analysis is not performed until the other forms of stability are determined for both players. Further, simultaneous stability is rare, and a quick analysis can be done on a conflict without even considering it; however, a thorough analysis will always involve checking for simultaneous stability.

Figure 1.2 Stability of outcome q for player A in a two-player game.

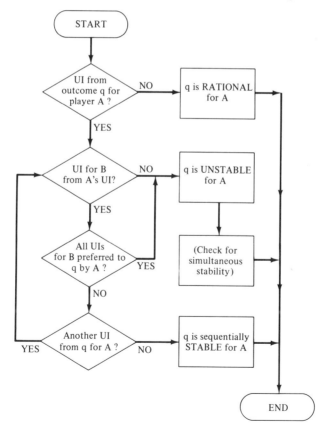

If an outcome possesses some type of stability for all the players in a game, it is called an *equilibrium*, and this outcome constitutes a possible resolution to the conflict. For example, outcome 4 is rational for the United States and sequentially stable for the USSR. This means that if the model represents the real world situation correctly, the scenario where the Soviets withdraw their missiles while the Americans perform no aggressive actions would be likely to persist, should it come about. Outcome 6, where the United States imposes a blockade and the Soviets withdraw their missiles, is also an equilibrium. All other outcomes are unstable for at least one of the players. Equilibriums are indicated by an *E* placed above the appropriate outcome for the topmost player in the stability analysis tableau. An outcome that is unstable for at least one player is marked with an ×.

1.3.4 Results of the Cuban Crisis Analysis

The results of Table 1.4 shed a significant amount of insight into the Cuban missile crisis. For example, a resolution to the conflict will clearly be one of the equilibriums, so the Russians are expected to withdraw their missiles from Cuba. To determine which of the two equilibriums one would expect to be the resolution, a valuable approach is to examine the current situation (*status quo*). The status quo on October 17, 1962 was no aggressive action by the US, and neither withdrawal nor escalation by the USSR. This corresponds to outcome 0. Note that outcome 0 is rational for the USSR, but that the US has a UI that it would be expected to take to outcome 2, which is rational for it. Outcome 2 is unstable for the USSR, however, and the UI from 2 leads to outcome 6. Outcome 6 is an equilibrium, and thus this would be the expected resolution to the conflict. The actions that correspond to this sequence of outcomes are that the United States imposes a blockade (0 to 2), after which the USSR withdraws its missiles (2 to 6).

Outcome 6 is of course exactly what happened in the real conflict. However, after the missiles were removed, the United States dropped its blockade of Cuba, since it did not expect the Soviets to return their missiles to Cuba. In the model, this would be a transition by the United States from outcome 6 to outcome 4. However, according to Table 1.4, outcome 6 is stable since the USSR has a credible sanction against the American UI from 6 to 4. The explanation is that the analysis is appropriate only for a single point in time, October 17, 1962. After that point the preferences of the players are likely to change, thus altering the stability of the outcomes. After withdrawing their missiles from Cuba, the USSR no longer would prefer to have (i.e., *return*) missiles there. This means that the UI from 4 to 0 would not exist, and the sanction on the

U.S. UI from 6 to 4 would no longer be credible. The United States would therefore remove its blockade. (A thorough analysis of this latter time would probably have different options and outcome numbers. An example of a conflict analyzed at more than one point in time is given in Chapter 3, and a more thorough development of the dynamic aspects of a conflict is presented in Chapter 6.)

Another important point to note is that the player's actions will not necessarily correspond to the outcome transitions evidenced in the analysis tableau. The players themselves are generally aware of the implications of the opponent's actions and of their own actions, and therefore may jump ahead in order to try and obtain the best resolution possible for themselves. For example, the USSR may note that of the two equilibriums to this game, it prefers outcome 4 to outcome 6. In the normal course of events, outcome 6 would occur and be the resolution, but the USSR could enforce 4 as the resolution by simply withdrawing the missiles. Consequently, both of the equilibriums possess important implications.

A conflict may have only one equilibrium, or it may have many, although in practice even very complex conflicts have only two or three equilibriums in total. It is very important to recognize that equilibriums are usually meaningful, even if it seems unreasonable to expect a particular one to be the final resolution to the conflict. Very frequently it happens that all equilibriums to a game occur in time: as a conflict progresses, the current equilibrium becomes unstable due to the changing preferences of the players. The conflict then moves to another inherently stable situation, which had appeared as an unrealized equilibrium in the game created for the earlier point in time. This is the situation in the Cuban crisis, and will be seen again in other examples in this book.

The fact that a conflict model is never as complex or as complete as the real world situation it represents must be carefully considered at every stage of conflict analysis. Not only does this mean that the results of a conflict analysis will always contain some degree of inaccuracy, but also that it may be difficult to develop an appropriate model. For example, occasionally outcomes are determined to be stable through strict application of the stability criteria, whereas an examination of them from an understanding of the actual conflict reveals that they are not stable. Often a more accurate model will solve a problem like this, and the approach presented in this chapter can accommodate special adjustments to a particular model.

For a conflict analysis a player's preferences need not be transitive: one is permitted to like outcome x more than y, and outcome y more than z, and simultaneously prefer z to x. (Transitivity of preferences is discussed thoroughly in Part II of this book.) Similarly, a player can prefer outcome x to outcome y while prefering y to x. The UIs listed under a preference vector can accommodate both these situations and indicate a preference vector that is not strictly ordinal. This is a great advantage over other approaches to conflict analysis, as is discussed in Chapter 10.

The definitions and algorithms presented in this book represent mathematical characteristics of game models that have been verified through experience. However, one of the benefits of these methods is their great flexibility in being able to handle a wide variety of special circumstances. The analyst should take advantage of this flexibility when it can aid in the understanding of a conflict problem.

1.4 Important Concepts from Chapter 1

The conflict analysis algorithm for analyzing simple two-player conflicts may be summarized as follows:

Modeling Process

1. Develop background information about the conflict (see Section 1.3.1).
2. Model the conflict (see Section 1.3.2)
   a. for a particular *point in time*,
   b. as a *game* with *players* and *options*,
   c. to create a *meaningful ordering of options*,
   d. to determine the feasible *outcomes* to the game, and
   e. to create *preference vectors* for both players in the game.
3. If considered necessary, a number of alternative models can be developed by repeating step 2. One or more of the most appropriate models is then analyzed at the stability analysis stage.

Stability Analysis *(see Section 1.3.3)*

4. For each model, construct the analysis tableau for the conflict:
   a. List the *decimal* preference vectors for both players.
   b. List *unilateral improvements* (*UIs*) under each outcome.
5. For each model, perform the stability analysis shown in Figure 1.2 for all feasible outcomes for each player:
   a. Mark as *rational* (*r*) all outcomes with no UIs.
   b. For each successive outcome determine if it is *sequentially sanctioned* (*s*) or *unstable* (*u*) by examining the UIs. If for all the UIs available for a given player from a particular outcome the other player can take a UI that results in an outcome less preferred than the particular outcome by the given player, the particular outcome is sequentially stable for that player. Otherwise it is unstable.
   c. If an outcome is unstable for both players, in a thorough analysis it is wise to check for *simultaneous stability*. Add together the decimal values of the outcomes to which the players have UIs and

subtract the original outcome value. If the result is less preferred to the original outcome for all of a player's unsanctioned UIs, the outcome is stable for that player and the u is slashed (i.e., u) to indicate that the outcome is simultaneously stable. Mathematically, the formula is

$$p = (a + b) - q \qquad (1.1)$$

where q is the outcome which is unstable for both players A and B, a is the outcome to which player A can improve from q, b is the outcome to which player B can improve from q, and p is the outcome that results when both players move simultaneously.

    d. If an outcome is stable for both players, it is an *equilibrium*, denoted by an *E*. All other outcomes are not equilibriums and are marked with an ×.

6. If the stability analysis results from one or more of the models suggest that model modifications are required, the appropriate sections from steps 1 to 5 can be repeated.

In this chapter all the terms italicized in the above outline were defined or explained through the analysis of the Cuban missile crisis of 1962. It was learned that more than one equilibrium can be predicted using the game model, but that examination of these can suggest the course of events that will bring about one of them. The *status quo* outcome can be of use in determining the resolution of a conflict from a number of equilibriums. More than one equilibrium can sometimes come to pass as preferences change in a conflict. It was also stressed that the conflict analysis approach allows special circumstances to be accommodated so that the model of the conflict is as close to the real world situation as possible.

Questions

1. Select a current conflict or controversy that is summarized clearly in a newspaper or magazine article. Examine how the writer describes the participants and their courses of action. Try to write down one or more possible conflict analysis models, including players and options. For each model, which outcomes are infeasible? How accurately do you feel you can order the outcomes to your models based on the information in the article?

2. Consider the game called "Chicken," where two thrill seekers drive toward one another at high speed, each driver hoping the other will swerve before they collide. Each player has the one option of swerving. By not selecting this option a given player does not swerve. The most preferred outcome for each player is where the other player swerves, followed by both swerving, the player himself swerving, and, least preferred, a collision. Model and perform a stability analysis of the game of Chicken.

3. Two suspects have been apprehended following a robbery. The district attorney

has insufficient evidence to book them for the crime, but could put them both in jail for a limited time. He offers each suspect the following deal: if one suspect confesses and the other does not, the confessor goes free and his partner goes to jail for 10 years. If they both confess, they both go to jail for 5 years. If neither confesses, they both go to jail for 1 year. Model and analyze this "Prisoner's Dilemma."

4. Llewellyn Thomson believed that Khrushchev might have wanted to escalate the Cuban conflict to nuclear war if Soviet personnel died in Cuba (Able, 1969, p. 53). Reconstruct the Russian preference vector to reflect this view, and perform a new stability analysis. Discuss the results thoroughly.

5. What if the Russians would prefer escalating to war rather than submitting to a blockade? Would nuclear war be expected to occur?

6. Outcome 6 in the U.S. preference vector of Table 1.4 for the Cuban missile crisis was considered stable for the United States because of the sanction of the USSR changing its strategy to produce outcome 0. However, it was later determined that outcome 4 was stable for the USSR, and thus the United States should not expect the sanction to come about, and outcome 6 would not be stable for the United States. Discuss how you think this situation should be handled and what meaning it has with respect to the real world conflict.

7. Why is it not necessary to look at improvements a player might make from the sequential sanctioning outcome formed by another player? For example, if the United States had a UI from outcome 0 that it preferred to outcome 6, would this make 6 unstable? Is it possible to find extra equilibriums by examining cycles of UIs in this manner?

8. Try to construct a game in which there are no equilibriums. If preferences are strictly ordinal, it means that they exhibit transitivity and no two outcomes are equally preferred. (Outcomes are transitive for a player who prefers outcome x to y, y to z, and also x to z.) Can you prove that there will be at least one equilibrium in any two-player game in which the preferences are strictly ordinal?

9. The phrase "the grass is always greener on the other side of the fence" represents a nonordinal set of preferences: a person on one side of the fence invariably wants to be on the other side. Think of a simple conflict between two players in which one of them exhibits nonordinal preferences, and perform a conflict analysis. Will there always be an equilibrium in a two-player game in which preferences can be nonordinal?

Chapter 2
Garrison Diversion Unit

2.1 Introduction

The methods introduced in Chapter 1 to analyze the Cuban missile crisis are equally suitable for the analysis of much more complex problems. In this chapter an international conflict of great complexity is presented and analyzed. The conflict concerns the Garrison Diversion Unit (GDU), a large water resources project in North Dakota that may eventually cause environmental damage in Canada and also in the United States. The major purposes of this chapter are to provide a comprehensive example of a complex conflict study and thereby introduce some important considerations and features in conflict analysis that were not discussed in Chapter 1. Readers who are not concerned with the details of this interesting conflict may wish to skip the historical information and proceed directly to Section 2.3.3, where techniques for outcome removal are discussed prior to performing a comprehensive stability analysis of the GDU conflict model. Using the GDU dispute, Hipel and Fraser (1982) have shown how risk can be realistically considered in the conflict analysis of environmental controversies.

2.2 Garrison Diversion Unit

The GDU is a partially constructed multipurpose water resources project involving the transfer of water from the Missouri River basin to areas in central and eastern North Dakota that are mainly located within the Hudson Bay drainage basin. Figure 2.1 illustrates the major regions affected by the project. When the system becomes operational, water will be pumped from Lake Sakakawea on the Missouri River along the McClusky

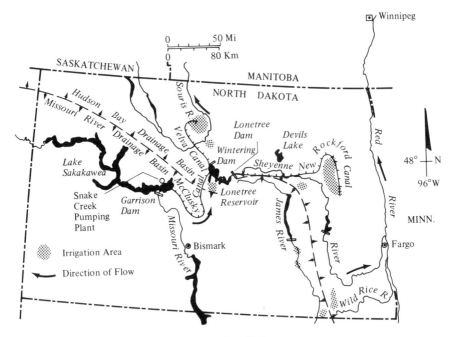

Figure 2.1 Map of the Garrison Diversion Unit.

Canal to the Lonetree Reservoir, which lies within the Hudson Bay drainage basin. From the Lonetree, water will proceed to the major irrigation areas via the Velva and New Rockford canals. The reservoir will also augment the flow in the James River for downstream irrigation. Runoff from the irrigated fields will make its way to either the Souris or Red rivers, which flow across the international border into the Canadian province of Manitoba.

The GDU has a long history, dating back beyond the turn of the century, when the first written request to Congress for construction of a Missouri diversion was made. Numerous other plans similar to the one in Figure 2.1 were proposed and then rejected (Environmental Impact Assessment Project, 1975). The Garrison Dam on the Missouri was completed by the Bureau of Reclamation of the U.S. Department of the Interior in 1955. The resulting creation of Lake Sakakawea inundated some 120,000 hectares of fertile valley land as well as enormous areas of valuable wildlife habitat (Mundry, in Leitch and Keleher, 1974), and apparently left a large unpaid political debt by the Bureau of Reclamation to the people of North Dakota. The Bureau of Reclamation seemed obliged to complete the entire GDU project so that the water from Lake Sakakawea could be used to restore by irrigation the agricultural land lost through the building of the Garrison Dam.

Diversion plans with benefit–cost ratios of 0.53:1 and 0.76:1 were proposed in 1957 and 1959, but were rejected. Finally, a plan with a claimed benefit–cost ratio of 2.51:1 received Congressional authorization in 1965 and construction was started by the Bureau of Reclamation in 1968 (EIAP, 1975). Kremers (1974) points out that this final plan converts 89,000 hectares of farmlands and wetlands into drains, ditches, service roads, and other facilities to irrigate 100,000 hectares that already support prosperous agriculture.

A major benefit of the water for the Americans is irrigation, but other benefits include the provision of municipal and industrial water supply, recreational and wildlife areas, and higher employment. The total economic value of the GDU for North Dakota was expected to reach $122 million per annum (Dorothy, 1973, p. 5).

The conflict over the GDU arises as a result of Canadian fears that the project may cause extensive environmental damage due to the runoff of the polluted irrigation waters, which flow via the Souris and Red rivers into Canada (Boyd, 1975). In addition, American environmentalists are concerned that the environmental damage caused by the project in the United States has been grossly underestimated (EIAP, 1975, p. v). This international conflict also involves the International Joint Commission (IJC), a nominally impartial political entity with special powers over political disputes between Canada and the United States, as specified in the Boundary Treaty of 1909 between the two countries (IJC, 1965).

The first official action on the part of the government of Canada was in April 1969, when questions regarding Garrison were raised by the Canadian embassy in Washington, D.C. This was followed in April 1970 by a diplomatic note crystallizing Canadian concerns (IJC, 1977, p. 7). Diplomatic notes reiterating these concerns were submitted to the American government in October 1971, October 1973, June 1975, October 1976, and April 1978. The October 1973 diplomatic note strongly requested a moratorium on construction of the GDU, and in a response in February 1974 the American government promised to halt all parts of the project affecting Canada. Evidently the determination of the sections of the project that affect Canada is not clear because the October 1976 diplomatic note protests the continuation of the project, and in particular objects to the building of the Lonetree Reservoir.

In February 1977 the Carter administration stopped all funds for portions of the project affecting Canada, including the Lonetree Reservoir (*Toronto Star,* 1977), and a diplomatic note from the U.S. State Department reiterated the commitment to undertake no construction of works affecting Canada. In spite of this, on June 22, 1977 the Senate approved "full funding" for the project (*Toronto Globe and Mail,* 1977). As of 1980 no water has actually entered the Hudson Bay drainage basin but the Snake Creek Pumping Plant and the Wintering Dam are complete, and the McClusky Canal is virtually finished. Construction continues relatively unhindered.

An international mediator exists between the United States and Canada in the form of the IJC, a commission composed of three members from Canada and three from the United States. It may make recommendations and judgments on boundary conflicts as detailed in the Boundary Treaty of 1909, and its powers in the Garrison conflict are outlined in Section 2.3.1. In 1975 the IJC was directed by the two governments to (IJC, 1977, p. 6)

1. report on existing conditions in the area to be affected by Garrison,
2. determine the impact of the GDU on these conditions,
3. make recommendations to ensure that Article IV of the Boundary Waters Treaty of 1909 is honored, and
4. estimate the costs involved.

The report of the commission was completed in August 1977, following submission of the report by its International Garrison Diversion Study Board (IGDSB), in October 1976.

Charges were brought against the builders of Garrison for violating U.S. environmental legislation at least as early as 1972 (EIAP, 1975, p. 5). In 1973 the Bureau of Reclamation was engaged in lawsuits by an environmental organization, an amalgamation of farmers, and a few professional people (Dorothy, 1973, p. 8). The controversial first Final Environmental Impact Statement (EIS) was released by the Bureau of Reclamation in January 1974 (Bureau of Reclamation, 1974). It was heavily criticized as being biased in support of a large diversion project (EIAP, 1975).

In May 1976 the National Audubon Society filed suit against the U.S. Department of the Interior (of which the Bureau of Reclamation is part). An agreement was reached in May 1977 between the two parties requiring a new EIS by January 1978. The resulting EIS presented six alternative plans, one of which was recommended by the U.S. Department of the Interior (1978b). A diplomatic note from the Canadian Department of External Affairs to the U.S. State Department dated April 4, 1978, notes that the revised EIS "does not address substantive Canadian concerns." More detailed background information about the GDU and the conflict that surrounds it can be obtained by referring to the research of Hipel and Fraser (1979, 1980) or the IJC (1977).

2.3 Modeling the Garrison Conflict

The IJC has said that the transboundary implications of the GDU constitute "one of the most difficult and intricate issues the Commission has ever been asked to consider" (IJC, 1978a, p. 18). This high degree of complexity makes it difficult for a decision maker to comprehend the problem fully and eventually reach a reasonable decision. Consequently, conflict analysis techniques are needed to provide a structure for systematically modeling the problem and predicting the possible resolutions or equilibriums to the dispute.

Background information for the following analysis was obtained from the large amount of published material concerning the GDU, although some preference information was developed directly from telephone conversations with individuals involved in the project. April 1976 is selected as the date for which the GDU project is analyzed. As noted in Chapter 1 and also in various publications (Radford, 1980; Bennett and Huxham, 1982; Hipel and Fraser, 1984), it is often advisable to entertain a number of possible alternative models for the conflict being studied. In the GDU dispute, there are actually more than 40 explicitly named participants in the conflict. Consequently, it would be possible to construct complex models for this dispute where there are many players and options. On the other hand, very simple models could be developed by considering the two main groups of players to be Canada and the United States. A number of possible models were actually considered; the model that possessed just enough complexity to represent the dispute realistically is described in this section and then analyzed in Section 2.4.

2.3.1 Players

The many participants in the Garrison conflict can be grouped into four main players, comprising similar interests, shared powers, and common goals. These four players will now be introduced.

United States Support for Garrison. Historically, the greatest support for the GDU has been given by the Bureau of Reclamation of the U.S. Department of the Interior. Friction within the Department of the Interior over this support resulted in the creation of a new entity, the aptly named Oversight and Management Group, to prepare the second EIS for the project (U.S. Department of the Interior, 1978b, p. 14).

The Garrison Diversion Conservancy District is a well-funded and politically powerful organization that also supports the GDU. The director of the Garrison Diversion Conservancy District firmly believes that the GDU will be completed.

Other parties that have expressed support for Garrison include the State of North Dakota, the Garrison Diversion Irrigation Council, the National Park Service, and the North Dakota State Game and Fish Department.

United States Opposition to Garrison. United States opposition to Garrison consists mostly of environmental organizations and private individuals. Environmental organizations include the National Audubon Society, the Environmental Protection Agency, the Bureau of Sport Fisheries and Wildlife (a sister Bureau to the Bureau of Reclamation in the Department of the Interior), and the President's Council on Environmental Quality (Kremers, 1974, p. 36). Relevant environmental legislation that could be used for altering or blocking construction of the GDU includes the National Environmental Policy Act, the Water Supply Act of 1958, the Federal Water Pollution Control Act, and the Migratory Bird Convention of 1916 (EIAP, 1975, pp. 80–89).

Other organizations that have expressed opposition to Garrison on various grounds include the Committee to Save North Dakota, the North Dakota Farmers' Union, the National Farmers' Union, the North Dakota Students' Organization, the National Water Commission, the State Department, the Office of Management and Budget, and the General Accounting Office (Kremers, 1974, p. 36).

Canadian Opposition to Garrison. Canadian organizations that have expressed opposition to Garrison include the Canadian Federal Government, Environment Canada (the Canadian federal environmental ministry), the Manitoba Provincial Government, the Manitoba Ministry of Mines, Resources, and Environmental Management, the Manitoba Environmental Council, the Manitoba Wildlife Federation, the Prairie Environmental Defense League, and a number of municipalities, industries, and professionals.

Legal tools available to oppose the Garrison project include the Boundary Treaty of 1909, the Doctrine of Equitable Utilization contained in the 1966 Helsinki Rules, and the Migratory Bird Convention of 1916. The most powerful of these legal agreements is the Boundary Treaty of 1909, which is discussed further in the next section. Carter (1975, p. 180) affirms that the Boundary Treaty confers legal rights to Canadian citizens in U.S. courts.

International Joint Commission (IJC). The IJC was formed as part of Article VI of the "Treaty Between the United States and Great Britain Relating to Boundary Waters and Questions Arising Between the United States and Canada," commonly called the Boundary Waters Treaty of 1909. The IGDSB, responsible for assessing the transboundary implications of the GDU, was an investigative board commissioned by the IJC on October 23, 1975.

The jurisdiction of the IJC is specified in Article VIII of the Boundary Waters Treaty as follows:

> The International Joint Commission shall have jurisdiction over and shall pass upon all cases involving the use or obstruction or diversion of the waters with respect to which under Articles III and IV of this Treaty the approval of this Commission is required [IJC, 1965, p. 16].

Article IX permits either of the two countries to refer any issue between them to the IJC for study and recommendation, but jurisdiction is automatic only for points mentioned in Articles III and IV. By joint approval of the U.S. Senate and the Canadian Parliament, the IJC can be called upon to give a binding judgment on a mutual concern, under Article X of the Treaty.

Article III says in part:

> It is agreed that . . . no . . . uses or obstructions or diversions, whether temporary or permanent, of boundary waters on either side of the line, affecting the natural level or flow of boundary waters on either side of the line shall be made except . . . with the approval . . . of . . . the International Joint Commission [IJC, 1965, p. 14].

Article IV reads in its entirety as follows:

> The High Contracting Parties agree that, except in cases provided for by special agreement between them, they will not permit the construction or maintenance on their respective sides of the boundary of any remedial or protective works or any dams or other obstructions in waters flowing from boundary waters or in waters at a lower level than the boundary in rivers flowing across the boundary, the effect of which is to raise the natural level of waters on the other side of the boundary unless the construction or maintenance thereof is approved by the aforesaid International Joint Commission.
>
> It is further agreed that the waters herein defined as boundary waters and waters flowing across the boundary shall not be polluted on either side to the injury of health or property on the other [IJC, 1965, p. 14].

The powers of the IJC in the Garrison conflict are based on Article IX of the Boundary Treaty of 1909 via the reference from the governments of the United States and Canada of October 22, 1975 (IJC, 1977, p. 130). Jurisdiction is not automatic because neither Article III or IV are relevant for the Garrison conflict. Article III is for boundary waters, whereas the waters involved in the Garrison conflict are transboundary waters. The jurisdiction given in Article VIII specifies those sections to which "the approval of the Commission is required." In the second paragraph of Article IV, it is not stated that the approval of the Commission is required for pollution problems, so that this paragraph does not provide automatic jurisdiction over the GDU for the IJC. The first paragraph of Article IV refers only to the raising of water levels and is taken to mean the situation where a dam backs up water across the international boundary.

Since the legal basis for the IJC's involvement in the Garrison conflict is Article IX, all recommendations are nonbinding to the two countries. However, the judicial authority for disputes between the two countries may be established by Article X of the treaty as also being the IJC, and consequently the recommendations indicate the direction a judgment would take if called for. However, it may be unrealistic to expect Article X ever to be invoked (it has never yet) because the U.S. Senate is not likely to give up such power.

Manley and Peterson (1975, p. 337) suggest that precedent does provide the IJC with mandatory jurisdiction over pollution in the Souris River. They cite the 1928 reference under Article IX, involving air pollution in the U.S. state of Washington from a smelter in British Columbia, Canada. Also, an IJC recommendation is considered to be the product of the efforts of the best minds from both countries, and so a more sound opinion is not practically obtainable elsewhere.

Because of the above considerations, the significance of an IJC recommendation in the Garrison conflict is unquestionable. Given the special powers of the IJC, and the fact that the IJC represents a unique point of view, it is wise to include the IJC as a separate player in this conflict.

2.3.2 Options

In April 1976, the point in time for which the analysis will be done, the IJC recommendations had been called for by the governments of the United States and Canada. The final IJC report would not be released for another nine months. The first EIS had been released by the Bureau of Reclamation more than two years earlier, and numerous comments on this had been published. Officially, parts of the project affecting Canada had been halted for over two years, although construction had been continuing unabated. The lawsuit by the National Audubon Society had not yet been filed.

Based primarily on the IJC final report (1977), the options found in Table 2.1 may be selected. Note that the players are amalgamated into the four major parties defined in the last section.

In Table 2.1, the player *U.S. support* is considered to be the builders of the GDU project. The options available to this player are much more varied than the three presented, but these reflect the three major types of projects that would determine the responses of the other players. The "full GDU" option represents projects that are not significantly different from the one approved by Congress in 1965. The project modified to reduce Canadian impacts includes undertakings similar to that suggested by the IGDSB in its report to the IJC (IGDSB, 1976). A GDU modified to appease environmentalists has not been clearly specified in the literature, but here would mean a project with which U.S. environmentalists would not find fault.

The single option for *U.S. opposition* represents legal action based on any of the environmental legislation listed in the previous section under this player. Legal action based on the Boundary Treaty was selected as

Table 2.1 Players and Options for the Garrison Conflict

Players	Options
U.S. support	1. Proceed to complete full GDU.
	2. Proceed to complete GDU modified to reduce Canadian impacts.
	3. Proceed to complete GDU modified to appease U.S. environmentalists.
U.S. opposition	1. Legal action based on environmental legislation.
Canadian opposition	1. Legal action based on the Boundary Treaty of 1909.
IJC (International Joint Commission)	1. Support completion of full GDU.
	2. Support completion of GDU modified to reduce Canadian impacts.
	3. Support suspension of the GDU except for the Lonetree Reservoir.
	4. Support complete suspension of the GDU.

the only option for the *Canadian opposition* because it is the most powerful legal tool at its disposal. Other options that might be brought to bear by the Canadians as potential sanctions do not appear in the literature and so have not been included in this analysis.

The options of the *IJC* are somewhat precognitive, but the other parties would be aware of these possible recommendations of the IJC. The first and second options listed for the IJC refer to the same projects described in the first two options, respectively, for U.S. support. The third IJC option is the support of a project incorporating irrigation areas only in the Missouri River basin. Although the Lonetree Reservoir is located in the Hudson Bay drainage basin, it is required for irrigation in the Missouri basin via the James River (see Figure 2.1). By invoking its fourth option, the IJC would support suspending the entire project.

2.3.3 Outcome Removal

Recall from Chapter 1 that outcomes are written as columns of 1s and 0s listed opposite an ordering of players and options, where a 1 indicates that an option is taken by a player in the outcome, whereas a 0 indicates that it is not taken. The outcomes are written horizontally in text, where the order of 1s and 0s is understood to correspond to some meaningful ordering of options. A strategy is a selection of the options under a player's control. Thus an outcome can be considered the situation where each of the players has selected a strategy.

For the Garrison conflict, the nine options in Table 2.1 mean that $2^9 = 512$ outcomes are mathematically possible. In the Cuban missile crisis model studied in Chapter 1, there were only 16 possible outcomes so that it was reasonable to write them down on a piece of paper and then examine them for feasibility. There were four that were not feasible, which were removed from the model before the subsequent stability analysis. Because the GDU conflict is much more complex than the Cuban missile crisis, removal of infeasible outcomes is not as straightforward. In practice it is preferable to end up with not more than 25–50 outcomes after removing various kinds of outcomes from the total set of those possible. This allows for exhaustive stability analyses to be conveniently done by hand, as demonstrated here and in Chapter 1, or else by computer, as shown in Chapter 7.

To explain a comprehensive outcome removal scheme, consider again the Cuban missile crisis model presented in Tables 1.1–1.4. The outcomes that were removed as infeasible are (00, 11), (10, 11), (01, 11), and (11, 11), representing the situations where the USSR removed its missiles and escalated the conflict at the same time. By letting a dash represent both a 0 and a 1, these four outcomes can be depicted more economically as (– –, 11). It is easy to develop sets of infeasible outcomes expressed this way from an understanding of the conflict: the specified options are represented by a 1 or a 0, whereas a dash indicates "doesn't matter." In the Garrison conflict, for example, the three options for the player U.S. support are all mutually exclusive. Therefore, no matter what the other players do, as long as U.S. support selects more than one of its options, the resulting outcomes are infeasible. All of these infeasible outcomes are contained in the three sets represented by (11 –, –, –, – – – –), (1–1, –, –, – – – –), and (–11, –, –, – – – –).

Table 2.2 lists all the outcomes that can be removed from the Garrison conflict model. The selection of outcomes to eliminate in a conflict can be challenging. Four different types of outcomes can be removed.

Type 1. The safest and easiest outcomes to identify for removal are those that are logically infeasible for a single player. Outcomes that involve mutually exclusive options are logically infeasible. For example, in the Garrison conflict the player U.S. support cannot build more than one kind of GDU. Similarly the IJC cannot make more than a single recommendation. Sometimes a certain option for a given player must be chosen in conjunction with one or more other options of the player in order to make sense. For instance, in the Cuban missile conflict of Chapter 1 the United States might have had a separate option called "invade," as well as their option of "air strike." Since a full invasion would under the circumstances necessarily include an air strike, all outcomes in which the option "invade" was selected but the option "air strike" was not would be logically infeasible. Logically infeasible outcomes for a single player pose no danger of loss of information and should be removed before any others.

Table 2.2 Outcomes Removed from the Garrison Model

Removable outcomes	Reasons	Outcomes remaining
Type 1		
(1 1 –, –, –, – – – –)	Mutually exclusive options	432 separate outcomes of
(1 – 1, –, –, – – – –)	for U.S. support	type 1 are removed to
(– 1 1, –, –, – – – –)		leave 512 – 432 = 80 outcomes
(– – –, –, –, 1 1 – –)	Mutually exclusive options	
(– – –, –, –, 1 – 1 –)	for IJC	
(– – –, –, –, 1 – – 1)		
(– – –, –, –, – 1 1 –)		
(– – –, –, –, – 1 – 1)		
(– – –, –, –, – – 1 1)		
Type 2		
(0 0 0, –, –, – – – –)	Some sort of diversion will be built.	32 type 2 outcomes are removed to leave
(– – –, –, –, 0 0 0 0)	The IJC will make a recommendation	80 – 32 = 48 outcomes
Type 3		
None		
Type 4		
(1 – –, 0, –, – – – –)	U.S. opposition will pursue legal action against full project	25 type 4 outcomes are removed to leave
(– – 1, 1, –, – – – –)	U.S. opposition will not pursue legal action if appeased	48 – 25 = 23 outcomes
(1, –, –, 0, 0, 0 –)	Canadian opposition will pursue legal action if any project is built that is larger than that approved by the IJC	

Type 2. The next surest outcomes for removal are those that are preferentially infeasible for one player because of the possible strategy choices for the player. These are outcomes that involve a strategy selection that a player would not be expected to take under any circumstances. For example, although it is possible for U.S. support not to build any project, there is no set of strategies of the other players which would deter U.S. support from building some kind of project. Therefore the outcomes where they do not build a project will not come about and can safely be removed. These outcomes are included in the set represented by (000, –, –, – – – –).

Type 3. Somewhat dangerous for removal are outcomes that are logically infeasible between players. For example, if the players are vying for some indivisible resource, the situations where they both acquire the resource are infeasible. Logically infeasible outcomes can also involve dependencies between players. For example, if an option for player A is to bribe player B and an option for player B is to accept a bribe from player A, then the outcomes where player B accepts a bribe that has not been offered are clearly infeasible and can be removed. The danger of removing outcomes of this nature is that the meaning of the options may be unintentionally restricted. In the bribery example above, the option to accept a bribe from player A may have been intended to mean "indicate a willingness to accept a bribe" rather than actually accepting one. Since a person can certainly indicate a willingness to take a bribe that has yet to be offered, information could inadvertently be lost.

Type 4. The most dangerous outcomes for removal are those involving specific strategy choices for two or more players that are preferentially infeasible for at least one player. For instance, if U.S. support proceeds with the full project, U.S. opposition would probably file legal action. Therefore, outcomes contained in the set $(1- -, 0,-, - - - -)$ are considered to be preferentially infeasible from the viewpoint of U.S. opposition. However, it might turn out that outcomes in this group could come about as the conflict unfolds to an eventual resolution, although none of them would be likely to be an equilibrium. Additionally, no matter how unlikely outcomes of this type may seem, under certain circumstances the possibility that one of them may occur could affect the actions of the players. Ideally, preferentially infeasible outcomes depending on the strategy choices of two or more players should only be removed if there are still a large number of feasible outcomes remaining after the first three kinds of outcomes have been eliminated. When more than 25–50 feasible outcomes are still remaining, outcomes of the fourth type should be removed carefully, keeping in mind the possible consequences upon the forthcoming analyses of the remaining outcomes.

As shown in Table 2.2, for the Garrison conflict, removal of 432 separate type 1 outcomes that involve mutually exclusive options for a given player leaves 80 outcomes. Further removal of 32 type 2 outcomes leaves 48 outcomes. This is still a fairly large number and it would be more convenient to work with fewer outcomes. However, there are no clearly infeasible outcomes left to remove. The remaining outcomes listed for removal in Table 2.2 are of type 4, and their removal may cause errors in the analysis. However, as will be seen, it is possible to compensate for such errors. Removal of the 25 type 4 outcomes leaves 23 outcomes.

Once infeasible outcomes are removed, it is necessary to ascertain the remaining feasible ones. For small conflicts, one method is to write down all the outcomes and then remove the infeasible outcomes, as was done for the Cuban missile crisis in Section 1.3.2. For large conflicts, the simplest and most versatile way is to use a computer program, as is presented in Chapter 7 of this book. However, it is also possible to perform outcome removal by hand for a large conflict using one of the following three methods.

One technique is to count sequentially through all the outcomes, and check them against the list of outcome sets that are to be removed. The ones that do not appear in the infeasible outcome sets are then written down as feasible outcomes. Counting is easy to do. The first 10 outcomes for the Garrison conflict are

$$(0\ 0\ 0\ 0\ 0\ 0\ 0\ 0\ 0)$$
$$(1\ 0\ 0\ 0\ 0\ 0\ 0\ 0\ 0)$$
$$(0\ 1\ 0\ 0\ 0\ 0\ 0\ 0\ 0)$$
$$(1\ 1\ 0\ 0\ 0\ 0\ 0\ 0\ 0)$$
$$(1\ 0\ 1\ 0\ 0\ 0\ 0\ 0\ 0)$$
$$(0\ 1\ 1\ 0\ 0\ 0\ 0\ 0\ 0)$$
$$(1\ 1\ 1\ 0\ 0\ 0\ 0\ 0\ 0)$$
$$(0\ 0\ 0\ 1\ 0\ 0\ 0\ 0\ 0)$$
$$(1\ 0\ 0\ 1\ 0\ 0\ 0\ 0\ 0)$$
$$(0\ 1\ 0\ 1\ 0\ 0\ 0\ 0\ 0).$$

With a little practice, the pattern is fairly simple to follow. The benefit of this method is that the sets of removable outcomes tend to be in blocks rather than spaced out randomly. For example, the above 10 outcomes can all be eliminated immediately because they are included in the set $(- - -, -, -, 0000)$ which is to be removed from the Garrison model on the basis that the IJC will make a recommendation. The first 32 (2 to the power of the number of initial dashes in the outcome set $= 2^5 = 32$) outcomes can thus be skipped without counting through them individually. Similarly, from Table 2.2 the last 128 $(= 2^7)$ outcomes are represented by the set $(- - -, -, -, - - 11)$ and can be skipped over without examining each outcome. The set $(- - -, -, -, -11-)$ represents two blocks of 64 outcomes $(2^6 = 64)$ each because it can be subdivided into the two sets given by $(- - -, -, -, -110)$ and $(- - -, -, -, -111)$.

A second way to perform outcome removal by hand is to subtract the sets of outcomes to be removed from the complete set of outcomes while retaining as many dashes as possible. For instance, consider a 7-option game. All the outcomes mathematically possible in this game can be represented as $(- - - - - - -)$. Subtracting the set of outcomes $(1 - - - - - -)$ clearly leaves the set $(0 - - - - - -)$. Similarly, subtracting $(10 - - - - -)$ from $(- - - - - - -)$ gives $(0\ 0 - - - - -)$, $(01 - - - - -)$, and $(11 - - - - -)$. Since the sets $(0\ 0 - - - - -)$, and $(01 - - - - -)$ can be combined as $(0 - - - - - -)$, subtracting $(10 - - - - -)$ from $(- - - - - - -)$ can also be expressed as the two sets of outcomes $(0 - - - - - -)$ and $(11 - - - - - -)$. They could also be expressed as $(-1 - - - - -)$ and $(0\ 0 - - - - -)$, but

not as (–1– – – – –) and (0 – – – – – –) because these last two sets contain outcomes in common.

To subtract a group of outcome sets from the complete set of outcomes,
simply proceed through the sets individually. For example, consider the
problem of subtracting (10 – – – – – –), (1 – – – 1 – –), (– – – 0 0 – –),
and (0 – – – – – 0) from (– – – – – – –). Subtracting (10 – – – – –) from
(– – – – – – –) gives

$$(0 - - - - - -)$$
$$(1\ 1 - - - - -).$$

Subtracting (1 – – –1– –) from each of the above two only affects the last
set because the first set has a 0 as its first entry. The result is

$$(0 - - - - - -)$$
$$(1\ 1 - - 0 - -).$$

Removing (– – – 0 0 – –) from the above two sets of outcomes gives

$$(0 - - 0\ 1 - -)$$
$$(0 - - 1\ 1 - -)$$
$$(0 - - 1\ 0 - -)$$
$$(1\ 1 - 1\ 0 - -),$$

which, after combining the second and third sets, simplifies to

$$(0 - - 0\ 1 - -)$$
$$(0 - - 1 - - -)$$
$$(1\ 1 - 1\ 0 - -).$$

Because the last of the above three sets has a 1 in the first location,
(0 – – – – – 0) can only be removed from the first two sets to produce
the result

$$(0 - - 0\ 1 - 1)$$
$$(0 - - 1 - - 1)$$
$$(1\ 1 - 1\ 0 - -).$$

The outcomes represented by these sets can now be easily obtained. Each
dash can be replaced by a 1 or a 0, so three dashes, as in the first outcome
set, mean it can be expanded into $2^3 = 8$ outcomes. Similarly, the second
set represents $2^4 = 16$, and third set another $2^3 = 8$. Because the sets
were developed so that there are no outcomes in common, this produces
a total of 32 remaining outcomes. Howard and Shepanik (1976) discuss
subtraction and other operations that can be done with sets of outcomes.

A third procedure for ascertaining which outcomes remain in the game
is to select the feasible strategies for each player and list all combinations
of these. In the Garrison conflict, U.S. support only has three feasible

strategies it can take, expressed as (100), (010), and (001). The U.S. opposition can choose strategy (0), which means to not pursue legal action based on environmental legislation, or else select strategy (1) by implementing legal action. In a similar fashion the Canadian opposition can select either (0) or (1), respectively, by not invoking or else taking legal action based on the Boundary Treaty of 1909. The *IJC* has the four feasible strategies given by (1000), (0100), (0010), and (0001). Because there are three, two, two, and four feasible strategies available to the U.S. support, U.S. opposition, Canadian opposition, and IJC, respectively, there are 3 × 2 × 2 × 4 = 48 possible feasible outcomes that can be formed when all possible combinations of strategy selections are considered.

A systematic procedure can be employed to write down these 48 outcomes. For example, set the strategy (100) for *U.S. support,* (0) for *U.S. opposition,* and (0) for the *Canadian opposition.* If all possible feasible strategy selections for *IJC* are considered while the other player's strategies remain fixed, the four resulting outcomes are

$$(100, 0, 0, 1000)$$
$$(100, 0, 0, 0100)$$
$$(100, 0, 0, 0010)$$
$$(100, 0, 0, 0001).$$

This process can be repeated, allowing each player's strategies to vary in turn, until all of the possible feasible outcomes are recorded.

After this procedure is employed for removing outcomes that involve strategy selection by one player alone, the remaining type 3 or 4 outcomes can be removed. Thus for the Garrison dispute, the removal of 25 type 4 outcomes results in a final count of 23 feasible outcomes.

These 23 remaining outcomes are displayed in Table 2.3. The players and options in Table 2.3 refer to those presented in more detail in Table 2.1. The binary form of each outcome has been converted to its decimal representation, as described in Section 1.3.3. Thus the outcome on the extreme left, written as (010, 0, 0, 1000) in binary notation, has a decimal equivalent of $0 \times 2^0 + 1 \times 2^1 + 0 \times 2^2 + 0 \times 2^3 + 0 \times 2^4 + 1 \times 2^5 + 0 \times 2^6 + 0 \times 2^7 + 0 \times 2^8 = 2 + 32 = 34.$

2.3.4 Preferences

The stability analysis tableau for the Garrison conflict is shown in Table 2.4. Recall from Section 1.3.2 that the decimal outcomes are ordered from most preferred on the left to least preferred on the right to form the preference vector for each player. UIs (unilateral improvements) are determined as the outcomes to which a player can improve by changing the

Table 2.3 Feasible Outcomes for the Garrison Conflict

	34	36	41	42	50	52	57	58	66	68	74	82	84	89	90	146	148	153	154	274	276	281	282
U.S. support																							
Full	0	0	1	0	0	0	1	0	0	0	0	0	0	1	0	0	0	1	0	0	0	1	0
Reduced	1	0	0	1	1	0	0	1	1	0	1	1	0	0	1	1	0	0	1	1	0	0	1
Appease	0	1	0	0	0	1	0	0	0	1	0	0	1	0	0	0	1	0	0	0	1	0	0
U.S. oppos.																							
Legal	0	0	1	1	0	0	1	1	0	0	1	0	0	1	1	0	0	1	1	0	0	1	1
Can. oppos.																							
Treaty	0	0	0	0	1	1	1	1	0	0	0	1	1	1	1	1	1	1	1	1	1	1	1
IJC																							
Full	1	1	1	1	1	1	1	1	0	0	0	0	0	0	0	0	0	0	0	0	0	0	0
Reduced	0	0	0	0	0	0	0	0	1	1	1	1	1	1	1	0	0	0	0	0	0	0	0
Lonetree	0	0	0	0	0	0	0	0	0	0	0	0	0	0	0	1	1	1	1	0	0	0	0
Suspend	0	0	0	0	0	0	0	0	0	0	0	0	0	0	0	0	0	0	0	1	1	1	1
Decimal.	34	36	41	42	50	52	57	58	66	68	74	82	84	89	90	146	148	153	154	274	276	281	282

Note: Best to list binary strategies when developing preference vectors.

Table 2.4 Stability Analysis Tableau for the Garrison Conflict

U.S. support

E	×	×	E^a	×	×	×	×	×	×	×	×	×	×	×	E	×	E^a	×	E	×	E^a	×
r	r	r	r	u	r	r	r	r	r	r	r	u	u	u	r	u	r	u	r	u	r	u
41	57	34	36	42	50	52	58	66	82	74	90	89	84	68	148	146	153	154	276	274	281	282
		36		41			57					90	82	66		148		153		276		281

U.S. opposition

r	r	r	r	r	r	r	r	r	u	u	u	r	r	r	r	s	s	r	r	r	r	r
276	148	84	68	52	36	282	154	148	90	74	58	42	89	153	281	50	58	146	274	282	90	84
274	154	68							74	66	66	68				34	42					

Canadian opposition

r	r	r	r	r	r	r	u	u	r	r	r	r	s	s	r	r	r	r	r	r	r	r
282	274	276	154	148	66	74	68	90	82	84	36	42	58	50	52	153	89	41	34	57	146	281

IJC

r	r	r	r	r	r	r	r	r	r	r	r	r	r	r	r	r	r	r	r	r	r	r
34	36	41	42	50	52	57	58	66	68	82	74	90	89	84	146	148	153	154	274	276	281	282

[a] Outcomes 36, 153, and 281 are false equilibriums.

options under his or her control, given that the other players' strategies remain the same. The UIs are listed under the outcomes in the preference vector as a column with the UI most preferred from the outcome listed on top. To interpret the meanings of the decimal outcomes in Table 2.4, it is convenient to refer to the binary translations given in Table 2.3.

A number of considerations determines the ordering of outcomes in the preference vectors in Table 2.3. First consider the preference structure of U.S. support. It is taken to be politically unacceptable for U.S. support for Garrison not to build some sort of diversion project involving irrigating areas in the Hudson Bay drainage basin. This is supported by Robinson (1966, p. 465), who says of the early days of the current diversion plan:

> Although [an economic analysis] raised serious doubts about irrigation in a region which received adequate rainfall in at least three years out of every four, it was given little attention. No one in North Dakota publicly questioned the benefits of diversion, any more than he would motherhood, virtue, or patriotism.

This view is maintained today, as evidenced through personal contact with individuals associated with the project. It is generally felt that the U.S. government has a binding contract to build the GDU and it is fully expected to do so.

The U.S. support would most prefer to build the full project, but there is no rationale available to distinguish preferences between a project modified to reduce Canadian impacts, as described in the IGDSB report (IGDSB, 1976), and one modified to appease environmentalists. Because of this, they are considered to be equally preferred, except that when the IJC supports a project for irrigation in the Hudson Bay drainage basin, U.S. support would prefer a project to match the IJC recommendation. Thus the first eight outcomes in the preference vector for U.S. support all involve the IJC supporting the full project. In the two most preferred outcomes, 41 and 57, the full project is built with the support of the IJC. Equally preferred outcomes are indicated by a *bridge* (overbar) drawn over the outcomes involved. The bridge over outcomes 34 and 36 indicates the indifference felt by U.S. support between a reduced project and one built to appease the environmentalist, given that the IJC is supporting a full project. When the IJC supports no project for irrigation in the Hudson Bay drainage basin, U.S. support would prefer to ease U.S. internal legal pressure by proceeding with a project that would appease environmentalists. Thus 148 is preferred to 146 and 276 is preferred to 274, but 34 and 36 are equally preferred as are outcomes 50 and 52. Note that bridges may also be used when modeling outcomes of unknown relative preferability, i.e., by treating them as equally preferred.

The U.S. opposition to Garrison has numerous powerful legislative tools at their disposal and is composed of many very motivated groups. It is reasonable to expect that one of these groups will press legal action as long as the project has any adverse and unmitigated effects on the environment. Thus U.S. opposition would invariably prefer to choose the option of legal action on environmental grounds if the full project were built, and would be likely to prefer to choose this option even if the reduced Canadian impacts project option were chosen by U.S. support. If U.S. support elects to modify the diversion project to appease environmentalists, U.S. opposition would prefer not to press legal action. The first six outcomes of U.S. opposition's preference vector in Table 2.4 are the outcomes where U.S. support chooses to build a project that appeases environmentalists. These are all equally preferred for U.S. opposition since this group is appeased and does not care what the IJC or the Canadians do. In the next two outcomes, 282 and 154, U.S. opposition is still appeased but is also taking legal action, which it prefers not to do in this circumstance.

The Canadian opposition prefers no diversion project to be built. However, it has no control in the matter other than to press legal action, via the Boundary Treaty of 1909. If any project were built, the Canadians would generally prefer to choose this option. On the other hand, if the IJC were to support a diversion project, the Canadian opposition would likely be wasting its time and money pursuing legal action because the IJC recommendation is relatively unassailable. Also there is nothing to indicate that the Canadians are likely to prefer the project with supposedly reduced Canadian impacts over one to appease the American environmentalists. Thus in the Canadian opposition preference vector the sets of outcomes given by 274 and 276, 146 and 148, 66 and 68, 82 and 84, and 50 and 52 constitute groups in which the two outcomes are equally preferred.

The IJC was created by a treaty that was to "prevent disputes . . . between the United States and Canada" (IJC, 1965, p. 13), so has an obligation to resolve conflicts between the two countries. According to the Reference of October 22, 1975, "Both the United States and Canada ascribe particular importance to the view of the Commission on this matter [the transboundary implications of Garrison]" (IJC, 1977, p. 132). This suggests that the recommendation of the IJC is expected to aid in the resolution of the conflict, a consideration borne out by an examination of the situation. Thus it would definitely be preferred by the IJC to make a recommendation. However, since the IJC would be expected to retain impartiality, the best *model* for the IJC's preferences among its possible recommendations is to consider them all equally preferred. This is indicated in Table 2.4 by the bridge that connects all the outcomes in its preference vector.

2.4 Stability Analysis

All of the outcomes in Table 2.4 must be analyzed for stability for each of the four players. The four types of stability presented in Section 1.3.3 for a two-player game also apply to games with more than two (say, n) players:

1. *Rational* (r). The player has no UIs from this outcome.
2. *Sequentially sanctioned* (s). The player is deterred from taking a UI from this outcome because credible actions by the other players could result in a less preferred outcome for each of the player's possible UIs from the particular outcome.
3. *Unstable* (u). The player has at least one UI that is not deterred by credible actions on the part of the other players.
4. *Simultaneously sanctioned* ($/$). This type of stability is calculated after the aforementioned three types have been determined for all of the outcomes for each player. When an outcome is unstable for at least two players, simultaneous action by more than one player could cause a less preferred outcome to occur, thereby inducing stability for an outcome previously thought to be unstable for a given player.

[handwritten margin note: find at least one UI which leaves you worse off]

The algorithm of the stability analysis of a conflict with n players is shown in Figure 2.2. The algorithm is very similar to the procedure outlined in Figure 1.2 for two-player conflicts except that a sequential sanction is determined as any outcome formed by the other players consistently improving themselves from the outcome under consideration. This means that not only do the UIs of the other players need to be examined, but all UIs leading from these UIs must also be assessed as possible sequential sanctions. As an example of how the stability analysis proceeds, consider outcome 50 for each of the players. For U.S. support and the IJC, 50 is rational because neither player has a UI available. To indicate this, an r is placed above 50 in the preference vectors of the two players.

The U.S. opposition has a UI from 50 to 58. From 58, U.S. support has a UI to 57, which is also preferred by U.S. opposition to outcome 50, and consequently no sanction has yet been found. From 57, Canadian opposition has a UI to 41, which is also preferred to 50 by U.S. opposition and is rational for all the players. Backtracking to 58, it can be seen that Canadian opposition has a UI from 58 to 42, which is also preferred by U.S. opposition to 50, and from 42 U.S. support can again go to 41. All possible outcomes brought about by consistent improvement by the other players have not resulted in an outcome less preferred to the original outcome by the U.S. opposition, and so 50 is unstable for this player. A u is placed above the 50 in the preference vector for U.S. opposition.

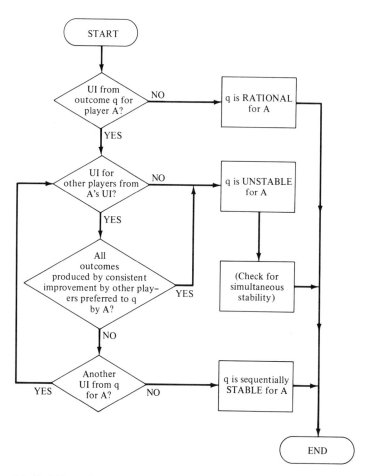

Figure 2.2 Stability of outcome *q* for player A in an *n*-player game.

Note that outcome 50 for U.S. opposition is the most complex search for sequential sanctions in the Garrison analysis.

Finally, consider the stability of outcome 50 for Canadian opposition. The Canadians have a UI from 50 to 34. The U.S. opposition can improve from 34 to 42, at which point U.S. support has a UI from 42 to 41. Outcome 41 is less preferred to 50 by Canadian opposition, and so 50 is sanctioned for the Canadians, as shown by the *s* written above it in Table 2.4. When checking for credible sanctions using the concept of consistent improvement, it is only necessary to find at least one credible sanction in order for sequential stability to be induced. Note that this ensures that no equilibriums are missed, although the dynamics of a conflict may indicate that a player may depart from an equilibrium in the hope that the expected sanction will not endure.

For a given player A, an outcome q possessing one or more UIs is stable only if all of the UIs can be blocked by credible actions levied by the other players. Consequently, in order for outcome q to be unstable it is only necessary to have at least one unsanctioned UI. The overall algorithm for determining whether or not outcome q for player A is sequentially stable is given by the following:

1. Label the most preferred UI for A from outcome q as outcome p.
2. Perform function check(p).
3. If a sanction has been found, UI is sequentially sanctioned. If a sanction has not been found, outcome q is unstable for player A.
4. If the UI is sanctioned and if all of the UIs below outcome q for player A have not been examined, replace p by the next most preferred UI and go to step 2. If all of the UIs are sequentially sanctioned, outcome q is sequentially stable.

The function check(*) consists of the following steps:

1. If a sequential sanction has been found, go to step 5.
2. Determine a UI from * for any player other than A that has not yet been assessed as a possible sanction. Label this outcome as r. If there are no UIs from * or all UIs have been assessed, go to 5.
3. If r is less preferred to q by A, the UI is sequentially sanctioned— go to step 5. If r is not less preferred to q by A, then perform function check(r).
4. Go to step 1.
5. End.

In practice it is a straightforward procedure to apply the above algorithm. After it has been used a few times the intricacies of the procedure becomes quite evident. Keep in mind that for a given UI from outcome q this algorithm checks all possible improvements by the other players from this outcome.

If an outcome is unstable for two or more players, one may check for simultaneous sanctioning. If the outcome is unstable for exactly two players, the simultaneous sanctioning calculation is the same as for the two-player game described in Section 1.3.3. When an outcome q is unstable for m out of n players in an n-player game, the simultaneous sanctioning calculation must be done for all possible combinations of two or more players for which q is unstable. Let a_i be the decimal value of the most preferred UI player i has from outcome q, where q is unstable for player i. When performing the computation for all m players, the formula to use is

$$p = \sum_{i=1}^{x} a_i - (x-1)q, \qquad x = 2, 3, \ldots, m. \tag{2-1}$$

In (2-1), x is replaced by 2,3, ..., m when checking for all possible combinations of players for which q is unstable. If during the calculations outcome p is less preferred to q for any player, then the outcome is stable for that player. This is indicated by putting a slash through the u above outcome q for that player. None of the outcomes in the Garrison conflict was found to be simultaneously stable, and none was unstable for more than two players. For example, in Table 2.4 consider outcome 84, which is unstable for U.S. support and also for Canadian opposition. The U.S. support has a UI from 84 to 82, whereas Canadian opposition has a UI from 84 to 68. The resulting outcome is given by (2-1) to be

$$p = (82 + 68) - [(2 - 1) \times 84]$$
$$= 150 - 84 = 66.$$

Since outcome 66 is preferred by both players over 84, outcome 84 is not simultaneously stable for either player. Occasionally when checking for simultaneous stability in models in which type 4 outcomes have been removed, the outcome p will not be found in the preference vector. An examination of the meaning of such an outcome and its proper location in the preference vectors of the players will determine whether simultaneous stability is induced.

Note also that if simultaneous stability is determined with respect to a particular UI available to a player, the next most preferred UI should be assessed for sequential sanctions. If this next UI is determined to be unstable, simultaneous stability must be checked again with the other unstable players. It is sufficient, however, only to consider the UIs that determine the instability of the relevant outcomes when calculating simultaneous stability.

The only special consideration required when performing an analysis in which equally preferred outcomes are included is in the assessement of sanctions. If a possible sanction, either sequential or simultaneous, is found to be equally preferred to the outcome for which stability is being checked, then the outcome is indeed sanctioned, since there is no advantage for the player to move from one equally preferred outcome to another. Thus, outcomes that are considered equally preferred when ordering preferences are considered as less preferred when examining them for sanctions against UIs. In the analysis, if a possible sanction is under the same bridge as the outcome being examined, the outcome is sanctioned, even if the possible sanction is physically located to the left of the outcome in the player's preference vector.

In order for an outcome to be a possible resolution or equilibrium in the conflict it must possess some type of stability for each player. In Table 2.4 outcome 36 is rational for all four players, and therefore an E is written above it in the preference vector for U.S. support. On the other hand, outcome 50 is unstable for U.S. opposition and therefore cannot constitute an equilibrium even though it is stable for the other players. To indicate this, a × is placed above it where it appears in the preference vector for U.S. support.

In Table 2.2 the type 4 outcomes (see Section 2.3.3) that were removed, though actually feasible, were eliminated in order to reduce the number of outcomes to examine for stability. However, removing realizable outcomes during outcome removal may result in the generation of *false equilibriums*. These are readily identifiable by examining the equilibriums individually. For a false equilibrium to exist, an unsanctioned outcome to which a player can unilaterally improve from the equilibrium must have been removed from the full set. For example, consider outcome 153 from Table 2.4. (Refer to Table 2.3 for a description of this outcome.) A consideration of the preferences of the four players reveals that there is an identifiable UI available for the player U.S. support from "build full GDU" to "appease environmentalists." The resulting outcome, (001, 1, 1, 0010), was one of the group of outcomes removed on the basis of the judgment that U.S. opposition would always oppose any project except one designed to appease them. This improvement is clearly unsanctionable because any combination of feasible strategies by the players U.S. opposition and Canadian opposition are still preferred to the original outcome, and the IJC has no UIs available.

After removing the three false equilibriums (001, 0, 0, 1000), (100, 1, 1, 0010), and (100, 1, 1, 0001), which are decimal outcomes 36, 153, and 281, four equilibriums remain: 41, 74, 148, and 276. The equilibrium given by 41 suggests that if IJC were to support the full GDU, U.S. support would proceed to build the full project in spite of legal action by U.S. opposition. The Canadian opposition would not pursue legal action. From the equilibrium outcome 74 it is evident that if the IJC were to support a project with reduced Canadian impacts, U.S. support would proceed with such a plan, U.S. opposition would pursue legal action but Canadian opposition would not.

In the situations where *IJC* supports a project including the Lonetree Reservoir only (148), or supports total suspension of the GDU (276), U.S. support would proceed to construct a project that appeases U.S. opposition, which would not pursue legal action. The Canadian opposition, however, *would* initiate legal action because of its IJC support.

As events turned out, this model predicts the conflict equilibrium well. The IJC recommended in its report of August 1977 that all portions of the project except the Lonetree Reservoir be discontinued (IJC, 1977, p. 121). This would suggest that the resolution to the GDU conflict, as assessed for April 1976, should be the corresponding equilibrium outcome 148, or (001, 0, 1, 0010). This represents U.S. support building a project designed to appease environmentalists, U.S. opposition not pursuing legal action, but Canadian opposition taking legal action.

The U.S. support appears to have reached its resolution strategy. The U.S. Department of the Interior released its Supplementary EIS to satisfy the May 1977 agreement to the May 1976 suit by the National Audubon Society (U.S. Department of the Interior, 1978a) in January 1978. However, this EIS "does not address substantive Canadian concerns" (diplomatic note, Canadian Department of External Affairs, Canada, April 4, 1978). The six alternative plans presented in this Statement all involve irrigation in the Hudson Bay drainage basin. The report on the plan recommended by the U.S. Department of the Interior (1978b) makes only a brief, one-page mention of the most significant Canadian concern, that regarding the introduction of exotic fish into the Hudson Bay drainage basin. Minimizing environmental damage was an explicitly stated main objective of the recommended plan; the "reduction" of interbasin biota transfer was accorded secondary consideration (U.S. Department of the Interior, 1978b, p. 1). Hence, this appears to be a plan designed to appease American environmentalists.

If U.S. support is successful in appeasing U.S. opposition, the current state of no significant legal action on environmental grounds is likely to continue. Because the suit by the National Audubon Society was settled by the release of the Supplementary EIS, U.S. opposition has now chosen its resolution strategy.

The Canadian opposition has not firmly reached its final strategy. The equilibrium suggests that Canada will pursue legal action based on the Boundary Treaty. Action in the form of protests via diplomatic notes has been continued to the present, but no explicit court action has yet been initiated. Court action may be expected as long as the game retains the format presented in this analysis.

2.5 Important Concepts from Chapter 2

The general conflict analysis algorithm for analyzing n-player conflicts is summarized as follows:

Modeling Process

1. Develop background information about the conflict.
2. Model the conflict:
    a. for a particular point in time,
    b. as a game with players and options,
    c. to create a meaningful ordering of options,
    d. to determine the feasible outcomes to the game by performing *outcome removal* (see Section 2.3.3), and
    e. to create preference vectors for each player in the game.
3. If deemed necessary, a number of alternative models can be developed

by repeating step 2. One or more of the most appropriate models are analyzed at the stability analysis stage.

Stability Analysis. For each model, perform steps 4 and 5:

4. Construct the analysis tableau for the conflict:
   a. List the decimal preference vectors for each player.
   b. List UIs under each outcome.
   c. Indicate equally preferred outcomes with a *bridge*.
5. Perform the stability analysis shown in Figure 2.2 (see Section 2.4).
   a. Mark as rational (*r*) all outcomes without UIs.
   b. For each successive outcome determine if it is unstable (*u*) or sequentially sanctioned (*s*) by examining the UIs (see algorithm in Section 2.4).
   c. If an outcome is unstable for two or more players, check for simultaneous stability (see Section 2.4). The formula is

$$p = \sum_{i=1}^{x} a_i - (x-1)q, \qquad x = 2, \ldots, m, \qquad (2\text{-}1)$$

number of players for instability

outcome q

   where a_i is the UI for the *i*th player from outcome *q*, and *q* is unstable for *m* players.
   d. Outcomes that are stable for all the players constitute equilibriums; all other outcomes do not. Outcomes are labeled with an *E* or × above the topmost player's preference vector to indicate that each posesses overall stability or instability, respectively.
6. If the stability analysis results from one or more models suggest that model modifications are required, the appropriate sections from steps 1–5 can be repeated.

The italicized words and phrases in the above algorithm were defined or discussed in this chapter while presenting the analysis of the conflict surrounding the GDU. It was explained that when an outcome is being checked for sanctions, equally preferred outcomes in a player's preference vector are considered to be less preferred to the one being checked.

Four kinds of outcomes that can be removed from a complete model were presented in Section 2.3.3. Written in the order in which they should be removed, they are the following:

1. logically infeasible for one player,
2. preferentially infeasible for one player,
3. logically infeasible for more than one player, and
4. preferentially infeasible with specific strategies for more than one player.

Four methods of removing outcomes were also detailed in Section 2.3.3:

1. writing down all the outcomes and crossing out the infeasible ones;
2. counting through the individual outcomes and only retaining those that are not included in the list of removable outcomes;
3. subtracting sets of removable outcomes from the set of all possible outcomes in the game; and
4. writing down all combinations of feasible strategies.

Method 1 is usually employed for small conflicts consisting of 32 or fewer possible outcomes, whereas the other techniques are valuable for large conflict models. Employing a microcomputer for removing infeasible outcomes is described in Chapter 7. The generation of false equilibriums because of removing type 4 removable outcomes was demonstrated to be easily handled by a critical examination of the analysis results.

Questions

1. Remove the following outcome sets from a complete model of the appropriate size. Describe the method that you use and show all calculations. *leaves 18... see notes.*
   (a) (–1–11), (0–1–0), (– –110), (00– –1), and (001– –);
   (b) (– – – – –11), (10– – – – –), (1– – –0– –), and (1–1–1– –);
   (c) (– – – – – – –1–), (– – –1– – –0–), and (– – –0– – –0–);
   (d) (– 1 – 1 – – – – – – –), (1 – – – – – – – – – 1),   (– – 1 1 – – – – – – –),
       (1 1 – – – – – – – – –), (0 0 0 0 0 – – – – – –),   (– – – – – – – 1 – – 1),
       (– – – – – 0 1 – – – –), (– 1 1 – – – – – – – –),   (1 – – – 1 – – – – – –),
       (– – – – – – – – 1 1 –), (1 – – 1 – – – – – – –), ·   (– – – 1 1 – – – – – –),
       (– 1 – – 1 – – – – – –), (– – – – – – – – – 0 0),   (– – – – – – – 0 0 – –),
       (– – – – – 0 0 – – – –), (1 – 1 – – – – – – – –), and (– – 1 – 1 – – – – – –).
2. Why are (001, 0, 0, 1000) and (100, 1, 1, 0001) false equilibriums in the Garrison conflict?
3. The IJC did eventually choose to recommend the suspension of the GDU project except for Lonetree. It could thus be argued that they preferred outcomes in which they select this option over outcomes in which they select other options. Perform a complete analysis of a game model that incorporates this preference information for the IJC.
4. Develop both a simpler and a more complex model for the GDU conflict. Explain the circumstances under which the proposed models would be more appropriate than the model analyzed in this chapter.
5. Will there always be an equilibrium in a game with more than two players (assuming strictly ordinal preferences)? *is There a game, where there is no stable*
6. Construct a game in which the UIs form a cycle between some of the players when using the algorithm of Section 2.4. Is the original outcome stable or unstable based on the original UI?
7. The stability analysis algorithm for the n-player case looks at possible sanctions produced by tracing the individual UIs performed by each of the players.

However, in the real world people do not always act independently. It is likely that two players cooperating with one another could sometimes come up with a joint strategy resulting in an outcome preferred by both of them to some other outcome, even though the individual changes of strategy would not be UIs for the players. Would it not be the case, then, that this joint UI could be a credible sanction against some improvement by a third player? Discuss the validity of this argument and suggest an approach for assessing the credibility of such sanctions.

8. Research and analyze a complex conflict as a major project.

Yes, could be assessed, more or less, like a budge.

Chapter 3
Hypergame Analysis

3.1 Introduction

Hypergames are conflicts in which one or more of the players are not fully aware of the nature of the conflict situation. The term was first coined by Bennett (1977), who with Dando also developed the first real world application of the approach in the analysis of the fall of France during World War II (1977, 1979). The fall of France is also briefly analyzed in the next chapter.

The players in a hypergame may

1. have a false understanding of the preferences of the other players,
2. have an incorrect comprehension of the options available to the other players,
3. not be aware of all the players in the game,
4. or have any combination of the above faulty interpretations.

Note that each player in the game has a particular perspective of how each of the other players views the game in terms of players, options, and preferences. A given player's actions reflect a specific understanding of the stability of the outcomes in the game; that is, they are determined according to the way that player perceives reality, which may not reflect the true state of affairs. However, bearing this in mind, the stability analysis algorithms from Chapters 1 and 2 can be applied to the analysis of hypergames. Stability of outcomes from a particular player's viewpoint is calculated according to the way that player perceives the game. Overall equilibriums are based on the stability results determined separately for each player.

In this chapter, two different real world conflicts are examined. First, the Cuban missile crisis described in Chapter 1 is considered as a simple or first level hypergame where the USSR has a faulty interpretation of U.S. preferences. In this situation the United States is unaware of the Soviet lack of information. Following this analysis, the general idea of a higher level hypergame is introduced. In higher level hypergames, perceptions by one or more players are built upon other players' misperceptions of the conflict. To demonstrate how a second level hypergame can be analyzed in practice, the Cuban missile crisis is analyzed for the case where the United States is aware that the USSR has a misperception about their preferences.

The second real world conflict analyzed in this chapter is the Allied invasion of Normandy on June 6, 1944. In this conflict the Allies misled the Germans into thinking that a major invasion of Europe was to take place at Calais whereas the actual invasion occurred at Normandy. Because the Normandy invasion involves three levels of perception (see Section 3.3.2), it is categorized as a third level hypergame. As is the case with any hypergame, the conflict analysis algorithm of Chapters 1 and 2 can be employed to analyze the Normandy invasion thoroughly. The fundamental concepts required for analyzing a hypergame can be determined by reading any of the three examples in this chapter or those in Chapter 4.

3.2 Cuban Missile Crisis Hypergame

One very common form of hypergame is the situation where one or more of the players misinterprets the preferences of one or more of the other players, yet none of the players realize that there are misperceptions occurring. For example, consider the Cuban missile crisis of Chapter 1. There is evidence to suggest that Khrushchev expected a weak response from the United States to the placement of missiles by the USSR in Cuba (Able, 1969; Allison, 1971). One possible manifestation of this expectation is the preference vector for the United States shown in Table 3.1, which represents the USSR's understanding of U.S. preferences. This preference vector can be compared to the true preference vector shown in Table

Table 3.1 Preference Vector for the United States as Perceived by the USSR in the Cuban Missile Crisis Hypergame

U.S.											
Air strike	0	0	0	0	1	1	1	1	1	1	0	0
Blockade	0	0	1	1	0	0	1	1	1	0	1	0
USSR											
Withdraw	1	0	1	0	1	0	1	0	0	0	0	0
Escalate	0	0	0	0	0	0	0	0	1	1	1	1
Decimal	4	0	6	2	5	1	7	3	11	9	10	8

1.2. A conflict in which the players are playing different games, but are unaware that misperceptions are involved, can be modeled as a first level hypergame.

3.2.1 First Level Hypergames

In conflict analysis, a game G can be defined by the set of preference vectors of all the players. For a game with n players this is denoted

$$G = \{V_1, V_2, \ldots, V_n\},$$

where V_i is the preference vector for player i. In games of complete perception, such as those presented in Chapters 1 and 2, all players perceive each others' preference vectors correctly and completely; hence are all playing the same game.

In a hypergame, one or more of the players perceive different games. Player q's game, defined as the game that player q perceives including any misperceptions that q may have about the conflict, is denoted

$$G_q = \{V_{1q}, V_{2q}, \ldots, V_{nq}\},$$

where V_{iq} is the preference vector of player i as perceived by player q. A hypergame H is defined as the set of games as perceived by each player:

$$H = \{G_1, G_2, \ldots, G_n\}.$$

A hypergame is shown in matrix form in Table 3.2 where the qth column represents G_q.

In some cases players' misperceptions may be so severe that the options and outcomes seen will not be the same. For example, one player's option to smile may be interpreted as a baring of teeth by another. In this case a mapping function is defined to relate the options and outcomes among the individual players' games. An algebraic description of this situation is given by Bennett (1980a), and Bennett et al. (1980) present an application. Although Bennett (1980a) has given equivalent definitions for

Table 3.2 Preference Vectors in a Hypergame

Player perceived	Game perceived by player			
	1	2	$\cdots$	n
1	V_{11}	V_{12}	$\cdots$	V_{1n}
2	V_{21}	V_{22}	$\cdots$	V_{2n}
$\vdots$	$\vdots$	$\vdots$	$\cdots$	$\vdots$
n	V_{n1}	V_{n2}	$\cdots$	V_{nn}
	G_1	G_2	$\cdots$	G_n

structuring hypergames, they are here defined in a manner that allows for ready analysis using the conflict analysis algorithm.

The stability analysis for a hypergame is done by treating each player's game separately. Intuitively, this corresponds to analyzing player q's game from q's point of view about the conflict. For q, the decisions made, and thus the strategies chosen, will depend only on how q interprets the situation, whatever the misperceptions.

As noted earlier some outcomes may not be perceived by a player. Since a player cannot make a unilateral change from an unperceived outcome, for stability analysis purposes such an outcome is considered stable for that player. Therefore, even though it is neither rational nor sequentially or simultaneously sanctioned, an outcome can be stable if it is unknown to a player. Hypergames that include an unknown option are presented in Chapter 4 as *strategic surprise*.

An outcome is an equilibrium in player q's game if it is stable in all the preference vectors of q's game. Thus the equilibriums that result from player q's game are those that q believes could resolve the conflict. An outcome is an equilibrium of a hypergame if it is stable in all the preference vectors that the players perceive *for themselves;* that is, the outcome must be stable in all the preference vectors that appear along the main diagonal of the hypergame matrix of preference vectors in Table 3.2. Intuitively, the equilibriums of a hypergame depend only upon the stability of the outcomes as each player perceives them. The equilibriums of each player's game are not needed for determining those of the hypergame, but they are useful in that they show the analyst what each player believes will happen.

3.2.2 Cuban Missile Crisis as a First Level Hypergame

Following the structure established in Table 3.2, Table 3.3 lists the four preference vectors implied by the possible perceptions in the Cuban missile crisis hypergame. In this conflict, the United States has no misinterpretation of the preferences of the USSR. This can be seen in Table 3.3 by noting that in the row corresponding to the USSR, both preference vectors are identical.

Table 3.3 Preference Vectors in the Cuban Missile Crisis Hypergame

Player perceived	U.S. perception	Soviet perception
U.S.	4 6 5 7 2 1 3 0 11 9 10 8	4 0 6 2 5 1 7 3 11 9 10 8
USSR	0 4 6 2 5 1 7 3 11 9 10 8	0 4 6 2 5 1 7 3 11 9 10 8

Recall that when performing a stability analysis for a given player, the preference vectors and UIs for the other players must be considered in order to see whether credible actions exist to block possible UIs by the particular player (see Sections 1.3.3 and 2.4). In a hypergame, the preference vectors that must be compared when performing a stability analysis are those that appear in a single player's view of the game. Thus the columns of Tables 3.2 and 3.3 are treated as distinct games that, for stability analysis calculations, are totally independent of one another.

Table 3.4 illustrates the stability analysis of the hypergame in which the United States does not know that the USSR lacks information about U.S. preferences. All four preference vectors from Table 3.3 are explicitly represented in Table 3.4. In this situation, the game perceived by each player is completely independent of the game perceived by the other since neither player is aware it is playing a hypergame. The first two preference vectors in Table 3.4 represent the game seen by the United States, which can be denoted G_a (a for America). It is exactly the same game presented

Table 3.4 Stability Analysis Tableau of the First Level Hypergame for the Cuban Missile Crisis[a]

American game (G_a)

×	E	×	×	×	×	×	×	×	×	×	×	overall
E	E	×	×	×	×	×	×	×	×	×	×	U.S.
r	s	u	u	r	u	u	u	r	u	u	u	
4	6	5	7	2	1	3	0	11	9	10	8	
	4	4	4		2	2	2		11	11	11	
		6	6			1	1			9	9	
		5					3				10	

												USSR
r	s	r	u	r	u	r	u	u	u	u	u	
0	4	6	2	5	1	7	3	11	9	10	8	
0			6	5		7	7	7	5	6	0	
								3	1	2	4	

Soviet game (G_s)

												U.S.
r	r	u	u	u	u	u	u	r	u	u	u	
4	0	6	2	5	1	7	3	11	9	10	8	
		4	0	4	0	4	0		11	11	11	
		6	2	6	2					9	9	
				5	1						10	

												USSR
E	×	×	×	×	×	×	×	×	×	×	×	
r	u	r	u	r	u	r	u	u	u	u	u	
0	4	6	2	5	1	7	3	11	9	10	8	
0			6	5		7	7	7	5	6	0	
								3	1	2	4	

[a]United States is unaware of hypergame.

in Tables 1.1–1.4, and the stability results are identical. For example, to assess the stability of outcome 6 in the U.S. preference vector, one examines the UI from 6 to outcome 4. The USSR as seen by the United States has a UI from 4 to 0. Since outcome 0 is less preferred to outcome 6 by the United States, outcome 6 is sequentially sanctioned for the United States. Note that the preference vectors indicating the preferences of the players as seen by the USSR are not referenced when determining the stability of outcomes for the United States. The equilibriums determined for the United States are placed immediately above the stability codes written above their preference vector.

The stability of outcomes for the USSR is determined by comparing the bottom two preference vectors in Table 3.4 for the Soviet game, denoted G_s. Note that one does not refer to the preferences perceived by the United States in G_a when assessing stability for the USSR, but only compares the two preference vectors in G_s. Equilibriums for the USSR are placed above the outcomes in their preference vector.

From Section 1.3.3, simultaneous stability must be calculated for any outcome that is unstable for both players in a two-player game. In a hypergame, simultaneous stability is calculated entirely with respect to each player's perception, since it is the *expected* simultaneous action that deters the player from a change in strategy. For example, in G_a in Table 3.4, outcome 1 is unstable in both the U.S. and Soviet preference vector. The calculation is

$$2 + 5 - 1 = 6.$$

Since, in G_a, outcome 6 is preferred to outcome 1 by both players, outcome 1 remains unstable for both in that game. This particular outcome also remains bilaterally unstable in G_s, though there the appropriate calculation is

$$0 + 5 - 1 = 4.$$

For the overall hypergame, a third set of equilibrium information must be ascertained. By comparing the stability results for the United States in G_a and the USSR in G_s in Table 3.4, or equivalently the cells along the diagonal in Table 3.3, these hypergame equilibriums can be found. In Table 3.4 the true, overall equilibriums are written above the U.S. equilibrium information.

The result for the overall hypergame is the single equilibrium 6, where the Soviet missiles are withdrawn due to an American blockade of Cuba. From the U.S. viewpoint in G_a in Table 3.4, both outcomes 6 and 4, which involve the USSR withdrawing its missiles from Cuba, are perceived as being resolutions. However, as interpreted by the USSR in G_s, the status quo position is the only equilibrium in the game. Even outcome 4 is not an equilibrium in G_s since the Soviets believe that the United States is not willing to use any of its aggressive options if the USSR maintains its missiles in Cuba. Thus, the UI from outcome 4 to outcome 0 is undeterred in the Soviet view, and outcome 4 is unstable for the USSR in the hypergame although it is an equilibrium in the game of complete perception presented in Chapter 1. The hypergame approach thus has provided a more complete and realistic model of the Cuban missile crisis.

3.2.3 Second Level Hypergames

Although modeling the Cuban missile crisis as a first level hypergame has provided a better model of the situation, there is historical justification for the idea that the United States was in fact aware of the Soviet misunderstanding (Able, 1969; Allison, 1971). If at least one player in a hypergame is aware that a hypergame is being played, this constitutes a second level hypergame. Such a situation can arise if one or more players perceive another player's misperception. Within a second level hypergame, *player q's hypergame* is defined as the (hyper)game that player q perceives. Player q's hypergame is denoted

$$H_q = \{G_{1q}, G_{2q}, \ldots, G_{nq}\},$$

where G_{iq} is player i's game as perceived by player q. (Player q may not be one of the players who knows that *hyper*game is being played.) In this case, each G_{iq} is identical. If some players' games are missing from the set H_q, it is because they are not perceived by q.

A *second level hypergame* is defined as the set of hypergames as perceived by each player:

$$H^2 = \{H_1, H_2, \ldots, H_n\}.$$

Table 3.5 shows a second level hypergame in matrix form where player p's hypergame appears as the pth column. Note that this matrix is actually a cube because each of the elements of the matrix is a game that consists of a preference vector for each player.

In a manner similar to first level hypergame analysis, analysis of second level hypergames begins by treating each player's game separately. This

Table 3.5 Second Level Hypergame in Matrix Form

Player perceived	Hypergame perceived by player			
	1	2	$\cdots$	n
1	G_{11}	G_{12}	$\cdots$	G_{1n}
2	G_{21}	G_{22}	$\cdots$	G_{2n}
$\vdots$	$\vdots$	$\vdots$	$\cdots$	$\vdots$
n	G_{n1}	G_{n2}	$\cdots$	G_{nn}
	$\overline{H_1}$	$\overline{H_2}$	$\cdots$	$\overline{H_n}$

step produces stability information for every preference vector in the conflict; this can be used to determine equilibriums for each game. Equilibriums for the first level hypergames in the overall second level hypergame are determined as explained in Section 3.2.2.

The equilibriums of the second level hypergame are determined only by the stability information from the preference vectors of each player's game within that player's hypergame as perceived by that player. Thus, they are determined by the stability information that appears along the main diagonal of the second level hypergame "cube" of preference vectors. Just as the equilibriums of a game within a hypergame are not needed to determine the equilibriums of that hypergame, so the equilibriums of a hypergame within a higher level hypergame are not needed to determine the equilibriums of that higher level hypergame.

To reiterate, a game is defined by a set of preference vectors. If all players are playing the same game, the conflict is simply a game G or a hypergame of level zero. If the players are playing different games, then the conflict is a hypergame H of level one. If the players are playing different hypergames, the conflict is a second level hypergame H^2. It is also possible to conceive of higher level hypergames H^l where l is the level. For example, the D-Day invasion of 1944, studied in detail in Section 3.3, is a third level hypergame H^3. The analytic procedure for these higher level hypergames is similar to that of the lower levels with the exception of dimension.

Although it is not necessary to determine the equilibriums of the lower levels in order to determine the equilibriums of a particular level, it is still worthwhile to go through the exercise, since many valuable insights may be found. By analyzing each level, one determines the players' expectations. Combining these results with the players' intentions at the various levels, the analyst has a clear view of each player's strategy. The tactics that a player uses to support those strategies then provide a means for checking the model. In addition, while performing an analysis, the analyst may discover that there is some information missing that should be known. This can then be procured before completing the analysis. Once the analysis is complete at all levels, the analyst has a complete and clear view of the structure of the conflict. Establishing this viewpoint is the primary objective of hypergame analysis.

3.2.4 Cuban Missile Crisis as a Second Level Hypergame

Table 3.6 illustrates the overall structure of the second level hypergame. Each of the two players perceives a different hypergame, labeled H_a and H_s for American and Soviet, respectively. Each hypergame contains two games, G_{aa} and G_{sa} in H_a, and G_{as} and G_{ss} in H_s. The games G_{sa}, G_{as},

Table 3.6 Cuban Missile Crisis as a Second Level Hypergame

Cuban missile crisis second level hypergame H^2	
American hypergame H_a	
American game G_{aa}	*Soviet game* G_{sa}
U.S. 4 6 5 7 2 1 3 0 11 9 10 8	4 0 6 2 5 1 7 3 11 9 10 8
USSR 0 4 6 2 5 1 7 3 11 9 10 8	0 4 6 2 5 1 7 3 11 9 10 8
Soviet hypergame H_s	
American game G_{as}	*Soviet game* G_{ss}
U.S. 4 0 6 2 5 1 7 3 11 9 10 8	4 0 6 2 5 1 7 3 11 9 10 8
USSR 0 4 6 2 5 1 7 3 11 9 10 8	0 4 6 2 5 1 7 3 11 9 10 8

and G_{ss} are identical since the Soviets do not realize that there is a mis-perception, and the United States correctly understands the Soviet view of the situation.

To perform a stability analysis of the conflict in Table 3.6 one could first individually analyze the four separate games denoted by G_{aa}, G_{sa}, G_{as}, and G_{ss}. To obtain the equilibrium results within each of these four games, only the stability results for the two preference vectors in each individual game are compared. Then, to ascertain the equilibriums in the U.S. first level hypergame H_a, the stability information for the U.S. preference vector in G_{aa} and the Soviet preference vector in G_{sa} are considered. In a similar fashion, the equilibriums in the first level hypergame H_s for the USSR is obtained by entertaining the stability results for the U.S. preference vector in G_{as} and the Soviet preferences in G_{ss}. Finally, to procure the equilibriums for the overall second level hypergame H^2, the stability results for the U.S. preference vector in G_{aa} and the USSR preference vector in G_{ss} are examined. In a complex higher order hypergame such as the Normandy invasion conflict analyzed later in this chapter, it is necessary to follow an elaborate analysis procedure similar to the one just described for the Cuban missile crisis. However, for a game like the Cuban missile crisis in Table 3.6 where most of the preference vectors are the same and only one player perceives a hypergame, the expression and analysis of the game is much simpler.

The short form of the hypergame stability analysis tableau for the Cuban missile crisis, given the situation where the United States is aware that the USSR perceives it to prefer a weak response, is shown in Table 3.7. Note that only the three distinct preference vectors in the hypergame are listed: the U.S. vector, the U.S. vector as perceived by the USSR, and that of the USSR. In order to analyze the stability of the outcomes in each preference vector, it is only necessary to relate the appropriate vectors.

In Table 3.7, possible sequential sanctions against UIs in the U.S. preference vector are determined by examining the Soviet preference vector, since the United States correctly sees the Soviet preferences. However, when assessing the stability of outcomes for the USSR, sanctions are checked with respect to its perception of the United States rather than against true U.S. preferences, since it has a misperception. Stability for outcomes in the preference vector representing the Soviet view of the United States is determined with respect to the preference vector of the USSR also. For example, consider outcome 4 for the USSR. It has a UI from outcome 4 to outcome 0. In the preference vector representing their perceptions of the US, there is no UI from 0, so outcome 4 is unstable for the USSR. The USSR does not know that the United States has a UI from 0 to 2, so the USSR cannot be deterred from moving from 4 to 0. This can be contrasted with the analysis for the game of Chapter 1, where it was determined that outcome 4 was stable for the USSR because of the credible sanction of the United States improving from outcome 0 to 2.

Table 3.7 Stability Analysis Tableau of the Second Level Hypergame for the Cuban Missile Crisis[a]

U.S.

×	E	×	×	×	×	×	×	×	×	×	×
×	E	×	×	×	×	×	×	×	×	×	×
r	s	u	u	r	u	u	u	r	u	u	u
4	6	5	7	2	1	3	0	11	9	10	8
	4	4	4		2	2	2		11	11	11
	6	6	6		1	1	1			9	9
	5					3					10

U.S. perceived by USSR

r	r	u	u	u	u	u	u	r	u	u	u
4	0	6	2	5	1	7	3	11	9	10	8
		4	0	4	0	4	0		11	11	11
		6		6	2	6	2			9	9
				5		5	1				10

USSR

E	×	×	×	×	×	×	×	×	×	×	×
r	u	r	u	r	u	r	u	u	u	u	u
0	4	6	2	5	1	7	3	11	9	10	8
	0		6		5		7	7	5	6	0
								3	1	2	4

[a]United States is aware of hypergame.

Simultaneous stability must be calculated for any outcome that is unstable for both players in each individual player's perception in the second level hypergame. Thus for the American preference vector in G_{aa} of Table 3.6, simultaneous stability is determined with reference to the stability of the Soviet preference vector in G_{ss}, because the United States is aware of the fact that the USSR is going to react according to their misunderstanding of the conflict. On the other hand, simultaneous stability for the USSR in G_{ss} is determined by looking at the U.S. preference vector in G_{ss} since the USSR is unaware that a hypergame is taking place. Similarly, if simultaneous stability calculations are desired for any other preference vector, one decides which preference vector in the overall hypergame reflects the player's perception of the conflict. For example, in G_{sa} simultaneous stability would be simply between the two preference vectors in the game because neither of these players is aware that a hypergame is being played.

In the short form analysis tableau, the important preference vectors for determining simultaneous stability are those displayed in Table 3.7, since these reflect the two players' perceptions of one another's preferences. Thus for the outcome 3, the simultaneous stability calculation for the USSR is $0 + 7 - 3 = 4$, rather than $2 + 7 - 3 = 6$, because in their perception of the United States, the United States would improve from 3 to 0 rather than from 3 to 2.

Equilibriums for the hypergame are determined by correctly relating the stability information. The equilibrium perceived by the United States is determined by comparing its stability information with the stability for the true preferences of the USSR, and this is listed immediately above the stability information above the U.S. preference vector. In this case the United States perceives one equilibrium, outcome 6. Similarly, the equilibrium envisioned by the USSR is determined by comparing the Soviet preference vector with the stability of their view of the U.S. preferences. This is given above the Soviet preference vector, and it can be seen in Table 3.7 that the USSR expects outcome 0 to occur. However, outcome 0 is unstable for the actual U.S. preference vector, whereas outcome G is stable (rational) for the USSR and is therefore the overall equilibrium. This is the same equilibrium given by the U.S. results because the United States perceives the true state of the situation.

Note that the analysis of the Soviet game in Table 3.7 provides the results for G_{sa}, G_{as}, and G_{ss} of Table 3.6. The analysis of the U.S. game in Table 3.7 gives the U.S. stability results for G_{aa}, but not the Soviet stability for this game. The Soviet stability in G_{aa} is not very important in understanding the overall hypergame, but if desired it can still be ascertained by comparing the preference vector for the USSR with the true preferences for the United States. Also observe that the equilibriums for

H_a are the same as the ones determined for the United States, and similarly the equilibriums for H_s are those found for the USSR.

The results in Table 3.7 provide a reasonable explanation for the activities of the players in the conflict. The USSR perceives the single equilibrium given by outcome 0 as being the status quo. It does not expect coercive action by the United States. In reality, however, the single equilibrium is 6, as seen by the United States. It should be noted that as soon as the United States invokes one of its options, the USSR immediately realizes its error, and the hypergame collapses into the simple game treated in Chapter 1.

The short form of a hypergame such as the one in Table 3.7 is convenient for analyzing less complicated second level hypergames. Three examples that employ this format are presented in Chapter 4. However, in more complex models it is still necessary to analyze each game within the hypergame in order to comprehend fully all of the important characteristics of the game. One such complex conflict is the Allied invasion of Normandy in 1944.

3.3 Hypergame Analysis of the Normandy Invasion

The Allied invasion of Normandy on June 6, 1944 (D-Day) was an important event since it provided the Allies with a beachhead in France, which eventually led to the end of World War II. Because this conflict can be conveniently modeled as a third level hypergame, it demonstrates the flexibility of hypergames for the analysis of complex levels of deception in real world problems. Additionally, the study clarifies historically why the Normandy invasion was successful in spite of the powerful German defenses.

Most of the historical information used in this chapter for the analysis of the D-Day invasion has been drawn from the authoritative book entitled *The Second Front* by D. Botting (1978). The interested reader may wish to refer to the substantial reference list contained in this book for more detailed information about the D-Day invasion. Also, the paper by Takahashi et al. (1984) provides a more detailed explanation of the analysis of the D-Day hypergame.

3.3.1 Historical Background

Until June 6, 1944, Germany had complete control of Western Europe, with the western coast heavily fortified against an Allied invasion. Even though Germany was pulling back on the Eastern Front, it also still occupied large sections of European Russia. Stalin demanded that the Allies, which included the United States, Britain, and Canada, begin an invasion of the European continent to draw some of the pressure away from the Soviet Union.

Germany's coastal defenses were very strong. Called the "Atlantic Wall," this front stretched for 3500 kilometers from Norway to Spain. At the most likely invasion locations, 15,000 permanent strong points were constructed and 300,000 troops were assigned to their defense. The heaviest concentration of defenses was placed at the narrowest part of the channel, between the Netherlands and Le Havre in Normandy. Along the channel coast, Dr. Fritz Todt and Reich minister Albert Speer placed half a million assorted antiinvasion obstacles and four million mines. Logs and steel beams were driven into the sand tipped with mines or metal cutters to gut landing craft. Concrete antitank obstacles lined the beaches. Large inland areas were flooded and antiglider obstacles were put up to impede airborne invaders. As well, Germany's air and land military forces (seven armored divisions and the seventh and fifteenth armies were in Western Europe) could be used to back up the coastal defences to repel any invasion back to the sea.

An Allied invasion would first have to overpower the German coastal defenses at some point. Then enough forces and supplies would have to be landed to establish a base from which continental military operations could be launched. The invasion and securement of a base would have to be accomplished before the German air and land forces could be brought to repel the invaders. Therefore, if an Allied invasion were to be successful, the German backup forces would have to be at a sufficient distance from the point of invasion to allow the Allies to establish a base. Because the invasion required a great deal of planning and preparation, the Allies had to commit themselves to one location and try to lead Germany into believing that the invasion was going to occur at another location. This plan was code-named "Operation Overlord" by the Allies, and a 95-kilometer stretch of the Normandy coast was chosen as the actual point of invasion.

The Allies had many factors in their favor. Their primary asset was that of information. The French Resistance was able to keep an accurate and timely account of Germany's military force movements. Also, the Allies had broken the German codes and were aware of Germany's intentions and movements. Finally, for the thrust of the invasion, the Allies had at their disposal 3467 heavy bombers, 1645 medium, light, and torpedo bombers, and 5409 fighters in the air, 5000 ships in the sea, and 170,000 assault troops for the land.

Germany, on the other hand, was not as well informed about the Allied power and movements. Additionally, its main coastal defenses were spread over hundreds of kilometers, and its support forces were scattered over a large area. A successful repulsion of an Allied invasion would require that sufficient backup forces be close to the point of invasion. Considering the potential size of the inevitable invasion and the time required to move support forces into action, Germany would have to anticipate the location of the invasion in order to be successful in preventing the Allies from building a base on the continent.

Both Germany and the Allies perceived Germany's need for preparation. Similarly, both Germany and the Allies perceived the Allies' need for deception. "Operation Fortitude" was the code name for the set of plans that the Allies developed to draw the German forces away from Normandy. The most important of these plans was the deception at Pas-de-Calais.

Both Calais and Normandy were acknowledged by Germany and the Allies as suitable Allied invasion points. Each of these locations met the many factors required to establish a base. Calais, being closer and more obvious, was more heavily defended. Topographically, Calais possessed high cliffs, narrow beaches, and restricting exits to the mainland. Also, the local ports and those in England opposite Calais had a small capacity. Normandy, on the other hand, was less heavily defended and had high capacity beaches that were sheltered from the prevailing winds. The inland terrain was suitable for airfield development and the port at Cherbourg and those opposite in England were large. Thus Normandy, though farther from England, was preferred by the Allies.

The deception at Calais was carried out in two overlapping phases. The first phase was to persuade Germany that the invasion was to occur at Calais. Some of the tactics that were employed to this end included the following:

1. Allied agents in neutral capitals began buying maps of Calais. Some of these agents would be under surveillance by German agents.
2. A false army group of 50 divisions, complete with fake camps, hospitals, tanks, planes, and an oil dock, were created in England for the Calais invasion.
3. Known German agents were persuaded that Calais would be the invasion point.

The second phase, which began just before the invasion and lasted for two days afterward, was aimed at persuading Germany that the main invasion was occurring at Calais and that the Normandy invasion was only a feint. It included a variety of tactics:

1. A diversionary force was sent to Calais. Airplanes dropped precisely cut strips of aluminum foil to fool the German radar operators into thinking that a huge fleet of fighter planes was approaching. Motor launches were fitted with balloons with reflectors to mimic large troop transports.
2. Dummies were dropped by parachute over Normandy to reinforce the idea that the Normandy invasion was only a feint.

3. Radio transmissions were jammed. German language broadcasts were made on Luftwaffe frequencies to direct pilots to Calais.

The Normandy invasion began with the bombardment of the coastal defenses and a paratroop and glider assault in the fields behind the front. The diversionary tactics at Calais worked so well that the German backup forces were all sent there to meet the imaginary fleet. As a result, the Normandy invasion forces met much less resistance and were able to establish a base of operations. The deception was so successful that Germany did not realize that the main invasion was occurring at Normandy until two days after the initial assault. By then the Allies were establishing the beach landings and were soon to capture Cherbourg. The Allies were able to land troops, tanks, and supplies faster than the German tank divisions could arrive from the east. In less than one year, Germany surrendered after Allied forces successfully invaded Germany itself.

3.3.2 Modeling D-Day as a Hypergame

The D-Day conflict is best modeled as a third level hypergame at the time immediately before the invasion. The Allies and Germany are the two players in the conflict. The Allies have the options of invading Normandy and invading Calais. Germany also possesses two options, which are to defend Normandy and defend Calais. Since neither player can exercise both its options at the same time, seven of the possible 16 outcomes are infeasible and can be removed. Table 3.8 illustrates the feasible outcomes for the conflict.

In the D-Day conflict, both players are aware of each other's existence and options. However, they do not both perceive each other's preferences correctly. It is a third level hypergame because the Allies have led the Germans into having a misperception of a second level hypergame.

Allies' Perception. The Allies have persuaded Germany into believing that Normandy is only a feint. The Allies will invade Normandy believing

Table 3.8 Feasible Outcomes for D-Day

Allies									
Invade Normandy	0	1	0	0	1	0	0	1	0
Invade Calais	0	0	1	0	0	1	0	0	1
Germany									
Defend Normandy	0	0	0	1	1	1	0	0	0
Defend Calais	0	0	0	0	0	0	1	1	1
Decimal	0	1	2	4	5	6	8	9	10

that Germany will defend Calais. In Germany's perception as seen by the Allies, the Allies will invade Calais and Germany will defend Calais. In other words, the feint has worked.

Germany's Perception. Germany believes that Normandy is a feint and that the Allies' true target is Calais. Germany, therefore, will defend Calais believing that the Allies will strike its forces head on. In the Allies' perception as seen by Germany, the Allies will invade Calais believing that Germany will defend Normandy. Germany believes that it has misled the Allies into believing that the feint at Normandy has worked.

Preference Vectors. Given the above description of the players' misperceptions, it can be seen that there are four distinct orderings of the outcomes in the hypergame. For the Allies, the outcomes are ordered according to their true preference of attacking at Normandy. However, a different preference ordering for the Allies is required to represent the possible German view of their preferences: the Germans expect the Allies to attack at Calais rather than Normandy. Similarly, the German preference vectors can either represent the Germans preferring a defense at Calais or at Normandy.

The four possible preference vectors that can be experienced or perceived by the players in the D-Day hypergame are presented in Table 3.9 along with a label to represent each one. The binary interpretation of the decimal outcomes in Table 3.9 can be formed by referring to Table 3.8. The following assumptions were made to complete the preference ordering of the outcomes in these preference vectors.

1. The Allies preferred to invade even if it meant they would meet a strong German defense at the point of invasion. This is a valid assumption because Stalin was pressuring the Allies for a second front and they did not want Stalin to occupy Germany on his own.

Table 3.9 Preference Vectors for D-Day

Allies prefer to invade at Normandy									
9	1	5	6	2	10	8	4	0	(INV NOR)
Allies prefer to invade at Calais									
6	2	10	9	1	5	4	8	0	(INV CAL)
Germany prefers to defend at Normandy									
4	5	6	0	1	2	8	10	9	(DEF NOR)
Germany prefers to defend at Calais									
8	10	9	0	2	1	4	5	6	(DEF CAL)

2. The Allies preferred to have Germany defend the wrong point than no defense at all. This is reasonable because being committed to a defense at the wrong point would mean less defense at the point of invasion.

3. Germany preferred not to defend at either point over defending at the wrong point, because the German forces would be concentrated out of position.

4. The Allies were committed to an invasion and, of the two choices of Normandy or Calais, they preferred Normandy no matter what Germany did.

5. Germany was convinced that the Allies would launch an invasion. They were committed to defend somewhere, and they preferred to defend where they believed the Allies would invade.

Note that at the moment chosen for analysis—immediately before the invasion—the two sides are committed to the strategy of attacking or defending either Normandy or Calais. Usually the Allies would prefer to attack at Calais and have the Germans defend at Normandy (outcome 6) rather than attack at Normandy and have the Germans defend Normandy (outcome 5). However, at a time close to the invasion, the Allies' preferences are *lexicographic:* they simply prefer Normandy over Calais, independent of Germany's actions. These lexicographic preferences on the part of both players are a consequence of the time and effort it takes to mount an attack or a defense at either location. It is possible for the Allies to change all its plans at the last minute and attack Calais instead, but it would prefer not to do so. Since the players are committed, in order to achieve their objectives they must mislead the opposition somehow. The Allies must convince the Germans that they prefer to attack Calais; the Germans must meet the Allies wherever they land. Hypergame analysis can be used to reveal the structure and implications of these deceptions.

3.3.3 Hypergame Structure

The information about the misperceptions of the players and the preference vectors that have been developed can now be put together into a formal hypergame model, shown in Table 3.10. In this table, A (or a) and G (or g) stand for the Allies and Germany, respectively. The preference vectors have been represented by labels denoting their main decision (compare Table 3.9). Thus, INV NOR represents the Allied preference vector in which the Allies commit their forces to invading at Normandy.

Table 3.10 clearly shows the hierarchical structure of the conflict in one tableau. The overall third level hypergame is comprised of two second level hypergames, one for each player. These second level hypergames

Table 3.10 D-Day Hypergame

D-Day third level hypergame H^3			
Allies' second level hypergame H_a^2			
Allies' hypergame H_{aa}		Germany's hypergame H_{ga}	
Allies' Game G_{aaa}	Germany's Game G_{gaa}	Allies' Game G_{aga}	Germany's Game G_{gga}
A INV NOR	A INV CAL	A INV CAL	A INV CAL
G DEF CAL	G DEF CAL	G DEF NOR	G DEF CAL
Germany's second level hypergame H_g^2			
Allies' hypergame H_{ag}		Germany's hypergame H_{gg}	
Allies' Game G_{aag}	Germany's Game G_{gag}	Allies' Game G_{agg}	Germany's Game G_{ggg}
A INV CAL	A INV NOR	A INV CAL	A INV CAL
G DEF NOR	G DEF NOR	G DEF NOR	G DEF CAL

are comprised of two hypergames, which in turn are comprised of two simple games. The objectives and intentions of each player at every level of the conflict are clearly laid out in a simple structure.

Consider the games in the Allies' second level hypergame denoted H_a^2. In the Allies' hypergame in H_a^2, denoted H_{aa}, there are two games, labeled G_{aaa} and G_{aaa}, for the Allies' game and the German game, respectively. In H_{aa}, the Allies have successfully duped the Germans into believing the attack is to take place at Calais, although their preference is to attack at Normandy. However, as demonstrated in the hypergame H_{ga}, the conflict is more complicated: the Germans think that the Allies' true preference is indeed to attack at Calais.

In H_g^2, there is a different second level hypergame seen by the Germans. The hypergame H_{ag} represents what the Germans think the Allies believe is happening in the conflict; namely, that the Allies have duped the Germans into defending Normandy when the true attack is to occur at Calais. However the Germans, in H_{gg}, believe they have perceived the deception and have every intention of defending Calais thoroughly.

3.3.4 Stability Analysis of the D-Day Hypergame

Given the overall structure of the hypergame developed in the Section 3.3.3, it is now possible to analyze it to determine the possible resolutions to the conflict. Each game in the hypergame is analyzed individually; the resulting stability information can then be used to draw conclusions about each level of the hypergame.

Consider the analysis of the hypergame H_{aa}. The complete stability analysis of this hypergame is presented in Table 3.11. The appropriate preference vectors from Table 3.9 have replaced the abbreviations used in Table 3.10, and UIs are listed below their proper outcomes.

Analyzing all the outcomes in the two games of the hypergame of Table 3.11 results in a stability determination for each outcome in every preference vector. Note that for simultaneous stability, one may have to consider the stability of vectors outside the game under consideration. For the Allies' preference vector in the game G_{aaa}, for example, it is necessary to compare the Germans' preference vector in G_{ggg} since the Allies are aware that the Germans are playing a hypergame. The Germans in G_{ggg}, on the other hand, would assess possible simultaneous deterrents with respect to their view of the Allies' stability, which would be found as the Allies' preference vector in G_{aag}.

For each game, an outcome has overall stability, or is an equilibrium, if it is stable for every player in the game. In the Allies' game in Table 3.11, there is a single equilibrium at outcome 9, where the Allies invade Normandy and the Germans defend Calais. In the German game the single equilibrium is outcome 10 where both players meet at Calais.

Table 3.11 Stability Analysis of the Hypergame H_{aa} for D-Day

Allies' game (G_{aaa})

									Hypergame equilibrium
E	×	×	×	×	×	×	×	×	Allies
E	×	×	×	×	×	×	×	×	
r	r	r	u	u	u	u	u	u	
9	1	5	6	2	10	8	4	0	
		5	1	9	9	5	1		
			10	6	2				Germany
r	r	r	u	u	u	u	u	u	
8	10	9	0	2	1	4	5	6	
		8	10	9	8	9	10		
			0	1	2				

Germany's game (G_{gaa})

									Allies
r	r	r	u	u	u	u	u	u	
6	2	10	9	1	5	4	8	0	
		10	2	6	6	10	2		
			5	9	1				Germany
×	E	×	×	×	×	×	×	×	
r	r	r	u	u	u	u	u	u	
8	10	9	0	2	1	4	5	6	
		8	10	9	8	9	10		
			0	1	2				

The equilibrium for the first level hypergame is, of course, based upon each player's stability according to that player's view of the situation. Consequently, in Table 3.11 this is determined by comparing the stability for the Allies in the Allies' game with the stability for the Germans in the German game. In this case there is again the single equilibrium at 9, where the invasion at Normandy takes place while the Germans defend Calais.

Each of the first level hypergames from Table 3.10 is analyzed in a similar manner, and the stability information at each level is valuable for understanding the conflict. Table 3.12 is similar to Table 3.10 and presents the equilibriums for each game and hypergame in the D-Day model. The equilibriums for the second level hypergames and the overall third level hypergame are also presented in Table 3.12. The second level hypergame equilibriums are calculated by comparing the true preference vector stability results for the players in the hypergame. For example, in H^2_a the preference vectors to compare are the Allies' vector in G_{aaa} and the German preference vector in G_{gga}. The overall, third level equilibrium is determined from the Allies' vector in G_{aaa} and the German preference vector in G_{ggg}.

It can be seen from Table 3.12 that the overall equilibrium for the D-Day conflict is again outcome 9, which is the historical resolution. The

Table 3.12 D-Day Hypergame Results

D-Day third level hypergame H^3 Equilibrium: 9			
Allies' second level hypergame H^2_a Equilibrium: 9			
Allies' hypergame H_{aa} Equilibrium: 9		Germany's hypergame H_{ga} Equilibrium: 10	
Allies' game	Germany's game	Allies' game	Germany's game
G_{aaa}	G_{gaa}	G_{aga}	G_{gga}
Equil: 9	Equil: 10	Equil: 6	Equil: 10
Germany's second level hypergame H^2_g Equilibrium: 10			
Allies' hypergame H_{ag} Equilibrium: 6		Germany's hypergame H_{gg} Equilibrium: 10	
Allies' game	Germany's game	Allies' game	Germany's game
G_{aag}	G_{gag}	G_{agg}	G_{ggg}
Equil: 6	Equil: 5	Equil: 6	Equil: 10

Allies' third level hypergame objective was to cause Germany to think that the Allies were playing a second level hypergame, $H^2{}_g$. In that hypergame, the Allies' objective was to persuade Germany into believing that Normandy was a feint. In response to the Allies' second level hypergame, Germany's second level hypergame objective was to allow the Allies to believe that the feint was working, which would result in the outcome 10. Since the Allies could sense Germany's defense movements, the Allies were able to deduce Germany's second level hypergame and to take advantage of that deduction by playing a third level hypergame. Remarkably, this complex stratagem worked and helped speed the end of World War II.

3.4 Important Concepts from Chapter 3

Conflicts that involve misperceptions by at least one of the participants are called hypergames. A player may not be aware of the correct players, options, or preferences in the game, or any combination of these. Because the participants often have some misunderstanding of the situation, hypergames are extremely important in the analysis of conflicts. As will be seen in Chapter 5, hypergames are also important in the study of the sensitivity of possible equilibriums in a conflict to suspected misinformation on the part of an analyst or a player.

To analyze a hypergame, the preference vectors representing each player's view of every other perceived player's preferences are developed. The games as seen by each player are analyzed to determine the true stability for each player, and this correct stability information is used to determine the equilibriums in the hypergame. The level of the hypergame is determined by the number of layers of perceptions, where the layers are constructed by misperceptions founded upon other misperceptions. Whatever the case, by comparing the appropriate preference vectors, the same stability analysis procedures that were presented in Chapters 1 and 2 can be employed to analyze any level of hypergame.

In this chapter, two conflicts were analyzed to demonstrate how to perform a hypergame analysis. First, analyses of the Cuban missile conflict revealed that viewing the conflict as a hypergame provides a realistic explanation for the historical events. The Cuban missile crisis was studied as both a first and a second level hypergame. For the second level hypergame, a short form of the stability tableau was presented that makes it easier to perform the analysis in cases where many preference vectors are the same. The second conflict studied in this chapter was the D-Day invasion in 1944, which was modeled as a third level hypergame. In practice, any level of hypergame can be thoroughly analyzed by employing the general hypergame structure presented in this chapter in conjunction with the conflict analysis algorithm.

Questions

1. Construct a hypothetical hypergame in which there are no equilibriums. Can you suggest a situation in which this might actually occur?
2. Adjust the Cuban missile crisis hypergame of Section 3.2 to model an additional misunderstanding on the part of the United States. Let the United States perceive the USSR's preferences to be given by the preference vector

$$(0\ 2\ 4\ 6\ 5\ 1\ 7\ 3\ 11\ 9\ 10\ 8).$$

Assume that the United States is not cognizant of the Soviet misunderstanding regarding the U.S. preference vector. Perform an analysis of this new hypergame.
3. In the Cuban missile crisis, it is likely that in addition to the USSR misunderstanding the preferences of the United States, they had not considered the possibility of the United States imposing a blockade. Perform a hypergame analysis of the Cuban missile conflict in which the USSR is unaware of a blockade option and does not expect the United States to perform any aggressive actions. Assume that the United States knows that the USSR has a misunderstanding of the conflict.
4. Perform the stability analyses for the hypergames H_{ga}, H_{ag}, and H_{gg} in Table 3.10. Clearly demonstrate how all of the equilibriums in Table 3.12 are obtained.
5. What would have happened if the Germans had found out about the plans for the Normandy invasion before D-Day? Present the structure and equilibrium results for this conflict in a table similar to Table 3.12.

Change options in USSR hypergame set,
They now know only do nothing or airstrike.

Chapter 4
Modeling Strategic Surprise Using Hypergames

4.1 Introduction

Many conflicts of great interest to an analyst involve *strategic surprise*, in which one or more of the participants in a conflict exploit a misperception of an opponent by invoking an unexpected strategy and thereby outwitting the opponent. In order to select a surprise strategy, there must be at least one option that is unknown to one or more players in the game. Consequently, strategic surprise constitutes a special kind of hypergame that can often arise in many types of practical applications.

In this chapter two conflicts that involve strategic surprise are thoroughly analyzed using the hypergame methods presented in Chapter 3: the fall of France in 1940, and the Suez crisis of 1956. In the fall of France, the French were unaware of one of the options available to the Germans, which was to attack the French through the almost impassable Ardennes region of Western Europe. The result was an overwhelming loss for the French and British forces. In the Suez crisis, President Nasser of Egypt unexpectedly nationalized the Suez canal on July 26, 1956 and removed it from British control. The surprise invasion of the canal zone by British, French, and Israeli troops three months later was equally unexpected to Nasser. Because one player was not aware of a secret option available to the other player and the other player knew this, each of the hypergames studied in this chapter is a second level hypergame.

4.2 Fall of France

The hypergame situation where a player is unaware of one or more of the options available to the other players proceeds in the same manner as the hypergame applications discussed in the previous chapter. Table

Table 4.1 Feasible Outcomes in the Fall of France Hypergame

Players	Options	Feasible outcomes					
France	Reinforce the Maginot Line	1	0	1	0	1	0
	Move into Belgium	0	1	0	1	0	1
Germany	Assault on the Maginot Line	1	1	0	0	0	0
	Attack in the north	0	0	1	1	0	0
	Attack through the Ardennes	0	0	0	0	1	1
	Decimal outcomes	5	6	9	10	17[a]	18[a]

[a]Not known by France.

4.1 illustrates the game model and feasible outcomes for a conflict that was first formulated as a hypergame by Bennett and Dando (1977, 1979), and later analyzed by Fraser and Hipel (1979a) using the conflict analysis method. The conflict is the fall of France in 1940, and the options represent battle strategies for the players. A map of northern Europe indicating the contested area is shown in Figure 4.1.

In May 1940 the German army mounted an offensive against the French and the British expeditionary forces in Europe. The French command had to predict whether the Germans would launch their main attack in the north through Belgium, in the south at the Maginot Line, or through

Figure 4.1 Troop placements in Northern Europe before May 10, 1940.

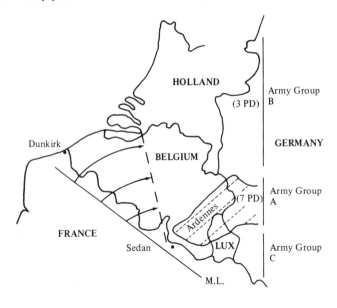

the Ardennes. The French would then move the bulk of their forces to a position that would block the main German thrust. Even though the Germans had three options available to them, the French military leadership under General Gamelin did not perceive the Ardennes route as being an option in the game because they considered the rugged terrain in the Ardennes region to be impassable for tanks (Bennett and Dando, 1977, 1979). This option was in fact the one selected by Germany, and the result was one of the most disastrous defeats in the history of warfare.

For the fall of France hypergame there are a number of outcomes that are not physically possible, and only the feasible outcomes are considered in Table 4.1 and 4.2. As is the case for the Cuban missile crisis in Section 3.3, where the United States is cognizant of the Soviet misunderstanding, the fall of France is also a second level hypergame. Germany is aware of the French misperception of not considering the possibility of a German invasion through the Ardennes. The preference vectors used in the stability analysis in Table 4.2 were developed from the research done by Bennett and Dando (1977, 1979). Notice that since France is unaware of the Ardennes option, outcomes 17 and 18, which incorporate the selection of this option, are not listed in either France's preference vector or France's interpretation of the German preference vector. However, Germany fully realizes that it can invoke strategic surprise by attacking through the Ardennes, and therefore all of the feasible outcomes are listed in its preference vector.

The stability analysis proceeds in a manner similar to the short form second level hypergame analysis of the Cuban missile crisis presented in Table 3.7. In Table 4.2, the first two preference vectors are compared to ascertain the stability for the outcomes for both vectors and also to find the single equilibrium of outcome 10 in the French game. France is under the impression that Germany considers the classical situation (outcome

Table 4.2 Stability Analysis of the Fall of France Hypergame

	×	E	×	×		
France	r	r	s	u		
	5	10	6	9		
			5	10		
Germany perceived	r	r	u	u		
by France	9	10	6	5		
			10	9		
	E	×	E	×	×	×
	r	r	s	u	u	u
Germany	18	9	17	10	6	5
			9	18	18	9
					10	17

10), which occurred in World War I. However, the German generals did not want to repeat the mistakes of the first World War where huge armies were trapped in trench warfare for many years. The secret option of a blitz through the Ardennes would preclude this.

By comparing the first and third preference vectors in Table 4.2, stability and equilibrium results can be obtained for Germany. Outcomes 17 and 18 are not listed in France's preference vector because France is unaware of them. Because France has no UIs available from these outcomes, like rational outcomes they are thus stable. Consider outcome 17, for example. Germany has a UI from outcome 17 to outcome 9. From outcome 9, France has a UI to 10, which is less preferred by Germany to outcome 17. The possibility that outcome 10 could occur induces sequential stability for outcome 17 for Germany, as indicated by the s written above its preference vector in Table 4.2. Outcome 17 is stable for Germany and unknown by France, and thus constitutes an equilibrium. No outcomes are simultaneously stable for either player in this conflict.

The two equilibriums indicated above Germany's preference vector, which result from the complete analysis, are both outcomes of which France is unaware. The options in this conflict involve the commitment of millions of troops and arms and are virtually impossible to change once selected. This means that the assumption that outcomes 17 and 18 are stable for France remains valid, because after France becomes aware of the extra option available to Germany, it is too late to make a possible improvement.

After the commencement of a German attack in the north of Belgium on May 10, 1940, France moved its main force northward into Belgium to counteract what was thought to be a major offensive. However, the Germans outflanked the French by concentrating the main German thrust through the Ardennes (see Figure 4.1). By the time the French realized the strategy of the Germans it was too late for their huge forces to block the flow of German panzers through the Ardennes. Outcome 18 in Table 4.2 resulted in an overwhelming victory for the Wehrmacht. If in a conflict situation it were possible for another player to react to a strategy that became known as the game progressed, then another analysis could be done for the point in time when that player's knowledge about the game was increased. This was certainly not the situation for the French in 1940.

The equilibrium in France's game is the outcome 10, and thus the strategy that could be expected from France by Germany would be the one found in that outcome. Based on this information and the fact that outcome 18 can be attained by Germany from outcome 10, outcome 18 is the expected result. This corresponds to the historical resolution where Germany launched an unexpected attack through the Ardennes and thereby gained complete control of Western Europe.

4.3 Suez Crisis

The Suez crisis of 1956 constitutes a fine example of a complex situation where strategic surprise is employed in two related disputes. During the summer of 1956, President Nasser of Egypt invoked the nonmilitary yet coercive action of unexpectedly nationalizing the Suez canal. In the fall of the same year, Britain, France, and Israel launched a surprise attack against the Egyptians. Following a presentation of the historical background to this conflict, it is modeled as two separate second level hypergames. Each of these hypergames exhibits strategic surprise. Hypergame analyses of the two Suez incidents were originally performed by Shupe et al. (1980) and Wright et al. (1980).

4.3.1 Historical Background

In the years before the Suez crisis of 1956, Egypt was becoming increasingly nationalistic and was trying to break away from the domination of Great Britain, which still controlled large parts of Africa. Britain's main concerns in the Middle East included prevention of Soviet interference, the safeguarding of the Suez Canal which handled a large amount of British and other Western marine traffic, and maintenance of a secure oil supply from the Middle East. Unfortunately for the British, the influence of Britain in Egypt was slowly deteriorating.

In 1954 Britain was pressured by the Egyptian nationalists into removing its last troops from Egyptian military bases by June 18, 1956. (The troops had been stationed in Egypt to protect the Middle East, particularly the Suez Canal.) The two countries confronted each other again over the development of the Baghdad Pact in 1955. The pact was a defense agreement among Turkey, Iran, and Britain (Pakistan and Iraq joined later) and encouraged by the United States. It was designed to protect the member countries from the perceived threat of the USSR. Nasser, however, was more concerned about Western influence (Bowie, 1974), and denounced the pact as another attempt at imperialist domination. He felt the pact would prevent the development of a strong united Arab league and would jeopardize the neutrality of the Arab nations by associating them, through Britain, with NATO (the North Atlantic Treaty Organization) (Nutting, 1972).

In February 1955, a series of raids between Egypt and Israel caused an increase in tensions between these two countries and both felt the need to strengthen their military forces. Nasser much preferred to get arms from the West rather than the USSR, but was unsuccessful (Bowie, 1974). France, Britain, and the United States were discouraged from supplying armaments by the Tripartite Declaration of 1950, which required that they maintain a balance of power in the area and limit arms deals. Nasser then approached the USSR and completed arrangements in late August, 1955, to obtain Soviet military equipment from Czechoslovakia.

Despite his need for arms, however, Nasser's overriding aim was to build the High Aswan Dam. Construction of the dam on the Nile River was central to Nasser's policy of social and economic development. It would create over one million acres of new farmland and provide hydroelectric power. The Egyptian government could not afford the project on its own and therefore required funds from outside sources—either the West or the USSR.

Britain and the United States feared that the USSR would seize this opportunity to develop friendly relations with Egypt through a display of generosity. This suspicion was particularly strong in view of the recent Soviet–Egyptian arms deal. Providing Western assistance for the dam project would eliminate this possibility. Britain saw it as an opportunity to regain some influence with Nasser after having refused him weapons. Offering foreign aid would be consistent with the U.S. policy of promoting independence of developing countries (Capitanchik, 1969) and of creating a favorable international environment for itself (Guhin, 1972). Accordingly, on December 16, 1955, Britain and the United States, along with the World Bank, proposed to help finance the dam through a series of loans and grants.

The feasibility of the dam project was investigated by Eugene Black, head of the World Bank, who declared it "good and sound." The cost of the project was estimated to be approximately $1.3 billion over 12–15 years (Bowie, 1974). An agreement was drafted by the British and the Americans in which they would provide 30% of the cost and Egypt 70%. The agreement involved a number of conditions including the following:

1. One-third of Egypt's internal revenue was to be diverted to the dam project for ten years.
2. Economic measures were to be taken by the Egyptian government to curb the growth of inflation due to the influx of money into Egypt.
3. Contracts for construction work were to be awarded on a competitive basis.
4. Help from the communist bloc countries was to be refused.

Nasser was insulted by these conditions and flatly rejected them. He felt they would be a threat to Egypt's independence and saw them as another Western attempt to dominate Egypt. Eugene Black then went to Cairo to discuss the conditions with Nasser and convince him that they were reasonable economic safeguards. Nasser was still not satisfied, however, and drafted an alternative proposal that toned down the wording of the agreement. This he sent to London and Washington on February 9, 1956. The Americans had already lost some interest in the loan [due primarily to

Nasser's continued anti-Western stance (Guhin, 1972) and also to other reasons including a change in U.S. domestic policies (Love, 1969; Nutting 1972)], whereas the British were still in favor of providing money (Love, 1969). However British Prime Minister Eden soon lost his enthusiasm for the loan when King Hussein of Jordan dismissed General Glubb, an Englishman, from his post as Commander-in-Chief of the Jordanian Army. Nasser had been maintaining a strong anti-imperialist campaign at this time, including broadcasting anti-Western propaganda on Arab radio. Thus, when Glubb was discharged, Eden held Nasser responsible for influencing Hussein's decision (Nutting, 1972). [King Hussein later claimed that the dismissal had nothing to do with Nasser (Love, 1969).] After this incident, the Americans and the British agreed to let the loan deal lapse (Guhin, 1972). Nasser did not force the matter for some months. He was either waiting for a reply (Nutting, 1972) or trying to improve his bargaining position (Guhin, 1972).

In April 1956, Israeli attacks again heightened Egypt's desire for more weapons. By May 16, however, Britain, the United States, and the USSR came to an agreement to limit the influx of arms into the Middle East (Love, 1969). Nasser, in order to find a source of armaments, then recognized Communist China. This move enraged both the United States and Britain and further jeopardized the loan offer.

Nasser, who had already begun to fear that Britain and the United States were backing down on the loan, decided to force the issue by withdrawing his objections to the original loan conditions and accepting the original proposal (Nutting, 1972). Ahmed Hussein, the Egyptian ambassador to the United States, went to Washington on July 19 to demand that the Americans reconsider the agreement. In the process, he referred to the availability of a Soviet loan in an attempt to persuade the Americans to sign. However, U.S. Secretary of State J. F. Dulles said, "The U.S. does not submit to blackmail" (Thomas, 1966), and retracted the U.S. offer for the loan. The Americans, followed two days later by the British, officially withdrew their offer with a statement saying that the ability of Egypt to devote adequate resources to ensure the success of the Aswan dam had become too uncertain. [The decision to reject the loan proposal was probably made easier by the growing belief among the Americans that the USSR could not afford to support the High Aswan Dam project (Nutting, 1972)]. Nasser was not surprised by the withdrawal but was insulted by the manner in which it occurred and the criticism of Egypt's economy (Goldman, 1967). He then turned to the USSR who denied having made any promise of a loan for the project (Robertson, 1965). [There is some confusion among sources as to whether the USSR did indeed make the offer.]

Nasser was now in need of money and a bold defiant gesture to rebuff the West. Seizure of the Suez Canal was an attractive possibility. Taking control of the canal would provide Egypt with a substantial income [U.S. $91 million gross and $32 million net in 1955 (Bowie, 1974)] and at the same time remove "the last vestige of Egypt's subordination to the West" (Bowie, 1974). The canal was already scheduled to become the property of the Egyptian government in 1968 when its concession came to an end, but Nasser could make a case for nationalization because Egypt's rights to a share of the profits from the canal had been denied earliers by the British. Because the British troops had been removed from the site since June 13 (five days earlier than had been required by the agreement), nationalization would pose no military problem.

Nasser had been considering nationalization of the canal for some time (Bowie, 1974; Nutting, 1972). In September 1954, the Egyptian government set up a committee to study the transition of the Suez Canal to government control in 1968 (Bowie, 1974). In June of 1956, Nasser spoke to Ahmed Hussein of nationalizing the canal when he contemplated the possibility of the United States withdrawing its offer. He did not, however, initiate a plan for the takeover until after the loan was withdrawn (Love, 1969). On July 23, Nasser and his cabinet considered delivering an ultimatum, stating that he would nationalize the canal if he were not granted a loan. This, it was reasoned, would just result in another ultimatum from the West and Egypt would be backed into a corner. The surprise takeover of the canal was preferred. This would enable Egypt to occupy the canal quickly and without bloodshed. Nasser reasoned that if the British were to launch an attack to retake the canal it would require about two months to prepare, and he thought a settlement would be reached before that time. Furthermore, he felt that the British would have to move cautiously for fear of jeopardizing their interests in the Middle East (Love, 1969). Consequently, on July 26, 1956 Nasser nationalized the canal and, as he did, broadcast a passionate speech, denouncing the West and asserting his government's right to the canal. This move deeply shocked the West and created immediate concern for the security of the canal. Among the Arab countries, however, Nasser was the champion of Arab nationalism.

Of the Western countries, Britain was vitally concerned over the flow of oil from the Middle East, and because of its high investments in the canal and its declining position in the area, it viewed Nasser's action as a critical threat. France considered the Suez Canal as a French undertaking since its construction was originally organized by a Frenchman. Furthermore, France already viewed Nasser with hostility because of his support of the Algerian rebels, who wanted Algeria to break away from France. Regaining control of the canal would guarantee a vital supply route and would serve to humiliate Nasser. Thus Britain and France immediately wanted urgent and decisive action against Egypt. An integrated British–French military command was soon established with the British in charge.

At this stage Britain and France assumed that the United States would be involved in their plans, but the United States has a developing and delicate position in the Middle East and negligible investments in the canal. The Americans were prepared neither to support nor to approve armed intervention. The maximum demand from the United States was the efficient operation of the canal and freedom of passage through it. The USSR wished to gain influence in the Middle East because of its concern over the West's attempts at containment (Kanet, 1974). Having made political advances in Egypt, the USSR wished to support that country in any negotiations concerning the Suez Canal.

On August 2, 1956 the British cabinet made the final decision that, although a negotiated settlement should be sought for the Suez situation, force would be used if the negotiations failed. In France, both the right and left political factions urged military action. The right did so because of French Algeria and the left because of its support of Israel. Also, the French military required a boost in morale after successive defeats in Algeria and Indochina. Success in Egypt would improve its military prestige.

From August 16 to 23, a conference of 22 maritime nations met in London to discuss international operation of the Suez Canal. (Egypt was invited but did not attend.) At the end, 18 nations (with Ceylon, India, Indonesia, and the USSR refraining) called for operation, maintenance, and development control to be vested in a Suez Canal Board. Egypt was to be represented on the Board and was to grant the Board all rights and facilities required for its function. Nasser denounced the proposal as a plan for "collective colonialism" (Nutting, 1972).

British Prime Minister Eden was under the impression that the United States would acquiesce to the use of force if Nasser rejected the conference's proposal, but the United States was merely playing for time. On September 3, U.S. President Eisenhower wrote to Eden that American public opinion flatly rejected force. Further, on a personal and professional level he did not see how a successful result could be achieved by forcible means (Guhin, 1972).

On September 4, in a further attempt for a negotiated settlement, U.S. Secretary of State Dulles presented a proposal to Britain for the Suez Canal User's Association (SCUA), which was vaguely defined as an organization that would hire pilots, receive transit dues, and supervise the canal's management without prejudice to Egypt's sovereignty. This move was seen by Dulles as a way of further delaying armed conflict in the event that Egypt continued not to cooperate. Eden, however, interpreted it as a means of depriving Nasser of the revenue from the canal by force, if necessary. On September 14, the proposal was made public, and on September 15 Nasser responded, "SCUA would lead to international anarchy. . . . It was designed to usurp Egypt's sovereignty and rights to control the Canal" (Nutting, 1972).

The U.N. Security Council debate on the Suez issue lasted from the 5th to the 14th of October, 1956. In spite of apparent headway, none of the parties were negotiating in good faith. As far as the British were concerned, their Secret Service had advised them "to discount anything agreed by Fawzi (the Egyptian Foreign Minister) on the grounds that he was too close a friend of Hammarskjold (the U.N. Secretary General)" (Thomas, 1966). Nasser later said, "I have no intention of removing the canal from Egyptian policies. We have used a conciliatory tactic in New York, that's all" (Robertson, 1965). Furthermore, the British and French were in the midst of planning a secret military operation with Israel against Egypt.

During the mid-1950s, France had been secretly supplying Israel with military weapons to gain Israel's support in the Middle East. Consequently, in late September, France suggested to Eden the idea of an alliance with Israel. His reaction was one of interest and caution. He let the French continue their discussions with Israel and advised the military command to develop a plan. For the Israelis, there were tremendous advantages to be gained. As Moshe Dayan, the Israeli commander, later told his general staff, "We should behave like the cyclist who is riding uphill when a truck chances by and he grabs hold" (Thomas, 1966).

On October 16, Eden went to Paris to discuss the joint operation with Mollet, the French Premier. The military plan called for the Israelis to launch a major attack on the Sinai on October 29. The objective of this attack, as described in the directives issued on October 25 by Dayan was "to create a military threat to the Suez Canal by seizing objectives in its proximity" (Thomas, 1966). This threat was to provide a pretext for the British–French forces to intervene. An ultimatum would then be issued on October 30. This was to be sent to Israel and Egypt and would call for an immediate ceasefire which, if not obeyed, would allow the British–French forces to occupy the canal zone (Beaufre, 1969).

During October 23–24, the French and Israeli Prime Ministers, Mollet and Ben-Gurion, and British Foreign Minister Lloyd secretly met in a private villa in France. There they signed a declaration of intent concerning the joint operation. The leaders (although apparently not their aides) swore that none would in the lifetime of the others reveal what they had witnessed (Thomas, 1966).

From October 16 to 30, there existed a communication blackout between Washington and London. The British were determined to use force and planned to present the United States with a fait accompli. The United States wanted to do everything possible to avoid the use of force and was aware, by the middle of October, that the Israelis were planning some military operation. Though it was thought that the action was to be against Jordan, the United States warned Israel that it would censure any military move. It was also apparent that Britain and France were becoming active.

In the midst of an election, the United States assumed that two of its closest allies would wait.

In both Britain and France, knowledge of the plan was severely restricted. The British and French Prime Ministers issued explicit orders which forbade information of any kind being given to anybody who had no direct need to know (Robertson, 1965). Consequently, vital information was not passed through the ordinary channels of communication upon which NATO, friendly military missions, and service attachés usually relied for intelligence. Starting on October 22, 1956, the USSR was involved with the popular uprising in Hungary. The British and French were assisted by this event since it focused diplomatic and public attention on this new crisis.

At dusk on October 29, Israel launched the attack on the Sinai. When Nasser learned of it, he thought it was an isolated action but decided to reinforce the defenses east of the canal. On October 30, Nasser received the British–French ultimatum. At this point, the Israeli forces were still a hundred miles from the canal. Since the ultimatum requested each side to retreat to positions ten miles east and west of the canal, it was actually demanding that the Egyptians retreat 110 miles and the Israelis advance 90 miles. This was so unusual that "Nasser believed that the ultimatum must be a bluff or a ruse to help Israel to achieve an easy victory in the Sinai by drawing Egyptian forces away from the Negev border to protect Port Said and the Canal" (Nutting, 1972). On October 31, learning of an Allied air attack on his airfields, Nasser realized he had been wrong and was in danger of having his main forces caught east of the canal. Nasser gave orders for a general retreat from the Sinai. On November 5, the British–French forces landed at Port Said and Port Fuad.

At this time Nasser received a reply from the Soviet leader, Khruschev, to his request for aid. Though not willing to intervene physically on behalf of Egypt and "risk getting involved in a third world war for the sake of the Suez Canal" (Nutting, 1972), the Soviet Union was prepared to call for a halt to hostilities. The USSR sent a threatening message to London saying, "What would be Britain's situation if stronger governments, possessing all forms of contemporary destructive arms, attacked her? If missile weapons were employed against Britain or France, you, no doubt, would call this a barbarous action. How, then, is the inhumane attack made by the British and French armed forces on an almost defenceless Egypt any different?" (Progress Publishers, 1975). Furthermore, Russian planes were detected flying over Turkey to an unknown destination. It was thought that the planes were either carrying "volunteers" or were bombers heading for the British–French fleet lying off Port Said. The USSR then asked Turkey for permission for a cruiser and three destroyers to pass through the Dardanelles.

The United States, in response to British and French requests for reassurance, said, "The Government of the United States will respect its obligations under the North Atlantic Treaty arrangements" (Robertson, 1965). This was interpreted to mean that the United States would support Europe in a nuclear attack but that it would not support European forces in the Mediterranean and Egypt against an attack from the USSR. In addition, Britain's oil supplies had been stopped and there was a run on the pound. Britain was in desperate need of American financial and oil support, which were denied. In order to avoid a severe financial crisis and devaluation, Britain needed a loan of 300 million pounds. As a result of this pressure from both the United States and the USSR, a ceasefire was imposed on the evening of November 6, 1956.

4.3.2 Hypergame Modeling and Analysis

There are clearly two distinct points in time where important conflict decisions were made in the Suez crisis. The first was sometime after February 9, 1956 when Nasser proposed an alternative loan agreement and before the United States and Britain were discouraged from making the loan. The principal players at this point (Egypt, Britain, the United States, and the USSR) had each made their objectives known and had each proposed a solution. Egypt was asserting its nationalism and trying to finance the Aswan Dam project. Britian wanted to maintain its influential status in the Middle East, prevent Soviet penetration, and appease Nasser after having refused him weapons. The United States also wanted to limit Soviet influence in the Middle East but wished to promote Egyptian nationalism without antagonizing Britain. Finally, the USSR was trying to gain a stronger foothold in the Middle East. These different objectives eventually led to the nationalization of the canal.

A second situation leads from the nationalization of the canal to the invasion of the Suez Canal region by the British, French, and Israeli forces. An appropriate moment to select for analysis is shortly after the British have been invited into the French–Israeli secret coalition in late September 1956.

The modeling and analysis of the Suez crisis at these two points are best done separately to provide distinct insights into the conflict. Both conflicts are modeled as second level hypergames because in each case of the two Suez controversies one of the two players is unaware of an option available to the other player, who is cognizant of this fact. In the first hypergame, Egypt misleads the West; in the second, Egypt is the one that is surprised.

Nationalization Hypergame. *Players and Options.* The final arrangement of players and options for the nationalization hypergame is shown in Table 4.3. Because Britain and the United States have to act together in the loan they can be considered as one player, labeled "The West."

Table 4.3 Players and Options in the Nationalization of the
Suez Canal Hypergame

Player	Option
The West	1. Offer loan with original conditions
	2. Offer loan on Nasser's terms
Egypt	3. Negotiate loan with original conditions
	4. Negotiate loan on Nasser's terms
	5. Appease Britain and the United States
	6. Pursue loan with USSR
	7. Pursue loan with USSR and, if this fails, nationalize the Suez Canal (secret option)

this causes
a strategy
appeal

They can offer to help to finance the project on their terms, subject to Nasser's conditions, or withdraw the loan altogether. Nasser can either negotiate the loan on the original terms or according to his own proposal. If he chooses either of these, he might improve his chances at getting the loan by toning down his harsh anti-Western campaign, and thereby appease the West. Alternatively, Egypt could try to obtain a loan from the USSR or postpone the dam project altogether. Further, Egypt can nationalize the Suez Canal as a surprise move.

Although the USSR has an important influence in the conflict, it was not an active participant and therefore is not represented as an independent player in the hypergame. However, the option that the Egyptians pursue the loan with the USSR is included as option 6 in Table 4.3 and also as part of option 7. If Egypt takes the Soviet loan option and the Russians agree, there is no need to nationalize the canal; hence option 6 will be chosen. On the other hand, if the Egyptians do not obtain a Soviet loan, they can nationalize the canal as shown in option 7. Finally, the option that the British and the Americans withdraw the loan altogether is represented by selecting neither option 1 nor 2. If Egypt decides to postponse the dam project, this is equivalent to not choosing any of options 3–7.

Outcome Removal. Table 4.4 lists the outcomes that can be removed from the complete list of outcomes. Most of the sets of outcomes listed in this table are removed on the basis of the mutual exclusiveness of certain options. (See Section 2.3.2 for a complete discussion of the types of outcomes that can be removed from a conflict model.) For example, the fact that the West cannot offer the original loan and agree to Nasser's terms simultaneously is indicated by the set of outcomes (11, – – – – –), which is listed vertically in the first outcome column of Table 4.4. The rightmost set of outcomes, (– 1, – 0 – – –), illustrates outcomes that can be removed because of a dependence between players. The West can only agree to Nasser's terms if he decides to offer them. The feasible

Table 4.4 Outcomes Removed in the Nationalization of the
                  Suez Canal Hypergame

The West									
Offer original loan	1	–	–	–	–	–	–	–	–
Agree to Nasser's terms	1	–	–	–	–	–	–	–	1
Egypt									
Negotiate original loan	–	1	1	1	–	–	–	0	–
Negotiate Nasser's terms	–	1	–	–	1	1	–	0	0
Appease West	–	–	–	–	–	–	–	1	–
Soviet loan	–	–	1	–	1	–	1	–	–
Soviet loan–nationalize	–	–	–	1	–	1	1	–	–

outcomes that remain after outcome removal are shown in Table 4.5.
Note that since the West is not aware of the nationalization option, there
are two outcomes that are not recognized by the West.

Preferences. All the preference vectors for the analysis of the nationalization of the Suez canal are shown in the stability analysis tableau in
Table 4.6. To interpret the decimal outcomes in the preference vectors
of Table 4.6, it is convenient to refer back to the binary forms of the
outcomes in Table 4.5. Two preference vectors are needed for Egypt
because of its secret nationalization option. One shows Egypt's preferences from the viewpoint of Britain and the United States; the other shows
Egypt's real set of preferences. The only difference between the two is
that Egypt's actual preference vector includes the secret nationalization
option, whereas the British–United States view does not.
    Egypt's true preference vector in Table 4.6 is determined according to

Table 4.5 Feasible Outcomes in the Nationalization of the
                  Suez Canal Hypergame

The West															
Original loan	0	1	0	1	0	1	0	0	1	0	1	0	0	1	0	1
Nasser's terms	0	0	0	0	0	0	1	0	0	0	0	1	0	0	0	0
Egypt																
Original loan	0	0	1	1	0	0	0	1	1	0	0	0	0	0	0	0
Nasser's terms	0	0	0	0	1	1	1	0	0	1	1	1	0	0	0	0
Appease West	0	0	0	0	0	0	0	1	1	1	1	1	0	0	0	0
Soviet loan	0	0	0	0	0	0	0	0	0	0	0	0	1	1	0	0
Nationalize	0	0	0	0	0	0	0	0	0	0	0	0	0	0	1	1
Decimal	0	1	4	5	8	9	10	20	21	24	25	26	32	33	64[a]	65[a]

[a]Unknown by West.

Table 4.6 Stability Analysis of the Nationalization of the Suez Canal Hypergame

(handwritten left margin: G_wwu, G_ew, G_we)

The West

×	×	×	×	×	×	×	×	×	E	×	E	E	×
r	s	r	r	r	r	r	r	r	s	s	r	r	u
21	20	24	25	0	1	4	8	9	5	26	32	33	10
	21								4	24			9
										25			8

Egypt perceived by the West   *(handwritten: NASSER'S TERMS)*

r	r	r	s	u	u	u	u	u	u	u	u	u	u
10	5	32	33	0	1	4	8	9	20	24	25	26	21
		5		32	5	32	32	5	32	32	5	10	5
					33			33	8	8	33		33
									4	4	1		1
											9		9
											25		

Egypt   *(handwritten: NATIONALIZATION)*

×	E	E	E	×	×	×	×	×	×	×	×	×	×	×	×
r	r	r	s	u	u	u	u	u	u	u	u	u	u	u	u
10	5	64	65	32	33	0	1	4	8	9	20	24	25	26	21
		5		64	5	32	64	64	5		64	64	5	10	5
		65		32		65	32	32	65	32	32	32	65		65
				33				33	8	8	33				33
									4	4	1				1
											9				9
											25				

(handwritten lower left: Nationalization Option →)

(handwritten right margin: Gee)

a number of principles. First, Nasser was determined to get money for the Aswan Dam. He would not, however, sacrifice the independence of Egypt to get the funds since this would violate his nationalistic principles. Second, Nasser preferred to deal with the West rather than with the USSR. Finally, nationalizing the Suez Canal was to be only a last resort. Thus Egypt's most preferred outcome is outcome 10, where Egypt receives a loan from the West under Nasser's terms. The second most preferred outcome is 5, in which Egypt receives a loan under the original agreement. This is reasonable in view of Egypt's attempts to deal with the West for weapons before going to the USSR and of the small difference between Nasser's counterproposal and the original deal.

The next four most preferred outcomes for Egypt in Table 4.6 (64, 65, 32, and 33) involve pursuing a loan from the USSR. Of these, the first two include nationalizing the canal if the loan does not come through. The only difference between these two outcomes is the status of the Western loan offer. Since this is irrelevant to Egypt's preferences between the outcomes, 64 and 65 are placed under a bridge to indicate that they are equally preferred. Note that in the United States and British view of Egypt's preference vector, these two outcomes are not included since they are unknown. However, the rest of the preference vector is identical to Egypt's real preference vector. Outcomes 32 and 33 in the preference vector for Egypt differ from outcomes 64 and 65 in that Egypt selects option 6 instead of option 7. The next five equally preferred outcomes in Egypt's preference vector (0, 1, 4, 8, and 9) represent situations in which the Egyptians cannot come to an agreement on the loan with the British and the Americans. The last five outcomes (20, 24, 25, 26, and 21) involve Egypt appeasing the West.

The worst outcome for Egypt is 21. However, as shown in the preference vector of Great Britain and the United States in Table 4.6, this is the best outcome for these players. The next most preferred outcomes for Britain and the United States are the equally preferred outcomes 20, 24, and 25, which involve Egypt's political cooperation without a loan settlement. These are followed by the equally preferred set of outcomes 0, 1, 4, 8, and 9, where Egypt does not appease the West and the two parties cannot come to an agreement on the loan. The remaining preference ordering is displayed in Table 4.6.

Stability Analysis. The stability analysis of the second level Suez hypergame can be executed by following the efficient procedures outlined in Section 3.3 for the Cuban missile crisis. Consequently, the complete short form hypergame stability analysis of the nationalization part of the Suez crisis is shown in Table 4.6. To determine the stability of the outcomes in the preference vectors for the West and for the West's view of Egypt, the first two preference vectors are compared. For example, the West has a UI to outcome 21 from outcome 20. In the preference vector of Egypt as seen by the West, Egypt has a UI from 21 to 5. Since outcome 5 is less preferred by the West to outcome 20, outcome 20 is sequentially sanctioned. As another example, consider outcome 1 in the preference vector of Egypt as seen by the West. From outcome 1, Egypt appears to have a UI to outcome 5. From outcome 5 the United States can improve to outcome 4. Even though outcome 4 is under the same bridge as 1, in terms of sanctioning outcome 4 is less preferred to 1 since there is no advantage to move from 1 to 4. Consequently, the UI from 1 to 5 is sequentially sanctioned. However Egypt as seen by the West has another UI to outcome 33, which cannot be blocked. Outcome 33 is rational for the West, so outcome 1 is unstable for Egypt as seen by the West.

When analyzing the outcomes in Egypt's true preference vector for stability, deterrents are found by checking the preference vector of the West. For example, Egypt has a UI from outcome 65 to 5. However, even though Britain and the United States do not realize 65 is possible (see Table 4.5) they do have a UI from outcome 5 to 4. Because 4 is less preferred by Egypt to 5, this sequential sanction may deter Egypt from moving from 65 to 5.

The overall equilibriums in the hypergame can be found by comparing the stability results for the vectors of Egypt and the West. These equilibrium outcomes are marked by an E above the Egyptian preference vector in Table 4.6. It can be seen that, at this point in time, outcomes 5, 64, and 65 constitute three possible resolutions to the Suez crisis. The equilibriums as seen by the West, and also by Egypt from the West's viewpoint, are determined by comparing the stability results of the first two preference vectors in Table 4.6. Because of the hypergame situation, Great Britain and the United States mistakenly think that outcome 5, 32, and 33 are the true equilibriums. Outcome 5 is an agreement on the Western loan with the original conditions. Outcomes 32 and 33 involve the Egyptians pursuing the Soviet loan (without a surprise nationalization of the canal if a loan is not forthcoming). It appears that outcome 5 is the equilibrium preferred by both players. This suggests that had Nasser recognized the wisdom of accepting the original loan offer at this time, an outcome preferred by all players to the nationalization option could have come about. However, the stability of outcome 5 for Great Britain and the United States in Table 4.6 is dependent on the deterrent effects of Egypt negotiating a Soviet loan. Since the British and Americans later felt that the USSR would not be able to supply the loan and other factors reduced the importance of the threat of Soviet influence, this deterrent would not turn out to be credible. Over the course of time, outcome 5 would therefore become unstable for Great Britain and the United States. This would leave only two possible equilibriums, 64 and 65, both of which involve the nationalization of the Suez Canal. Outcome 64 is what occurred historically.

Invasion Hypergame. *Players and Options.* The invasion hypergame is analyzed for the point in time shortly after the British have been invited into the French–Israeli secret coalition in late September 1956. At that time, Britain could join the secret French–Israeli alliance or negotiate guarantees for the Suez Canal through SCUA or Egypt. If Britain chose to negotiate SCUA, it could also exert economic pressure and threaten military action to force the Egyptians to accept the conditions of SCUA. Egypt did not realize the attack option existed but it was fully aware of the other options. Alternatively, Britain could opt to do nothing. This would mean conceding the canal to Egypt and recognizing Egyptian nationalism.

France could proceed with Britain and Israel in the secret alliance or, if Britain chose not to join, France could proceed in the alliance with Israel only. It also had the option of complying with a negotiated settlement. Finally, France could choose to do nothing and thereby accept

Egypt's new position. Similarly, Israel could proceed with an alliance that included France and Britain or just France. It could also choose to attack Egypt by itself or do nothing.

Egypt had the choice of negotiating SCUA guarantees for the operation of the canal or negotiating its own guarantees. It could also choose to do nothing and ignore any attempts at negotiation.

The United States could pressure Egypt to accept SCUA or pressure Britain to accept Egyptian guarantees. It could also choose to do nothing and thereby remain neutral in the negotiations. Regardless of the options chosen by the United States, it would continue to discourage Britain and France from attacking Egypt. Since it had been doing this since Nasser had first nationalized the canal, this action was not viewed as a decisive option.

The USSR could either support Egypt in the negotiations or support the decision resulting from the negotiations. Finally, the USSR could choose to do nothing and allow the West to settle the conflict. At this juncture the USSR was probably not aware of its eventual role in the final standoff with the West over the canal.

There was only one realistic military option in the conflict and that was an invasion by Britain, France, and Israel. The French possibility of proceeding only with Israel can be ignored because without Britain the two countries lacked the necessary strength. France was able to provide only 30% of the troops in the joint invasion force (Beaufre, 1969). The closest base from which a joint attack could be launched was located in Cyprus and was a British base. Furthermore, only the British had the long range bombers required to attack the Egyptian airfields. For these reasons, it is realistic to suggest that France would not have proceeded against Egypt without Britain. Therefore Britain and France can be represented as one player without distorting the analysis.

Israel need not be considered as a separate player because its only feasible option, to attack in conjunction with Britain and France, is automatically included in the British–French option. Israel had other possible options including attacking with just France and attacking by itself. The former has already been shown to be unrealistic and the latter is even more so: Israel could not have launched a full scale attack without leaving itself vulnerable to an attack from Jordan or Syria.

The options of the United States have no significant effect on the conflict since shortly after France invited Britain into the secret alliance, Britain had just about reached a decision to ignore the United States. Eden assumed that the United States would be dormant, at least until the national election in early November (Love, 1969). Soviet support of Egypt was sufficiently vague so that it could also be ignored by Britain. Since the United States and the USSR played a largely passive role at this time, they have not been represented in the game. Therefore, the principal players are Britain–France and Egypt. Their options are shown in Table 4.7.

Outcome Removal. The outcomes removed from the set of all possible outcomes in the hypergame are listed in Table 4.8; the remaining feasible outcomes are listed in Table 4.9. The eight leftmost columns of outcomes in Table 4.8 are all either logically or preferentially infeasible for one of the players (see Section 2.3.2). The fourth and fifth columns from the right contain outcomes that are logically infeasible between players. Egypt cannot negotiate SCUA if Britain and France do not; nor can Britain and France negotiate Egyptian guarantees if Egypt does not. The last three columns of outcomes on the right are removed on the basis of preferential infeasibility for more than one player. It is felt that these outcomes are unlikely to come about during the course of the conflict.

Preferences. To interpret the outcomes in the preference vectors of Table 4.10, it is convenient to refer back to the binary forms of the outcomes in Table 4.9. As shown in Table 4.10, Britain and France favor outcome 34 the most because this enables them to place the canal under international control without resorting to hostile measures. The next outcomes in their preference vector are 38, 42, and 46, involving an escalation of hostile action ranging from economic pressure to military threats in order to force the Egyptians to negotiate SCUA. Outcomes 18, 22, 82, and 86 are concerned with a stalemate in negotiations and a joint invasion of the canal zone. Outcomes 82 and 86 involve Egypt insisting on negotiating its own guarantees, whereas in outcomes 18 and 22 Egypt refuses to negotiate at all. Outcomes 18 and 22 are grouped together as are 82 and 86. Within each group, the only difference in the Western strategies is the use of economic pressure in negotiations (in outcomes 22 and 86), and this is irrelevant to the preferences of the outcomes whose key element is an invasion. These four outcomes involving an invasion are placed after the first four outcomes in the preference vector of Britain

Table 4.7 Players and Options in the Invasion of the Suez Canal Hypergame

Player	Option
Britain and France	1. Negotiate Egyptian guarantees
	2. Negotiate SCUA
	3. Use economic pressure
	4. Threaten military action
	5. Invade (secret)
Egypt	6. Negotiate SCUA
	7. Negotiate Egyptian guarantees

Table 4.8 Outcomes Removed in the Invasion of the Suez Canal Hypergame

Britain and France	
Negot. Egyptian guarantees	– 1 1 1 1 – – – 1 – – 0 0
Negotiate SCUA	– 1 – – – 0 0 – – 0 – 0 0
Apply economic pressure	– – 1 – – 1 – – – – – 0 0
Threaten force	– – – 1 – – 1 1 – – – 0 0
Invade	– – – – 1 – – 1 – – 1 0 0
Egypt	
Negotiate SCUA	1 – – – – – – – – 1 1 1 –
Negot. Egyptian guarantees	1 – – – – – – – 0 – – – 1

and France because these countries prefer to put the canal under international control without having to resort to force. However, invasion outcomes are preferred over those outcomes where the Allies (Britain and France) neither use force nor succeed. They are also preferred over not negotiating at all while planning a secret invasion since the Allies wish to keep up the appearance of at least trying to seek a peaceful solution.

The next two sets of outcomes, (78, 74, 70, 66) and (14, 10, 6, 2), involve a stalemate in negotiations. The Allies would prefer a stalemate with Egypt insisting on its own guarantees (78, 74, 70, and 66) over a stalemate where Egypt refuses to negotiate at all (outcomes 14, 10, 6 and 2). Note that within these two groups, options are ordered differently than in the first set of four outcomes in the Allies' preference vector. The four most preferred outcomes are ordered with escalating hostile action viewed as less preferable. The groups of outcomes involving stalemates, however, are ordered with decreasing magnitude of hostile acts because the Allies would most likely be in a stalemate after exhausting all means of coercion.

After outcome 2 the most preferable outcome for the Allies is 16, which involves no negotiations while Britain and France plan an invasion. Out-

Table 4.9 Feasible Outcomes in the Invasion of the Suez Canal Hypergame

Britain and France																				
Egypt. guar.	0	0	0	0	0	0	0	0	0	1	0	0	0	0	0	0	0	0	0	0
SCUA	0	1	1	1	1	1	1	1	1	0	1	1	1	1	0	1	1	0	1	1
Economic	0	0	1	0	1	0	1	0	1	0	0	1	0	1	0	0	1	0	0	1
Threaten	0	0	0	1	1	0	0	1	1	0	0	0	1	1	0	0	0	0	0	0
Invade	0	0	0	0	0	0	0	0	0	0	0	0	0	0	1	1	1	1	1	1
Egypt																				
SCUA	0	0	0	0	0	1	1	1	1	0	0	0	0	0	0	0	0	0	0	0
Egypt. guar.	0	0	0	0	0	0	0	0	0	1	1	1	1	1	0	0	0	1	1	1
Decimal	0	2	6	10	14	34	28	42	46	65	66	70	74	78	16[a]	18[a]	22[a]	80[a]	82[a]	86[a]

[a]Unknown by Egypt.

Table 4.10 Stability Analysis of the Invasion of the Suez Canal Hypergame

Britain and France

```
×   ×   ×   ×   E   E   E   E   ×   ×   ×   ×   ×   ×   ×   ×   ×   ×   ×   ×
r   s   s   s   r   r   r   r   u   u   u   u   u   u   u   u   u   u   u   u
34  38  42  46 ⌈18  22⌉⌈82  86⌉ 78  74  70  66  14  10   6   2  16  80  65   0
    34  34  34                  82] 82] 82] 82] 18] 18] 18] 18] 18] 82] 82] 18]
        38  38                  86] 86] 86] 86] 22] 22] 22] 22] 22] 86] 86] 22]
            42                  78  78  78      14  14  14  14  78  78  14
                                74  74          10  10  10  74  74  10
                                70               6   6  70  70   6
                                                 2  66  66   2
                                                80  16
```

Britain and France perceived by Egypt

```
r   s   s   s   r   u   u   u   r   u   u   u   u   u
34  38  42  46  78  74  70  66  14  10   6   2  65   0
    34  34  34      78  78  78      14  14  14  78  14
        38  38          74  74          10  10  74  10
            42          70               6  70   6
                                        66   2
```

Egypt

```
×   ×   ×   ×   ×   ×   ×   ×   E   E   ×   ×   ×   ×
r   r   r   r   r   r   r   r   r   r   u   u   u   u
0  65  ⌈2  66⌉⌈6  70⌉ 10  74  14  78  34  38  42  46
                              2]  6] 10  78
                             66] 70] 74  14
```

overall equilibriums

18, 22, 82, 86

involve invasion...
which don't exist
in Egyptian game.

come 16 is preferred to outcome 80, in which the Allies do not negotiate but Egypt does. This is due to the fact that outcome 80 would result in more world criticism of Britain and France (since Egypt at least is trying to negotiate). Because of the Allies' strong feelings against Egypt and their unwillingness to concede to Egyptian demands, both outcomes 16 and 80 are preferred over outcome 65, where both players negotiate Egyptian guarantees. The last outcome is 0, which involves Egypt's refusal to negotiate any guarantees. This was viewed as least preferable by the Allies because of the possible threat to Allied shipping.

The preference vector in Table 4.10 for Egypt's view of the Allies' position is the same as the preference vector for Britain and France except that the outcomes involving an invasion have been removed. Egypt is not aware of outcomes 18, 22, 82, 86, 16, and 80 since these outcomes are formed by the Allies choosing the secret invasion option.

The last preference vector in Table 4.10 orders the outcomes according to Egypt's preferences. The most preferred outcome is 0 because it gives Nasser the most credibility: the Allies concede the canal to him without protest. Outcome 65 is the next most preferred outcome since the Allies negotiate an Egyptian guarantee. This concedes the canal to Egypt and also boosts Nasser's prestige. The next eight outcomes (2, 66, 6, 70, 10, 74, 14, and 78) deal with stalemates in negotiations. These are ordered from most to least preferred according to an increase in threatening measures from the Allies. If the only difference between two outcomes is Egypt selecting the option to negotiate Egyptian guarantees, the outcomes are considered equally preferred since none of these eight outcomes involves the Allies also negotiating Egyptian guarantees. A stalemate is preferable to a return to the original situation where the canal is controlled by an external agency. If Nasser were to allow external control, his political standing would almost certainly be threatened. The outcomes where this occurs (34, 38, 42, and 46) are hence least preferred by Egypt.

Stability Analysis. The preference vectors in Table 4.10 are used to determine which outcomes are possible resolutions to this second level hypergame. A *vertical bar* joining UIs under a given outcome indicates that these USs are equally preferred by the player being considered. To analyze the outcomes in the preference vector of Britain and France for stability, deterrents are formed by checking the preference vector of Egypt. Likewise, when analyzing the outcomes in Egypt's preference vector for stability, credible sanctions against UIs are found in the Allies' preference vector. For instance, in Table 4.10 the Allies have a UI from outcome 38 to outcome 34. In Egypt's preference vector there is a UI from 34 to 2. Returning to the preference vector for Britain and France, it can be seen that outcome 2 is less preferred than 38. Hence, outcome 38 is stable for the Allies. The overall equilibriums in the hypergame are obtained by comparing the stability results in the first and third preference vectors. As can be seen in Table 4.10, the outcomes that have an *E* written above them in the Allies' preference vector are outcomes 18, 22, 82, and 86.

By comparing the second and third preference vectors in Table 4.10, stability results and equilibriums can be obtained for the outcomes in the preference vector for Egypt's view of Britain and France and also in the preference vector for Egypt. The equilibriums for Egypt's mistaken interpretation of the game are outcomes 14 and 78. From Table 4.9, outcome 78 is a stalemate where the Allies are negotiating SCUA and using economic and military pressure while Egypt is negotiating its own guarantees. Outcome 14 is the same except that Egypt does not negotiate. As shown in the Allies' actual preference vector, Britain and France have UIs from 78 to the equilibriums 82 or 86. Since Egypt is not aware of the surprise invasion, that country possesses no deterrents to stop it. Likewise, the UIs for the Allies from outcome 14 result in an invasion of Egypt according to either equilibrium 18 or 22. No outcomes need to be checked for simultaneous stability in this analysis.

The four possible resolutions to the second part of the Suez conflict provided by this analysis all involve an invasion of the canal by the Allies after a stalemate in negotiations. They differ trivially according to whether the Allies apply economic pressure or whether Egypt attempts to negotiate Egyptian guarantees. Outcome 18, where neither of these occurs, is the historical resolution to this conflict.

4.4 Important Concepts from Chapter 4

In a hypergame, one or more of the players have misperceptions regarding the dispute. Strategic surprise constitutes a special type of hypergame where at least one player possesses one or more options that are unknown to the others. By choosing a strategy for which an unknown option is selected, a player can often attain a more advantageous position.

As demonstrated by the fall of France and the Suez crisis applications, strategic surprise is of great importance for analyzing conflicts that can happen in the real world. Along with the Cuban missile crisis studied in Section 3.2, these strategic surprise disputes can be modeled as second level hypergames. They can be conveniently analyzed using a compact version of hypergame analysis (see Tables 3.7, 4.2, 4.6, and 4.10).

Questions

1. Suppose France knew about Germany's Ardennes option but Germany did not know this. France could than have defended at the Ardennes. Model this situation as a third level hypergame.
2. Develop a model for the Suez invasion conflict in which there are three players: the Allies, Egypt, and the USSR. Assume that both the USSR and Egypt know that the USSR is a player in the conflict, but the Allies do not. One Soviet option would be military action in defense of Egypt. Selecting a reasonable preference ordering for each player, perform a complete hypergame analysis.
3. Research a historical case of strategic surprise and perform a thorough analysis of a hypergame model of the conflict.

Chapter 5
Sensitivity and Coalition Analysis

5.1 Introduction

The goal of *sensitivity analysis* is to be able to assess the relative validity of the results of a conflict analysis even if the information being used is erroneous. Ideally, a sensitivity analysis should also indicate in what manner the results are most sensitive to errors in information. In this chapter a number of different approaches that can be used for sensitivity analysis are described. These include performing the analysis with different preferences for the players, considering the conflict as a hypergame, and adopting a more conservative criterion for sequential stability.

Another consideration that can be used for sensitivity analysis is the effect of players forming coalitions in a conflict. A *coalition* is a group of players who chose to act together in the game for their mutual benefit. As described in Chapter 2, when performing an analysis that involves more than two players, sanctions are formed by actions of consistent improvement by the individual players. However, often players do act together. By changing a strategy in conjunction with other players, a member of a coalition can attain a preferred outcome that could not be attained by unilateral improvement. Coalition analysis determines the effect of a coalition on the stability calculated for a game model. To explore the use of coalition analysis in the study of a conflict thoroughly, the methodology is employed for studying the 1979 Lancaster Peace Talks concerning the civil war in Zimbabwe. These were originally analyzed by Kuhn et al. (1983).

5.2 Techniques for Sensitivity Analysis

5.2.1 Multiple Analyses

One technique of sensitivity analysis consists of performing a stability analysis a number of times. One can then observe the results for various different models and see how the conclusions can differ. Players, options, or preferences can all be changed, or any combination of these.

For example, Table 5.1 lists four different possible preference vectors that Khrushchev might have developed for the United States in the Cuban missile crisis of Chapter 1, as well as the associated stability analysis results. In spite of a variety of preference orderings for the United States, the conflict analysis results do not change very much. The only major change occurs when it is assumed that the United States would prefer to launch an air strike on Cuba rather than a blockade. In this circumstance the equilibrium where the United States imposes a blockade while the USSR has withdrawn the missiles is replaced by a similar equilibrium

Table 5.1 Sensitivity of the Analysis of the Cuban Missile Crisis to Changes in U.S Preferences

Preference Vectors with Stability and equilibriums[a]													Explanation
	E	E	×	×	×	×	×	×	×	×	×	×	Preference ordering
U.S.	r	s	r	u	u	u	u	u	r	u	u	u	used in Chapter 1.
	4	6	5	7	2	1	3	0	11	9	10	8	U.S. willing to fight, but prefers blockade.
USSR	r	s	r	u	r	u	r	u	u	u	u	u	
	0	4	6	2	5	1	7	3	11	9	10	8	
	E	E	×	×	×	×	×	×	×	×	×	×	U.S. will permit missiles
U.S.	r	s	u	u	r	u	u	u	r	u	u	u	rather than strike
	4	6	5	7	2	0	1	3	11	9	10	8	Cuba in air attack.
USSR	r	s	r	u	r	u	r	u	u	u	u	u	
	0	4	6	2	5	1	7	3	11	9	10	8	
	E	E	×	×	×	×	×	×	×	×	×	×	U.S. prefers air strike to
U.S.	r	s	u	u	r	u	u	u	r	u	u	u	a blockade.
	4	5	6	7	1	2	3	0	11	9	10	8	
USSR	r	s	r	s	r	u	r	u	u	u	u	u	
	0	4	6	2	5	1	7	3	11	9	10	8	
	E	E	×	×	×	×	×	×	×	×	×	×	U.S. does not want to
U.S.	r	s	r	u	u	u	u	u	r	u	u	u	strike Cuba by air.
	4	6	2	0	5	7	1	3	11	9	10	8	
USSR	r	s	r	u	r	u	r	u	u	u	u	u	
	0	4	6	2	5	1	7	3	11	9	10	8	

[a]UIs not shown.

where the United States attacks the missile bases by air and the USSR withdraws from Cuba.

A problem with this approach to sensitivity analysis is that it can be tedious, especially if players or options are changed in addition to the preferences. Computer assistance, discussed in Chapter 7, can be of aid in this respect since it speeds up the model development and stability analysis of a conflict.

5.2.2 Hypergame Analysis

Hypergame analysis, discussed thoroughly in Chapters 3 and 4, provides for the inclusion of misinformation into a conflict analysis. Hypergames can clearly be used to model various situations that are similar to the conflict problem in order to do a sensitivity analysis in the manner of the previous section.

However, note that a hypergame analysis provides an additional advantage. A hypergame sensitivity analysis not only permits the analysis of the nature of the game stability for various changes of preference vector, but also demonstrates the results of acting in belief of a player's preferences where those beliefs are in error. For example, Khrushchev could have performed a hypergame analysis of the Cuban missile crisis to see the results of himself acting on the belief that the United States would not be aggressive in its response to missiles in Cuba, whereas in reality the United States would prefer to be aggressive. This is exactly the hypergame analyzed in Section 3.2 of this book.

5.2.3 Conservative Sanction Criterion

Many preference vectors will have groups of outcomes that have been "bridged" by the analyst to indicate that they are best considered as equally preferred outcomes, as described in Section 2.3.4. Recall that as a consequence of two outcomes being equally preferred, there is normally no UI from one to the other, since a player would not be expected to change strategy if no improvement would result. However, a more conservative attitude can be adopted when examining for sanctions by considering that players might change outcomes within equally preferred blocks. Since such changes within a block of outcomes are not improvements for a player, they are called *unilateral changes* (UCs). Thus players have two kinds of unilateral movements: UIs, where a player can improve unilaterally to a more preferred outcome, and UCs, where a player can change to an equally preferred outcome. A third unilateral movement, the *unilateral disimprovement,* is not utilized in the conflict analysis methods dealt with in this book.

For example, consider a two-player game where each player has two options:

Player A					
option a		0	1	0	1
Player B					
option b		0	0	1	1
decimal		0	1	2	3

A completed stability tableau for this game might be the following:

		×	E	×	×
		r	r	r	u
Player A		0	1	3	2
					3
		r	u	r	u
Player B		1	3	2	0
			1		2

Noting that player A can change (not improve) strategies by moving either from outcome 0 to 1 or from outcome 1 to 0, the more conservative criterion for sequential sanctioning can be implemented by first listing these possible changes of strategy as UCs in A's preference vector. With the understanding that UCs within an equally preferred block are used *for sanctions alone*, the stability analysis is completed in the conventional manner, giving:

	×	E	E	×
	r	r	r	u
Player A	0	1	3	2
	1	0		3
	r	s	r	u
Player B	1	3	2	0
		1		2

Because Player A's UC of outcome 1 to 0 sanctions the UI by B from outcome 3, it is determined that the stability of outcome 3 is very sensitive to the preference that player A has between outcomes 0 and 1. If both UIs and UCs are to be considered within an equally preferred block, they can be written below each other in separate groups under each outcome. This is illustrated in Table 5.10 for the Zimbabwe conflict, which is also analyzed using the conservative sanction criterion in Section 5.3.

This conservative criterion for sanctions reflects a lack of certainty on the part of the players about the preferences of their opponents when the analyst has represented groups of outcomes as equally preferred. For this reason, outcomes under a bridge that have been given UCs for use in sanctioning are better handled as *unknown preferences* rather than as equally preferred. Sensitivity analysis using unknown preferences is very convenient since it can be done by simply adding the UCs to the original stability analysis tableau and noting how they change the analysis. The nature of the changes resulting from adopting a conservative criterion for sanctions demonstrates how sensitive the analysis is to small changes in player preference.

There are certain circumstances where it is necessary to include UIs, as opposed to UCs, within a block of equally preferred outcomes. For example, when constructing coalitions, this will often occur, as will be discussed in the analysis of the Zimbabwe conflict presented in Section 5.3. For this reason, the bridge used above certain sets of outcomes is best considered to be an indication of outcomes that do not conform to the conventional, strictly ordinal ordering of outcomes, rather than just of those that are equally preferred. Outcomes under a bridge may be equally preferred, may have unknown preferences, or may have UIs among them. Generally, the UIs alone will indicate the exact nature of the preferences under a bridge, except when the conservative sanction criterion is being used.

5.2.4 Coalitions

Coalition Characteristics. There are several characteristics that are usually found when coalitions are significant in a conflict. First, there must be at least three players in the game: it takes at least two players to form a coalition, and for there to continue to be a conflict, there must be another opposing player. Second, individual parties who form a coalition do not forfeit their independence, as they would if the coalition were considered as a single player in the ordinary sense. Each member of the coalition is able to choose from their available options without serious interference from other members of the coalition. If this is not the case, and a party in a conflict is totally dominated by another, then the two participants would best be considered as a single ordinary player rather than as a coalition. For example, in the Cuban missile crisis examined in Chapter 1, the player Cuba was completely absorbed by the player USSR. Because Cuba was unable to act independently, the player comprising the USSR and Cuba was not a coalition.

Third, coalitions are also characterized by shared goals. The members of the coalition generally have a common objective although they may differ on details. For example, in the GDU conflict of Chapter 2 it might make sense for the U.S. opposition and the Canadian opposition to form a coalition because they both want to stop the project. It would not be reasonable, however, for a coalition to be formed by U.S. support and Canadian opposition.

Fourth, the formation of coalitions is made easier when a similarity in the structure or characteristics of the individual members exists. For example, in the GDU conflict the player IJC is unlikely to form a coalition w₁.h any of the other players because it is clearly structurally different from them.

Coalitions in Sensitivity Analysis. When performing a stability analysis for a game with more than two players as described in Section 2.4, a credible sanction can be any outcome generated as a result of the players other than the one under consideration consistently improving themselves from the outcome being examined. This means that the players are acting independently, each trying to obtain a preferred outcome without cooperating among themselves. However, in the real world, players do cooperate, especially when they share the same general objectives with respect to a specified conflict. Thus as a form of sensitivity analysis for games of more than two players, coalition analysis is invaluable. It allows the determination of the change in the nature of the game stability when a player or a player's opposition cooperates.

The conflict analysis of a game where a coalition preference vector has been developed from former individual players proceeds in the same manner as a standard conflict analysis, with the coalition being treated as a single player. Certain UIs may be determined in a coalition preference vector that lead from one outcome to another that is bridged to (or in the same block as) the first. Unilateral improvements between bridged outcomes are treated as any other UI; that is, they can make an outcome unstable for the coalition as well as induce sequential stability for another player.

The underlying principle for determining the coalition preference vector is that an outcome is not preferred by the coalition to another outcome if any member of the coalition does not prefer it (Howard, 1971). Equivalently, in order for an outcome to be preferred to a particular outcome by the coalition, all members of the coalition must prefer it. In order to develop thoroughly an algorithm that employs this principle, the following sections of this chapter are devoted to the presentation and analysis of the Zimbabwe conflict. Following a presentation of the history of the problem and a conventional conflict analysis, the coalition analysis algorithm is described and then applied to the Zimbabwe conflict.

5.3 Historical Description of the Zimbabwe Conflict

Zimbabwe is a relatively prosperous country located in the interior of southern Africa and has a total area of $391,000$ km^2, which is about three times the size of England. Of the almost seven million people who live in Zimbabwe, the vast majority, approximately 95%, are black Africans; the rest are mainly of European descent. Throughout its history, the country has been known by a number of names including Southern Rhodesia (1889–1965), Rhodesia (1965–1979), Zimbabwe–Rhodesia (1979–1980), and Zimbabwe as of March 1980.

In spite of its prosperity, based on an economy of agriculture, mining, and manufacturing, Zimbabwe has recently had a turbulent history. Black nationalist groups, under patriotic front leaders Mugabe and Nkomo, had been fighting in earnest since the early 1970s to topple the white minority government headed by Rhodesian Front (RF) leader and Prime Minister Ian Smith. In addition, world opinion was against the whites and, as a result, Rhodesia was not diplomatically recognized by many other countries and international economic sanctions were brought against it. During the discussions held at Lancaster House in London from September to December of 1979, the country of Zimbabwe–Rhodesia (as it was known at the time) confronted the question of how to end a seven-year-old civil war, remove economic sanctions, and gain international recognition as a majority rule government.

Zimbabwe's political troubles and, ironically, economic prosperity began in 1889 when Cecil Rhodes and other white settlers secured for the South African Company a royal character for the area now known as Zimbabwe. Rhodes quickly subjugated the Matabele and Mashona people who were living there and in 1895 named the area Southern Rhodesia, "but it was not recognized by the British Government till the Southern Rhodesian Order in Council in 1898" (Blake, 1977). In 1923, the white settlers voted for Southern Rhodesia to become a British colony. As part of the dominion of the United Kingdom, however, Britain insisted upon universal suffrage, and consequently a black majority rule government. The white minority obstinately resisted this British suggestion because

> the settlers had voted to accept "a constitution which save for a pretended and probably illusory reservation to the Imperial authority of control over native affairs, established local Responsible Government" [Mutambirwa, 1980, p. 211].

In the late 1940s and early 1950s, movement toward a Central African Federation of Southern and Northern Rhodesia and Nyasaland was apparent because of

> Economic arguments—the dollar-earning capacity of copper and tobacco— and strategic considerations—the danger of South Africa drawing territories north of Limpopo into her orbit [Blake, 1977, p. 247].

On October 23, 1953, Britain allowed the formation of the soon-to-be-apparent white-dominated Federation. The Federation did not last, though, because of

> the alienation of African nationalists from the European electorate, which gathered momentum after 1958. By the end of 1962, all three Territorial Governments had ceased to support the continuation of the Federation.

Succession had already been in principle conceded to Nyasaland and it was only a matter of time before the coalition government of Northern Rhodesia under Kaunda and Nkumbuda would follow the same course [Blake, 1977, p. 345].

The formal dissolution of the federation occurred on January 1, 1964.

In 1961, the whites tightened their control on the government of Southern Rhodesia by creating a single 65-member legislature in which only those of "superior means and education" (the whites and a few blacks) had the right to vote for 50 seats in parliament.

By many, and not only Rhodesian Front [a political party consisting of a group of prominent white farmers headed by Ian Smith] supporters, it was claimed that the granting of the 1961 Constitution implied acceptance of Rhodesian independence if and when the Federation ceased to exist [Clements, 1969, p. 186].

Indeed, on November 11, 1965, a year after the demise of the Federation, the Southern Rhodesian people elected Ian Smith as their Prime Minister. Britain immediately imposed economic sanctions on Rhodesia and declared the government illegal. It was not until December 1966 that Ian Smith and British Prime Minister Harold Wilson finally met on the ship H.M.S. Tiger in the Mediterranian off the Rock of Gilbraltar for talks on the normalization of relations between the two countries. Wilson presented Smith with a lenient "Five-Principle" proposal that essentially allowed Rhodesia a British-recognized independence for a promise of eventual majority rule in the country. Smith refused these proposals and, as a result, the United Nations Security Council imposed international economic sanctions on the country (Encyclopedia Britannica, 1979, vol. 15, p. 815).

For the next five years, Smith's regime became more and more entrenched in its minority rule. The October 1968 H.M.S. Fearless talks, at which British terms were similar to those given to Rhodesia in 1966, failed due to Smith's intransigency (Legum, 1969). In June 1969, the RF party held a referendum restricted to whites only, which overwhelmingly approved a Rhodesian constitution based on the 1961 revisions to the government (Legum, 1972). In March 1971, the RF swept all 50 seats in the legislature. In spite of growing criticism (13 bordering or near-bordering African states issued the Lusaka Manifesto denouncing the Rhodesian Front's 1969 referendum), guerrilla activity remained sporadic and the United Nations sanctions proved frustratingly ineffectual because of merchants operating out of countries violating the international sanctions.

By late 1971, however, the ailing Rhodesian economy, hurt by a serious drop in mineral prices and a poor foreign exchange, forced some white Rhodesian concessions. In November of 1971, Britain and Rhodesia reached an agreement based on the Five Principles (Legum, 1972). However, the Pearce Commission, created by the British government to test the opinion of all segments of the Rhodesian population, found the agreement unacceptable to the majority. The black Rhodesian population wanted actual majority rule and not merely the promise of it as set out in the Five Principles. As a result of the Pearce Commission's findings, international sanctions were retained and recognition withheld from Rhodesia.

Military, political, and economic pressures against Rhodesia intensified between 1972 and 1978. December 1972, when a white Rhodesian farm was subjected to rocket fire by guerrillas, is generally considered as the start of the Rhodesian civil war (Legum, 1973). In late 1974, the Portuguese surrendered a once impartial Mozambique to black nationalists (Legum, 1975). By 1976, President Samora Marcel of Mozambique closed his borders and communications with Rhodesia in a show of displeasure of Rhodesian racist policies (Legum, 1977). A marked decline in the white population due to emigration left a shortage of personnel in agriculture and industry during this period. Also, the oil embargo significantly affected the fuel hungry industry of Rhodesia.

During the early 1970s many black opposition parties emerged.

On December 8, 1974, an agreement was concluded at Lusaka, Zambia, by Bishop Abel Muzorewa of the African National Council (ANC), Joshua Nkomo of the Zimbabwe African People's Union (ZAPU), Ndabaningi Sithole of the Zimbabwe African National Union (ZANU), and James Chikerema of the Front for the Liberation of Zimbabwe (Frolizi), whereby the latter three would join an enlarged ANC executive under Bishop Muzorewa. On September 1976, Sithole announced that ZANU had withdrawn from the ANC, which, since its formation in December 1974, had been split into two wings led by Bishop Muzorewa and ZAPU leader Nkomo. Collaterally, Mugabe claimed the leadership of ZANU and the Sithole group within Rhodesia became known as ANC–Sithole, while the Muzorewa group became known as the United African National Council (UANC). [Furthermore,] Mugabe . . . announced the formation of a Patriotic Front (PF) linking ZANU and ZAPU military units [Banks, 1979, p. 559].

Thus, the black opposition can be broken down into the moderate black African parties (UANC, ANC–Sithole, and ZAPU lead by Muzorewa, Sithole, and Chirau, respectively) and overtly insurgent black African groups (ZAPU and ZANU, united under the PF lead by Nkomo and Mugabe, respectively).

Reacting to the intensified pressures, Smith held secret talks with moderate black leader Bishop Muzorewa throughout 1973 and early 1974 (Legum, 1975). These discussions proved to be futile. However, due to political pressure not only from Zambian president Kaunda but also from Rhodesian ally South Africa Prime Minister Vorster, Ian Smith and patriotic front leader Nkomo met on August 25, 1975. Unfortunately, by March 1976, these talks had also broken down (Legum, 1976).

In March 1978 "inside talks" between Ian Smith and the three moderate black African leaders (Muzorewa, Sithole, and Chirau) concluded the so-called Internal Settlement (IS). At the same time, "outside talks" were conducted among British and American emissaries, leaders of the PF (Nkomo and Mugabe), and the "Front Line Presidents" of Tanzania, Zambia, Mozambique, Botswana, and Angola. These outside talks concluded that the IS did not command sufficient authority to bring the war or international sanctions to an end (Legum, 1979).

In spite of world opinion, Zimbabwe–Rhodesia was created out of the IS on May 31, 1979. This ended 88 years of white domination, but a true majority ruled independent government had not yet emerged. In essence, the 65-man Rhodesian legislature was increased to 100 with only 28 seats reserved for the whites; however, special privileges and powers were still retained by the whites. Muzorewa, after a campaign viewed by many blacks with extreme skepticism, gained a majority in the new government; Ian Smith became a cabinet minister without portfolio (Legum, 1979).

White Rhodesian hopes for recognition of their IS settlement faded quickly in 1979. The Zimbabwe–Rhodesian army now faced about 40,000 guerrillas, 13,000 of whom were now thought to operate within the country (double the previous year). Throughout early 1979 Muzorewa shuttled between the African United Organization (an organization representing many African countries), the United States, and Britain to gain international recognition for his government, but he was unsuccessful (New York Times Index, 1979).

A hopeful breakthrough for the Zimbabwe conflict appeared on August 5, 1979, at the Commonwealth's 22nd Conference in Lusaka, where new proposals were approved calling for a ceasefire, a new constitution, and an election supervised by the British government. Continuing the impetus, Britain formally invited the representatives of Muzorewa's government and the PF to Lancaster House, London. Finally, on September 11, 1979, with British Foreign Secretary Lord Carrington presiding, the Zimbabwe–Rhodesians and guerrillas met (New York Times Index, 1979). The three participants sought a way to end the fighting, remove economic sanctions, and achieve international recognition for Zimbabwe–Rhodesia.

5.4 Stability Analysis of the Zimbabwe Conflict

5.4.1 Modeling the Conflict

September 11, 1979, the date the talks began at Lancaster House, London, is selected as the time and place to proceed with the conflict analysis for the Zimbabwe dispute. As shown in Table 5.2, the three players in the

Table 5.2 Feasible Outcomes in the Zimbabwe Conflict

Rhodesians																				
Advocate IS	0	1	0	1	0	0	1	0	1	0	0	1	0	1	0	0	1	0	1	0
Escalate war	0	0	1	1	0	0	0	1	1	0	0	0	1	1	0	0	0	1	1	0
Compromise	0	0	0	0	1	0	0	0	0	1	0	0	0	0	1	0	0	0	0	1
PF																				
Accept IS	0	0	0	0	0	0	0	0	0	0	0	0	0	0	0	0	0	0	0	0
Escalate war	1	1	1	1	1	0	0	0	0	0	1	1	1	1	1	0	0	0	0	0
Compromise	0	0	0	0	0	1	1	1	1	1	0	0	0	0	0	1	1	1	1	1
British																				
Accept IS	0	0	0	0	0	0	0	0	0	0	0	0	0	0	0	0	0	0	0	0
Support PF	1	1	1	1	1	1	1	1	1	1	0	0	0	0	0	0	0	0	0	0
Compromise	0	0	0	0	0	0	0	0	0	0	1	1	1	1	1	1	1	1	1	1
Decimal	144	145	146	147	148	160	161	162	163	164	272	273	274	275	276	288	289	290	291	292

Zimbabwe conflict are the Rhodesians, Patriotic Front (PF), and Britain. The Rhodesian player, or actually the Zimbabwe–Rhodesians as they were known in September 1979, represents not only Ian Smith's Rhodesian Front and the white minority in Zimbabwe–Rhodesia, but also the moderate black leaders (Muzorewa, Sithole, and Chirau) and their following. The PF is composed of the Patriotic Front guerrilla group led by Mugabe and Nkomo, which is influenced by the Front Line Presidents. Britain includes only itself but is influenced by the United States.

As can be seen in Table 5.2, the Rhodesian's options would be to try to convince the PF and Britain to accept the Internal Settlement (advocate IS), escalate the war, and, if these two options are not possible, entertain serious conciliatory discussion with the PF on black majority rule (compromise). The PF desire to gain control of Zimbabwe–Rhodesia and thus their two most preferable options would be either to escalate the war or compromise. There is also the remote possibility that due to pressure from the Front Line Presidents, the PF may choose to accept the IS as another option. Britain's main objective is to convince the Rhodesians and PF to settle the dispute peacefully. The British options, therefore, are to take a position supporting the Rhodesians (accept IS), supporting the PF (support PF), or one that is unbiased (compromise).

Each column in Table 5.3 represents a set of outcomes that can be removed. The total number of removable outcomes contained in all the columns in Table 5.3 is 492. When these are removed, the 20 feasible outcomes appearing in Table 5.2 remain.

The decimal preference vectors for each of the players in the Zimbabwe conflict are shown in Table 5.4. The Rhodesian preference vector can be broken into four main blocks, reading from left (most preferred) to right (least preferred) in Table 5.4: the PF and British compromise (292, . . ., 291), the PF compromise with British support (160, . . ., 163), the PF

Table 5.3 Outcomes Removed from the Zimbabwe Conflict

Rhodesia													
Advocate IS	–	–	–	–	–	–	–	1	–	–	–	–	–	–
Escalate war	–	–	–	–	–	–	1	–	–	–	–	–	–	–
Compromise	–	–	–	–	–	–	1	1	–	–	–	–	1	–
PF													
Accept IS	–	–	–	–	1	1	–	–	–	0	1	0	1	1
Escalate war	–	–	–	1	–	1	–	–	–	–	0	–	–
Compromise	–	–	–	1	1	–	–	–	–	0	–	–
Britain													
Accept IS	–	1	1	–	–	–	–	–	0	1	0	–	–	–
Support PF	1	–	1	–	–	–	–	–	0	–	–	–	–	–
Compromise	1	1	–	–	–	–	–	–	0	–	–	–	–	–

Table 5.4 Decimal Preference Vectors for Zimbabwe Dispute

Preference vector position

	1	2	3	4	5	6	7	8	9	10	11	12	13	14	15	16	17	18	19	20
Rhodesia	292	288	289	290	291	160	161	164	162	163	272	273	276	274	275	144	145	148	146	147
PF	292	164	148	276	160	161	288	289	163	162	291	290	144	145	147	146	272	273	275	274
Britain	292	164	276	148	288	289	160	161	291	290	163	162	272	273	275	274	144	145	147	146

escalates the fighting at the same time the British are trying to act un-
biasedly in the talks (272, . . ., 275) and, least preferred, the PF escalates
the civil war with British support (144, . . ., 147). Similarly, the PF's
preference vector may be subdivided into three main blocks, from most
to least preferred: the Rhodesians compromise (292, . . ., 276), the PF
compromises (160, . . ., 144) and, last, the PF escalates the war (145,
. . ., 274). Finally, Britain has three sets of outcomes that are quite similar
to those of the PF's preference vector. In fact, the only consistent difference between the two preference vectors is that, within each of the
outcome sets, the British prefer mediating the talks impartially as opposed
to supporting the PF politically. (Naturally, the PF would prefer the reverse of this.) Thus, the outcome pair (148, 276) in the PF preference
vector appears as (276, 148) in the British preference vector in Table 5.4.
Outcomes 292 and 164, in which the PF and Rhodesians both compromise,
are considered equally preferred.

5.4.2 Stability Analysis

Each of the outcomes listed in the preference vector in Table 5.5 is analyzed for stability for each player separately and also across the players.
Note that outcome 276 in the PF preference vector is simultaneously
sanctioned, as indicated by a ⋈. The calculation is:

$$(292 + 272) - 276 = 288$$

Since 288 is less preferable to 276 by the PF, 276 is simultaneously
sanctioned.

Outcome 292, which is stable for all three players, is the only equilibrium
for the Zimbabwe conflict. Thus outcome 292 represents all three parties
in the conflict seriously discussing black majority rule in Zimbabwe–Rhodesia. In fact, this is exactly what occurred historically and
by December 23, 1979, the three parties hammered out an agreement for
transition to black majority rule. This agreement entailed reducing the
seats reserved for whites from 28 to 20 out of a total of 100 seats in the
legislature and eliminating most special privileges and powers held by the
whites since the IS settlement. On March 4, 1980, ex-guerrilla leader
Robert Mugabe's party took 57 of 100 seats to give him an absolute
majority in the Parliament of the country now named Zimbabwe.

5.5 Coalition Analysis of the Zimbabwe Conflict

5.5.1 Ordinality in Coalition Formation

Coalition analysis for the Zimbabwe dispute is performed on ordinal preference vectors. The algorithm used to combine the individual preference

Table 5.5 Stability Analysis of the Zimbabwe Conflict Without a Coalition

Rhodesian Preference Vector

Overall stability	E	×	×	×	×	×	×	×	×	×	×	×	×	×	×	×	×	×	×	×
Rhodesian stability	r	u	u	u	u	r	u	u	u	u	r	u	u	u	u	r	u	u	u	u
Rhodesian preference vector	292	288	289	290	291	160	161	164	162	163	272	273	276	274	275	144	145	148	146	147
Most preferred UIs		292	292	292	292		160	160	160	160		272	272	272	272		144	144	144	144
Next most preferred UIs			288	288	288			161	161	161			273	273	273			145	145	145
Third most preferred UIs				289	289				164	164				276	276				148	148
Least preferred UIs					290					162					274					146

PF's Preference Vector

PF stability	r	r	s	u	r	r	r	r	r	u	u	u	u	u	u	u	u	u	u
PF preference vector	292	164	148	276	160	161	288	289	162	163	290	144	145	273	274	272	275	146	147
UIs	164	292			160	161	288	289	162	163	290	144	145	273	274	272	275	146	147

British Preference Vector

British stability	r	u	r	s	r	u	r	r	r	u	r	u	u	u	r	u	u	u
British preference vector	292	164	276	148	288	160	289	161	290	162	291	163	272	273	144	145	274	275
UIs	292		276		288	160	289	161	290	162	291	163	272	273	144	145	274	275

vectors of all the merging players into a single coalition preference vector, therefore, must take into account the ordinality of each player's preference vector. When the outcomes in different individual coalescing preference vectors are ordered in a similar manner, these outcomes are ordered in the same fashion in the coalition preference vector. However, when outcomes in different individual coalescing preference vectors are ordered differently from one another, then these outcomes are considered nonordinal in the coalition preference vector.

Nonordinality occurs when *some* outcomes in a preference vector are both more *and* less preferable than a particular outcome. For example, consider the PF and British preference vectors given in Tables 5.4 and 5.5. Both the PF and Britain prefer outcome 148 over outcome 288; thus, in the coalition preference vector of these two players, 148 is assumed to be preferred to 288. However, a question arises as to what the ordering of outcomes 148 and 276 would be in a coalition preference vector for these two players. Outcome 276 is preferred to 148 by Britain; the reverse ordering holds for the guerrillas (PF). Thus, in the coalition preference vector, outcomes 148 and 276 would be nonordinal.

However, not *all* outcomes within a group of nonordinal outcomes are both more and less preferable than a particular outcome. Consider outcomes 288 and 289 in Table 5.6 where the preference vectors of the PF and British are combined to form a coalition preference vector by following two main steps. Outcome 288 is preferred to outcome 289 for both the PF and the British in Table 5.6 (part 1), yet both appear in the nonordinal region of the PF–British coalition preference vector (part 2). Recall from section 5.2.3 that nonordinal regions are designated by drawing a line across the top of the affected outcomes. Thus, a degree of *order—* agreement among coalition members about the preference ordering of some outcomes—exists in nonordinal regions. Those nonordinal outcomes with the same ordering for all coalition members are referred to as *ordered* nonordinal outcomes; those with conflicting ordering among coalition members are known as *unordered* nonordinal outcomes.

Equally preferred outcomes are considered to be a special case of unordered nonordinal outcomes. Although the latter outcomes may be unordered with respect to only some of the other outcomes in the nonordinal region, the former are considered unordered with respect to all other outcomes in the equally preferred region. For example, outcome 288 is unordered with respect to outcomes 160 and 161 but ordered with respect to outcome 289 in the (288, 289, 160, 161) nonordinal region (Table 5.6, part 2). If these four outcomes were to appear in an equally preferred region, they would all be unordered with respect to each other. Since equally preferred outcomes are a special case of nonordinal outcomes, both are notationally indicated in the same manner in coalition analysis by a connecting bridge placed above the appropriate outcomes. Thus,

Table 5.6 Coalition Analysis Between PF and Britain

Preference vector position	1	2	3	4	5	6	7	8	9	10	11	12	13	14	15	16	17	18	19	20
Individual preference vectors																				
First Above: PF	292	164	148	276	160	161	288	289	163	162	291	290	144	145	147	146	272	273	275	274
Baseline: Britain	292	164	276	148	288	289	160	161	291	290	163	162	272	273	275	274	144	145	147	146
1. Individual bridge removal																				
First Above: PF	292	164	148	276	160	161	288	289	163	162	291	290	144	145	147	146	272	273	275	274
Baseline: Britain	292	164	276	148	288	289	160	161	291	290	163	162	272	273	275	274	144	145	147	146
2. Coalition bridge creation																				
PF–British coalition	292	164	276	148	288	289	160	161	291	290	163	162	272	273	275	274	144	145	147	146
3. Unilateral movements (UIs and UCs)																				
PF–British coalition	292	164	276	148	288	289	160	161	291	290	163	162	272	273	275	274	144	145	147	146
UIs	292	292	292	292									288	289	291	290	288	289	291	290
			164	164									160	161	163	162	160	161	163	162
UCs	148		148	276	160	161	288	289	163	162	291	290	144	145	147	146	272	273	275	274

although outcomes (292,164) are equally preferred before the coalition process and outcomes (276,148) are nonordinal after the coalition in Table 5.6, a single line or 'bridge' is drawn across both these pairs of outcomes to indicate their nonordinality.

A couple of questions arise concerning ordinal coalition analysis. First, it is not known by how much one player prefers one outcome over another. If Britain strongly prefers 276 to 148 and the PF only mildly prefers 148 to 276, then perhaps the outcomes should be ordered in favor of Britain and not be designated as nonordinal in the coalition preference vector. The implicit assumption made is that, although differing strengths of preference may exist for one outcome over another among partners in a coalition preference vector, the cold hard truth of disagreement remains. Whether the partners disagree on ordering by a lot or by a little, disagreement inevitably leads to these outcomes (e.g., 276 and 148 for the PF–British coalition) being designated nonordinal.

A second question arises concerning the insensitivity of the analysis to the relative strengths among players. For instance, if the PF were the stronger member of the coalition supporting outcome 148 over 276 and the British favored outcome 276 over 148, it is possible that the PF retain its ordering of outcomes in the coalition preference vector. However, it is reasoned that the strengths of other players are taken into account in the ordering of an *individual's* preference vector. For example, Britain ordered their 276 and 148 outcomes by taking into account the strength of the PF. That is, the British could have (276,148) in both of which the PF escalates the war, not at position (3,4) in Table 5.4 and 5.6 but further down their preference vector, say at (11,12). However, because they figure they are strong enough relative to the PF, they have located the (276,148) outcomes at their more preferred positions.

The three-part method presented in the next section is used to create a coalition preference vector suitable for stability analysis. This coalition preference vector may be derived from any number of individual coalition preference vectors that are *equal in length*. The first two parts describe the implementation of a coalition algorithm to identify the nonordinal outcomes in the coalition preference vector. In the third part the appropriate UIs (and UCs if desired) for the coalition preference vector are determined before executing a stability analysis of the game containing a coalition. Following these, there is a presentation of a possible metric for indicating the compatibility of coalescing members.

5.5.2 Coalition Algorithm

The coalition algorithm is a systematic method used to compare the ordering of every combination of outcome pairs among two or more players' equally long preference vectors in order to obtain a single coalition preference vector. Although a rather lengthy description is required to explain properly how the algorithm works, one familiar with it would find the process simple to perform and quick. The coalition preference vector is created from the preference vector of one of the merging players which, once stripped of its bridges, is referred to as the *baseline*. The ordering of the coalition baseline preference vector is founded upon designating each contained outcome pair as ordinal or nonordinal. (Ordinal outcomes are those not found beneath a bridge.) Each baseline outcome pair is compared to another *nth-above* player's preference vector. In Table 5.6, Britain's preference vector is the baseline and the PF's is the *first-above* preference vector. (A third player who was to be merged with Britain and the PF would have the *second-above* vector.)

The coalition algorithm contain three parts. The first involves removing wherever possible the nonordinal bridges from the individual preference vectors. Removal of these bridges simplifies the second part of the algorithm which is to determine the nonordinal bridges for the coalition preference vector. The third part involves determining the coalition preference vector's UIs.

Part 1 of Coalition Algorithm: Individual Bridge Removal. The first part of the algorithm involves removing as many bridges as possible from the preference vectors of coalescing players. In essence, a bridge is removed if the outcomes it covers are able to be moved within one player's preference vector so as to permit matching the identical outcome ordering in another player's preference vector. They can be moved in this way because the bridged player treats the affected outcomes with indifference and thus will order them according to another's order. This other player's preference order will be in one of three conditions with respect to the first player's ordered bridged outcomes:

1. Ordinal and aligned (i.e., in the same positions as);
2. Equally preferred and aligned; or
3. simply not aligned with the first's outcomes.

These three cases are described below in greater detail.

Equally Preferred–Ordinal Outcome. An equally preferred–ordinal case arises when an equally preferred outcome in an individual preference vector is so positioned as to be moved to the position of the identical (but ordinal) outcome of another player's preference vector. For example, consider outcomes 292 and 164 in the PF preference vector of Table 5.6. Both outcomes can be moved within the designated equally preferred region and thus could be located either at preference vector positions (1,2) or (2,1). In this example, (292,164) just happens to be positioned at (1,2) and therefore lines up with the position of the ordinal outcomes (292,164) in the British preference vector. However, if outcomes (292,164) had been at positions (2,1) rather than (1,2) for the PF (as in Table 5.7, case 1), this revised situation would still be an equally preferred–ordinal case. Either way, once the outcomes are reshuffled, all affected bridges are removed. Thus, the bridge above (1,2) in the PF preference vector is removed in part 1 of the algrithm.

Equally Preferred–Equally Preferred Outcome. This second case arises when a pair of outcomes are equally preferred in both the baseline and *n*th-above preference vectors. In this situation, the individual preference vector bridges are removed in part 1 of the algorithm, but the appropriate pair of coalition preference vector outcomes are designated equally preferred in part 2. In other words, the affected outcomes are initially de-bridged during the first part of the coalition algorithm but automatically rebridged in the second part. Consider the hypothetical example in Table 5.7, case 2, where it is imagined outcomes 292 and 164 are equally preferred for both the PF and British. In this case, the bridges over both these outcomes would be removed in the preference vectors in part 1 of the coalition algorithm and a bridge automatically reinstated over (292,164) in the coalition preference vector in part 2.

No Match (Unaligned). The third case arises when the equally preferred outcomes are not able to match up with corresponding ordinal outcomes. In this situation, the equally preferred bridges are removed, leaving the revealed outcomes in their unordered positions. This case

Table 5.7 Part 1 of Coalition Analysis Algorithm: Individual Bridge Removal Examples

From this . . .				to this			
Case 1: Equally preferred–ordinal example (hypothetical)							
position	1	2	. . .	position	1	2	. . .
PF	⌐164	292⌐	. . .	PF	292	164	. . .
Britain	292	164	. . .	Britain	292	164	. . .
Br. baseline	292	164	. . .	Br. baseline	292	164	. . .
Case 2: Equally preferred–equally preferred example (hypothetical)							
position	1	2	. . .	position	1	2	. . .
PF	⌐164	292⌐	. . .	PF	292	164	. . .
Britain	⌐292	164⌐	. . .	Britain	292	164	. . .
Br. baseline	292	164	. . .	PF–British	⌐292	164⌐	. . .

Case 3: No match example (hypothetical)										
position	1	2	. . .	6	7	position	1	2	. . .	6	7
PF			. . .	292	164	PF			. . .	292	164
Britain	⌐292	164⌐	. . .			Britain	292	164	. . .		
Br. baseline	292	164	. . .			Br. baseline	292	164	. . .		

occurs when the position in one preference vector of the equally preferred region, in which a particular outcome occurs, does not cover an equivalent region that contains the same ordinal outcome in the merging preference vector. Since the particular outcome cannot move outside its equally preferred region and the equally preferred region cannot move to another position in the preference vector, a match in position between the particular equally preferred outcome and the ordinal outcome is not possible. When the equally preferred bridge is removed, the outcomes affected are left in their unordered positions and the number of strictly ordered outcomes remain the same. An example of this case does not appear for the PF–British coalition in the Zimbabwe dispute. However, consider the simple hypothetical example given in Table 5.7, case 3, where the British have equally preferred outcomes (292,164) at the (1,2) positions and the PF have their ordinal outcomes (292,164) at positions (6,7). In this instance, all outcomes would remain in their individual preference vector positions when the equally preferred bridge is removed from above the British (292,164) outcomes in the first step of the algorithm.

This completes the description of the first half of the coalition algorithm. In summary, the three cases are as follows:

1. *Equally preferred–ordinal outcome.* The equally preferred bridges are removed and the affected outcomes in the individual preference vectors are designated ordinal.
2. *Equally preferred–equally preferred outcome.* The equally preferred bridges are removed from the affected individual preference vector outcomes and the appropriate outcomes in the coalition preference vector are designated equally preferred.
3. *No match (unaligned).* The equally preferred bridges are removed and the affected outcomes remain unchanged in position in the individual preference vectors.

Part 2 of Coalition Algorithm: Coalition Bridge Creation. The determination of the placement of the nonordinal bridges in the coalition preference vector is undertaken in the second part of the algorithm. The coalition vector is constructed in three steps: 1. Leave the previously designated equally preferred outcomes (part 1, case 2) algorithm as is. 2. Regard all individual preference vector outcomes whose order and position is exactly the same for each of the players (*strictly ordered*) as ordinal in the coalition preference vector. 3. Designate all other outcomes as nonordinal.

In the Zimbabwe conflict, the final preference vector contains no previously designated equally preferred sections. However, continuing with the hypothetical example for part 1, case 2, (see Table 5.7), where equally preferred bridges for the PF and British individual preference vectors have been removed and a bridge automatically placed over (292,164) in the coalition preference, one finds, as shown in Table 5.8, case 1 that the bridge over (292,164) in the PF–British coalition simply remains intact.

Only two sets of individual outcomes, 292 and 164, are strictly ordered in the Zimbabwe conflict. As can be seen in part 2 of Table 5.6 (highlighted in Table 5.8, case 2) these outcomes are located in the first and second positions of the PF–British coalition preference vector because they are located in the same positions of both the individual PF and British preference vectors.

The third situation arising in a merging process involves a *bridge expansion* technique. This is amply represented in the PF–British preference vector of the Zimbabwe conflict since the rest of the outcomes in this coalition are nonordinal. Consider outcomes 276 and 148 in part 2 of Table 5.6. As indicated previously, the PF and British prefer these outcomes in an opposite manner to one another. More specifically, note that the location of the (148,276) outcome pair for the PFs is position (3,4) and for the British is (4,3). If one of these players were to interchange this outcome pair each by one position, outcome pair (276,148) for both would

Table 5.8 Part 2 of Coalition Analysis Algorithm: Coalition Bridge Creation Examples

From this . . .				to this				
Case 1. Coalition equally preferred[a]								
position	1	2	. . .	position	1	2	. . .	
PF	292	164	. . .	PF	292	164	. . .	
Britain	292	164	. . .	Britain	292	164	. . .	
PF–Br. coalition	⌐292	164⌐	. . .	PF–British	⌐292	164⌐	. . .	
					(no change)			
Case 2. Individual strictly ordered[b]								
position	1	2	. . .	position	1	2	. . .	
PF	292	164	. . .	PF	292	164	. . .	
Britain	292	164	. . .	Britain	292	164	. . .	
Br. baseline	292	164	. . .	PF–British	292	164	. . .	
					(no change)			
Case 3. Nonordinal outcomes[b]								
position	5	6	7	8	position	5	6	7	8
PF	160	161	288	289	PF	160	161	288	289
Britian	288	289	160	161	Britain	288	289	160	161
Br. baseline	288	289	160	161	PF–British	⌐288	289	160⌐	161
						and then			
						⌐288	289	160	161⌐

[a]Continued from Table 5.7, case 2.
[b]Taken from Table 5.6, part 2.

become strictly ordered. Thus, (276,148) is only *slightly disordered* for the PF–British coalition. This is shown by a short nonordinal line extending across the top of only these two outcomes.

In general, the larger the distance between identical outcomes in different preference vectors, the larger the nonordinal area. Consider outcomes 288, 289, 160, and 161 shown in Table 5.8, case 3 (taken from Table 5.6, part 2). In particular, notice outcome 288. The nonordinal line must extend at least from outcome 288, at position 5 in the baseline preference vector, to outcome 160 at position 7, because outcome 288 occurs at position 7 of the first-above preference vector. The PF–British partnership is unable to decide whether to position outcome 288 in position 5 or 7 of its coalition preference vector as indicated by the nonordinal line drawn between outcomes 288 and 160. The search for nonordinal outcome does not end here, as the question arises as to how outcome 289, inadvertently enclosed by the nonordinal line between outcomes 288 and 160, is to be classed in the coalition preference vector. Outcome 289 appears at position 8 of the PF preference vector, aligned with outcome 161 in the British preference vector. The disagreement between the PF and British about the positioning of outcome 289 entails the extension of the nonordinal line from outcome 288 to outcome 161 at position 8 in the coalition preference vector (hence the term *bridge expansion technique*). In regard to outcome 160, the PF and British disagree once again about the position of this outcome. However, this time, the position of outcome 160 for both players (positions 5 and 7 for the PF and British, respectively) falls within the previously developed nonordinal area (positions 5–8). Thus, the nonordinal line remains the same length. Similarly, the coalescing partners disagree about the position of outcome 161 (positions 6 and 8 for the PF and British, respectively) but once again, it falls within the previous nonordinal area. At this point the nonordinal region stops growing to remain at four outcomes in length.

Once a nonordinal area has stopped expanding, a few things may happen: another nonordinal area can begin (as is the case for outcome 291, the next outcome after 161 as shown in Table 5.6, part 2; an ordinal region may appear; or the end of the coalition preference vector may be reached. A coalition preference vector consisting of a mixture of ordinal and nonordinal outcomes emerges once the end of the coalition preference vector is reached.

Comparing and resolving two outcome pairs across more than two preference vectors is merely an extension of the above coalition technique. Instead of progressing through the baseline preference vector and looking above to only the first-above outcome, the search is extended to all *n*th-above preference vectors. The preference vector that has the outcome furthest out of place with respect to the position of the baseline preference vector is chosen as the extent of the growing nonordinal area.

With the exception of this modification, the coalition algorithm for more than two players are exactly the same as for two players.

In summary, the steps involved in the second part of the coalition algorithm are as follows:

1. Previously designated equally preferred outcomes from part 1, case 2 of the algorithm are left as is.
2. All strictly ordered individual outcomes in part 1 of the coalition algorithm are designated ordinal in the part 2 coalition preference vector.
3. All other outcomes are designated nonordinal according to the above described bridge expansion technique.

Part 3 of Coalition Algorithm: UI Determination. This section describes a simple method to determine the UIs from the outcomes in any coalition preference vector. The determination of UIs within coalition preference vectors is very similar to those in individual preference vectors. The analyst must be careful to recognize that when dealing with the unilateral movements of individual players, all other strategies except the one for the player making the movement remain fixed. In contrast, when dealing with coalitions all other strategies except those of the merging (more than one) players making the movement remain fixed. Consider Table 5.6, part 3. The PF–British coalition player at the bottom of Table 5.6 can make a UI from outcome 148 (0001, 010, 010) to outcome 292 (001, 001, 001) because only strategy (001) of the Rhodesians—the one player outside the coalition—remains the same for both these outcomes.

Coalition preference vectors can have nonordinal outcomes that have UIs. The unilateral movements of nonordinal outcomes are designated either UIs or UCs (see Section 5.2.3) according to whether the outcomes are ordered or unordered, respectively. Ordered nonordinal outcomes (outcomes having the same ordering for all coalition members) treat their unilateral movements as UIs. Unordered nonordinal outcomes (outcomes having conflicting ordering among the coalition members) are treated similarly to equally preferred outcomes and have their unilateral movements treated as UCs if desired by the analyst.

For Zimbabwe, the conservative sanction criterion is invoked; consequently both UIs and UCs are written in Table 5.6, divided into different lines below the coalition preference vector. The unilateral movement 292 for nonordinal outcome 148 (taken from Table 5.6, part 3) and highlighted in Table 5.9, case 1), has been designated a UI because, for both PF and Britain, outcome 292 is preferred to outcome 148. On the other hand, the unilateral movement 276 for nonordinal outcome 148 (also taken from Table 5.6, part 3 and highlighted in Table 5.9, case 2), has been designated a UC because of the reversed ordering of outcomes 276 and 148 in the PF and British preference vectors.

Table 5.9 Part 3 of Coalition Analysis Algorithm: Unilateral Moves Determination Example

Case						Comment
1: Unilateral improvement[a]						
position	1	2	3	4	...	
PF–British	292	164	276	148	...	Outcome 292 is a UI because it is
				292		preferred to 148.
2: Unilateral change[a]						
position	1	2	3	4	...	
PF–British	292	164	276	148	...	Both 276 and 148 are UCs because
			148	276		they are equally preferred.

[a]Taken from Table 5.6, part 3.

In summary, here are the steps involved in the third part of the coalition algorithm:

1. Unilateral movements for ordered nonordinal outcomes are UIs.
2. Unilateral movements for unordered nonordinal outcomes are UCs if the conservative sanction criterion is being used.

5.5.3 Stability Analysis for the Coalition Preference Vector

Once the coalition preference vector for the PF and the British is determined along with UIs and UCs, another stability analysis can be performed as shown in Table 5.10. Indeed, comparing Tables 5.5 and 5.10, the equilibrium results of the stability analysis before the PF and British

Table 5.10 Stability Analysis of the PF–British Coalition

Rhodesia

E	×	×	×	×	E	×	×	×	×	×	×	×	×	×	×	×	×	×	×
r	u	u	u	u	r	u	u	u	u	r	s	s	u	u	r	u	u	u	u
292	288	289	290	291	160	161	164	162	163	272	273	276	274	275	144	145	148	146	147
	292	292	292	292		160	160	160	160		272	272	272	272		144	144	144	144
		288	288	288			161	161	161			273	273	273			145	145	145
			289	289				164	164				276	276				148	148
				290					162					274					146

PF–British coalition

r	u	u	u	r	r	r	r	r	r	r	u	u	u	u	u	u	u	u	u	
292	164	148	276	288	289	160	161	291	290	163	162	272	273	275	274	144	145	147	146	
	292	292	292																	
		164	164									288	289	291	290	288	289	291	290	UIs
												160	161	163	162	160	161	163	162	
		276	148	160	161	288	289	163	162	291	290	144	145	147	146	272	273	275	274	UCs

merge can be seen to differ from the results of the stability analysis after they merge. In particular, there is a new equilibrium at outcome 160, the situation in which the Rhodesians do nothing, the PF indicates a willingness to compromise, and the British support the PF. The consequence of this analysis is that the British, who were sympathetic to the goals of the PF, could not form an overt coalition with it lest, by so doing, the coalition's behavior might result in the less preferred, stalemate situation of outcome 160. By acting independently, however, Britain would ensure that the resolution to the conflict was their favored equilibrium, outcome 292. Thus the PF and Britain should not have coalesced, and this is what happened historically.

5.5.4 Compatibility of Coalition Members

This section describes the use of the number of ordinal outcome groups in a coalition as a metric indicating the compatibility between players. An *ordinal outcome group* is defined as either a single outcome that is not under a bridge or a group of outcomes joined by a bridge in a coalition preference vector.

It is assumed that the more members in a coalition are compatible with each other, the greater the amount of agreement they have over preference vector ordering, The greater the agreement over ordering the greater the number of ordinal outcome groups that appear in the coalition preference vector. Consider Table 5.11 where the preference vectors appear for the three Zimbabwe conflict players, as well as for the three possible coalitions between players. In the PF–British coalition preference vector, there are actually only two single ordinal outcomes (292 and 164). However, each block of nonordinal or equally preferred outcomes could be counted as one ordinal outcome group because each nonordinal block is preferred to the next nonordinal block. (For example, the nonordinal block of outcomes 276 and 148 is preferred to the nonordinal block of outcomes 288, 289, 160, and 161.) Thus, the PF–British coalition preference vector has a total of six ordinal outcome groups. Similarly, the Rhodesians–British and Rhodesians–PF coalition preference vectors have three and two ordinal outcome groups, respectively.

Since the largest number of ordinal outcome groups of the three coalitions is six, the PF–British coalition, according to the metric, is the most compatible of the coalitions. The least likely merger according to the metric occurs for the Rhodesian–PF coalition. These insights gained from the strictly ordered outcome group measure conform to historical events. The PF and British were more closely related to one another than either was to the Rhodesians because both essentially wished majority rule in Zimbabwe. Their means to attain this end, however, differed—the PF were more ready to seek a military solution than the British.

Table 5.11 Ordinal Outcome Group Metric[a]

Preference vector position	1	2	3	4	5	6	7	8	9	10	11	12	13	14	15	16	17	18	19	20	
1. Individual preference vectors																					
Rhodesia	292	288	289	290	291	160	161	164	162	163	272	273	276	274	275	144	145	148	146	147	
PF	292	164	148	276	160	161	288	289	163	162	291	290	144	145	147	146	272	273	275	274	
Britain	292	164	276	148	288	289	160	161	291	290	163	162	272	273	275	274	144	145	147	146	
2. Coalition preference vectors																					
Rhodesian–PF	292	164	148	276	160	161	288	289	163	162	291	290	144	145	147	146	272	273	275	274	→2[a]
Rhodesian–British	292	164	276	148	288	289	160	161	291	290	163	162	272	273	275	274	144	145	147	146	→3
PF–British	292	164	276	148	288	289	160	161	291	290	163	162	272	273	275	274	144	145	147	146	→6

[a]Total number of ordinal outcome groups.

5.6. Other Coalition Research

Previous work in coalition analysis is reviewed in order to explain how it relates to the coalition algorithm presented in this chapter. First, the major difference between this and most other coalition analysis work is outlined. Second, Brams' (1975) "winning" concept of coalitions and Arrow's (1963) General Possibility Theorem are discussed.

Ordinal vs Cardinal Approaches. The single major distinction between the coalition algorithm in this chapter and many other works in the co-alition analysis field (Caplow, 1956; Kelly and Arrowood, 1960; Gamson, 1961; Riker, 1962; Komorita, 1974; Medlin, 1976; Michener et al., 1976; Komorita and Kravitz, 1978; Rapoport et al., 1979; Guiasu and Malitza, 1980) is that the former is based on an ordinal approach whereas the latter are based on a cardinal approach. In the *ordinal approach*, players coalesce based on their knowledge of the relative ranking of the feasible outcomes. In the *cardinal approach*, on the other hand, players coalesce based on their knowledge of the distribution of weights representing such things as resources, votes, and power; consequently a real number or utility value can be assigned to each outcome.

Thus the ordinal approach necessitates only knowing relative ordering whereas the cardinal approach demands detailed data on the distribution of weights. Since it may often be unrealistic to attain the detailed infor-mation required by the cardinal approach, the ordinal approach is the only practical means of performing coalition analysis. Its accurate de-scriptive ability is demonstrated in this text by its successful application to the Zimbabwe dispute.

Brams' and Arrow's Work. Brams, who views coalition formation in a political context related specifically to voting, suggests that coalitions are formed for the sole purpose of winning. A player searches not for a partner who has a similar preference ordering but who provides that player with a greater chance of winning. Indeed, Brams advocates Riker's (1962) *size concept*—that the winning coalitions will be no larger than necessary to be effective. Furthermore, Brams disagrees with coalitions formed by minimum ideological distance because of circular reasoning:

> Ideological compatibility is determined from the history of previous party alignments, which is information then used to predict what coalitions will form that are ideologically compatible (Brams, 1975, p 228).

The principle that coalitions form (and only to the degree required) to win appears to be a valid and logical argument given in the voting context described by Brams. It is clear that when one party or group merges with another party, it probably does so in order to obtain a majority of votes. However, the winning coalition concept loses its intrinsic value when given in the broader and nonquantitative political context used in this text. Specifically, a player does not simply win or lose but may, as a result of forming a coalition, obtain an equilibrium more preferable in his (or her) preference vector, relative to the vectors of the other players. To call this winning would not be as accurate as saying that this player's situation improves. Thus, although it seems logical to assume that coalitions do form to win in voting situations as described by Brams, this reasoning does not appear to be applicable to the coalition algorithms given in this chapter.

Brams also argues that coalitions do not form to minimize ideological differences because these coalitions are based on previous party alignments. At first glance, Brams appears to contradict directly the ordinal outcome group metric described in this chapter (i.e., that players are more likely to merge if their preference vectors are arranged in a similar manner). However, a closer inspection of the algorithms reveals that although the players may order their preferences according to ideology, they more probably order their preferences specifically according to the problem at hand. For example, two ideologically dissimilar players, the British and PF, are seen to be more likely to coalesce than other players in the Zimbabwe conflict. The PF and the British order their vectors in a similar manner because both share the goal of converting Zimbabwe–Rhodesia to a black majority rule government rather than both sharing a particular political persuasion. Thus, because ideological similarity is not the sole reason for the construction of each player's preference vector, the algorithms described in this chapter avoid this problem.

Arrow (1963), another writer in the field of coalition formation, constructed the General Possibility Theorem. Essentially, this states that two axioms and five conditions he has postulated cannot all hold true at once for any coalition. Indeed, in their present state, the coalition algorithm given in this chapter seems to violate Arrow's Condition of Independence of Irrelevant Alternatives; basically, that if an arrangement of outcome pairs for two different sets of preference vectors is exactly the same, then the outcome pairs of the two coalition preference vectors resulting from these two sets of vectors must be the same. For example, consider outcomes 3 and 2 in cases 1 and 2 for players A, B, and C in Table 5.12. In both cases the ordering of outcomes 3 and 2 for all players remains constant which, according to Arrow's condition, should result in two identical coalition orderings for 3 and 2. However, in case 1 the coalition preference vector is nonordinal between outcomes 2 and 3, whereas in case 2 outcome 3 is always preferred to outcome 2. Note, though, that cases 1 and 2 are treated exactly the same in stability analysis because of the UI given

Table 5.12 Arrow's Condition of the Independence of Irrelevant Alternatives

Player	Case 1	Case 2
A	1 3 2	3 2
B	3 2 1	3 2
C	3 1 2	3 2
Coalition	1 2 3	3 2
	3 UI	

by outcome 3. (The net affect of this UI on the stability analysis of case 1 is to treat outcome 3 as preferred to outcome 2.) Thus, if outcome 1 were removed, case 1 would simply dissolve into case 2. Thus Arrow's condition is, in fact, avoided; indeed, it appears as though all five of Arrow's conditions are somehow satisfied.

In order to satisfy Arrow's five conditions, however, the concept of nonordinality was introduced into the coalition algorithm. Specifically, Arrow's axiom constraining coalition analysis to transitive relations between outcomes was expanded to allow intransitivities into the coalition preference vector. For example, consider outcomes 288, 289, and 160. Outcome 288 is indifferent to outcome 160 as indicated by their respective UCs (Table 5.10) and shown by their reverse ordering in the PF and British individual preference vectors (Table 5.5). Similarly, outcome 160 is indifferent to outcome 289. If transitivity held, outcome 288 should have been indifferent to outcome 289. Inspection of the PF and British individual preference vectors shows, however, that outcome 288 is actually preferred to outcome 289 in the coalition preference vector (though there it is bridged). Therefore intransitivity exists for these three outcomes and, in general, can be shown to exist for other outcomes in a coalition preference vector.

Allowing intransitivity into the coalition preference vector seems valid because it probably more realistically describes a player's preference ordering. For example, an individual may prefer apples to oranges and prefer oranges to grapes, but may or may not prefer apples to grapes. Assuming transitivity implies a requisite preference of apples to grapes, whereas the assumption of intransitivity allows for the preference ordering to be either way or indifferent between the two items. Thus, intransitivity is probably the more effective assumption to make.

Thus, in summary, the basic difference between the algorithm presented in this chapter and other research is that the former is ordinally based and the latter is cardinally based. It has also been shown that restrictions on coalitions proposed by other writers either do not apply to the present study or are indeed satisfied by the algorithm.

5.7. Important Concepts from Chapter 5

Four ways of determining the sensitivity of the results of a conflict analysis were presented:

1. Do the analysis again using various conceivable preference vectors.
2. Perform hypergame analyses.
3. Adopt a conservative sanction criterion by considering equally preferred outcomes as unknown preferences.
4. Perform coalition analyses.

A coalition is a group of players who act together in order to obtain a preferred outcome for themselves. In sensitivity analysis, a conflict analysis incorporating coalitions can be used to gauge the effect of opponents cooperating against a particular player, or the advantages of a player joining a coalition.

Coalitions form in cicumstances where:

1. there are at least three players in the game;
2. the players do not forfeit their independence;
3. players have shared goals; and
4. the players have a similar structure.

In Section 5.5.4 a metric was presented for determining which coalitions are most likely to form.

A coalition preference vector can be obtained from the preference vectors of the coalition's members by using the principle that an outcome is less preferred than another for a coalition if the outcome is less preferred by any coalition member. The basic steps of the algorithm are as follow:

1. individual bridge removal,
2. coalition bridge creation, and
3. UI development.

In this chapter, a thorough analysis was made of the environment preceding the Lancaster Peace Talks over the civil war in Zimbabwe. Coalition analysis elucidated the similarities between the British and the Patriotic Front in their activities concerning this conflict, and it was concluded that the best course of action for the British and PF players was for each to act independently.

A short review was made of important ideas about coalitions from the literature. It was pointed out that most previous research on coalitions utilized cardinality as the basis of preference ordering, and that the methodology presented in this chapter avoids problems related to Arrow's Possibility Theorem.

Questions

1. Check the sensitivity of the analysis of the Cuban missile crisis of Chapter 1 for changes in the preferences of the USSR, as was done for the preferences of the United States in section 5.2.1 and Table 5.1. Discuss your results.
2. Perform a sensitivity analysis of the Garrison Diversion Unit of Chapter 2 from the point of view of the player U.S. opposition. Try to incorporate all of the sensitivity analysis techniques presented in this chapter. Is there any advantage for U.S. opposition in forming a coalition with Canadian opposition?
3. Is it possible to form a coalition, using the algorithm in this chapter, among players who have ordered nonordinal outcomes? For example, this may arise when bringing previously developed coalition preference vectors into some larger coalition. Identify the crux of the problem that arises when performing a coalition of coalitions, and propose a workable solution.
4. What is the difference between performing a stability analysis with or without UCs? Discuss the effect on the Zimbabwe conflict if UCs are not incorporated into the analysis.
5. Perform all the calculations needed to develop the Rhodesian–PF and Rhodesian–British coalitions given in Table 5.11.

Chapter 6
Dynamic Models
and Probability Considerations

6.1 Introduction

The conflict analysis methods examined so far in this book handle most situations that arise in practice. However, there are two drawbacks that limit the information that can be rigorously used. First, the technique does not provide an algorithmic manner in which to incorporate information about the *dynamics* of the conflict; it is limited to the analysis of a conflict for one point in time alone. Second, no procedure has been given to include probabilistic information about the conflict.

There are two approaches to these problems, each of which has certain advantages. Both are primarily methods of denoting the dynamics of a conflict, as opposed to an abstract model formulation. One is the *extensive form* of the game, which is a classical technique from game theory (see, e.g., Luce and Raiffa, 1957). The extensive form is suitable for simple games with few players, strategies, and outcomes, and is very useful to show graphically how a sequential game proceeds. The other method is the *state transition approach* (Fraser and Hipel, 1983c), developed in this chapter, which provides a medium for the analysis of very complex situations that have dynamic and probabilistic factors. The state transition method, although less graphic than the extensive form, is much more compact and has a mathematically useful structure. Both techniques follow easily from the previous methods presented in this book.

In this chapter the conflict surrounding former U.S. President Richard Nixon over the Watergate tapes is described and initially modeled using the techniques of conflict analysis presented so far, which can be called *static* (i.e., like the "snapshot" example of Chapter 1). The Watergate tapes conflict is then studied using both the extensive and the state transition forms. These methods are analogous to taking a "motion picture" of the conflict as it evolves over time. The Watergate model presented in this chapter is based on one originally developed by Meleskie et al. (1982).

Following the presentation of the Watergate tapes conflict, a hypothetical military situation is presented to demonstrate the incorporation of probabilistic information into a conflict analysis. Finally, the Cuban missile crisis is analyzed using the state transition model.

6.2 Watergate Tapes Conflict

The arrest of five men caught breaking into an office building on June 17, 1972 was to mark the beginning of one of the most famous political scandals in the history of the United States. Initially, "Watergate" (the name of the building) was used by journalists to refer to the burglary itself, but as the scandal snowballed it came to represent much more. As stated by Dickenson:

> Nothing in the way of education or experience adequately prepared the national audience for the sorry recitation of intrigue, purjury, deception, burglary and hubris that made Watergate a generic term symbolizing the greatest political crisis since the Civil War [*Congressional Quarterly*, 1973, p. 1].

The most dramatic consequence of the Watergate scandal was the resignation of U.S. President Richard M. Nixon on August 8, 1974. The turning point in the downfall of his presidency was the revelation of the existence of a taping system that recorded all conversation that took place in the Oval Office of the White House. The Watergate investigators surmised that the contents of the tapes would substantiate the accusations made against the Watergate participants and the president himself. Consequently, the investigators demanded that the tapes be made available to them, but the Nixon Administration refused. Howard H. Baker Jr., Vice Chairman of the Senate Select Committee investigating Watergate, described the ensuing struggle as "an historic conflict between the legislative and executive branches of the government" (*Congressional Quarterly*, 1973, p. 208).

6.2.1 History of the Watergate Conflict

Newspaper reporters, most notably Woodward and Bernstein of *The Washington Post*, were credited with initially spearheading the investigation into the break-in at the Watergate complex. The *Post* reported one of the first damaging revelations linking the president to the burglary. A check for $25,000 that was intended for Nixon's re-election campaign had been deposited in the bank account of Bernard Baker, one of the men arrested at the Watergate buildings (Congressional Quarterly, 1973, p. 5). Also, the newspapers uncovered a "slush fund" that was used for various espionage expenses (Dean, 1976, p. 161; Nixon, 1978, vol. II, p. 315).

Following these disclosures the Justice Department pledged that the Federal Bureau of Investigation would make a full inquiry into the Watergate situation. A Senate investigation committee was also established on February 7, 1973 by Senate vote (New York Times Staff 1974, p. 3), and was headed by Senator Sam Ervin. The Ervin committee's mandate as outlined in a Senate resolution gave the committee the right to conduct an investigation into improper or unethical activities during the 1972 presidential election. The committee would then recommend new congressional legislation to safeguard the electoral process (Congressional Quarterly, 1973, p. 46).

During this time Nixon yielded to pressure from the Senate and Congress by giving the Attorney General, Elliot Richardson, power to name a Special Prosecutor who would investigate the Watergate allegations. On May 18, 1973 Archibald Cox, a Harvard law professor who was the former Solicitor General to the Kennedy and Johnson administrations, was appointed to the position. The Special Prosecutor's Office could "investigate, subpoena and bring suit in court against anyone suspected of criminal wrongdoing in the campaign of 1972" (White, 1975, p. 320). Cox and his office would be "nominally attached to the Department of Justice, . . . would act in the name of the Federal Government but would in fact operate independently of the Nixon Administration—virtually an autonomous regulatory agency" (Ben-Veniste and Frampton, 1977, p. 12).

By far the most damaging accusations about Nixon's involvement in Watergate came from John Dean, Special Counsel to President Nixon. Dean had the task of keeping the White House informed on Watergate developments. On August 19, 1972, Nixon announced that Dean had conducted an investigation when no such investigation had taken place (Dean 1976, p. 125). Dean believed that he was becoming too involved in the affair and that even his own actions amounted to obstruction of justice. He felt he should go public with what he knew. After refusing to resign, Dean was essentially fired by Nixon when Nixon announced his resignation anyway. Dean believed he was being made a scapegoat by the White House. Because of his intimate knowledge about the President and Watergate, Dean even feared for his life (Dean 1976, pp. 279–292). He made the following charge in his testimony before the Ervin committee on June 25, 1973:

"I left," said Dean, speaking of his meeting with Nixon on September 15, 1972, "with the impression that the President was well aware of what had been going on regarding the success of keeping the White House out of the Watergate scandal" [White, 1975, p. 302].

On July 13, 1973, during preliminary questioning of Alexander Butterfield, a former aid of Nixon's Chief of Staff H.R. (Bob) Haldeman, the existence of tape recordings of presidential conversations became known. The system had been in place and maintained from 1971 until it was taken out after Butterfield formally disclosed it before the Ervin committee on July 16, 1973 (Dash 1976, p. 177). The recording system was installed in the Oval Office, the President's office in the Executive Office Building, and on three of the telephones the President usually used. Because the recorders were voice activated and ran automatically, all of the conversations were recorded. Secret Service personnel had the task of logging the conversations and changing the tapes daily (White, 1975, pp. 248–550).

The tape revelation created quite a furor in Washington. Senator Ervin, when he first heard the news, said it was "the most remarkable discovery of evidence that I have learned in my entire experience in the practice of law" (Dash 1976, p. 179). It suddenly became possible to prove or disprove statements made, especially Dean's, about the President's involvement in Watergate or its cover-up.

> What the tapes added up to was the first concrete evidence that could resolve the dispute over what had happened at the White House during the months before and after the Watergate burglary [Lukas, 1976, p. 382].
>
> Without the tapes, there was no evidence against the President personally except John Dean's word [White, 1975, p. 314].

When the existence of the tapes had been made public, Nixon decided that to destroy the tapes "would forever seal an impression of guilt in the public mind" (Nixon, 1978, vol. II, p. 451). Also, his lawyers were unsure of the legal aspects of destroying the tapes. Furthermore, Nixon says he believed at this time that the tapes would disprove Dean's charges (Nixon, 1978, vol. II, p. 452). On July 16, 1973, the day Butterfield testified, Senator Ervin wrote Nixon a letter requesting all relevant tapes and presidential documents. In a letter on July 6, Nixon had previously denied access to presidential papers, and on July 23 he again gave a written refusal to relinquish the tapes (Congressional Quarterly, 1973, pp. 196, 225). On July 18, Special Prosecutor Archibald Cox also requested eight specific tapes of presidential conversations for his criminal investigations. Charles Wright, Consultant to White House Counsel, replied on behalf of the President and refused to release the tapes (Congressional Quarterly, 1973, p. 224).

Nixon's arguments to both investigative bodies was that the principle of separation of powers and of executive privilege allowed him to withhold the tapes (Congressional Quarterly, 1973, p. 209). On July 23 both Cox and Ervin decided to pursue the matter in court and promptly subpoenaed

President Nixon. The conflict now threatened to test directly the constitutional powers entrusted to the President.

This moment was chosen for the conflict analysis of the situation since
it seemed to be the turning point in the downfall of the Nixon Administration. As Nixon states in his memoirs:

> I now believe that from the time of the disclosure of the existence of the
> tapes and my decision not to destroy them, my presidency had little chance
> of surviving to the end of its term (Nixon, 1978, vol. II, p. 454).

6.2.2 Players and Options

President Nixon is considered the first player in the game, and his options
concern the release of the Watergate tapes. Nixon personally took control
of the tapes following their revelation (Congressional Quarterly, 1973, p.
225) and therefore had the option of releasing all the tapes. Another option
of Nixon's was partial compliance to the subpoenas—releasing some of
the tapes requested while withholding others. A third option was some
sort of compromise involving the tapes. This could take the form of transcripts, with non-Watergate-related matters omitted, verified for authenticity by a third party. A final alternative for Nixon was to refuse to
release any of the tapes. Haldeman, Nixon's former Chief of Staff, recalls
a 1972 conversation regarding Nixon's position:

> He didn't want transcripts made at any time,. . . . Nobody was to listen to
> those tapes, ever, except himself. Then he added, ''I'll never even have Rose
> Woods [Nixon's private secretary of many years] listen to them. Rose doesn't
> even know I'm making the tapes. I say things in this office I don't want even
> Rose to hear'' [Haldeman and Dimona 1978, p. 196].

Two investigating bodies can be identified that have an important role
in the conflict: the Ervin committee and the Special Prosecutor's office.
These two can be joined to form the second player in the game. Although
they are widely different in certain respects, one must consider only their
views concerning the important factor in this game—the disposition of
the presidential tapes. Their options and preferences in this matter are
essentially identical. Both groups are seeking evidence for their particular
investigations, and the tapes are the best potential evidence to be uncov-
ered. Nixon, in his actions, must consider the two bodies as one player:
he cannot consider relinquishing the tapes to one body while refusing
access to the other because he cannot be sure that the Ervin committee
and the Special Prosecutor's office would not cooperate in that event.

The Investigators had the option of going to court to enforce their subpoenas. The Ervin committee had the right to do this under "the federal statutory offense of Contempt of Congress which requires a grand jury indictment against the President" (Dash 1976, p. 188). They could also sue the President in federal district court. Cox, of course, had the right to go to court since he was seeking the tapes for a criminal investigation.

Another option for the investigators to consider was to accept partial compliance to the subpoenas by being satisfied with only some of the tapes, thereby recognizing that some of the tapes could be too sensitive and could damage the Presidency. A third option would be to accept some sort of third-party arbitration. This could take the form of the White House supplying transcripts of the tapes verified by some respected official as to omissions for National Security reasons. The players and their options are listed on the left in Tables 6.1 and 6.2.

6.2.3 Outcome Removal

Table 6.1 lists sets of outcomes that can be removed from the full game model. (Refer to Section 2.3.2 for a complete discussion of outcome removal.) The three leftmost (vertical) sets of outcomes are situations in which selected options are mutually exclusive. The next two sets from the left represent dependencies the investigators have on actions taken by Nixon: the investigators cannot accept some tapes without Nixon having released them, nor can they accept arbitration unless Nixon proposes it. The three sets of outcomes on the right reflect the consideration that the investigators will take none of their options if Nixon releases the tapes.

6.2.4 Preferences

For the Watergate conflict there are 13 feasible outcomes in the game, shown in Table 6.2. The preference vectors for the two players can be seen in the static stability analysis tableau of Table 6.3. Consider the

Table 6.1 Infeasible Outcome Sets in the Watergate Tapes Conflict

Nixon								
Release all tapes	1	1	–	–	–	1	1	1
Release some tapes	1	–	–	0	–	–	–	–
Arbitrate	–	1	–	–	0	–	–	–
Investigators								
Go to court	–	–	1	–	–	1	–	–
Accept some tapes	–	–	–	1	–	–	1	–
Accept arbitration	–	–	1	–	1	–	–	1

Table 6.2 Feasible Outcomes to the Watergate Tapes Conflict

Nixon													
Release all tapes	0	1	0	0	0	0	0	0	0	0	0	0	0
Release some tapes	0	0	0	1	0	1	1	1	1	1	0	1	1
Arbitrate	0	0	0	0	1	1	0	1	0	1	1	1	1
Investigators													
Go to court	0	0	1	1	1	1	0	0	1	1	0	0	0
Accept some tapes	0	0	0	0	0	0	1	1	1	1	0	0	1
Accept arbitration	0	0	0	0	0	0	0	0	0	0	1	1	1
Decimal	0	1	8	10	12	14	18	22	26	30	36	38	54

rationale underlying Nixon's preferences among the feasible outcomes. Nixon had a personal interest in keeping the tapes secret. He had listened to some of them on June 4, 1973 and realized the political ramifications of releasing them. Nixon claimed to have firmly believed that releasing the tapes would have created a legal precedent that would forever weaken the principle of executive privilege (Nixon, 1978, vol. II, p. 453). He also believed it would be a breach of presidential privacy that would make it impossible for himself or any president to function properly (Sirica, 1979, p. 145). Nixon's lawyers argued that to uphold the subpoenas would be an assertion of power from the court, and the executive would no longer be an equal and coordinate branch of the government as provided in the Constitution (Sirica, 1979, p. 145). Based upon these arguments, Nixon most preferred the strategy of not releasing any of the tapes regardless

Table 6.3 Stability Analysis

Nixon												
×	*E*	×	×	×	×	×	*E*	×	×	×	×	×
r	*r*	*r*	*r*	*s*	*s*	*r*	*r*	*u*	*u*	*u*	*u*	*u*
0	8	36	18	38	22	54	26	30	10	12	14	1
				36	18			26	8	8	8	0
										10	10	
											12	
Investigators												
r	*r*	*r*	*r*	*u*	*r*	*u*	*u*	*u*	*u*	*u*	*u*	*u*
1	26	30	8	10	12	14	54	36	18	38	22	0
			26		30		30	12	26	30	30	8
							14		10	14	14	
										54	54	
											38	

of the investigators' strategies. Consequently, outcomes 0 and 8 are the most desirable outcomes for Nixon.

Since arbitration would retain some confidentiality for the president, outcome 36 is the third most preferred outcome for Nixon. He preferred this to releasing any of the tapes outright because of his belief that "if only one tape was yielded, it would only heighten the desire for two more" (Nixon 1978, vol. II, p. 453). Nixon did in fact propose what has been called the "Stennis Compromise" after Judge Sirica and the Court of Appeals ruled Nixon must turn over the tapes. Nixon claimed he suggested that Senator Stennis verify third-person summaries of the tapes and attest to valid omissions (Nixon, 1978, vol. II, p. 487). Senators Ervin and Baker maintained that Nixon offered them verbatim transcripts prepared under the supervision of Stennis (Dash, 1976, p. 21; Mankiewicz, 1975, p. 31). Over these misunderstandings, the compromise fell through.

Outcome 38 also represents Nixon releasing some tapes as well as arbitrating the rest of the subpoenaed tapes. This outcome is less preferred to releasing only some of the tapes in outcome 18 since, with the latter, at least some of the tapes remain secret. The next most preferred outcomes after 38 are outcomes 22 and 54, respectively.

When the investigators' strategies are considered, outcomes where court action is involved (i.e., 26, 30, 10, 12, and 14) are less preferred by Nixon, but not at the expense of releasing the tapes. If Nixon did agree to some sort of partial compliance to the subpoenas in his strategy, he would prefer that the investigators accept what he is offering since it would show that he is indeed interested in having the truth brought out. For example, outcome 26 is preferred to outcome 10.

The least preferred outcome for Nixon is outcome 1 where he releases all the tapes; however, this is the most preferred outcome for the investigators, as can be seen in their preference vector in Table 6.3. Next most preferred for the investigators are the six outcomes that involve going to court to force Nixon to honor the subpoenas if he does not comply totally (i.e., 26, 30, 8, 10, 12, and 14). This was because, without the tapes, "if any of the possible defendants were to be indicted, they could claim with justification that the government (prosecutors) had not considered all the available evidence (Mankiewicz, 1975, p. 27). Within this block of six outcomes, those where the investigators' accept only some of the tapes (outcome 26, 30) are more preferred, since then they could at least ascertain the credibility of their witnesses (Dash, 1976; Jaworski, 1976). Four outcomes of the block of six outcomes are all equally preferred because the investigators refuse to accept anything Nixon offers. The remaining outcomes in the investigators' preference vector (54, 36, 18, 38, 22, and 0), are those concerned with not going to court. Without court proceedings, the investigators would try to get as much information as possible from what Nixon offered.

6.3 Static Analysis

From the completed stability analysis of Table 6.3 it can be seen that outcomes 8 and 26 are the two equilibriums in the game. (Refer to Section 1.3.3 for a presentation of the stability analysis method.) Outcome 8 refers to Nixon not releasing any of the tapes and the investigators taking the President to court. In outcome 26, Nixon releases some of the tapes while the investigators accept these tapes and go to court to obtain the others. Although two possible equilibriums are predicted by the analysis, only one equilibrium outcome can actually occur. Because of the dynamics of the conflict, Nixon is the one who makes the first move; he therefore would select outcome 8, which he prefers to 26. Outcome 8 is the one that occurred historically.

> Nixon promptly refused to honor the subpoena for the tapes claiming executive privilege. . . . The committee decided that its best course of action was to sue the President in district court. Cox had gone to court earlier to enforce his subpoena [Dash, 1976, pp. 188–189].

The Ervin committee subsequently lost its suit in court, on grounds that the tapes released would prejudice legal proceedings (Dash, 1976, p. 190). However, Cox won his suit, and the Court of Appeals upheld Judge Sirica's decision on a Nixon appeal. Sirica ordered Nixon to turn over the tapes to him and he, as a federal court judge, would decide which parts should be omitted for security reasons (Mankiewicz, 1975, p. 26; Dash, 1976, p. 209).

It is clear in the static analysis of this game that a viable model can be developed and used to increase one's understanding of the conflict. However there is at least one vital piece of information that could not be rigorously incorporated into the analysis: the fact that Nixon selects his strategy first. Although outcome 26 has special significance in this conflict, it is clearly not a possible resolution in the same way as outcome 8. Both the extensive form and the state transition form of the game provide a medium for incorporating this information about the dynamics of the conflict situation.

6.4 Extensive Form

The extensive form of the game is represented by a tree graph, as illustrated for the Watergate conflict in Figure 6.1. Each *node* of the tree corresponds to one of the players and represents the moment at which the player can select a strategy or make a decision in the conflict. Each *branch* of the tree corresponds to possible decisions that could be made by the player. In Figure 6.1, Nixon (N) can choose from five initial strat-

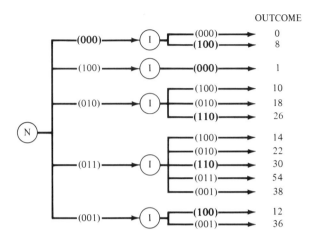

Figure 6.1 Game tree of the Watergate Tapes Conflict

egies, which are indicated using 1s and 0s (written horizontally) to correspond to the option ordering used in Tables 6.1 and 6.2:

(0 0 0)—Nixon releases no tapes, arbitrates none.

(1 0 0)—Nixon releases all the tapes.

(0 1 0)—Nixon releases some tapes, does not arbitrate the rest.

(0 1 1)—Nixon releases some tapes, arbitrates the rest.

(0 0 1)—Nixon arbitrates the tapes.

The five strategies available to Nixon lead to the limited responses of the investigators (I). Their six strategies are as follow:

(0 0 0)—Investigators do not go to court and accept no tapes.

(1 0 0)—Investigators go to court, accept no tapes.

(0 1 0)—Investigators do not go to court, accept some tapes.

(1 1 0)—Investigators go to court, accept some tapes.

(0 1 1)—Investigators accept some tapes, arbitrate the rest.

(0 0 1)—Investigators accept arbitration.

However, only the combinations of these strategies that are feasible (Table 6.2) appear in Figure 6.1. For example, there are two outcomes in Table 6.2 that involve a strategy of (000) by Nixon: outcomes (000, 000) and (000, 100). Thus the two possible strategy choices available for the investigators in the game tree, following a selection of the strategy (000) by Nixon, are strategies (000) and (100). The decimal representation of the resulting outcome after both Nixon and the investigators have chosen a strategy is shown at the far right in Figure 6.1.

If it was felt that Nixon was likely to change his strategy after the investigators had selected theirs, a third set of nodes would be placed to the right of the investigator nodes in Figure 6.1. Final outcomes are determined as the union of the final strategy selection by each of the players.

Note that in Figure 6.1, at any of the investigators' nodes, *they* have the sole choice over the resulting outcome because Nixon has already chosen his strategy. Thus in the topmost node for the investigators, they can choose between outcome 0 and outcome 8. Since they prefer 8 to 0, at this node they would be expected to choose the strategy (100). In other words, if Nixon decided not to release any tapes, the investigators would be expected to go to court.

The most preferred strategy for the investigators, given a strategy by Nixon, is shown in boldface in Figure 6.1 at each of the investigators' nodes. Since Nixon can be expected to know the preferences of the investigators, he will be aware that a selection of, for example, strategy (000) will lead to outcome 8. In effect, Nixon's strategy selection determines his choice of outcome 8, 1, 26, 30, or 12. Since he prefers 8 from all these possibilities, the expected resolution to this conflict is outcome 8, where Nixon does nothing and the investigators take him to court. The strategy selection by Nixon that leads to this outcome is also shown in boldface in Figure 6.1. By following from Nixon's decision node through the preferred strategies, the course of events can be traced from Nixon's decision neither to release any tapes nor arbitrate, to the investigators' choice of going to court. Note that the extensive form does not differentiate outcome 26 from other outcomes that the investigators might select. This represents an important loss of information, since the static analysis determined 26 to be an equilibrium, and thus of special importance in this conflict.

The main advantage to the game tree is that an entire conflict can be presented in one clear diagram. The actions and responses of the players can easily be assessed and the expected resolution can be determined. The chief disadvantages of the extensive form are the following:

1. The extensive form is not generally very compact. It requires the explicit representation of all the strategies available for each player as branches in the game tree. Commonly games have a very large number of possible strategies for each player, making the game tree very large. The Watergate model is small and is about the maximum size desired for an extensive form representation.
2. To develop a game tree, one has to think up possible strategies by the players for each decision node, and it is easy to miss some strategies.
3. Often conflicts are too complex to be meaningfully presented in a game tree. The Watergate tapes conflict involves two clearly sequential decisions, first by Nixon, then by the investigators. Most

conflicts involve simultaneous moves, misinformation on the part of one of the players, or other complications that are hard to represent graphically.

6.5 State Transition Approach

6.5.1 State Transition Model

The state transition model is a matrix representation of the conflict that provides much the same information as the extensive form, yet offers a number of advantages. Consider a conflict with f feasible outcomes. The state transition model of this conflict has the form

$$Y = TX, \tag{6-1}$$

where Y and X are vectors of dimension $f \times 1$, and T is an $f \times f$ matrix. Each row of Y, T, and X is associated with a particular outcome, and each column of T is associated with the same outcome as its corresponding row. The vector X represents the status quo, and has values corresponding to the outcomes that have a probability of being the status quo. For example, a conflict with four feasible outcomes may have a 20% chance of being in the second outcome, and an 80% chance of being in the fourth outcome at some time of interest. In this case

$$X = \begin{bmatrix} 0 \\ 0.2 \\ 0 \\ 0.8 \end{bmatrix}.$$

The matrix T contains outcome transition information. As is the case for the X vector, the elements of each column in T sum to one, and each entry in a column represents the probability that the column outcome under consideration will change to the particular row outcome. An outcome that does not change has a 1 opposite the row representing the same outcome as represented by the column. Such an outcome is called an *absorbing state*. For example, if 40% of the time this conflict were in the second state it stayed in the second state, but otherwise went to the fourth state, and all other states were absorbing, the matrix would be

$$T = \begin{bmatrix} 1 & 0 & 0 & 0 \\ 0 & 0.4 & 0 & 0 \\ 0 & 0 & 1 & 0 \\ 0 & 0.6 & 0 & 1 \end{bmatrix}.$$

Y is the state resulting from T operating on X. In this case the vector Y

is calculated from (6-1) to be

$$Y = \begin{bmatrix} 0 \\ 0.08 \\ 0 \\ 0.92 \end{bmatrix}.$$

To determine the succeeding state distribution, Y becomes the new status quo vector, and the matrix T is applied again using (6-1). A steady-state solution is determined by repetitively applying the transition matrix until either the status quo remains constant or a cycle is identified.

The transition information for the Watergate conflict can be developed from an understanding of the conflict directly, or can be derived from the stability analysis tableau using a simple algorithm. In general, matrices T_A, T_B, . . . can be created for each of the players in the game model, where A, B, . . . are the players. Given an outcome q in the preference vector for player A, the element of the column corresponding to outcome q in T_A will have a 1 in the row associated with either:

1. outcome q if the outcome is stable, or
2. outcome a, where a is the most preferred UI determining instability, if q is unstable for A.

For example, outcome 0 for Nixon is rational, so he would not cause a transition from outcome 0 to another outcome. As shown in Table 6.4, outcome 0 is thus an absorbing outcome in Nixon's transition matrix. Outcome 30 is unstable for Nixon, leading to outcome 26, so Nixon's transition matrix indicates a transition from 30 to 26. Finally, although

Table 6.4 Transition Matrix for Nixon

	0	1	8	10	12	14	18	22	26	30	36	38	54
0	1	1	0	0	0	0	0	0	0	0	0	0	0
1	0.	0	0	0	0	0	0	0	0	0	0	0	0
8	0	0	1	1	1	1	0	0	0	0	0	0	0
10	0	0	0	0	0	0	0	0	0	0	0	0	0
12	0	0	0	0	0	0	0	0	0	0	0	0	0
14	0	0	0	0	0	0	0	0	0	0	0	0	0
18	0	0	0	0	0	0	1	0	0	0	0	0	0
22	0	0	0	0	0	0	0	1	0	0	0	0	0
26	0	0	0	0	0	0	0	0	1	1	0	0	0
30	0	0	0	0	0	0	0	0	0	0	0	0	0
36	0	0	0	0	0	0	0	0	0	0	1	0	0
38	0	0	0	0	0	0	0	0	0	0	0	1	0
54	0	0	0	0	0	0	0	0	0	0	0	0	1

Nixon has a UI from outcome 38 to 36, this improvement is sequentially sanctioned; thus 38 is also an absorbing state in his matrix. A transition matrix for the investigators can be similarly developed and is shown in Table 6.5.

In the two-player case, the overall transition matrix T can be developed from T_A and T_B by examining each column outcome using the following algorithm:

1. If both matrices have an entry on the main diagonal, the T matrix has the entry on the main diagonal.
2. If one matrix has the entry on the main diagonal, and the other does not, the T matrix has an entry in the position corresponding to the off-diagonal entry.
3. If both entries are off the main diagonal, the T matrix has an entry corresponding to the outcome with decimal representation given by $(a + b) - q$, where q is the outcome being considered, a is the improvement by player A, and b is the improvement by player B.

Since if $a = q$, $(a+b)-q = b$, and if $b = q$, $(a+b)-q = a$, a 1 will always be placed in the row given by

$$(a + b) - q, \tag{6-2}$$

where q is the decimal outcome number associated with the column under consideration, a is the row of the corresponding column in T_A in which an entry is found, and b is the row of the corresponding column in T_B in which an entry is found. The similarity to simultaneous sanctioning presented in Section 1.3.3 should be noted.

Table 6.5 Transition Matrix for the Investigators

	0	1	8	10	12	14	18	22	26	30	36	38	54
0	0	0	0	0	0	0	0	0	0	0	0	0	0
1	0	1	0	0	0	0	0	0	0	0	0	0	0
8	1	0	1	0	0	0	0	0	0	0	0	0	0
10	0	0	0	0	0	0	0	0	0	0	0	0	0
12	0	0	0	0	1	0	0	0	0	0	1	0	0
14	0	0	0	0	0	0	0	0	0	0	0	0	0
18	0	0	0	0	0	0	0	0	0	0	0	0	0
22	0	0	0	0	0	0	0	0	0	0	0	0	0
26	0	0	0	1	0	0	1	0	1	0	0	0	0
30	0	0	0	0	0	1	0	1	0	1	0	1	1
36	0	0	0	0	0	0	0	0	0	0	0	0	0
38	0	0	0	0	0	0	0	0	0	0	0	0	0
54	0	0	0	0	0	0	0	0	0	0	0	0	0

For n players, the entry is determined from the following formula:

$$t = \sum_{i \in U}(a_i) - (m-1)q, \qquad (6\text{-}3)$$

where U is the set of matrices that have off-diagonal entries for outcome q, a_i are the row outcomes, m is the number of elements in U, and t is the row into which a 1 is to be entered. Clearly the two-player situation is a special case of the n-player rule. Again the similarity to simultaneous sanctioning for n players, discussed in Section 2.4, should be noted.

The situation where both players have an off-diagonal entry is somewhat special. The outcome that results from the application of (6-2) or (6-3) will actually only occur if both players take their strategies simultaneously. This is a fair approximation; however, in practice one of the strategies will be taken before the other and a different state will in fact result. For this reason, it is wise to examine situations in which there is an off-diagonal entry for more than one player and carefully assess the resulting transition. It may be to the outcome produced by (6-2) or (6-3), to any of the individual player's transition outcomes, to a combination of some of the player's strategies, or to a probabilistic distribution among these.

A direct algorithmic development of the state transition matrix from a stability analysis tableau results in a model that will provide exactly the same results as the static form of the game. However, new information about the dynamic or probabilistic nature of the game can be incorporated into the transition matrix. Information about the dynamics of the game are usually physical or logical constraints against some particular transitions occurring. For example, in the Watergate situation, Nixon cannot logically take back any tapes that have been released, so the transitions from outcome 1 to 0, 10 to 8, and 14 to 8 cannot take place. Outcomes 0 and 10 are actually absorbing states, and 14 leads to 10 instead of 8. The transition matrix for Nixon that reflects these constraints appears in Table 6.6. The investigators have no such constraints on their actions.

Also, note carefully that the calculations of (6-2) and (6-3) assume that the time to actually change a strategy in the real world situation is equal for all players, since if one player changes strategy first, an outcome will be produced that is different from the one that occurs after all players have changed their strategies. For example, suppose that in the Watergate conflict (given a different order of preferences) Nixon decided to improve from outcome 0 (doing nothing) to outcome 1 (releasing the tapes). Assume that outcome 0 was also unstable for the investigators because they would take a UI to outcome 8 from 0. The above formula (6-2) indicates that the resulting transition from 0 would be to outcome $1 + 8 - 0 = 9$. However, Nixon can take his strategy immediately, whereas natural delays would mean that the investigators would hardly have begun imple-

Table 6.6 Modified Transition Matrix for Nixon

	0	1	8	10	12	14	18	22	26	30	36	38	54
0	1	0	0	0	0	0	0	0	0	0	0	0	0
1	0	1	0	0	0	0	0	0	0	0	0	0	0
8	0	0	1	0	1	0	0	0	0	0	0	0	0
10	0	0	0	1	0	1	0	0	0	0	0	0	0
12	0	0	0	0	0	0	0	0	0	0	0	0	0
14	0	0	0	0	0	0	0	0	0	0	0	0	0
18	0	0	0	0	0	0	1	0	0	0	0	0	0
22	0	0	0	0	0	0	0	1	0	0	0	0	0
26	0	0	0	0	0	0	0	0	1	1	0	0	0
30	0	0	0	0	0	0	0	0	0	0	0	0	0
36	0	0	0	0	0	0	0	0	0	0	1	0	0
38	0	0	0	0	0	0	0	0	0	0	0	1	0
54	0	0	0	0	0	0	0	0	0	0	0	0	1

menting their strategy before outcome 1 was the actual new status quo. Thus the more correct transition from 0 in the transition matrix would be to outcome 1 rather than 9.

Using (6-2) to develop the overall transition matrix results in Table 6.7. Note that there are three entries on the diagonal in this matrix. These absorbing states correspond to possible resolutions to the conflict in the same manner as an equilibrium in a static analysis because they represent situations that are stable once achieved. Two of the entries in Table 6.7 are outcomes 8 and 26, calculated to be equilibriums in the static analysis

Table 6.7 Overall Transition Matrix for the Watergate Tapes Conflict

	0	1	8	10	12	14	18	22	26	30	36	38	54
0	0	0	0	0	0	0	0	0	0	0	0	0	0
1	0	1	0	0	0	0	0	0	0	0	0	0	0
8	1	0	1	0	1	0	0	0	0	0	0	0	0
10	0	0	0	0	0	0	0	0	0	0	0	0	0
12	0	0	0	0	0	0	0	0	0	0	1	0	0
14	0	0	0	0	0	0	0	0	0	0	0	0	0
18	0	0	0	0	0	0	0	0	0	0	0	0	0
22	0	0	0	0	0	0	0	0	0	0	0	0	0
26	0	0	0	1	0	1	1	0	1	1	0	0	0
30	0	0	0	0	0	0	0	1	0	0	0	1	1
36	0	0	0	0	0	0	0	0	0	0	0	0	0
38	0	0	0	0	0	0	0	0	0	0	0	0	0
54	0	0	0	0	0	0	0	0	0	0	0	0	0

of the Watergate conflict. Outcome 1 is a new possible resolution developed using the state transition approach. This is the situation where Nixon releases all the tapes while the investigators perform none of their options. In the static analysis, outcome 1 is unstable because Nixon could improve to a more preferred outcome. However, the dynamics of the game do not permit Nixon to take back the tapes once released; thus if outcome 1 is achieved, it must remain. In fact, like outcome 26, outcome 1 did eventually occur over time, as the ultimate resolution of the conflict.

Using (6-1) and the transition matrix of Table 6.7, the expected progression of the conflict can be traced from a given status quo. In the Watergate conflict the sole choice for status quo is the outcome (000, 000), decimal outcome 0, in which neither player has selected any of the available options. This is represented as the state vector (1000000000000). Applying the transition matrix to this state vector once using (6-1) results in the state vector (0010000000000), indicating that outcome 8 is the new state. Since 8 is an absorbing state, applying the transition matrix again does not change the state vector, and outcome 8 is the expected resolution to the conflict. This is the same conclusion generated through the static analysis; however, in this case the dynamics of the conflict have been absorbed into a more complete model rather than applied subjectively after completing the analysis.

Finally, notice that if the status quo is 0, 8, 12, or 36, the resulting steady-state outcome is 8. However, if the status quo outcome is 10, 14, 18, 22, 26, 30, 38, or 54, the result is outcome 26. This reinforces the importance of outcome 26 in this conflict.

6.5.2 Probability Considerations: The Afghan Battle

The Watergate conflict did not have any probabilistic considerations, which can also be handled using the state transition approach. Consider a hypothetical military situation concerning a strategic pass in Afghanistan between Afghan rebels and Soviet invaders. The pass is held by a small camp of Soviets, and the Afghans wish to secure the pass so that valuable Chinese arms and supplies can be brought through it. The Afghans expect to overwhelm the Soviets easily, given that there is sufficient snow on the ground to inhibit the mobility of the mechanized Soviet forces. The Soviets, on the other hand, can move in airborne reinforcements to hold the pass against any conceivable opposition by the Afghan rebels.

The model for this conflict consists of three players: the Afghans, the Soviets, and a player representing nature. The Afghans have the option of attacking the Soviet encampment, and the Soviets have the option of moving in reinforcements. Nature can either provide or prevent enough snow to support an attack by the Afghans. All possible outcomes for this game model are shown in Table 6.8.

Table 6.8 Afghan Battle Model

Players	Options	Outcomes							
Afghans	Attack	0	1	0	1	0	1	0	1
Soviets	Reinforce	0	0	1	1	0	0	1	1
Nature	Snow	0	0	0	0	1	1	1	1
Decimal		0	1	2	3	4	5	6	7

Consider further that in this situation the preferences of the players are such that if there is snow and the encampment has not been reinforced, the Afghans will attack and hold the pass until Soviet reinforcements arrive. The Soviets will move in reinforcements if the pass is in rebel hands, and once the pass has been reinforced, it will remain so. Snow does not critically restrict the reinforcements.

The Soviets sometimes have intelligence about the rebel's plans, so that in this case they have a probability of knowing in advance whether or not the Afghans plan an attack. In this conflict, assume that previous experience indicates that the Soviets have a 40% chance of knowing the Afghan plans. Also, the probability that there will be snow or any particular occasion is known in advance. Let p be the probability of there being sufficient snow for the Afghans to carry out their attack.

Extensive Form. The game tree for the Afghan battle game is shown as Figure 6.2, where A denotes the player Afghans, S is the Soviets, and P_0 is Nature. The dotted line enclosing the two Afghan nodes is called an *information set* and indicates that the Afghans do not know which strategy the Soviets have selected when they chose their strategy from this node.

In the extensive game tree, a chance situation, such as whether there will be a certain amount of snow, is usually represented by the *chance player* P_0. Recall from Section 6.4 that branches from each player node correspond to possible strategies by the players. If the players have a probability associated with a strategy, this probability labels the branch

Figure 6.2 Game tree of the Afghan battle.

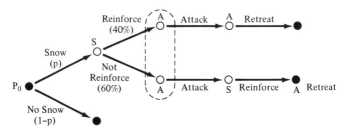

representing the strategy. Thus in Figure 6.2 the chance player P_0, representing nature, has two branches: one indicating a p chance of sufficient snow and the other a $(1-p)$ chance of insufficient snow. Similarly, the Soviets have a probability of reinforcing their camp to take advantage of their intelligence information, and this is reflected in probability labels on the two branches from their first node.

From this diagram it is clear that there will be three possible final outcomes to this conflict. There is a probability of $(1-p)$ that there will be insufficient snow, and so there will be no reinforcement of the Soviet camp and no attack by the Afghans. With a probability of $0.4 \times p$, the Afghans will attack a reinforced Soviet camp and be repelled. Finally, there is a probability of $0.6 \times p$ that the Afghans will attack a vulnerable camp and get their arms through the pass before the Soviets bring in new forces.

Note that in this example of the game tree, not all possible strategies at each node have been listed. Only strategies that the players are expected to take have been included, in order to clarify the tree, so that the probabilistic elements are emphasized. Also, note that if the Soviets did not want to keep its reinforcements at the pass, this conflict would become cyclic, with the Afghans attacking, the Soviets moving in reinforcements, the Afghans retreating, the Soviets moving out their reinforcements, the Afghans attacking again, and so on. The extensive form of this game would be infinite.

State Transition Form. Developing individual transition matrixes for players whose preferences are probabilistic can be done by performing more than one static analysis. In the Afghan conflict, the preferences of the Soviets are dependent on whether or not they have received intelligence about the Afghan raid. If they have not received information, they would prefer not to reinforce the camp because the troops could be better used elsewhere. On the other hand, if they do know the Afghans are going to attack, they would definitely prefer to tighten up their defenses. Transition matrixes can be developed for the USSR to reflect the transitions associated with each set of preferences. To calculate the final individual transition matrix for the USSR, each of these possibilities is multiplied by the probability of its occurrence and added together.

The player Nature is not considered a separate player when developing the state transition form of this conflict. The existence of enough snow for an attack or not is an element of the conflict that is best represented as part of the status quo.

When probabilistic information is included in the players' transition matrixes, (6-2) or (6-3) can be used for developing an overall transition matrix by multiplying the appropriate probabilities. For example, let $\mathbf{T}_A$ have two entries in rows a_1 and a_2 in the qth column such that $p(a_1) =$

0.2 and $p(a_2) = 0.8$, whereas $\mathbf{T}_B$ has entries $p(b_1) = 0.7$ and $p(b_2) = 0.3$ in its qth column. Using (6-2), the calculations are as follow:

Row outcome	Probability value
$a_1 + b_1 - q$	$0.2 \times 0.7 = 0.14$
$a_1 + b_2 - q$	$0.2 \times 0.3 = 0.06$
$a_2 + b_1 - q$	$0.8 \times 0.7 = 0.56$
$a_2 + b_2 - q$	$0.8 \times 0.3 = 0.24$

The fact that the probabilities will not be independent in general qualifies the validity of algorithmically developing the overall transition matrix. This is especially true when there are a lot of constraints on transitions in the conflict. In practice, an overall transition matrix can often be developed directly from the preference vectors, or even from an understanding of the conflict, and ad hoc probability assignments can be made as desired. In most conflicts involving probability information this is the sensible approach to take.

The final transition matrix for the Afghan conflict is given in Table 6.9. The probability of there being sufficient snow determines the status quo, which is thus $((1-p)000p000)$. When this transition matrix is repetitively applied to each new status quo (former state vector), the following sequence of state vectors occurs:

$$
\begin{matrix}
(1\text{-}p) & (1\text{-}p) & (1\text{-}p) & (1\text{-}p) & (1\text{-}p) \\
0 & 0 & 0 & 0 & 0 \\
0 & 0 & 0 & 0 & 0 \\
0 & 0 & 0 & 0 & 0 \\
p & 0 & 0 & 0 & 0 & \cdots \\
0 & 0.6p & 0 & 0 & 0 \\
0 & 0 & 0.4p & p & p \\
0 & 0.4p & 0.6p & 0 & 0 \\
\end{matrix}
$$

Note that there are three sections to this sequence. The first vector is the status quo, which has already been defined. The next two vectors represent the *transient response*, because they represent temporary situations leading to a stable resolution. The last two vectors, which are identical, denote the *steady-state solution*, since as long as the model retains the same structure, no further change of state will occur.

The progression of the conflict can clearly be traced through these state vectors. On a given day, $(1\text{-}p) \times 100$ percent of the time there will not be enough snow to support an attack, and in this situation neither will the Afghans attack nor the Soviets move in reinforcements. In the $p \times 100$ percent of the time in which there is sufficient snow, the Afghans will attack, but since the Soviets are sometimes cognizant of their plans, $p \times 40$ percent of the time the Soviets simultaneously move in reinforcements.

Table 6.9 Afghan Battle Transition Matrix

	0	1	2	3	4	5	6	7
0	1	1	0	0	0	0	0	0
1	0	0	0	0	0	0	0	0
2	0	0	1	1	0	0	0	0
3	0	0	0	0	0	0	0	0
4	0	0	0	0	0	0	0	0
5	0	0	0	0	0.6	0	0	0
6	0	0	0	0	0	0	1	1
7	0	0	0	0	0.4	1	0	0

In the third state vector, the Afghans retreat in the $p \times 40$ percent of the time that the Soviets already have reinforcements, and in the other $p \times 60$ percent of the time in which it snows sufficiently the Soviets move in reinforcements. Finally in all cases in which the Afghans attack they have retreated, and a steady-state solution has the Soviets reinforcing the camp $p \times 100$ percent of the time, and nothing at all happening $(1-p) \times 100$ percent of the time. This thoroughly corresponds with an intuitive appreciation for this conflict, and presents the dynamic structure in a useful and easily understood manner.

Although the state transition model of conflict is primarily descriptive, it can be used to determine a correct course of action. For example, say it costs the Afghans \$10,000 (they use U.S. dollars to buy the Chinese weapons) to prepare for an attack, and the probability of sufficient snow p for any particular day is known to reasonable accuracy. Say the value of an attack on the unreinforced camp is \$150,000 but the loss of an attack for which the Soviets were prepared is \$20,000 (life is cheap). Also, let the cost of leaving the pass reinforced be \$50,000. What should p be before an attack is profitable? By an examination of the transient response this is given by p such that

$$-10,000 + (0.6p \times 150,000) - (0.4p \times 20,000) - 50,000p > 0.$$

This leads to a p greater than 0.31, meaning that if the probability of sufficient snow is greater than about one-third, the Afghans should attack. Although in this case this calculation could be carried out from the information provided without developing the state transition model, in a more complicated circumstance it would not be easy to do so.

6.5.3 Further Discussion of the State Transition Model

Although the state transition model is primarily descriptive, it does not suppose that the parties represented by players will act in the manner indicated. A player who has knowledge of the other players' preferences may select an inducement strategy. This is a strategy that does not improve the player's position, given that the other players maintain their strategies, but that is pursued in the hope that the other players will subsequently improve to an outcome that is preferred by the first player. This could be a reasonable strategy to take if the desired steady-state or equilibrium outcome would not be reached in the ordinary course of events. However, if it is known in advance that a player can be expected to select an inducement strategy in this manner (or has a probability of doing so), this information can be incorporated into the transition matrix. Further, the state transition model is the ideal medium for determining the result of selecting an inducement strategy. This would be done by choosing as the status quo the outcome produced by the inducement strategy and examining the transient and steady-state response of the game model.

An important benefit of the state transition approach is that it is suitable for implementation on a computer, whereas the extensive form is not. Also, as will be seen in Chapter 7, a computer can be used to calculate a state transition matrix from a static analysis automatically.

6.6 State Transition Analysis of the Cuban Missile Crisis

The Cuban missile crisis was analyzed as a static game of complete perception in Chapter 1, first and second level hypergames in Chapter 3, and for sensitivity in Chapter 5. However, none of the models used captured the dynamic nature of this conflict in a formal manner. The state transition form provides a realistic model of this conflict and fully demonstrates how the conflict evolves over time.

The individual transition matrices for the United States and the USSR for the Cuban missile crisis are constructed using the preference vectors and stability results of Table 1.4 (see p. 15). For example, consider outcome 3 in the U.S. preference vector in Table 1.4. The United States has a undeterred UI to outcome 2. This is indicated in the matrix in Table 6.10 as the 1 in the column under outcome 3 opposite the row labeled 2. Similarly, in the Soviet individual transition matrix in Table 6.11, there is a 1 in the (4,4) position to indicate that outcome 4 is stable for the USSR in the static stability analysis.

After the initial transition matrices are determined, the dynamic constraints in the conflict can be incorporated in order to come up with the final transition matrices for each player. This is done for the Cuban missile crisis game by noting that either an air strike by the United States or an escalation by the USSR could not be withdrawn, once invoked. Thus the changes by the United States from outcome 1 to 2 or from outcome 3 to 2 are considered dynamically infeasible in the final transition matrix. Therefore, outcomes 1 and 3 are designated absorbing states, as seen in Table 6.12.

Table 6.10 Individual Transition Matrix for the United States in the Cuban Missile Crisis

	0	1	2	3	4	5	6	7	8	9	10	11
0	0	0	0	0	0	0	0	0	0	0	0	0
1	0	0	0	0	0	0	0	0	0	0	0	0
2	1	1	1	1	0	0	0	0	0	0	0	0
3	0	0	0	0	0	0	0	0	0	0	0	0
4	0	0	0	0	1	0	0	0	0	0	0	0
5	0	0	0	0	0	0	0	0	0	0	0	0
6	0	0	0	0	0	1	1	1	0	0	0	0
7	0	0	0	0	0	0	0	0	0	0	0	0
8	0	0	0	0	0	0	0	0	0	0	0	0
9	0	0	0	0	0	0	0	0	0	0	0	0
10	0	0	0	0	0	0	0	0	0	0	0	0
11	0	0	0	0	0	0	0	0	1	1	1	1

On the other hand, the United States would be expected to release their blockade after the Soviet missiles were withdrawn from Cuba since the USSR would not be expected to try to get away with installing the missiles again. Thus the sanctions on the UIs to outcome 4 from outcomes 6 and 7 in the U.S. preference vector in Table 1.4 are in fact now not considered credible. This is denoted in Table 6.12 by the state changing from 6 to 4. However, outcome 7 involves an air strike, the undoing of what is considered infeasible. The UI from 7 to 5 is feasible and shown in the table.

Table 6.11 Individual Transition Matrix for the USSR in the Cuban Missile Crisis

	0	1	2	3	4	5	6	7	8	9	10	11
0	1	0	0	0	0	0	0	0	1	0	0	0
1	0	0	0	0	0	0	0	0	0	0	0	0
2	0	0	0	0	0	0	0	0	0	0	0	0
3	0	0	0	0	0	0	0	0	0	0	0	0
4	0	0	0	0	1	0	0	0	0	0	0	0
5	0	1	0	0	0	1	0	0	0	1	0	0
6	0	0	1	0	0	0	1	0	0	0	1	0
7	0	0	0	1	0	0	0	1	0	0	0	1
8	0	0	0	0	0	0	0	0	0	0	0	0
9	0	0	0	0	0	0	0	0	0	0	0	0
10	0	0	0	0	0	0	0	0	0	0	0	0
11	0	0	0	0	0	0	0	0	0	0	0	0

Table 6.12 Final Transition Matrix for the United States in the Cuban Missile Crisis

	0	1	2	3	4	5	6	7	8	9	10	11
0	0	0	0	0	0	0	0	0	0	0	0	0
1	0	1	0	0	0	0	0	0	0	0	0	0
2	1	0	1	0	0	0	0	0	0	0	0	0
3	0	0	0	1	0	0	0	0	0	0	0	0
4	0	0	0	0	1	0	1	0	0	0	0	0
5	0	0	0	0	0	1	0	1	0	0	0	0
6	0	0	0	0	0	0	0	0	0	0	0	0
7	0	0	0	0	0	0	0	0	0	0	0	0
8	0	0	0	0	0	0	0	0	0	0	0	0
9	0	0	0	0	0	0	0	0	0	0	0	0
10	0	0	0	0	0	0	0	0	0	0	0	0
11	0	0	0	0	0	0	0	0	1	1	1	1

Outcome 5 is an absorbing state for the United States because it involves only the air strike.

The changes to the Soviet matrix of Table 6.11 to result in the final transition matrix of Table 6.13 involve outcomes 8, 9, 10, and 11. These four outcomes have a transition that involves de-escalation, which is not considered dynamically feasible. Consequently, as shown in Table 6.13, these outcomes are all made into absorbing states in the final Soviet matrix.

Using the procedure given in Section 6.5.1, the matrixes of Tables 6.12 and 6.13 are combined to give the overall conflict transition matrix shown

Table 6.13 Final Transition Matrix for the USSR in the Cuban Missile Crisis

	0	1	2	3	4	5	6	7	8	9	10	11
0	1	0	0	0	0	0	0	0	0	0	0	0
1	0	0	0	0	0	0	0	0	0	0	0	0
2	0	0	0	0	0	0	0	0	0	0	0	0
3	0	0	0	0	0	0	0	0	0	0	0	0
4	0	0	0	0	1	0	0	0	0	0	0	0
5	0	1	0	0	0	1	0	0	0	0	0	0
6	0	0	1	0	0	0	1	0	0	0	0	0
7	0	0	0	1	0	0	0	1	0	0	0	0
8	0	0	0	0	0	0	0	0	1	0	0	0
9	0	0	0	0	0	0	0	0	0	1	0	0
10	0	0	0	0	0	0	0	0	0	0	1	0
11	0	0	0	0	0	0	0	0	0	0	0	1

in Table 6.14. For example, consider transitions from outcome 6. The United States has a transition from outcome 6 to 4, whereas for the USSR outcome 6 is absorbing. Thus, in the overall transition matrix there is a transition from outcome 6 to 4. Using (6-2) with $a = 4$ and $b = 6$,

$$(4 + 6) - 6 = 4,$$

mathematically gives the same result.

Using the basic state transition equation given by

$$Y = TX,\qquad\qquad (6\text{-}1)$$

where T is the transition matrix, X is the status quo vector, and Y is the output vector, one can trace the events of the conflict. In the Cuban missile crisis, the status quo on October 17, 1962 was outcome 0, where the United States had neither performed an air strike nor blockaded Cuba, while the USSR had neither withdrawn its missiles nor escalated the conflict. The X vector is then written horizontally as (100000000000). Multiplying the matrix T given in Table 6.14 by this vector X gives the first output vector Y, which is (001000000000).

By applying the state transition equation repetitively, one can determine the transient and steady-state response of the system. These are shown in Table 6.15. The transient response is the sequence of outcomes $0 \to 2 \to 6 \to 4 \to 4$. This means that from the status quo, the United States will impose a blockade. Subsequently, the USSR will withdraw its missiles, after which the United States will remove its blockade. Steady-state outcome 4 remains the same once it has been achieved, so it can be said that the ultimate resolution to the conflict is that the USSR will remove its missiles.

Table 6.14 Overall Transition Matrix for the Cuban Missile Crisis

	0	1	2	3	4	5	6	7	8	9	10	11
0	0	0	0	0	0	0	0	0	0	0	0	0
1	0	0	0	0	0	0	0	0	0	0	0	0
2	1	0	0	0	0	0	0	0	0	0	0	0
3	0	0	0	0	0	0	0	0	0	0	0	0
4	0	0	0	0	1	0	1	0	0	0	0	0
5	0	1	0	0	0	1	0	1	0	0	0	0
6	0	0	1	0	0	0	0	0	0	0	0	0
7	0	0	0	1	0	0	0	0	0	0	0	0
8	0	0	0	0	0	0	0	0	0	0	0	0
9	0	0	0	0	0	0	0	0	0	0	0	0
10	0	0	0	0	0	0	0	0	0	0	0	0
11	0	0	0	0	0	0	0	0	1	1	1	1

Table 6.15 Transient and Steady-State Response

State (outcome)	Status quo	Transient response				Steady state
0	1.0	0	0	0	0	0
1	0	0	0	0	0	0
2	0	1.0	0	0	0	0
3	0	0	0	0	0	0
4	0	0	0	1.0	1.0	1.0
5	0	0	0	0	0	0
6	0	0	1.0	0	0	0
7	0	0	0	0	0	0
8	0	0	0	0	0	0
9	0	0	0	0	0	0
10	0	0	0	0	0	0
11	0	0	0	0	0	0

In Chapter 1 it was observed that one could trace the dynamics of the conflict through the analysis tableau by following UIs from the status quo outcome to an equilibrium. However, this is not generally a valid technique because UIs are not necessarily actions but may only be in the mind of the player. As executed by the state transition form, the dynamics of the game must take into account the constraints on the actions of the players.

6.7 Important Concepts from Chapter 6

There are two approaches to analyzing and presenting dynamic and probabilistic aspects of a conflict. These are the extensive and state transition forms of the game. In the extensive form the conflict is represented as a tree graph with the nodes being players and the branches strategies. The extensive form allows the graphic display of the dynamics of a conflict and easily accommodates probabilistic information. However, it is suitable for only very simple conflicts.

The state transition model also permits the inclusion of dynamic and probabilistic information about a conflict into an analysis and can handle very complex situations. The state transition form of the game considers a conflict as a sequence of states, where each state is an outcome or set of outcomes with a probability of occurrence for each outcome. A new state is determined by applying a transition matrix to the original state, using (6-1). The transition matrix for a conflict can be calculated from the results of a static analysis, as described in Section 6.5.1, or can be developed from an understanding of the conflict.

The extensive and state transition form of the game were demonstrated through the analysis of the Watergate tapes conflict and a hypothetical military example. In the Watergate tapes conflict, the static analysis determined two equilibriums, one of which was the immediate resolution to the conflict. The extensive form of the game demonstrated how the resolution determined in the static analysis was due to the dynamics of the game, but failed to indicate the second equilibrium as a special outcome. The state transition form of the game correctly identified the resolution to the game and the equilibrium found in the static analysis, and also revealed a new stable outcome that was due to the dynamics of the conflict.

In the hypothetical military conflict, the extensive form of the game provided a reasonable representation of the situation by including only the outcomes that the participants would be expected to take. The state transition form of the game was used to develop a transient response and a steady-state solution to the conflict, which provided a meaningful and useful method of examining the problem.

The final conflict analyzed in this chapter is the Cuban missile crisis, which was first introduced in Chapter 1. The state transition form was used to model the dynamics of the conflict, and the results clearly demonstrated how the missile crisis changed over time.

Questions

1. Construct an extensive game tree for the Watergate tapes conflict for which it is assumed that Nixon will change his strategy in some cases after the investigators have selected their strategy. Does this alter the conclusions from the analysis?
2. Construct a reasonable extensive model for the Cuban crisis.
3. Is it possible to have a state transition matrix with no entry on the main diagonal?
4. Is there any information contained in a game tree (the extensive form of the game) that cannot be obtained from the transition matrix? What about the other way around?
5. Explain the similarity between the formula for simultaneous sanctioning and the calculation for determining the row entry in the overall transition matrix. Derive (6-3).
6. Develop a state transition matrix to model the infinite game mentioned at the end of the subsection on the extensive form of the game in Section 6.5.2. Write out the transient response for this situation.
7. Develop a dynamic model to present the GDU conflict of Chapter 2.

Chapter 7

Computer Assistance in Conflict Analysis

7.1 Introduction

Even though a conflict analysis can be easily performed completely by hand with pencil and paper, computer assistance provides a valuable convenience. Many real world conflicts are best modeled as having a large number of players and options, which may make the analysis fairly complex. Also, an analysis will often be performed many times before a suitable model is developed. Similarly, a sensitivity analysis may require repeated analyses of a final model. Conflicts that require a large model and those in which many analyses are performed benefit most from computer assistance.

One of the most tedious tasks when performing a conflict analysis is outcome removal, and efficient algorithms for outcome removal have been previously implemented in FORTRAN (Trustees of the University of Pennsylvania, 1969b; Shepanik, 1971, 1974) and in APL. There are also other aspects of a conflict analysis that are usefully performed by computer. These are presented in this chapter through an analysis of the Poplar River conflict using the Conflict Analysis Program (CAP) (Fraser and Hipel, 1979b, 1980a,c). This program is an interactive, microcomputer-based aid to decision making that is exceptionally useful and easy to use. It was originally developed on a Compucolor-II microcomputer and a new version is available for the IBM PC microcomputer. Information on acquiring CAP can be obtained from the publishers.

7.2 Poplar River Conflict

7.2.1 History of the Conflict

The Poplar River Basin lies in the southern part of the Canadian province of Saskatchewan and the northern part of Montana. The river and its tributaries flow southward to join the Missouri River near Poplar, Montana. The Poplar watershed encompasses an area of 8620 km², which is about the same size as the basin of the Thames River in England. The northern third of the Poplar watershed is in Saskatchewan. The remainder is in Montana, with the southern third in the Fort Peck Indian Reserve. Except for a few small towns the area is rural, with a population of about 7000 or 8000. The Poplar River region has been subject to severe droughts that have lasted as long as a decade. The Poplar River has an average annual flow of 42,000 cubic decameters at the international boundary, three-quarters of which occurs in the spring runoff that may last from ten days to three weeks (IJC, 1978b). This can be compared with a flow of 1,000,000 cubic decameters annually at the mouth of the Thames.

In 1971 a coal exploration program was initiated by the Saskatchewan Power Corporation (SPC), a provincial Crown (government-owned) corporation responsible for meeting Saskatchewan's energy needs. An economically recoverable source of lignite coal was discovered near Coronach, within the Poplar basin. A thermal generating station built to use this coal would require a constant supply of water, a great deal of which would be lost through forced evaporation cooling. It was estimated that the coal reserves were sufficient to support a generating station of at least 1200 megawatts (MW) (SPC, 1974).

On March 24, 1972, the SPC made a formal application to the Saskatchewan government for water rights on the Poplar River. All required authorization was obtained, and construction was started in August 1975 (SPC, 1975). Completion date of the initial 300 MW stage was estimated in the SPC 1976 annual report as 1979, at a cost of $150 million (SPC, 1976).

Political activity associated with the project commenced shortly after the first public announcement in 1974. Parties in the United States were concerned about loss of water from the Poplar River. On September 15, 1974, Environment Canada informed the International Souris—Red Rivers Engineering Board of the project (IJC, 1978b). The Board was established in 1948 by the International Joint Commission (IJC) to advise it regarding water uses and requirements in the part of the United States—Canada international boundary that includes the Poplar basin. (See Section 2.3.1 for more information about the IJC.)

On April 8, 1975, the IJC instructed its International Souris–Red Rivers Engineering Board to undertake a study of the Poplar River Basin with a view to preparing recommendations for the apportionment of flows. The

Board's report on water apportionment in the Poplar River Basin became available on February 27, 1976, and was followed by an IJC publication entitled *Water Apportionment in the Poplar River Basin* (IJC, 1978b). This report is the key source used in the ensuing analysis although it actually presents two issues: those of water apportionment and air and water quality. The information available in the report dates from late 1977, which determines the time at which the analysis takes place.

7.2.2 Players

Eight interested parties are mentioned in the IJC report as being significant in this conflict.

Saskatchewan Power Corporation. At the time of the IJC report, the SPC had a large investment in the power project as well as commitments for the energy produced. Also, it would be very much in the SPC's interest to be able to expand beyond the 300 MW initial phase. The SPC had thus expressed its desire for an apportionment of 70% of the water for Canada and 30% for the United States (IJC, 1978b).

If water were not available from the Poplar River for the power plant, it would be possible to import water from Lake Diefenbaker, 140 miles away. However, this would be extremely expensive (Province of Saskatchewan, 1976).

Province of Saskatchewan. The Province of Saskatchewan was advised by its Board of Inquiry that the Poplar River power project was the best source of electrical energy to meet the future needs of the people of Saskatchewan (Province of Saskatchewan, 1976). The Province expressed support for a larger share than 50% of the water in the Poplar River to be available to the SPC, and insisted upon not less than 50%. The Province believed this was justified by the Helsinki Rules of 1966 and by precedent (Province of Saskatchewan, 1976).

Government of Canada. The Canadian Government indicated an interest in air and water quality issues (IJC, 1978b).

Fort Peck Indian Tribes. The Fort Peck Indian Tribes strongly expressed their desire for a major portion of the water from the Poplar River. A project for irrigating a large number of acres on the reservation was not compatible with heavy use of water from the Poplar River by Saskatchewan. They supported a minimum apportionment at the international boundary of 70% for the United States and 30% for Canada, based on prior use or on the *Winters Doctrine*. The Winters Doctrine predates the Boundary Waters Treaty and guarantees the right to sufficient water to meet the present and future needs of the reservation (IJC, 1978b). In addition, the Fort Peck Tribes claim to be a quasi-sovereign territory with corresponding powers and privileges (IJC, 1978b).

State of Montana. The expressed concerns of the State of Montana were over air and water quality. Montana indicated that it would support a 50–50 apportionment split, subject to further air and water quality negotiations (IJC, 1978b).

Department of State. The U.S. Department of State had taken the position that an Environmental Impact Statement would be required by the U.S. federal government before it could enter into an apportionment agreement with Canada (IJC, 1978b, p. 30). However, the State Department also expressed unqualified support for any apportionment agreement, thus contradicting its environmental concerns (IJC, 1978b, p. 31).

U.S. Government. The U.S. government indicated an interest in air and water quality issues (IJC, 1978b).

International Joint Commission (IJC). The IJC was directed by Canada and the United States to "secure the interests of both countries" (IJC, 1978b). In this respect the Commission can take on some of the aspects of an active player in the conflict because it is in the interests of both countries to have the conflict resolved. Thus the Commission must choose a strategy based to a certain extent upon the responses of the other parties.

The legal basis for the IJC's involvement in the Poplar conflict is Article IX of the Boundary Treaty of 1909, similar to the Garrison conflict of Chapter 2. No IJC recommendation is binding to the two countries (IJC, 1965), but all have a great deal of political significance, as described in Section 2.3.1.

7.2.3 Options

The players and options suggested in Section 7.2.2 are summarized in Table 7.1. This table presents the situation as recorded in the IJC report (IJC, 1978b) for the chosen time of late 1977. In 1977 the IJC, the Canadian and U.S. governments, and the State of Montana had all indicated that water and air quality studies were underway. Until these studies were completed these parties could not express positions on the conflict relating to water and air quality. The other player that expressed concern about environmental quality was the U.S. State Department, but it had also indicated that it was in support of any apportionment agreement (IJC, 1978b).

Table 7.1 Players and Options for the Poplar Conflict

Player	Option
Saskatchewan Power Corporation	Build initial power plant
	Build extended power plant
	Build to full capacity
	Import water
Province of Saskatchewan	Legal action based on Boundary Treaty and Helsinki Rules
Fort Peck Indian Tribes	Build full irrigation project
	Build reduced irrigation project
	Legal action based on Boundary Treaty
	Legal action based on Winters Doctrine
State of Montana	Legal action based on environmental concerns
U.S. State Department	Legal action based on environmental concerns
Canadian government	Action based on environmental concerns
U.S. government	Action based on environmental concerns
International Joint Commission	Support apportionment favoring Canada
	Support apportionment favoring U.S.
	Support 50–50 apportionment
	Action based on environmental concerns

The aforesaid would suggest that the two aspects of the Poplar conflict, apportionment and environmental concerns, can effectively be separated. They are of course interdependent but, because of the time factor, expressed options relating to environmental concerns cannot be freely chosen by the participants to have bearing on the apportionment conflict. This separation reduces the number of significant players in the conflict. Further simplification can be made by noting that the interests of the Province of Saskatchewan and the SPC are identical. They are then considered as one player, whose total options include the options of both. The list of players and options for the apportionment conflict as adjusted in this manner may be found as Table 7.2.

Note that the options listed in Tables 7.1 and 7.2 do not represent instantly selectable actions, but activities that the parties have indicated are likely under certain circumstances. Also, some fairly complex activities have been coalesced into single options. For example, the 50–50 IJC apportionment actually is a very complex apportionment plan and was chosen from 22 similar ones (IJC, 1978b). In the same manner, the option

Table 7.2 Players and Options for the Apportionment Conflict

Player	Option
Saskatchewan Power Corporation	Build initial power plant
	Build extended power plant
	Build to full capacity
	Import water
Fort Peck Indian Tribes	Build full irrigation project
	Build reduced irrigation project
	Legal action based on Boundary Treaty
	Legal action based on Winters Doctrine
International Joint Commission	Support apportionment favoring Canada
	Support apportionment favoring U.S.
	Support 50–50 apportionment

of legal action encompasses a number of activities, from formal protests to litigation.

The three listed sizes of power plant have been chosen to represent the full range of possibilities available to the SPC. The initial plant represents the 300-MW plant that was under construction at the time of the analysis. It is assumed that there will be enough water to support this plant if a minimum 70–30 apportionment favoring the United States is carried out. The extended plant represents a plant developed to take advantage of a 50–50 apportionment. The complete plant requires a 70–30 apportionment favoring Canada.

For the Fort Peck Tribes, two options include all the possible irrigation projects that are available. It is assumed that there will be enough water to support the full irrigation project with a 70–30 split favoring the United States, and the partial project with either a 70–30 split favoring Canada or else a 50–50 apportionment.

7.2.4 Preferences

In the Poplar conflict, the SPC would prefer as large a power plant as possible, but would prefer not to import water because of the great expense involved. The Fort Peck Tribes would prefer a full irrigation project to a partial one.

A general assumption can be made concerning the decision on the parts of the SPC and the Fort Peck Tribes to initiate legal action. It is reasonable to say that a party would favor legal action if it anticipated winning, but would not favor legal action if it expected to lose. In some situations this would not be true (e.g., in a suit advanced to satisfy political pressure), but in the Poplar River conflict it is reasonable to determine the players' preferences for court action on this basis. Since the IJC's recommendation can be expected to parallel a judgment made by it should such a judgment be required, and since the opinion of the IJC represents the most sound analysis available, it is assumed that legal action based on the Boundary Waters Treaty will fail unless supported by the IJC recommendation. Thus either the SPC or the Fort Peck Tribes are likely to initiate legal action when supported by the IJC, but not otherwise. The Fort Peck Tribes indicated that they may initiate legal action under the Winters Doctrine under any circumstances other than a 70–30 split favoring the United States (IJC, 1978b).

Because the IJC must "secure the interests of both countries" (IJC, 1978b), and it is in the interests of both Canada and the United States to have the conflict resolved, the IJC would prefer to make a recommendation. However, beyond this no preferences are permissible for the IJC (as in the case of the Garrison conflict of Chapter 2).

7.2.5 Model Entry

The model of the Poplar River conflict for December 1977 has three players and 12 options for a total of 4096 outcomes. The players and options are entered into CAP in the model entry stage of the program. Table 7.3 is similar to the outcome removal screen display from CAP. On the left are found the players and short expressions representing the options available to the players in this conflict.

Table 7.3 Outcome Removal Screen Display for the Poplar River Conflict

```
OUTCOME REMOVAL
                                       22 OUTCOMES LEFT
1.  SPC
      INITIAL       - - - - - 1 1 - - - - - - - - - - - 0 - -
      EXTENDED      - - - - 1 - 1 1 - - - - - - - - - - 0 - -
      COMPLETED     - - - - 1 1 - - 1 1 - - - - - - - - 0 - -
      IMP. WATER    - - - - - - - - 0 0 - - - - - - - - - 1
      LEGAL B       - - - - - - - - - - - - 1 - - - - - - -
2.  FORT PECK
      FULL PROJ     - - - 1 - - - - - - - 1 1 - - - - - - 0 -
      PART PROJ     - - - 1 - - - - - - - - - - - - - - - 0 -
      LEGAL B       - - - - - - - - - - - - - - 1 - - - - - -
      LEGAL W       - - - - - - - - - - - - - - 0 0 - - - -
3.  IJC
      30-70 CAN     - 1 1 - - - - - - - 1 - - 1 1 - 0 - - -
      30-70 USA     1 - 1 - - - - 1 1 - - - 1 - - - 0 - - -
      50-50         1 1 - - - - - - - 1 - 1 - - - 1 0 - - -
```

7.3 Outcome Removal

For outcome removal, sets of outcomes are entered vertically on the microcomputer display. Thus, the first outcome on the left in Table 7.3 represents the 1024 infeasible outcomes where the player IJC supports a 30–70 appropriation and a 50–50 appropriation at the same time. The removal of the outcomes listed in Table 7.3 reduces the outcomes which remain in the model to only 22 from the original $2^{12} = 4096$.

One convenient data structure for the storage of a set of outcomes is an $N \times 2$ array, where N is some experimentally obtained value related to the available storage and the number of options expected in the conflict model. The original version of CAP uses $N = 100$. As always, outcomes may be considered as binary numbers and thus may also be expressed in decimal form, as described in Section 1.3.3. Outcomes in the array are stored as blocks of outcomes in decimal fashion. For example, the set of all outcomes of a 12-option conflict model would employ one row of the outcome matrix, and would appear as

$$(0 \quad 4095).$$

The remaining 99 rows of the matrix would not be used. If one were now to remove the outcome (10011,0100,010) (decimal 1113), the new matrix would be

$$\begin{pmatrix} 0 & 1112 \\ 1114 & 4095 \end{pmatrix}$$

with the remaining 98 rows empty. Removing the outcome with decimal value 1115 will result in

$$\begin{pmatrix} 0 & 1112 \\ 1114 & 1114 \\ 1116 & 4095 \end{pmatrix}$$

In practice, outcome removal tends to remove outcomes that fall into ordered blocks, thus keeping the size of the storage array relatively small. For example, consider the situation of removing outcomes from a 12-option model where the ninth and tenth options are mutually exclusive. This can be indicated by the vector $(- - - - -, - - -1,1- -)$. In decimal form, this generalized vector represents outcomes 768–1023, 1792–2047, 2816–3071, and 3840–4095. Removing these 1024 outcomes from the full model leaves the following outcome matrix:

$$\begin{pmatrix} 0 & 767 \\ 1024 & 1791 \\ 2048 & 2815 \\ 3072 & 3839 \end{pmatrix}$$

It is clear that more dashes to the left of the first specified option results in fewer blocks of decimalized outcomes. For this reason CAP users are advised to enter first generalized outcomes that have specified options of high order. This increases the speed of processing and ensures that the reserved memory for the outcome matrix is not exceeded.

The algorithm that employs this data structure counts through each specific outcome in the group of outcomes that is to be removed. Blocks of outcomes are identified and passed to a routine that correctly updates the outcome matrix to reflect the block's removal. This routine also maintains a *pointer* to the last row altered in the outcome matrix. Since the outcomes to be removed are numerically increasing, the pointer ensures the rapid location of an outcome. The stopping condition is either the end of the possible blocks or an attempt to remove a block of outcomes whose smallest member is greater than the largest element in the outcome matrix.

7.4 Preference Vector Development

A second way in which the computer offers valuable assistance in conflict analysis is in the ordering of outcomes by the preferences of the individual players. One very convenient technique is to use a *lexicographic* ordering scheme. Lexicographic means in the pattern of a dictionary, where words are ordered by the first letter in each word, and within this ordering, by the second letter in the word, and so on. In conflict analysis, outcomes are very often ordered by option. Consider this statement: "The SPC would prefer to build an initial power plant (option 1) even if the Fort Peck Tribes pursue legal action based on the Winters Doctrine (option 9), but the SPC does not want the Fort Peck Tribes to pursue legal action." This is a lexicographical ordering on taking option 1 and rejecting option 9. This would mean that all outcomes with a 1 for the first option would be more preferred for the SPC than outcomes with a 0 in this position. Within this ordering, outcomes are ordered with regard to rejection of the ninth option. Thus all outcomes with a 0 corresponding to the ninth option would be preferred to outcomes with a 1 in this position, subject to the priority given the ordering based on the first option.

The method of preference vector development used in CAP is the specification of a lexicographic ordering as a vector of option numbers, where the sign of the option number can indicate whether the ordering is forward or reverse. In this manner the statement under consideration would be expressed as $(1, -9)$. This *lexicography vector* can be interpreted as an implicit pseudo-Boolean preference function (Shepanik, 1971; Ragade et al., 1976a). A pseudo-Boolean preference function weights options according to their preference by a player. The index of the elements in the lexicography vector can be interpreted as a weight for the corresponding option, and a value representing the desirability of any outcome for a player can be easily calculated. The preference vector can then be reordered according to the functional value provided by the lexicography vector. In cases where the preferences are not fully lexicographic, outcomes can subsequently be adjusted individually.

In CAP, the following specific implementation is used. Let the ith element of the lexicography vector be indicated by $l(i)$, and let the jth element of an outcome be indicated by $o(j)$. Let n be the length of the lexicography vector. The value of an outcome can then be calculated as

$$\sum_{i=1}^{n} \{\text{sgn}[l(i)]\, o(|l(i)|)\, 2^{n-1}\} \qquad (7\text{-}1)$$

where $\text{sgn}(x)$ has the value 1 if x is positive and -1 if x is negative. For example, consider the following four outcomes from a two-option model, where the outcomes are written vertically as in the tables rather than horizontally as in the text:

$$\begin{array}{cccc} 0 & 1 & 0 & 1 \\ 0 & 0 & 1 & 1. \end{array}$$

It is determined that the lexicography vector $(2, -1)$ accurately reflects the preferences of one of the players, and it is desired to order the outcomes according to this lexicography vector. From (7-1), the value of the first outcome from the left is

$$(0 \times 2) - (0 \times 1) = 0.$$

Similarly, the remaining three outcomes have values of:

$$(0 \times 2) - (1 \times 1) = -1,$$
$$(1 \times 2) - (0 \times 1) = 2,$$
$$(1 \times 2) - (1 \times 1) = 1.$$

Reordering the outcomes from highest functional value on the left to lowest functional value on the right gives

$$\begin{array}{cccc} 0 & 1 & 0 & 1 \\ 1 & 1 & 0 & 0, \end{array}$$

which is the desired ordering.

Table 7.4 is similar to the preference development screen display for the player SPC in the Poplar River conflict. The outcomes that remained after outcome removal have been ordered based on published information about the player, using a lexicographic ordering scheme. The specific lexicographic vector used for the outcomes in Table 7.4 was $(3, 2, 10, -11, -6, -5, -8, -9)$. The equals signs above outcomes in the CAP screen display shown in Table 7.4 indicate that the the grouped outcomes are all equally preferred by this player (as do bridges in earlier tables).

Table 7.4 Preference Ordering Screen Display for the SPC in the Poplar River Conflict

PREFERENCE ORDERING

PREFERENCES FOR SPC

																	=	=	=	=	=	=
1. SPC																						
INITIAL	0	0	0	0	0	0	0	0	1	1	1	1	1	1	1	1	1	1	1	1	1	1
EXTENDED	0	0	1	1	1	1	1	1	1	0	0	0	0	0	0	0	0	0	0	0	0	0
COMPLETED	1	1	0	0	0	0	0	0	0	0	0	0	0	0	0	0	0	0	0	0	0	0
IMP. WATER	0	0	0	0	0	0	0	0	0	0	0	0	0	0	0	0	0	0	0	0	0	0
LEGAL B	0	1	0	1	0	0	1	1	0	1	0	0	1	1	0	0	0	0	0	0	0	0
2. FORT PECK																						
FULL PROJ	0	0	0	0	0	0	0	0	0	0	0	0	0	0	0	0	0	0	1	1	1	1
PART PROJ	1	1	1	1	1	1	1	1	1	1	1	1	1	1	1	1	1	1	0	0	0	0
LEGAL B	0	0	0	0	0	1	0	1	0	0	0	1	0	1	0	0	1	1	0	0	1	1
LEGAL W	1	1	1	1	1	1	1	1	1	1	1	1	1	1	0	1	0	1	0	1	0	1
3. IJC																						
30–70 CAN	1	1	1	1	0	0	0	0	1	1	0	0	0	0	0	0	0	0	0	0	0	0
30–70 USA	0	0	0	0	0	0	0	0	0	0	0	0	0	0	0	1	1	1	1	1	1	1
50–50	0	0	0	0	1	1	1	1	1	0	0	1	1	1	1	0	0	0	0	0	0	0

The newer versions of CAP have a more sophisticated scheme for entering lexicographic preference information. This consists of an ordered set of *preference masks* that indicates preferences in a more detailed manner than a lexicography vector. Using preference masks, the equivalent to the lexicography vector 2, -3, 1 is given by:

$$\begin{array}{ccc} - & - & 1 \\ 1 & - & - \\ - & 0 & - \end{array}$$

Unlike lexicographic ordering, however, preference masks need not be mutually exclusive. These masks reflect how players would naturally prioritize their objectives with respect to their own options and those of the opponents. At one end of the set is specified the ideal set of option selection from the viewpoint of a given player, and at the other, the least preferred case.

In order to determine the resulting ordering of outcomes from a set of preference masks, a weighting scheme is used. Each mask m is assigned a weight of $2^{(n-m)}$, where n is the number of preference masks. Hence an outcome that matches a given mask is assigned a weight higher than that of an outcome that matches any of the subsequent masks. In the case of equally preferred groups of preference masks, each member of the group is given the weight of the mask farthest to the left.

For example, consider a three-option game with the following set of preference masks:

	Mask No. (m)			
	1	2	3	4
Option 1	0	—	—	—
Option 2	—	0	1	1
Option 3	0	1	0	—
Weight	8	4	4	1

This says that the player would most prefer outcomes in which options 1 and 3 were not selected. A weight of $2^{(1-4)} = 2^3 = 8$ is added to any outcome that is a member of this set, as shown in the last row of the table. The line joining masks 2 and 3 indicates equal preference; consequently the weighting factor is the same for these two masks, at $2^{(2-4)} = 2^2 = 4$. All other things being equal, the player prefers the situation where option 2 is selected. Table 7.5 demonstrates the results of applying this lexicographic information to the complete three-option game.

7.5 Stability Analysis

A third valuable contribution of computer assistance is the actual analysis of a fully developed conflict model. One of the key operations in the analysis of a conflict is the assessment of deterrents players may have against other players' UIs. Recall that a unilateral improvement may be

Table 7.5 Applying Preference Masks

Preference masks								
Option 1	0	—	—	—				
Option 2	—	0	1	1				
Option 3	0	1	0	—				
Weight	8	4	4	1				
Weight Calculation								
	0	1	0	1	0	1	0	1
	0	0	1	1	0	0	1	1
	0	0	0	0	1	1	1	1
Mask 1	8		8					
Mask 2					4	4		
Mask 3			4	4				
Mask 4			1	1			1	1
Total weight	8	0	13	5	4	4	1	1
Resulting preference ordering								
	0	0	1	0	1	0	1	1
	1	0	1	0	0	1	1	0
	0	0	0	1	1	1	1	0

deterred by a credible sequential sanction (see Section 1.3.3). This means that in order to check for deterrents one must check all outcomes that may be produced by players improving their positions not only from the initial improvement, but also from outcomes produced by improvements made by other players. (Refer to Section 2.4 for a thorough discussion of this requirement.)

The algorithm used by CAP for stability analysis is a recursive one. Although BASIC allows subroutines to call themselves, it does not support local variables; therefore in the original version of CAP a table of local variables was built and maintained. The routine used in CAP was limited to ten recursions so that if a less preferred outcome is not found after 10 separate improvements by the other players, the improvement is considered to be undeterred. This realistic limitation also forestalls any problems with the program inescapably looping among improvements for different players.

Table 7.6 shows a screen display for the stability analysis of the Poplar River conflict. CAP constantly displays the overall stability of the outcomes near the bottom of the screen. An E means that the outcome is an equilibrium; × means that at least one player has an undeterred improvement available from the corresponding outcome. (Compare *E* and × in earlier chapters.) The stability of the outcomes for each player is shown below the overall stability. The letter R indicates that the corre-

Table 7.6 Stability Analysis Screen Display for the Poplar River Conflict

ANALYSIS

PREFERENCES FOR SPC

1. SPC																					=	=	=	=	=	=
INITIAL	0	0	0	0	0	0	0	0	1	1	1	1	1	1	1	1	1	1	1	1	1	1		
EXTENDED	0	0	1	1	1	1	1	1	1	0	0	0	0	0	0	0	0	0	0	0	0	0	0	0
COMPLETED	1	1	0	0	0	0	0	0	0	0	0	0	0	0	0	0	0	0	0	0	0	0	0	0
IMP. WATER	0	0	0	0	0	0	0	0	0	0	0	0	0	0	0	0	0	0	0	0	0	0	0	0
LEGAL B	0	1	0	1	0	0	1	1	0	1	0	0	1	1	0	0	0	0	0	0	0	0	0	0
2. FORT PECK																								
FULL PROJ	0	0	0	0	0	0	0	0	0	0	0	0	0	0	0	0	0	0	1	1	1	1		
PART PROJ	1	1	1	1	1	1	1	1	1	1	1	1	1	1	1	1	1	1	0	0	0	0		
LEGAL B	0	0	0	0	0	1	0	1	0	0	0	1	0	1	0	0	1	1	0	0	1	1		
LEGAL W	1	1	1	1	1	1	1	1	1	1	1	1	1	0	1	0	1	0	1	0	1			
3. IJC																								
30–70 CAN	1	1	1	1	0	0	0	0	1	1	0	0	0	0	0	0	0	0	0	0	0	0		
30–70 USA	0	0	0	0	0	0	0	0	0	0	0	0	0	0	1	1	1	1	1	1	1	1		
50–50	0	0	0	0	1	1	1	1	0	0	1	1	1	1	0	0	0	0	0	0	0	0		
STABILITY:	E	X	X	X	E	X	X	X	X	X	X	X	X	X	X	X	X	X	E	X	X	X		
SPC	R	U	U	U	R	R	U	U	U	U	U	U	U	U	R	R	R	R	R	R	R	R		
FORT PECK	S	R	R	R	R	U	R	U	R	R	S	R	R	S	U	U	U	U	R	U	U	U		
IJC	R	R	R	R	R	R	R	R	R	R	R	R	R	R	R	R	R	R	R	R	R	R		

sponding outcome is rational, S indicates that the player has a deterred improvement from this outcome, which makes the outcome stable for the player, and U indicates that the player has an undeterred improvement from the outcome, which makes the outcome unstable. (Compare *r*, *s*, and *u* in earlier chapters.) This means that the stability of an individual outcome can be traced as a succession of individual strategy selections and deterrents among the players. At all times the significance of an outcome can be determined by comparing the vector of 1s and 0s to the player and option list. The program also checks for simultaneous stability, so that the results are the same as would be calculated by hand.

For the Poplar River conflict, the analysis determines that there are three equilibriums. There is an equilibrium associated with each of the strategies available to the IJC, and these correspond to the other two players taking full advantage of all the water allotted to them in the allocation scheme supported by the IJC. This analysis also predicts that no legal action based on the Boundary Treaty would be pursued, but that the Fort Peck Tribes would pursue legal action based on the Winters Doctrine unless the IJC supported a water allocation scheme favoring them. For example, the leftmost outcome in Table 7.6 is the equilibrium where the IJC supports an apportionment scheme that favors Canada. The analysis predicts that in this situation the SPC would proceed to build a large power plant, the Fort Peck Tribes would proceed with a partial irrigation project and only pursue legal action based on the Winters Doctrine.

The final IJC recommendation was a 50–50 split, with modifications to accommodate Saskatchewan, although an apportionment agreement could not be signed until the U.S. government submitted an Environmental Impact Statement. The initial phase finally went on line in 1981, following several years of legislative and political bickering. As of February 1984, a second 300 MW unit is in operation, and the Fort Peck Tribes have not followed through with any legal action based on the Winters Doctrine, although they may do so in the future.

7.6 State Transition Form

The state transition model of Chapter 6 is suitable for implementation on a computer and will eventually be incorporated into CAP. For one thing, the transition matrix is generally very sparse and can economically be stored and processed as a linked list requiring very little computer memory. Another point is that rows in the transition matrix that have only 0s in them generally correspond to outcomes that are unlikely to occur in real life. If these outcomes are not in any status quo to be considered (including transient states), they can be removed from the analysis and will not affect the result. This means that although the number of outcomes in a conflict model may mathematically be very large, the transition matrix is likely to remain a reasonable size. In fact, outcomes that have only 0s in their row of the transition matrix correspond to outcomes that are removed from the conflict model during a static conflict analysis. The algorithms for outcome removal developed earlier in this chapter can be used for reducing a state transition model. Also, since the state transition model and the static model both have the same structure in terms of players, options, outcomes, and preferences, and both consider the same subset of the mathematically possible outcomes, it is a natural progression to provide a state transition analysis capability as an extension to CAP.

Use of a computer will make possible a number of further enhancements to the state transition approach. For example, in some circumstances a player's preferences can change with an awareness of the options or preferences of the other players. This is a hypergame situation that has been discussed in Chapters 3 and 4. For example, at one time in the conflict a player may improve, say, from outcome 22 to 28; but once aware that another player can implement a certain option, the first player would prefer not to make the improvement. Since the player would be made aware of the other player's option when the other player selects a strategy that includes that option, it is easy to instruct the program to update the transition matrix to reflect the first player's new knowledge. Other events could be specified to trigger an update of the transition matrix where it is thought that this would represent the real world situation most accurately, such as the performance of a particular improvement by a player or repeated entering of a particular state.

7.7 Important Concepts from Chapter 7

Some of the contributions that a computer can make in the analysis of conflict are discussed. A computer is especially valuable when:

1. many models are to be tried in an effort to determine the most appropriate representation of the real world situation;
2. the game model has a large number of players and options; or
3. many sensitivity analyses are to be done.

The computer is helpful for the following:

1. *Outcome removal.* Outcomes are stored as a matrix of decimal numbers, with only the upper and lower values of a contiguous set of numbers actually being retained. Outcomes expressed in this generalized form are similarly removed in blocks, thus keeping the storage array small in size.

2. *Preference ordering*. A lexicographic ordering scheme makes it easy to order rapidly a large number of outcomes for a player.
3. *Stability analysis*. The program analyzes the stability of each outcome in the identical manner as is done by hand.

All of these computer features are part of the Conflict Analysis Program (CAP) and have been demonstrated through the analysis of the conflict surrounding the allocation of water on the Poplar River.

Questions

1. In what circumstances is it unwise to use a computer to analyze a conflict?
2. Will simultaneous stability ever occur in a conflict in which all preferences are purely lexicographic? If not, why not?
3. If CAP or another computer program for conflict analysis is available, use it to analyze thoroughly one of the example conflicts in this book.

Chapter 8
Conflict Analysis and Bargaining

8.1 Introduction

Bargaining and negotiation involve special kinds of conflicts where the participants attempt to reach mutually acceptable contracts. As presented in this chapter, bargaining and negotiation situations are different from conventional conflicts in a number of ways. However, the basic ideas of conflict analysis as discussed in the previous chapters of this book can equally well apply to bargaining and negotiation problems.

The terms "bargaining" and "negotiation" have almost identical meanings in everyday English usage. However, they have taken on somewhat special meanings in the literature. Nierenberg (1973), for example, views bargaining as something that can be modeled and analyzed, but negotiation as defying analysis because there are no rules and everything is possible in negotiation. Rubin and Brown (1975) see bargaining as something done between individuals whereas negotiations are conducted among groups. They also note that experimental work in the field is usually termed "bargaining". Stevens (1963) points out that one can "strike a bargain" without negotiating, but usually bargaining is involved when one does negotiate. He sees negotiation as the "extra information" that is sometimes brought into a bargaining situation. Kennedy et al. (1980) view bargaining as the act of making tradeoffs and concessions during the negotiation process. Ponssard (1981) sees the bargaining process as being flexible, whereas in negotiation, once a player has reached an agreement, he or she is bound to it. In general, mathematicians and scientists prefer the term "bargaining," and lawyers and other practitioners prefer "negotiation," to refer to approximately the same process.

In this text, the terms "bargaining" and "negotiation" are used in a specific manner. *Bargaining* is taken to be the technical process by which two or more parties attain a mutually agreeable contract concerning limited resources. It is usually used in terms of the *bargaining problem*, which is the determination of an appropriate mutually agreeable contract, and can be fully modeled in some mathematical way.

Negotiation, on the other hand, involves the human interactions that form the environment of the bargaining process. Negotiation tends to be heuristic and can be considered as an art rather than a science. For example, in a labor–management situation, bargaining concerns the bids or concessions that lead to the final contract whereas negotiation involves the personal interactions of the labor boss and the company president.

The bargaining problem is primarily descriptive. The question to be answered is, "What will be the best or expected agreement to a particular bargaining situation?" Negotiation, however, is primarily normative or prescriptive: "What should a particular player do in order to achieve his or her best outcome?"

The negotiation process can be further broken down into two distinct time frames. Negotiation that occurs over a long period of time, so that the participants have time to reflect and decide on their courses of action, can be called *strategic* negotiation. On the other hand, negotiation that is very rapid and requires quick decisions by the negotiators is called *tactical* negotiation.

Figure 8.1 illustrates the structure of bargaining and negotiation as defined in this text. In this figure, there are two types of negotiation, tactical and strategic. The jagged line indicates that there is no easy way

Figure 8.1 Bargaining and negotiation.

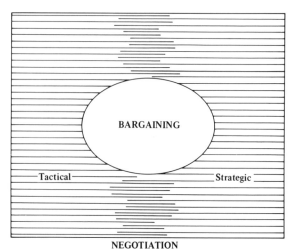

NEGOTIATION

to distinguish between the two in some circumstances. Bargaining is shown as contained within negotiation. This is not meant to indicate that bargaining is a subset of negotiation, but rather that negotiation is the environment in which bargaining is found.

In this chapter a case study is introduced regarding the pollution of the Holston River. Following this, the remainder of the chapter is devoted to an extension of conflict analysis for use in bargaining situations. Chapter 9 is concerned with the application of conflict analysis techniques to negotiation situations. Readers interested in background information about bargaining and negotiations may refer to Appendixes A and B, which present historical approaches to bargaining and negotiation, respectively.

8.2 Holston River Negotiations

In 1972 the U.S. Congress passed the Federal Water Pollution Control Act (FWPCA) Amendments which, among other things, specify that a permit is required to discharge any pollutants into receiving waters. The issuance of these National Pollution Discharge Elimination System (NPDES) permits, which specifically indicate the kind and quantity of allowable discharges, is administered by the EPA. The Holston River problem concerns the negotiations that took place between the Environmental Protection Agency (EPA) and the Tennessee Eastman Company (TEC) prior to the issuance of a NPDES permit. All of the information presented about this dispute is taken from the book by Bacow and Wheeler (1982), supplemented by personal contact with one of these authors, Michael Wheeler. The conflict analysis of the Holston River negotiations was previously presented by Fraser (1983).

8.2.1 Participants

The two major participants in the Holston River situation are the EPA and the TEC. A third participant, the Tennessee Water Quality Control Division (TWQCD), also had some influence. In order to understand the position and role of each of these parties in the negotiations, a short description of each is useful.

EPA. The EPA is foremost of a number of agencies within the executive branch of the U.S. federal government with authority to enforce federal environmental legislation. It was created under Reorganization Plan Number 3 in 1970, bringing together the Federal Water Quality Administration, the National Air Pollution Control Administration, the Environmental Control Administration, the Pesticides Research and Standards Setting Program of the Federal Department of Agriculture, and the Pesticides Registration Authority of the Department of Agriculture.

The mandate of the EPA is to set and enforce standards of environmental quality and to support research and monitoring in all areas of environmental assessment and control (Heer and Hagerty, 1977). Sufficient funding is provided to ensure that the EPA can provide technical assistance to other federal, state and, local agencies and to support an extensive infrastructure throughout the United States.

The role of the EPA in the Holston River situation is a consequence of its responsibility to set and enforce standards of environmental quality. Various pieces of legislation specify the particular standards to be met and the ways in which these standards are to be enforced. The FWPCA Amendments of 1972 allows a negligent company to be held liable for all damages resulting from pollution caused by it. Furthermore, the simple failure to use the *best current practice* is judged to be sufficient grounds to prove negligence (Heer and Hagerty, 1977).

TEC. The TEC is a large chemical manufacturing company located on the Holston River in the northeast corner of the state of Tennessee. The manufacturing complex occupies more than 400 acres on the outskirts of Kingsport, Tennessee. It employs about 12,000 people, including more than 1800 engineers and scientists in five research and development laboratories. About 15,000 tons of chemicals are produced daily, resulting in more than 250 tons of liquid chemical waste. This chemical waste is currently incinerated or processed in a wastewater treatment facility.

The plant products include Kodel polyester fibers and Tennite plastics. The company also produces electricity and steam for the chemical processing at three powerhouses. It has facilities for equipment fabrication, concrete mixing, and industrial gas production and operates its own railway, garages, and other services.

According to the EPA, before water quality controls were placed on the company, the TEC discharged effluents equivalent to that produced by a city of five million inhabitants. Furthermore, of all major sources of pollution on the area of the Holston river near Kingsport, Tennessee, the TEC was by far the largest polluter. By one common measurement method, the TEC was responsible for 62% of the pollution in the river.

TWQCD. The TWQCD is the Tennessee state authority that sets water quality standards. In addition to the NPDES permit from the EPA, the TEC was also required to get a state permit from the TWQCD. However, the EPA water quality standards were stricter in this case than the state standards.

8.2.2 History of the Negotiations

The first step of the negotiation process occurred in September 1972, when the EPA started testing the waste disposal discharges from the TEC plant. At this time the TEC indicated that it was duplicating the EPA's tests. This was a signal that the TEC was preparing to react to any proposed EPA limitations on technical grounds.

The next step of the negotiation process occurred in April 1973, when the EPA issued a report entitled "Waste Source Investigations—Kingsport, Tennessee." This document contained the result of previous investigations by the EPA to determine the effluent limitations for the TEC, but did not at this time specify the proposed limits. The TEC responded to this report by emphasizing the complex nature of the setting of effluent standards. The company also insisted, and continued to insist in the following months, that the permit process not be made public until after the EPA and the company came to some sort of agreement between themselves.

In June 1973, the EPA sent the TWQCD a preliminary draft of the NPDES permit. The EPA and the state had some communication and cooperation but on the whole functioned independently in their permit granting processes, in spite of the fact that the permits were virtually identical. The resulting lack of coordination made the negotiations more difficult for all parties.

In July 1973, the EPA communicated to the TEC the details of the proposed limitations. The TEC responded with outrage, claiming that it was impossible with current technology to meet them. The TEC also reiterated its desire that the public still not be made aware of the information about the situation. A staff meeting between the TEC and the EPA was proposed within which technical issues alone were to be discussed. It should be noted that the TEC had a strong argument against severe restrictions on nontechnical grounds because the Holston river is inaccessible to the public (only military and industrial installations border it). Consequently invoking strict effluent limitations would constitute a misallocation of resources. This social choice argument could be sufficient to challenge a number of the FWPCA provisions effectively. However, the TEC chose to negotiate on technical grounds alone.

A closed meeting between the EPA and the TEC was subsequently held and it was agreed at this time that the TEC was to develop a counter proposal specifying what it felt were feasible effluent limits. The resulting report, "Water Borne Effluent Limits" (TEC, 1973), suggested effluent limitations that were substantially higher than those proposed either by the EPA or the TWQCD. However, it is clear in retrospect (Bacow and Wheeler, 1982) that the limitations proposed by the TEC were inflated to allow for later compromise.

To bolster its position, the TEC hired the highly respected consultants Peter A. Krenkel and Vladimir Novotny who wrote a report (Krenkel and Novotny, 1973) in which the mathematical model that forms the basis of the EPA limitations was challenged. An alternative was proposed that unsurprisingly indicated that the river could accept more effluent than estimated by the EPA.

The negotiations by this time had centered between the TEC and the EPA. The TWQCD had been put in the position of being towed along behind the EPA in its dealings with the TEC. From an outsider's point of view (Backow and Wheeler, 1982), it was clear at this time that the EPA would have been in a better bargaining position had it formed a team with the TWQCD rather than worked independently.

On October 2, 1973 the TEC presented the EPA with its two reports. Both sides gave the impression of being entrenched and unwilling to give ground. The TEC did not get a trade association to try to defend its interests or apply extensive political pressure. It did, however, invest a great deal in technical expertise on the scientific basis for effluent limitations. There is some indication that this expertise was being developed for use as evidence in court should the situation result in litigation. However, the TEC did not want to go to court because control would be lost to the lawyers and to points of law.

Similarly, the EPA did not want to go to court. A protracted legal battle could last years, during which the effluent discharge would be uncontrolled. The EPA had a great deal of latitude as to exactly what limitations it invoked and was more concerned with getting some kind of acceptable control in place. The EPA had in the past issued permits without negotiating with the affected company and had then to wage court battles since there was no recourse to an out-of-court agreement.

After the EPA received the TEC reports, there was discussion between the parties and also with other experts concerning the various technical issues. The EPA threatened to release its draft NPDES permit to the public, but the TEC convinced them to refrain until after a scheduled technical meeting. The technical meeting occurred on March 4, 1974 where the two parties hammered out a number of compromises, although they had not reached full agreement. There was significant indication that the two parties were approaching a common ground for agreement.

In April 1974, one month later, the EPA brought the process to the public by announcing a public hearing to be held on May 29, 1974. One effect of this was to place a time limit on the negotiations since the EPA is required to issue the permit within a certain time following the public hearing. The announcement was greeted with apparent dismay by the TEC, although it indicated that it wished to continue the negotiation process which had proved somewhat successful at the March 4 meeting.

At the public hearing, the EPA and the TEC both presented their cases. The EPA had only two persons speaking for it other than its own staff. The TEC not only had special technical representatives at the hearing, but a number of local business and political personalities presented the company favorably. Two weeks after the hearing, following a small amount of communication with the TEC, the EPA accepted in full the previous TEC proposal. It abandoned any idea of going for a final compromise and instead allowed the TEC everything that it had originally specified. The explanation for this by the EPA was that the proposal by the TEC was adequate to protect the river and that the marginal cost of achieving a permit with better limitations was too high for the EPA to justify. Also, if the EPA had pushed harder, the case may have gone to court for which the EPA was unprepared.

A final NPDES permit, which corresponded to the TEC's proposal, was issued on July 28, 1974. This permit was met with disappointment and bitterness by the TWQCD, which felt that it was weak and had undermined its entire permit process. In fact, the NPDES did eventually replace the state permit. The TWQCD felt that if the EPA had cooperated with it better, such a poor result would not have occurred.

Subsequent to the original granting of the permit, some of the limits were even adjusted upward to correspond to practical considerations. However, fortuitously a production process was able to be changed, at little cost to the company, to reduce emission of a specific dangerous pollutant. Furthermore, the company's assessment of appropriate limits, rather than the EPA's, proved to be more correct, so that good water quality was indeed maintained. Consequently, the negotiation process eventually achieved a successful resolution for both the EPA and the TEC.

8.3 Bargaining Analysis

In spite of the vast amount of work that has been conducted on the bargaining process, there remains little in the way of practical tools to aid individuals or groups involved in bargaining situations. Conflict analysis, which is nonquantitative in nature, has shown itself to be highly robust as a method of studying conflicts, and the specific requirements of the bargaining problem can be approached in a manner similar to conflict analysis.

The key characteristic that distinguishes the bargaining problem from a conventional conflict analysis is that the players in a bargaining situation are not strictly competitive. Usually they would prefer to come to an agreement on a contract or result rather than do nothing. Also, they cannot unilaterally achieve agreement. They must act in concert, whether by signing a contract, concluding a peace treaty, or offering and accepting a bribe. As previously developed in Chapter 5, one way of incorporating the ideas of cooperation and acting in concert is to consider coalitions that can be formed by two or more players in a game. However, this approach ignores the competitive aspects of the bargaining situation.

In the Holston River conflict, the two participants are battling over a number of significant issues. In order to demonstrate the application of the bargaining algorithm, a simple but enlightening version of this conflict will be presented. It is not intended that this example be a comprehensive study of the complex problems involved in environmental negotiations. The reader who feels he or she has more facts about the conflict is urged to perform a new analysis using the method developed in this chapter.

8.3.1 Modeling the Holston River Negotiations

For the Holston River conflict, the game is modeled with two players— the EPA and the TEC. The TWQCD is not considered as a separate player because it took no active part in the negotiations, but rather trailed along the EPA.

Consider the situation early in the conflict during the initial round of negotiations in July 1973. Let the EPA have three options:

1. *Compromise* on technical issues with the TEC,
2. Follow a *hard line* policy on all items, and
3. Call for debate in a *public forum*

The TEC, on the other hand, has two options.

1. Try for a *compromise* on technical grounds, or
2. Follow a *hard line* policy

In this model it is assumed that for a compromise to be possible, it must be accepted by both parties. Each player and its options are listed on the left-hand side of Table 8.1.

Outcome Removal. As discussed in Chapter 2, in conventional conflict analysis there are four types of outcomes that may be removed from a game model.

1. Logically infeasible for a single player. For example, it is not possible for the EPA to compromise on technical issues and at the same time adopt a hard line stance. The outcomes that include this strategy can be removed from the model, and are indicated as the first column

Table 8.1 Feasible Outcomes for the Holston River Negotiations

Player	Option	Feasible outcomes									
EPA	Compromise	0	0	0	0	1	1	0	0	0	0
	Hard line	0	1	0	1	0	0	0	1	0	1
	Public forum	0	0	1	1	0	1	0	0	1	1
TEC	Compromise	0	0	0	0	1	1	0	0	0	0
	Hard line	0	0	0	0	0	0	1	1	1	1
	Decimal	0	2	4	6	9	13	16	18	20	22

on the left in Table 8.2. Similarly, the second column in Table 8.2 represents the outcomes where the TEC also compromises and follows a hard line.

2. Preferentially infeasible for one player. No examples of this kind of outcome removal appear in the Holston River game.
3. Logically infeasible between players. No examples of this kind of outcome removal appear in the Holston River game.
4. Outcomes that involve specific strategy choices for two or more players that are preferentially infeasible for at least one player. No examples of this kind of outcome removal appear in the Holston River game.

The inclusion of *cooperative* options, like the option to compromise for both players, requires a fifth criterion for removing outcomes. These outcomes are strictly logically infeasible, and thus are similar to both types 1 and 3 above. However, they are distinct from either of these, and thus are considered a separate type:

5. For a compromise on technical grounds to be reached, all players must agree to compromise. One player cannot unilaterally compromise while the others do not. Any outcomes in which the players do not either all select the option or all reject the option is infeasible. This is indicated by the two rightmost sets of outcomes listed in Table 8.2.

Like type 1 outcomes, type 5 outcomes are completely safe for removal. However, whereas type 1 outcomes are infeasible for a single player, type 5 outcomes always concern at least two players. Type 3 outcomes involve independent options by the players, and not cooperative ones like those found in type 5 outcomes.

The Holston River model requires the removal of the type 1 and 5 outcomes listed in Table 8.2. The result of removing these infeasible outcomes is to reduce the number of possible outcomes in the game from 32 to only 10. Outcomes that involve the selection of only cooperative options are referred to as *cooperative outcomes*. The term 'cooperative'' is used differently in game theory, as discussed in Chapter 10.

Table 8.2 Removable Outcomes for the Holston River Negotiations

Player	Option	Sets of removed outcomes			
EPA	Compromise	1	–	0	1
	Hard line	1	–	–	–
	Public forum	–	–	–	–
TEC	Compromise	–	1	1	0
	Hard line	–	1	–	–

Preferences. The decimal preference vectors for the EPA and the TEC appear in Table 8.3. As shown by outcome 6 in the EPA preference vector in this table, the EPA would most prefer to adopt a hard line and have a public debate without the TEC also following a hard line. Next to this, it would like outcome 2 where it simply takes a hard line. The third most preferred outcome for the EPA is outcome 13 where it compromises on technical issues with the TEC while still making the process public. The other outcomes making up the preference ordering for the EPA can similarly be examined, down to the least preferred outcome, outcome 16, where the TEC adopts a hard line attitude without similar action by the EPA.

For the TEC, the most preferred outcome is outcome 16 which is the least preferred for the EPA. Second to this, the TEC would prefer outcome 9 where it compromises with the EPA. Third on the TEC preference ordering is outcome 13 which involves a compromise even if the EPA calls for a public forum. Least preferred for the TEC is the most preferred outcome for the EPA, outcome 6, where the EPA adopts a hard line and calls for a public forum while the TEC does nothing.

Note that in ordering both the EPA and the TEC preference vectors no distinction is made between the cooperative and non-cooperative outcomes. However, in order to distinguish them for the analysis, in which they are treated differently, a bridge is drawn above the outcomes in which the option compromise is taken by both players. Thus in Table 8.3 the outcomes 9 and 13 are cooperative outcomes.

8.3.2 Stability Analysis of the Holston River Negotiations

For any given feasible outcome in a bargaining situation there are five types of stability which can be determined for a game with n players where each player can have any finite number of options at his disposal. Four of these kinds of stability are the same as those used in a conventional conflict analysis described in Chapters 1 and 2; rational, sequentially

Table 8.3 Stability Analysis of the Holston River Negotiations

×	×	E	E̶	×	E̶	E̶	×	×	×	
r	s	c	s	u	s	r	u	u	u	
6	2	⌐13⌐	4	⌐9⌐	0	22	18	20	16	EPA
	6		6	13	6		22	22	22	
			2		2			18	18	
					4				20	
r	c	c	s	r	s	r	r	u	u	
16	⌐9⌐	⌐13⌐	0	20	4	18	22	2	6	TEC
			16		20			18	22	

sanctioned, unstable, and simultaneously sanctioned (see Section 1.3.3).When considering bargaining situations where cooperative outcomes are present, a fifth type of stability—stability by cooperation—can be determined. If a cooperative outcome without UIs is preferred by the player to the least preferable equilibrium outcome that does not exhibit the selection of the cooperative option, it is stable by cooperation for the player. Stability by cooperation is denoted c. Similarly, all cooperative outcomes that are less preferable than the least preferable noncooperative equilibrium outcome are unstable, even if they were previously determined to be sequentially or simultaneously stable. Other cooperative outcomes retain the instability or stability assigned them before stability by cooperation was assessed.

Note that if cooperative outcomes are not present, the types of stability are identical to conventional conflict analysis. Consequently the bargaining analysis is a generalization of conflict analysis.

The procedure for determining the foregoing types of stability is quite straightforward. First, check in the preference vector tableau for noncooperative outcomes that have no UIs listed under them; these are rational and can be immediately marked r. For example, outcome 6 for the EPA is a noncooperative outcome since there is no line drawn above it, and rational because it has no UIs.

Next, proceed through each of the remaining (cooperative and noncooperative) outcomes with UIs and assess their stability according to the other criteria except stability by cooperation. To demonstrate sequential sanctioning, consider outcome 4 for the EPA in Table 8.3. The EPA can unilaterally improve from outcome 4, where it is calling for a public forum only, to outcome 6, where it is also adopting a hard line policy. However, the TEC would be likely to retaliate by also being hard line (outcome 22). Because outcome 22 is less preferred than the original outcome 4 by the EPA, the UI from 4 to 6 is sanctioned. Similarly, the UI from 4 to 2 is sanctioned since the TEC could subsequently improve from 2 to 18, which is less preferred by the EP to outcome 4. Since all the UIs available to the EPA from outcome 4 are credibly sanctioned, the outcome is sequentially sanctioned and marked with an s.

As an example of an unstable outcome, consider outcome 18 for the EPA. From outcome 18, the EPA can unilaterally improve to outcome 22, which is rational for the TEC. Thus outcome 18 is unstable for the EPA and marked with a u.

An outcome can also be unstable for a player if the other player has a UI whose outcome is preferred to the original outcome by the first player. For instance, the TEC has a UI from outcome 2 to 18, and the EPA has a UI from 18 to 22; however, since 22 is preferred by the TEC to outcome 2, the latter is unstable.

Cooperative outcomes are unstable if they have an undeterred UI. For example, consider outcome 9 for the EPA. If the EPA is compromising on technical issues, it would prefer additionally to call for a public forum (outcome 13). The TEC has no credible deterrent to this improvement, and therefore outcome 9 is unstable for the EPA. Cooperative outcomes can also exhibit sequential stability and simultaneous stability.

After all outcomes, except cooperative outcomes without UIs, are labeled appropriately as *r, s,* or *u* for the players, simultaneous stability is calculated for each outcome that is unstable for both players (see Section 1.3.3). In the EPA–TEC conflict no outcomes are unstable for both players, so this form of stability does not have to be checked.

The noncooperative equilibriums are now assessed to be outcomes 4, 0, and 22. (Only the noncooperative outcomes have the *E* or X written above them at this point in the analysis.) Once these have been identified, the stability of the cooperative outcomes can be determined. Cooperative outcomes that are preferred to the least preferable noncooperative equilibrium outcome are stable by cooperation, except those that are unstable due to undeterred UIs. Cooperative outcomes that are less preferable than the least preferable noncooperative equilibrium are unstable, even if all UIs are deterred. This criterion can make cooperative outcomes that were deemed to be stable previously become unstable, but will not make unstable cooperative outcomes stable.

The rationale behind the stability criterion for cooperative outcomes is based upon the concept of *conflict point* from bargaining theory (see Appendix A). Players are only interested in bargaining contracts that offer more than they can achieve without bargaining. If they can get a better bargain through cooperation, they are likely to pursue a cooperative outcome. The least preferable equilibrium outcome for player can be interpreted as the worst thing that could occur if no bargain were struck. Obviously, any cooperative outcome that is less preferable than this default situation will not be tenable to the player. On the other hand, any stable contract preferred to the least preferable noncooperative equilibrium might be a plausible arrangement for the player and is thus a viable stable outcome.

For example, outcome 13 for the EPA is preferred to the least preferable noncooperative equilibrium for the EPA (outcome 22) and thus is stable by cooperation for the EPA. Similarly, outcomes 13 and 9 are stable by cooperation for the TEC because they are preferred to the TEC's least preferable noncooperative equilibrium, which is also outcome 22. However, outcome 9 does not become stable for the EPA because it was previously judged to be unstable. None of the cooperative outcomes in this conflict happened to be less preferable than the least preferable noncooperative equilibrium. If there were any, they would be unstable even if previously judged to be stable. This would be indicated by a slash through the *s* if the outcome was previously sequentially sanctioned, or a reverse slash if the outcome was simultaneously sanctioned.

Similar to noncooperative equilibriums, cooperative equilibriums are formed when an outcome is stable for both players. Consequently, outcome 13 is the only cooperative equilibrium in this conflict.

A summary of the procedure for the stability analysis of a single outcome q for player A in a game in which there are two players A and B is shown as Figure 8.2. In this figure the assessment of simultaneous stability and the determination of cooperative stability are parenthesized

Figure 8.2 Stability of outcome q for player A in a two-player game with cooperative outcomes.

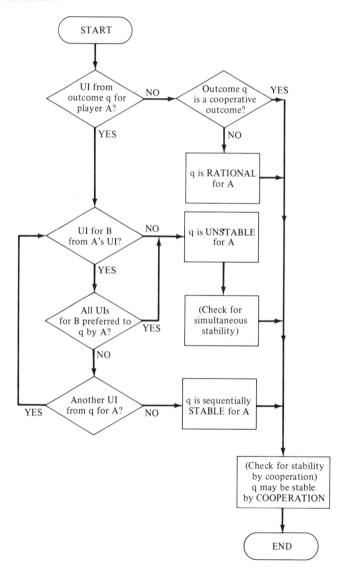

188

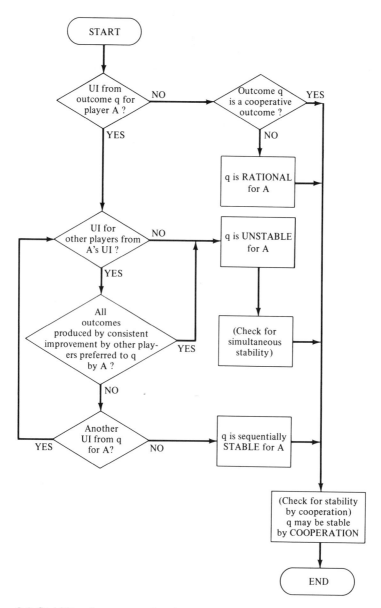

Figure 8.3 Stability of outcome *q* for player A in an *n*-player game with cooperative outcomes.

to indicate that these phases of the stability analysis are not done until the other forms of stability are determined for both players in the game.

Extension of the algorithm to include any finite number of players and options is a straightforward procedure. The basic principles are the same. First perform the stability analysis on all outcomes that are not cooperative and without UIs. Then determine the cooperatively stable outcomes as those that are preferred to the least preferable noncooperative equilibrium. A diagram of the complete stability analysis algorithm for the n-player case is presented in Figure 8.3.

Fraser (1983) proves that even when cooperative outcomes are present in a game with ordinal preferences, there will always be at least one equilibrium. Additionally, there may be other equilibriums brought about due to the introduction of the cooperative options.

In general, the equilibriums that are determined as a result of the complete stability analysis form the negotiation set (see Appendix A) for the bargaining or conflict situation. In some circumstances, there will be no clear indication which of the equilibriums will be the eventual resolution to the problem. In other cases, various techniques can be used to identify a likely candidate.

In the Holston River dispute, a case can be made to identify a single equilibrium as the likely resolution. This is because any equilibrium that is less preferable than cooperative equilibrium by both players is not likely to be stable in a game in which cooperation is a viable factor. These less preferable outcomes are called *Pareto suboptimal*. (Pareto optimality is generally considered to be an important consideration in games in which the players can communicate.) If the players can together improve to an outcome that is preferred by both of them, they will do so if they are in a position to cooperate. Since the model of the situation includes the cooperative outcome 13, there is the implication that these players may indeed cooperate.

The Pareto suboptimal outcomes are indicated in Table 8.3 by putting a slash through the E above the outcome in the EPA preference vector. The result is that there is only one Pareto optimal equilibrium in this game, which constitutes the apparent resolution to the Holston River dispute. This is outcome 13, where the EPA and the TEC compromise on technical issues while the EPA calls for a public forum. Historically, this is exactly what happened.

8.4 Important Concepts from Chapter 8

The bargaining problem concerns the fact that bargainers want to achieve some sort of agreement as well as get the best outcome for themselves. The use of a generalization of conflict analysis to model and analyze situations involving bargaining was demonstrated through the analysis of the Holston River negotiations. This example demonstrated the flexibility of the generalized conflict analysis method to assist in the study of bargaining situations.

A model of a bargaining situation requires the use of *cooperative options,* which constitute a special kind of option that is in common to more than one player. An outcome that includes players taking a cooperative option is called a *cooperative outcome.*

In order to eliminate infeasible outcomes correctly, a new type of removable outcome is introduced (type 5). This reflects the fact that all players must simultaneously select or not select a cooperative option.

The basic principle of the generalized conflict analysis algorithm that includes bargaining is that a cooperative outcome is unstable for a player if it is less preferable than the least preferable noncooperative equilibrium, but is stable for a player if it is preferred to the least preferable noncooperative equilibrium outcome. The principle of Pareto optimality can be used to distinguish preferred equilibriums in bargaining conflicts.

Questions

1. Consider a union–management bargaining conflict in which the players have the following options:

Union	Sign contract
	Go on strike
	Work to rule

Management	Sign contract
	Lock out the union

   The option to sign a contract is a cooperative option. Deduce from the following preference vectors the five outcome sets that were removed from the complete set of mathematical options. Indicate the type of each of the five, and explain the rationale for removing it. Then for each of the following sets of preference vectors perform a bargaining conflict analysis.

   In each case describe the general preferences of the players, and the consequences of these preferences as revealed in the bargaining analysis.

   (a) Union   9   13   4   2   0   20   16   18
       Mgt.   0   9   16   4   13   20   18   2
   (b) Union   9   13   4   2   0   20   16   18
       Mgt.   0   16   4   9   13   20   18   2
   (c) Union   4   9   13   2   0   20   16   18
       Mgt.   0   16   4   9   13   20   18   2

2. Prove that when cooperative outcomes are present there will always be at least one equilibrium.

Chapter 9
Conflict Analysis
and Negotiation

9.1 Introduction

Negotiation, as defined in this text, is different from bargaining in that it is more difficult to model as a mathematical process. According to Nierenberg (1973), negotiation is not amenable to mathematical analysis because there are no rules and anything is possible. It may not even involve competition (Praitt, 1981). Although negotiation forms the environment in which bargaining can occur, as illustrated in Figure 8.1 (p. 176) it may not involve any bargaining at all.

However, bargaining is central to negotiation, and in this text negotiation is seen as the actions, techniques, skills, and capabilities that allow a player to achieve a favorable bargain. Nierenberg (1973) says that "in a successful negotiation, everybody wins," but Karrass (1972) points out that "in a successful negotiation both parties gain, but more often than not one party gains more than the other." The goal of the application of conflict analysis to negotiation is to help ensure that both parties gain optimally and that the party who uses the decision aid is the one that gains the most.

Negotiation can be considered to occur in two distinct time frames. Negotiation that occurs over a long period of time, and in which the participants have time to reflect and decide on their courses of action, can be called *strategic negotiation*. On the other hand, negotiation that is very rapid and where negotiators must make fast decisions is called *tactical negotiation*. As shown in this chapter, conflict analysis methods are applicable to both types of negotiations. Previously developed concepts regarding negotiation are outlined in Appendix B.

9.2 Strategic Negotiation

Strategic negotiation concerns the planning and strategy selection for a negotiation in the situation where the negotiator has enough time to examine a variety of possibilities. The negotiator's problem is to arrange a superior position for those he or she represents (possibly himself) while at the same time ensuring that some sort of contract will be achieved. Techniques of conflict analysis are directly applicable to strategic negotiation, with or without the bargaining extensions of the approach presented in Chapter 8.

In this section a simple strategic negotiation problem is looked at using a static conflict analysis (see Chapters 1 and 2), a hypergame analysis (see Chapter 3), and a state transition model (see Chapter 6). A similar application of conflict analysis techniques to a labor–management negotiation was reported by Fraser and Hipel (1980d).

9.2.1 Static Conflict Analysis

Consider the Holston River conflict at an early point in time where the EPA is considering how to approach the problem of dealing with the TEC. For example, in April 1973 the EPA had just completed its study entitled "Waste Source Investigations—Kingsport Tennessee." The EPA was aware from this study that the TEC would be required to control its effluent discharge, and from previous experience the EPA also realized that the company would contest any imposed limitations. The TEC was also aware of the impending confrontation because of its knowledge of the EPA investigations. As shown in Table 9.1 this can be modeled as a game in which each player has two options. The EPA can follow a noncooperative policy (hard line) and may additionally go to court in order to secure a legislated settlement (litigation). The TEC can also follow a

Table 9.1 Preference Vector for the EPA with the Stability Analysis

EPA												
Hard line	1	0	1	0	1	0	1	0	1	1	1	1
Litigation	0	0	0	0	0	0	0	0	1	1	1	1
TEC												
Hard line	0	0	1	1	0	0	1	1	0	1	0	1
Concessions	1	1	1	1	0	0	0	0	1	1	0	0
Stability	×	×	×	×	×	×	E	×	×	×	×	×
EPA	r	s	r	s	r	s	r	u	u	u	u	u
TEC	u	u	u	u	u	u	r	r	r	u	u	u
Decimal	9	8	13	12	1	0	5	4	11	15	3	7

hard line policy or concede on some points (concessions). There are no cooperative outcomes in this model.

In Table 9.1, the 12 feasible outcomes in this conflict are listed in order of preference for the EPA. (The four outcomes in which the EPA goes to court but does not take a hard line have been removed on the basis of preferential infeasibility.)

The EPA preference vector reflects the EPA's strong disinclination to go to court, the desire on the part of the EPA for concessions, and the preference of pursuing a hard line policy while the TEC pursues a soft line policy. The same outcomes are ordered according to the TEC's preferences in Table 9.2. The considerations here are that the TEC does want litigation, prefers a hard line policy, and does not want to concede points unnecessarily. The TEC also does not want the EPA to follow a hard line policy.

A conflict analysis determines that in this simple conflict there is a single equilibrium: the deadlock situation of both the EPA and the TEC following a hard line policy (10,10). Given that the actual preferences of these two parties are accurately represented by the indicated preference vectors, and given that both sides have accurate information about one another, this suggests that the negotiations should be expected to end up as a deadlock with both players following a hard line policy. If this were true, another analysis could be done where specific hard line tactics are assessed; but if the two sides have misleading or incomplete information about each other, a deadlock need not occur, as demonstrated in the next section.

Use of a static conflict analysis for a negotiation situation like this one is to accomplish the following:

1. Impose a structure on the problem in order to facilitate the consideration of the players, their power, the activities they can perform, and their preferences among possible outcomes to the negotiation.

Table 9.2 Preference Vector for the TEC with the Stability Analysis

EPA												
Hard line	0	1	0	1	0	1	0	1	1	1	1	1
Litigation	0	0	0	0	0	0	0	0	1	1	1	1
TEC												
Hard line	1	1	1	1	0	0	0	0	0	0	1	1
Concessions	0	0	1	1	0	0	1	1	1	0	1	0
Stability	×	E	×	×	×	×	×	×	×	×	×	×
EPA	u	r	s	r	s	r	s	r	u	u	u	u
TEC	r	r	u	u	u	u	u	u	r	u	u	u

2. Identify where more information is required.
3. Predict the possible results of the parties proceeding with the negotiation.

9.2.2 Hypergames in Negotiation

In the Holston River model of the previous section, imagine that the EPA wants to mislead the TEC in order to obtain a preferred resolution to the conflict. One thing that the EPA might do is to make the TEC believe that the EPA is very interested in going to court. Consider the case where the EPA is successful in causing the TEC to think that the EPA's preferences are as shown in Table 9.3. Here the EPA most prefers to get concessions, followed by the TEC taking the soft line. Next to this, the EPA prefers to take the hard line and then, all other things being equal, it would prefer to go to court. The deceptive preference vector in Table 9.3 can be compared to the true preferences of the EPA, displayed in Tables 9.1 and 9.4. Table 9.4 is the same hypergame display as Table 9.3 except that in Table 9.4 the outcomes are ordered according to the true preferences of the EPA rather than preferences of the EPA as seen by the TEC.

The analysis of the hypergame using the conflict analysis algorithm appears at the bottom of both Tables 9.3 and 9.4. The equilibriums for the hypergame are determined by comparing the true stability vectors of the two players: the EPA as seen by the EPA (fifth line from the bottom) and the TEC as seen by the TEC (the bottom line). Since the stability of the outcomes for the TEC is determined by its mistaken view of the problem, the overall equilibrium results are different from the game in the previous section. The seven overall equilibriums for the hypergame are indicated opposite "stability." By comparing Table 9.4 with Table

Table 9.3 Forced Hypergame Analysis Where Outcomes Are Ordered According to the TEC's View of the EPA's Preferences

EPA												
Hard line	1	1	0	1	1	0	1	1	0	1	1	0
Litigation	1	0	0	1	0	0	1	0	0	1	0	0
TEC												
Hard line	0	0	0	1	1	1	0	0	0	1	1	1
Concessions	1	1	1	1	1	1	0	0	0	0	0	0
Stability	×	E	E	×	E	E	×	E	E	×	E	×
EPA	×	E	E	×	E	E	×	E	E	×	E	×
EPA	u	r	s	u	r	s	u	r	s	u	r	u
TEC	r	s	s	u	s	s	u	s	s	u	r	r
TEC	E	×	×	×	E	E	×	×	×	×	×	×
EPA	r	u	u	r	s	s	r	u	u	r	u	u
TEC	r	s	s	u	s	s	u	s	s	u	r	r

Table 9.4 Forced Hypergame Analysis Where Outcomes Are Ordered According to the EPA's True Preferences

EPA												
Hard line	1	0	1	0	1	0	1	0	1	1	1	1
Litigation	0	0	0	0	0	0	0	0	1	1	1	1
TEC												
Hard line	0	0	1	1	0	0	1	1	0	1	0	1
Concessions	1	1	1	1	0	0	0	0	1	1	0	0
Stabililty	E	E	E	E	E	E	E	×	×	×	×	×
EPA	E	E	E	E	E	E	E	×	×	×	×	×
EPA	r	s	r	s	r	s	r	u	u	u	u	u
TEC	s	s	s	s	s	s	r	r	r	u	u	u
TEC	×	×	E	E	×	×	×	×	E	E	E	E
EPA	u	u	s	s	u	u	u	u	r	r	r	r
TEC	s	s	s	s	s	s	r	r	r	u	u	u

9.1, both of which have the outcomes ordered according to the true preferences of the EPA, it can be seen that every equilibrium in the hypergame is actually preferred by the EPA to the original single equilibrium. Thus the EPA can only possibly improve its position by such a deception.

Meanwhile, the TEC only perceives the three equilibriums written horizontally as (11,01), (00,11), and (10,11), because these are the only outcomes that are stable for both the TEC and the TEC's view of the EPA (the bottom two rows of Table 9.3 or 9.4). These equilibriums indicate a lowering of expectations for the TEC from the situation where it has a correct understanding of the conflict. If the equilibrium outcome most preferred of those perceived by the TEC occurs, which is (00,11), the TEC will likely be highly satisfied. Yet this outcome is clearly preferred by the EPA to the single true equilibrium outcome.

Consequently, the EPA can secure for itself a more preferred outcome by pretending to the TEC that it is prepared to go to court to get its way. Note that the hypergame analysis approach clearly indicates the nature of the required deception and the reasons for the reaction of the TEC. The tremendous value of hypergame analysis is clearly presented in this example, which emphasizes the importance of this technique for studying real world conflicts.

9.2.3 State Transition Model in Negotiation

The importance of the state transition model in negotiation lies in the fact that bargaining is a dynamic process that can lead to more than one possible solution where all parties are satisfied. This is indicated by the multiple equilibriums that arose in the hypergame analysis, which correspond to members of the negotiation set, or set of mutually acceptable contracts. Only one contract can be attained, however, and the goal of the negotiator is to achieve one that is favorable to his or her side. The state transition model permits the negotiator to predict the resulting contract given the conflict situation in the form of the transition matrix, and an initial strategy in the form of the status quo vector. There are other dynamic models of negotiation such as the differential game model of Leitmann and Liu (1974). The continuous time state transition model presented in Chapter 14 can also be applied to negotiation problems.

A transition matrix for the Holston River negotiation situation can be developed from the previous models using the algorithms detailed in Chapter 6, or directly from an understanding of the game. A transition matrix for the forced hypergame of Section 9.2.2 is presented as Table 9.5. There is no probabilistic information in this game model, so the matrix is very sparse and consists of 1 and 0 only. Along the top of the matrix and down the left-hand side appear the decimal numbers for each outcome in the model. The correspondence between the decimal values and the binary outcomes can be determined by referring to Table 9.1.

Consider the problem of an initial strategy selection by the EPA in this conflict. It has three strategies available to it: soft line–no litigation; hard line–no litigation; and hard-line–litigation. Assume that the EPA is not sure whether the TEC will initiate a hard line or soft line policy, but is reasonably sure that the TEC will not start out offering concessions. Assuming an equal probability between the strategies of hard and soft line for the TEC, the three possible status quos under EPA control are shown here horizontally:

$$(0.5, \quad 0, \quad 0, \quad 0.5 \; 0, \quad 0, \quad 0, 0 \; 0, 0, 0, 0t,$$
$$(\quad 0, \quad 0.5, \quad 0, \quad 0, \quad 0.5, \quad 0, \quad 0, 0, 0, 0, 0, 0t,$$
$$(\quad 0, \quad 0, \quad 0.5, \quad 0, \quad 0, \quad 0.5, 0, 0, 0, 0, 0, 0),$$

These vectors are the transposes of the $\mathbf{X}$ vector from equation (6.1). The 12 elements in each correspond to the 12 outcomes ordered as they are in the transition matrix in Table 9.5. The first of these vectors is determined by a soft line–no litigation strategy for the EPA, the second by a hard line–no litigation strategy, and the third by a hard line–litigation strategy.

The course of events of the negotiation session can be predicted by iteratively applying the transition matrix to each possible status quo using (6.1), under the assumption that the TEC will not realize its misperception of EPA's preferences too quickly. The first status quo possibility listed above leads to the resolution outcome (00,00), where no option is taken, 50% of the time. The other half of the time outcome (10,10), the hard line stalemate, is the resolution. Applying the second status quo leads to (10,00) half the time, where only the EPA follows a hard line policy, and otherwise to (10,10). However the third status quo leads invariably to the

Table 9.5 State Transition Model

	0	1	3	4	5	7	8	9	11	12	13	15
0	1	0	0	0	0	0	0	0	0	0	0	0
1	0	1	0	0	0	0	0	0	0	0	0	0
3	0	0	0	0	0	0	0	0	0	0	0	0
4	0	0	0	0	0	0	0	0	0	0	0	0
5	0	0	0	1	1	0	0	0	0	0	0	0
7	0	0	0	0	0	0	0	0	0	0	0	0
8	0	0	0	0	0	0	1	0	0	0	0	0
9	0	0	0	0	0	0	0	1	1	0	0	0
11	0	0	1	0	0	1	0	0	0	0	0	1
12	0	0	0	0	0	0	0	0	0	1	0	0
13	0	0	0	0	0	0	0	0	0	0	1	0
15	0	0	0	0	0	0	0	0	0	0	0	0

resolution (10,01), which is the situation where the EPA follows a hard line policy and the TEC gives the EPA concessions. This happens to be the most preferred outcome for the EPA, and it can be attained by initiating the negotiating session with the highly coercive strategy of pursuing a hard line policy and threatening or intending legal action. The TEC is likely to be reasonably pleased with this result because it is preferred by the TEC to the worst of its expectations, as can be verified by reference to Table 9.2. Of course, the TEC may well undertake similar considerations in its development of a strategy for the negotiations, and this consideration can be implemented through the proper development of the model. Similarly, the change in the stability of outcomes for the TEC as it becomes aware of the true preferences of the EPA can also be included within the state transition structure.

9.2.4 Discussion

It is particularly interesting in the analyses in Section 9.2 that the actions of the players did not correspond with the historical results. The EPA did not threaten to invoke litigation in the Holston River situation, and in fact negotiated fairly poorly throughout. It failed to team up with the TWQCD, for example, and effluent limitations resulting from the negotiations were essentially those proposed by the TEC. The implication of this is that the EPA should have been more conscientious in its approach to this negotiation, and similar ones, in order to secure a more socially beneficial resolution.

The three techniques of examining strategic negotiation presented in this section demonstrate the flexibility of conflict analysis for assisting in this kind of study. The static method is useful for a model of conflict at a specific point in time. It is easy to use and provides a good model of the strategic considerations of negotiation. Hypergame models allow the effective representation of situations where one or more players have a misperception. These models are excellent for planning a deception. The state transition model is useful when the dynamics of a negotiation are important. It allows the determination of how a conflict will change over time, and thus predicts the consequence of some particular action.

9.3 Tactical Negotiation

Tactical negotiation concerns decision making that is required in the heat of negotiation where choices must be made without the opportunity for any time-consuming analysis. The face-to-face negotiator is not able to enter a negotiation model on a computer or often even write anything down on paper. He (or she) must react to perhaps totally unexpected actions by his adversary in an intelligent and productive manner. He must use his brain alone, and any decision aids that may be developed must be able to assist him in this environment. Probably most day-to-day "bargaining" as the word is commonly used would be referred to as tactical negotiation in this text.

Historically, tactical negotiation has been a skill developed from native talent and experience. The available literature presents heuristics derived from the wisdom of the seasoned negotiator (see e.g., Ilich, 1973; Nierenberg, 1973 or from social science experiments (e.g., Karrss, 1972; and Cummings, 1980). However, a decision aid should go beyond the advice of experience or experiments and involve some basic understanding of the underlying structure and dynamics of the process.

Certainly, familiarity with some of the established concepts like aspiration level, power, coercion, threats, and others presented in Appendix B enable the more rapid consideration of facts and the quick development of tactics. Also, the modeling structures of conflict analysis are useful for thinking about a situation. The ideas of player, options, outcomes, and preferences aid in the comprehension of a complex problem involving more than one interacting party. Further, ideas about the stability of outcomes and hypergames are valuable for developing and proposing viable resolutions.

Ideally, however, decision aids for tactical negotiation should go beyond these valuable contributions. Fraser (1983) presents a development of models for tactical negotiation that may be of interest to the reader. In addition to a conflict analysis model of players, options, and preferences, he also proposes a process model and an environment model. The *process model* consists of six interrelated steps:

1. pre-negotiation preparation,

   2. initial contact,
   3. information exchange,
   4. handling objections,
   5. getting commitment, and
   6. following through.

The *environment model* considers that each negotiator is either warm or hostile in personality, while at the same time either dominating or submissive. Consequently there are four different personality types, and a negotiation environment is characterized by the combination of personality types present. Fraser (1983) also uses the Holston River negotiations as a case study to explain his points.

9.4 Important Concepts from Chapter 9

Negotiation forms the environment for most practical bargaining situations, which were analyzed using conflict analysis in Chapter 8. Within Chapter 9, conflict analysis methods were also used in the study of a strategic, or long term, aspect of the Holston River negotiations. In addition to a static conflict analysis, hypergame analysis and the state transition form were also demonstrated to be of assistance in strategic negotiation. Hypergame analysis permitted the study of how one might achieve a more preferred contract or resolution by passing misinformation to one's opponent. This is referred to as a *forced hypergame*. The state transition form showed that a particular future scenario can be achieved through the consideration of how a negotiation can change over time.

Tactical negotiation concerns the moment-by-moment decision making that must be done in face-to-face negotiations. Reference was made to other models of use in dealing with tactical negotiation.

Questions

1. Consider the Cuban missile crisis in Chapter 1 as a forced hypergame, with the United States making the USSR believe it was prepared to attack Cuba if the USSR did not remove its missiles. Do you think this is a possible explanation of the historical events?
2. Assume in the Holston River conflict of this chapter that the TEC sees the true preferences of the EPA and the EPA is not playing a forced hypergame. Select a suitable forced hypergame by the TEC to mislead the EPA, and draw conclusions from the results. Develop a state transition matrix to represent this situation, and determine a suitable initial strategy selection for the TEC.
3. Refer to recent newspaper articles involving a labor–management conflict. Should certain aspects of the conflict be catagorized as bargaining, strategic negotiation, or tactical negotiation? Employ appropriate tools from Chapters 8 and 9 to analyze the problem.

PART II
CONFLICT ANALYSIS
IN THEORY

Chapter 10
Development of Metagame Analysis

10.1 Introduction

Part I presented techniques of conflict analysis that seem intuitively reasonable and work well in practice. The purpose of Part II is to show that these methods are also firmly grounded in well-developed mathematical principles. Conflict analysis is a set of practical methods for applying ideas from game theory to real world conflicts. Game theory is a study of the mathematical properties of conflicts that has been developed primarily in the past 30 years (Luce and Raiffa, 1957). A broad introduction to game theory is given in Appendix C, and discussions of certain aspects of game theory are made in Chapters 12 and 13.

Part II of this book links up conflict analysis with the ideas from game theory that contributed to its development, and also explores the relationship of conflict analysis to other ideas from game theory. An appealing feature of the conflict analysis tools developed in Part I is that the entire underlying theory is based upon fairly elementary concepts from set theory and logic. These branches of mathematics are often referred to as the "mathematics of relationships," and they constitute a nonquantitative approach for realistically modeling the sociological and psychological properties inherent in conflict situations. Therefore, in addition to academics and students, some practitioners may wish to peruse the appropriate sections of Part II in order to appreciate fully the power of the conflict analysis methods due to the proper mathematical and scientific design.

The branch of game theory known as metagame theory (Howard, 1971) is of particular importance in the development of conflict analysis. In this chapter, ideas from game theory that led to the development of metagame theory are presented. On this basis, metagame theory is introduced. Both

of these techniques are presented in the context of analyzing a hypothetical attack by the USSR on Europe.

10.2 Normal Form

A military conflict presented by Richelson (1979), and extensively analyzed by Fraser et al. (1983a,b), is shown as a game in *normal form* in
Table 10.1. A game is a situation where two or more decision makers
have to choose among several strategies. The decision makers, known as
players, are in this case the United States, which is called player 1, and
the USSR, which is called player 2. In Richelson's description of this
game each player has three strategies from which to choose. The rows
of the normal form matrix correspond to the U.S. strategies and the
columns to the Soviet strategies. The Soviet strategies are three: a conventional attack on Western Europe, labeled strategy C; a limited nuclear
strike below the total war threshold, labeled L; and a full nuclear attack
on Western Europe and the United States, labeled S. Similarly, in reaction
to a Soviet invasion of Western Europe, the United States would have
the choice to use any of the same three types of attacks against the USSR.

An outcome is formed in Table 10.1 by each player choosing a strategy,
and hence is presented by a cell in the matrix. The first number in each
cell shows the preference order of the outcome for the United States; the
second gives the Soviet order. The higher the number, the more preferable
the outcome. For example, in this game the most preferred outcome for
the United States is the outcome (L,C). This is the case when the United
States reacts with limited nuclear strikes to a conventional attack on
Europe by the Soviet Union, and thereby avoids the loss of Europe and
causes some damage to the USSR. Likewise, the Soviets' most preferred
outcome is when the United States chooses not to go beyond a conventional counterattack in response to their limited nuclear operation on
Europe [outcome (C,L)]. As a result of this, Europe is lost and the United

Table 10.1 U.S.–USSR Confrontation in Normal Form

U.S. (Player 1)	USSR (Player 2)		
	C	L	S
C	5 , 8	R_2 4 , 9	1 , 7
L	R_1 9 , 4	R_2 6 , 6	2 , 5
S	8 , 1	R_1 7 , 2	$R_1 R_2$ 3 , 3

States suffers some nuclear damage. For a complete explanation of the ordinal preferences for each country refer to Richelson's (1979) article.

Game theory provides a mathematical framework for analyzing games based upon the definition of rationality (Luce and Raiffa, 1957, Section 12.3). An outcome is *rational* for a player if it is that player's best outcome given the other players' strategy choices. For example, in this specific conflict one can see that given a conventional attack by the Soviet Union the rational outcome for the United States is formed by the U.S. choice of strategy L. The symbol R_1 is written in the cell (L,C) in Table 10.1 to indicate that the outcome is rational for the United States. Likewise, the other rational outcomes for player 1 are the outcomes (S,L) and (S,S), the best outcomes for the United States when player 2 chooses strategies L and S, respectively. The best outcomes for player 2, given a fixed strategy choice for player 1, are the outcomes (C,L), (L,L), and (S,S). These rational outcomes are designated by entering R_2 in the appropriate cells in Table 10.1. An outcome that is rational for all players forms an *equilibrium* and therefore is a possible solution to the conflict. From Table 10.1 it can be seen that the outcome (S,S) is the only equilibrium in the nuclear conflict.

If both countries select (L,L) they would do better than with the equilibrium outcome (S,S) which is chosen according to rationality. Instead of a nuclear war with fatal consequences for both nations and for the rest of the world, both countries would improve their situation if they decided to use only limited nuclear strikes. The outcome (L,L) is a *cooperative* solution to the game, as are (C,C), (C,L), and (L,C) (Luce and Raiffa, 1957). In all of these cases the outcome is preferred by both players to the single noncooperative equilibrium outcome (S,S). One method that assists in detecting cooperative solutions is the metagame theory of Howard (Trustees of the University of Pennsylvania, 1969a; Howard, 1971). Metagame theory is the basis of the conflict analysis technique known as metagame analysis or the analysis of options (Howard, 1971; Hipel et al., 1974, 1976a).

10.3 Metagame Theory

A metagame is a game that takes into account the possible reactions of a particular player to the other players' known strategies in the basic game (such as that shown in Table 10.1). For example, in the hypothetical nuclear war conflict the United States has a set of possible reactions or metagame strategies $x/y/z$ that can be defined as follows:

The United States will select x if the USSR chooses C.

The United States will select y if the USSR chooses L.

The United States will select z if the USSR chooses S.

A game where one analyzes the U.S. reaction patterns to the initial strategies of the USSR can be represented in normal form, as seen in Table 10.2. The United States has $3^3 = 27$ possible strategies for this metagame. For example, one U.S. strategy would be represented by L/L/L, meaning that the United States will respond with a limited nuclear attack no matter how the USSR invades Europe. Another strategy would be C/L/S, which represents a U.S. counterattack with the same strength used by the USSR. Because the United States has 27 strategies and the USSR has three, there are $27 \times 3 = 81$ possible outcomes in the complete metagame in Table 10.2. The outcome (C/L/L,C), for example, describes a Soviet strategy of C to attack conventionally, coupled with the U.S. strategy of C/L/L where the United States counteracts a conventional strike and uses limited nuclear armament only if the Soviet Union uses some kind of nuclear weapons. Since the USSR is employing strategy C, this leads the United States also to choose a conventional attack. This corresponds to outcome (C,C) in the original game in Table 10.1. Consequently, in Table 10.2 the outcome (C/L/L,C) is given the same preference numbers as outcome (C,C) in Table 10.1. In a similar fashion, the preference numbers for all of the outcomes in Table 10.2 can be ascertained.

By employing the same definitions for rationality that were used in Table 10.1, the rational outcomes for players 1 and 2 in the metagame of Table 10.2 can be found. The rational outcomes for each player in Table 10.2 are known as *metarational outcomes* for the corresponding outcomes in Table 10.1. Outcomes that are rational for both players in the metagame

Table 10.2 Metagame from the U.S.–USSR Confrontation

U.S. (Player 1)	USSR (player 2)		
	C	L	S
C/C/C	5 , 8	R_2 4 , 9	1 , 7
C/C/L	5 , 8	R_2 4 , 9	2 , 5
C/C/S	5 , 8	R_2 4 , 9	R_1 3 , 3
C/L/C	R_2 5 , 8	6 , 6	1 , 7
C/L/L	R_2 5 , 8	6 , 6	2 , 5
C/L/S	R_2 5 , 8	6 , 6	R_1 3 , 3
C/S/C	R_2 5 , 8	R_1 7 , 2	1 , 7

(continued)

Table 10.2 (*continued*)

U.S. (Player 1)	USSR (player 2) C	L	S
C/S/L	R_2 5 , 8	R_1 7 , 2	2 , 5
C/S/S	R_2 5 , 8	R_1 7 , 2	R_1 3 , 3
L/C/C	R_1 9 , 4	R_2 4 , 9	1 , 7
L/C/L	R_1 9 , 4	R_2 4 , 9	2 , 5
L/C/S	R_1 9 , 4	R_2 4 , 9	R_1 3 , 3
L/L/C	R_1 9 , 4	6 , 6	R_2 1 , 7
L/L/L	R_1 9 , 4	R_2 6 , 6	2 , 5
L/L/S	R_1 9 , 4	R_2 6 , 6	R_1 3 , 3
L/S/C	R_1 9 , 4	R_1 7 , 2	R_2 1 , 7
L/S/L	R_1 9 , 4	R_1 7 , 2	R_2 2 , 5
L/S/S	$R_1\,R_2$ 9 , 4	R_1 7 , 2	R_1 3 , 3
S/C/C	8 , 1	R_2 4 , 9	1 , 7
S/C/L	8 , 1	R_2 4 , 9	2 , 5
S/C/S	8 , 1	R_2 4 , 9	R_1 3 , 3
S/L/C	8 , 1	6 , 6	R_2 1 , 7
S/L/L	8 , 1	R_2 6 , 6	2 , 5
S/L/S	8 , 1	R_2 6 , 6	R_1 3 , 3
S/S/C	8 , 1	R_1 7 , 2	R_2 1 , 7
S/S/L	8 , 1	R_1 7 , 2	R_2 2 , 5
S/S/S	8 , 1	R_1 7 , 2	$R_1\,R_2$ 3 , 3

METAEQUILIBR...

of Table 10.2 form equilibriums in this game and *metaequilibriums* for the corresponding outcomes in Table 10.1. One of the two metaequilibriums in Table 10.2 corresponds to the outcome (S/S/S,S). This is the situation where the USSR starts with a large scale nuclear operation and the U.S. strategy is to do likewise. Thus the equilibrium outcome (S/S/S,S) boils down to the metaequilibrium outcome (S,S) in the basic game. The second equilibrium in Table 10.2 is (L/S/S,C) and this corresponds to the meta-equilibrium outcome (L,C) in Table 10.1.

Analyzing how the USSR reacts to the U.S. reaction to the initial Soviet strategies leads to a higher level metagame. This game would be composed of 3^{27} possible strategies for the Soviet Union and 27 for the United States. The idea of reactions to reaction patterns can be carried on indefinitely to form a hierarchy of metagames, referred to as the *metagame tree* (Howard, 1971).

Figure 10.1 illustrates a metagame tree for a game with n players. The circle at the top of Figure 10.1 refers to the basic game G, that is, the game in Table 10.1 for the military conflict. From the basic game G, n first level metagames labeled $1G$, $2G$, ..., nG can be formed. In the game iG player i chooses a policy or function set with the knowledge of the strategy choices of the other players in game G. In a similar manner, second level metagames of the form $1iG$, $2iG$, ..., niG could be constructed from each first level metagame iG. This process can be carried out to infinity to produce the infinite metagame tree shown in Figure 10.1. Because the metagame tree is composed of an infinite number of metagames, it is impossible to analyze exhaustively every metagame in normal form.

The infinite metagame tree forms the backbone of metagame theory. Behavior in G is interpreted as behavior in the metagame tree since players will in some fashion think in terms of metagames (Howard, 1971). Using

Figure 10.1 Infinite metagame tree.

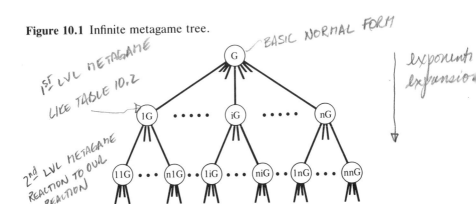

set theory and logic, Howard (1971) systematically derived the various mathematical properties from the infinite metagame tree. The resulting theory was checked by experiment to see if it actually described what happens in real life situations. Experimental results (Howard, 1971) and actual applications to political conflicts (Howard, 1970a; Alexander, 1975; Fraser and Hipel, 1980b; Hipel and Fraser, 1980) support the value of the metagame approach.

Richelson used metagame theory to examine the reaction patterns of the United States and the USSR to metastrategy declarations by the other player, and thus looked at the metagames explicitly. To permit a rigorous metagame study to be performed in spite of the infinite number of possible metagames, Howard (1971) developed the Characterization Theorem (see Appendix D). This theorem allows one to look automatically at all possible metagames by analyzing only the initial game.

10.4 Mathematical Description of Metagame Theory

10.4.1 Strategies and Outcomes

Let S_i represent the strategy set of player i. In the basic game of the nuclear conflict, C, L, and S form the strategy set for each of the players. A typical element of S_i is denoted by s_i (i.e., $s_i \in S_i$). Let the set of n players be denoted by N. If K is a subset of N, s_K is a joint strategy choice by the players in set K, and S_K the corresponding set of joint strategies. Then s_{N-K} is the joint strategy of the players other than those contained in set K and S_{N-K} the corresponding set of strategies.

The complete set of outcomes Q in an n-player game is formed by the Cartesian product of all the players' strategy sets.

$$Q = S_1 \times S_2 \times \cdots \times S_n. \tag{10-1}$$

The Cartesian product contains all combinations formed by selecting one element from each strategy set S_i. A typical element of Q is q (i.e., $q \in Q$).

$q = (\bar{s}_i, \bar{s}_{n-i})$ is outcome where player i selects strategy $\bar{s}_i$ and player $n-i$ pick strategy $\bar{s}_{n-i}$. BAR MEANS STRATEGY IS FIXED.

Example: In the nuclear conflict in Table 10.1,

$$S_1 = S_2 = \{C, L, S\}.$$

The Cartesian product is

$$Q = S_1 \times S_2 = \{(C,C), (C,L), (C,S), (L,C),$$
$$(L,L), (L,S), (S,C), (S,L), (S,S)\}.$$

This is simply all the outcomes for the basic game G in the military dispute shown in Table 10.1.

10.4.2 Preference Functions

The Boolean of Q, written $B(Q)$, is the set of all subsets of Q. For each player i let the preference function M_i stand for a function from the set Q to the set $B(Q)$. The function M_i does not have to be ordinal as is the case for the nuclear conflict of Table 10.1, but can also obey the properties of a general or partly ordinal game (Howard, 1971). In particular,

$M_i^+(q)$ is the set of outcomes preferred by player i to q;
$M_i^-(q)$ is the set of outcomes not preferred by player i to q
(set includes q).

Note that $M_i(q) = \{(M_i^+(q), M_i^-(q), \forall q \in Q)\}$. For $q = (\bar{s}_i, \bar{s}_{N-i})$, where the bar denotes the fact that the indicated strategy is fixed,

$$m_i(q) = (s_i, \bar{s}_{N-i})$$

is the set of outcomes accessible unilaterally from q by player i (includes q). Define

$$m_i^+(q) = m_i(q) \cap M_i^+(q) \quad \text{(this is a UI),} \quad \textit{could} \quad (10\text{-}2)$$
$$m_i^-(q) = m_i(q) \cap M_i^-(q). \quad \textit{be more than 1.} \quad (10\text{-}3)$$

Note that $m_i(q) = m_i^+(q) + m_i^-(q)$.

An outcome q is not preferred by i to an outcome p if and only if

$$M_i^-(q) \subseteq M_i^-(p). \quad \textit{(subset)} \quad (10\text{-}4)$$

This means that

$$q \in M_i^-(p). \quad (10\text{-}5)$$

Example: Consider outcome (L,L) from Table 10.1 for the nuclear conflict where the United States is player 1 and the USSR is player 2.

M_1^+ (L,L) = {(S,L), (S,C), (L,C)},
M_1^- (L,L) = {(L,L), (C,C), (C,L), (S,S), (L,S), (C,S)},
m_1 (L,L) = {(S,L), (L,L), (C,L)},
m_1^+ (L,L) = m_1 (L,L) $\cap$ M_1^+ (L,L) = {(S,L)},   .
m_1^- (L,L) = m_1 (L,L) $\cap$ M_1^- (L,L) = {(L,L), (C,L)}.

For outcome (S,L),

M_1^+ (S,L) = {(S,C), (L,C)},
M_1^- (S,L) = {(S,L), (L,L), (C,C), (C,L), (S,S), (L,S), (C,S)}.

Because M_1^-(L,L) $\subseteq$ M_1^-(S,L) this means that (L,L) $\in$ M_1^-(S,L); therefore outcome (L,L) is not preferred to outcome (S,L).

10.4.3 Game Definition

A game G is an object described by the strategy sets and preference functions of all the players.

$$G = (S_1, S_2, \ldots, S_n; M_1, M_2, \ldots, M_n), \tag{10-6}$$

where $n \geq 2$ and each S_i has at least two elements.

10.4.4 Metarational Outcomes

The theory of rationality predicts that an outcome that is rational for i is also stable for i. Using metagame theory it is possible to find rational outcomes in each metagame for player i. These are called *metarational outcomes* for player i in the basic game. Metarationality implies that an ✗ outcome that is metarational for player i is also stable for i.

An rth level metagame L is written

$$L = k_1 k_2 \ldots k_r G, \tag{10-7}$$

where each k_i is a player. The metagame kG will be used to illustrate and define aspects of a metagame.

10.4.5 Metagame kG

The metagame kG is formed from G by replacing k's strategy set S_k with the set F of all functions f from S_{N-k} to S_k. Metagame kG is then an object described by the strategy sets and preference functions of all players in kG.

$$kG = (S_1, S_2, \ldots S_{k-1}, F, S_{k+1}, \ldots, S_n; M_1', \ldots, M_n'), \tag{10-8}$$

where S_{N-k} is the set of joint strategies other than the strategies of player k; F is termed the set of the first level policies of player k in kG; and M_i' is the preference function of player i in kG. A typical outcome in kG is (f, s_{N-k}), where $f \in F$. The set of all outcomes in kG is the Cartesian product $F \times S_{N-k}$. Therefore, *a typical outcome is*

$$(f, s_{N-k}) \in F \times S_{N-k}. \tag{10-9}$$

10.4.6 β Operator

The β operator takes any outcome from a metagame L to a unique outcome in the immediate ancestor of L (the metagame one level lower than L in the metagame tree). If L is an rth level metagame, the β operator applied r times (i.e., β^r) yields an outcome in G. The symbol β^* means application of the β operator enough times to get back to G. For kG,

$$\beta(f, s_{N-k}) = (f(s_{N-k}), s_{N-k}). \tag{10-10}$$

e.g. outcome $(L/s/s, c)$ *in* $1G$ *is* (L, c) *in* G
or $\beta(L/s/s, c) = (f(c), c) = (L, c)$

10.4.7 Metagame Preferences

Preferences in metagame L are obtained from the preferences in G. For example, preferences in kG are related to G by

$$p \in M_i^{-\prime}(q) \Leftrightarrow \beta p \in M_i^{-} \beta(q). \qquad (10\text{-}11)$$

10.4.8 Metarational Outcomes

An outcome $q \ [=(\bar{s}_i, \bar{s}_{N-i})]$ is rational (i.e., $q \in R_i$) for player i if, for a fixed strategy choice $\bar{s}_{N-i}$ of the other players and for all possible strategy choices for i ($\forall s_i$), player i cannot find an outcome preferred to q. Thus

$$R_i = \{q \mid \forall s_i, (s_i, \bar{s}_{N-i}) \in M_i^{-}(q)\}. \qquad (10\text{-}12)$$

A metarational outcome for i in G is an outcome derived from an outcome rational for i in a metagame. For example, if $q \in R_i(kG)$ (outcome q is rational for i in kG), then q is metarational for player i in the game G. In the metagame L the β operator is applied enough times to the set of rational outcomes in L to obtain the set $\beta^* R_i(L)$ of metarational outcomes in G. This set is also denoted by $\hat{R}_i(L)$. Of course, in kG the operator only has to be applied once and

$$\beta R_i(kG) = \hat{R}_i(kG). \qquad (10\text{-}13)$$

The union of all metarational outcomes from all metagames with the rational outcomes in the basic game is denoted by R_i^* for player i. Thus

$$R_i^* = \bigcup_j \hat{R}(L_j) \cup R_i(G), \qquad (10\text{-}14)$$

where j takes on all possible values.

The set of equilibriums $E(L)$ in some metagame L is the set of outcomes rational for all players in L. The β operator relates equilibriums in L to the appropriate metaequilibriums $\beta^* E(L)$ in G. This set of metaequilibriums is also denoted by $\hat{E}(L)$. In metagame kG,

$$\beta E(kG) = \hat{E}(kG). \qquad (10\text{-}15)$$

Example: In the nuclear war conflict in Table 10.1 there are two players, and therefore $N = \{1,2\}$. Consider the metagame $1G$ shown in Table 10.2. The set F of all 27 functions f going from S_2 to S_1 is

$$F = \{C/C/C, C/C/L, \ldots, S/S/S\},$$

which is the left column of functions in Table 10.2 and forms the strategy set of player 1 in $1G$. The strategy set S of player 2 in the metagame $1G$ is $S = \{C,L,S\}$, which is the same strategy set in G presented in Table 10.1.

Figure 10.2 illustrates how the functions f map strategies from player 2's strategy set to player 1's strategy set for three examples. The strategy set for player 1 is called the *domain,* and the strategy set for player 2 is called the *codomain* in this case, although in general this would depend on the particular metagame being studied.

Outcome (L/S/S,C) is one of the 81 possible outcomes in $1G$ shown in Table 10.2. The outcome (L/S/S,C) in $1G$ yields (L,C) in G because

$$\beta(L/S/S,C) = (f(C),C) = (L,C).$$

Since (L,C) has the preference structure (9,4) in G, outcome (L/S/S,C) in $1G$ possesses the preference (9,4) in $1G$. The outcome (L,C) is meta-rational for players 1 and 2 in G since (L/S/S,C) is rational for both players

Figure 10.2 Mapping of strategy sets.

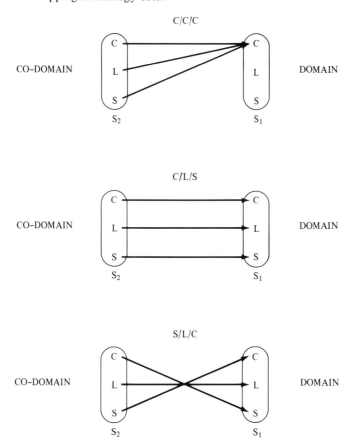

in 1G. Consequently, (L/S/S,C) is one of the two equilibriums in 1G and (L,C) forms a metaequilibrium in G.

10.4.9 Types of Metarational Outcomes

It would appear that in order to determine R_i^* for all players i one would have to go through the infinite metagame tree to find all metarational outcomes. However, there is an extremely powerful theorem called the Characterization Theorem for Metarational Outcomes that enables one to identify the set R_i^* for any given i from an examination of the basic game G. Knowing the metarational outcomes by examining G, the theory of metarationality can then be checked by experiment and practical application (Howard, 1971).

The Characterization Theorem and its corollaries are explained in detail in Howard (1971). A proof of the Characterization Theorem is presented in Appendix D. There are three types of metarational outcomes specified by the Characterization Theorem that are used to analyze conflicts: rational, symmetric metarational, and general metarational.

Rational Outcomes. Rational outcomes are metarational from every metagame. To check whether an outcome q is rational for i in G, one checks for the absence of strategies, called *unilateral improvements*, which are described mathematically by

$$\exists s_i: \qquad (s_i, \bar{s}_{N-i}) \in M_i^+(q). \tag{10-16}$$

The outcomes produced by unilateral improvements are also called unilateral improvements, and are abbreviated UI. Given $q = (\bar{s}_i, \bar{s}_{N-i})$, a UI $p \in P$ from q would be given by

$$p \in \{(s_i, \bar{s}_{N-i}) : (s_i, \bar{s}_{N-i}) \in M_i^+(q)\}. \tag{10-17}$$

Thus, from (10-2), a UI from q is a member of the set $m_i^+(q)$.

When an outcome q is not rational, player i can find an outcome preferable to q by a change of strategy. In this case one checks for symmetric metarationality.

Symmetric Metarational Outcomes. A symmetric metarational outcome is formed when a given player has one or more UIs from a particular outcome but the other players have joint strategy selections by which they can guarantee that, regardless of the particular player's strategy choice, the resulting outcome is not preferred by the particular player to the one being analyzed. In terms of the metagame tree, a symmetric metarational outcome is metarational from some descendant of every metagame. To check whether an outcome q is symmetric metarational for i in G, one checks for the presence of *inescapable sanctions* which are represented mathematically as

$$\exists s_{N-i} \quad \forall s_i: \quad (s_i, s_{N-i}) \in M_i^-(q). \tag{10-18}$$

An outcome formed from a UI by a player invoking a sanction is also called a sanction or a sanctioning outcome. Because of the inescapable sanctions, player i is unlikely to move away from outcome q. If no inescapable sanctions exist, one checks to see whether the outcome is general metarational.

General Metarational Outcomes. A general metarational outcome arises when a particular player has a UI, but the other players can choose a joint strategy to move the given player to a less preferred outcome. In turn, however, the particular player can use a different strategy to improve his or her situation once again. This cycle can continue indefinitely, therefore suggesting that it might be better for the particular player to remain with the original outcome. Consequently, the original outcome is general metarational and in terms of the metagame tree it is metarational from at least one metagame. To check whether outcome q is general metarational for i in G, one checks for the absence of an *inescapable improvement*, described by

$$\exists s_i \quad \forall s_{N-i}: \quad (s_i, s_{N-i}) \in M_i^+(q). \tag{10-19}$$

If an outcome is either rational, symmetric metarational, or general metarational for a player, the outcome is said to be stable for that player. An outcome that is stable for all players can be a possible solution or equilibrium to the conflict.

The preceding terminology for metagame theory is useful for describing the mathematical characteristics of metagames. The procedure for applying relevant concepts from metagame theory to practical problems is called *metagame analysis* or the *analysis of options*.

10.5 Metagame Analysis

Although Ragade et al. (1976b) describe a method for determining metarational outcomes directly from the normal form, the *tabular form* of the game (Howard, 1971) provides a much more flexible medium for performing a metagame analysis than the rather restrictive normal form. As shown in Table 10.3 for the nuclear conflict, each player's options are written in a column on the left-hand side of the table. The United States and USSR each have the three options C, L, and S, defined in Section 10.2.

As in Chapter 1, a 1 placed opposite an option means that the option is taken by the player controlling it, whereas a 0 indicates that the option is rejected. Any combination of 1s and 0s opposite all the options of a given player is called a *strategy*. Note that for the nuclear conflict the three options for each player are all mutually exclusive, making the number of options equal to the number of strategies. In general, however, the maximum number of strategies available to a player is 2^m, where m is the number of options available to the player. After each player chooses a strategy, the result is an *outcome;* outcomes thus appear as columns opposite the listed options. For example, the first column from the left in Table 10.3 indicates the outcome where the United States selects the strategy of a conventional attack, while the USSR performs a limited nuclear strike. Table 10.4 provides a convenient translation between the normal form and metagame notations for outcomes.

The metagame algorithm to discover stable outcomes is displayed in Figure 10.3, and is based upon the Characterization Theorem defined by Howard (1971) and the conditions for stability discussed in Section 10.4.9. One of the relevant outcomes of the set, the particular outcome q, is chosen to be analyzed first, from player i's point of view. As shown in Table 10.3, all other feasible outcomes are listed as preferable or not preferable for player i relative to the particular outcome q. The first step in the stability analysis consists of checking whether any UIs exist for the player. If there is none, the outcome is rational and stable for the particular player. When UIs exist for the player, the particular outcome may still be stable if there are some actions the other players can take to deter this player from selecting any of the UIs. If sanctioning puts i in a less preferable position with respect to outcome q no matter what i does, the sanction is inescapable and the outcome is symmetric metarational

Table 10.3 Metagame Analysis of Outcome (010, 100) for the USSR

		Preferable				Particular outcome		Not preferable	
U.S.:									
C	1	1	1	0	0	0	0	0	0
L	0	0	0	1	1	1	0	0	0
S	0	0	0	0	0	0	1	1	1
USSR:									
C	0	1	0	0	0	1	0	0	1
L	1	0	0	1	0	0	0	1	0
S	0	0	1	0	1	0	1	0	0

Unilateral improvements

Inescapable sanctions

Table 10.4 Comparison of Different Outcome Notations

Notation	Outcomes								
Metagame analysis									
U.S.:									
C	1	0	0	1	0	0	1	0	0
L	0	1	0	0	1	0	0	1	0
S	0	0	1	0	0	1	0	0	1
USSR:									
C	1	1	1	0	0	0	0	0	0
L	0	0	0	1	1	1	0	0	0
S	0	0	0	0	0	0	1	1	1
Normal form	(C,C)	(L,C)	(S,C)	(C,L)	(L,L)	(S,L)	(C,S)	(L,S)	(S,S)

Figure 10.3 Metagame analysis algorithm for the stability of outcome q for player A.

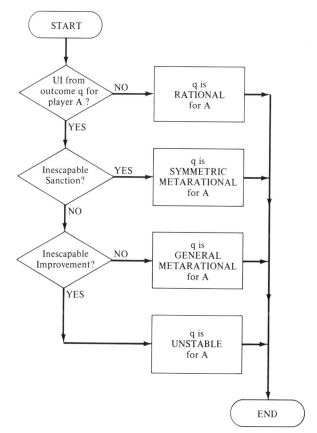

for i. When there is a cyclic pattern in the sanctioning, as was described for general metarational outcomes, stability can also be induced. An outcome will be unstable for player i if i has available a strategy that, if taken, will form an inescapable improvement and put i in a preferred position relative to the particular outcome no matter what the other players do. The above analysis is applied to every player in the game, for all the outcomes to be considered. Note that an outcome is unstable in only one circumstance: when the player has an inescapable improvement to another more preferable outcome. The improvement is inescapable because the other players cannot select strategies to put the particular player in a less preferable position.

The equilibriums resulting from the application of the above criterion are subject to *credibility assessment*. This is done by examining the credibility, or reasonableness, of the sanctions responsible for stability. A sanction not likely to occur in the real world conflict situation is said to be *noncredible*. Equilibriums based only on noncredible sanctions are not stable, and thus are not true equilibriums. The identification of noncredible sanctions is not a trivial procedure in metagame analysis, and the fact that an algorithmic method of credibility determination has not been included in metagame analysis sometimes makes it difficult to use. Strict application of metagame analysis to a complex conflict may result in a substantial number of equilibriums that are based on noncredible sanctions.

The outcome where the United States pursues strategy L and the USSR selects C can be represented horizontally by (010, 100). The analysis of this particular outcome in the nuclear war conflict is shown in Table 10.3. This outcome is rational for the United States since it is its most preferable outcome (see Table 10.1). Therefore the United States cannot improve its position by changing its strategy while the Soviet strategy remains the same. When analyzing the same outcome from the Soviet viewpoint, one must first check for UIs. As shown in Table 10.3 the USSR can "move" to (010, 010) or (010, 001) to be in a more preferable position. In terms of the real conflict, this means that the Soviet Union prefers to use at least the same level of nuclear strength as the United States does in a counterattack. Even though the USSR has UIs, the particular outcome may still be stable if the United States can take some other action to deter the USSR from moving to the preferred outcome. Table 10.3 shows how the United States can sanction the USSR by moving to outcome (001, 010) or (001, 001), depending on the improvement chosen by the USSR. These sanctions are inescapable because the USSR does not then possess any option to select in order to move to an outcome that is more preferred than the particular outcome. Hence, outcome (010, 100) is symmetric metarational for the USSR and its stability relies on the credibility that the United States will sanction the Soviet improvements. Since the USSR would not like to see strategic nuclear war, the sanctions are credible, and outcome (010, 100) is stable for the USSR. Because the outcome is stable for both the USSR and the United States it forms an equilibrium and is a possible solution for this conflict.

Using the metagame analysis algorithm outlined in Figure 10.3 one can obtain the results shown in Table 10.5 for all nine feasible outcomes defined by Richelson (1979). This requires 18 metagame tableaux to be completed, one for each outcome from the point of view of every player. In Table 10.5 the type of stability is indicated, and from this the overall stability is ascertained. Notice that the equilibrium of total nuclear war is rational for both players whereas the other four equilibriums depend upon the credibility of sanctions because of symmetric metarationality. Also note that these equilibriums correspond to the solutions to the game indicated by the normal form analysis, when cooperative solutions are considered.

10.6 Important Concepts from Chapter 10

The normal form of the game consists of a matrix, as shown in Table 10.1. Each dimension of the matrix is labeled according to one of the players in the game. The rows and columns relate to strategies that are available to the corresponding players. The elements in the matrix are outcomes in the game.

Table 10.5 Results of Metagame Analysis on U.S.–USSR Confrontation

	Stability		
Outcome	U.S.	USSR	Overall
(100, 100)	Symmetric metarational	Symmetric metarational	Equilibrium (if credible)
(100, 010)	Symmetric metarational	Rational	Equilibrium (if credible)
(100, 001)	Unstable	Symmetric metarational	Unstable
(010, 100)	Rational	Symmetric metarational	Equilibrium (if credible)
(010, 010)	Symmetric metarational	Rational	Equilibrium (if credible)
(010, 001)	Unstable	Symmetric metarational	Unstable
(001, 100)	Symmetric metarational	Unstable	Unstable
(001, 010)	Rational	Unstable	Unstable
(001, 001)	Rational	Rational	Equilibrium

An outcome in the normal form is *rational* for a player if it is the best outcome that can be achieved by that player given that the other players do not change their strategies. An outcome that is rational for all players is called an *equilibrium*.

If strategies are selected that take into account the possible reactions of the players, more complex games are formed, called *metagames*. These games can be represented in the normal form, and the rationality criterion can also be applied to them. An example metagame is shown in Table 0.2. Each metagame has its corresponding simple or basic game, and outcomes that are rational in a metagame are said to be *metarational* in the basic game. Metarationality is an important consideration when determining the stability of an outcome.

The metarationality of an outcome can be determined in the basic game alone because of the Characterization Theorem. There are three types of stability:

1. *Rationality* is determined from the absence of unilateral improvement strategies, which are mathematically described as

$$\exists s_i: \qquad (s_i, \bar{s}_{N-i}) \in M_i^+(q). \tag{10-16}$$

2. *Symmetric metarationality* applies to an outcome if for every unilateral improvement strategy available for a player, the other player or players have a joint strategy that results in a less preferable outcome for the particular player. The other players' strategy is referred to as *sanctioning strategy* and is denoted

$$\exists s_{N-i} \ \forall s_i: \qquad (s_i, s_{N-i}) \in M_i^-(q). \tag{10-18}$$

3. *General metarationality* applies to all remaining outcomes if there are no inescapable improvement strategies available for the particular player. An inescapable improvement strategy is denoted

$$\exists s_i \ \forall s_{N-i}: \qquad (s_i, s_{N-i}) \in M_i^+(q). \tag{10-19}$$

The method of application of metagame theory is called *metagame analysis*. A flowchart of the metagame analysis procedure is shown in Figure 10.3. Metagame analysis is very convenient to use because one can have any number of players or options. This is difficult to do in normal form. An example of the metagame analysis of a single outcome is seen in Table 10.3. A hypothetical nuclear war conflict was analyzed using both the normal form and metagame analysis. Both methods yielded similar results.

Questions

1. Analyze a simple three-player game in normal form. Do you think you could analyze a five-player game in normal form?

2. Will there always be an equilibrium in the normal form? Prove your answer.
3. Calculate the following sets for the nuclear conflict:
   (a) $M_2^+(C,C)$, (b) $m_2^-(L,S)$, (c) $M_2^-(S,S)$,
   (d) $m_2^+(L,C)$, (e) $M_2^+(S,C)$.
4. Suppose a game in the normal form is given as follows:

		Player 2	
		Don't	Confess
Player 1	Don't	3,3	1,4
	Confess	4,1	2,2

This game is called Prisoner's Dilemma. Let q represent a given outcome and i a particular player. For all four outcomes and both players calculate the following sets:
   (a) Q, (b) $M_i^+(q)$, (c) $M_i^-(q)$,
   (d) $m_i(q)$, (e) $m_i^+(q)$, (f) $m_i^-(q)$.
   (g) Show mathematically that outcome (D,D) is not preferred to outcome (C,C) by both player 1 and player 2.
5. For the basic game G in normal form given in question 4, determine $1G$, $2G$, $12G$, and $21G$. For each of these metagames ascertain the rational outcomes for both players and the equilibriums. Relate the rational outcomes and equilibriums back to the basic game G. Discuss the results.
6. If the statement

$$\exists s_i \ \forall s_{N-i}: \quad (s_i, s_{N-i}) \in m_i^-(q)$$

is true, does it mean that outcome $q = (\bar{s}_i, \bar{s}_{N-i})$ is the most preferable outcome for player i? How many strategies are available to the $(N-i)$ players? Can q be unstable for i?
7. Develop the metagame tableau for both the United States and the USSR for the outcome (010, 001) in the nuclear war conflict.

Chapter 11
Conflict Analysis Methods

11.1 Introduction

Although the metagame analysis method of Howard (1971) discussed in Chapter 10 provided one of the first approaches for the rigorous study of a complex conflict situation, it has a number of flaws that render it difficult to use in practice:

1. Metagame analysis requires a large number of tables. In a thorough analysis, each player requires a separate table for each outcome. Thus the total number of tables required is the number of players multiplied by the number of outcomes in the game. For the nuclear conflict, at least 18 different tables are required.

2. Metagame analysis merely determines the metaequilibriums in a game. It is up to the analyst to distinguish the outcomes that are based on credible sanctions and that might thus be resolutions to the conflict. Since often most of the outcomes in a given conflict form meta-equilibriums, metagame analysis does not really provide much information other than a convenient notation.

3. Metagame analysis cannot be readily used for the analysis of games in which information is incomplete or misleading.

4. Metagame analysis is not easy to computerize, although efforts have been made to do so (Shepanik, 1974, 1975).

The conflict analysis method used throughout this book and derived in this chapter has been developed by adapting traditional metagame analysis to the study of practical problems. In the course of doing·so, the faults listed above have been overcome.

This chapter first presents the theoretical development of the conflict method for the case of two players only. The theoretical basis for the analysis of a game with more than two players is then presented. This is brought into perspective by the analysis of the hypothetical nuclear war example introduced in Chapter 10.

11.2 The Two-Player Game

11.2.1 Credibility Assumption

In chapter 10, metagame criteria for the determination of stability through metarationality were derived. The following sets of outcomes were defined:

$M_i^+(q)$ is the set of outcomes preferred by player i to q;

$M_i^-(q)$ is the set of outcomes not preferred by player i to q (set includes q);

$m_i(q)$ is the set of outcomes accessible unilaterally from q by player i (set includes q);

$m_i^+(q) = m_i(q) \cap M_i^+(q)$ is the set of UIs from q for i;

$m_i^-(q) = m_i(q) \cap M_i^-(q)$.

Consider a conflict involving two players, A and B. For metagame analysis, the only condition under which a given outcome q will be unstable is an inescapable improvement. An inescapable improvement was described as

$$\exists s_i \quad \forall s_{N-i} : \quad (s_i, s_{N-i}) \in M_i^+(q) \tag{10-19}$$

or, for two players,

$$\exists s_A \quad \forall s_B : \quad (s_A, s_B) \in M_A^+(q). \tag{11-1}$$

The conditions for membership in the set R_A^* of "stable" outcomes for player A in a metagame analysis can then be re-expressed as

$$(\exists p \in m_A^+(q) : m_B(p) \cap M_A^-(q) = \emptyset) \Leftrightarrow q \notin R_A^*. \tag{11-2}$$

The outcome within the set R_B^* are determined in a similar fashion.

If the assumption is made that the credibility of a sanction is related to the preferences of the sanctioning players among the possible outcomes of the conflict, a far simpler and more convenient algorithm than traditional metagame analysis can be developed. The authors contend that an action on the part of a player or group of players is credible if and only if the action results in an outcome more preferred for the player or players who are levying the action. Thus the only outcomes that could credibly deter a player from improving from an outcome are those that can be achieved by the other players improving their position from either the possible UI available to the player, or from the outcome under consideration. These two possibilities may be examined separately.

11.2.2 Sequential Stability

When considering sequential moves, metagame analysis indicates that an outcome can be made stable for a particular player if another player has a change in strategy from the particular player's UI that results in a less preferred outcome for the particular player. In order to discard noncredible actions on the part of the other player from the possible UI by the particular player, the preferences of the other player can be incorporated into (11-2). Recall that the set $m_i(q)$ is composed of $m_i^+(q) + m_i^-(q)$. However, the outcomes in the set $m_i^-(q)$ are not credible, and hence should not be considered as viable sanctions. Consequently, (11-2) can be reformulated as

$$(\exists p \in m_A^+(q) : m_B^+(p) \cap M_A^-(q) = \emptyset) \Leftrightarrow q \notin R_A^* \qquad (11\text{-}3)$$

The algorithm for determining stability for player A implied by the above condition is portrayed in Figure 11.1. The first box in Figure 11.1 is an examination for rationality. It proceeds on the basis of the definition for rational outcomes as expressed in (10-16) (see p. 214). If there are no unilateral improvements from an outcome, the outcome is stable for the player under consideration. For an outcome q to be unstable, a UI for B from A's UI must be less preferred by A to q. If B has no UI, as questioned in the second box in the flowchart, $m_B^+(p)$ is empty and q is unstable for A. The third box checks whether

$$m_B^+(p) \subseteq M_A^+(q),$$

which also results in q being unstable for A. Finally, if all UIs from q for A have been checked (since $\exists p \cdots$) and instability has not occurred, the outcome must be stable by credible sanction.

11.2.3 Simultaneous Stability

The foregoing algorithm permits the determination of the stability of outcomes based upon the deterrent effect of another player improving from the improvement made by a player. However, the deterrent effect of improvements from the original outcome must also be assessed. If the outcome that results from the changes made by both players improving simultaneously is less preferred for a player, then it is a credible sanction against the possible improvement and the original outcome may be considered stable. Since simultaneous stability can only occur when an outcome can be improved upon by more than one player, it is sufficient to

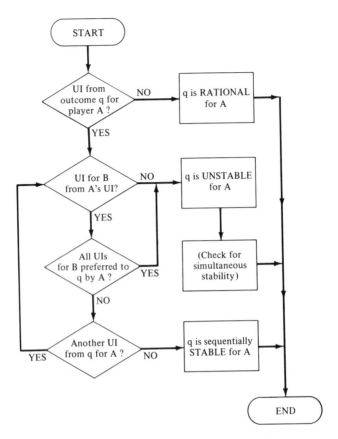

Figure 11.1 Stability of outcome q for player A in a two-player game.

search for this kind of stability after the previous algorithm has been carried out. In Figure 11.1, this is indicated by the box that follows the determination of instability of the outcome q. The process is parenthesized to indicate that it occurs only if the outcome q is unstable for both players.

The mathematics used for examining simultaneous stability works as follows: Let q be the outcome under consideration. Let a be the outcome to which player A can improve from q, and let b be the outcome to which B can improve. When a, b, and q are considered as numbers (either decimal or binary), $(a - q)$ is the value of the net change made by A on q, and $(b - q)$ is the value of the net change made by B on q. The resulting outcome is then:

$$q + (a - q) + (b - q) = q - 2q + a + b = (a + b) - q. \quad (11\text{-}4)$$

The rule is thus to add the values of the outcome to which the players have UIs, and from this subtract the value of the original outcome (compare Section 1.3.3) If the resulting outcome is not preferred for a player, it is a credible sanction, and q is stable for that player.

11.2.4 Analysis Consequences

This new analysis algorithm invariably leads to the determination of at least one equilibrium in a conflict, as is rigorously proven in Theorem 13.23 (see p. 269). Consider a game with players A and B. Assume initially that every outcome is unstable for one or both of the players. Let q be the most preferable unstable outcome for player A. From (11-3),

$$\exists p: \quad m_B^+(p) \cap M_A^-(q) = \emptyset, \qquad \text{where} \quad p \in m_A^+(q). \qquad (11\text{-}5)$$

Now p must be stable for A since q is the most preferred unstable outcome for A and p is preferred to q by A. If $m_B^+(p)$ is empty, p is stable for B and thus forms an equilibrium. If $m_B^+(p)$ is not empty, then any improvement y for B must be a member of $M_A^+(q)$ and stable for A. If the preferences of player B are strictly ordinal, at least one of the improvements available to B will be rational for B (say, y_j) and therefore form an equilibrium. Thus in this game there is at least one equilibrium outcome, either p or y_j, contradicting the original assumption that all outcomes were unstable for one or both of the players. This means that the original assumption was false, and all two-person games with strictly ordinal preferences must have at least one equilibrium.

This stability algorithm, although based on the mathematical foundation of metagame analysis, also has a clear commonsense interpretation. To determine whether an outcome is stable, one simply finds out if the player can expect to achieve an improved position by performing some action. If the other players are likely to alter their actions, either later than or at the same time as the player under consideration, and thereby cause a worse situation for the player under consideration, then that player is not likely to take an action. This principle is clearly a form of rationality since the player in question is doing the best he or she can under the circumstances. This point is explored in more detail in Chapter 12.

Since the modeling of real world conflicts is a complex problem, sometimes the resulting models strain the tidy mathematical structures imposed by theory. The variations and special cases that occur often require judgment on the part of the analyst as to the best manner in which to assess the stability of the outcomes. Application of the above rationality principle, coupled with conservatism with regard to the degree of threat that might induce stability, results in a workable manner of dealing with unusual situations. However, the techniques presented throughout this book are flexible enough to accommodate any algorithm for the assessment of stability. The reader is encouraged to incorporate any beliefs he or she may have regarding criteria for stability in game models of conflicts.

11.3 n-Player Games

For the case of n players, an algorithm may be developed in a fashion similar to that of the two-player case. Although the complexity of the analysis increases, it generally remains possible to perform by hand. In generalizing Howard's criteria (1971) for metagame stability to the n-player case, no distinction needs to be made for the actions of the individual players in assessing an inescapable sanction: the sanction exists irrespective of the individual players' preferences. When players' preferences are considered, a sanction can only be considered credible if it can be achieved through credible (self-improving) actions on the part of the other players.

When considering n players, let $\hat{m}_{N-i}^{+}(q)$ be the set of outcomes that can be generated by the players in the set $N-i$ consistently improving their individual positions from q and subsequent outcomes. This means that

$$m_j^{+}(q) \subseteq \hat{m}_{N-i}^{+}(q), \qquad \forall j \neq i,$$
$$m_k^{+}(m_j^{+}(q)) \subseteq \hat{m}_{N-i}^{+}(q), \qquad \forall k \neq j \neq i, \quad \forall j \neq i,$$
$$m_l^{+}(m_k^{+}(m_j^{+}(q))) \subseteq \hat{m}_{N-i}^{+}(q), \qquad \forall l \neq k \neq i, \quad \forall k \neq j \neq i, \quad \forall j \neq i,$$

The new criterion for instability in an n-player game is then

$$(\exists p \in m_i^{+}(q) : \hat{m}_{N-i}^{+}(p) \cap M_i^{-}(q) = \emptyset) \Leftrightarrow q \in R_i^{*}. \qquad (11\text{-}6)$$

An examination of (11-6) reveals that the algorithm for an n-player conflict is then very similar to that for a two-player conflict. For the n-player conflict, if any outcomes that result from consistent improvement on the part of the other players are not preferable for a particular player to the outcome under consideration, the outcome is sequentially stable for that player. In practice, the outcomes possible through consistent improvement are not very numerous, and the stability of an outcome for a player may be very quickly established. The complete algorithm for determining the stability of an outcome q for player i in an n-player game is shown in Figure 11.2.

To determine if an outcome is sequentially sanctioned, one must examine all possible improvements made by the other players individually. This can be done for player i and a given outcome q using the following recursive algorithm:

1. Label the most preferred UI for i from outcome q as outcome p.
2. Perform function check(p).
3. If a sanction has been found, UI is sanctioned. If a sanction has not been found, outcome q is unstable for player i.
4. If the UI is sanctioned and if all of the UIs below outcome q for player i have not been examined, replace p by the next most pref-

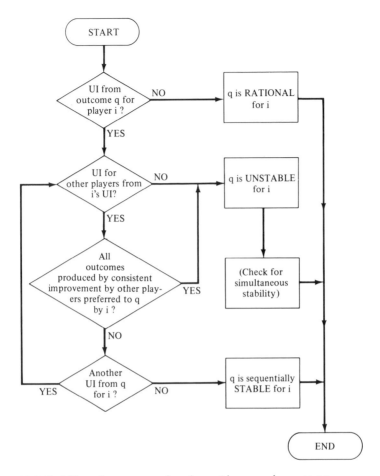

Figure 11.2 Stability of outcome *q* for player *i* in an *n*-player game.

erable UI and go to step 2. If all of the UIs are sanctioned, outcome *q* is sequentially stable.

The function check(*) consists of the following steps:

1. If a sanction has been found, go to step 5.
2. Determine a UI from (*) for any player other than *i* that has not yet been assessed as a possible sanction. Label this outcome as *r*. If there are no UIs from (*) or all UIs have been assessed, go to step 5.
3. If *r* is less preferable than *q* for *i*, the UI is sanctioned—go to step 5. If *r* is not less preferable than *q* for *i*, then perform function check(*r*).

4. Go to step 1.
5. End.

In practice, application of the above algorithm is a straightforward procedure. After it has been used a few times, its intricacies become quite evident. Bear in mind that for a given UI from outcome q this algorithm checks all possible improvements by the other players from this outcome. Another way of expressing consistent improvement is detailed in Definition 13.9 (p. 265).

An equilibrium is guaranteed for games in which ordinality of preferences is assumed, as can be proven by contradiction. Consider a game in which every outcome is unstable for at least one player. Label the most preferable unstable outcome for the first player outcome q_1, and let the UI be to outcome p_1. Now call one of the players for whom p_1 is unstable the second player, and call q_2 the most preferable unstable outcome in the second player's preference vector that can be formed by all players consistently improving from p_1. Note that q_2 must be stable for the first player, since it must be to the left of (more preferable than) outcome q_1. Continue in this manner developing p_2, q_3, p_3, ..., q_n, p_n. Each q is stable for every player that has previously been considered. The outcome p_n, where n is the number of players, is an equilibrium, contradicting the original assumption. Therefore all strictly ordinal games must have at least one equilibrium.

If an outcome is unstable for two or more players, one must check for simultaneous stability. If the outcome is unstable for exactly two players, the calculation is the same as for the two-player game described in the previous section. When an outcome q is unstable for m out of n players in an n-player game, the simultaneous stability calculation must be done for all possible combinations of two or more players for which q is unstable. Let a_i be the decimal value of the most preferable UI player i has from outcome q. When performing the computation for all m players, the formula to use is

$$p = \sum_{i=1}^{x}(a_i) - (x-1)q, \qquad x = 2, 3, \ldots, m. \qquad (11\text{-}7)$$

In the above formula, x is replaced by 2, 3, . . ., m when checking for all possible combinations of players for whom q is unstable. If during the calculations outcome p is less preferable than q for any player, then the outcome is stable for that player.

Note also that if simultaneous stability is determined with respect to a particular UI available to a player, the next most preferable UI should be assessed for sequential sanctions. If this next UI is determined to be unstable, simultaneous stability must be checked again with the other unstable players. It is sufficient, however, to consider only the UIs that determine the instability of the relevant outcomes when calculating simultaneous stability.

11.4 Nuclear Conflict

The complete decimal preference vector (see Section 1.3.3) for the United States in the nuclear conflict, as developed from the preference ordering given by Richelson (1979), is

[10 12 20 18 9 17 36 34 33].

Likewise, the Soviet preference vector is

[17 9 33 18 34 10 36 20 12]

Table 11.1 relates the three different notational conventions for outcomes used in this chapter, and can be used to determine the meaning of each decimal outcome.

To employ the procedure of Figure 11.1 in the nuclear conflict, first consider outcomes from Table 11.2 that have no UIs and therefore are rational (r) for a given player. For the United States, these are outcomes 10, 20, and 36; for the USSR, outcomes 17, 18, and 36.

Next look for credible sanctions that deter each player from implementing a UI. In Table 11.2, for example, consider outcome 12 for the United States. There is a U.S. UI to outcome 10, but the Soviet Union can improve from 10 to either 18 or 34, which are less preferred by the United States than outcome 12. Consequently outcome 12 is sequentially stable (s) for the United States. On the other hand, consider outcome 20 for the Soviet Union. It has a UI to outcome 36, from which the United States cannot improve. Therefore there is no sanction on this Soviet improvement, and outcome 20 is unstable (u) for the USSR.

Table 11.1 A Comparison of Different Outcome Notations

Notation	Outcomes								
Metagame analysis									
U.S.:									
C	1	0	0	1	0	0	1	0	0
L	0	1	0	0	1	0	0	1	0
S	0	0	1	0	0	1	0	0	1
USSR:									
C	1	1	1	0	0	0	0	0	0
L	0	0	0	1	1	1	0	0	0
S	0	0	0	0	0	0	1	1	1
Normal form	(C,C)	(L,C)	(S,C)	(C,L)	(L,L)	(S,L)	(C,S)	(L,S)	(S,S)
Decimal	9	10	12	17	18	20	33	34	36

Table 11.2 Stability Analysis for the Nuclear Conflict

	E	×	, ×	E	E	×	E	×	×
	r	s	r	s	s	u	r	u	u
U.S.	10	12	20	18	9	17	36	34	33
		10		20	10	20		36	36
					12	18			34
	r	s	s	r	s	s	r	u	u
USSR	17	9	33	18	34	10	36	20	12
		17	17		18	18		36	36
			9			34			20

The last criterion is simultaneous stability. This need only be checked for outcomes that are unstable for more than one player, and is calculated according to (11-7). Simultaneous stability (/) does not appear in the nuclear conflict (see the Zimbabwe conflict analyzed in Chapter 5 for an example of this form of stability).

After stability for each outcome and each player has been determined the final analysis step is to determine all outcomes that are either rational or stable for both participants—the equilibriums (E). By inspection of Table 11.2, only four outcomes are equilibriums and thus possible solutions for the overall conflict. As in the metagame analysis the only outcome that is rational for both players is 36 [equivalently, (001, 001) or (S,S)]; however, there is one less equilibrium than was found using the metagame analysis algorithm (see Table 10.5, p. 219).

The missing equilibrium is outcome 17 (100, 010), where the USSR attacks Europe using only limited nuclear strikes, and the United States responds with a conventional counterattack. From Table 11.2 it is evident that this outcome is stable for the USSR but unstable for the United States. When the United States makes a UI to outcome 20, by increasing the level of the counterattack to the S level, the USSR could sanction by matching the strength of the U.S. operation (outcome 36). This sanction would be credible for the USSR, because outcome 36 is preferred by it to 20. Alternatively, if the United States decides to improve from 17 to outcome 18, the Soviet Union cannot improve from this outcome; consequently it does not possess a credible sanction. This is why outcome 17 is unstable for the United States. Metagame analysis indicated that the USSR could sanction the U.S. UI (outcome 18) by moving to outcome 34 (010, 001). This strategy is not credible since it will put the USSR in a position less preferable than the original one. Conflict analysis automatically recognizes this important consideration.

Table 11.3 lists the results of the three kinds of stability analysis that have been applied to the nuclear war conflict. Only the conflict analysis technique was successful in identifying that outcome 17 was in fact un-

Table 11.3 Summary of Results Obtained Using the Three Methods

	Result		
Outcome	Normal form	Metagame analysis	Conflict analysis
9 (C,C) (100, 100)	Cooperative solution	Equilibrium	Equilibrium
10 (L,C) (010, 100)	Cooperative solution	Equilibrium	Equilibrium
12 (S,C) (001, 100)	—	—	—
17 (C,L) (100, 010)	Cooperative solution	Equilibrium	—
18 (L,L) (010, 010)	Cooperative solution	Equilibrium	Equilibrium
20 (S,L) (001, 010)	—	—	—
33 (C,S) (100, 001)	—	—	—
34 (L,S) (010, 001)	—	—	—
36 (S,S) (001, 001)	Equilibrium	Equilibrium	Equilibrium

stable; otherwise, the results were the same. Conflict analysis also offers other advantages to metagame analysis, including the ability to handle hypergames (Bennett, 1977; Shupe et al., 1980; Wright et al., 1980) and its amenability to computer implementation (Fraser and Hipel, 1980b).

11.5 Important Concepts from Chapter 11

If the assumption is made that credibility of a sanction is related to the preferences of the players, a convenient method of analyzing the stability of outcomes is derived from metagame analysis. Based upon the stability requirements for metagame analysis, this assumption results in straightforward algorithms for the analysis of conflict. The algorithm for the analysis of a two-player game is shown in Figure 11.1. The general algorithm for an *n*-player game, where $n \geq 2$, is available in Figure 11.2.

These algorithms are supported by a new notation that facilitates the manipulation of the conflict information. This notation consists of converting the binary expressions of Howard (1971) into decimal numbers. In addition to making the outcomes easier to work with, this transformation preserves certain mathematical properties that are useful when calculating the stability of the outcomes. The efficacy of the approach was reinforced by further developing the nuclear war.

Questions

1. For each of the following four simple games, perform a normal form analysis, a metagame analysis, and a conflict analysis. In each case, compare and contrast the results of each form of analysis. Each of these games is well known because of certain interesting theoretical characteristics.

(a)

	Player B	
Player A	3, 3	1, 4
	4, 1	2, 2

(b)

	Player B	
Player A	1, 2	2, 1
	2, 1	1, 2

(c)

	Player B	
Player A	3, 3	2, 4
	4, 2	1, 1

(d)

	Player B	
Player A	2, 2	4, 3
	1, 1	3, 4

Chapter 12

Theory and Implications of Conflict Analysis

12.1 Introduction

Conflict analysis is the branch of game theory that can be utilized for solving real world problems. Because of the many new developments in conflict analysis that have been presented in this book and elsewhere, it can now be considered as a separate and distinct field in decision making. Although conflict analysis as discussed in this text centers around the method of Fraser and Hipel (1979a), it also involves many other ideas and techniques that are independent of the particular stability analysis algorithm employed. For instance, the technique presented in Section 5.5.3 for forming a single coalition preference vector from two or more players' preference vectors is not dependent upon the stability analysis algorithm used to ascertain the equilibrium after the formation of a coalition. Following the creation of a coalition preference vector, any suitable stability analysis algorithm can be employed to determine the equilibriums in the game. For reasons that are to be clarified in the course of this chapter and in Chapter 13, the authors firmly believe that the conflict analysis algorithm is the most realistic and useful approach for studying real world conflicts. However, this does not preclude an analyst from using stability analysis algorithms such as the traditional metagame method of Howard (1971), or Von Stackelberg's approach (Von Stackelberg, 1952; Henderson and Quandt, 1971) in conjunction with coalition analysis.

In Table 12.1 a variety of valuable techniques are listed that can be used with any desired stability analysis algorithm where ordinal preference information is assumed. A conflict can be conveniently modeled as a game with players and options, and a binary notation can be utilized to represent strategies and outcomes economically. Infeasible outcomes can be re-

Table 12.1 Techniques That Are Independent of the Stability
Analysis Algorithm

Technique	Discussed in . . .
Players and options	Section 1.3.2
Binary notation for strategies and outcomes	Section 1.3.2
Outcome removal to eliminate infeasible outcomes	Section 2.3.3
Preference vector for each player to display the ordinal preference information among the feasible outcomes	Section 1.3.2
Decimalization of outcomes for easy manipulation	Section 1.3.3
Forming coalition preference vectors	Section 5.5.3
Sensitivity analysis	Chapter 5
Hypergames	Chapters 3, 4
Bargaining	Chapter 8, Appendix B
State-transition form	Section 6.5

moved from the total set of possible outcomes in the game by using either
one of the methods presented in Section 2.3.3 or else a microcomputer.
Subsequently, a preference vector can be developed for each player by
ordering the feasible outcomes from most to least preferred. Although
the binary notation is convenient for understanding what an outcome
means in the real world situation, the decimal version of the binary outcome is more convenient for manipulation purposes when performing a
stability analysis with a specified algorithm. As described in Section 5.5.3
and also by Kuhn et al. (1983), a coalition technique is available for
forming a single coalition preference vector from two or more players'
preference vectors given in decimal form. In addition to coalition analysis,
other types of sensitivity analysis are presented in Chapter 5. When there
are mistaken interpretations by one or more players in a game, the conflict
can be modeled as a hypergame where a suitable stability analysis method
can be used to predict the equilibriums. Bargaining and negotiation constitute a general class of situations that can often be modeled as games
with and without mistaken information. Consequently, various stability
analysis methods can also be utilized in bargaining and negotiation. Even
though the state-transition model described in Chapter 6 for modeling the
dynamics of a conflict is based upon conflict analysis, it would also be
possible to express that model using other stability criteria. Finally, although all of the methods in Table 12.1 can be executed by hand, they
can also be programmed for convenient use on a microcomputer. The
algorithms required for programming conflict analysis in conjunction with
the techniques listed in Table 12.1 are described in Chapter 7.

The conflict analysis algorithm possesses a sound theoretical foundation. Some of the theoretical ideas can be traced back to concepts de-

veloped in game theory. However, as presented in this book, conflict analysis avoids one of the basic assumptions of game theory—that of *cardinality*—and has as its mandate the modeling and analysis of real world phenomena for which it is usually only feasible to obtain *ordinal* preference information. Game theory is generally involved with the study of abstract mathematical constructs, which are sometimes loosely related to real situations. Conflict analysis is highly descriptive, whereas game theory in general tends towards the normative approach. This means that conflict analysis endeavors to describe what is happening in a useful way, whereas game theory often attempts to determine what *should* happen or what one *should* do.

As a consequence of these differences between game theory and conflict analysis, a number of questions may arise as to how some of the ideas that are common in game theory literature fit in with the conflict analysis approach taken in this book. These issues are the subject of both this chapter and Chapter 13. This chapter is devoted to an overview of how various ideas from game theory relate to conflict analysis. After a brief discussion of the structural basis of the conflict analysis method, some of the basic concepts of game theory are presented and discussed in light of this new technique. After this, four famous games that have been studied in the game theory literature are presented. Each of these games possesses unique features that can be used for demonstrating the characteristics of various *solution concepts*. A thorough mathematical comparison of solution concepts is the subject of Chapter 13.

12.2 Foundations of Conflict Analysis

The conflict analysis method of Fraser and Hipel (1979a) presented in this book is the result of repeated attempts at trying to model and analyze real world problems. When studying actual situations using other techniques, one finds that there is generally not the sort of information available that is required for calibrating the given game theory model. In other words, many game theory techniques have not been designed specifically to reflect what happens in the real world, but rather to be mathematically tractable. For many actual problems, there is usually little or no quantitative information, and probabilities are often subjective. In practice, conflicts involve nonquantitative information, and one of the most difficult aspects of assessing a conflict is simply organizing the available information.

Historically, the idea of modeling a game in terms of players, strategies, and outcomes was a great contribution to formalizing the modeling of conflicts. These concepts of classical game theory allowed people to think about a complex situation in a natural and intuitively reasonable manner. Similarly, the idea of rationality, discussed later in this chapter, made sense and helped analysts come to conclusions about conflict problems.

Howard's metagame analysis (1971) constituted a significant contribution in the modeling of conflicts. It allowed the easy display of numerous players, and the idea of options made even more sense than thinking about strategies alone. Expressing a given outcome as a set of binary digits was also more sensible than portraying it as a position in a matrix, as was usually done in game theory.

As demonstrated by the famous games that are analyzed in Section 12.6, the type of classical game theory presented by Von Neumann and Morgenstern (1953) and Nash (1951) clearly cannot properly model many situations that could arise in practice. Consequently, classical game theory has been largely ignored by decision makers. Although metagame analysis possesses a firm theoretical foundation, further changes are required to enhance certain theoretical definitions and greatly improve the method of application of the techniques for solving real world problems. However, neither classical game theory nor metagame analysis is adequate for the analysis of complex conflicts. The model components and basic theory are sound, but neither approach offers a practical analysis method. The basic problem with the metagame method is that Howard (1971) was careful to make his analysis method fit his elegant theory exactly, rather than make allowances for practicality.

The changes the authors have made to transform metagame analysis into conflict analysis will be taken up next. In every case the change does not alter the underlying mathematical basis for the technique.

Credible Sequential Sanctions. For a two-player game, a credible sequential sanction is defined as an outcome that is formed by a player improving his or her position from the UI of another player, and that is less preferable to the other player than the original (pre-UI) outcome. The threat of the imposition of a credible sequential sanction deters the other player from taking advantage of the UI. When all UIs from the given outcome are blocked by credible sequential sanctions the outcome is considered to be sequentially stable for the other player. As discussed in Section 2.4, this concept can easily be extended to the n-player case. The assumption that sanctioning a UI is credible for a player if it results in an improved outcome for that player is the fundamental improvement made upon metagame analysis by the authors. This is an empirical assumption based upon the manner in which credibility of sanctions is actually determined in metagame analysis. Thus this assumption is not a change in the underlying theory, but merely a variation in its implementation. Furthermore, it is consistent with the idea of rationality, discussed in Section 12.3. As discussed in Chapter 11, simultaneous stability properly accounts for the sequentiality inherent in this viewpoint.

Transitivity. All metagame tables have been combined into a single, decimal tableau in the improved method, within which a complete stability

analysis can conveniently be performed. Consequently, the decimaliza-
tion of outcomes greatly simplifies the stability analysis calculations. However, the fact that each player possesses a preference vector may imply
transitivity of preferences, which is not an underlying assumption of metagame theory. Transitivity requires that if outcome p is preferred to q,
and q is preferred to r, then p must be preferred to r.

In practice, although people do tend to have transitive preferences,
occasionally they may not. A preference vector as presented in this text
is transitive by default, but a bridge can be used to indicate variations
from strict ordinality, as described in Chapter 5. The lack of transitivity
is then indicated by both the bridge and the UIs available from each
outcome under the bridge. Thus, the use of additional notation in the
preference vector allows for intransitivities to be properly taken into account in the analysis.

Equally Preferred Outcomes. Howard (1971), as a consequence of his
requirement for outcomes to be reflexive, stipulated that an outcome is
not preferred to itself. An outcome q is reflexive if it is not preferred to
itself. This point, although not stressed in the description of the analysis
methods in the first part of this book, is carefully followed. For example,
if a player has a UI and the only sanction that is available to the other
players is to an outcome that is equally preferred, it may seem more
reasonable to consider this a noncredible sanction than a credible one.
However, it is better to consider this a credible sanction since this is the
more conservative point of view. It is seen in the analysis of the naval
conflict in Section 12.6.2 that this consideration is important for determining an equilibrium in some kinds of conflict situations.

On the other hand, when the conservative sanction criterion presented
in Section 5.2.3 is used, a player is considered to have UIs among outcomes that are said to be equally preferred. However, noting that these
UIs are used for sanctioning purposes only, it can be seen that this criterion is actually part of the credibility assumption rather than the definition of preferences.

In coalition analysis, on the other hand, the conflict analysis technique
does vary from Howard's (1971) work since, when equally preferred outcomes are coalesced with strictly ordinal outcomes, the result is strictly
ordinal. Howard assumes that "a coalition outcome is preferred by the
coalition only if it is preferred by all players in the coalition"; hence,
according to Howard, when equally preferred outcomes are coalesced
with strictly ordinal outcomes the coalition preference vector is equally
preferred. The result obtained using the coalition algorithm in Chapter 5
is based upon common sense. If two people want to go to a movie, and
one of them does not care which movie they see whereas the other has
a definite preference, then clearly the pair will go to the movie preferred

by the latter. However, the important consideration is that variations on Howard's principle have been invoked not in the conflict analysis, but only in the coalition algorithm.

The consequence of the foregoing discussion is that there are no fundamental theoretical changes to metagame analysis in the conflict analysis method. The modifications are simply the inclusion of credibility assessment into the analysis, and changes in notation.

Metagame analysis has been a controversial contribution to game theory (Harris, 1969a; 1969b; 1970; Howard 1969; 1970b; Rapoport, 1969b; 1969c; 1970a), but it unquestionably provides a very firm foundation for the highly practical techniques presented in this book. However, since Howard only assesses credibility subjectively, one can indeed claim a strong theoretical basis for any method that incorporates only some sort of automatic credibility assessment into a metagame analysis. In fact, the basis for the credibility criterion used in the technique presented in this book was originally purely empirical. Nevertheless, it is quite consistent with the idea of rationality as it is presented throughout game theory.

12.3 Rationality

Rationality can be defined as behavior that is characterized as follows: "Of two alternatives which give rise to outcomes, a player will choose the one which yields the more preferred outcome" (Luce and Raiffa, 1957). As Luce and Raiffa point out elsewhere in their well-known book, rationality means many different things in various theories. The above quote is their own loose way of defining it, and is consistent with most approaches to rationality in the literature.

Many game theorists put great stock in the concept of rationality, and without doubt it is the central tenet upon which most of game theory is built. Indeed, metagame analysis has at its heart the idea of rationality. However, rationality can vary from a straightforward criterion to very subtle concept with complex ramifications. In Section 12.6, where a number of famous games are examined, it is made clear where simple rationality fails to indicate fully the possible behavior of game players.

Conflict analysis, as well as having rationality as its foundation because of its roots in metagame theory, is also patently rational in practice. An examination of every situation that arises in the conflict analysis method clearly demonstrates this.

1. *Rational outcomes.* This category of outcomes is named "rational" because it arises as a consequence of the simplest interpretation of rationality. An outcome is rational for a given player who cannot unilaterally move to a more preferable outcome by a change in strat-

egy. Given the alternatives of maintaining the current outcome or changing strategy to create a less preferable one, rationality prescribes that the player maintain the present strategy. Because the conflict analysis method considers this outcome to be rational and therefore stable for the player, it is thus consistent with rationality.

2. *Sequential stability.* In sequentially stable outcomes, the particular player has two alternatives: maintain current strategy, or change strategy to cause a sequence of events that may lead to a less preferable outcome for himself. Rationality dictates no change, as does the conflict analysis method. Also, the expected sanction is based on a sense of the other player's rationality. A sanction is said to be credible if it leads to an outcome more preferred by the player imposing it; that is, if it conforms to the other player behaving rationally.

3. *Simultaneous stability.* Here, as is also the case for sequential stability, the particular player has two alternative courses of action for any outcome that is simultaneously stable: maintain the current strategy, or change strategy and risk a less preferable outcome for himself caused by another player or group of players simultaneously changing strategy. Again, rationality indicates that the current strategy be maintained, and conflict analysis likewise predicts that the threat of simultaneous sanctioning will cause a player to preserve the original outcome.

4. *Unstable.* In the case of an unstable outcome, the player can either stay at that outcome or change strategy to result in a preferable outcome. A rational player would, of course, change strategy, and this is also predicted by the conflict analysis algorithm.

In summary, the conflict analysis method is not only rooted in the basic rationality assumption through its mathematical foundation in metagame analysis, but is also inherently rational in practice.

12.4 Utility and Transitivity

The idea of *utility*, though at the heart of much of game theory, is not used in conflict analysis at all. Utility is very conventient from a theoretical point of view, but in practice there are many problems with this approach.

A *utility function* for a particular player maps each outcome into the real number space. Consequently, the preferences of a given player for the feasible outcomes in the game are expressed as cardinal numbers. A utility value for a given outcome is a real number that expresses the worth of the outcome for a particular player. The units for the utility value may be in terms of money or any other appropriate unit.

Rationality, in terms of utility, can then be defined as behavior that is characterized as follows: "Of two alternatives which give rise to outcomes, a player will choose the one which maximizes his expected utility" (Luce and Raiffa, 1957). A complex logical and qualitative problem is thus translated into a constrained maximization exercise that can be conveniently solved mathematically by well developed optimization methods. The effect of the introduction of utility into the study of games has been to foster a wide literature dealing with implications derived from mathematical relationships that appear under these circumstances. However, in most situations where both intangible and quantitative information may affect the preferences of the players, it is reasonable to obtain only ordinal preference information. Consequently, utility theory has limited scope for solving this type of real world problem.

Luce and Raiffa use the game of poker to emphasize one of the problems with the idea of utility.

> Poker, when it is played for money, is a game with numerical payoffs assigned to each of the outcomes, and one way to play the game is to maximize one's expected monetary outcome. But there are players who enjoy the thrill of bluffing for it's own sake, and they bluff with little or no regard to the expected payoff [1957, p. 5].

Clearly, often the obvious expression of the utility of outcomes is not necessarily always the correct one. Game theorists generally counter this observation with the point of view that there will be some measure of utility, however derived, that validly represents the preferences of the player.

On the other hand, the use of utility has been of great benefit in the clarification of a number of key concepts in game theory. Some of the basic results of the use of utility are described in Appendix C. Also, these ideas can have useful application in certain types of real world problem solving. For instance, in cases where only costs are considered, utility theory can be used for equitably allocating costs among the participants in a project. [See, for example, Young et al. (1982) for an application of utility theory to cost allocation.] A number of books concerned with modeling real problems using classical game theory are available (Williams, 1954, Brams, 1975; Hamburger, 1981).

The concept of transitivity, like utility, is an essential assumption in much of game theory. As Luce and Raiffa point out:

> No matter how intransitivities arise, we must recognize that they exist, and we can take only little comfort in the thought that they are anathema to most of what constitutes theory in the behavioral sciences today. We may say that we are only concerned with behavior which is transitive, adding hopefully that we believe this need not always be a vacuous study. Or we may contend that the transitive description is often a "close" approximation to reality. Or we may limit our interest to "normative" or "idealized" behavior

in the hope that such studies will have a metatheoretic impact on more realistic studies. In order to get on, we shall be flexible and accept all of these as possible defenses, and to them the traditional mathematicians hedge: transitive relations are far more mathematically tractable than intransitive ones [1957, p. 25].

Conflict analysis, like metagame analysis, does not require transitivity of preferences. Thus it is more consistent with the observable preferences of humans.

12.5 Equilibriums and Solution Concepts

The practical consequence of conflict analysis is the determination of stable outcomes and equilibriums that are somewhat different than those suggested by other approaches. In Chapter 13, all of the known non-cooperative solution concepts are compared in a mathematically rigorous manner in order to determine the relationships among them. In the present chapter, the same stability concepts are introduced and qualitatively compared.

Other stability analysis algorithms generally result in equilibriums that are a subset of equilibriums found using conflict analysis. Consequently, an analyst who has been accustomed to employing a particular kind of stability algorithm can be assured that the types of equilibriums found by his or her method will not be overlooked by the more comprehensive conflict analysis algorithm. Furthermore, reasonable equilibriums that that technique may fail to discover will be detected by conflict analysis.

The idea of Pareto optimality and inducement are also discussed in this section.

12.5.1 Nash Equilibriums and Metagame Analysis

Nash (1951) equilibriums are outcomes that are rational for all players. Since such outcomes are also conflict analysis equilibriums, all Nash equilibriums are a subset of the equilibriums found using the conflict analysis approach. However, there are equilibriums in conflict analysis that are not Nash equilibriums. Clearly, since an outcome can be stable for a player due to sanctioning, Nash equilibriums are not general enough to apply to many real world situations.

Traditional metagame analysis (Howard, 1971), on the other hand, generally results in far more equilibriums than does conflict analysis. This is because a determination of the credibility of sanctions is not automatically performed in the technique. However, if sanctions were determined according to common practice and consistent with the assumptions used in conflict analysis, then the resulting equilibriums would be identical to those that would result from a direct application of conflict analysis.

12.5.2 Nonmyopic Equilibriums

Nonmyopic equilibriums (Brams and Wittman, 1984) have only been defined for a game with two players where each player possesses two strategies. This type of equilibrium is determined by assessing the extensive game tree that results from imagining that two players alternately change from one strategy to the other in a two-strategy game. The players will change strategy if the change will eventually lead to a better outcome. This is determined using the backward induction assessment method introduced in the study of the Watergate conflict in Section 6.4. An outcome from which both players will not deviate under this criterion is a nonmyopic equilibrium.

By exhaustive enumeration, or using the theorems in Section 13.5, it can be proven that the nonmyopic equilibriums are always a subset of the equilibriums found using conflict analysis when considering games with strict ordinal preferences (i.e., when there are no equally preferred outcomes for any player). Of the 78 possible 2 × 2 games with strict ordinal preferences described by Rapoport et al. (1976), each of the nonmyopic equilibriums is a Nash equilibrium in every game except Prisoner's Dilemma and Chicken. Because *something* must happen in every game, a serious drawback of nonmyopic theory is that 41 of the 78 games possess no nonmyopic equilibriums. In Prisoner's Dilemma, the second nonmyopic equilibrium is the cooperative solution, which is also an equilibrium according to conflict analysis. In Chicken, the single nonmyopic equilibrium is the outcome that is simultaneously stable for both players. Both of these games are covered in more detail in Section 12.6.

Kilgour (1984) extended the nonmyopic concept by allowing the extensive game trees formed by the players alternating their moves to be of any arbitrary length, rather than the limit of four moves each imposed by Brams and Wittman (1984). If a player will end up at a particular outcome for any tree over a particular length, the outcome is said to have *extended nonmyopic stability*. Occasionally, extended nonmyopic equilibriums are different from those determined using conflict analysis (see Sections 13.4 and 13.5, Appendixes E and F).

12.5.3 Stackelberg Equilibriums

The Stackelberg concept of stability (Von Stackelberg, 1952; Henderson and Quandt, 1971) is one that has recently gained popularity. Consider a two-player game in which one player is arbitrarily called the leader and the other is labeled the follower. Assume the leader can optimize his or her strategy selection on the basis of the follower's best response, whereas the follower simply responds to the strategy selection of the leader by choosing the strategy that results in his or her best outcome. The best outcome the leader can obtain under these circumstances is called a *Stackelberg equilibrium*. If the equilibrium is the same regardless of which player is the leader, the outcome is called a *dual Stackelberg equilibrium*.

A Stackelberg equilibrium is always a subset of the set of conflict analysis equilibriums, as proved in Chapter 13. This can be shown easily by contradiction. First, assume there is an outcome (s_{1A}, s_{1B}) in a game with two players A and B, where s_{1A} refers to a particular initial strategy for player A and s_{1B} indicates a first strategy choice for player B. Let (s_{1A}, s_{1B}) be a Stackelberg equilibrium, but not a conflict analysis equilibrium. Let A be the leader, and B be the follower. Since (s_{1A}, s_{1B}) is a Stackelberg equilibrium, it is rational for B. Therefore, it cannot be rational for A because then it would be a conflict analysis equilibrium.

Since (s_{1A}, s_{1B}) is not rational for A, there must be an outcome (s_{2A}, s_{1B}) that is more preferable to A than (s_{1A}, s_{1B}). Let the outcome (s_{2A}, s_{2B}) be the outcome that is rational for B and incorporates the strategy s_{2A} for player A. Since (s_{1A}, s_{1b}) is not a conflict analysis equilibrium, (s_{2A}, s_{2B}) must be more preferable to A than (s_{1A}, s_{1B}); otherwise (s_{1A}, s_{1B}) would be sequentially stable for A.

Consequently, if there is an outcome (s_{1A}, s_{1B}) that is a Stackelberg equilibrium while at the same time not a conflict analysis equilibrium, there must be an outcome (s_{2A}, s_{2B}) that is rational for player B and more preferable to player A than (s_{1A}, s_{1B}). However, this means that (s_{2A}, s_{2B}) is the Stackelberg equilibrium in the game rather than (s_{1A}, s_{1B}), which contradicts the original assumption that outcome (s_{1A}, s_{1B}) is a Stackelberg equilibrium. Thus all Stackelberg equilibriums must also be metagame equilibriums.

In the nuclear conflict of Chapters 10 and 11, an analysis reveals that the two Stackelberg equilibriums are outcomes (L,L) and (L,C), which can also be expressed as (010,010) and (010,100) or decimal outcomes 18 and 10. Consider Table 10.1 and select the United States as the leader. If the United States selects C, the best the USSR can do is L. A U.S. choice of L leads to the USSR also performing L. If the United States takes S, the most preferred choice for the USSR is also S. Consequently the United States has the choice of outcomes (C,L), (L,L), or (S,S). Of these three, (L,L) is most preferred for the United States, and this constitutes one of the Stackelberg equilibriums; the other, (L,C), is calculated similarly but with the USSR as the leader. From Table 11.3 it can be seen that these two Stackelberg equilibriums are elements of the set of conflict analysis equilibriums for the nuclear conflict.

12.5.4 Pareto Optimality

An idea that has gained wide popularity in the game theory literature is *Pareto optimality*. An outcome is Pareto optimal if there is no other outcome that is either equally or more preferable to every player in the game. Some definitions of stability require that the game equilibriums possess Pareto optimality; conflict analysis does not. Pareto optimality fails to take into account the route that might be required to get from an outcome less preferable to the players taken as a group, to the one most preferable. If the game is not fully cooperative, non-Pareto optimal outcomes could indeed be stable and constitute possible resolutions to the conflict.

For example, in the nuclear conflict (Table 10.1), outcome (S,S) is not Pareto optimal, though clearly a possible resolution to the conflict, because there are obtainable outcomes that are preferred by both players over (S,S). These are (C,C), (C,L), (L,C), and (L,L), each of which *is* Pareto optimal, however.

12.5.5 Inducement

One point of view about conflicts suggests the following: sometimes a player will initially select a strategy that results in an outcome that is less than optimal in the hope that the other player or players will subsequently change strategy to bring about another outcome that is more preferable to the first player than any outcome he could obtain directly. This is called *inducement*. Although an example of this has not been discussed earlier in this book, it is similar to the position of the USSR in the Cuban missile crisis of Chapter 1. As seen in Table 1.4, from the status quo outcome 0, the USSR could perceive that the United States would improve to outcome 2 by imposing a blockade. The eventual equilibrium would be 6, where the United States has imposed a blockade and the USSR has removed the missiles. However, if the USSR initially "disimproves" from outcome 0 to outcome 4, it would achieve an equilibrium superior to that at outcome 6. If the United States were then to make a UI from 4 to some (hypothetical) outcome more preferable to the USSR than 0, this would be a true case of inducement.

With regard to stability, however, inducement can at most reduce the number of equilibriums in a game and never result in new equilibriums. This is because if an outcome is unstable for a player, the ability to change strategy and produce a less preferable outcome that may lead to a more preferable one cannot make the original outcome stable. On the other hand, inducement may actually make a stable outcome unstable, reducing the number of equilibrium outcomes. Therefore all equilibriums that can be explained as being caused by inducement are always a subset of the conflict analysis equilibriums.

12.6 Famous 2 × 2 Games

In this section, four simple games that have become well known because of their interesting theoretical characteristics are presented. It has become traditional to employ simple but interesting games for comparing the relative merits and disadvantages of different stability analysis concepts. Each of these four games is analyzed using classical game theory in normal form, traditional metagame analysis, and conflict analysis. The results for the cooperative, Stackelberg, and nonmyopic approaches are also provided. For a detailed explanation of how to perform normal form analysis, traditional metagame analysis, and conflict analysis, the reader can refer to Sections 10.2, 10.5, and 11.4, respectively.

The first game, *Prisoner's Dilemma,* has long been used to demonstrate the "breakdown of rationality," because an obviously sound resolution to the dispute is not detected. In the *Naval conflict* game, the Nash approach fails to result in any equilibriums. Due to this intuitively unsettling result, this game exhibits what is called the "second breakdown of rationality" (Howard, 1971). The game of *Chicken* is probably most frequently used as an example in the game theory literature because it is not satisfactorily modeled by any game theory approach except for conflict analysis. (This game is discussed at length in Chapter 14.) The final famous game presented in this chapter is the *Cookie Conflict,* which demonstrates the breakdown of metagame analysis.

12.6.1 Prisoner's Dilemma

There is a story attributed to A.W. Tucker (Brams, 1975), in which two persons suspected of being partners in a crime are arrested and placed in separate cells so that they cannot communicate with one another. The district attorney does not have enough evidence to convict them for the crime, so to obtain a confession he presents each suspect with the following offers:

1. If one of them confesses and the other does not, the one who confesses can go free for cooperating with the state while the other gets a stiff 10-year sentence.
2. If both prisoners confess, both get reduced sentences of 5 years.
3. If both suspects keep silent, both go to prison for 1 year on a lesser charge of carrying a concealed weapon.

Table 12.2 shows the Prisoner's Dilemma as a game in normal form. The preferences for each player are determined according to the aforementioned offers. For instance, the most preferred outcome for each player is confessing without the partner confessing, and this outcome is given an ordinal value of 4. Thus outcomes (confess, don't confess) and (don't confess, confess) are those most preferred by players A and B, respectively.

Table 12.2 Prisoner's Dilemma in Normal Form

	Player B	
Player A	Don't confess	Confess
Don't confess	3, 3	R_B 1, 4
Confess	R_A 4, 1	R_A R_B 2, 2

The rational outcomes for players A and B are denoted by R_A and R_B, respectively. Recall that to ascertain a rational outcome in normal form one simply holds one player fixed at a given strategy; the outcome that is then most preferred for the other player is rational. For instance, when player B stays at the strategy "don't confess," the outcome (confess, don't confess) is rational for player A. As shown in Table 12.2 the outcome (confess, confess) is the outcome rational for both players and is therefore an equilibrium. Nevertheless, a much more appealing strategy for both players would be not to confess, if each could be sure that the other would not confess.

The metagame analysis results of this conflict are shown in Table 12.3. According to this analysis, the cooperative outcome where both players do not confess is symmetric metarational for both and can be a possible final resolution for this conflict depending on the credibility of inescapable sanctions. This is demonstrated in Table 12.4, which shows the individual analysis tables for the two players for this outcome.

The application of the conflict analysis algorithm indicates whether or not the sanctions are credible. Table 12.5 displays the decimal preference vectors for the two prisoners and their possible unilateral improvements. Prisoner A has a unilateral improvement from outcome 0 (don't confess, don't confess) to outcome 1 where A confesses and B does not. However,

Table 12.3 Metagame Analysis of Prisoner's Dilemma

	Stability		
Outcome	Player A	Player B	Overall
Don't confess, don't confess	Symmetric metarational	Symmetric metarational	Equilibrium (if credible)
Confess, don't confess	Rational	Unstable	No
Don't confess, confess	Unstable	Rational	No
Confess, confess	Rational	Rational	Equilibrium

Table 12.4 Metagame Analysis of the Cooperative Equilibrium Outcome in Prisoner's Dilemma

	Preferable	Particular outcome	Not preferable	
Player A:				
Player A Confess	1	0	1	0
Player B Confess	0	0	1	1
	unilateral improvement inescapable sanction			
Player B:				
Player A Confess	0	0	1	1
Player B Confess	1	0	1	0
	unilateral improvement inescapable sanction			

prisoner B can in turn sanction this improvement by moving to outcome 3 which is less preferable to prisoner A than the initial outcome 0. Similarly, if prisoner B decides to unilaterally move to the more preferable outcome 2, A would sanction this by moving to outcome 3. Therefore, based upon the theory of metarationality, outcome 0 is a possible solution since the credibility of the sanctions has been assessed.

This is called a "breakdown of rationality" because from practical

Table 12.5 Conflict Analysis of Prisoner's Dilemma

Model				
Player A Confess	0	1	0	1
Player B Confess	0	0	1	1
Decimal	0	1	2	3
Stability analysis	×	E	E	×
Player A	r 1 1	s 0 0	r 3 1	u 2 3
Player B	r 2 2	s 0 0	r 3 3	u 1 3

experience we all know that outcome 0, where neither player confesses, is a reasonable outcome to this game, whereas straightforward rationality as used by Nash (1951) does not determine this outcome to be a solution. In Table 12.6 the equilibrium results for Prisoner's Dilemma are summarized for six different stability analysis methods. As can be seen, outcome 0 is a cooperative solution and a nonmyopic equilibrium, but not a Stackelberg solution. Outcome 3, where both players confess, is not a cooperative solution but is a nonmyopic equilibrium and a dual Stackelberg solution.

12.6.2 Naval Conflict

This game represents the situation where a foreign trawler has been reportedly fishing illegally in territorial waters. The Coast Guard patrol tries to capture it but, as shown in Figure 12.1, an island is separating them. Each ship has to choose whether to go north or south. The foreign trawler wishes to travel in a route opposite to the Coast Guard patrol boat in order to escape; the Coast Guard patrol wants to travel in the same direction to capture the foreign trawler.

By applying a classical game theory analysis one cannot find any equilibriums to the game, as indicated in Table 12.7 for the normal form. Nevertheless, by performing a metagame analysis on this naval conflict quite different results could be obtained. It can be shown that the outcomes in which the ships go in opposite directions are rational for the trawler and general metarational for the Coast Guard patrol. The corresponding analysis of the boats traveling in the same direction shows how these outcomes are rational for the Coast Guard and general metarational for the foreign trawler. These results are summarized in Table 12.8.

Table 12.6 Summary of Stability Results for Prisoner's Dilemma

Outcome	Decimal	Nash	Metagame analysis	Conflict analysis	Non-myopic	Stackelberg
			Solution concept			
Don't confess, don't confess	0	Coop.	Equil. (if cred.)	Equil.	Equil.	—
Confess, don't confess	1	—	—	—	—	—
Don't confess, confess	2	—	—	—	—	—
Confess, confess	3	Rat'l.	Equil.	Equil.	Equil.	Dual equil.

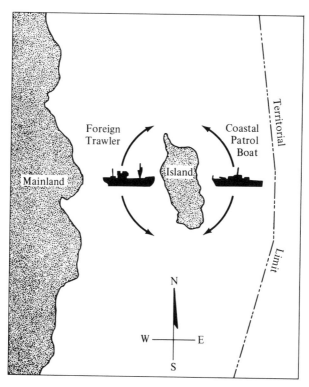

Figure 12.1 Naval Conflict.

To establish the stability of the general metarational outcomes one needs to demonstrate that the sanctions available to each player are credible by employing the conflict analysis method. This analysis is presented in Table 12.9. The bridges placed across pairs of outcomes in both preference vectors indicate that these outcomes are equally preferred by that player. Unilateral improvements do not exist between members of the equally preferred outcome sets. To perform the stability analysis in Table 12.9, the procedure presented in Chapters 1 and 2 can be used. As an example, consider the stability analysis of outcome 3 (north, north). The foreign trawler has a unilateral improvement to outcome 2. The patrol has a credible sanction to this improvement by moving from outcome 2 to outcome 0, which is equally preferred by the trawler to the initial outcome 3, thereby deterring the trawler from moving away from the particular outcome 3. A similar analysis of the rest of the outcomes show that they are also stable since all the sanctions are credible.

Table 12.7 Naval Conflict Game in Normal Form

Trawler	Coast Guard	
	North	South
North	R_B 1, 2	R_A 2, 1
South	R_A 2, 1	R_B 1, 2

Note that the stability of all the equilibriums is dependent on the idea of reflexivity presented in Section 12.2. If reflexivity were not required, all of the outcomes would be unstable, and there would be no equilibriums to the game. Reflexivity helps to ensure that this condition never occurs.

In Table 12.10 the stability results are summarized for all the techniques. There are no cooperative solutions to the game, none are nonmyopic equilibriums, and all are Stackelberg equilibriums. One concludes that any of the outcomes is a possible resolution to the naval conflict, and the actual outcome will depend on one of the players making a mistake. However, since a solution concept should always determine at least one resolution to a game, metagame analysis, conflict analysis, and Stackelberg stability all are better in this respect than the other approaches listed in Table 12.10.

12.6.3 Chicken

The game of Chicken, which has been studied extensively in game theory literature, takes its name from a daredevil automobile duel. Two drivers race directly toward one another at high speed. Each has the choice of

Table 12.8 Metagame Analysis of Naval Conflict

Outcome	Stability		
	Player A	Player B	Overall
S,S	General metarational	Rational	Equilibrium (if credible)
N,S	Rational	General metarational	Equilibrium (if credible)
S,N	Rational	General metarational	Equilibrium (if credible)
N,N	General metarational	Rational	Equilibrium (if credible)

Table 12.9 Conflict Analysis of Naval Conflict

Model				
Trawler				
North	0	1	0	1
Coast Guard				
North	0	0	1	1
Decimal	0	1	2	3
Stability analysis	E	E	E	E
	r	r	s	s
Trawler	⌐1	2⌐	⌐0	3⌐
			1	2
	r	r	s	s
Coast Guard	⌐0	3⌐	⌐1	2⌐
			3	0

either swerving and avoiding a collision or continuing straight. The game in normal form is shown in Table 12.11. There are four possible outcomes:

1. The first player does not swerve and wins; the second does swerve and is disgraced.
2. The second player does not swerve and wins; the first one does swerve and is disgraced.
3. Both drivers swerve. They both suffer some loss of prestige but the loss is less than that endured by a driver who alone plays it safe by swerving.

Table 12.10 Summary of Stability Results for the Naval Conflict

			Solution concept			
Outcome	Decimal	Nash	Metagame analysis	Conflict analysis	Non-myopic	Stackelberg
S,S	0	—	Equil. (if cred.)	Equil.	—	Equil.
N,S	1	—	Equil. (if cred.)	Equil.	—	Equil.
S,N	2	—	Equil. (if cred.)	Equil.	—	Equil.
N,N	3	—	Equil. (if cred.)	Equil.	—	Equil.

Table 12.11 Chicken in Normal Form

	Player B	
Player A	Swerve	Don't swerve
Swerve	3, 3	R_A R_B 2, 4
Don't swerve	R_A R_B 4, 2	1, 1

4. Both drivers refuse to swerve and thus have a head-on collision. This is the worst outcome for both.

Studies by Rapoport et al. (1976) indicate that under particular experimental conditions the outcomes appear as resolutions to the conflict in the following proportions:

43%: the first player swerves;

41%: the second player swerves;

5%: both players swerve; and

10%: the players crash.

The only explanation for the discrepancy between the percentages for the first and second players swerving alone is experimental error. The experiment involved multiple trials with 10 pairs of players.

When making a normal form analysis, two outcomes are found to be rational for both players, as seen in Table 12.11. These are the situations

Table 12.12 Metagame Analyses of Chicken

	Stability		
Outcome	Player A	Player B	Overall
Don't swerve, don't swerve	Unstable	Unstable	No
Swerve, don't swerve	Rational	Rational	Equilibrium
Don't swerve, swerve	Rational	Rational	Equilibrium
Swerve, swerve	Symmetric metarational	Symmetric metarational	Equilibrium (if credible)

Table 12.13 Conflict Analysis of Chicken

Model				
Player A				
Swerve	0	1	0	1
Player B				
Swerve	0	0	1	1
Decimal	0	1	2	3
Stability analysis	E	E	E	×
	r	~~r~~	r	u
Player A	2	3	1	0
		2		1
	r	~~r~~	r	u
Player B	1	3	2	0
		1		2

in which only one of the drivers swerves and the other continues on the road. The case where both players decide to swerve is not rational since each one has the incentive to remain on course and win the game. The traditional metagame analysis of Chicken suggests three possible resolutions which are described in Table 12.12. In addition to the two outcomes that are rational for both players, the third outcome of (swerve, swerve) is also suggested as an equilibrium. The outcome is symmetric metarational for both players due to the idea that each player would not improve from the outcome to the condition of "don't swerve" because of the sanction of the other player also changing strategy, resulting in the least

Table 12.14 Summary of Stability Results for Chicken

		Solution Concept				
Outcome	Decimal	Nash	Metagame analysis	Conflict analysis	Nonmyopic	Stackelberg
Don't swerve, don't swerve	0	—	—	—	—	—
Swerve, don't swerve	1	Rat'l.	Equil.	Equil.	—	Equil.
Don't swerve, swerve	2	Rat'l.	Equil.	Equil.	—	Equil.
Swerve, swerve	3	—	Equil. (if cred.)	Equil.	Equil.	—

Table 12.15 Cookie Conflict in Normal Form

		Child B	
Child A		Hit A	Don't hit A
Take cookie		R_A 2, 2	R_A R_B 4, 3
Don't take cookie		1, 1	R_B 3, 4

preferable outcome of a crash. This sanction may be considered either credible or noncredible, depending on the point of view of the analyst.

Table 12.13 contains the complete stability analysis of Chicken using the conflict analysis technique. Note that outcome 3 (swerve, swerve) in the analysis of Table 12.13 was initially unstable for both players, and so simultaneous stability was checked. The outcome resulting from both players simultaneously improving from outcome 3 is calculated from equation (1-1) or (11-4) to be $2 + 1 - 3 = 0$. Since outcome 0 is not preferred by either of the players over 3, outcome 3 is simultaneously stable for both, as indicated by the $\cancel{/}$ above the 3 in each player's preference vector in Table 12.13. As opposed to the traditional metagame analysis of this outcome, here the credibility of this outcome is not ambiguous. It is a possible equilibrium since each player may indeed be credibly deterred from moving back on course by the fact that the other player could also change strategy, resulting in the collision.

In Table 12.14 the results of all the approaches can be seen. Note that each outcome is rejected as a resolution to the conflict by at least one of the solution concepts. Chicken is a very subtle game that is not suitably modeled by any of these approaches, as can be seen in the experimental results. In Chapter 14, another model is proposed for Chicken that is much better at presenting this problem.

Table 12.16 Metagame Analyses of Cookie Conflict

		Stability	
Outcome	Player A	Player B	Overall
Don't take, don't hit	Symmetric metarational	Rational	Equilibrium (if credible)
Take, don't hit	Rational	Rational	Equilibrium
Don't take, hit	Unstable	Unstable	No
Take, hit	Rational	Unstable	No

12.6.4 Cookie Conflict

In this conflict there are two children, one of whom has a cookie that the other child wants (Fraser and Hipel, 1979a). Child A would prefer to obtain the cookie as long as it does not entail being hit by child B. Child B would like to retain the cookie but would rather let A have it than hit him (or her). The normal form of this game is shown in Table 12.15, where it can be seen that the only Nash equilibrium is when child A takes the cookie and child B does not hit him.

The results of the traditional metagame analysis of this conflict are shown in Table 12.16. Using metagame analysis one can find that the outcome where child A does not take the cookie and child B does not hit him is a second possible equilibrium. The analysis of this outcome indicates that this outcome is the most preferred for child B and hence is stable for him (or her). Child A has a UI from (don't take, don't hit) to (take, don't hit), but child B has an inescapable sanction by changing strategy and deciding to hit A. Thus (don't take, don't hit) is symmetric metarational for child A, and is an overall equilibrium if the sanction is credible.

The use of the new technique shows that the sanction described above is not credible, since it takes into account that child B prefers not to hit even when child A takes the cookie (Fraser and Hipel, 1979a). From Table 12.17 one sees that child A can improve from outcome 0 (don't take, don't hit) by moving to outcome 1 (take, don't hit), and that child B does not have any credible sanction from 1 to deter child A from taking this improvement. The results shown in Table 12.17 indicate that the only equilibrium is outcome 1, in which child A takes the cookie and is not hit by B.

Table 12.17 Conflict Analysis of Cookie Conflict

Model				
Child A				
Take	0	1	0	1
Child B				
Hit	0	0	1	1
Decimal	0	1	2	3
Stability analysis	E	×	×	×
Child A	r	u	r	u
	1	0	3	2
	1			3
Child B	r	r	u	u
	0	1	3	2
		1	1	0

The stability results for all the techniques used to analyze the Cookie Conflict are displayed in Table 12.18. All of the solution concepts except metagame analysis agree that outcome 0 is not a resolution to the conflict. For this reason, the Cookie Conflict is said to show the "breakdown of metarationality."

12.7 Important Concepts from Chapter 12

Conflict analysis is the practical application of mathematical game theory to real world problems. The conflict analysis method was developed directly from the mathematical basis of metagame theory and incorporates only procedural and notational changes. Also, the approach is inherently rational since the analysis always assumes that the players will act in such a manner as to secure for themselves the most preferable outcomes possible.

Conflict analysis avoids two of the basic assumptions that have held back the practical application of much of game theory. The first assumption is that of *utility*, a number attached to an outcome to represent the worth of the outcome to a player. Conflict analysis requires only an ordinal ranking of outcomes, which is much easier to determine in real world problems.

The second assumption is that of *transitivity*, which requires that if outcome p is preferred to q and q is preferred to r, then p is preferred to r. This type of preference structure is not always found in the real world, and conflict analysis can easily handle any intransitivities that may arise.

A number of solution concepts for predicting equilibriums have been developed from game theory, including the following:

1. *Nash equilibriums* (outcomes that are rational for all players);
2. *Metagame equilibriums* (see Chapters 10 and 11);
3. *Nonmyopic equilibriums* (determined by imagining an extensive game tree showing the players alternating their strategies, and then determining the solution using backward induction); and

Table 12.18 Summary of Stability Results for the Cookie Conflict

Outcome	Decimal	Nash	Solution concept Metagame analysis	Conflict analysis	Non-myopic	Stackelberg
Don't take, don't hit	0	—	Equil. (if cred.)	—	—	—
Take, don't hit	1	Rat'l.	Equil.	Equil.	Equil.	Dual equil.
Don't take, hit	2	—	—	—	—	—
Take, hit	3	—	—	—	—	—

4. *Stackelberg equilibriums* (outcomes that are the best choice for a player given that the best response of the other player is known).

The set of equilibriums determined using conflict analysis generally includes all reasonable equilibriums defined by these stability concepts. It was shown that for practical reasons conflict analysis equilibriums are not always Pareto optimal. Also, equilibriums based on inducement will always be included in the set of conflict analysis equilibriums.

Four games that have often been discussed in the game theory literature—the Prisoner's Dilemma, the Naval Conflict, Chicken, and the Cookie Conflict—were analyzed in detail using the normal form, metagame analysis, and conflict analysis. The results for nonmyopia and Stackelberg equilibriums were also presented. The results for each of these games for the various approaches are detailed in Tables 12.6, 12.10, 12.14, and 12.18, respectively. From these tables it is evident that overall the most realistic and comprehensive approach to use for solving any of the famous games is the conflict analysis technique.

Questions

1. Determine the Nash and Stackelberg equilibriums for the Cuban missile crisis of Chapter 1. Are these solutions Pareto optimal?
2. Consider a game in which there are two players, A and B. If A has a UI from outcome q to outcome p, and B has a UI from p to r such that r is less preferable to A than q, then q is judged to be stable if A has no more UIs available from q. However, imagine that A also has a UI from r to outcome s, which is more preferable to A than q. Similarly to inducement, A could take the original deterred UI from q to p in the expectation of achieving outcome s.

   Explain why this logic will never result in more equilibriums being determined in a stability analysis.

Chapter 13
Solution Procedures
for Noncooperative Games

13.1 Introduction

Because of the great need to study conflict in many different fields, various game theoretical techniques have been developed for modeling disputes and their resolutions. Since the pioneering work of von Neumann and Morgenstern (1953), a number of interesting solution concepts have been formulated. However, the exact mathematical relationships among many of the procedures used in noncooperative game theory have not been previously available, and as a result both mathematicians and practitioners are sometimes unsure which techniques are most promising for theoretical study and practical application. Accordingly, the main purpose of this chapter is to compare rigorously the solution concepts from noncooperative game theory that were introduced in Chapter 12.

In the ensuing sections, individual and group stability concepts are defined, compared mathematically, and evaluated for ordinal and strict ordinal preferences in n-person, 2-person, and 2×2 noncooperative games. For n-person games, solution procedures from classical game theory (Von Neumann and Morgenstern, 1953), metagame analysis (Howard, 1971), and conflict analysis (Fraser and Hipel, 1979a) are compared. In addition to the types of stability considered for n-person games, the method of Stackelberg (Basar and Olsder, 1982; Henderson and Quandt, 1971) is also studied in 2-person games. The other stability approaches that are discussed for 2×2 games are the nonmyopic (Brams and Wittman, 1984) and extended nonmyopic (Kilgour, 1984) methods. Appendix E presents lists of games that constitute examples of the existence assertions made during the course of the chapter. Appendix F includes an examination of all of the solution concepts in the context of no-conflict games and games of complete opposition, where their results can be compared with pre-conceived notions of what should constitute a resolution. Further details about the results in this chapter and Appendix F are given in the paper by Kilgour et al. (1984).

13.2 Definitions and Conventions

A conventional view of a conflict situation consists of a group of decision makers who have different objectives and who can take actions that to-gether determine the outcome. To set up a frame of reference for the various mathematical concepts that have been used to model stability in conflict situations, it is first necessary to define terms. These definitions all correspond to general usage in the game theory literature and have been chosen to facilitate the comparison among the stability concepts.

If $n \geq 2$ is an integer, an n-person (or n-player) *game* is a finite ordinal noncooperative game defined by

$$G = (S_1, \ldots, S_n; v_1, \ldots, v_n),$$

where the n-person game G has the player set $N = \{1, 2, \ldots, n\}$. For each player $i \in N$, S_i is a finite nonvoid set called i's *strategy set*. Each player i controls the choice of his (or her) strategy $s_i \in S_i$. If $H \subseteq N$, where $H \neq \emptyset$, the set of strategies of the players of H is $S_H = \underset{i \in H}{\mathsf{X}} S_i$.

The set of *outcomes* is $S = S_N$. When every player $I \in N$ has indepen-dently selected a strategy $s_i \in S_i$, an outcome $s = (s_1, s_2, \ldots, s_n) \in S$ is specified. For each $i \in N$, player i's *payoff function* is $v_i: S \to \mathbb{R}$ so that the worth of outcome s to player i is indicated by $v_i(s)$. Thus, i prefers $s^1 \in S$ to $s^2 \in S$, or is indifferent between s^1 and s^2, if and only if (iff) $v_i(s^1) \geq v_i(s^2)$. Note that although a player's preferences among outcomes are specified by his payoff function, cardinal utilities are not assumed. The payoff function is simply a mathematical convenience for indicating preference ordering. For the purposes of this chapter, the payoff function definition is a more convenient way of expressing preferences than the set definition $[M_i^+(q)$, etc.] used in previous chapters.

The distinction between the general case of ordinal games and the special case of strict ordinal games will sometimes be important. For $i \in N$, the game G is *strict ordinal for i* iff i is never indifferent between distinct outcomes [i.e., $v_i(s^1) = v_i(s^2)$ iff $s^1 = s^2$]. G is *strict ordinal* iff it is strict ordinal for i for each $i \in N$. Consequently, games that are ordinal may have outcomes that are equally preferred by some players; games that are strict ordinal never do.

One further notational convenience will be useful. If $s \in S$ and $H \subseteq N, H \neq \emptyset$, the *projection* of s on S_H is denoted by s_H, and s can be written as $s = (s_H, s_{N-H})$. Thus, if the outcome is $s \in S$, the joint strategy of the players in H is $s_H \in S_H$, and so on. If $i \in N$, the distinction between *i* and {*i*} is suppressed so that $s = (s_i, s_{N-i})$. Also, $v_i[(s_H, s_{N-H})] = v_i(s_H, s_{N-H})$.

13.3 Stability Concepts in *n*-Person Games

The most general kind of ordinal game to be treated here allows any finite number of players and any finite number of strategies for each player. These games are generally called *n-person games*. There is a limited number of stability concepts that have been developed for these games.

For an outcome to be stable for a player (i.e., individually stable), it must possess specific characteristics as required by some stability criterion. For an outcome to be stable for the game (i.e., group stable), it must be stable according to the criterion for every player in the game. A group stable outcome is sometimes be called an *equilibrium*. The two aspects of stability are examined separately.

13.3.1 Individual Stability Concepts

Three distinct groups of stability criteria have been developed for *n*-person games. The first idea was based on a simple view of *rationality*, which can be defined as behavior characterized as follows: "Of two alternatives which give rise to outcomes, a player will choose the one which yields the more preferred outcome" (Luce and Raiffa, 1957). As Luce and Raiffa (1957) point out elsewhere in their well-known book, rationality means many different things in various theories, but the above phrase is consistent with most approaches to rationality in the literature. Nash (1950b, 1951) formalized this concept into an individual stability criterion.

Definition 13.1. For a player $i \in N$ and an outcome $\bar{s} \in S$, a strategy $s_i \in S_i$ is a *unilateral improvement* (UI) for *i* from $\bar{s}$ iff $v_i(s_i, \bar{s}_{N-i}) > v_i(\bar{s})$.

Definition 13.2. For $i \in N$, an outcome $\bar{s} \in S$ is *rational* (R) *for i* iff there exists no UI for *i* from $\bar{s}$ (Nash, 1951).

Equivalently, $\bar{s}$ is R for *i* iff $v_i(s_i, s_{N-i}) \leq v_i(\bar{s}) \ \forall \ s_i \in S_i$.

Thus an outcome is R for a player if and only if it is the best that he (or she) can achieve, given the strategies of the other players. Therefore, outcomes that are not R are unstable since the player can unilaterally improve his position.

While there is considerable appeal in the notion that an outcome is stable for a player who has no UIs from it, the converse is not so easy to accept. Rationality, as defined in Section 13.2, entails a very short-sighted viewpoint since it does not take into account the possible responses to a unilateral improvement by a player. Howard (1971) argued that not only would such reactions be important to players, but that they would take such considerations into account in advance of selecting a strategy in the game. His *metagame analysis* formalized these considerations into two additional criteria for stability, called *symmetric metarationality* and *general metarationality*. Both criteria imply that a player can find certain outcomes not to be rational (R) and yet stable nonetheless. The first idea from Howard's metagame analysis is general metarationality.

Definition 13.3. If $i \in N$, $\bar{s} \in S$, and s_i is a UI for i from $\bar{s}$, then $s_{N-i} \in S_{N-i}$ is a *sanction* against s_i iff $v_i(s_i, s_{N-i}) \leq v_i(\bar{s})$ (Howard, 1971).

Definition 13.4. Let $i \in N$. An outcome $\bar{s} \in S$ is *general metarational* (GMR) *for i* iff for every UI, s_i, for i from $\bar{s}$ there exists a sanction against s_i (Howard, 1971).

Equivalently, $\bar{s}$ is GMR for i iff

$$\forall s_i \in S_i: \; \exists \; v_i(s_i, \bar{s}_{N-i}) > v_i(\bar{s}),$$
$$\exists \; s_{N-i} \in S_{N-i}: \; \exists \; v_i(s_i, s_{N-i}) \leq v_i(\bar{s}).$$

Define player i's *maximin* value to be

$$\text{maxmin}_i = \max_{s_i \in S_i} \; \min_{s_{N-i} \in S_{N-i}} \; v_i(s_i, s_{N-i}).$$

Then Howard (1971) showed

Theorem 13.5. $\bar{s}$ *is GMR for* i *iff* $v_i (\bar{s}) \geq maxmin_i$.

Howard's second stability concept is symmetric metarationality.

Definition 13.6. Let $i \in N$. An outcome $\bar{s} \in S$ is *symmetric metarational* (SMR) *for i* iff there exists $s^*_{N-i} \in S_{N-i}$ such that $v_i (s_i, s^*_{N-i}) \leq v_i (\bar{s})$ for every $s_i \in S$ (Howard, 1971).

Equivalently, $\bar{s}$ is SMR for i iff there is an "inescapable sanction" s^*_{N-i} against every possible strategy of i, including those that are not UIs from $\bar{s}$. Define player i's *minimax* value to be

$$\text{minmax}_i = \min_{s_{N-i} \in S_{N-i}} \; \max_{s_i \in S_i} \; v_i (s_i, s_{N-i}).$$

It is not difficult to show that $\text{maxmin}_i \leq \text{minmax}_i$. Howard (1971, p. 106) observed

Theorem 13.7. $\bar{s}$ *is SMR for* i *iff* $v_i (\bar{s}) \geq minmax_i$.

An outcome is general metarational for a player when, for each of his (or her) UIs, if any, the other players have a joint response that puts him in a position no better for him than the original outcome. An outcome that is symmetric metarational for the player has the additional feature that the player has no subsequent strategy selection that can result in an outcome he prefers to the original outcome after the other players have sanctioned the original UI.

Theorem 13.8. *Let* i $\in$ N *and* $\bar{s}$ $\in$ S. *If* $\bar{s}$ *is* R *for* i, *then* $\bar{s}$ *is SMR for* i, *and if* $\bar{s}$ *is SMR for* i, *then* $\bar{s}$ *is GMR for* i *(Howard, 1971).*

PROOF: If $\bar{s}$ is R for *i*, then choose $s^*_{N-i} = \bar{s}_{N-i}$ to show that $\bar{s}$ is SMR for *i*. If $\bar{s}$ is SMR for *i* and s_i is a UI for *i* from $\bar{s}$, than s^*_{N-i} is a sanction against s_i so that $\bar{s}$ is GMR for *i*. Equivalently, this can be proved using the results of Theorems 13.5 and 13.7, and the fact that maxmin$_i$ $\leq$ minmax$_i$. $\square$

Metarationality, both general and symmetric, postulates that a player may choose to stay at an outcome, even when he has a UI available, for fear that the other players will act together to put him ultimately in a less preferred position. No formal procedure is provided for determining whether a sanction would in fact be carried out, particularly if it actually hurt the player or players who might invoke it. From a practical point of view, this results in the empirical fact that most outcomes in a game are R, SMR, or GMR for at least some players.

Fraser and Hipel (1979a) proposed stability concepts in which players consider whether sanctions are reasonable. Their stability criterion includes R outcomes, *sequentially stable* outcomes, and *simultaneously stable* outcomes. Unlike the other stability concepts presented here, simultaneous stability exists as a group stability concept only, and its definition is deferred to Section 13.3.2. The development of sequential stability begins with the definition of a credible response.

Definition 13.9. For $\bar{s}$ $\in$ S and H $\subseteq$ N, H $\neq$ $\emptyset$, a *credible response of* H *to* $\bar{s}$ is a member of $C_H(\bar{s})$ $\subseteq$ S, defined inductively by

(i) $\bar{s}$ $\in$ $C_H(\bar{s})$;
(ii) if s $\in$ $C_H(\bar{s})$, i $\in$ H, and s'_i is a UI for *i* from s, then (s'_i, s_{N-i}) $\in$ $C_H(\bar{s})$ (Fraser and Hipel, 1979a).

A credible response by an individual player to an outcome is simply the outcome resulting from a UI by that player. Thus, when a player makes a UI, a credible response by a second player to the outcome resulting from that UI is the subsequent outcome after a UI by the second player. In a two-person game, every credible response by a player after a UI by his opponent is the result of a subsequent UI by the responding player. When a player in a game with more than two players makes a UI, a credible response by a set of several of the other players to the outcome resulting from the original UI is the result of any sequence of UIs by some or all of the players in the set. Note that in this sequence the same player may make UIs more than once. The key principle is that each player who acts must act unilaterally to improve his own position. Two useful observations follow directly from Definition 13.9.

Theorem 13.10. *If* s $\in$ S, H' $\subseteq$ H $\subseteq$ N *and* H' $\neq$ $\emptyset$, *then* $C_{H'}$ (s) $\subseteq$ C_H(s).

Theorem 13.11. *Let* s $\in$ S *and* H $\subseteq$ N, H $\neq$ $\emptyset$. *If* s' $\in$ C_H(s), *then* C_H(s') $\subseteq$ C_H(s).

Definition 13.12. Let $i \in N$, $\bar{s} \in S$, and suppose that $s_i \in S_i$ is a UI for i from $\bar{s}$. Then $s_{N-i} \in S_{N-i}$ is a *credible sanction* against s_i iff s_{N-i} is a sanction against s_i and (s_i, s_{N-i}) is a credible response of $N - i$ to $(s_i, \bar{s}_{N-i})$ (Fraser and Hipel, 1979a).

Thus a sanction s_{N-i} against a UI s_i from $\bar{s}$ is a credible response iff $(s_i, s_{N-i}) \in C_{N-i}(s_i, \bar{s}_{N-i})$.

Definition 13.13. Let $i \in N$. An outcome $\bar{s} \in S$ is *sequentially stable* [FHQ (Fraser-Hipel seQuential)] *for* i iff for every UI, s_i, for i from $\bar{s}$ there exists a credible sanction against s_i (Fraser and Hipel, 1979a).

Accordingly, an outcome is FHQ for a player if and only if, for each of the player's UIs, the other players can, by a sequence of individual unilateral improvements, attain an outcome that is not preferred to the original outcome by the first player.

The relationships between FHQ and the previous stability concepts are given by

Theorem 13.14. *Let* i $\in$ N *and* $\bar{s} \in$ S. *If* $\bar{s}$ *is R for* i, *then* $\bar{s}$ *is FHQ for* i, *and if* $\bar{s}$ *is FHQ for* i, *then* $\bar{s}$ *is GMR for* i.

PROOF: If $\bar{s}$ is R for i, then Definition 13.13 is satisfied trivially since i has no UIs. Since a credible sanction is a sanction, an outcome that is FHQ for i must also be GMR for i. $\qquad\square$

An additional concept related to sequential stability will be useful below:

Definition 13.15. Let $i \in N$, $\bar{s} \in S$, and suppose that $s_i \in S_i$ is a UI for i from $\bar{s}$. Then s_i is an *inescapable improvement* (II) for i from $\bar{s}$ iff there exists no credible sanction against s_i (Howard, 1971; Fraser and Hipel, 1979a).

Theorem 13.16. *Let* i ∈ N *and* s̄ ∈ S; *then* s̄ *is not FHQ for* i *iff there exists an II for* i *from* s̄.

PROOF: Immediate from Definitions 13.13 and 13.15. ☐

The consequences of Theorems 13.8 and 13.14 are illustrated in Figure 13.1. It is easy to show that the results of Theorems 13.8 and 13.14 cannot be improved using the examples given in Appendix E, which illustrate that there are no inclusion relationships among stability types other than those given in Theorem 13.8 and 13.14. Note that for every player in every game there is an outcome, namely *i*'s most preferred outcome, that is R for *i*, and therefore FHQ, SMR, and GMR for *i*.

Note on Metagame Analysis: In Definitions 13.5 and 13.7, GMR and SMR outcomes are defined. These definitions are presented simply as assumptions about how an individual might find a particular outcome of a conflict situation to be stable. As described in Chapter 10, Howard (1971) developed an elaborate theory to arrive at, and justify, these definitions. For a basic game *G*, Howard considered how one player could "react" to the possible strategies of the other players to form a first level metagame. Since reactions could be built upon other players' reactions, an infinite metagame tree could be constructed. By considering rational (R) outcomes for each player in a given metagame in the tree, Howard firmly connected his theory to the classical idea of rationality. The mapping of the rational outcomes for player *i* in any metagame back to *G* allows the determination of the metarational outcomes in *G* for *i*. According to the Characterization Theorem (Howard, 1971; Appendix D),

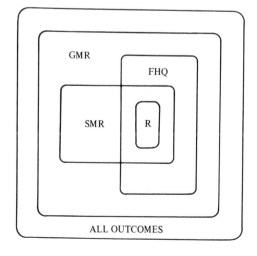

Figure 13.1 Individual stability concepts in *n*-person games.

it is necessary only to examine G to find all the metarational outcomes for i that can be R, SMR, or GMR.

The conflict analysis algorithm is not derived from some type of infinite metagame tree since this step is unnecessary. Rather, a reasonable definition for a credible response in Definition 13.9, followed by what is meant by a credible sanction in Definition 13.12, are all that is required to define FHQ in Definition 13.13. To complete the conflict analysis, simultaneous sanctioning is defined next.

13.3.2 Group Stability Concepts

If an outcome is individually stable for a player according to some stability criterion, the player is then content, according to that criterion, to remain at the outcome rather than to move unilaterally to another outcome. However, for an outcome to be stable overall, it must be individually stable for every player in the game. Thus an outcome has group stability of a particular type if and only if it has individual stability of that type for every player.

Definition 13.17. An outcome $\bar{s} \in S$ is *rational* (R) iff it is R for i for each $i \in N$; $\bar{s}$ is *general metarational* (GMR) iff it is GMR for i for each $i \in N$; $\bar{s}$ is *symmetric metarational* (SMR) iff it is SMR for i for each $i \in N$; $\bar{s}$ is *sequentially stable* (FHQ) iff it is FHQ for i for each $i \in N$.

Then Theorems 13.8 and 13.14 yield

Theorem 13.18. *Let* $\bar{s} \in S$. *If* $\bar{s}$ *is R, then* $\bar{s}$ *is SMR, and if* $\bar{s}$ *is SMR, then* $\bar{s}$ *is GMR.*

Theorem 13.19. *Let* $\bar{s} \in S$. *If* $\bar{s}$ *is R, then* $\bar{s}$ *is FHQ, and if* $\bar{s}$ *is FHQ, then* $\bar{s}$ *is GMR.*

Fraser and Hipel (1979a) introduced a form of stability defined only at the group level, induced by credible sanctions that occur simultaneously, rather than in sequence.

Definition 13.20. For $i \in N$ and $\bar{s} \in S$, let $S_i^*(\bar{s}) \subseteq S_i$ denote the set of all inescapable improvements for i from $\bar{s}$. Let $M(\bar{s}) = \{i \in N : S_i^*(\bar{s}) \neq \emptyset\}$, and, if $H \subseteq M(\bar{s})$, $H \neq \emptyset$, define $S_i^*(\bar{s}) = \underset{i \in H}{X} S_i^*(\bar{s})$.

Observe that, by Theorem 13.16, $S_i^*(\bar{s}) = \emptyset$ iff $\bar{s}$ is FHQ for i. Thus $M(\bar{s})$ is the set of all players for whom $\bar{s}$ is not FHQ.

Definition 13.21. An outcome $\bar{s} \in S$ is *simultaneously stable* [FHM (Fraser-Hipel siMultaneous)] iff $|M(\bar{s})| \geq 2$ and, whenever $i \in M(\bar{s})$, then for all $s_i \in S_i^*(\bar{s})$, there exists $H \subseteq M(\bar{s}) - i$, $H \neq \emptyset$, such that for some $s_H \in S_H^*(\bar{s})$, $v_i(s_i, s_H, \bar{s}_{N-H-i}) \leq v_i(\bar{s})$ (Fraser and Hipel, 1979a).

To determine whether an outcome is FHM first verify that there are two or more players for whom the outcome is not FHQ. This is because if simultaneous actions are to represent sanctions, there must be at least two players who could improve simultaneously. Then, for each II of each player who has one, examine the outcomes that could result from that II together with every possible combination of the IIs of every possible combination of the other players who have them. If some outcome produced by these strategy combinations is not preferred to the original outcome by the original player, then the original II is simultaneously sanctioned. If every II of every player who has one is simultaneously sanctioned, then the outcome is FHM.

Theorem 13.22. *Let* $\bar{s} \in S$. *If* $\bar{s}$ *is FHM, then* $\bar{s}$ *is GMR but* $\bar{s}$ *is not FHQ.*

PROOF: That $\bar{s}$ is not FHQ for at least two players is evident from Definition 13.21 and the remarks following Definition 13.20. Now if $i \notin M(\bar{s})$, $\bar{s}$ is GMR for i by Theorem 13.14. Suppose that $i \in M(\bar{s})$ and that s_i is a UI for i from $\bar{s}$. If $s_i \notin S_i^*(\bar{s})$, then there exists a credible sanction against s_i, and therefore a sanction, by Definition 13.12. If $s_i \in S_i^*(\bar{s})$, then $s_{N-i} = (s_H, \bar{s}_{N-H-i}) \in S_{N-i}$ is a sanction against s_i by Definition 13.21. Thus $\bar{s}$ is GMR for $i \in M(\bar{s})$, so that $\bar{s}$ is GMR. $\qquad\square$

Figure 13.2 illustrates the findings of Theorems 13.18, 13.19, and 13.22. Notice that the relationships among group stability concepts are identical to those among the corresponding individual stability concepts, so that the distinction between Figures 13.1 and 13.2 lies only in the appearance of the new group stability concept FHM in Figure 13.2. It is shown by example in Appendix E that the results of Theorems 13.18, 13.19, and 13.22 cannot be improved. It is easy to show that there are games with no SMR outcomes (and therefore no R outcomes) and that there are games with no FHM outcomes. The next result shows that every game has at least one outcome that is FHQ (and therefore GMR).

Theorem 13.23. *Every game has an FHQ outcome.*

PROOF: (Fraser and Hipel, 1979a). There must be a player, $i_1 \in N$, and an outcome $s \in S$, such that s is not FHQ for i_1 (otherwise there would be nothing to prove). Let q^1 denote an outcome most preferred by i_1 [i.e., maximizing $v_{i_1}(\cdot)$] among all those that are not FHQ for i_1. By definition

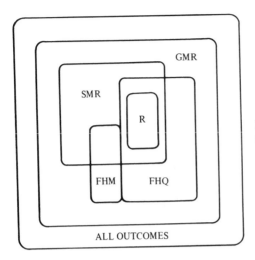

Figure 13.2 Group stability concepts in n-person games.

13.15, an II for i_1 from q^1, say $\bar{s}_{i_1} \in S_{i_1}$, must exist. Let $p^1 = (\bar{s}_{i_1}, q^1_{N-i_1})$. Since p^1 is preferred by i_1 to q^1, p^1 is FHQ for i_1. Define $N_1 = N - i_1$. If, for every $k \in N_1$, p^1 if FHQ for k, then the proof is complete. Otherwise a player $i_2 \in N_1$ can be identified such that p^1 is not FHQ for i_2. It is now shown that if $s \in C_{N_1}(p^1)$, then s is FHQ for i_1. If $s = p^1$, this has already been shown; otherwise, note first that $v_{i_1}(s) > v_{i_1}(q^1)$. (If this inequality were false, then s_{N-i_1} would be a credible sanction against the II $\bar{s}_{i_1}$.) Since s is preferred by i_1 to get q^1, s is FHQ for i_1.

Now assume that, for $1 \leq j < n$, there are distinct players $i_1, i_2, \ldots,$ i_{j+1} and an outcome p^j such that p^j is not FHQ for i_{j+1} and, if $N_j = N - i_1 - i_2 - \cdots - i_j$ and $s \in C_{N_j}(p^j)$, then s is FHQ for i_h, for $h = 1, 2, \ldots, j$. Let q^{j+1} denote an outcome of $C_{N_j}(p^j)$ most preferred by i_{j+1} among all those that are not FHQ for i_{j+1}. There is at least one such outcome in $C_{N_j}(p^j)$, namely p^j. By Definition 13.15, an II for i_{j+1} from q^{j+1}, say $\bar{s}_{i_{j+1}} \in S_{i_{j+1}}$, must exist. Let $p^{j+1} = (\bar{s}_{i_{j+1}}, q^{j+1}_{N-i_{j+1}})$. Observe that $p^{j+1} \in C_{N_j}(p^j)$ because $q^{j+1} \in C_{N_j}(p^j)$ and $p^{j+1} \in C_{i_{j+1}}(q^{j+1}) \subseteq C_{N_j}(q^{j+1}) \subseteq C_{N_j}(p^j)$, by Theorems 13.10 and 13.11. Since $v_{i_{j+1}}(p^{j+1}) > v_{i_{j+1}}(q^{j+1})$, p^{j+1} is FHQ for i_{j+1}, and by the induction hypothesis, p^{j+1} is FHQ for i_h, for $h = 1, 2, \ldots, j$. Let $N_{j+1} = N_j - i_{j+1}$. If either $j = n - 1$ or p^{j+1} is FHQ for k, for every $k \in N_{j+1}$, the proof is complete. Otherwise there is a player $i_{j+2} \in N_{j+1}$ such that p^{j+1} is not FHQ for i_{j+2}. To complete the induction, it is necessary to show that if $s \in C_{N_{j+1}}(p^{j+1})$, then s is FHQ for i_h, for $h = 1, 2, \ldots, j + 1$. That this assertion is true when $s = p^{j+1}$ has already been shown. If $h = 1, 2, \ldots, j$,

$$s \in C_{N_{j+1}}(p^{j+1}) \subseteq C_{N_j}(p^{j+1}) \quad \text{(by Theorem 13.10)}$$
$$\subseteq C_{N_j}(p^j) \quad \text{(by Theorem 13.11)},$$

[since $p^{j+1} \in C_{N_j}(p^j)$], so that s is FHQ for i_h by the induction hypothesis. Now assume that $h = j + 1$ and $s \neq p^{j+1}$. Since

$$s \in C_{N_{j+1}}(p^{j+1}) \subseteq C_{N-i_{j+1}}(p^{j+1}) \qquad \text{(by Theorem 13.10)},$$

then $v_{i_{j+1}}(s) > v_{i_{j+1}}(q^{j+1})$, because, if this inequality were false, then $s_{N-i_{j+1}}$ would be a credible sanction against $s_{i_{j+1}} = \bar{s}_{i_{j+1}}$, which has no sanctions. Since $s \in C_{N_j}(p^j)$ and s is preferred by i_{j+1} to q^{j+1}, s is FHQ for i_{j+1}. $\qquad \Box$

This existence proof for FHQ outcomes is quite significant. Any procedure that attempts to describe the behavior of players of a game should determine at least one group stable outcome. This is because, in the real world situation that the game models, some outcome presumably does occur. The sequential stability (FHQ) approach is the most restrictive basic stability concept known that guarantees at least one group stable outcome for n-person games where the players have ordinal preferences.

13.4 Stability Concepts in Two-Person Games

When more restrictive assumptions are made about the game model being used, some additional stability concepts can be defined. The majority of these are limited to games that involve two players each having a choice between two strategies, for a total of four possible outcomes. These 2×2 games are the subject of Section 13.5. Besides the stability concepts from Section 13.3, there is one stability criterion that applies to games involving only two players but any number of strategies (or options). This is attributed to von Stackelberg (Henderson and Quandt, 1971; Basar and Olsder, 1982) and is often referred to as *Stackelberg stability*.

For 2-person games, additional conventions are introduced for convenience. If a player $i \in N$ has been identified, i's coplayer is denoted by j (rather than $N-i$). The definitions and theorems of Section 13.3 are easily specialized to the case $n = 2$. For example, there is considerable simplification in the notion of a credible response in Definition 13.9 since $s \in C_{N-i}(\bar{s}) = C_j(\bar{s})$ iff $v_j(s) > v_j(\bar{s})$ or $s = \bar{s}$.

To define Stackelberg stability formally, the idea of an optimal reaction must first be introduced.

Definition 13.24. Let $i \in N$ and $s_i \in S$. An *optimal reaction of j against s_i* is a member of $R_j(s_i) \subseteq S_j$, defined by

$$R_j(s_i) = \{s_j : v_j(s_i, s_j) \geq v_j(s_i, s_j') \ \forall \ s_j' \in S_j\}.$$

Observe that if $\bar{s} \in S$, then $s_j \in R_j(\bar{s}_i)$ implies $(\bar{s}_i, s_j) \in C_j(\bar{s})$ iff either $\bar{s}_j \notin R_j(\bar{s}_i)$ or $|R_j(\bar{s}_i)| = 1$. in other words, every optimal reaction to $\bar{s}_i$

is a credible response to $\bar{s}$ unless $\bar{s}_j$ is already an optimal reaction and there are other optimal reactions.

Von Stackelberg's stability concept depends crucially on the principle of an optimal reaction.

Definition 13.25. Let $i \in N$. An outcome $\bar{s} \in S$ is *stable in the sense of von Stackelberg* (ST) *for* i iff

(i) $\bar{s}_j \in R_j(\bar{s}_i)$ and
(ii) $\min\limits_{s_j \in R_j(\bar{s}_i)} v_i(\bar{s}_i, s_j) = \max\limits_{s_i \in S_i} \min\limits_{s_j \in R_j(s_i)} v_i(s_i, s_j)$.

To determine Stackelberg stability for i, consider i to be the *leader* and j the *follower*. The leader will choose his (or her) best strategy, bearing in mind that the follower will optimize his position subject to the strategy chosen by the leader. In other words, the leader selects his best strategy knowing what the reaction of the follower will be to his move. Additionally, if the follower has a number of reactions available that are of equal value to him, the leader conservatively assumes that the follower will choose the optimal reaction least preferred by the leader.

Originally, Stackelberg stability was defined only for strict ordinal games (Henderson and Quandt, 1971). However, to be consistent with the other stability concepts presented in this chapter, the original definition for Stackelberg stability has been extended to apply to games that are not strict ordinal as well. This has been done in a manner consistent with many game theoretic definitions in that it assumes that the players act conservatively. Other ways to extend Stackelberg for ordinal games are possible. Basar and Olsder (1982) discuss analogous extensions of Stackelberg stability to the n-person case.

Theorem 13.26. *Let* $i \in N$ *and* $\bar{s} \in S$, *and suppose that* $\bar{s}$ *is ST for* i. *Then* $\bar{s}$ *is GMR for* i *and* $\bar{s}$ *is R for* j. *Further* $\bar{s}$ *is FHQ for* i *if G is strict ordinal for* j.

PROOF: That $\bar{s}$ is R for j follows from Definition 13.25(i). Now suppose that s_i' is a UI for i from $\bar{s}$. Choose $s_j^* \, R_j(s_i')$ so that

$$v_i(s_i', s_j^*) = \min\limits_{s_j \in R_j(s_i)} v_i(s_i', s_j).$$

Then s_j^* is a sanction against s_i', since

$$v_i(s_i', s_j^*) = \min\limits_{s_j \in R_j(s_i)} v_i(s_i', s_j) \le \max\limits_{s_i \in S_i} \min\limits_{s_j \in R_j(s_i)} v_i(s_i, s_j)$$
$$= \min\limits_{s_j \in R_j(\bar{s}_i)} v_i(\bar{s}_i, s_j) \le v_i(\bar{s}_i, \bar{s}_j).$$

by Definition 13.25(ii). Thus $\bar{s}$ is GMR for i. If G is strict ordinal for i, then $|R_j(s_j')| = 1$ and the observation following Definition 13.24 implies that s_j^* is a credible sanction against s_i'. It follows that $\bar{s}$ is FHQ for i in this case. □

Figure 13.3 illustrates the results from Theorems 13.8, 13.14, and 13.26. Examples in Appendix E show that in general these results cannot be improved. It is trivial to show that for a player i in a game there is always at least one outcome that is R for i and at least one outcome that is ST for i.

If an outcome is ST for both players, it is referred to as a *dual Stackelberg equilibrium*. An outcome that is ST for one player possesses a form of group stability since it also must be R for the coplayer. However, group ST stability is a composite stability concept analogous to the others presented in this chapter.

Definition 13.27. An outcome $\bar{s} \in S$ is ST iff it is ST for i for each $i \in N$.

Theorem 13.28. *Let* $\bar{s} \in S$. *If* $\bar{s}$ *is ST, then* $\bar{s}$ *is R.*

PROOF. Follows from Theorem 13.26. □

Figure 13.4 illustrates the findings of Theorems 13.18, 13.19, 13.22, and 13.28. Examples in Appendix E show that, in general, these results cannot be improved. By Theorem 13.23, every 2-person game has a FHQ outcome (and therefore a GMR outcome); it can be shown by example that none of the other group stability (equilibrium) concepts are always present in every 2-person game.

Figure 13.3 Individual stability concepts in two-person games.

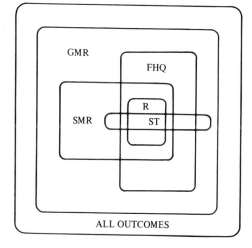

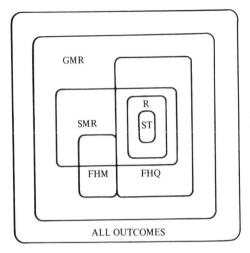

Figure 13.4 Group stability concepts in two-person games.

13.5 Stability Concepts in 2 × 2 Games

The most restrictive game model for which stability criteria have been developed are games of two players where each player must choose between two strategies. Thus it is assumed that $n = 2$ and $|S_1| = |S_2| = 2$. Two additional stability concepts are introduced that are of interest because of their assumption of extreme foresight on the part of the players.

When one considers whether some outcome $s^0 = (s_1^0, s_2^0) \in S$ is stable for a farsighted player $i(i = 1$ or $2)$, one can, because one is dealing with only 2×2 games, define s^1 to be the outcome that would result from s^0 if i were to change strategy while j's remained fixed. Similarly, define s^2 to be the outcome resulting from s^1 when j changes strategy, and s^3 to be the outcome resulting from s^2 when i changes strategy. Based upon the definitions for $s^0, s^1, \ldots, s^m$, let G_m denote the extensive game shown in Figure 13.5. G_m is called the *departure game of length m*. A *D-move* is the decision to depart from an outcome; a *$\overline{D}$-move* is the decision to stay at (i.e., not to depart from) an outcome. Let T_m be the final outcome of G_m, obtained by the usual backward induction process (Owen, 1980, pp. 6–8), with the additional stipulation that a player choose a $\overline{D}$-move over a D-move when both are of equal value to him. Thus it is assumed that a player stays at an outcome unless he (eventually) gains by departing. Observe that the "game" G_0 is degenerate; its outcome is $T_0 = s^0$.

Define an outcome $\bar{s} \in S$ to be *best for player i* iff $v_i(\bar{s}) \geq v_i(s)$ for every $s \in S$. If the initial outcome s^0 is best for i, it is obvious that s^0 should be stable for i since i could never gain by departing from s^0. Now suppose that s^1 is best for j, and that i prefers s^0 to s^1, or is indifferent between s^0 and s^1. Then s^0 should again be stable for i, since i has the choice of staying at s^0 or departing to s^1, and i can foresee that j would never make

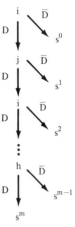

Figure 13.5 The departure game G: Player h, who makes the last move, is $h = i$ if n is odd and $h = j$ if n is even.

a countermove from s^1. (Observe that the assumptions have implied a strict move–countermove framework, so that, if i were to depart form s^0 to s^1 and j were to choose to stay at s^1, the sequence of moves would end at s^1 since i would have no further opportunity to move.) The next definition enables the further extension of this concept of "stability by foresight."

Definition 13.29. The outcome s^0 is *of type k for i*, where $k = 0, 1, 2,$ or 3, iff

   (i) s^k is best for the player with the opportunity to move from s^k (i.e., i if k is even, j if k is odd), and

   (ii) s^0 is not of type k' for $k' < k$.

The outcome s^0 is *noncyclic for i* iff it is of type 0, 1, 2, or 3 for i, and is *cyclic for i* otherwise. The stability concept is based on the idea that if s^0 is of type k for i, then a departure from s^0 by i cannot possibly progress further than s^k.

Definition 13.30. An outcome $\bar{s} \in S$ is *nonmyopically stable* (NM) *for i* iff $\bar{s}$ is noncyclic for i, and, if $\bar{s}$ is of type k for i, then the departure game of length k, G_k, has outcome $T_k = \bar{s}$ (Brams and Wittman, 1984).

The concept of NM stability is limited by its inability to assign a final outcome to any cyclic departure. Zagare's (1984) recent limited-move equilibrium definitions remedy this problem, but at the cost of some foresight. Brams and Hessel (1982) suggest outcomes that might be stable when none are NM. Kilgour (1984) extends NM stability by making "cycling back" to outcomes already achieved a possibility. For this extension, define $s^m = s^{m-4}$ for $m = 4, 5, 6, \ldots$. Now the departure of i from s^0 can be studied in terms of all the departure games $G_0, G_1, G_2, \ldots$.

Definition 13.31. An outcome $s^0 \in S$ is *determinate for i* iff there exists a nonnegative integer m such that $T_h = T_m$ for every $h \geq m$. In this case, the *final outcome* of the departure of i from s^0 is $T = T_m$ (Kilgour, 1984).

Thus a departure is determinate for i if every sufficiently long departure game results in the same outcome, the final outcome. Kilgour (1984) provides a finite algorithm for deciding whether an outcome is determinate for i, and if so, identifying the final outcome. In particular, he shows that if s^0 is noncyclic of type k for i, then s^0 is determinate for i and $T = T_k$.

Definition 13.32. An outcome $\bar{s} \in S$ is *nonmyopically stable in the extended sense* (XNM) *for i* iff $\bar{s}$ is determinate for i and $T = \bar{s}$ (Kilgour, 1984).

Thus an outcome is XNM for i if, whenever i has sufficient foresight, he chooses not to depart from that outcome. For brevity, the inclusion results below are given without proof.

Theorem 13.33. *If $\bar{s}$ is NM for* i, *then $\bar{s}$ is XNM for* i, *and if $\bar{s}$ is XNM for* i, *then $\bar{s}$ is SMR for* i *(Kilgour, 1984).*

Figure 13.6 illustrates the results from Theorems 13.8, 13.14, 13.26, and 13.33 on individual stability concepts applicable to 2×2 games. As

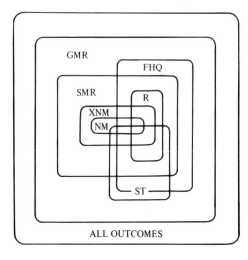

Figure 13.6 Individual stability concepts in 2×2 games.

is shown, NM outcomes are XNM, which in turn are SMR. All of the stable outcomes are GMR. Examples in Appendix E show that, in general, these results cannot be improved. It is easy to show that in any 2 × 2 game there is always at least one outcome that is NM (and therefore XNM) for some player.

From the individual nonmyopic stability concepts, group stability concepts can be synthesized in the usual way:

Definition 13.34. An outcome $\bar{s} \in S$ is NM iff it is NM for each player $i \in N$; $\bar{s}$ is XNM iff it is XNM for each player $i \in N$.

The following inclusion results for group stability can be proven.

Theorem 13.35. *Let $\bar{s} \in S$. If $\bar{s}$ is NM, then $\bar{s}$ is XNM. If $\bar{s}$ is XNM, then $\bar{s}$ is SMR.*

Theorem 13.36. *Let $\bar{s} \in S$. If $\bar{s}$ is FHM and XNM, then $\bar{s}$ is NM.*

Theorem 13.37. *Let $\bar{s} \in S$. If $\bar{s}$ is R and XNM but not ST, then $\bar{s}$ is NM.*

Figure 13.7 illustrates the findings of Theorems 13.18, 13.19, 13.22, 13.28, 13.35, 13.36, and 13.37 on group stability concepts in 2 × 2 games. Examples in Appendix E show that in general these results cannot be improved. It is easy to show by example that a 2 × 2 game need not have an XNM (and therefore an NM) outcome.

Figure 13.7 Group stability concepts in 2 × 2 games.

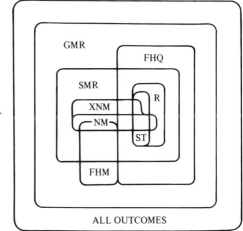

13.6 Strict Ordinal Games

Some features of the interrelationships among the stability concepts presented in this chapter in fact occur only in games with outcomes that are equally preferred by one or more players. Although the class of ordinal games includes that of strict ordinal games, the smaller class is of considerable interest since, in practice, most conflicts are appropriately modeled as strict ordinal games. Even when a conflict can be modeled only by an ordinal game, often there are only a few equally preferred outcomes for only one of the players, and the game is strict ordinal for the rest (Fraser and Hipel, 1979a). Consequently, a study of how the stability concepts interrelate in strict ordinal games has practical advantages. In addition, all of the individual and group stability approaches can be compared and contrasted according to their behavior in games of this important class.

Recall that an n-person game is strict ordinal for a player $i \in N$ iff $v_i(s^1) = v_i(s^2)$ implies $s^1 = s^2$, and that G is strict ordinal iff it is strict ordinal for every $i \in N$. When G is strict ordinal, certain of the inclusion results of Sections 13.3 to 13.5 for individual stability can be strengthened. For example, in Theorem 13.26 it was shown that

Theorem 13.38. *If* G *is a strict ordinal 2-person game and* s̄ $\in$ S *is ST for a player* i $\in$ N, *then* s̄ *is FHQ for* i.

Also it is not hard to demonstrate

Theorem 13.39. *If* G *is a strict ordinal 2* × *2 game,* i $\in$ N, *and* s̄ $\in$ S *is NM for* i *and ST for* i, *then* s̄ *is R for* i.

Figure 13.8 illustrates the results of Theorems 13.8, 13.14, 13.26, 13.33, 13.38, and 13.39 on individual stability concepts in strict ordinal games. Figure 13.8 shows that in strict ordinal games ST outcomes are always FHQ. This is not the case for ST outcomes in either 2-person or 2 × 2 games as shown in Figures 13.3 and 13.6, respectively. It is shown by example in Appendix E that these results cannot be improved. Each type of individual stability is exhibited by some outcome for some player in every strict ordinal game for which the stability is defined.

When the group stability concepts of Sections 13.3–13.5 are considered in the context of strict ordinal games, two new relationships appear:

Theorem 13.40. *If* G *is a strict ordinal 2* × *2 game, and* s̄ $\in$ S *is R and NM, then* s̄ *is ST.*

Theorem 13.41. *If* G *is a strict ordinal 2* × *2 game and* s̄ $\in$ S *is NM and not FHQ, then* s̄ *is FHM.*

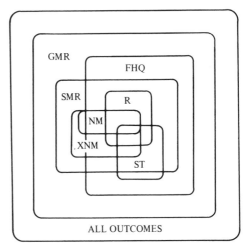

Figure 13.8 Individual stability concepts in strict ordinal games: Note that ST is defined only in two-person games, NM and XNM only in 2 × 2 games.

In Figure 13.9, the results of Theorems 13.18, 13.19, 13.22, 13.28, 13.35, 13.36, 13.37, 13.40, and 13.41 for group stability concepts in strict ordinal games are shown. Figures 13.8 and 13.9 show that NM outcomes are not always FHQ outcomes. In fact, the single exception is in the game of Chicken [game No. 66 in Rapoport et al. (1976); see Section 12.6.3] in which the so-called "cooperative" outcome is NM and FHM rather than FHQ. Other examples in Appendix E show that the results of these theorems cannot be improved. Every strict ordinal game contains an outcome that is FHQ (and therefore GMR); however, it need not possess an outcome exhibiting any other group stability concept.

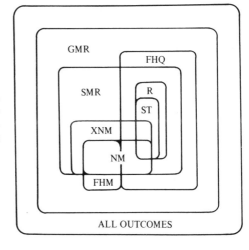

Figure 13.9 Group stability concepts in strict ordinal games: Note that ST is defined only in two-person games, NM and XNM only in 2 × 2 games.

Note that there are two sets of outcomes that have disappeared between Figure 13.7, which depicts stability concepts in general, and Figure 13.9, which displays the stability concepts in the class of strict ordinal games. The sets not observed in the strict ordinal cases are (1) FHM and SMR but not NM and (2) NM and R but not ST. In addition, there is only one instance of an outcome that is NM but not FHQ in the class of strict ordinal games.

The resulting simplification of the relationships between the stability concepts brings forward the importance of the approach of Fraser and Hipel (1979a). Recall that their approach includes both FHQ and FHM. In fact for strict ordinal games, FHQ and FHM together include every other stability concept except one 2 × 2 game [No. 55 in Rapoport et al. (1976)] where a particularly far-sighted XNM outcome is observed, and except of course for the very broad concepts of general and symmetric metarationality. Furthermore, in practice it is observed that FHQ and FHM outcomes are generally few in number for even very large game models. In addition to this, Theorem 13.23 proves that at least one FHQ outcome will exist for any game model. These three points together provide strong support for the Fraser–Hipel approach as an essential game analysis procedure, particularly in strict ordinal games.

13.7 Important Concepts from Chapter 13

Extensive mathematical results have clearly shown the interrelationships of the various stability concepts used in noncooperative game theory. For n-person, 2-person, and 2 × 2 games, individual and group stability concepts were defined, compared, and evaluated for ordinal games in general and for the special case of strict ordinal games. The application of these concepts to no-conflict games and games of complete opposition is also examined in Appendix F.

For the n-person case, the two main groups of stability concepts are traditional metagame analysis (Howard, 1971), which defines R, SMR, and GMR outcomes, and conflict analysis (Fraser and Hipel, 1979a), involving R, FHQ, and FHM outcomes. The main difference between these two groups is that the credibility of sanctions is important only in the conflict analysis approach. In the traditional metagame analysis, the preferences of the other players are not considered when determining whether a player's UIs from an outcome are sanctioned. Therefore in applications where the preferences of the other players are not known or for some reason not to be considered, metagame analysis is a reasonable method of assessing stability.

In conflict analysis, only credible sanctions against a player's UIs are considered. A sanction is credible if it can arise as a result of some of the other players acting individually to improve their positions, either in sequence (yielding FHQ outcomes) or simultaneously (yielding FHM outcomes). Because the preferences of the other players are considered when assessing FHM and FHQ stability, the conflict analysis procedure is widely applicable to practical problems.

As illustrated by Figures 13.1 and 13.2, all stability concepts for the n-person case define outcomes that are subsets of the GMR outcomes for individual and group stability, respectively. From Theorem 13.23, there is always an outcome that has group FHQ stability, and FHQ and GMR stability are the only group stabilities that occur in every n-person game. Although this chapter and Appendix F deal exclusively with ordinal games, it should be pointed out that both metagame analysis and conflict analysis can handle intransitive preferences where a player may prefer outcome x to y, y to z, but z to x. This is because when stability is assessed, preferences among outcomes are compared only pairwise.

Besides the stability methods for n-person games, the ST approach applies to 2-person games. In Figure 13.8 it can be seen that, for individual stability, outcomes that are ST are always FHQ when the game is strict ordinal but, as shown in Figure 13.3, this relationship does not hold in general. Figure 13.4 demonstrates that, for group stability, ST outcomes are automatically R outcomes, which in turn are FHQ, SMR and GMR.

The additional stability principles introduced for 2×2 games are the two nonmyopic approaches, which are based on the assumption of "farsighted" players who can envision a long sequence of interactive moves by the players. From Figures 13.6 and 13.7 it can be seen that for both individual and group stability, respectively, NM outcomes are always XNM outcomes, which are in turn always SMR outcomes. Except for one case, Figures 13.8 and 13.9 show that for strict ordinal games NM outcomes are always FHQ outcomes for both individual and group stability, respectively. The only exception is in the game of Chicken [game No. 66 in Rapoport et al. (1976); see Section 12.6.3] in which an outcome that is NM is also FHM rather than FHQ. However, as can be seen in Figures 13.5 and 13.7, the relationships among NM, XNM, and FHQ outcomes are more complicated in the general case.

Questions

1. Suppose that there are intransitive preferences present in a game. Will there always be an equilibrium when conflict analysis is employed as the solution concept? Will an equilibrium always exist for games with intransitive preferences when metagame analysis is employed?
2. Can the extended nonmyopic solution concept handle intransitive preferences? Clearly explain the reason for your response.
3. In the FHQ approach, the meaning of a credible action is explicitly defined. Construct an alternative way of defining the credibility of a response. Prove

whether or not an equilibrium always exists when the new definition for credibility is employed.

4. Suggest a general taxonomy for classifying solution concepts from noncooperative game theory. For example, can you develop a taxonomy that reflects how far into the future players can contemplate moves and countermoves?

5. As discussed in Chapter 5, when at least two players are playing a game, coalitions can be formed. Suppose that a game of five players is first analyzed using conflict analysis and three equilibriums are detected. If a coalition of three of the players is formed, what can be concluded about the number of equilibriums that will be present in the resulting game when it is analyzed using conflict analysis?

6. Can you suggest alternative ways to define Stackelberg stability when equally preferred outcomes are present?

7. Suggest an approach for extending Stackelberg stability for handling n-player games.

Chapter 14
Advanced Dynamic Modeling

14.1 Introduction

Conflict is by its very nature a dynamic phenomenon. In most of this book the emphasis has been on analyzing conflicts from a static point of view because this type of analysis is useful for obtaining a "snapshot" of the conflict at one point in time. Furthermore, this is much easier than studying the entire "motion picture" of the conflict as it evolves over time. However, as presented in Chapter 6, approaches to looking at the dynamics of a conflict are available and can provide useful insight into the study of real world problems.

This chapter is concerned with the further development of the dynamic approaches to conflict analysis that were introduced in Chapter 6. First, the idea of a supergame is presented. Following this, the study of the nuclear conflict of Chapters 10–12 is concluded by an analysis using two dynamic methods—the extensive and state transition models. Finally, an extension of the state transition method is presented that allows for the explicit inclusion of continuous time as an important element of a conflict analysis. For both the presentation on supergames and that on continuous-time state transition modeling, the game of Chicken described in Section 12.6.3 is used as an example conflict.

14.2 Supergames

A *supergame* is a set of static games developed to represent the way in which a conflict changes over time (Rapoport, 1967; 1969a; Snyder and Diesing, 1977). One example used by Snyder and Diesing (1977) is constructed as a concatenation of 2×2 games. Each cell in one of the

2 × 2 subgames provides a payoff to the players and a pointer to the next
2 × 2 subgame to consider. In this manner the conflict changes its nature
as it is played out, with payoffs being accrued at each stage of play. This
concept can be extended to any size or format of game, with the key idea
that outcomes in one game may lead to a different game as they are
achieved.

For example, consider again the game of Chicken, which was presented
in Section 12.6.3. Recall that in this game each of two players is driving
a car towards the other player, and each player possesses the strategies
to swerve (in order to avoid a collision) or not to swerve. The model
presented in Section 12.6.3 indicated that each player would prefer to
swerve rather than collide. However, when the contest begins and the
cars are still far apart there is no danger that they will collide. Consequently, at the start of the game it makes sense that the outcome where
both players do not swerve is the only equilibrium at that time. As the
cars come closer together and there is a real danger of collision, the players
start to prefer swerving over not swerving and new equilibriums appear:
namely, those predicted using the conflict analysis algorithm.

Clearly, the preferences of each player in the game of Chicken change
over time. Consider the conflict at the very beginning, when the two
drivers are far away from each other. The players and options for the
game are the same as shown in Table 12.11 or 12.13 (pp. 254, 255), but
the preferences are different. Both players, at this point in time, do not
wish to swerve since there is no danger of crashing until the cars are
closer. The normal form and conflict analysis tableau of this early part of
the game are shown in Table 14.1. As expected, there is a single equilibrium given by both approaches: neither player swerves at the start of
Chicken.

Table 14.2 displays a possible supergame model for Chicken based on
the two static representations of Chicken found in Tables 12.11 and 14.1.
Two normal form games labeled 1 and 2 are presented in Table 14.2.
Every outcome in these two games has a payoff for each player, and an
instruction on how to proceed once an outcome has been achieved. For
example, in game 1 the outcome (swerve, don't swerve) has a payoff of
− 100 units for player A and a payoff of 10 units for player B. This means
that if player A swerves at the start of Chicken, it is very unpleasant for
A, but rewarding for player B, who wins the game. Note that these numbers are cardinal utilities rather than numbers indicating preference orderings. The instruction from this outcome is to stop the supergame since
a player has won. On the other hand, the instruction from the outcome
(don't swerve, don't swerve) is to proceed to game 2.

This supergame permits the analysis of various supergame strategies.
For example, referring to Table 14.2, suppose player A considered that
there was a 10% chance that player B would swerve in the early part of

Table 14.1 Conflict Analysis of Chicken Early in Game

Normal form			
		Player B	
Player A		Swerve	Don't swerve
Swerve		2, 2	R_B 1, 4
Don't swerve		R_A 4, 1	R_A R_B 3, 3

Conflict analysis tableau				
Model				
Player A				
Swerve	0	1	0	1
Player B				
Swerve	0	0	1	1
Decimal	0	1	2	3
Stability analysis	×	E	×	×
Player 1	r 2	r 0	u 3 2	u 1 0
Player 2	r 1	r 0	u 3 1	u 2 0

the game, and a 50% chance of swerving in the second game. If A decided not to swerve under *any* circumstances, his (or her) expected payoff can be calculated as

$$(0.1 \times 10) + (0.9 \times 1) + \{0.9 \times [(0.5 \times 10) + (0.5 \times -1000)]\} = -452.6,$$

whereas if A follows the strategy of never swerving in the first part of the game and always swerving in the second part, the calculation is

$$((0.1 \times 10) + (0.9 \times 1) + \{0.9 \times [(0.5 \times -1) + (0.5 \times -20)]\}) \times (1 + 0.45 + 0.45^2 + 0.45^3 + \cdots) = -14.9.$$

Consequently A would be wiser to follow the second strategy.

Rather than being a true dynamic model, a supergame is much like a group of static games that have been linked together to cover a specific period of time. Also, such a model is highly dependent upon cardinal payoffs, which are often arbitrary or difficult to determine. The state transition and extensive approaches described in Chapter 6 possess a better design for expressing the changing nature of a conflict. These methods are discussed in Section 14.3 in the context of the nuclear conflict.

Table 14.2 Supergame Model of Chicken

	Player B	
Player A	Swerve	Don't swerve
Game 1		
Swerve	−5, −5 go to game 1	−100, 10 stop game
Don't swerve	10, −100 stop game	1, 1 go to game 2
Game 2		
Swerve	−1, −1 go to Game 1	−20, 10 stop game
Don't swerve	10, −20 stop game	−1000, −1000 stop game

14.3 Nuclear Conflict

As explained in Section 10.2, the nuclear conflict originally presented by Richelson (1979) involves a potential nuclear war between the United States and the USSR. The USSR has the strategies of launching a conventional war upon Western Europe (strategy C in Table 10.1, p. 204), starting a limited nuclear war within Europe (strategy L), or commencing an intercontinental nuclear war with the United States (strategy S). Likewise, the United States can respond to Soviet aggression by selecting one of the same three strategies (i.e., C, L, or S). In this section, the nuclear conflict is examined using the extensive and state transition forms in order to provide an improved understanding.

14.3.1 Extensive Form Analysis

As explained in Section 6.4 for the Watergate conflict, in the extensive form of a game the conflict is represented as a *game tree*. Each node of the tree refers to one of the players, and the branches leaving a node correspond to decisions the player can make at that time. Also, since the environment for decision making at any node is developed by previous decisions, a particular outcome can be associated with the node, and a specific strategy is represented by each branch emanating from the node. For a detailed explanation of the extensive form see, for example Luce and Raiffa (1957).

The extensive form representation for the nuclear conflict is shown in Figure 14.1. In this figure, the game progresses horizontally from left to right as opposed to the vertical branching that is utilized by some authors. Each node is labeled either USSR or USA with the outcome it represents, and each branch is tagged with one of the strategies C, L, or S. The

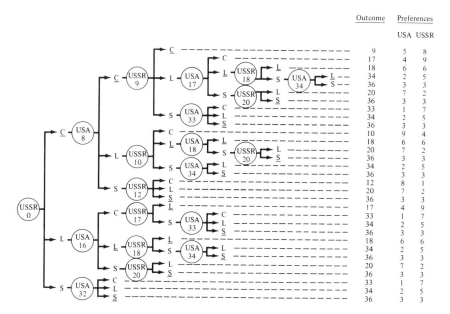

Figure 14.1 Extensive form of nuclear conflict.

extensive form represents the changes in a conflict over time so that physical constraints on changes in strategy can be included. For example, the USSR cannot realistically change its mind from the strategy of using atomic weapons to using conventional weapons once battle has commenced. In general, it is unreasonable for either side to de-escalate in the course of the conflict, and this is the principle used in the development of the game tree appearing in Figure 14.1. Also, if a player has not changed strategy following a change of strategy by the other player, it is assumed that the conflict resolution has been reached.

It should be noted that this extensive form model also requires the inclusion of four outcomes that did not appear in the normal form of the game in Table 10.1. Since there must be a status quo or starting position, the outcome 0 must be included, represented by the node farthest to the left in Figure 14.1. Similarly, since the USSR moves first according to the game presented by Richelson (1979), there must be outcomes corresponding to a strategy selection by the USSR, but with no options yet taken by the United States. These are the three nodes corresponding to the decimal outcomes 8, 16, and 32. The reader can refer to Table 11.1 (p. 231) to translate outcome numbers into the exact options selected by each player.

The extensive form can readily be analyzed to determine the expected actions of the players in the conflict. For example, consider the bottom three outcomes that appear in Figure 14.1. The final decision node that applies to these is that of the United States. The United States must choose either strategy C for outcome 33, strategy L for outcome 34, or strategy S for outcome 36. An examination of the preferences provided in Table 10.1, (p. 204) where a higher number means the outcome is more preferable, reveals that the United States would prefer 36 over the other two outcomes. Thus at this decision node, the United States would be expected to choose strategy S, which has been underlined to indicate this result. The most preferable strategies leading out of each node in Figure 14.1 has also been underlined.

The node previous to the one discussed in the above paragraph corresponds to a decision by the USSR at node 0. Assuming the USSR correctly understands United States preferences, the USSR can recognize that a strategy selection of S, leading to the node just analyzed, will result in outcome 36 because of the expected United States action. Similar considerations permit the USSR to select a strategy at node 0 with only one outcome being the expected result of each possible choice. A comparison of the value of each result determines the best strategy selection. In this case, the USSR can choose either strategy C (which can be expected to lead to outcome 9), strategy L (leading to 18), or strategy S (resulting in the nuclear holocaust outcome 36). Of these three outcomes, the Soviet preference is 9, and since the USSR is both the initiator and perpetuator of the conflict, the expected resolution is a conventional war.

The extensive form is a very valuable method for presenting conflict information and can also model probabilistic decisions, simultaneous moves, and conditions of incomplete information. Its major fault lies in its notational inefficiency, which leads to unnecessary complexity and size. As explained in Sections 6.4 and 6.5, these difficulties can be overcome by employing the state transition method.

14.3.2 State Transition Model

The state transition model is of the form

$$Y = TX, \tag{14-1}$$

where X is the status quo vector, T is the transition matrix, and Y is the output vector. Recall from Chapter 6 that the state transition matrix can be developed algorithmically from individual transition matrices for each player. The individual transition matrices can be taken from the static stability analyses. The overall transition matrix is calculated from the individual matrices using:

$$t = \sum_{i \in U} (a_i) - (m - 1)q, \tag{14-2}$$

where U is the set of matrices that have off-diagonal entries for outcome q, a_i are the row outcomes, m is the number of elements in U, and t is the row into which a 1 is to be entered.

In the nuclear conflict, the matrix T does not involve probabilistic information, so it is composed of 1s and 0s only. The individual transition matrix T_{US} for the United States is developed by carefully examining the stability for the US as determined for its preference vector in Table 11.2 (p. 232). First, the transition information from this preference vector can be put directly into a matrix, as shown Table 14.3. This is done by noting that the United States only changes states for outcomes that are unstable. Thus the matrix in Table 14.3 consists of ones on the main diagonal except in the columns corresponding to outcomes 17, 34, and 33 since these are the only unstable outcomes in the United States preference vector in Table 11.2. The UI for the United States from outcome 17 to 20 (Table 11.2) is sanctioned by the Soviet UI from 20 to 36, but the United States UI to 18 is not sanctioned. Thus, a 1 is placed in the column of Table 14.3 corresponding to outcome 17 in the row for outcome 18, indicating that the United States will "move" from outcome 17 to 18 should 17 come about. Similarly, Table 14.4 is the initial transition matrix T_{USSR} representing the Soviet transition information.

Note that further information about the dynamics of the conflict should be considered for inclusion in the model. However, the example of dynamic constraints used in the previous section—that once the conflict has escalated there is no turning back—is not important here since none of the UIs involve de-escalation of the conflict. The final T_{US} and T_{USSR} are illustrated in Tables 14.5 and 14.6, respectively. The major difference between these tables and Tables 14.3 and 14.4 is that the set of outcomes in Tables 14.5 and 14.6 have been expanded as in Section 14.3.1 for the extensive form to include situations where no offensive action is taken

Table 14.3 Initial Transition Matrix T_{US} for the United States in the Nuclear Conflict

	9	10	12	17	18	20	33	34	36
9	1	0	0	0	0	0	0	0	0
10	0	1	0	0	0	0	0	0	0
12	0	0	1	0	0	0	0	0	0
17	0	0	0	0	0	0	0	0	0
18	0	0	0	1	1	0	0	0	0
20	0	0	0	0	0	1	0	0	0
33	0	0	0	0	0	0	0	0	0
34	0	0	0	0	0	0	0	0	0
36	0	0	0	0	0	0	1	1	1

Table 14.4 Initial Transition Matrix T_{USSR} for the USSR in the Nuclear Conflict

	9	10	12	17	18	20	33	34	36
9	1	0	0	0	0	0	0	0	0
10	0	1	0	0	0	0	0	0	0
12	0	0	0	0	0	0	0	0	0
17	0	0	0	1	0	0	0	0	0
18	0	0	0	0	1	0	0	0	0
20	0	0	0	0	0	0	0	0	0
33	0	0	0	0	0	0	1	0	0
34	0	0	0	0	0	0	0	1	0
36	0	0	1	0	0	1	0	0	1

by the United States (outcomes 8, 16, and 32). The interpretation of the other decimal outcomes can be found by referring to Table 11.1.

The only other variation imposed on the individual transition matrices concerns outcome 10. Outcome 10 is stable for the USSR in Table 11.2, but is shown having a transition to outcome 18 in Table 14.5. Notice in Table 11.2 that the stability of outcome 10 for the USSR is dependent on the UI by the United States from outcome 18 to 20. However, this UI is itself sanctioned by the Soviet UI from 20 to 36. Thus although stability for 10 is required in the static game, when the dynamics of the conflict are considered it is recognized that the outcome should be considered unstable. The distinction is that the dynamic model permits the establishment of preferences throughout the duration of the conflict, rather than at a single point in time.

Table 14.5 Final Transition Matrix T_{US} for the United States in the Nuclear Conflict

	8	9	10	12	16	17	18	20	32	33	34	36
8	0	0	0	0	0	0	0	0	0	0	0	0
9	1	1	0	0	0	0	0	0	0	0	0	0
10	0	0	1	0	0	0	0	0	0	0	0	0
12	0	0	0	1	0	0	0	0	0	0	0	0
16	0	0	0	0	0	0	0	0	0	0	0	0
17	0	0	0	0	0	0	0	0	0	0	0	0
18	0	0	0	0	1	1	1	0	0	0	0	0
20	0	0	0	0	0	0	0	1	0	0	0	0
32	0	0	0	0	0	0	0	0	0	0	0	0
33	0	0	0	0	0	0	0	0	0	0	0	0
34	0	0	0	0	0	0	0	0	0	0	0	0
36	0	0	0	0	0	0	0	1	1	1	1	1

Table 14.6 Final Transition Matrix T_{USSR} for the USSR in the Nuclear Conflict

	8	9	10	12	16	17	18	20	32	33	34	36
8	1	0	0	0	0	0	0	0	0	0	0	0
9	0	1	0	0	0	0	0	0	0	0	0	0
10	0	0	0	0	0	0	0	0	0	0	0	0
12	0	0	0	0	0	0	0	0	0	0	0	0
16	0	0	0	0	1	0	0	0	0	0	0	0
17	0	0	0	0	0	1	0	0	0	0	0	0
18	0	0	1	0	0	0	1	0	0	0	0	0
20	0	0	0	0	0	0	0	0	0	0	0	0
32	0	0	0	0	0	0	0	0	1	0	0	0
33	0	0	0	0	0	0	0	0	0	1	0	0
34	0	0	0	0	0	0	0	0	0	0	1	0
36	0	0	0	1	0	0	0	1	0	0	0	1

Given the final transition matrices for the two players in Table 14.5 and 14.6, the overall transition matrix for the conflict is calculated using equation (14-2). The result is presented in Table 14.7. It can be observed that there are three nonzero elements on the main diagonal in this matrix, which means that there are three stable outcomes in the game given by outcomes 9, 18, and 36.

Rows of the transition matrix that consist of all zeros correspond to outcomes that will not come about in the progression of the conflict unless they appear in the status quo, and thus can be neglected in the model. Since the status quo is logically composed of outcomes 8, 16, or 32, the rows and columns of the matrix of Table 14.7 corresponding to outcomes

Table 14.7 Overall Transition Matrix T for the Nuclear Conflict

	8	9	10	12	16	17	18	20	32	33	34	36
8	0	0	0	0	0	0	0	0	0	0	0	0
9	1	1	0	0	0	0	0	0	0	0	0	0
10	0	0	0	0	0	0	0	0	0	0	0	0
12	0	0	0	0	0	0	0	0	0	0	0	0
16	0	0	0	0	0	0	0	0	0	0	0	0
17	0	0	0	0	0	0	0	0	0	0	0	0
18	0	0	1	0	1	1	1	0	0	0	0	0
20	0	0	0	0	0	0	0	0	0	0	0	0
32	0	0	0	0	0	0	0	0	0	0	0	0
33	0	0	0	0	0	0	0	0	0	0	0	0
34	0	0	0	0	0	0	0	0	0	0	0	0
36	0	0	0	1	0	0	0	1	1	1	1	1

10, 12, 17, 20, 33, and 34 can be removed, leaving only the reduced transition matrix of Table 14.8.

Richelson (1979) indicated in his presentation of this conflict that the USSR is the aggressor, so in terms of this model the USSR has complete control over the status quo. It can determine a status quo composed of outcomes 8, 16, 32, or any probabilistic combinations thereof. Either by performing the necessary matrix multiplications using (14-1) or simply by inspection of Table 14.8, it can be shown that a choice of 8 by the USSR leads to the steady-state solution 9, 16 leads to 18, and 32 leads to 36. Since the USSR prefers 9 to both 18 and 36, the reasonable Soviet choice would be the strategy associated with outcome 8—a conventional attack on Europe. This is identical to the result provided by the extensive form.

14.3.3 Concluding Discussion of the Nuclear Conflict

The progressive refinement of the model used for analyzing the nuclear conflict has resulted in a more thorough representation of the problem. The conflict was first presented as a conflict in normal form in Section 10.2. In Section 10.5 a metagame analysis of the conflict was performed, and a conflict analysis was done in Section 11.4. Stackelberg solutions were mentioned in Section 12.5.5. In this chapter the nuclear conflict was analyzed using the extensive form in Section 14.3.1 and then employing the state transition approach in Section 14.3.2. Table 14.9 summarizes the results of the seven modeling methods used for studying this confrontation.

It can be seen in Table 14.9 that the normal form and metagame analysis provide for five possible solutions, one of which is discarded using the conflict analysis technique. As explained in Section 11.4, outcome 17 is not an equilibrium since stability for one of the players is based upon a noncredible sanction. The Stackelberg equilibriums are found to correspond to two of the cooperative equilibriums. The extensive form identifies the single expected resolution to the game. The state transition form reveals three possible stable states and also detects the expected resolution.

Table 14.8 Reduced Transition Matrix for the Nuclear Conflict

	8	9	16	18	32	36
8	0	0	0	0	0	0
9	1	1	0	0	0	0
16	0	0	0	0	0	0
18	0	0	1	1	0	0
32	0	0	0	0	0	0
36	0	0	0	0	1	1

Table 14.9 Summary of Solution Concept Results[a] for the Nuclear Conflict

			Solution Concept			
Outcome	Nash	Metagame analysis	Conflict analysis	Stackelberg	Extensive form	State matrix
9 (C, C) (100, 100)	Coop.	Equil.	Equil.	—	Expected	Expected
10 (L, C) (010, 100)	Coop.	Equil.	Equil.	Equil.	—	—
12 (S, C) (001, 100)	—	—	—	—	—	—
17 (C, L) (100, 010)	Coop.	Equil.	—	—	—	—
18 (L, L) (010, 010)	Coop.	Equil.	Equil.	Equil.	—	Stable
20 (S, L) (001, 010)	—	—	—	—	—	—
33 (C, S) (100, 001)	—	—	—	—	—	—
34 (L, S) (010, 001)	—	—	—	—	—	—
36 (S, S) (001, 001)	Equil.	Equil.	Equil.	—	—	Stable

[a]Coop. = cooperative solution; Equil. = equilibrium; Expected = expected resolution; Stable = stable outcome.

The various approaches to determining the resolution outcome of a conflict have been performed and compared using the nuclear conflict. It can be seen that conflict analysis is very useful for rigorously selecting equilibriums for further study. The state transition method is ideal for refining the selection down to a single expected resolution. Thus the conflict analysis and state transition techniques of Fraser and Hipel (1979a, 1983c) have been demonstrated to constitute a comprehensive approach to the modeling and analysis of conflicts. Together they form a framework within which virtually all information pertaining to a conflict can be retained and assessed. To enhance the comprehensive nature of these techniques further, the manner in which preference changes over continuous time can be modeled is explained in Section 14.4.

14.4 Time-Dependent Transition Matrices

14.4.1 Introduction

In general, the nature of a conflict is likely to change continuously as time passes. The players' preferences may change, or their understanding of the game may become more complete. In fact, changes can occur in the players, options, and preferences in a game or any combination thereof. Although the state transition method is useful for studying the way conflicts can progress over time, up to this point in the book a procedure has not yet been presented for explicitly including time in the model. In this section, a method for permitting the conflict model itself to change is presented. This is done by making the **T** matrix in the state transition formula in equation (14-1) a function of time. The game of Chicken, discussed in Sections 12.6.3 and 14.2, is the particular example used in this section.

Chicken is developed in game theory literature as a verbal description of a mathematical phenomenon. The preference structure in Chicken is the main item of interest in game theory; the story of the car drivers merely adds color and intuition (sometimes misleadingly) to the analysis.

Conflict analysis, as opposed to game theory, is more concerned with determining an adequate model for describing the real world phenomenon. In this regard, neither the normal form nor the conflict analysis method, nor any of the other stability analysis methods presented in the previous chapter suitably represent what is happening in the game of Chicken. For example, as explained in Section 14.2, at the start of the game (don't swerve, don't swerve) is the only equilibrium; however, as the cars come closer together, the players start to prefer swerving over not swerving and new equilibriums appear. However, the multiple static game approach used in a supergame is not appropriate when the preferences change continuously, as they do over time in the game of Chicken.

Assuming that the model of Table 12.13 (p. 255) correctly represents the conflict as the players are approaching a crash, and that Table 14.1 truly models the situation as the conflict begins, the problem remains of devising a single model that includes and relates these two components of this confrontation into a single continuous representation. This can be done by considering a state transition form of the game in which the matrix **T** from equation (14-1) is a function of time.

14.4.2 Time-Dependent State Transitions

In equation (14-1)

$$\mathbf{Y} = \mathbf{TX}, \tag{14-1}$$

Y is an $f \times 1$ output vector, **T** is an $f \times f$ transition matrix, and **X** is an

$f \times 1$ status quo vector for a conflict with f feasible outcomes. In this equation nothing is mentioned about how long a period of time t is involved for the players to change strategies to form the state vector $\mathbf{Y}$ from the state vector $\mathbf{X}$. Define $T(t,t+h)$ to be a transition matrix with elements $\tau_{ij}(t,t+h)$. Each $\tau_{ij}(t,t+h)$ is the probability of state j changing to state i during the period h from t to $t+h$. Equation (14-1) then becomes

$$\mathbf{X}(t+h) = \mathbf{T}(t,t+h)\mathbf{X}(t) \tag{14-3}$$

Now, assume that for a particular transition matrix $\mathbf{T}(t,t+h)$ there exists a matrix $\mathbf{A}(t)$ with elements a_{ij} defined by two sets of functions. For each state i;

$$a_{ii}(t) = \lim_{h \to 0} \left\{ \frac{1}{h} [\tau_{ii}(t,t+h) - 1] \right\}; \tag{14-4}$$

and for each pair of states i and j, where $i \neq j$;

$$a_{ij}(t) = \lim_{h \to 0} \left\{ \frac{1}{h} [\tau_{ij}(t,t+h)] \right\}. \tag{14-5}$$

Note that this means that the probability $1 - \tau_{ii}(t,t+h)$ of a transition from a state i to some other state during the time interval $(t,t+h)$ is equal to $h(-a_{ii}(t))$ plus a remainder that tends to 0 as h does. Similarly, the probability $\tau_{ij}(t,t+h)$ of transition from i to j during the time interval $(t,t+h)$ is equal to $h(a_{ij}(t))$ plus a remainder that tends to 0 as h does. When discussing Markov chains, $-a_{ii}(t)$ is called the *intensity of passage;* $a_{ij}(t)$ is the *intensity of transition* (Parzen, 1962). In matrix form, (14-4) and (14-5) are written

$$\lim_{h \to 0} \left\{ \frac{1}{h} [\mathbf{T}(t,t+h) - \mathbf{I}] \right\} = \mathbf{A}(t), \tag{14-6}$$

where I is the unit matrix of appropriate dimension and $\mathbf{A}(t)$ has elements a_{ij}.

Kolmogorov used the assumption in (14-6) in the development of his "forward" and "backward" equations for determining the transition probability functions of a Markov chain (Kolmogorov, 1931; Parzen, 1962). However, by an alternative approach, a differential equation can be developed that can be used to determine directly the state trajectory for the conflict. The *trajectory of a state* gives the value of the state at each point in time, or in other words the probability that the conflict will be in any particular outcome at any time t.

Define $\mathbf{T}(t)$ to have elements $\tau_{ij}(t)$ such that

$$\tau_{ij}(t) = \lim_{h \to 0} \left\{ \frac{1}{h} \tau_{ij}(t,t+h) \right\}, \tag{14-7}$$

so that $\tau_{ij}(t)$ is the transition probability per unit time at time t. Thus, for small h,

$$h(-a_{ii}(t)) = h(1 - \tau_{ii}(t))$$

and

$$h(a_{ij}(t)) = h(\tau_{ij}(t)).$$

This means that

$$-a_{ii}(t) = 1 - \tau_{ii}(t)$$

or

$$a_{ii}(t) = \tau_{ii}(t) - 1 \qquad (14\text{-}8)$$

and

$$a_{ij}(t) = \tau_{ij}(t). \qquad (14\text{-}9)$$

Thus,

$$\mathbf{A}(t) = [\mathbf{T}(t) - \mathbf{I}]. \qquad (14\text{-}10)$$

Now, subtracting $\mathbf{X}(t)$ from both sides of (14-3) gives

$$\mathbf{X}(t+h) - \mathbf{X}(t) = \mathbf{T}(t,t+h)\mathbf{X}(t) - \mathbf{X}(t) \qquad (14\text{-}11)$$

or

$$\mathbf{X}(t+h) - \mathbf{X}(t) = [\mathbf{T}(t,t+h) - \mathbf{I}]\mathbf{X}(t). \qquad (14\text{-}12)$$

Premultiplying both sides by $1/h$ results in

$$\frac{1}{h}[\mathbf{X}(t+h) - \mathbf{X}(t)] = \frac{1}{h}[\mathbf{T}(t,t+h) - \mathbf{I}]\mathbf{X}(t). \qquad (14\text{-}13)$$

Taking the limit of both sides gives

$$\lim_{h \to 0}\left\{\frac{1}{h}[\mathbf{X}(t+h) - \mathbf{X}(t)]\right\} = \lim_{h \to 0}\left\{\frac{1}{h}[\mathbf{T}(t,t+h) - \mathbf{I}]\mathbf{X}(t)\right\}. \qquad (14\text{-}14)$$

Noting that

$$\lim_{h \to 0}\left\{\frac{1}{h}[\mathbf{X}(t+h) - \mathbf{X}(t)]\right\} = \frac{d\mathbf{X}(t)}{d\mathbf{t}} \qquad (14\text{-}15)$$

and that, from equation (14-6),

$$\lim_{h \to 0}\left\{\frac{1}{h}[\mathbf{T}(t,t+h) - \mathbf{I}]\right\} = \mathbf{A}(t), \qquad (14\text{-}6)$$

equation (14-14) can be rewritten

$$\frac{d\mathbf{X}(t)}{dt} = \mathbf{A}(t)\mathbf{X}(t) \qquad (14\text{-}16)$$

or, equivalently,

$$\dot{\mathbf{X}}(t) = \mathbf{A}(t)\mathbf{X}(t). \tag{14-17}$$

Note that equation (14-17) requires the specification of an initial condition or status quo vector $\mathbf{X}_0$. Substituting equation (14-10) into (14-17) gives a practical formula for determining the state trajectories for a conflict that changes over time:

$$\dot{\mathbf{X}}(t) = [\mathbf{T}(t) - \mathbf{I}]\mathbf{X}(t). \tag{14-18}$$

Equation (14-18) is the expression of the time-dependent state transition equation used in the remainder of this chapter.

14.4.3 Dynamic Analysis of Chicken

To develop the matrix $\mathbf{T}(t)$ for the Chicken game, first one must determine the matrices $\mathbf{T}_A(t)$ and $\mathbf{T}_B(t)$ similar to those required for conventional state transition conflict analysis. Examining Tables 12.13 and 14.1 for player A, it can be seen that outcome 2 is stable at both the beginning and at the end of the game. Outcome 1 has a transition to outcome 0 while the drivers are far apart; the transitions are reversed in the latter part of the game. Outcome 3 is determined to be unstable in the early part of the conflict, but eventually becomes stable as the drivers approach one another. Let $f_A(t)$ represent the probability at time t that player A will swerve while the status quo is outcome 0, and $g_A(t)$ be the chance that player A will not swerve at time t given that the current situation is outcome 3. The transition matrix $\mathbf{T}_A(t)$ for player A is then given by the Table 14.10. Similarly, $\mathbf{T}_B(t)$ is calculated and presented in Table 14.11. In $\mathbf{T}_B(t)$, the function $f_B(t)$ represents the chance at time t that player B will swerve given that the current state is outcome 0, whereas $g_B(t)$ is the probability that player B will decide not to swerve given that outcome 3 is occurring.

The dynamic confrontation has at this point been considered as two games: the early game of Table 14.1 and the late game of Table 12.13. Thus when the preferences in Tables 14.10 and 14.11 indicate that the conflict is leaving the first game the preferences must symmetrically show the game becoming like the situation at the end of the race. For example, in the conflict of Table 14.1, outcome 1 is unstable for player A, who has

Table 14.10 Initial Transition Matrix for Player A in Chicken

	0	1	2	3
0	$1 - f_A$	$1 - f_A$	0	0
1	f_A	f_A	0	0
2	0	0	1	g_A
3	0	0	0	$1 - g_A$

Table 14.11 Initial Transition Matrix for Player B in Chicken

	0	1	2	3
0	$1 - f_B$	0	$1 - f_B$	0
1	0	1	0	g_B
2	f_B	0	f_B	0
3	0	0	0	$1 - g_B$

an undeterred UI to outcome 0. In Table 12.13, the late game, there is an undeterred UI for player A from 0 to 1. Thus the sum of the probability of transition from outcome 1 to outcome 0 and the probability of transition from outcome 0 to outcome 1 at any time t for player A must equal 1.0. This is why the matrix of Table 14.10 has the entry $f_A(t)$ for the element corresponding to the probability of transition from outcome 1 to itself in spite of the fact that $f_A(t)$ was defined as a different transition probability.

At this point, dynamic constraints can be incorporated into the model. In the nuclear conflict, an example of a dynamic constraint is that neither the United States nor the USSR could de-escalate the confrontation. A similar situation occurs in the Chicken game in that neither player, after each has swerved, could possibly go back on course and still win the game: a player who has "chickened out" and swerved has irrevocably lost the contest. Thus outcome 1 is purely absorbing for player A, as is outcome 2 for player B. However, if both players swerve together (outcome 3), they have "lost face" equally, so the various transitions from outcome 3 are justifiable. [In fact, they have very little effect for most realistic selections of $g_A(t)$ and $g_B(t)$.] The final transition matrices for players A and B in the Chicken conflict are shown in Tables 14.12 and 14.13, respectively.

The overall transition matrix shown in Table 14.14 is calculated from Tables 14.12 and 14.13 using equation (14-2) in the same manner as for a transition matrix that does not change over time. For example, consider the transition from outcome 0 to 1 in Table 14.14. In Table 14.12, player A has a probability of f_A of moving from outcome 0 to 1; in Table 14.13, player B has no chance of making that transition. However, player B will

Table 14.12 Final Transition Matrix for Player A in Chicken

	0	1	2	3
0	$1 - f_A$	0	0	0
1	f_A	1	0	0
2	0	0	1	g_A
3	0	0	0	$1 - g_A$

Table 14.13 Final Transition Matrix for Player B in Chicken

	0	1	2	3
0	$1 - f_B$	0	0	0
1	0	1	0	g_B
2	f_B	0	1	0
3	0	0	0	$1 - g_B$

make no change in strategy with a chance of $1-f_B$, given by the value in Table 14.13 in the row and column corresponding to outcome 0. Thus the overall probability of the conflict going from outcome 0 to 1 is the probability of player A making the change in strategy multiplied by the chance of player B not changing options at all. This is given by $f_A (1-f_B)$, as shown in Table 14.14.

The system of differential equations that results from the application of the **T** matrix in Table 14.14 to the formula in (14-18) is not generally solvable in closed form. In the special case of equation (14-17) where $A(t)$ and $\int_0^t A(s)\, ds$ commute, a closed form solution is given by Kailath (1980);

$$X(t) = \exp\left[\int_0^t A(s)\, ds\right] X,$$

where "exp" denotes the exponential function. In certain other situations, equation (14-18) will result in directly solvable equations, and in all cases numeric methods can be used to determine the state trajectory. For the Chicken game, CSMP (the Continuous System Modeling Program) was used to determine the state trajectories for various values of $f_A(t)$, $f_B(t)$, $g_A(t)$, and $g_B(t)$. A complete example solution of equation (14-18) using the final $T(t)$ defined for the Chicken conflict is presented in Fraser (1981).

The functions $f_A(t)$, $f_B(t)$, $g_A(t)$, and $g_B(t)$ respectively represent the probability that player A will move from outcome 0 to 1, player B will change from 0 to 2, player A will change from 3 to 2, and player B will move from 3 to 1. Realistic functions that are used to represent these

Table 14.14 Overall Transition Matrix for Chicken

	0	1	2	3
0	$(1 - f_A)(1 - f_B)$	0	0	$g_A g_B$
1	$f_A (1 - f_B)$	1	0	$(1 - g_A) g_B$
2	$(1 - f_A) f_B$	0	1	$g_A (1 - g_B)$
3	$f_A f_B$	0	0	$(1 - g_A)(1 - g_B)$

probabilities are displayed in Figures 14.2 and 14.3. The functions $f_A(t)$ and $f_B(t)$ are first expressed as cumulative probability distributions; the derivatives of these functions are then taken to provide the desired probability distribution values. The cumulative probability distributions and their derivatives are illustrated for player A in Figure 14.2, whereas Figure 14.3 shows the functions for player B. Cumulative probability distributions are an easy way to express the change in preferences in this particular conflict, but are not appropriate in general unless the preferences change in a uniform manner. The functions $g_A(t)$ and $g_B(t)$ are not illustrated in figures. Both $g_A(t)$ and $g_B(t)$ are given a value of 0 for $t<40$ and a value of 1 for $t>40$ in the detailed example in Fraser (1981).

The resulting state trajectories determined by CSMP applying the input functions in Figures 14.2 and 14.3 to the differential equations for Chicken are shown in Figure 14.4. They are labeled x_0, x_1, x_2, and x_3 to correspond to decimal outcomes 0, 1, 2, and 3. Note that for each state, time is the horizontal axis; the probability of the conflict being in that state is the vertical axis.

The results support the mathematical development presented in this chapter. For the Chicken conflict, a selection of reasonable preference functions resulted in state trajectories that indicated that about 40% of the time one of the players would swerve off course and be the chicken, and about 40% of the time the other player would be the loser. The situations of both players swerving or the outcome of a collision occur

Figure 14.2 Transition functions $\int_0^t f_A(s)\, ds$ and $f_A(t)$ for player A in Chicken.

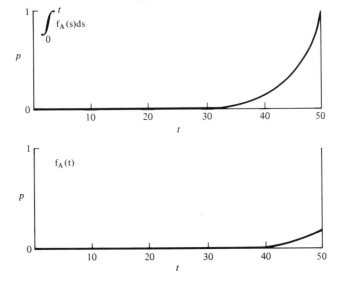

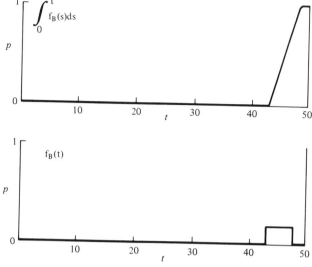

Figure 14.3 Transition functions $\int_0^t f_B(s)\, ds$ and $f_B(t)$ for player B in Chicken.

less frequently. The simulation results are not significantly different from what is expected intuitively or in comparison with experimental results (Rapoport et al., 1976).

14.4.4 Further Remarks Concerning Time-Dependent State Transition Functions

The remarkable result of equation (14-18) opens up a wealth of possibilities in the study of conflicts. Not only does it provide a formula for determining the state of the conflict at any point in time given the preferences of the players as they change over time, but it provides an avenue for controlling conflicts dynamically. The form of equation (14-17) is the same as for the state–space equation used in the study of systems and control theory. There is a body of knowledge in these disciplines that can now be applied to the analysis of conflicts.

For example, for the Chicken conflict a function $h(\mathbf{X},t)$ could be defined to provide a certain desired weighting of states with respect to time. The problem of finding an optimum strategy for the first player could be formulated as

$$\min_{f_A, g_A} \left\{ J = \int_{t=t_o}^{t=t_1} h(X,t)\, dt \right\},$$

$$\text{subject to} \quad \dot{\mathbf{X}}(t) = \mathbf{A}(f_A, f_B, g_A, g_B, t)\, \mathbf{X}(t); \; \mathbf{X}_0. \tag{14-19}$$

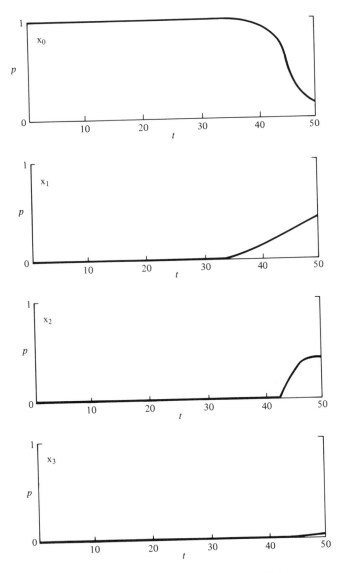

Figure 14.4 State trajectories for the dynamic model of Chicken.

This is a constrained optimization problem similar to those solved using the technique of variational calculus. Other possible applications of ideas from systems and control theory can be found in the references (Kailath, 1980; Kwakernaak, 1972).

The consideration that a player will often change preferences in response to the state of the conflict has not been represented in the time-dependent formulation developed in this chapter. For example, a particular player may be unaware of a possible option in the game. This hypergame situation will continue until the state of the conflict includes the selection of that particular option. Thus the transition matrix is a function of the state of the conflict as well as of time. This circumstance can easily be handled on an individual basis using a simulation computer program like CSMP.

There are techniques available from game theory for assessing conflict situations that involve continuous actions by the participants. These methods are called *differential games* (Leitmann, 1974; Hajek, 1975). In a differential game, a set of differential equations is developed to model a problem; these are then solved to answer some specified questions. For example, one situation that appears in the literature is the *pursuit problem* (Hajek, 1975). If there is a pursuer and a quarry on an x–y plane, the possible motions of both the quarry and the pursuer can be defined as differential equations. These can then be used to determine the optimal actions of the pursuer to allow him (or her) to catch the quarry, or the best strategy by the quarry in order to delay capture as long as possible.

The major differences between differential games and the formulation presented in this chapter are as follow:

1. For differential games, a set of differential equations must be set up for each new conflict to be studied. For the state transition form, one simply inserts one's knowledge of the conflict into a standard form.

2. The differential games approach is primarily *normative*. This means it endeavors to show how people in conflict situations should act by trying to determine some essential characteristic of certain types of games. The state transition form is more *descriptive* in orientation. It models a real world conflict, and provides insight specifically for a particular problem.

14.5 Important Concepts from Chapter 14

The dynamics of a conflict can be important in the study of a real world problem. In this chapter it is demonstrated that, based upon concepts from the conflict analysis algorithm, comprehensive tools can be developed for modeling a game over time. Of particular importance are the state transition model in equation (14-1) and the continuous model in equation (14-18).

A supergame is a set of games linked so that an outcome achieved in one game results in a different game, which must then be played out. A supergame is not truly dynamic, however, because it is a set of linked static games. Furthermore, a cardinal payoff rather than an ordinal preference is associated with each outcome for each player.

The nuclear conflict was analyzed using the extensive and state transition form. Although both of these methods enabled the expected resolution to the conflict to be ascertained, the example showed that the state transition model is simpler and more flexible than the extensive form. It was concluded that the conflict analysis method and the state transition approach together constitute a comprehensive set of conflict analysis tools.

An extension of the state transition approach that incorporates time explicitly was mathematically derived to obtain the formula in equation (14-18). For the analysis of Chicken, this formula was shown to be particularly useful. In general, (14-18) can be employed for procuring a basic understanding of any conflict under study. Furthermore, in conjunction with concepts from systems and control theory, there is great potential for analyzing more complex problems.

Questions

1. In the Chicken supergame, which of the following strategies is the best for player A if A thinks that player B will swerve in both games 10% of the time?
   (a) Player A never swerves.
   (b) Player A never swerves in game 1, but always swerves in game 2.
   (c) Player A swerves 10% of the time in game 1, 10% of the time in game 2.
2. In the Prisoner's Dilemma (see Section 12.6.1), a case can be made that each prisoner would be less likely to confess at the start of his interrogation. Design a reasonable supergame for Prisoner's Dilemma.

Appendix A
Bargaining Problem

A.1 Introduction

The bargaining problem concerns determining which of a number of possible contracts will be expected to occur or which will be best for the players involved (Luce and Raiffa, 1957; Rapoport, 1970b). A number of mathematical models of bargaining have been proposed in the literature. The value of these models generally lies in pointing something out about the mathematical nature or the structure of bargaining situations.

Early models of bargaining were highly quantitative in orientation and strived to determine a numerical solution to the bargaining problem. Although experiments have shown that bargainers make better decisions if they have quantitative rather than qualitative information (Ulvila, 1979), more recent models are generally nonquantitative. The major drawbacks of quantitative formal models include (Young, 1975):

1. the consideration of models that are too constrained to represent the real world,
2. the problems of acquiring accurate information,
3. requiring an assessment of the utility of outcomes,
4. assuming values for parameters that are unattainable in real life,
5. assuming rationality by the players,
6. neglecting the interactions among many issues, and
7. ignoring the dynamic aspects of the situation.

A *cooperative game* is a game in which the players have complete freedom of preplay communication to make joint binding agreements (Luce and Raiffa, 1957). A *noncooperative game* allows no preplay communication. Historically, cooperative games have generally required quantitative methods of analysis. On the other hand noncooperative games can be effectively analyzed using nonquantitative models. Because of the foregoing problems with quantitative bargaining models, the most promising avenue for dealing with bargaining problems is to utilize a noncooperative game theory model such as conflict analysis where at most ordinal preferences are assumed. This Appendix is concerned with various approaches to the modeling of bargaining situations using both cooperative and noncooperative concepts.

A.2 Cooperative Game Solutions

When outcomes are assigned utilities, or payoffs, for the players, schemes can be used to establish an optimal contract, under the general model of a cooperative game. Consider a space of utility payoffs in a two-player game to be represented by the region R in Figure A.1. The symbols u_1 and u_2 represent the utility payoffs for players 1 and 2, respectively. Any of the possible agreements must lie in R, so obviously the optimal final contract will lie along the northeast boundary of R, because these agreements are most beneficial to both players considered together. This boundary is called the *negotiation set* (Luce and Raiffa, 1957), alternatively referred to as the "contract zone" (Bacharach and Lawter, 1981), or the "bargaining arena" (Kennedy et al., 1980). The problem is to come up with some way to define a particular resolution within this set.

A.2.1 Nash Solution

Nash (1950a) presented four seemingly reasonable assumptions that a bargaining solution should fulfill:

1. The solution should be the same even if the units or origins of the utilities are transformed.
2. The solution should be Pareto optimal; that is, there should be no other point in R that is preferred by both players.
3. If there are two different bargaining games with the same status quo, and the region R of game 1 is completely contained in the region R of game 2, then the solution of game 2 must be the same as the solution of game 1, or it must not be in the region R of game 1.
4. If the bargaining game places the players in completely symmetric roles, then they should receive the same payoff.

Given these assumptions and a status quo or conflict point (u_1^0, u_2^0), Nash (1950a) showed that there is a unique bargaining solution to the game. This is given by (u_1^*, u_2^*) such that

$$(u_1^* - u_1^0)(u_2^* - u_2^0) \geq (u_2 - u_1^0)(u_2 - u_2^0)$$

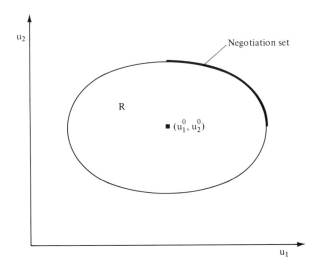

Figure A.1 Utility Space and the Negotiation Set

for all u_1, u_2 in R. This solution is independent of any interpersonal comparisons of utility, and Nash proved that it is the only solution procedure that satisfies the assumptions he put forward (Nash, 1950a; Luce and Raiffa, 1957).

A.2.2 Zeuthen's Principle

Zeuthen's Principle provides a compelling reinforcement for the Nash solution. Zeuthen (1930) argued that at a particular point in a bargaining situation the player that will make a concession is the player that is less willing to risk a conflict. When outcomes are assigned utilities, Zeuthen's Principle allows the assessment of which player should make a concession in the bargaining situation by determining a quantitative expression for his or her risk. The risk r_i for player i is given by

$$r_i = \frac{u_i\,(A_i) - u_i\,(A_j)}{u_i\,(A_i) - u_i\,(C)}$$

where $u(\cdot)$ is the utility of the parenthesized agreement, A_i is an agreement proposed by player i, and C is the situation of no agreement (Harsanyi, 1977). If $r_j \leq r_i$, then player i should make the next concession. As a result of that concession, player i's risk will be lowered to a value less than or equal to that for player j, so that player j should make the following concession. The players will alternately make concessions until a final agreement is reached. This final agreement mathematically coincides with the Nash solution for a two-player game (Harsanyi, 1977).

A.2.3 Shapley Value

The Shapley value is a payoff calculated to be an expression of the expected utility of a player in a game (Shapley, 1953). It is especially useful in games where coalitions play a major role. Shapley described the value of a game using three conditions, and showed that these conditions uniquely determined a single evaluation function:

1. Value is a property of the abstract game, so that the value of the game to a player is the same no matter how the game is formatted.
2. The individual values to the players in the game sum to the value of the whole game.
3. The value of two games taken together is the sum of the values of each game considered separately.

These conditions uniquely lead to an expression that amounts to a weighted sum of the incremental additions made by a player to all the coalitions of which he or she can possibly be a member. It can be shown that the Shapley value is a generalization of the minimax value of a game, and that the payoffs for the Nash solution correspond to the Shapley value in two-person games in which the conflict point corresponds to the non-cooperative solution (Luce and Raiffa, 1957).

A.2.4 Other Quantitative Game Models

There are innumerable other models and approaches to the bargaining problem to be found in the literature that require some form of utility assessment. Once numbers have been assigned to real world phenomena, any variety of mathematical procedures can be developed. Some are realistic but, unfortunately, most are not.

If the objectives and constraints of a problem can be expressed by algebraic functions, mathematical programming can be used to ascertain the optimal solutions. When there is more than one objective function, the problem is referred to as *multiobjective programming* (see, e.g., Haimes, 1977; Cohen, 1978; Goicoechea et al., 1982). For cases where there are more than one decision maker, the desires or objectives of each player can be expressed as one or more algebraic objective functions. An overall *objective function* can be formed by somehow combining the individual objective functions. The objective function is a function of "decision variables"—variables that represent some quantification of real world phenomena. For example, consider negotiations that concern the pollution of the Holston River (see Chapter 8). Some of the important decision variables in this problem would include water quality and cost of effluent treatment. Both of these parameters can be represented quantitatively by decision variables expressed by real number values using appropriate units. The objective function of these decision variables is selected so that minimizing (or maximizing) the objective function appropriately optimizes the decision variables—in this case increasing the water quality and decreasing the price. Since it costs money to increase water quality, the decision variables are not independent.

When there is more than one party involved in the problem, the optimization process must be performed for all parties simultaneously. Central to this multiobjective decision analysis is the concept of Pareto optimality, which is exhibited by solutions for which any improvement for one objective function can be achieved only at the expense of another (Haimes, 1977). One common technique for solving multiobjective decision problems is to give each objective function a weight, and then optimize the weighted average of the objective functions as a scalar optimization problem. Normally in a multiobjective problem more than a single solution will result.

As is the case for any quantitative scheme, the major drawback of the objective function approach is determining the numerical values of the decision variables and the relationships among them. In the solution procedure, the use of the surrogate worth trade-off method (Haimes, 1977) can assist in partially overcoming this difficulty because it requires only ordinal decision making once a minimum set of objective levels have been attained.

A.3 Nonquantitative Game Models

Noncooperative game theory provides the richest avenue for the nonquantitative analysis of the bargaining problem. This form of analysis is assessed in detail in Chapter 8. However, there are two special cases that merit particular examination because they can be distinguished from more conventional approaches to noncooperative games.

A.3.1 2 × 2 Games

One of the simplest expressions of any conflict situation is a game in which there are two players each of whom has two mutually exclusive strategies. These 2 × 2 games are usually expressed in normal form. [See Luce and Raiffa (1957) or Chapter 10 for a complete description of games in normal form.] Unquestionably, very little detail about the interactions between the participants can be modeled in such a game, and it is of course limited to only two players. On the other hand, bargaining situations do commonly concern two major adversaries, and the selection by each player between two loosely defined strategies may not be an unrealistic constraint.

Snyder and Diesing (1977) view 2 × 2 game models as providing optimal structural information for studying a conflict. They use a 2 × 2 game model that does not employ many of the traditional assumptions about games in normal form. For example, their 2 × 2 model does not require the payoffs being known by the players or being fixed for the duration of the game, and does not have restrictions about whether single or simultaneous moves are made by the players. These authors see the bargaining process as a procedure of searching and modifying the cells of a 2 × 2 matrix. A player in a conflict initially may have an incomplete or mistaken impression of the structure and payoffs of the game. He (or she) acts based upon the game as he sees it, and his view of the game changes as he observes the actions of the opponent. Tentative probes will be made to assess the possibility of a cooperative solution to the conflict, as well as to determine whether there is a dominant strategy that can impose a preferred outcome. In this manner, the dynamics of the conflict can be traced out over time. The value of this technique is brought out in a number of real world examples presented in Snyder and Diesing's (1977) book.

Rapoport et al. (1976) have done an exhaustive study of 2 × 2 games. They have shown that the four cells of a 2 × 2 game can be ordinally ordered, when transposition of players and strategies are taken into account, in only 78 different ways. They have classified and cross-indexed these games and their cardinal variations so that a great deal of information about a particular game model can be accessed very easily. Their examination of these games includes subdividing them into groups of games with similar characteristics, exploring the logical and philosophical implications of particular games and their variations, and presenting the results of extensive experimentation to find out how humans behave when playing games designed to be similar to the game models. Their results can provide insight into the structural analysis of bargaining situations that can best be modeled using 2 × 2 games.

A.3.2 Supergames

Another possibility explored by Rapoport (1967, 1969a) and Snyder and Diesing (1977) is the supergame, a concatenation of games (Section 14.2). Each cell in one of the subgames provides a payoff to the players and a pointer to the next subgame to consider. In this manner the conflict will change its nature as it is played out, with payoffs being accrued at each stage of play. The supergame thus provides for the dynamic nature of bargaining situations without abandoning the rigor of a formal game model.

Appendix B
Negotiation Concepts

B.1 Introduction

In Chapter 9 the manner in which conflict analysis can be employed in negotiation is described. The aim of this appendix is to detail some of the other considerations that previous writers have identified as being of importance in the study of negotiation.

B.2 Negotiation Moves

Radford (1977) characterizes negotiation as a sequence of moves in which the adversaries attempt to arrive at a favorable agreement. He points out that negotiation moves can be either communicative or structural. A *communicative move* informs the opponents of either the truth or a deception about the preferences or intentions of the player, whereas a *structural move* is an overt action, commitment, or proposal. Simultaneously, a negotiation move can be accommodative or coercive. An *accommodative move* is one that strives for an agreement, is cooperative, and usually involves adjusting demands in the direction of compromise. A *coercive move*, on the other hand, is aggressive and often involves an escalation of conflict.

A plane in which the x coordinate represents degree of activity and the y axis represents accommodation can be used to present the range of negotiation move possibilities. In Figure B.1, point a, which is very communicative and highly coercive, would be the situation of a verbal threat. For example, in the environmental conflict described in Chapter 8, the EPA threatened to go to public notice; this constituted a coercive communicative move. Point b might be the situation where the EPA actually called for the public meeting. Point c would involve an accommodative

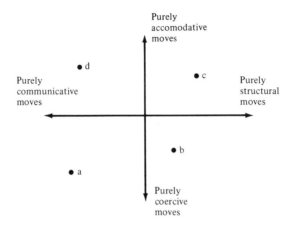

Figure B.1 Negotiation moves

structural move such as the EPA's concessions regarding the limitations during the March 4, 1974 technical meeting. An example of a move at point *d* would be where the EPA indicated its willingness to compromise by permitting the TEC to submit a counterproposal to the effluent limitations.

B.3 Commitment

A number of considerations are important in the making of a negotiation move. Schelling (1960) in his classic "Essay on Bargaining" makes a very good case for the value of commitment as a coercive communicative tactic. Consider a situation in which players A and B are negotiating over a house currently owned by player A. Player A wants a price of $50,000 or more, and is currently asking $60,000. Player B wants a price of $60,000 or less, and is currently offering $50,000. At this point, both players would prefer to make a contract, since there minimum requirements have been met, but they are left with the problem of how to establish the final price. The negotiation set in this situation is the range of contracts from $50,000 to $60,000. The Nash solution to this problem (see Appendix A) is $55,000.

Schelling points out that player B can commit to the lower price in such a manner that A's only reasonable choice is to agree to the $50,000 selling price. Suppose B made a contract with player C to the effect that if B did not achieve an agreement from A to sell the house for $50,000, B would give C $10,000. This would mean that if B bought the house for anything more than $50,000, it would actually cost B more than $60,000, which is more than B is willing to pay. Once B tells of this commitment, A has the choice of accepting the $50,000 offer or giving up the deal altogether. Since taking the offer is preferable to giving up the deal, he can be expected to accept the offer, and B has made a very good bargain.

In real life, commitments can be made in a more reasonable manner than actually making a third-party contract. One manner is to deal through an agent, who cannot make independent decisions. In the house purchasing situation, if B's agent is instructed to offer no more than $50,000, player A again must accept the offer or give up the deal. Another form of commitment is the use of publicity. A union negotiator who proclaims to the rank and file that he or she will hold out for a 20% increase has too much to lose to be expected to accept less.

In the Holston River negotiations of Chapter 8, commitment is part of the entire permit process. Once the permit is issued, it is a legal commitment and is not negotiable. Consequently, within weeks after the public hearing, the EPA had to issue the permit. It was then the responsibility of the TEC to secure an acceptable permit; otherwise, the only recourse was litigation.

B.4 Threats and Ambiguity

Threats are a useful and popular tactic when negotiating. The degree to which one negotiator can harm an opponent without hurting himself too much provides a corresponding power over the selection of a final contract. The EPA frequently threatened public notice to the TEC during the Holston River negotiations.

An important aspect of communicative moves such as threats is the decision of being ambiguous as opposed to expressing the intended information clearly (Radford, 1977). Ambiguity has the value of the ability to be re-expressed, clarified, reinterpreted, or denied at a later date, but on the other hand can be misconstrued. A clear communication reflects careful thinking (Fisher, 1970) and can be expected to lead more positively to a final agreement. It also reinforces credibility and resolve.

B.5 Bounds of Negotiation

Another important consideration is being able to take advantage of the structure or bounds of the negotiating environment. For example, if the problem can be broken up into a number of smaller parts, concessions made by one bargainer in one part can be compensated for by the other player in a different part. Similarly, negotiation often takes place repetitively over time. A concession at one point in time can be exchanged for a future concession of a similar nature. Finally, an additional negotiation situation can be introduced for which an exchange of concessions can be made. Imagine the company president and the union president negotiating over a union pay raise. Imagine further that they are respectively players A and B of the house-for-sale situation discussed in Section B.3. It would be a reasonable tactic for the union leader to offer the company president $60,000 for his house.

B.6 Power

Karrass (1972) feels that power is a very important characteristic of negotiation. A party with power in a negotiation is one that has more freedom to act. Power is the "capacity of a party to produce an agreement on its own terms" (Bacharach and Lawler, 1981). Karrass (1974) lists some sources of power for a negotiator:

1. *Commitment,* in the sense of having a single firm goal or loyalty.
2. *Legitimacy*—a form or legal document carries more power than a statement or opinion.
3. *Knowledge*—the negotiator who knows the most about the opposition can negotiate better.
4. *Risk taking and having courage*—a person who has more possible actions available due to his or her ability to operate under apparent uncertainty is more flexible and responsible.
5. *Time and effort*—the party that is more constrained by time limits or available resources is in a weaker position.

Both Bacharach and Lawler (1981) and Gruder (1970) believe that power is the key characteristic that determines the success of a negotiation. Further, Karrass (1972) has shown through experimentation that there is a direct correlation between power and success in negotiation.

In the Holston River negotiations, the TEC made effective use of power in its negotiations. First, it was willing to spend time and effort in order to secure the best result for the company. The EPA, on the other hand, was restricted by staff and budget limitations. Second, the power of legitimacy was on the side of the TEC because of its position as an expert in chemistry as well as its use of exceptionally qualified outside consultants. Third, the TEC had the power of commitment. Although the EPA was also committed, it had many battles to fight and could not be totally committed to one. The TEC had just one opponent on which to concentrate, and the result of the negotiations was of substantial economic interest to it.

B.7 Level of Aspiration

The success experienced by a participant in a negotiation as sufficient to meet his or her expectations is a critical characteristic of negotiation. This expectation, called the player's *level of aspiration,* may be verbalized or may simply be the anticipated result of a negotiation based upon the experience of previous similar negotiations. The level of aspiration can be seen as the goal of negotiation for a party, as opposed to a party's *limit* or level of benefit beyond which it is unwilling to concede (Praitt, 1981).

Experiments (Karrass, 1972; Praitt, 1981) have illustrated that if participants only aspire to a certain level of success, they will rarely achieve beyond it. On the other hand, individuals who have an unrealistic level of aspiration often succeed beyond anyone's imagination. Bacharach and Lawler (1981) present the generally accepted theory that the effect of one negotiator expressing high aspirations and tough behavior is to reduce the aspirations of the other negotiator. However, they point out that there is only marginal evidence to support this theory.

It is clear that the level of aspiration was fairly high for the TEC. Its original proposal for effluent limits was set very high so that even after considerable compromise had taken place favorable agreement resulted for the TEC.

B.8 Needs

One view of the negotiation process is that the resulting contract or resolution must meet a variety of needs by all parties. Neirenberg (1973) presents a comprehensive view of negotiation that identifies seven types of needs and how to handle them. From most basic to least basic, the seven types of needs are as follow (Maslow, 1954).

1. physiological (homeostatic),
2. safety and security,
3. love and belonging,
4. esteem,
5. self-actualization (inner motivation, to become what one is capable of becoming),
6. knowledge and understanding, and
7. aesthetic.

Neirenberg (1973) also identifies three different levels at which negotiation takes place:

1. interpersonal,
2. interorganizational (excluding nations), and
3. international.

Finally, Neirenberg (1973) presents six ways in which a negotiator can behave with regard to his (or her) needs and the needs of the opponent:

1. Negotiator works for the opponent's needs.
2. Negotiator lets the opponent work for the negotiator's needs.
3. Negotiator works for the opponent's and his own needs.
4. Negotiator works against his needs.
5. Negotiator works against the opponent's needs.
6. Negotiator works against the opponent's and his own needs.

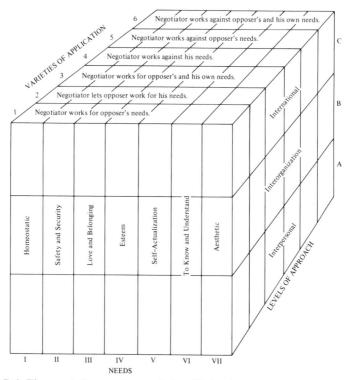

Figure B.2 The need theory of negotiating (Neirenberg, 1973).

These three aspects of negotiation—kinds of needs, levels of negotiations, and negotiator behavior—are summarized in Figure B.2.

Neirenberg's intention in presenting his Need Theory is to provide the negotiator with a structure for developing strategies and tactics in negotiating. For example, in the Holston River situation the level was clearly interorganizational. For the TEC, the needs involved were homeostatic since the cash flow and profit of the company were involved. The EPA's needs were less basic and probably self-actualization needs; in other words, doing its job. During negotiation, the EPA probably worked for both players' needs while the TEC worked solely for its own.

Appendix C

Summary of Classical Game Theoretic Techniques

C.1 Introduction

All game theory depends on the original work of von Neumann in the 1920s and 1930s (Von Neumann, 1928, 1937), but it first achieved wide acceptance following the 1944 publication of *Theory of Games and Economic Behavior* by Von Neumann and Morgenstern. Since this time, game theory has developed along many fascinating lines, but this appendix concerns some of the basic, thoroughly accepted concepts of game theory developed in the 1940s and 1950s. This is commonly called *classical game theory*.

C.2 Games and Extensive Forms of Games

Game theory injudiciously borrows some of its terminology from parlor games. The participants in a game are called *players,* and at each stage of the game they make *moves* according to some *rules*. The moves made by players are called *personal* moves, and moves that are controlled by some probabilistic device are called *chance* moves (Venttsel', 1963). At the conclusion of the game, there is some sort of reward for the players, called the *payoff.*

Consider the game called simplified two-finger morra (Hillier and Lieberman, 1974). There are two players, each of which can choose to display either one finger or two fingers. If they both display the same number of fingers, player 1 (P1) gets \$1 from player 2 (P2). If they do not display the same number of fingers, P2 gets \$1 from P1. This game can be displayed as a *game tree* as shown in Figure C.1.

Game trees have a number of properties. Each node of the game tree is associated with a player, or with chance. Each branch of the tree is associated with a move which can be made according to the rules of the game. The branches are directed, and each node has only one branch directed into it. The endpoints of the tree have a vector of payoffs associated with them. For example, $(1, -1)$ means that P1 gets $1 while P2 loses $1. A node representing a chance play has a probability associated with each outwardly directed branch such that the sum of the probabilities is 1.

In the game of simplified two-finger morra, the two players are not aware of the choices being made by the other player, so if the game is represented by P1 moving first, as it is in Figure C.1, the fact that P2 does not know whether P1 has chosen one finger or two is represented by enclosing the two nodes in a dotted line. This is called an *information set*. If all information sets in a game contain only one node, the game is called one of *perfect information* (Luce and Raiffa, 1957).

A completed game tree is also called the *extensive form* of the game. The extensive form of the game is a useful representation of the moves that must be made in the course of a game, but is very large except for the simplest of games, and thus its usefulness is limited.

The game of two-finger morra is an example of a *zero-sum game* because a win for one player incurs a corresponding equal loss for the other player. Two-person zero-sum games, although they do not represent many real world situations, form an important segment of game theory because they are amenable to analysis using the extensive form, or the normal form, discussed in the Section C.3.

C.3 Strategies, the Normal Form, and Utilities

A *strategy* is a complete description of how a player will behave under every possible circumstance (Davis, 1970). Thus even for simple games the number of possible strategies may be large. Strategies can often be generalized, however, and this leads to a compact method for presenting the game information, called the *normal* form of the game.

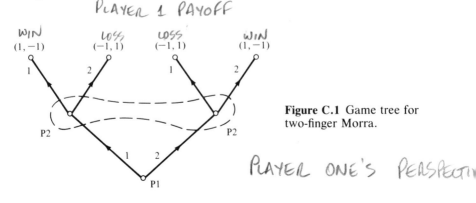

Figure C.1 Game tree for two-finger Morra.

In two-finger morra, the players each have two strategies: to show one finger or show two fingers. The normal form can be represented as a matrix, the strategies of the first player being the rows and the strategies of the second player being the columns, as illustrated in the top of Table C.1. Each pair of strategies forms an *outcome* of the game. The elements of the matrix are the vectors of payoffs for the players for each outcome. For two-person zero-sum games the matrix can be represented as having scalar entries giving the payoff to P1 only without any loss of information, as shown in the bottom of Table C.1

Usually real conflict situations do not have payoffs in easily manageable units like money. To express the value of an outcome to a player, the theory of *utility* has been developed. Basically, utility is a numerical value assigned to an outcome for a player. It is determined in such a manner that a higher utility means a more preferred outcome. Also, the utility of a *lottery*, or probabilistic occurrence of an outcome from a specific group, is derivable and comparable to the utility of other outcomes or lotteries. The goal of players in a game is then to *maximize their utility*.

C.4 Two-Person Zero-Sum Games

C.4.1 Equilibriums

A player will choose a strategy that he (or she) believes will maximize his utility, bearing in mind that his opponent desires to do the same for himself. If there is an ordered pair of strategies such that neither player can improve his utility payoff by a change in strategy, this outcome constitutes an *equilibrium*.

Consider Table C.2, which represents some game situation. The entries in the matrix are payoffs for player 1, and so player 2 gets the negative of these entries. The outcome formed from the strategies S11 and S21 forms an equilibrium because any change from S11 by P1 results in a smaller payoff for him, and any change from S21 by P2 results in less utility for him since the numbers presented in the matrix are the payoffs for P1. An equilibrium can be found by examining the outcomes for those

Table C.1 Normal Form of Two-Finger Morra

	P2	
P1	1 finger	2 fingers
1 finger	$(1, -1)$	$(-1, 1)$
2 fingers	$(-1, 1)$	$(1, -1)$
1 finger	1	-1
2 fingers	-1	1

Table C.2 Game with an Equilibrium

		P2	
P1	S21	S22	S23
S11	0	1	1
S12	-1	-2	3
S13	-2	2	-3

that are simultaneously the maximum in their column and the minimum in their row. Because of this, equilibriums are also referred to as *saddle points*.

C.4.2 Mixed Strategies

Consider the game presented in Table C.3 (Luce and Raiffa, 1957). If P1 chooses the strategy S12, the minimum payoff he (or she) is guaranteed no matter what P2 does is 2. If he chooses S11 he may get only 1. The payoff 2 is P1's *security level*, and if he chooses his strategy correctly he is guaranteed at least a payoff of 2. P2's security level—where his maximum loss is minimized—is 3 (representing a loss of 3), which is attained by choosing strategy S21. A security level is also called the *maximin* level or *lower value* of the game for P1, and the *minimax* level, or *upper value*, of the game for P2 (Venttsel', 1963). Since game theory assumes P1 is aware of the nature of the game, in the game of Table C.3 P1 can realize that P2 will choose S21, and thus P1 can improve his payoff by selecting strategy S11 instead of S12. P2 may be aware of this strategem, and can thus improve his position by selecting S22 instead of S21. This cyclic train of thought can continue forever, and leads to the concept of strategy selection through probabilistic means.

Consider the expected utility for P1 when he flips a coin and selects one of the two strategies available to him on the basis of whether heads or tails occurs. If P1 does this and P2 selects S21, the expected payoff is

$$(\tfrac{1}{2} \times 3) + (\tfrac{1}{2} \times 2) = \tfrac{5}{2}.$$

If P2 selects S22, the expected payoff is

$$(\tfrac{1}{2} \times 1) + (\tfrac{1}{2} \times 4) = \tfrac{5}{2}.$$

Thus P1 can expect to get $\tfrac{5}{2}$ of a dollar (or whatever the utility represents) in the long run by using this *mixed strategy* as compared to getting a minimum of 2 or 1 dollars by playing either *pure strategy*.

Table C.3 Game with No Equilibrium

		P2	
P1		S21	S22
S11		3	1
S12		2	4

If P2 plays a mixed strategy composed of $\frac{1}{2}$ S21 and $\frac{1}{2}$ S22, the payoff is

$$(\tfrac{1}{2} \times 3) + (\tfrac{1}{2} \times 1) = 2$$

when P1 plays S11, and

$$(\tfrac{1}{2} \times 2) + (\tfrac{1}{2} \times 4) = 3$$

when P1 plays S12. Thus this mixed strategy gives P2 only a sure payoff of 3, which is no better than the security level of playing the pure strategy of S21 alone. However, if the mixed strategy of $(\frac{3}{4}, \frac{1}{4})$ is used, where the ordered pair indicates that S21 is chosen $\frac{3}{4}$ of the time and S22 is chosen $\frac{1}{4}$ of the time, the payoff is

$$(\tfrac{3}{4} \times 3) + (\tfrac{1}{4} \times 1) = \tfrac{5}{2}$$

when P1 plays S11, and

$$(\tfrac{3}{4} \times 2) + (\tfrac{1}{4} \times 4) = \tfrac{5}{2}$$

when P1 plays S12.

Note that the payoffs for the mixed strategies $(\frac{1}{2},\frac{1}{2})$ for P1 and $(\frac{3}{4},\frac{1}{4})$ for P2 are the same at $\frac{5}{2}$. Von Neumann (1928) showed that for all two-person zero-sum games that there is at least one mixed strategy for each player such that the first player is guaranteed at least some amount, and the second player is guaranteed to lose no more than the same amount. This amount is called the *value* of the game, and if there is an equilibrium in the game, the value of the game is equal to the value of the payoff at the equilibrium.

The strategies (either pure or mixed) for P1 and P2 that yield the value of the game are called *optimal* strategies. A *solution* to a game consists of the set of optimal strategies for the players and the value of the game. The solution to the game of Table C.3 may be written

$$\langle\ (\tfrac{1}{2},\tfrac{1}{2}),\ (\tfrac{3}{4},\tfrac{1}{4});\ \tfrac{5}{2}\ \rangle$$

C.4.3 Solutions

There are many methods for finding some or all of the solutions for two-person zero-sum games. If one is just looking for a single solution, many games can be simplified through the use of *dominance arguments*. This is the principle that if a row (column) of the game matrix is always greater (less) than or equal to another row (column), then P1 (P2) will invariably prefer to use the strategy with the greater (lesser) payoff, and the *dominated* strategy need not appear in the solution. A row or column can also be dominated by a linear combination of other rows or columns. An illustration of how a large matrix can be reduced to a smaller matrix is given as Table C.4.

There is a simple method for finding a solution for square nonsingular

Table C.4 Reducing Matrices Through Dominance

	P2		
P1	S21	S22	S23
S11	1	1	3
S12	−1	3	2
S13	3	1	2

Now, $\frac{1}{2}$ (S21) + $\frac{1}{2}$ (S22) ≤ S23; therefore S23 is dominated, and the matrix reduces to

	P2	
P1	S21	S22
S11	1	1
S12	−1	3
S13	3	1

Since $\frac{1}{2}$ (S12) + $\frac{1}{2}$ (S13) ≥ S11, S11 is dominated, and the matrix reduces to

	P2	
P1	S21	S22
S12	−1	3
S13	3	1

This has the solution

$$\langle\, (\tfrac{1}{3},\tfrac{2}{3}),\ (\tfrac{1}{3},\tfrac{2}{3});\ \tfrac{5}{3}\, \rangle,$$

which means that the solution of the original problem is

$$\langle\, (0,\tfrac{1}{3},\tfrac{2}{3}),\ (\tfrac{1}{3},\tfrac{2}{3},0);\ \tfrac{5}{3}\, \rangle$$

matrix games such as the reduced game from Table C.4. It is given by

$$\left\langle \frac{J^T A^*}{J^T A^* J}, \frac{A^* J}{J^T A^* J}; \frac{|A|}{J^T A^* J} \right\rangle$$

where J is a vector of 1s to the dimension of A, J^T its transpose, A is a square matrix game, and A^* is the adjoint matrix of A (Dresher, 1961). This assumes that A has no saddle point.

A geometric method of solution can be handy for $2 \times n$ matrix games where dominated strategies are not obvious. Consider the matrix game and corresponding illustration given as Figure C.2 (Venttsel', 1963). The illustration is constructed by drawing lines from the values associated with the strategies for P2 when P1 chooses his first strategy on the abscissa to the values associated with the strategies for P2 when P1 chooses his second strategy on the line $x = 1$. The lower boundary of this set of lines, indicated by the heavy line in the diagram, indicates the payoffs to P1 for the corresponding mixed strategy read off the ordinate axis. An optimal strategy will be at the maximum of this boundary, and the value of the game corresponds to the Y value at this maximum.

For this game, P1 has many optimal strategies in which the probability

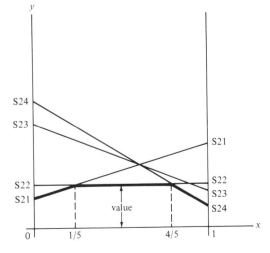

Figure C.2 Geometric solution to 2×2 matrix games.

of selecting pure strategy S12 may be from $\frac{1}{5}$ to $\frac{4}{5}$. P2 has a pure optimal strategy of S22, and the value of the game is 4.

Other methods of finding a solution include trial and error (Luce and Raiffa, 1967), successive approximation of the solution by repeated plays of the game (Luce and Raiffa, 1967; Dresher, 1961), and transformation of the game into a linear programming problem (Vadja, 1956). The problem of finding all solutions to a game is more challenging. The technique of Shapely and Snow is one method (Shapely and Snow, 1950).

Let $\hat{X}$ and $\hat{Y}$ be the sets of optimal strategies for P1 and P2, respectively. Shapely and Snow show that these sets are convex, and thus can be fully expressed by determining the extreme points of each set. The extreme points can be obtained by examining each square submatrix $\mathbf{M}$ of the original matrix $\mathbf{A}$. If $\mathbf{J}^T\mathbf{M}^*\mathbf{J} \neq 0$, let

$$\bar{x} = \frac{\mathbf{J}^T\mathbf{M}^*}{\mathbf{J}^T\mathbf{M}^*\mathbf{J}}, \; \bar{y} = \frac{\mathbf{M}^*\mathbf{J}}{\mathbf{J}^T\mathbf{M}^*\mathbf{J}},$$

where $\mathbf{J}$ is a vector of 1s and $\mathbf{M}^*$ is the adjoint matrix of $\mathbf{M}$. If the x and y obtained from $\bar{x}$ and $\bar{y}$ by inserting 0s in the relevant locations are both optimal, then they are extreme points.

If, for example, the extreme points found for some 3×3 game turned out to be

$$x_1 = (1,0,0), \qquad x_2 = (0,0,1)$$
$$y_1 = (1,0,0), \qquad y_2 = (\tfrac{1}{2},\tfrac{1}{2},0),$$

it would follow that

$$\hat{X} = \{(\alpha,0,(1-\alpha)), \; 0 \leq \alpha \leq 1\}$$
$$\hat{Y} = \{(\beta,(1-\beta),0), \; 0 \leq \beta \leq \tfrac{1}{2}\}$$

C.5 Two-Person Nonzero-Sum Games

Two person nonzero-sum games reflect the real world more accurately than zero-sum games, but they have the disadvantage that they generally have no universally accepted solution (Davis, 1970). One basic consideration in nonzero-sum games is that of *cooperation*. Consider the matrix game presented in Table C.5. Notice that in nonzero-sum games it is necessary to give the payoffs for both players, since the payoff for P2 can no longer be deduced from the payoff for P1. The first entry in the matrix is the payoff for P1 and the second is the payoff for P2. Two-person nonzero-sum games are also called *bimatrix* games because the matrix can be considered an ordered pair of matrices, each representing the payoffs to one of the players.

If the matrices corresponding to the players payoffs from Table C.5 are solved for each player in the manner of zero-sum games, the optimal

Table C.5 Bimatrix Game with Cooperative Solutions

		P2	
P1	S21		S22
S11	(0,0)		(10,5)
S12	(5,10)		(0,0)

mixed strategies are $(\frac{1}{3},\frac{2}{3})$ for P1, $(\frac{1}{3},\frac{2}{3})$ for P2, and a value in both cases of $\frac{10}{3}$. A nonzero-sum game best analyzed in this fashion is called a *noncooperative* game.

However, imagine now that the two players can communicate their choice of strategy before they select it. In this case, they can both do better by agreeing on one of the nonzero payoffs, which give both players a payoff of at least 5. A nonzero-sum game best analyzed in this fashion is called a *cooperative* game.

Many complications arise in nonzero-sum games because they are usually not purely cooperative or noncooperative. Real world conflicts are usually *mixed motive* games in which the players have some common interests and some competing ones (Dresher, 1961). Also, in a cooperative game there may be more than one good cooperative outcome, as is the case in the example of Table C.5. The problem of selecting a cooperative outcome is called the *bargaining* problem.

C.6 *n*-Player Games

n-player games are usually too complex for classical game theory to provide clear answers (Davis, 1970). There are developments in *n*-player game theory that are useful for real world problems, however, such as the development of voting schemes (Hamburger, 1979), but are usually application dependent and have been developed on an ad hoc basis.

One key principle in *n*-player game theory is that of the *coalition*. Single players often do not have much individual power to control the selection of an outcome and a good corresponding payoff, but groups of players working together can obtain preferred outcomes for each player through cooperation. Possible solutions to *n*-player games may involve many different coalition arrangements.

Two assumptions that are often basic to *n*-player game solutions are those of Pareto optimality and individual rationality. *Pareto optimality* means that there must be no outcome that gives every player the same or a larger payoff than the solution. *Individual rationality* means that every player must obtain at least as great a payoff as he or she could achieve unilaterally (Davis, 1970).

Appendix D
Characterization Theorem

D.1 Introduction

In Chapter 10, metagame theory was described and the metagame analysis procedure was introduced. The key principle linking metagame theory and metagame analysis is the Characterization Theorem. This theorem permits the assessment of metarationality by looking at characteristics of outcomes in the basic game alone. In this appendix, the Characterization Theorem is proven.

D.2 Definitions

The Characterization Theorem is a key theorem given by Howard (1971) in the theoretical development of metagame analysis. As noted in Chapter 10, an rth level metagame may be indicated by

$$L = k_1 k_2 \cdots k_r G,$$

where each k_i represents a player, and G is some given basic game. Setting $r = 0$, the zero level metagame or the basic game G is represented. For $r \neq 0$, L represents a proper metagame.

This notation can be continued to describe the ancestors and descendants of a given metagame. A metagame of the form

$$L_a = k_s k_{s+1} \cdots k_r G,$$

where $s \geq 1$ is called an *ancestor* of L. The particular metagame $L_{ia} = k_2 k_3 \cdots k_r G$ is the *immediate ancestor* of L. Note L is an ancestor of itself and the zero level metagame G has no ancestors.

In parallel, the *descendants* of L are of the form

$$L_d = j_1 \cdots j_s k_1 \cdots k_r G, \quad \text{where } s > 0.$$

An *immediate descendant* of L is of the form $L_{id} = j k_1 \cdots k_r G$. In particular L is not a descendant of itself. A metagame $L = k_1 k_2 \cdots k_r G$ is called a *prime metagame* if and only if each player occurs at most once in the list $k_1 k_2 \cdots k_r$. A *complete prime metagame* is a metagame in which all players occur once. The *prime representative* of any metagame L is defined to be the prime metagame obtained by striking out all but the rightmost listing of each player from L. For example, the prime representative of $L = 6563112G$ is $56312G$.

A player k "follows" a player j "last" in the prime representative of L if the rightmost listing of k is further to the right than occurrences of j's name, or if j does not appear in L but k does. To quote Howard (1971):

> These conditions mean that there exists an ancestor of L in which k's metastrategy is a function from j's basic strategy, so that we may imagine that j makes his basic choice first being followed by k, who chooses his basic strategy in knowledge of j's basic strategy.

D.3 Characterization Theorem for Metarational Outcomes

Theorem D.1. *A basic outcome $\bar{s}$ is metarational for player* i *from metagame* L *if and only if*

$$\exists s_P \; \forall s_i \; \exists \, s_F: \quad (\bar{s}_U, s_{S-U}) \in M_i^- \bar{s},$$

where U *is the set of players other than* i *unnamed in* L; F *is the set of players who follow* i *last in the prime representative of* L; P = N − U − F − {i} *is the set of players who precede* i *in the prime representative of* L; N *is the set of all players in the basic game* G; *and* M_i^- *is* i's *preference function which defines the set of outcomes not preferred by player* i *to any given outcome in the game* G.

For example, if L is the basic game G, the theorem reduces to

$$\forall s_i: \quad (\bar{s}_{N-i}, s_i) \in M_i^- \bar{s},$$

which is the condition necessary for $\bar{s}$ to be rational for player i in G.

Using the following lemma, based on the fundamental assumption of the Axiom of Choice, it is possible to proceed to prove Theorem D.1.

Lemma D.2. *Let* $Q^0, Q^1, \ldots, Q^r$ *be* r + 1 *quantifiers (e.g.,* $\exists$ *or* $\forall$*), and let* $S^*, S_1, \ldots, S_r$ *be* r + 1 *nonempty sets. Let* s* *be an element of* S*,

s_i *be an element of* S_i, s *be an element of* $S = S_1 \times S_2 \cdots \times S_r$, *and* f *stand for a function from* $S \rightarrow S^*$.

$$Q^1 s_1 \cdots Q^{k-1} s_{k-1} Q^0 f Q^k s_k \cdots Q^r s_r: \qquad (s, fs) \in P$$

is equivalent to

$$Q^1 s_1 \cdots Q^r s_r Q^0 f: \qquad (s, fs) \in P$$

or to

$$Q^1 s_1 \cdots Q^r s_r Q^0 s^*: \qquad (s, s^*) \in P.$$

Theorem D.1 is now proved by induction. Let L be a given metagame $k_1 k_2 \cdots k_r G$. As noted earlier for $r = 0$, Theorem D.1 reduces to

$$\forall s_i: \qquad (s_{N-i}, s_i) \in M_i^- \bar{s},$$

the condition necessary for $\bar{s}$, to be rational in the basic game G. Therefore Theorem D.1 is true when no players are named in the metagame, i.e., when $r = 0$ the metagame is reduced to G. Following proof by induction, Theorem D.1 is assumed true for the case where r players are named in the metagame and then proved true for the $r + 1$ case. For r named players the condition for an outcome s of G to be in the set of meta-rational outcomes from L [e.g., the set $\hat{R}_i(h) = \beta^r R_i(k_1 \cdots k_r G)$] is assumed to be

$$\exists s_P \ \forall s_i \ \exists s_F: \qquad (\bar{s}_U, s_P, s_i, s_F) \in M_i^- \bar{s},$$

where U, P, and F are the sets of unnamed, preceding, and following players, respectively, as determined from the prime representative of L. Note that the function M_i^- defines the set of outcomes not preferred by player i to the given outcome s in the basic game G.

To prove Theorem D.1 for $r + 1$ named players, the basic game is assumed to be a metagame of the form kG. The condition for an outcome $(\bar{f}, \bar{s}_{N-k})$ of the metagame kG to be in the set of metarational outcomes $\beta^r R_i(k_1 \cdots k_r(kG))$ is as follows. The player k in kG must be an element of U, P, i, or F.

If $k \in U$,

$$\exists s_P \ \forall s_i \ \exists s_F: \qquad (\bar{f}, \bar{s}_{U-k}, s_P, s_i, s_F) \in M_i^{-*}(\bar{f}, s_{N-k});$$

if $k \in P$,

$$\exists f \ \exists s_{P-k} \ \forall s_i \ \exists s_F: \qquad (\bar{s}_U, f, s_{P-k}, s_i, s_F) \in M_i^{-*}(\bar{f}, \bar{s}_{N-k});$$

if $k \in i$,

$$\exists s_P \ \forall f \ \exists s_F: \qquad (\bar{s}_U, s_P, f, s_F) \in M_i^{-*}(\bar{f}, s_{N-k});$$

if $k \in F$,

$$\exists s_P \ \exists s_i \ \exists f \ \exists s_{F-k}: \qquad (\bar{s}_U, s_P, s_i, f, s_{F-k}) \in M_i^{-*}(\bar{f}, \bar{s}_{N-k}):$$

where U, P, and F are defined from the prime metagame representation of the metagame $k^1 \cdots k_r G$ and where M_i^{-*} is player i's preference function, which defines the set of outcomes not preferred to any given outcome $(\bar{f}, \bar{s}_{N-k})$ in the game kG. Note that due to the reflexive condition $(\bar{f}, \bar{s}_{N-k}) \in M_i^{-*}(\bar{f}, \bar{s}_{N-k})$.

Since M_i^{-*} defines player i's preferences for outcomes in the game kG, the necessary conditions for an outcome s in the game G to be an element of the set of metarational outcomes for player i from metagame $k_1 \cdots k_r(kG)$: [i.e., $s \in \beta^{r+1} R_i(k_1 \cdots k_r(kG))$] are as follow.

$$\text{If } k \in U, \quad \exists \bar{f} \begin{cases} \exists s_P \quad \forall s_i \quad \exists s_F: \quad \beta(\bar{f}, \bar{s}_{U-k}, s_P, s_i, s_F) \in M_i^- \bar{s} \\ \bar{f}\bar{s}_{N-k} = \bar{s}_k, \end{cases} \tag{D-1}$$

where M_i^- defines the set of outcomes not preferred to $\bar{s}$ by player i in game G.

Again quoting Howard (1971):

Now although [(D-1)] requires an $\bar{f}$ to exist satisfying both conditions, in fact an $\bar{f}$ satisfying both conditions will exist if one exists satisfying the first condition. For if f^* satisfies the first condition then consider the function $f_{\bar{s}}^*$ identical to f^* except that $f_{\bar{s}}^* s_{N-k} = \bar{s}_k$. This will satisfy the second condition by definition and the first condition because $\bar{s} \in M_i^- \bar{s}$ always.

Therefore the second condition may be deleted and (D-1) reduces to the following:

If $k \in U$, $\quad \exists f \quad \exists s_P \quad \forall s_i \quad \exists s_F: \quad \beta(\bar{f}, \bar{s}_{U-k}, s_P, s_i, s_F) \in M_i^- \bar{s}.$

Applying the β operator and using Lemma D.2 results in

$\exists s_P \quad \forall s_i \quad \exists s_{FUk}: \quad (\bar{s}_{U-k}, s_P, s_i, s_{FUk}) \in M_i^- s,$

which is the required condition from Theorem D.1 for $s \in R_i(k_1 \cdots k_r(kG))$ when player k belongs to the set U obtained from $k_1 \cdots k_r G$ and obviously "follows" player i "last" in the metagame $k_1 \cdots k_r(kG)$.

Similarly, the following is obtained:

If $k \in P$, $\quad \exists f \quad \exists s_{P-k} \quad \forall s_i \quad \exists s_F: \quad \beta(\bar{s}_U, f, s_{P-k}, s_i, s_F) \in M_i^- \bar{s}.$

Applying the β operator and using Lemma D.2 results in

$\exists s_{P-k} \quad \forall s_i \quad \exists s_{FUk}: \quad (\bar{s}_U, s_{P-k}, s_i, s_{FUk}) \in M_i^- \bar{s},$

which is the necessary condition of Theorem D.1 if $k \in P$ determined from metagame $k_1 \cdots k_r G$.

If $k = i$, $\quad \exists s_P \quad \forall f \quad \exists s_F: \quad \beta(\bar{s}_U, s_P, f, s_F) \in M_i^- \bar{s}$

or

$$\exists s_{PUF} \; \forall s_i: \qquad (\overline{s}_U, s_{PUF}, s_i) \in M_i^- \overline{s},$$

the necessary condition of Theorem D.1 if $k = i$. Finally:

$$\text{If } k \in F, \quad \exists s_P \; \forall s_i \; \exists f \; \exists s_{F-k}: \qquad \beta(\overline{s}_U, s_P, s_i, f, s_{F-k}) \in M_i^- \overline{s}$$

or

$$\exists s_P \; \forall s_i \; \exists s_F: \qquad (\overline{s}_U, s_P, s_i, s_F) \in M_i^- \overline{s},$$

which is the necessary condition from Theorem D.1 in the final case where $k \in F$ as determined from metagame $k_1 \cdots k_r G$.

This completes the proof for the case $r + 1$. Since the theorem holds for $r = 0$ and for $r + 1$, by induction Theorem D.1 holds for all r and thus all metagames.

Five important corollaries follow from the Characterization Theorem. They can be stated as follow (Howard, 1971):

Corollary D.3.1 *If* L′ *is a descendant of metagame* L, *then* $\hat{R}_i$ (L′) $\supseteq \hat{R}_i$ (L).

Thus all outcomes s in game G that are metarational from L will also be metarational from the metagame descendant L'.

Corollary D.4. *If* L* *is the prime representative of* L, *then* $\hat{R}_i$ (L) $=$ $\hat{R}_i$ (L*).

Note that in particular since U, P, and F are all defined in Theorem D.1 from the prime representative of a metagame L, the condition of Theorem D.1 will be the same for any two metagames having the same prime representative. In fact, any prime representatives of metagames that define the same sets U, P, and F will also have the same condition for Theorem D.1. Corollary D.4 has the added significance that if L^* is a complete prime representative, the set $\hat{R}_i(L^*)$ will contain all possible metarational outcomes for the game G.

Corollary D.5.

$$\hat{R}_i(iL) = \hat{R}_i(L).$$

The significance of Corollary D.5 is that it indicates that player i does not expand his (or her) set of metarational outcomes by choosing a pattern of reactions to other player's strategies. He may only expand the set of metarational outcomes of the other players.

Corollary D.6. *The necessary and sufficient conditions for* s *to be general metarational for a player* i *are* $\Gamma_i = \bigcup_L \hat{R}_i(L)$ *or as follow:*

1. s *is metarational for* i *from some metagame;*
2. s *is metarational for* i *from some complete metagame;*
3. s *is metarational for* i *from some and every metagame in which all of the other players follow* i *last;*
4. i *does not possess a basic strategy that will guarantee that regardless of the other player's choices,* i *will obtain an outcome preferred by him to* s *(i.e., no inescapable improvements).*

Corollary D.7 *The conditions for an outcome* s *to belong to the set of symmetric metarational outcomes are as follow:*

1. s *is metarational for* i *from some descendant of any metagame;*
2. s *is metarational for every compete metagame;*
3. s *is metarational for* i *from some metagame in which* i *follows every other player last;*
4. *the other players possess a joint basic strategy by which they can guarantee that regardless of* i*'s strategy choice the outcome will not be preferred by* i *to* s *(i.e., all UIs are sanctioned).*

Appendix E
Examples to Illustrate Existence

E.1 Introduction

The purpose of this appendix is to cite specific examples of games that lie within many of the intersections for the solution concepts shown in the figures in Chapter 13. The various ways in which the solution concepts intersect imply certain existence theorems, which means that there exist games that fit into the sets indicated by the diagrams. Some of these theorems are explicitly stated in Chapter 13. The remaining existence assertions implied in these diagrams are proved by example in this appendix. If an example game exists for each illustrated category, the set cannot be empty.

The reproduced figures of Chapter 13 are altered in this appendix by numbering each distinct set contained in each diagram. Following each figure, the various sets are listed, and an example game is given. These games are in normal form and are all 2 × 2 games. The location in the game is given in terms of rows (R) and columns (C), with the row or column number immediately following the R or C. For example, the outcome in row 2 and column 1 is indicated as R2C1. If there is a particular player, it is indicated following the outcome position as either 1 for the row player or 2 for the column player. The number of the example game, corresponding to the numbering system used by Rapoport et al. (1976), is also given for strict ordinal examples.

E.2 Existence Examples for Figure E.1

Set	Game		Outcome	Player	No.
1	4,4	3,3	R1C1	1 or 2	1
	2,2	1,1			
2	2,2	4,1	R2C2	1 or 2	12
	1,4	3,3			
3	3,4	2,1	R1C1	1	70
	4,2	1,3			
4	4,4	3,3	R1C2	2	1
	2,2	1,1			
5	3,4	1,2	R1C2	1	33
	2,2	1,1			

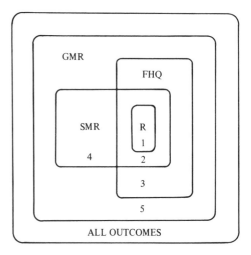

Figure E.1 Individual stability concepts in n-person games (cf. Figure 13.1).

E.3 Existence Examples for Figure E.2

Set	Game		Outcome	Player	No.
1	4,4 3,3 2,2 1,1		R1C1		1
2	2,2 4,1 1,4 3,3		R2C2		12
3	3,4 2,1 4,2 1,3		R1C1		70
4	4,4 3,3 2,2 1,1		R1C2		1
5	3,3 2,4 4,2 1,1		R1C1		66
6	4,4 2,3 1,1 3,2		R1C2		58
7	3,4 1,2 2,3 4,1		R2C1		33

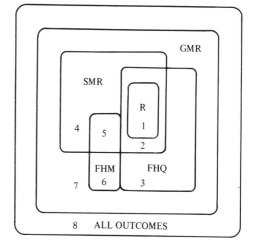

Figure E.2 Group stability concepts in *n*-person games (cf. Figure 13.2).

E.4 Existence Examples for Figure E.3

Set	Game		Outcome	Player	No.
1	4,4	3,3	R1C1	1 or 2	1
	2,2	1,1			
2	2,4	4,1	R2C2	1	44
	1,2	3,3			
3	2,4	4,1	R2C2	1	44
	1,2	3,3			
4	2,2	4,1	R2C2	1 or 2	12
	1,4	3,3			
5	2,4	3,1	R1C1	1	74
	4,2	1,3			
6	3,3	1,1	R1C1	1	
	4,2	2,2			
7	2,3	4,1	R1C1	2	
	3,2	1,2			
8	2,4	4,1	R2C1	2	44
	1,2	3,3			
9	4,4	3,3	R1C2	2	1
	2,2	1,1			
10	3,4	1,2	R2C1	1	33
	2,3	4,1			

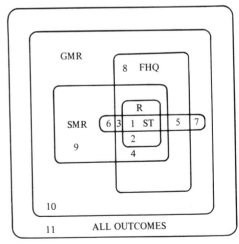

Figure E.3 Individual stability concepts in two-person games (cf. Figure 13.3).

E.5 Existence Examples for Figure E.4

Set	Game		Outcome	Player	No.
1	4,4 3,3 2,2 1,1		R1C1		1
2	2,4 4,1 1,2 3,3		R1C1		44
3	2,2 4,1 1,4 3,3		R2C2		12
4	3,4 2,1 4,2 1,3		R1C1		70
5	4,4 3,3 2,2 1,1		R1C2		1
6	3,3 2,4 4,2 1,1		R1C1		66
7	4,4 2,3 1,1 3,2		R1C2		58
8	3,4 1,2 2,3 4,1		R2C1		33

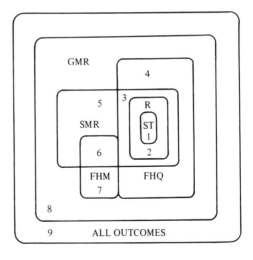

Figure E.4 Group stability concepts in two-person games (cf. Figure 13.4).

E.6 Existence Examples for Figure E.5

Set	Game		Outcome	Player	No.
1	4,4 3,3 2,2 1,1		R1C1	1	1
2	2,2 4,1 3,3 1,4		R2C2	1	77
3	2,2 2,2 3,1 1,2		R1C1	1	
4	2,2 4,1 1,4 3,3		R2C2	1	12
5	2,2 2,2 3,1 1,1		R1C1	1	
6	3,3 2,4 4,2 1,1		R1C1	1	66
7	3,4 4,2 2,3 1,1		R1C1	1	13
8	2,4 4,3 1,3 3,1		R2C1	2	17

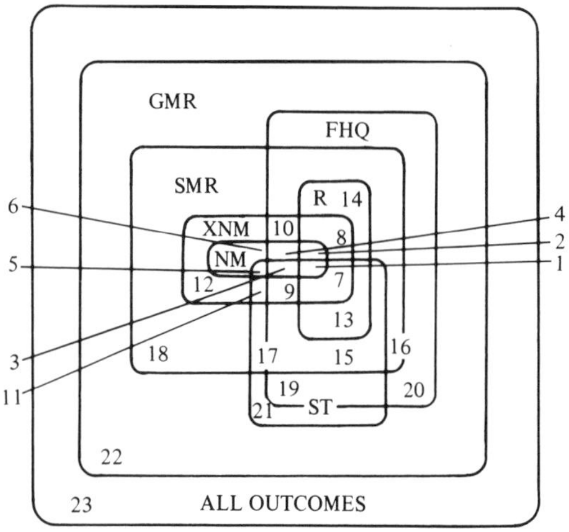

Figure E.5 Individual stability concepts in 2 × 2 games (cf. Figure 13.6).

Set	Game		Outcome	Player	No.
9	2,4	4,1	R2C2	1	44
	1,2	3,3			
10	3,2	4,1	R2C1	2	45
	2,3	1,4			
11	3,3	2,2	R1C2	1	
	4,1	1,1			
12	2,4	4,3	R1C2	2	55
	1,1	3,2			
13	3,4	4,3	R1C1	1	19
	1,2	2,1			
14	2,4	4,1	R1C1	1	44
	1,2	3,3			
15	3,4	2,1	R1C1	1	70
	4,2	1,3			
16	2,2	4,1	R2C1	2	48
	1,3	3,4			
17	3,3	2,1	R1C1	1	
	4,2	1,2			
18	2,4	4,3	R1C2	2	21
	1,2	3,1			
19	2,4	3,1	R1C1	1	74
	4,2	1,3			
20	2,4	4,1	R2C1	2	44
	1,2	3,3			
21	2,3	4,1	R1C1	1	
	3,2	1,2			
22	3,4	1,2	R2C1	1	33
	2,3	4,1			

E.7 Existence Examples for Figure E.6

Set	Game		Outcome	Player	No.
1	4,4	3,3	R1C1		1
	2,2	1,1			
2	3,4	4,2	R2C2		13
	2,3	1,1			
3	3,4	4,3	R1C1		49
	2,1	1,2			
4	3,3	1,3	R1C1		
	2,2	2,1			
5	2,3	4,1	R1C1		47
	1,2	3,4			
6	2,2	4,1	R2C2		12
	1,4	3,3			
7	2,3	4,1	R2C2		47
	1,2	3,4			

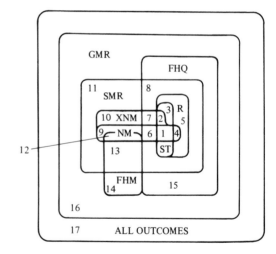

Figure E.6 Group stability concepts in 2 × 2 games (cf. Figure 13.7).

Set	Game		Outcome	Player	No.
8	2,4 4,1	1,2 3,3	R2C2		44
9	3,3 2,3	4,2 1,1	R1C1		
10	2,4 4,3	1,1 3,2	R1C2		55
11	4,4 3,3	2,2 1,1	R1C2		1
12	3,3 2,4	4,2 1,1	R1C1		66
13	4,4 2,2	1,1 3,3	R1C2		59
14	4,4 2,3	1,1 3,2	R1C2		58
15	3,4 2,1	4,2 1,3	R2C1		70
16	3,4 1,2	2,3 4,1	R2C1		33

E.8 Existence Examples for Figure E.7

Set	Game		Outcome	Player	No.
1	4,4 3,3 2,2 1,1		R1C1	1	1
2	2,2 4,1 3,3 1,4		R2C1	1	77
3	2,2 4,1 1,4 3,3		R2C2	1	12
4	3,3 2,4 4,2 1,1		R1C1	1	66
5	3,4 4,2 2,3 1,1		R1C1	1	13
6	2,4 4,3 1,3 3,1		R2C1	2	17
7	2,4 4,1 1,2 3,3		R2C2	1	44

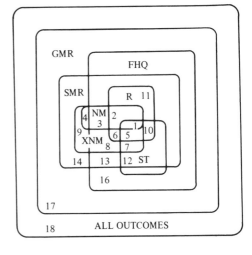

Figure E.7 Individual stability concepts in strict ordinal games (cf. Figure 13.8).

Set	Game		Outcome	Player	No.
8	3,2 4,1 2,3 1,4		R2C1	2	45
9	2,4 4,3 1,1 3,2		R1C2	2	55
10	3,4 4,3 1,2 2,1		R1C1	1	19
11	2,4 4,1 1,2 3,3		R1C1	1	44
12	3,4 2,1 4,2 1,3		R1C1	1	70
13	2,2 4,1 1,3 3,4		R2C1	2	48
14	2,4 4,3 1,2 3,1		R1C2	2	21
15	2,4 3,1 4,2 1,3		R2C1	2	74
16	2,4 4,1 1,2 3,3		R2C1	1	44
17	3,4 1,2 2,3 4,1		R2C1	1	33

E.9 Existence Examples for Figure E.8

Set	Game		Outcome	Player	No.
1	4,4 3,3		R1C1		1
	2,2 1,1				
2	3,4 4,2		R1C1		13
	2,3 1,1				
3	3,4 4,3		R1C1		49
	2,1 1,2				
4	2,3 4,1		R1C1		47
	1,2 3,4				
5	2,2 4,1		R2C2		12
	1,4 3,3				
6	2,3 4,1		R2C2		47
	1,2 3,4				

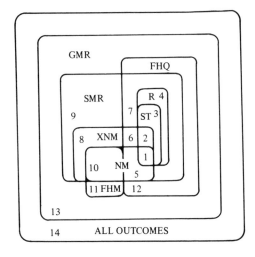

Figure E.8 Individual stability concepts in strict ordinal games (cf. Figure 13.9).

Set	Game		Outcome	Player	No.
7	2,4	4,1	R2C2		44
	1,2	3,3			
8	2,4	4,3	R1C2		55
	1,1	3,2			
9	4,4	3,3	R1C2		1
	2,2	1,1			
10	3,3	2,4	R1C1		66
	4,2	1,1			
11	4,4	2,3	R1C2		58
	1,1	3,2			
12	3,4	2,1	R2C1		70
	4,2	1,4			
13	3,4	1,2	R2C1		33
	2,3	4,1			

Appendix F
Special Classes of Games

F.1 Introduction

In Chapter 13 the focus is on the definitions of the various stability concepts, on their interrelationships, and on questions of existence. Within this appendix, the concepts are compared in the context of two particularly interesting classes of games. In *no-conflict* games there is clearly a best outcome for all players, and any good stability criterion should find it stable. In a *game of complete opposition,* there are two players in total conflict. These games are the ordinal analogue of two-person zero-sum games, for which there are well-developed notions of solutions. Together these two classes of games are the extremes of a spectrum of conflict relationships. Both allow a critical examination of the various stability approaches.

F.2 No-Conflict Games

A *no-conflict game* is a game in which there is at least one outcome that is best for all players. It is to be expected that any such outcome will show a high degree of stability. Further, a good stability criterion should find few if any of the outcomes that are not best to be stable. Because the concept of a best outcome and therefore the concept of a no-conflict game are essentially group concepts, the discussion will be restricted to group stability.

Definition F.1 If $i \in N$ and $\bar{s} \in S$, then $\bar{s}$ is *best for i* iff $v_i(\bar{s}) \geq v_i(s)$ for every $s \in S$. If $B \subseteq N$, then $\bar{s}$ is *best for B* iff $\bar{s}$ is best for i for each $i \in B$. The outcome $\bar{s}$ is *best*, or a *best outcome*, iff $\bar{s}$ is best for N. If $\bar{s}$

is not a best outcome, then $\bar{s}$ is *partially best* iff there exists $B \subseteq N$, $B \neq \emptyset$, such that $\bar{s}$ is best for B. The game G is a *no-conflict* (NC) *game* iff there exists a best outcome. If an outcome $\bar{s} \in S$ in an NC game G is neither best nor partially best, then $\bar{s}$ is *inferior*.

It is easy to show that the best outcomes in an NC game are central to the group stability concepts of Chapter 13.

Theorem F.2 *If* G *is an NC game and* $\bar{s} \in S$ *is a best outcome, then* $\bar{s}$ *is* R, SMR, FHQ, and GMR, and $\bar{s}$ is not FHM.

PROOF: If $i \in N$, then i has no UI from $\bar{s}$ by Definition F.1. By Definitions 13.2 and 13.8 and Theorem 13.14, $\bar{s}$ is R for i, SMR for i, FHQ for i, and GMR for i. The result follows from Definition 13.17 and Theorem 13.22.   □

Unfortunately, however, there exist NC games in which a partially best outcome, or even an inferior outcome, has the same stability properties as any best outcome. In fact, it is possible to find NC games in which there is a partially best outcome or an inferior outcome possessing any of the possible combinations of stabilities determined by Theorems 13.18, 13.19, and 13.22 and illustrated in Figure 13.1 (p. 267).

Now consider the question of stability in the sense of Von Stackelberg (ST) in two-person NC games. Surprisingly, a best outcome may fail to be ST. This failure is illustrated by the four 2×2 NC games shown in Figure F.1. These games are presented in normal form in which one player has row strategies and the other player has column strategies. Thus each element of the matrix is an outcome. The numbers in the cells denote the preference of the player for the outcome, where the row player's preferences are indicated by the first number and the column player's by the second number. A higher number denotes a more preferred outcome.

In game 1 of Figure F.1, there are two best outcomes of which only one is ST. In game 2, only a partially best outcome is ST, and in game 3, only an inferior outcome has this stability. Game 4 has no ST outcome. This anomalous behavior of ST stability is a reflection of the presence of partially best outcomes. As the next two theorems show, when there are no partially best outcomes, an outcome is ST if and only if it is best.

Theorem F.3. *In a two-person NC game* G, *let* i = *1 or 2 and suppose there exists* $\bar{s}_i \in S_i$ *such that, if* $s_j \in R_j (\bar{s}_i)$, *then* $(\bar{s}_i, s_j)$ *is best for* i. *Then, for each* $s_j \in R_j (\bar{s}_i)$, $(\bar{s}_i, s_j)$ *is ST for* i, *and, furthermore, if* s* ∈ S *is ST for* i, *then* s* *is best for* i.

PROOF: By hypothesis

$$\min_{s_j \in R_j(\bar{s}_i)} v_i (\bar{s}_i, s_j) = \max_{s \in S} v_i (s).$$

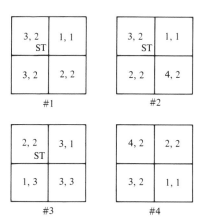

Figure F.1 Examples illustrating group ST outcomes in NC games.

It follows that

$$\max_{s_i \epsilon S_i} \min_{s_j \epsilon R_j(s_i)} v_i (s_i, s_j) = \min_{s_j \epsilon R_j(\bar{s}_i)} v_i (\bar{s}_i, s_j)$$

and so, by Definition 13.25, $(\bar{s}_i, s_j)$ is ST for i whenever $s_j \epsilon R_j (\bar{s}_i)$. If s^* is ST for i,

$$v_i (s^*) \geq \min_{s_j \epsilon R_j(s_i^*)} v_i (s_i, s_j) = \min_{s_j \epsilon R_j(\bar{s}_i)} v_i (\bar{s}_i, s_j) = \max_{s \epsilon S} v_i (s)$$

by Definition 13.25(ii), so that $v_i (s^*) = \max_{s \epsilon S} v_i(s)$, and s^* is best for i.

$\square$

Theorem F.4. *If G is a two-person NC game with no partially best outcomes, then* $\bar{s} \epsilon S$ *is ST iff it is best.*

PROOF: Let $\bar{s} \epsilon S$ be a best outcome of G and choose $i = 1$ or 2. Observe that $s_j \epsilon R_j (\bar{s}_i)$ iff $(\bar{s}_i, s_j)$ is a best outcome, as a consequence of the hypothesis. Since $\bar{s}_j \epsilon R_j (\bar{s}_i)$, $\bar{s}$ is ST for i by Theorem F.3. It follows that $\bar{s}$ is ST. Now assume $s^* \epsilon S$ is ST. Then application of Theorem F.3 twice shows that s^* is a best outcome. $\square$

In summary, Theorem F.4 shows that stability in the sense of Von Stackelberg is an "ideal" stability concept when there are no partially best outcomes, and in particular in strict ordinal games. However, the examples in Figure F.1 show that ST stability is very unreliable in the presence of partially best outcomes.

Stability of the NM and XNM types in 2×2 NC games is even closer to the coincidence of stable and best outcomes. It is easy to show that every outcome in a 2×2 NC game is noncyclic, so that every best outcome is either both NM and XNM, or neither.

Theorem F.5. *If* G *is a* 2×2 *NC game, every best outcome is NM (and XNM). If, further,* G *contains at most one partially best outcome, then* G *has no other NM (or XNM) outcomes (Kilgour, 1983).*

It can be shown by example that if a 2×2 NC game contains more than one partially best outcome, then a partially best outcome or an inferior outcome can be NM (and XNM).

F.3 Games of Complete Opposition

Individual and group stability concepts are now investigated in the context of games of complete opposition, which, as the ordinal analogues of two-person zero-sum games, are in a sense the opposite extreme to no-conflict games.

A two-person game $G = (S_1, S_2; v_1, v_2)$ is a game of *complete opposition* (CO) iff for every $s^1, s^2 \in S$, $v_1 (s^1) \leq v_1 (s^2)$ iff $v_2 (s^1) \geq v_2 (s^2)$. Thus player 2's preferences over the outcomes of S are exactly the reverse of player 1's.

Minimax and maximin values play an important role in the analysis of games of complete opposition. One useful result is the following theorem:

Theorem F.6. *Let* G *be a game of CO. Let* $\bar{s} \in S$ *and fix* $i = 1$ *or* 2. *Then* $v_i (\bar{s}) = maxmin_i$ *iff* $v_j (\bar{s}) = minmax_j$ *and* $v_i (\bar{s}) > maxmin_i$ *iff* $v_j (\bar{s}) < minmax_j$ *(Howard, 1971).*

It is an easy consequence of Theorem F.6 that $maxmin_1 = minmax_1$ iff $maxmin_2 = minmax_2$. This observation is the basis of the division of games of CO into two types.

Definition F.7. If G is a game of CO, then G is *strictly determined* iff $maxmin_i = minmax_i$ for $i = 1$ and 2, and G is *nonstrictly determined* iff $maxmin_i < minmax_i$ for $i = 1$ and 2 (Von Neumann and Morgenstern, 1953, p. 106).

The stability properties of games of CO will be shown to be vastly different in strictly determined and nonstrictly determined games. Strictly determined games can be characterized using the following:

Definition F.8. If G is a game of CO and $\bar{s} \in S$ is R, then $\bar{s}$ is a *saddle* of G (Von Neumann and Morgenstern, 1953, p. 95). The set of all saddles of G is denoted Sad(G).

Theorem F.9. *Let G be a strictly determined game of CO and let $\bar{s} \in S$. Then $\bar{s} \in Sad (G)$ iff*

$$v_1 (s_1, \bar{s}_2) \leq v_1 (\bar{s}_1, \bar{s}_2) \leq v_1 (\bar{s}_1, s_2) \qquad \forall s_1 \in S_1, \quad \forall s_2 \in S_2$$

Furthermore, if $\bar{s}$, $s^* \in Sad(G)$, then $v_i (\bar{s}) = v_i (s^*)$ for $i = 1$ and 2 (Von Neumann and Morgenstern, 1953, p. 95).

The relationship between saddles and strictly determined games is the following:

Theorem F.10. *Let G be a game of CO. Then G is strictly determined iff $Sad(G) \neq \emptyset$ (Von Neumann and Morgenstern, 1953, p. 95). In this case, $maxmin_i = minmax_i = v_i (\bar{s})$ for any $\bar{s} \in Sad(G)$, where $i = 1$ and 2.*

In strictly determined games of CO there are certain outcomes that are *not* saddles but that seem to be saddles.

Definition F.11. Let G be a strictly determined game of CO. An outcome $\bar{s} \in S$ is a *shadow* of G iff $\bar{s} \notin Sad(G)$ but $v_1 (\bar{s}) = v_1 (s^*)$ for $s^* \in Sad(G)$. A shadow $\bar{s}$ is a *shadow for 1 (2) only* iff $\bar{s}$ is R for 1 (2); $\bar{s}$ is a *double shadow* iff $\bar{s}$ is not R for either player. Denote the sets of shadows, shadows for 1 only, shadows for 2 only, and double shadows by Shad(G), Shad$_1$(G), Shad$_2$(G), and Shad$_{12}$(G), respectively. Since a shadow cannot be R for both players,

$$Shad(G) = Shad_1(G) \cup Shad_2(G) \cup Shad_{12}(G).$$

A characterization of the various types of shadows will be useful below.

Theorem F.12. *In a strictly determined game of CO G, let $\bar{s} \in Shad (G)$ and let $i = 1$ or 2. Then $\bar{s} \in Shad_i(G)$ iff there exists $s^* \in Sad(G)$ such that $s_j^* = \bar{s}_j$.*

PROOF: Assume that $i = 1$. Suppose there exists $s^* \in Sad(G)$ such that $s_2^* = \bar{s}_2$. Then for any $s_1 \in S_1$, $v_1 (s_1, \bar{s}_2) = v_1 (s_1, s_2^*) \leq v_1 (s_1^*, s_2^*) = v_1 (\bar{s}_1, \bar{s}_2)$ by Theorem F.9 and Definition F.11. Thus $\bar{s}$ is R for 1, and hence a shadow for 1 only.

Now suppose that $\bar{s} \in Shad_1(G)$ and let $s^* \in Sad(G)$. It will be shown that $(s_1^*, \bar{s}_2) \in Sad(G)$. By Theorem F.9 and Definition F.11, $v_1 (\bar{s}_1, \bar{s}_2) = v_1 (s_1^*, s_2^*) \leq v_1 (s_1^*, \bar{s}_2) \leq v_1 (\bar{s}_1, \bar{s}_2)$, so that $v_1 (s_1^*, \bar{s}_2) = v_1 (s_1^*, s_2^*) = v_1 (\bar{s}_1, \bar{s}_2)$. For any $s_2 \in S_2$, $v_1 (s_1^*, \bar{s}_2) = v_1 (s_1^*, s_2^*) \leq v_1 (s_1^*, s_2)$ by Definition F.8. Finally, $v_1 (s_1, \bar{s}_2) \leq v_1 (\bar{s}_1, \bar{s}_2) = v_1 (s_1^*, \bar{s}_2)$ for any $s_1 \in S_1$, and $(s_1^*, \bar{s}_1)$ is R for both players. Thus $(s_1^*, \bar{s}_2) \in Sad(G)$ by Definition F.8. The proof for $i = 2$ is similar. $\qquad\square$

Thus, for example, $\bar{s} \in \text{Shad}(G)$ is a shadow for 1 if and only if there is a saddle in the same column as $\bar{s}$. Now define $\text{SaS}(G) = \text{Sad}(G) \cup \text{Shad}(G)$ for any strictly determined game of CO G. From Theorem F.10 and Definition F.11 follows:

Theorem F.13. *Let* G *be a strictly determined game of CO. Then* $\bar{s} \in S$ *satisfies* $v_i(\bar{s}) = maxmin_i = minmax_i$ *for* i $= 1$ *or* 2 *iff* $\bar{s} \in SaS(G)$ *(Von Neumann and Morgenstern, 1953).*

It has been argued extensively [see for instance Von Neumann and Morgenstern (1953), pp. 98–112] that only outcomes in $\text{Sad}(G)$ are stable for rational players in a strictly determined game of CO G. However, a reasonably far-sighted player would be equally content at any outcome in $\text{SaS}(G)$, since any such outcome has the same payoff: far-sighted players would realize that, from such an outcome, neither player can effect any eventual gains by strategic maneuvering. Indeed several group stability concepts will determine the set of group stable outcomes as $\text{SaS}(G)$ in this instance.

The relationship of the individual stability concepts of Chapter 13 to the player's maximin and minimax values will be determined first. In addition to Theorems 13.5 and 13.7 there is the following:

Theorem F.14. *In a game of CO* G, *let* $\bar{s} \in S$ *and* i $= 1$ *or* 2. *Then* $\bar{s}$ *is FHQ for* i *iff* $\bar{s}$ *is GMR for* i.

PROOF: In light of Theorem 13.14, it suffices to show that, if i has a UI s_i from $\bar{s}$, and j has a sanction s_j against s_i, then j has a credible sanction against s_i. Now $v_i(s_i, \bar{s}_j) > v_i(\bar{s}_i, \bar{s}_j)$ and $v_i(s_i, s_j) \leqslant v_i(\bar{s}_i, \bar{s}_j)$ so that $v_i(s_i, s_j) < v_i(\bar{s}_i, \bar{s}_j)$. However, by the defining property of games of CO, $v_j(s_i, s_j) > v_j(s_i, \bar{s}_j)$, so that s_j is a credible sanction for j against s_i. $\square$

Theorem F.15. *In a game of CO* G, *let* $\bar{s} \in S$ *and* i $= 1$ *or* 2. *Then if* $\bar{s}$ *is ST for* i, $v_i(\bar{s}) = maxmin_i$.

PROOF: For any $s_i \in S_i$ it follows from Definition 13.24 that

$$R_j(s_i) = \{s_j^* \in S_j : v_j(s_i, s_j^*) \geqslant v_j(s_i, s_j) \ \forall s_j \in S_j\}.$$

By the defining property of games of CO,

$$R_j(s_i) = \{s_j^* \in S_j : v_i(s_i, s_j^*) \leqslant v_i(s_i, s_j) \ \forall s_j \in S_j\}.$$

Therefore,

$$s_j^* \in R_j(s_i) \quad \text{iff} \quad v_i(s_i, s_j^*) = \min_{s_j \in S_j} v_i(s_i, s_j). \tag{F-1}$$

If $\bar{s}$ is ST for i, then, by Definition 13.25(i) and relation (F-1),

$$v_i\,(\bar{s}_i,\,\bar{s}_j) = \min_{s_j \in S_j} v_i\,(\bar{s}_i,\,s_j) = \min_{s_j \in R_j(\bar{s}_i)} v_i\,(\bar{s}_i,\,s_j).$$

Then, using Definition 13.25(ii) and relation (F-1) again,

$$\begin{aligned}
v_i\,(\bar{s}_i,\,\bar{s}_j) &= \max_{s_i \in S_i}\ \min_{s_j \in R_j(s_i)} v_i\,(s_i,\,s_j) \\
&= \max_{s_i \in S_i}\ \min_{s_j \in S_j} v_i(s_i,\,s_j) = \text{maxmin}_i. \qquad \square
\end{aligned}$$

Theorem F.16. *In a game of CO G, let $\bar{s} \in S$ and* $i = 1$ *or 2. Then, if $\bar{s}$ is R for* i *and $\bar{s}$ is ST for* i, $\bar{s} \in Sad(G)$.

PROOF: Immediate, using Theorem 13.26 and Definition F.8. $\qquad \square$

Theorem F.17. *In a strictly determined game of CO G, let $\bar{s} \in S$ and* $i = 1$ *or 2. Then $\bar{s}$ is ST for* i *iff either $\bar{s} \in Sad(G)$ or $\bar{s} \in Shad(G)$.*

PROOF: Suppose that $\bar{s}$ is ST for i. By Theorems F.6 and F.15 and Definition F.7, $v_k(\bar{s}) = \text{minmax}_k$ for $k = 1$ and 2. By Theorem F.13, $\bar{s} \in Sas(G) = Sad(G) \cup Shad(G)$. If $\bar{s} \in Shad(G)$, Theorem 13.26 and Definition F.11 show that $\bar{s} \in Shad_j(G)$.

It will now be shown that if $\bar{s} \in Sad(G) \cup Shad_j(G)$, then $\bar{s}$ is ST for i. By hypothesis, $\bar{s}$ is R for j, so that $\bar{s}_j \in R_j(\bar{s}_i)$ and

$$v_j(\bar{s}_i,\,\bar{s}_j) = \max_{s_j \in S_j} v_j\,(\bar{s}_i,\,s_j).$$

This is equivalent to

$$v_i(\bar{s}_i,\,\bar{s}_j) = \min_{s_j \in S_j} v_i\,(\bar{s}_i,\,s_j),$$

and Theorem F.13 and relation (F-1) imply that

$$\begin{aligned}
\min_{s_j \in R_j \bar{s}_i} v_i(\bar{s}_i,\,s_j) &= v_i(\bar{s}_i,\,\bar{s}_j) = \text{maxmin}_i \\
&= \max_{s_i \in S_i}\ \min_{s_j \in S_j} v_i\,(s_i,\,s_j) \\
&= \max_{s_i \in S_i}\ \min_{s_j \in R_j(s_i)} v_i(s_i,\,s_j),
\end{aligned}$$

so that s is ST for i by Definition 13.25 $\qquad \square$

Figures F.2 and F.3 illustrate the interrelationships among individual stability concepts in strictly determined and nonstrictly determined games of CO, respectively. These Figures are based on Theorems 13.5, 13.7, 13.8, 13.14, 13.26, F.10, and F.14–F.17. For strictly determined games of CO in Figure F.2, the GMR, SMR, and FHQ outcomes are identical

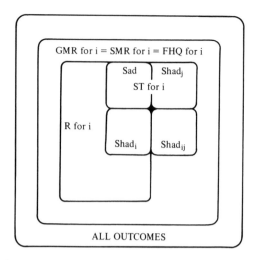

Figure F.2 Individual stability concepts in strictly determined games of complete opposition.

and by Theorem F.10 there must be a saddle. When there is no saddle and the game of CO is nonstrictly determined, Figure F.3 shows that the GMR and FHQ outcomes are the same and the SMR, R, and ST outcomes are subsets of these.

Now consider the group stability concepts of Chapter 13 in the context of games of complete opposition. From Theorem 13.22 and F.14 follows:

Figure F.3 Individual stability concepts in nonstrictly determined games of complete opposition.

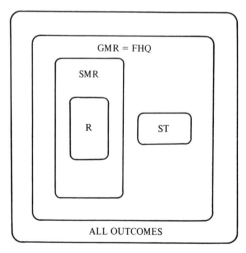

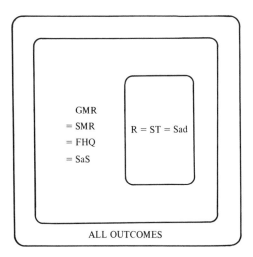

Figure F.4 Group stability concepts in strictly determined games of complete opposition.

Theorem F.18. *Let* G *be a game of CO and let* $\bar{s} \in S$. *Then* $\bar{s}$ *is FHQ iff* $\bar{s}$ *is GMR. Furthermore,* S *contains no FHM outcomes.*

Theorem F.19. *Let* G *be a strictly determined game of CO and let* $\bar{s} \in S$. *Then* $\bar{s}$ *is ST iff* $\bar{s} \in Sad(G)$.

Figure F.5 Group stability concepts in nonstrictly determined games of complete opposition. Note that in 2×2 games there are no NM or XNM outcomes that are group stable.

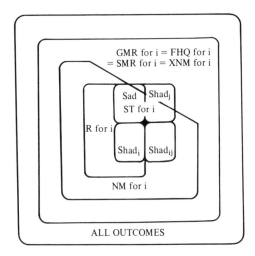

Figure F.6 Individual stability concepts in strictly determined 2 × 2 games of complete opposition.

PROOF: Because of 13.28 and F.8, it is necessary only to show that if $\bar{s} \in Sad(G)$, then $\bar{s}$ is ST. This follows from F.17.   □

Theorem F.20. *Let G be a strictly determined game of CO and let $\bar{s} \in S$. The following are equivalent: (a) $\bar{s}$ is GMR; (b) $\bar{s}$ is FHQ; (c) $\bar{s}$ is SMR; (d) $\bar{s} \in SaS(G)$.*

PROOF: Taking into account Theorems 13.5, 13.7, 13.17, F.7, F.12, and F.18, it is necessary only to show that if $v_i(\bar{s}) \geq$ maxmin$_i$ = minmax$_i$ for $i = 1$ and 2, then $\bar{s} \in SaS(G)$. However, if for some player i, $v_i(\bar{s}) >$ maxmin$_i$, then $v_j(\bar{s}) <$ minmax$_j$ by Theorem F.6, and the theorem follows from Theorem F.12.   □

Theorem F.21. *If G is a nonstrictly determined game of CO, then no outcome in S is SMR, R, or ST.*

PROOF: By Theorems 13.18 and 13.28, it is necessary only to show that there are no SMR outcomes. Suppose that $\bar{s} \in S$ satisfies, for some $i = 1$ or 2, $v_i(\bar{s}) \geq$ minmax$_i$. By Theorem F.6, $v_j(\bar{s}) \leq$ maxmin$_j <$ minmax$_j$ by Definition F.7. By Theorem 13.7 no outcome is SMR.   □

Figures F.4 and F.5 illustrate the results of Theorems F.18–F.21 on group stability in strictly determined and nonstrictly determined games of CO, respectively. Observe that each group stability concept illustrated

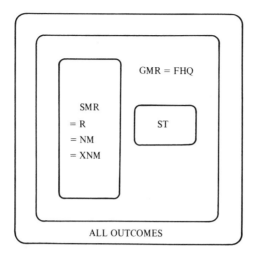

Figure F.7 Individual stability concepts in nonstrictly determined 2 × 2 games of complete opposition.

always occurs in any game of CO of the indicated type. In particular, an outcome $\bar{s} \in S$ in a nonstrictly determined game of CO is GMR (and FHQ) if and only if it satisfies $\text{maxmin}_1 \leq v_1(\bar{s}) \leq \text{minmax}_1$. There are at least two such outcomes.

For 2 × 2 games of complete opposition there are several special results:

Figure F.8 Group stability concepts in strictly determined 2 × 2 games of complete opposition.

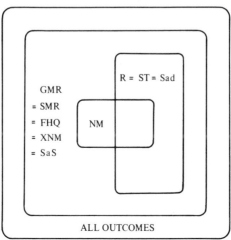

Theorem F.22. *Let* G *be a strictly determined* 2 × 2 *game of CO, let* $\bar{s}$ ∈ S *and let* i = *1 or 2. If* $\bar{s}$ ∉ *Sad*(G) *but either* $\bar{s}$ ∈ *Shad*$_{12}$(G) *or* $\bar{s}$ *is R for* i, *then* $\bar{s}$ *is NM for* i.

Theorem F.23. *Let* G *be a nonstrictly determined* 2 × 2 *game of CO, let* $\bar{s}$ ∈ S, *and let* i = *1 or 2. The following are equivalent: (a)* $\bar{s}$ *is SMR for* i; *(b)* $\bar{s}$ *is R for* i; *(c)* $\bar{s}$ *is NM for* i.

Theorem F.24. *Let* G *be a* 2 × 2 *game of CO and let* $\bar{s}$ ∈ S. *If* i = *1 or 2, then* $\bar{s}$ *is SMR for* i *iff* $\bar{s}$ *is XNM for* i. *Furthermore,* $\bar{s}$ *is SMR iff* $\bar{s}$ *is XNM.*

Note that F.23 asserts, in part, that an outcome in a nonstrictly determined 2 × 2 game of CO must be R for a player *i* if it is SMR for *i*. That this part of F.23 is false when the game is not 2 × 2 is easily shown by example.

The conclusions of Theorems F.22–F.24 in combination with previous theorems are shown in Figures F.5–F.8. Examples show that the results on which these Figures are based cannot be improved. Figure F.6 and F.7 illustrate the various sets of individual stabilities for strictly determined and nonstrictly determined 2 × 2 games of complete opposition, respectively. Figure F.6 is different from the other figures in this appendix because the solutions illustrated are specific to player *i* (*i* might equal 1 or 2) rather than for any player. Note that the shadows for *j* are rational for *j* but not for *i*, whereas the double shadows are not rational for either player. NM outcomes curiously include the double shadows but fail to include all the saddles. All the criteria that involve larger sets are identical. In Figure F.7, note that the ST set and R set cannot intersect because if they did, a saddle would be formed by Theorem F.16; this is impossible in a nonstrictly determined game.

Figure F.5 and F.8 illustrate the group stability concepts of nonstrictly determined and strictly determined 2 × 2 games of complete opposition. It was not necessary to reproduce Figure F.5 for 2 × 2 games because there are no nonstrictly determined outcomes that are group XNM or NM, due to Theorems F.21, F.23, and F.24. Figure F.8 illustrates that the criteria that involve larger sets than R, ST, and NM are all identical, as occurs in general in strictly determined games of CO.

Note on Pareto Optimality. In any game, an outcome is *Pareto optimal* if there is no other outcome that is at least as preferable for every player and strictly preferred for at least one player. An outcome that is not Pareto optimal is *Pareto inferior*. The study of NC games and games of CO clarifies the relationship of Pareto optimality with the various solution concepts.

It can be demonstrated by example that Pareto inferior outcomes can possess each of the types of stability defined in Chapter 13. These examples can be chosen from NC games, because from Definition F.1 any inferior outcome for NC games is Pareto inferior. As noted following Theorem F.2, inferior outcomes in NC games can exhibit any of the stability combinations illustrated in Figure 13.1, (p. 267) and examples for the other stability concepts are easy to construct.

Similarly, Pareto optimal outcomes can fail to be stable according to any chosen stability criterion. Examples illustrating this failure abound in games of complete opposition. In this class, every outcome of every game is Pareto optimal, by definition.

Bibliography

Able, E. (1969). *The Missiles of October: The Story of the Cuban Missile Crisis, 1962*. London: MacGibbon and Kee Ltd.

Alexander, J. M. (1975). An operational analysis of conflict in Northern Ireland: An American perspective. Presented to the Northern Ireland Constitutional Convention, Belfast.

Allison, G. T. (1971). *Essence of Decision: Explaining the Cuban Missile Crisis*. Boston: Little, Brown and Co.

Arrow, K. J. (1963). *Social Choice and Individual Values*, 2nd ed. New Haven, Conn.: Yale University Press.

Bacharach, S. B., and E. J. Lawler (1981). *Bargaining—Power, Tactics and Outcomes*. San Francisco: Jossey-Bass Publishers.

Bacow, L., and M. Wheeler (1982). *Resolving Environmental Disputes*. New York: Plenum Publishers.

Banks, A. S., ed. (1979). *Political Handbook of the World*. New York: McGraw-Hill Company.

Basar, T., and G. J. Olsder (1982). *Dynamic Non-Cooperative Game Theory*. New York: Academic Press.

Beufre, A. (1969). *The Suez Expedition 1956*. New York: Frederick A. Praeger.

Bennett, P. G. (1977). Toward a theory of hypergames. *OMEGA* 5 (6), 749–751.

Bennett, P. G. (1980a). Hypergames, the development of an approach to modelling conflicts. *Futures* 12, 489–507.

Bennett, P. G. (1980b). Bidders and dispensers: Manipulative hypergames in a multinational context. *European Journal of Operational Research* 4, 293–306.

Bennett, P. G., and M. R. Dando (1977). "Fall Gelb" and other games: A hypergame perspective of the fall of France, 1940. *Journal of the Conflict Research Society* 1 (2), pp. 1–32.

Bennett, P. G., and M. R. Dando (1979). Complex strategic analysis: A hypergame perspective of the fall of France. *Journal of the Operational Research Society* 30(1), 23–32.

Bennett, P. G., M. R. Dando, and R. G. Sharp (1980). Using hypergames to model difficult social issues: An approach to the case of soccer hooliganism. *Journal of the Operational Research Society* 31, 621–635.

Bennett, P. G., and C. S. Huxham (1982). Hypergames and what they do, *Journal of the Operational Research Society* 33, 41–50.

Ben-Veniste, R., and G. Frampton , Jr. (1977). *Stonewall*. New York: Simon and Schuster.

Blake, R. (1977). *A History of Rhodesia*. London: Eyre Metheun.

Botting, D. (1978). *The Second Front*. New York: Time-Life Books.

Bowie, R.R. (1974). *Suez 1956*. New York: Oxford University Press.

Boyd, D. H. (1975). *A Scientific and Policy Review of the Final Environmental Statement for the Initial Stage, Garrison Diversion Unit*, Volume II, *The Impacts of the Garrison Diversion Unit on Canada*. Manitoba Environmental Council, January.

Brams, S. J. (1975). *Game Theory and Politics*. New York: The Free Press.

Brams, S. J. (1977). Deception in 2 × 2 games. *Journal of Peace Science* 2, 171–203.

Brams, S. J. and Hessel, M. (1928). Absorbing outcomes in 2 × 2 games. *Behavioral Science* 27, 393–400.

Brams, S. J., and D. Muzzio (1977). Unanimity in the Supreme Court: A game-theoretic explanation of the decision in the White House tapes case. *Public Choice* (Winter), 67–83.

Brams, S. J., and D. Wittman (1981). Nonmyopic equilibria in 2 × 2 games. *Conflict Management and Peace Science* 6(1), 39–62.

Brams, S. J., and F. C. Zagare (1977). Deception in simple voting games. *Social Science Research* 6, 257–272.

Bureau of Reclamation (1974). *Final Environmental Statement—Initial Stage Garrison Diversion Unit*. Billings, Montana: U.S. Department of the Interior.

Canadian Department of External Affairs, Diplomatic Notes, October 23, 1973; June 23, 1975; October 12, 1976; April 4, 1978.

Capitanchik, D. B. (1969). *The Eisenhower Presidency and American Foreign Policy*. London: Routledge and Kegan Paul.

Caplow, T. A. (1956). A theory of conflict formation. *American Sociological Review* 21, 489–493.

Carter, A. T. (1975). The Boundary Treaty of 1909: Does it provide an environmental cause of action? *South Dakota Law Review* 20, 147–180.

Chacko, C. J. (1968). *The International Joint Commission Between the United States and Canada*. New York: AMS Press.

Chatterjee, K., and J. W. Ulvila (1982). Bargaining with shared information. *Decision Sciences* 13(3), 380–404.

Clements, F. (1969). *Rhodesia, A Study of the Deterioration of a White Society*. New York: Frederick A. Praeger.

Cohen, J. L. (1978). *Multiobjective Programming and Planning*. New York: Academic Press.

Congressional Quarterly (1973). *Watergate: Chronology of a Crisis*, Vol. 1. Washington, D.C.: Congressional Quarterly.

Dando, M. R. (1977). On taking a broad view: Strategic surprise and adequate analysis in complex conflicts. Unpublished paper, Operations Research Department, University of Sussex, Brighton, England.

Dash, S. (1976). *Chief Counsel*. New York: Random House.

Davis, M. D. (1970). *Game Theory—A Non-technical Introduction*. New York: Basic Books.

Dean, J. W., Jr. (1976). *Blind Ambition*. New York: Simon and Schuster.

Dorothy, R. E. (1973). Some engineering, environmental and social aspects of the Garrison Diversion Unit, North Dakota. Paper presented at the annual meeting, North Central Region American Society of Agricultural Engineers, Regina, Saskatchewan, Canada, October 12.

Dresher, M. (1961). *Games of Strategy*. Englewood Cliffs, NJ: Prentice-Hall.

Dufournaud, C. M. (1982). On the mutually beneficial cooperative scheme: Dynamic change in the pay-off matrix of international river basin schemes. *Water Resources Research* 18, 764–762.

Encyclopaedia Britannica (1979). Chicago: Encyclopaedia Britannica.

Environmental Impact Assessment Project of the Institute of Ecology (1975). *A Scientific and Policy Review of the Final Environmental Statement for the Initial Stage, Garrison Diversion Unit*, Vol. I, *United States Impacts*, January.

Environmental Protection Agency (1973). *Waste Source Investigations-Kingsport, Tennessee*; Washington D.C., April.

Fisher, R. (1970). *International Conflict for Beginners*. New York: Harper and Row.

Fraser, N. M. (1980). A state transition model for conflict analysis, in *Systems Design Workshop Symposium*, Department of Systems Design Engineering, University of Waterloo, Waterloo, Ontario, Canada, pp. IV. 2.1–IV.2.6.

Fraser, N. M. (1981). *Advances in Conflict Analysis*. M.A.Sc. Thesis, Department of Systems Design Engineering, University of Waterloo, Waterloo, Ontario, Canada.

Fraser, N. M. (1983). *New Perspectives in Bargaining and Negotiation*. Ph.D. Thesis, Department of Systems Design Engineering, University of Waterloo, Waterloo, Ontario, Canada.

Fraser, N. M., and K. W. Hipel (1979a). Solving complex conflicts. *IEEE Transactions on Systems, Man and Cybernetics* SMC9 (12), 805–815.

Fraser, N. M., and K. W. Hipel (1979b). Computer assistance in conflict analysis. *Proceedings of the 1979 International Conference on Cybernetics and Society*, sponsored by the IEEE Systems, Man and Cybernetics Society. Conference held at Denver, Colorado, October 8–10, pp. 205–209.

Fraser, N. M., and K. W. Hipel (1980a). Computational techniques in conflict analysis. *Advances in Engineering Software* 2(4), 181–185.

Fraser, N. M., and K. W. Hipel (1980b). Metagame analysis of the Poplar River conflict. *Journal of the Operational Research Society* 31, 377–385.

Fraser, N. M., and K. W. Hipel (1980c). The conflict analysis program, Technical Report No. 64-SFW070580, Department of Systems Design Engineering, University of Waterloo, Waterloo, Ontario, Canada.

Fraser, N. M., and K. W. Hipel (1980d). Conflict analysis and bargaining, *Proceedings of the 1980 International Conference on Cybernetics and Society*, sponsored by the IEEE Systems, Man and Cybernetics Society. Conference held at Boston, Mass., October 8–10, pp. 225–229.

Fraser, N. M., and K. W. Hipel (1980e). Computer analysis of a labor–management conflict, Technical Report No. 71-SM-270880, Department of Systems Design Engineering, University of Waterloo, Waterloo, Ontario, Canada.

Fraser, N. M., and K. W. Hipel (1981). Computer assistance in labor-management negotiations. *Interfaces* 11(2), pp. 22–30.

Fraser, N. M., and K. W. Hipel (1982). Developments in conflict analysis, invited paper in *General Survey of Systems Methodology*, Proceedings of the 26th Annual Meeting of the Society for General Systems Research with the American Association for the Advancement of Science. Len Troncale, ed. Washington, D.C.: Society for General Systems Report Vol. 2, pp. 976–986. (Paper presented at Washington, D.C., January.)

Fraser, N. M., and K. W. Hipel (1983a). Conflict analysis techniques in Strategic Choice, in *Decision Making with Uncertainty*. Proceedings of the NATO Research Workshop held at Maratea, Italy, July 4–17, 1982. L. Wilkin, A. Sutton, and A. Hickling, eds.

Fraser, N. M., and K. W. Hipel (1983b). Conflict analysis and bargaining. Paper presented at the International Studies Association 24th Annual Convention, Mexico City, April 4–9.

Fraser, N. M., and K. W. Hipel (1983c). Dynamic modelling of the Cuban missile crisis. *Journal of Conflict Management and Peace Science* 6 (2), 1–18.

Fraser, N. M., and K. W. Hipel (1983d). A continuous time state model for dynamic conflicts. Unpublished paper, Department of Systems Design Engineering, University of Waterloo, Waterloo, Ontario, Canada.

Fraser, N. M., K. W. Hipel, and J. del Monte (1983a). Algorithmic approaches to conflict analysis, *Proceedings of the International Symposium on Research on Social Conflict and Harmony*, Erasmus University, Rotterdam, The Netherlands, January 17–18.

Fraser, N. M., K. W. Hipel, and J. del Monte (1983b). Studying nuclear war using game theory. *Journal of Policy Modeling*, in press.

Funk and Wagnells Standard Dictionary (1974). Toronto: Fitzhenry and Whiteside.

Gamson, W. A. (1961). An experimental test of a theory of coalition formation. *American Sociological Review*, 26, 565–573.

Glubb, Sir J. B. (1969). *The Middle East Crisis: A Personal Interpretation*. London: Hodder and Stroughton.

Goicoechea, A., D. R. Hansen, and L. L. Duckstein (1982). *Multiobjective Decision Analysis with Engineering and Business Applications*. New York: John Wiley and Sons.

Goldman, M. I. (1967). *Soviet Foreign Aid*. New York: Frederick A. Praeger.

Gruder, C. L. (1970). Social power in interpersonal negotiation, in *The Structure of Conflict*, P. Swingle, ed. New York: Academic Press.

Guhin, M. A. (1972). *John Foster Dulles, A Statesman and His Times*. New York: Columbia University Press.

Guiasu, S., and M. Malitza (1980). *Coalition and Connection in Games*. Oxford: Pergammon Press.

Haimes, Y. Y. (1977). *Hierarchical Analysis of Water Resources Systems*. New York: McGraw-Hill.

Hajek, O. (1975). *Pursuit Games*. New York: Academic Press.

Haldeman, B. and J. Dimona (1978). *The Ends of Power*. New York: New York Times Book Co.

Hamburger, H. (1979). *Games as Models of Social Phenomena*. San Francisco: W. H. Freeman and Co.

Harnett, D. C., and L. L. Cummings (1980). *Bargaining Behavior—An International Study*. Houston, Texas: Dame Publications.

Harris, R. J. (1969a). Note on Howard's theory of metagames. *Psychological Reports* 25, 849–850.

Harris, R. J. (1969b). Comments on Dr. Rapoport's comments. *Psychological Reports*, 25, 825.

Harris, R. J. (1970). Paradox regained. *Psychological Reports*, 26, 264–266.

Harsanyi, J. C. (1977). *Rational Behavior and Bargaining Equilibrium in Games and Social Situations*. Cambridge: Cambridge University Press.

Heer, J. E., Jr. and D. J. Hagerty (1977). *Environmental Assessments and Statements*. New York: Van Nostrand Reinhold.

Henderson, J. M., and R. E. Quandt (1971). *Microeconomic Theory: A Mathematical Approach*. Second Edition. New York: McGraw-Hill.

Hillier, F. S., and G. J. Lieberman (1974). *Operations Research*. San Francisco: Holden-Day.

Hipel, K. W. (1981). Operational research techniques in water resources. *Canadian Water Resources Journal* 6(4), 205–226.

Hipel, K. W., and N. M. Fraser (1979). The historical and political aspects of the Garrison Diversion Unit, Technical Report No. 60-SM-051179, Department of Systems Design Engineering, University of Waterloo, Waterloo, Ontario, Canada.

Hipel, K. W., and N. M. Fraser (1980). Metagame analysis of the Garrison conflict. *Water Resources Research* 16 (4), 629–637.

Hipel, K. W., and N. M. Fraser (1982). Socio-political implications of risk, in *Technological Risk*. N.C. Lind, ed. University of Waterloo, Waterloo, Ontario, Canada, pp. 41–72.

Hipel, K. W., and N. M. Fraser (1983). Conflict analysis in systems management, in *Encyclopedia of Systems and Control*, M. G. Singh, ed. Oxford: Pergmon Press.

Hipel, K. W., and N. M. Fraser (1984). Modelling political uncertainty using improved metagame analysis. *Experimental Studies in Politics*, in press.

Hipel, K. W., R. K. Ragade, and T. E. Unny (1974). Metagame analysis of water resources conflicts. *Journal of the Hydraulics Division, American Society of Civil Engineers* 100 (HY10), 1437–1455.

Hipel, K. W., R. K. Ragade, and T. E. Unny (1976a). Metagame theory and its application to water resources. *Water Resources Research* 12 (3), 331–339.

Hipel, K. W., R. K. Ragade, and T. E. Unny (1976b). Political resolution of environmental conflicts. *Water Resources Bulletin* 12 (4) 813–837.

Howard, N. (1969). Comments on Harris' "Comments on Rapoport's comments." *Psychological Reports* 25, 826.

Howard, N. (1970a). The Arab–Israeli conflict: A metagame analysis, Technical Report, Department of Systems Design Engineering, University of Waterloo, Waterloo, Ontario, Canada.

Howard, N. (1970b). Note on the Harris–Rapoport controversy. *Psychological Reports* 26, 316.

Howard, N. (1971). *Paradoxes of Rationality*. Cambridge, Mass.: MIT Press.

Howard, N. (1975). Metagame analysis of business problems, *INFOR* 13, pp. 48–67.

Howard, N., and I. Shepanik (1976). Boolean algorithms used in metagame analysis, University of Ottawa Working Paper 76–4, Ottawa, Canada.

Ilich, J. (1973). *The Art and Skill of Successful Negotiation*. Englewood Cliffs, N. J.: Prentice-Hall.

International Garrison Diversion Study Board (1976). *Report to the International Joint Commission*, October.

International Joint Commission (1965). *Rules of Procedure and Text of Treaty*. Ottawa, Canada–Washington D.C.

International Joint Commission (1977) *Transboundary Implications of the Garrison Diversion Unit*. Report to the Governments of Canada and the United States, Ottawa, Canada–Washington, D.C.

International Joint Commission (1978a). *Annual Report—1977*. Ottawa, Canada–Washington, D.C.

International Joint Commission (1978b). *Water Apportionment in the Poplar River Basin*. Report to the Governments of Canada and the United States, Ottawa, Canada–Washington, D.C.

Jaworski, L. (1976). *The Right and Power*. New York: Reader's Digest Press.

Kailath, T. (1980). *Linear Systems*. Englewood Cliffs, N.J.:Prentice-Hall.

Kanet, R. E. (1974). *The Soviet Union and the Developing Nations*. Baltimore: John Hopkins University Press.

Karrass, C. L. (1972). *The Negotiation Game*. New York: World Publishing.

Karrass, C. L. (1974). *Give and Take—The Complete Guide to Negotiating Strategies and Tactics*. New York: Thomas Y. Crowel Company.

Kelly, H. H., and A. J. Arrowood (1960). Coalitions in the triad: Critique and experiment. *Sociometry* 23, 231–244.

Kennedy, G., J. Benson, and J. McMillan (1980). *Managing Negotiations*. London: Business Books.

Kilgour, D. M. (1984). Equilibria for far-sighted players. *Theory and Decision*, in press.

Kilgour, D. M., K. W. Hipel, and N. M. Fraser (1984) Solution concepts in noncooperative games. *Large Scale Systems*, Vol. 6.

Kolmogorov, A. N. (1931). Uber die analytischen Methoden in der Wahrscheinlichkeitsrechnung. *Mathematische Annalen* 104, 415–458.

Komorita, S. S. (1974). A weighted probability model of coalition formation. *Psychological Review* 81, 242–256.

Komorita, S. S., and D. Kravitz (1978). Some tests of four descriptive theories of coalition formation, in *Beitrage Zur Experimentellen Wirtschaftsforscheing*, Vol. 8, H. Saurman, ed. Tubingen: Mohr.

Kremers, O. (1974). Garrison Diversion Unit, Manitoba Environmental Council Annual Report Two. Winnipeg: Manitoba Environmental Council.

Kremers, O. (1977). Submission to the Presidential Panel on the Garrison Diversion Project. Winnipeg: Manitoba Environmental Council, April 1.

Krenkel, P. A., and V. Novotny (1973). *The Assimilative Capacity of the South Fork Holston River Below Kingsport, Tennessee*. Kingsport, Tennessee: The Tennessee Eastman Company.

Kuhn, J., K. W. Hipel, and N. M. Fraser (1983). A coalition analysis algorithm with application to the Zimbabwe conflict, *IEEE Transactions on Systems, Man and Cybernetics* SMC-13 (3), 338–352.

Kwakernaak, H. (1972). *Linear Optimal Control Systems*. New York: Wiley-Interscience.

Legum, C. ed. (1969–79). *African Contemporary Records*. London: William Chirdley & Son.

Leitch, W. G., and J. J. Keleher, eds. (1974). *Garrison Diversion Project Presentations*. Winnipeg: Manitoba Environmental Council.

Leitmann,G. (1974). *Cooperative and Non-cooperative Many Player Differential Games*. New York: Springer-Verlag.

Leitmann, G., and P. T. Liu (1974). A differential game model of labor–management negotiation during a strike. *Journal of Optimization Theory and Applications* 13 (4), 427–435.

Love, K. (1969). *Suez: The Twice Fought War*. Toronto: McGraw-Hill.

Luce, R. D., and H. Raiffa (1957). *Games and Decisions*. New York: John Wiley and Sons.

Lukas, J. A. (1976). *Nightmare, The Underside of the Nixon Years*. New York: Viking Press.

Mankiewicz, F. (1975). *U.S. vs. Richard M. Nixon: The Final Crisis*. New York: New York Times Book Co.

Manitoba Environmental Council (1975). Submission to the International Joint Commission hearings on the Garrison Diversion Unit. Winnipeg, November 20.

Manley, R. L., and J. J. Peterson (1975). Selected environmental law aspects of the Garrison Diversion Project. *North Dakota Law Review*, 329–358.

Maslow, A. H. (1954). *Motivation and Personality*. New York: Harper & Row.

Medlin, S. M. (1976). Effects of grand coalition payoffs on coalition analysis formation in 3-person games. *Behavior Science* 21, 48–61.

Meleskie, M. F., K. W. Hipel, and N. M. Fraser (1982). The Watergate tapes conflict: A metagame analysis. *Political Methodology*, 8 (4), 1–23.

Michener, H. A., J. A. Fleishman, and J. J. Vaske (1976). A test of the bargaining theory of coalition formation in four-person groups. *Journal of Personality and Social Psychology* 34, 1114–1126.

Mutambirwa, J. A. (1980). *The Rise of Settler Power in Southern Rhodesia (Zimbabwe) 1898–1928*. London: Farleigh Dickinson University Press.

Nash, J. F. (1950a). The bargaining problem. *Econometrica* 18, 155–162.

Nash, J. F. (1950b). Equilibrium points in *n*-person games. Proceedings of the National Academy of Sciences of the U.S.A. 36, 48–49.

Nash, J. F. (1951). Non-cooperative games. *Annals of Mathematics* 54, 286–295.

New York Times Index (1979). New York: New York Times Company, Vol. 67.

New York Times Staff (1974). *The End of a Presidency*. New York: Bantam Books.

Nierenberg, G. I. (1973). *Fundamentals of Negotiating*. New York: Hawthorn Books.

Nixon, R. M. (1978). *Memoirs of Richard Nixon*. New York: Warner Books.

Nutting, A. (1963). *No End of a Lesson*. Liverpool: C. Tinling and Co.

Nutting, A. (1972). *Nasser*. Tiptree: Anchor Press.

Owen, G. (1980). *Game Theory*, 2nd edition, New York: Academic Press.

Parzen, E. (1962). *Stochastic Processes*. San Francisco: Holden-Day.

Ponssard, J. P. (1981). *Competitive Strategies*. Amsterdam: North-Holland Publishing Company.

Praitt, D. G. (1981). *Negotiation Behavior*. New York: Academic Press.

Progress Publishers (1975). *The Policy of the Soviet Union in the Arab World and Short Collection of Foreign Policy Statements*. Moscow.

Province of Saskatchewan (1976). A brief respecting water apportionment in the Poplar River Basin. Coronach, Saskatchewan, May 27.

Radford, K. J. (1977). *Complex Decision Problems*. Reston, VA: Reston Publishing Company.

Radford, K. J. (1980). *Strategic Planning—An Analytic Approach*. Reston, VA: Reston Publishing Company.

Radford, K. J. (1981). *Modern Managerial Decision Making*. Reston, VA: Reston Publishing Company.

Radford, K. J., and B. Fingerhut (1980). Analysis of a complex Decision Situation—the Simpson/Simpsons–Sears merger proposal. *OMEGA* 8 (4), 421–431.

Ragade, R. K., K. W. Hipel, and T. E. Unny (1976a). Nonquantitative methods in water resources management. *Journal of the Water Resources Planning and Management Division, American Society of Civil Enginnering* 20 (WR2), 297–309.

Ragade, R. K., K. W. Hipel, and T. E. Unny (1976b). Metarationality in benefit–cost analysis. *Water Resources Research* 12 (6) 1069–1076.

Raiffa, H. (1982). *The Art and Science of Negotiation*. Cambridge, Mass.: Harvard University Press.

Rapoport, A., J. P. Kahan, S. G. Funk, and A. D. Horowitz (1979). *Coalition Formation by Sophisticated Players*. Berlin: Springer-Verlag.

Rapoport, A., M. J. Guyer, and D. G. Gordon (1976). *The 2 × 2 Game*. Ann Arbor: The University of Michigan Press.

Rapoport, A. (1967). Optimum policies for the prisoner's dilemma. *Psychological Review* 74, 136–148.

Rapoport, A. (1969a). Effects of payoff information in multi-stage mixed motive games. *Behavioral Science* 14, 204–215.

Rapoport, A. (1969b). Comments on Dr. Harris' "Note on Howard's theory of metagames." *Psychological Reports* 25, 765–766.

Rapoport, A. (1969c). Reply to Dr. Harris' comments on my comments. *Psychological Reports* 25, 857–858.

Rapoport, A. (1970a). Comments on "Paradox Regained." *Psychological Reprts* 26, 272.

Rapoport, A. (1970b). Conflict resolution in the light of game theory and beyond, in *The Structure of Conflict*, P. Swingle, ed. New York: Academic Press.

Richelson, J. T. (1979). Soviet strategic doctrine and limited nuclear operations. *Journal of Conflict Resolution* 23 (2), 326–336.

Riker, W. H. (1962). *The Theory of Political Coalitions*. New Haven: Yale University Press.

Robertson, T. (1965). *Crisis: The Inside Story of the Suez Conspiracy*. London: Hutchinson and Co.

Robinson, E. B. (1966). *History of North Dakota*. Lincoln, Nebraska; University of Nebraska Press.

Rubin, J. Z., and B. R. Brown (1975). *The Social Psychology of Bargaining and Negotiation*. New York: Academic Press.

Saskatchewan Power Corporation (1974). *Annual Report*. Regina, Saskatchewan.

Saskatchewan Power Corporation (1975). *Annual Report*. Regina, Saskatchewan.

Saskatchewan Power Corporation (1976). *Annual Report*. Regina, Saskatchewan.

Savich, P., K. W. Hipel, and N. M. Fraser (1983). The Alaskan gas pipeline conflict. *Energy–the International Journal* 8 (3), 213–224.

Schelling, T. C. (1960). *The Strategy of Conflict*. Cambridge, Mass.: Harvard University Press.

Shapely, L. S. (1953). A value for *n*-person games. In *Contributions to the Theory of Games II*, H. W. Kuhn and A. W. Tucker, eds. Princeton, N.J.: Princeton University Press.

Shapley, L. S., and R. W. Snow (1950). Basic solutions of discrete games, in *Contributions to the Theory of Games I*, H. W. Kuhn and A. W. Tucker, eds. Annals of Mathematical Studies No. 24, Princeton, N.J.: Princeton University Press, pp. 27–35.

Shepanik, I. (1971). Pseudo-boolean preference functions in metagame analysis, M.A.Sc. Thesis, Department of Systems Design, University of Waterloo, Waterloo, Ontario, Canada.

Shepanik, I. (1974). Design for an interactive computer program for metagame analysis. Ottawa, Canada: The Conan Institute.

Shepanik, I. (1975). MGAME: An interactive computer program for metagame analysis: User's manual. Ottawa, Canada: The Conan Institute.

Shupe, M., W. Wright, K. W., Hipel, and N. M. Fraser (1980). The nationalization of the Suez Canal—A hypergame analysis. *Journal of Conflict Resolution* 24 (3), 477–493.

Sirica, John J. (1979). *To Set the Record Straight*. New York: W.W. Norton and Company.

Snyder, G. H., and P. Diesing (1977). *Conflict Among Nations*. Princeton, N.J.: Princeton University Press.

Steele, J. L. (1976). Conflict resolution. *Operations Research Quarterly* 27 (1), 221–230.

Stevens, C. M. (1963). *Strategy and Collective Bargaining Negotiation*. Westport, Conn.: Greenwood Press.

Stokes, N. W., and K. W. Hipel (1983). Conflict analysis of an export credit trade dispute. *OMEGA* 11 (4), 365–376.

Stokes, N. W., K. W. Hipel, and P. H. Roe (1984). The New York subway car dispute. *INFOR* 22, in press.

Takahashi, M. A., N. M. Fraser, and K. W. Hipel (1984). Hypergames, European Journal of Operations Research, in press.

Tennessee Eastman Company (1973). *Water Borne Effluent Limits*. Kingsport, Tennessee.

Thomas, H. (1966). *The Suez Affair*. London: Wiedenfed and Nicholson.

Toronto Globe and Mail (1977) Associated Press article datelined Bismarck, North Dakota, "Full Funding Approach for Garrison Prject." 23 June, p. 2.

Toronto Star (1977). Associated Press article datelined Bismarck, North Dakota, "U.S. Halts Work on Disputed Dam Affecting Canada." 19 February, p. 1.

Trustees of the University of Pennsylvania (1969a). Conflicts and their escalation: Metagame analysis, mimeographed report ACDA ST-149, Vol. 1, U.S. Arms Control and Disarmament Agency, Washington, D.C.

Trustees of the University of Pennsylvania (1969b). The analysis of options: A computer aided method for analyzing political problems, mimeographed report ACDA ST-149, Vol. 2, U.S. Arms Control and Disarmament Agency, Washington, D.C.

Ulvila, J. W. (1979). *Decision with Multiple Objectives in Integrative Bargaining*. D.B.A. thesis, Cambridge, Mass.: Harvard University Graduate School of Business Administration.

U.S. Department of the Interior (1978a). *Garrison Diversion Unit—Draft Supplementary Environmental Statement*, January.

U.S. Department of the Interior (1978b). *Report on Recommended Plan—Garrison Diversion Unit*, February.

U.S. State Department, Diplomatic Notes, February 5, 1974; February 18, 1977.

Vadja, S. (1956). *Theory of Games and Linear Programming*. New York: John Wiley and Sons.

Venttsel', E. S. (1963). *An Introduction to the Theory of Games*. Translated from the Russian by J. Kristian and M.B.P. Slater. Boston: D.C. Heath and Co.

Von Neumann, J. (1928). Zer Theorie der Gesellschaftsspiele. *Mathematische Annalen* 100, 295–320.

Von Neumann, J. (1937). Uber ein okonomisches Gleichungssystem und eine Verallgemeinerung des Brouwerschen Fixpunktsatzes. *Ergebnisse eines Mathematik Kolloquims* 8, 73–83.

Von Neumann, J., and O. Morgenstern (1953). *Theory of Games and Economic Behavior*, 3rd ed. Princeton, N.J.: Princeton University Press.

Von Stackelberg, H. (1952). *The Theory of the Market Economy*. Oxford: Oxford University Press.

White, T. H. (1975). *Breach of Faith*. New York: Atheneum Publishers.

Williams, J. D. (1954). *The Compleat Strategyst*. New York: McGraw-Hill.

Wright, W., M. Shupe, N. M. Fraser, and K. W. Hipel (1980). A conflict analysis of the Suez Canal invasion of 1956. *Conflict Management and Peace Science* 5 (1) 27–40.

Young, H.P., N. Okada, and T. Hashimoto (1982). Cost allocation in water resources development—a case study in Sweden. *Water Resources Research*
463–475.

Young, O. R., ed. (1975). *Bargaining*. Urbana IL: University of Illinois Press.

Zagare, F. C. (1984). Limited move equilibria in 2×2 games. *Theory and Decision*
16, pp. 1–19.

Zeuthen, F. (1930). *Problems of Monopoly and Economic Warfare*. London:
Routledge and Kegan Paul.

Index